P9-CRP-180

Peru

Rob Rachowiecki, Charlotte Beech

Contents

Destination: Peru

The quintessential South American country, Peru fires the imagination like few other places. A land of magnificent lost cities, rich cultural heritage and dizzying historical upheavals, it has long drawn treasure-hunters and travelers alike, united in their search to uncover the secrets and wealth of remarkable, sometimes remote civilizations. Peru played host to the fabulous Inca Empire that flourished 500 years ago, but this was just the last of dozens of complex pre-Columbian civilizations, including those that built massive pyramids or drew immense and indecipherable shapes on the desert floor. Explorers are only just beginning to comprehend the sheer scope of the country's archaeological assets, continually discovering new and ever-more exciting ancient sites.

Peru is also a country of astounding natural diversity. Climb from parched expanses of dusty desert to the cool sapphire-blue waters of Lake Titicaca or descend from the jaw-dropping glaciated pinnacles of the Andes to lush jungles replete with wildlife. Outdoor adventurers will be itching to try the multitude of walking and wildlife-watching activities available. Culturally, the country is equally diverse. From the wild Afro-Peruvian music of the coast to the deeply ingrained traditions of the ancient cultures of the highlands; or from the modern beat of Lima nightlife to the timeless sounds of Amazonian Indian dance – wherever they go, travelers are welcomed by curious, big-hearted folk that tackle their underlying poverty with gusto and a lust for life.

Add to all of this the most strikingly familiar image in South America – the awesome, cloud-topping Inca city of Machu Picchu – and you have a simply unmissable destination.

GRANT DIXON

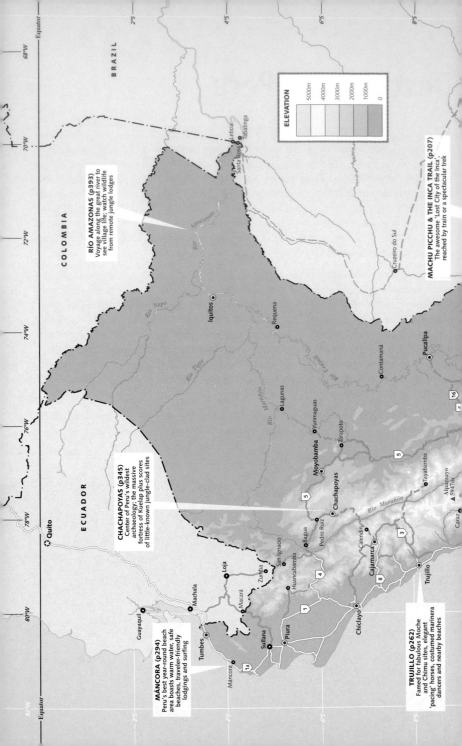

RÍO AMAZONAS (p393)
Voyage along the great river to see village life; watch wildlife from remote jungle lodges

MACHU PICCHU & THE INCA TRAIL (p207)
The awesome 'Lost City of the Inca', reached by train or a spectacular trek

CHACHAPOYAS (p345)
Center of Peru's wildest archaeology; the massive fortress of Kuelap plus scores of little-known jungle-clad sites

MÁNCORA (p294)
Peru's best year-round beach area boasts warm water, safe beaches, traveler-friendly lodgings and surfing

TRUJILLO (p262)
Famed for fabulous Moche and Chimu sites, elegant 'pacing' horses, costumed marinera dancers and nearby beaches

ELEVATION

5000m
4000m
3000m
2000m
1000m
0

BRAZIL

COLOMBIA

ECUADOR

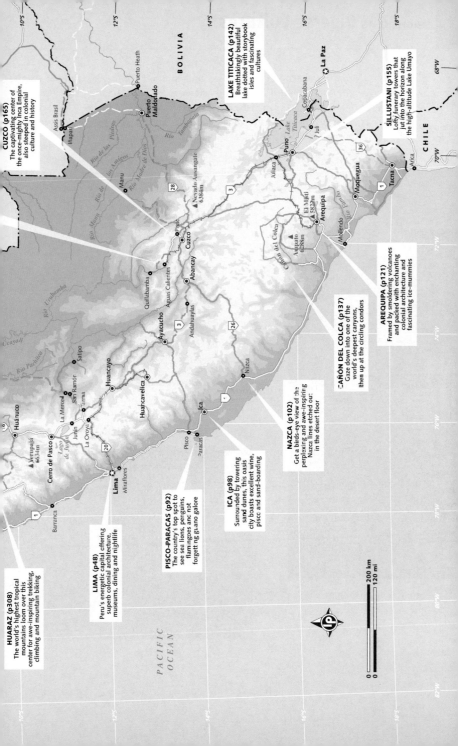

HUARAZ (p308)
The world's highest tropical mountains loom over this center for awe-inspiring trekking, climbing and mountain biking

LIMA (p48)
Peru's energetic capital offering superb colonial architecture, museums, dining and nightlife

PISCO-PARACAS (p92)
The country's top spot to see sea lions, penguins, flamingos and not forgetting guano galore

ICA (p98)
Surrounded by towering sand dunes, this oasis city boasts excellent wine, pisco and sand-boarding

NAZCA (p102)
Get a birds-eye view of the perplexing and awe-inspiring Nazca lines etched out in the desert floor

CAÑON DEL COLCA (p137)
Gaze down into one of the world's deepest canyons, then up at the circling condors

AREQUIPA (p121)
Framed by smoldering volcanoes and packed with enchanting colonial architecture and fascinating ice-mummies

CUZCO (p165)
The captivating center of the once-mighty Inca Empire, also steeped in colonial culture and history

LAKE TITICACA (p142)
Breathtakingly beautiful lake dotted with storybook isles and fascinating cultures

SILLUSTANI (p155)
Lofty funerary towers that jut into the horizon along the high-altitude Lake Umayo

PACIFIC OCEAN

BOLIVIA

CHILE

0   200 km
0   120 mi

From the 3000-year-old Andean underground temples of **Chavín de Huántar** (p327) to the lavish 21st-century **museums** (p284) around Chiclayo, Peru's cultural attractions span many fascinating civilizations. Much of what is known of Peru's history comes from ancient ceramics and jewelry now on view in Peru's museums, and in traditional textiles, still woven in the highlands.

As well as colonial architecture, archaeological sites abound – enigmatic designs on desert floors, huge adobe cities, the massive **pyramids of the Sun and the Moon** (p274) protecting untold artistic treasures, and exquisite Inca stonework.

Get to know stylish Peruvians in local attire in the **Central Highlands** (p225)

RICHARD I'ANSON

Take in the facade of the **cathedral** (p60) in Lima

JOHN BORTHWICK

KRZYSZTOF DYDYNSKI

Stroll along charming colonial back streets in **Cuzco** (p167)

CHRIS BEALL

Fly over the Condor, one of the many figures on the plains near **Nazca** (p104)

PAUL KENNEDY

Have a look at *totora* (reed boats) stored upright on the beach in **Huanchaco** (p275)

Spot the fish sculptures symbolizing the ocean currents in the ancient adobe city of **Chan Chan** (p269)

PAUL KENNEDY

The glaciated peaks of the **Cordillera Blanca** (p318) and Cordillera Huayhuash are the world's highest tropical mountains. They sharply separate Peru's Pacific coastal desert from the rain-drenched forests of the Amazon basin, giving Peru bragging rights for the greatest geographical and biological diversity on the planet.

The topographical changes across the country are bewildering and stunning, as evidenced by some of the world's deepest canyons. With so many ecological niches, Peru is a natural draw for birders and other wildlife-watchers seeking unforgettable encounters.

JASON EDWARDS

Look up into the forest canopy in the **Amazon basin** (p354)

Sit and take in the stunning river gorge in the depths of the **Cañón del Colca** (p137)

GRAN

DAVID TIPLING

Creep silently to get close to the cock-of-the-rock in the cloud forest in the **Manu area** (p369)

PAUL KENNEDY

Shrug; it's just another perfect peak in the **Cordillera Huayhuash** (p326)

JASON EDWARDS

Spot a poison arrow frog, an inhabitant of the **Amazon basin** (p354)

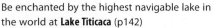

Be enchanted by the highest navigable lake in the world at **Lake Titicaca** (p142)

ERIC WHEATER

Long to be a frog and bound across the wide water lilies on the Río Yanayacu in the Amazon basin near **Iquitos** (p393)

LEANNE WALKER

It all started in the many mountains of the Cordillera Blanca, which became increasingly appreciated by foreign climbers in the 1960s. When international adventure travel began to boom in the 1970s, Peru was ripe to host travelers looking for the best of the best. Trekking was soon added to many adventure itineraries, followed by river running. Then came the curiously Peruvian sport of sand-boarding, followed by mountain biking and more extreme sports. Nevertheless, it is still the fantastic mountain climbing and trekking for which Peru is deservedly world-famous.

Walk on past a double-peaked mountain in the **Cordillera Huayhuash** (p326)

ROB RACHOWIECKI

GRANT DIXON

Climb a snowcapped summit ridge in the **Cordillera Blanca** (p318)

Ride the rapids on the **Río Urubamba** (p177)

RICHARD

Sand-board down the dunes near
Huacachina (p102)

Camp on a glacier below **Alpamayo**
(p323) in the Cordillera Blanca

Take a breather at the base camp by a mountain lake in the **Cordillera Huayhuash** (p326)

Peruvians love a fiesta, and they happen in the tiniest hamlets as well as in the cities. Every hotel in town is full during festival time and, at smaller places, locals rent out floor space for determined fiesta-goers.

There is never a week in Peru without a festival somewhere. Easter celebrations are among the most fervent, with those of **Ayacucho** (p241) and **Tarma** (p229) considered among the nation's finest, but fiestas in the smallest villages, sometimes stumbled upon by accident, are often the most intriguing.

ANTHONY PIDGEON

Admire the pageantry of the **Inti Raymi** (p196) at the monolithic ruins of Sacsayhuamán

Follow masked dancers at Paucartambo festival of **Virgen del Carmen** (p220)

BRUCE BI

Watch paraders in traditional dress at a festival in **Lima** (p69)

Getting Started

Peru has it all. Spectacular archaeological sites, amazing Amazon rainforests, the world's highest tropical mountains and an endless desert coastline will keep you traveling for months. A diverse and welcoming population, an even more diverse wildlife, and some of the continent's best food await the adventurous visitor. Best of all, transportation is efficient and relatively inexpensive, and accommodations to suit every budget are available, from cheapo backpackers' hostels to beautifully converted colonial mansions.

WHEN TO GO

Peru's climate has two main seasons – wet and dry – though the weather varies greatly depending on the geographical region. Temperature is mostly influenced by elevation – the higher you climb the cooler it becomes.

A Peruvian weather site, in Spanish, is www.senamhi.gob.pe.

See Climate Charts (p404) for more information.

The high tourist season is from June to August, which coincides both with the dry season in the highlands and summer vacation in North America and Europe. Certainly, this is the best time to go if you are interested in hiking the Inca Trail (see p212) to Machu Picchu, or climbing, trekking or mountain biking elsewhere. People can and do visit the highlands year-round, though the wettest months of January to April make trekking and backpacking a wet and muddy proposition. If you aren't planning on spending any time trekking, however, you shouldn't have any major problems visiting in the rainy season. Many of the major fiestas, such as Virgen de la Candelaria, Carnaval and Semana Santa, occur in the wettest months and continue undiminished even during heavy rain.

On the arid coast, Peruvians visit the beaches during the hottest time of the year, from late December through March. In central and south Peru, the coast is cloaked in *garúa* (coastal mist) for the rest of the year and, although their beaches don't attract visitors, the coastal cities can be visited at any time. In the north, however, the coast sees more sun, so beach lovers can hang out year-round.

DON'T LEAVE HOME WITHOUT...

- Yellow-fever, tetanus and typhoid **vaccinations**; make sure they are less than 10 years old before setting off.

- A copy of your **travel insurance** policy details.

- **Earplugs** – buses and many hotels insist on ear-splitting entertainment at all hours.

- A Swiss Army–style **penknife** – but remember to place it in your checked luggage when flying or it'll be confiscated.

- A **hat** – it'll keep you warm when it's cold, shade your eyes when it's sunny, and keep your head dry when it rains. A great deal!

- A roll of **toilet-paper** – essential as public toilets and most restaurants don't supply it. It works for your nose as well.

- Spare **shoes** if you have large feet; anything over size 43 (10½ US; 9½ UK) can't be found.

TOP 10S

OUTDOOR ADVENTURES

The variety of trails to trek is staggering (see Lonely Planet's *Trekking in the Central Andes* for more details on the possibilities). Most gear can be hired, but your own broken-in boots will save you from horrific blisters inflicted by poorly fitting rental boots. But why stop with trekking? There's plenty more to do!

- **Trekking in the Cordillera Blanca** (p311)

  Prime trekking past 50 glaciated peaks exceeding 5700m

- **Trekking in the Cordillera Huayhuash** (p326)

  Similar to the Blanca, but less visited and more remote

- **Trekking the Ausangate Circuit** (p220)

  Six days of high-altitude trekking alongside alpacas

- **Wandering in the Cañón del Colca** (p137)

  Get down into one of the world's deepest canyons

- **Trekking the Inca Trail to Machu Picchu** (p212)

  Deservedly world-famous guided trek

- **Reaching remote archaeological sites in the Northern Highlands** (p332)

  Hire a guide, machete and pack mule to thrash through cloud forest

- **River running in the Manu Area** (p369) **and near Arequipa** (p135)

  Multi-day Andes-to-Amazon descents or through deep canyons

- **Mountaineering around Huaraz** (p311)

  Huascarán (6768m) is for experts but easier peaks abound

- **Mountain biking around the Cordillera Blanca** (p312)

  Rent and ride! Easy trails and demanding single-track await

- **Sand-boarding at Huacachina** (p102)

  Slide down humungous dunes in the desert

- **Surfing on the north coast** (p277)

  Adventurers don't stop at 10! – there are radical waves up north

FLORA & FAUNA

Peru has over 1700 bird species (more than any country except Colombia). No wonder ornithologists flock to Peru. Wildlife enthusiasts also come to see sea-lion colonies, pink freshwater dolphins, creepy crocodiles, adorable anteaters and, with luck, jaguars. With coastal, mountain and rainforest habitats, there is so much to spot. Bring your binoculars.

- **Parque Nacional Manu** (p371)

  Remote and remarkable – your best chance of seeing a jaguar

- **Reserva Nacional de Paracas** (p95)

  Coastal reserve with penguins, Inca terns, flamingos, seals and sea lions

- **Reserva Nacional Pacaya-Samiria** (p386)

  Little-known rainforest awaiting exploration

Parque Nacional Huascarán (p318)

Andean condors, giant *Puya raimondii*, vicuñas and viscachas

Tambopata Research Center (p367)

Capybara sightings are highly likely while cruising to a macaw lick

Cruz del Condor (p139)

The single best place to see Andean condors daily

Reserva Nacional Pampas Galeras (p106)

A vicuña sanctuary with a round-up and shearing in May

Iquitos Area (p386)

A 500m-long canopy walkway, jungle lodges and river cruises

Yarinacocha (p382)

Pink dolphins, huge iguanas, fabulous birdlife and camping expeditions

Reserva Nacional Salinas y Aguada Blanca (p137)

Llamas, alpacas, vicuñas and flamingos

ARCHAEOLOGY, HISTORY & MUSEUMS

Check out the legacy of the Incas – definitely! But don't forget the string of civilizations going back many hundreds of years earlier. Here are our picks.

Machu Picchu (p207)

The world-famous mountaintop 'Lost City of the Inca'

Nazca Lines (p104)

Ancient designs covering vast areas of the southern pampa

Huaca de la Luna (p274)

Watch archaeology in action at this 1400-year-old Moche pyramid

Museo Santuarios Andinos (p125)

Home to the frozen Inca sun-bride Juanita

Monasterio Santa Catalina (p123)

Fascinating colonial convent and 'city within a city'

Museo de la Nación (p57)

Best overview of Peru's mind-bogglingly long list of bygone cultures

Sacsayhuamán (p195)

Awesome fortress and site of the festival of Inti Raymi

Kuélap (p348)

Massive Chachapoyan site in the cloud forest with no crowds

Museo Tumbas Reales de Sipán (p284)

Fabulous world-class museum showcasing 'The Lord of Sipán'

Trujillo (p262)

Colonial architecture and colorful parades

In the eastern rainforests it rains, of course. The wettest months are December through April, as in the highlands, but tourism continues undiminished because it rarely rains for more than a few hours at a time, so there are plenty of bright sunny periods to enjoy. Follow the locals' example – they are used to briefly taking cover during the heaviest downpours. It's not a big deal.

COSTS & MONEY

Shoestring travelers watching their céntimos – sleeping in dormitory rooms, traveling by cheaper buses, eating set menus – can easily get by on well under US$20 a day, and even under US$15 if frugality is one of their strong points. Visitors who prefer private hot showers, à-la-carte meals in moderately priced restaurants, comfortable buses and occasional flights will find that US$50 a day should meet their needs. As soon as you start looking at top-range restaurants and hotels, you can spend up to several hundred dollars a day, especially if you're doing your trip by organized tour or staying in the main centers of Lima and Cuzco.

You can stretch your travel budget by looking for a traveling partner as double rooms are normally much less expensive than two singles. Many restaurants offer good-value three-course set lunches for US$2 or even less, while eating à la carte will triple your meal cost. Hone your bargaining skills – taxi cabs don't have meters, and drivers routinely overcharge gringos. Hotels often give discounts if you ask for a promotional, student or business rate. Pay with cash rather than credit cards, which frequently attract a surcharge of 6%. Above all, keep your money stashed safely in a money belt and a neck pouch – that economical trip will get expensive fast if you are pickpocketed!

Adventurers on a tight budget will be dismayed at the high costs of hiking the famed Inca Trail to Machu Picchu – unguided trips are now illegal (and this is heavily enforced) and the cheapest four-day trips start around US$200 per person. The alternative train trip isn't cheap either – see Getting There & Away under Cuzco (p191).

TRAVEL LITERATURE

The White Rock, by Hugh Thomson, describes an explorer's search for Inca archaeological sites throughout the Peruvian Andes, ending at Machu Picchu. It includes a lot of background about earlier travelers and explorers.

Trail of Feathers, by Tahir Shah, seeks to uncover what lies behind the 'birdmen' legends in the Peruvian desert, eventually leading the author into the remote Amazon. It's an amusing, insightful look into Peruvian culture, beliefs and peoples.

Inca-Kola, by Matthew Parris, is a hilarious, tongue-in-cheek account of the backpacking author's travels in Peru.

At Play in the Fields of the Lord, by Peter Matthiessen, is a classic, superb and believable novel about the conflict between the forces of 'development' and indigenous peoples.

Running the Amazon, by Joe Kane, provides an exciting and insightful personal account of an expedition from the source of the Amazon (high in the Peruvian Andes) to the Atlantic. Much of the action takes place in Peru.

Touching the Void, by Joe Simpson, a harrowing account of surviving a terrifying mountaineering accident in Peru's Cordillera Huayhuash, was being made into a BBC film when this book was researched.

HOW MUCH?

Local phone call
US$0.15

Short taxi ride
(not in Lima)
US$1

Pisco sour – the national
cocktail
US$2.50

Room with bathroom
and TV
US$20

Flight between most
cities
US$79

**LONELY PLANET
INDEX**

Liter of gas/petrol
US$0.80

Liter of bottled water
US$0.80

Beer – 650ml Crystal
US$2

Souvenir T-shirt
US$7

Street treat – ¼ chicken
and fries
US$1.80

The Peru Reader: History, Culture, Politics, edited by Orin Starn, Carlos Iván Degregori and Robin Kirk, contains essays, poems, short stories and autobiographies in a wide-ranging look at everything from the conquest of the Incas to cocaine production, guerrilla warfare and gay activism.

Horrible Histories: The Incredible Incas, by Terry Deary, is a great book for primary-school-age children, with some meaty history mingled with the juicy bits.

INTERNET RESOURCES

Andean Travel Web (www.andeantravelweb.com/peru) Travel site with hundreds of links to hotels, tour companies etc.

Latin America Network Information Center (www.lanic.utexas.edu/la/peru/) The University of Texas provides hundreds of good links from academics to sport.

Magic Country (www.magicperu.com) Lots of links on everything from Peruvian astronomy to gastronomy.

Peru Links (www.perulinks.com) Over 2500 links covering a wide range of topics, many in Spanish, some in English. Editor's picks and top 10 sites are always good.

PromPerú (www.promperu.gob.pe) The official government tourist office, in Spanish, English and German.

Itineraries
CLASSIC ROUTES

GRINGO TRAIL
Two weeks / Lima to Cuzco & Machu Picchu

The loop from Lima, along the coastal deserts, up to Lake Titicaca and ending at Machu Picchu, is one of the most popular routes on the continent.

Leaving **Lima** (p81), journey south along the coast to **Paracas** (p92) where there are boat tours to the wildlife-rich **Islas Ballestas** (p93). Then it's on to **Ica** (p98), Peru's wine and pisco capital, and perhaps do some sand-boarding. Next is **Nazca** (p102) for a flight over the mysterious Nazca Lines. You then climb to get to the 'white city' of **Arequipa** (p121), with its relaxed atmosphere and colonial architecture. While there, take an excursion to **Cañón del Colca** (p137), among the world's deepest, and maybe climb **El Misti** (p136), a breathless 5822m high.

It's upwards to **Puno** (p148), Peru's port on **Lake Titicaca**, the world's highest navigable lake, for a visit to traditional **Isla Taquile** (p157), which has no roads or vehicles, and a side-trip to **Sillustani** (p155). Then a fast bus or slow train takes you to **Cuzco** (p165), the archaeological capital of the Americas. The adventurous can trek the **Inca Trail** to **Machu Picchu** (p207), which can also be visited less strenuously by comfortable trains from Cuzco.

A traveler could do this trip in two weeks. However, a meandering month is ideal and will help with acclimatization – spend a few days in Arequipa before hitting the heights of Lake Titicaca (3830m). Finish the loop with a quick Cuzco–Lima flight.

NORTH COAST

Two weeks / Lima to Tumbes

Straight as an arrow, the Panamericana Norte passes fabled archaeo-logical sites, great beaches, colonial cities and modern museums with fascinating artefacts. Hemingway liked it – you will too.

The first stop from **Lima** could be tiny **Casma** (p259), near the gruesome site of 1600 BC **Sechín** (p259), although many travelers prefer to con-tinue to **Trujillo** (p262), Peru's third city. Attractions here include a well-preserved colonial center, the world's largest adobe city at the Chimu capital of **Chan Chan** (p269), dating from AD 1300, ongoing excavations at the huge Moche pyramids, the **Temples of the Sun and Moon** (p274) and restful beaches at **Huanchaco** (p275) where local fishermen still use *totora*-reed canoes to paddle out beyond the breakers, as they have done for thousands of years. On the way to Chiclayo is **Puerto Chicama** (p277), which boasts the world's longest left-handed wave, attracting interna-tional surfers from May to August. Then it's cosmopolitan **Chiclayo** (p278), surrounded by several minor towns that contain world-class museums, and the important archaeological site of **Sipán** (p284).

Further north, **Piura** (p286) is the jumping-off point for a visit to the witchdoctors of **Huancabamba** (p291), eight hours by bus to the east. Beach lovers, though, should continue to **Máncora** (p294), with sunny weather and warmer water year-round and good surfing from December to March. The journey ends at **Tumbes** (p299), site of Peru's only mangroves, protected in a national park. It's just a few minutes from here by taxi to the Ecuador border.

A nonstop Lima to Tumbes bus can cover the 1270km along the Panamericana Norte in about 18 hours, but unless you are in a hurry to reach Ecuador, you'll want to spend a minimum of a week, or two weeks if beach relaxation and taking in the sights is to be part of your journey.

ROADS LESS TRAVELED

TO THE AMAZON BY ROAD & RIVER   Two weeks / Chiclayo to Iquitos

This route crosses the Northern Highlands by road and ends at Amazonian Iquitos, the world's largest city that cannot be reached by road.

Leaving **Chiclayo** (see the North Coast route), head for **Chachapoyas** (p345), the base for visiting the untouristed fortress of **Kuélap** (p348), dating from AD 1000, and many other remote, barely known, archaeological sites. Chachapoyas is easily reached in 10 hours from Chiclayo via the highland jungle town of **Jaén** (p344). Hardier travelers will take a longer route to first visit **Cajamarca** (p333), a lovely, highland provincial town where the Inca, Atahualpa, was imprisoned by the conquistadors. Continue on the slow, spectacular route to **Celendín** (p343) on the scenic but kidney-busting drive to Chachapoyas. Your choice.

From Chachapoyas, take the scenic unpaved road to **Pedro Ruiz** (p348) where transport is readily available to **Tarapoto** (p349). A break here provides opportunities to hike to high jungle waterfalls. The last road section to **Yurimaguas** (p383) is a six-hour, unpaved, gut-wrencher. Cargo boats leave here most days on the two-day trip via **Lagunas** (p385), a good entry village for the **Pacaya Samiria Reserve** (p386), to **Iquitos** (p386); hammock or cabin space is readily available. Don't expect comfort but enjoy watching how people live on the world's greatest river. At Iquitos you can arrange boat trips that go deep into the Amazon basin or Brazil.

From Chiclayo, choose the easier, quicker, paved northern road or tough it out on the wild, unpaved track through Celendín. Hurrying locals get from Chiclayo to Iquitos in three days, without visiting Chachapoyas. Curious travelers might take weeks or months.

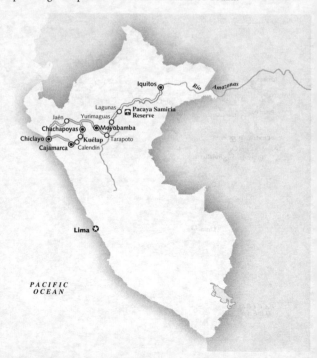

TAILORED TRIP

HIGH & MIGHTY

Spin the globe and you'll see that Peru has the highest tropical mountains in the world. Don't miss them. Trips can centre around Huaraz, Arequipa and Cuzco.

An eight-hour bus ride takes you from **Lima** to **Huaraz** (p308) from where you can see many of these tropical summits, including the highest, **Huascarán** (6768m, p322). Travelers don't need to climb that high – hiking, mountain biking or even simply riding a bus can bring you closer to the peaks than your camera lens can handle. Travelers not into tents and breathlessly high camp sites can take day trips out of Huaraz to visit pristine lakes, 10m-high bromeliads, ice caves, and 3500-year-old archaeological sites, all dominated by the spectacular peaks of the **Cordillera Blanca** (p307).

The classic and favorite trekking route is the four-day **Llanganuco to Santa Cruz trek** (p322), climbing the 4750m Punta Union pass surrounded by ice-clad peaks. Allow a few days for acclimatization first. Longer treks include the northern route around **Alpamayo** (p323) or the **Cordillera Huayhuash** (p308), both needing almost two weeks.

In the south of Peru, there is no shortage of highs. **Arequipa** (p121) offers the possibility of scaling **El Misti** (5822m, p136), which, despite its height, is basically a very long, tough walk-up. Near **Cuzco** (p165), a six-day trek around awesome **Ausangate** (6384m, p220) will take you over 5000m passes, through huge herds of alpacas, and past tiny hamlets unchanged in centuries. Or, if you are looking for an easier trek, the four-day trek on the **Inca Trail** (p205) to Machu Picchu might be the way to go.

The Authors

ROB RACHOWIECKI
Coordinating Author, Central Highlands, North Coast, Huaraz & the Cordillera Blanca, Northern Highlands, Amazon Basin

Over 20 years of visits to Peru has impressed one thing upon Rob: he is crazy about this country. With a masters degree in ecology, he is excited about all things Amazonian and he reveled in roaming the Amazon for this book. He also enjoyed covering the less-traveled northern and central parts of the country. He authored Lonely Planet's previous four *Peru* guides and coordinated *Trekking in the Central Andes*. He also leads adventure tours in the Peruvian Andes. When not on the road, Rob lives in Arizona and treasures spending time with his three children, Julia, Alison and David.

My Favorite Trip

On a ride up the Río Tambopata (p366), I saw *capybara* often; the sixth sighting was ho-hum. Suddenly my guide made frantic gestures at the boatman to stop. A jaguar! There he was, a fully grown male relaxing on the riverbank about 4m above the water, his eyes fixed on us. Then the big cat yawned elaborately, slowly arose and turned before melting into the forest. Barely five minutes later we had great views of three giant river otters on the bank. On a forest hike nearby we glimpsed a herd of over 100 peccaries. Abruptly, the herd divided and ran around us, like a thunderstorm of wild pigs in the forest. Fantastic!

Río Tambopata

CHARLOTTE BEECH
Lima, South Coast, Arequipa & Canyon Country, Lake Titicaca Area, Cuzco & the Sacred Valley

Ever since studying archaeology at Cambridge University, Charlotte has dreamt of exploring lost Andean cities. And so in 2001, after shelving a promising career editing travel books, she set off for South America. A year later, she jumped at this chance to write about a country she had fallen for so heavily on her travels. Charlotte thoroughly enjoyed researching sections covering the gringo trail from Lima to Cuzco for this book, and has also worked on Lonely Planet's *South America on a shoestring*. When not traveling, she lives in London with her Latin American partner.

My Favorite Trip

Choosing favorite moments in a country so full of surprises as Peru is very difficult, but my first trip saw some incredible hiking in the Cordillera Blanca (p318), sneaking into glistening ice caves and camping under a moon and starlit sky so bright you could read a book by it. Back on the coast, I love the chilled beachside town of Huanchaco (p275), and I couldn't resist dwelling in Huacachina (p102) down south for some sand-boarding. However, for their sheer awe factor, nothing surpasses the Nazca Lines (p104) for me, while the pristine grandeur of the Cañón de Cotahuasi (p140) makes it my favorite off-the-beaten-track destination.

Huanchaco

Cordillera Blanca

Huacachina

Cañón de Cotahuasi

Nazca

Snapshot

The average Peruvian today is economically far better off than a decade ago. Nevertheless, a teacher in Peru makes only US$200 a month. It's hardly surprising, then, that protests and strikes for higher wages happen quite often, not just by teachers, but by farmers, doctors, government workers and others. In mid-2003, teachers went on strike for a US$60 monthly raise, were offered US$29, and responded by closing major highways with demonstrations, treetrunks and burning tires. President Toledo imposed a 30-day state of emergency, allowing police and the armed forces to forcibly move the protestors and open roads to traffic. As the June to August high season for international tourism progressed, protests died down somewhat, perhaps as workers concentrated on the income derived from tourists. This unrest can be tiresome for travelers, who may find that their road trip is delayed by a day or two. It's not really a big deal to Peruvians, though, who have seen strikes on a regular basis. Some travelers wonder if they are in any danger. Most probably none.

While travelers sit around, waiting for transport, the conversation can turn to politics. Why is the first indigenous president of an Andean country receiving 10% approval ratings from a country in which the majority of the population is Indian? It's fairly simple – he promised jobs and he hasn't delivered. No work – no vote of confidence. Peruvians look back with mixed feelings to the days of ex-President Fujimori, now exiled in Japan. Fujimori straightened out the country's economy, but his right-hand man, Vladimiro Montesinos, was caught on film bribing a Peruvian congressman. After an international chase, Montesinos was captured and is now being tried in Peru. About 2700 films, popularly dubbed *Vladi-videos*, were discovered showing the man in politically scandalous action. Peruvians follow his rise and fall with all the slack-jawed, wide-eyed interest of Americans when they followed the OJ Simpson trials.

Perhaps the single biggest topic that foreign visitors carp about currently, though, is the Inca Trail (p205). It's the most famous trek in South America, and yet it has suddenly become supremely regulated. Backpackers, even those with much outdoor experience, cannot hike the trail without hiring a guide and a porter. Phooey! Where's the adventure in a guided trip, some ask? And it costs so much, others add. Well, that's the way it is today, as Peruvians attempt to control the trekking boom with bureaucracy. While the money raised may lead to better protection of the trail, this remains to be seen.

While waiting on a strike-bound bus, some travelers simply put their seats into full recline and go to sleep. Double-decker bus-camas with comfortable reclining seats to rival those of 1st-class airplane cabins are the latest rage to hit Peru's roads. No more chicken buses. Now you can travel with a cabin crew serving you drinks and snacks as you put your feet up and watch a video. Enjoy!

History

For many travelers, the first word that comes to mind when thinking of Peruvian history is 'Inca'. Certainly, the Inca civilization is the best known and most studied of South America's pre-Columbian cultures and the one that travelers are most likely to encounter. But the Incas are merely the tip of the archaeological iceberg. Peru had many pre-Columbian cultures, some preceding the Incas by millennia.

What we know of Peru's pre-Columbian civilizations has been gleaned almost entirely from archaeological excavation.

Peru is unequaled in South America for its archaeological wealth, and many archaeologists find Peru's ancient sites and cultures as exciting as those of Mexico, Egypt or the Mediterranean. Learning about and visiting these centuries-old ruins is one of the highlights of most travelers' journies as well, and even visitors with little interest in archaeology usually enjoy seeing some of the main sites.

With no written records available, archaeologists had to derive historical information from the realistic and expressive decoration found on the ceramics, textiles and other artefacts of Peru's pre-Columbian inhabitants. These relics often depict everyday life in detail and are worth examining in Peru's museums.

PRECERAMIC (STONE AGE) PERIOD

Humans are relatively recent arrivals in the New World, probably spreading throughout the Americas after migrating across the Bering Strait about 20,000 years ago. Peru's first inhabitants were nomadic hunters and gatherers who roamed the country in loose-knit bands, living in caves and hunting fearsome (and now extinct) animals such as giant sloths, saber-toothed tigers and mastodons.

Hunting scenes were recorded in cave paintings made by Peru's early inhabitants at Lauricocha near Huánuco and Toquepala near Tacna.

Domestication of the llama, alpaca and guinea pig had begun by about 4000 BC, though some sources claim that Camelid domestication may have begun as early as 7000 BC. Around the same time, people began planting seeds and learning how to improve crops by simple horticultural methods such as weeding. The coastal strip of Peru was wetter than today's desert, and a number of small settlements were established, thus changing the way of life of people living there from nomadic hunters and gatherers to settled agriculturists and fisherfolk. The inhabitants fished with nets or bone hooks, sometimes using rafts, and collected food such as shellfish, sea urchins, seabird eggs and even sea lions. Various crops were cultivated, including beans and cotton, which appeared at least as early as 3000 BC, as well as chilies, squashes and, by about 1400 BC, corn. Cotton was used to make clothing, mainly by using simple twining techniques and, later, by weaving. Manioc (also called cassava) and sweet potatoes appeared on the coast early on, indicating trade links with the Amazon basin. The coastal people lived in simple one-room dwellings, lined with stone or made from branches and reeds. Ceramics and metalwork were still unknown, although jewelry made of bone and shell has been found. Burial pyramids were constucted during this period.

Roughly contemporary with the later Preceramic Period coastal settlements was the enigmatic site of Kotosh near Huánuco, one of the

12,000 BC	4000 BC
Pikimachay caves, near Ayacucho, is used by hunters and gatherers; today it's the oldest archaeological site in Peru	Construction of the coastal burial pyramids

earliest ruins in highland Peru. Little is known about the people who lived there, but their buildings were the most developed for that period. Various forms of the Andean staple, the potato, began to be grown as a crop around 3000 BC.

INITIAL PERIOD

This period extended from approximately 2000 to 1000 BC. What is known about it today has been gleaned from remains found in the Virú valley and Guañape area, about 50km south of Trujillo on the north coast. More recently, large ceremonial temples from this period have been discovered in the Rímac valley above Lima and other coastal sites. Funerary offerings were made at many of them. During this time, ceramics developed from basic undecorated pots to sculpted, incised and simply colored pots of high quality. Weaving, fishing and horticulture also improved, the latter particularly through the development of irrigation. Toward the end of this time, agricultural terraces were constructed in the highlands.

Prior to the Incas, there were scores of different cultures and civilizations dating back to 1500 BC. *The Ancient Kingdoms of Peru*, by Nigel Davies, covers them all.

EARLY HORIZON

Lasting roughly from 1000 to 300 BC, this period has also been called the Chavín Horizon, after the site of Chavín de Huántar, 40km east of Huaraz. It's termed a 'horizon' because artistic and religious phenomena appeared, perhaps independently, within several cultures in different places at about the same time, indicating some kind of interchange of ideas and increasing cultural complexity. This horizon extended throughout much of the northern and central highlands and the northern and southern coast.

The salient feature of the Chavín influence is the repeated representation of a stylized jaguar face with prominently religious overtones. Other animal faces, some mythical, and human faces are also found. Most importantly, this period represents the greatest early development in weaving, pottery, agriculture, religion and architecture – in a word, culture. During this time, methods of working with gold developed on the northern coast.

Many archaeologists see the Early Horizon as the most important period of cultural development in pre-Columbian Peru.

EARLY INTERMEDIATE PERIOD

Around 300 BC, the Chavín culture inexplicably lost its unifying influence. Over the next 500 years, several cultures became locally important, of which the best known is the unusually named Paracas Necropolis (named after the burial site discovered south of Lima), which produced cotton and wool textiles considered to be the finest pre-Columbian textiles of the Americas.

From about AD 100 to 700 pottery, metalwork and weaving reached a pinnacle of technological development in several regions. Two distinct cultures are particularly noted for their exceptional pottery: the Moche from the Trujillo area produced pottery from molds, and the Nazca from the south coast introduced polychrome techniques. These cultures recorded their life in intricate detail on their ceramics.

Many of Peru's museums have good collections of Nazca and Moche pottery.

These two cultures also left some interesting sites that are worth visiting. The Moche built massive platform mounds (popularly called 'pyramids') such as the Huacas del Sol y de la Luna (Temples of the Sun and Moon) near Trujillo and at Sipán near Chiclayo. Sipán contains a series of tombs that have been under excavation since 1987 and are considered the

1000–300 BC	300 BC–AD 1100
Period of the Chavín Horizon; several cultures share developments in weaving, pottery, agriculture, religion and architecture	The Paracas create the finest textiles; the Moche build huge platform mounds; the Nazca construct the Nazca Lines

most important archaeological discovery in South America since Machu Picchu. The Temple of the Moon iscurrently under excavation, and amazing friezes have recently been uncovered. The Nazca made giant geometric designs in the desert, known as the Nazca Lines. These enigmatic designs are best appreciated from an overflight in a small airplane.

MIDDLE HORIZON

Most of the latter half of the 6th century was marked by a catastrophic drought along the coast, contributing to the demise of the Moche. From AD 600 to about 1000, the Wari emerged as the first expansionist peoples known in the Andes.

The ruins of the Wari capital, the highland city of Wari (Huari), are found 22km north of Ayacucho.

Unlike the earlier Chavín, expansion was not limited to the diffusion of artistic and religious influence. The Wari were vigorous military conquerors who built and maintained important outposts throughout much of Peru.

The Wari attempted to subdue the cultures they conquered by emphasizing their own values and suppressing local oral traditions and regional self-expression. Thus from about AD 700 to 1100, Wari influence is noted in the art, technology and architecture of most areas in Peru. More significantly, from an archaeologist's point of view, any local oral traditions that may have existed were discouraged by these conquerors and slowly forgotten. With no written language and no oral traditions to study, archaeologists must rely entirely on the examination of excavated artefacts to gain an idea of what life was like in early Peruvian cultures. The Wari too, in their turn, were replaced by other cultures.

LATE INTERMEDIATE PERIOD

Because of their cultural dominance and oppressive rule, it is not surprising that the Wari were generally not welcomed, despite the improvements they made in urban development and organization. By about AD 1000, their governance had been replaced by individual groups in local areas. These separate regional states thrived for the next 400 years, the best known being the Chimu kingdom in the Trujillo area. Its capital was Chan Chan, famous as the largest adobe city in the world.

The Chimu ruins of the adobe city of Chan Chan can easily be visited from Trujillo.

Roughly contemporary with the Chimu was the Chachapoyas culture which built Kuélap, one of the most intriguing and significant of the highland ruins, and reasonably accessible to travelers. Also contemporary with the Chimu were the Chancay people from the Chancay valley just north of Lima. The best collection of Chancay artefacts is at the excellent Museo Amano in Lima. Further south was the Ica-Chincha culture, whose artefacts can be seen in the Ica's Museo Regional. There were also several small altiplano kingdoms situated near Lake Titicaca that frequently warred with one another. They left impressive *chullpas* (circular funerary towers) dotting the bleak landscape – the best are to be seen at Sillustani.

INCA EMPIRE

The Inca Empire, for all its greatness, existed for barely a century. Prior to 1438, the Incas, whose emperor was believed to have descended from the sun, ruled over only the valley of Cuzco. The Cuzqueños and their rivals, the Chankas, were at war for some time, eventually culminating in the

600–1100	1000–1470
The expansionist, militaristic Wari culture emerges and spreads throughout the central Andes	The Chimu build Chan Chan, the world's largest adobe city; the Chachapoya people construct massive Kuélap

1430s with a major victory for the Cuzqueños. This marked the beginning of a remarkably rapid military expansion. The Inca Empire, known as Tahuantinsuyo (Land of Four Quarters), conquered most of the cultures in the area stretching from southern Colombia to central Chile (including also the Andean regions of Bolivia and northern Argentina). Like the Wari before them, the Incas imposed their way of life on the peoples they conquered. Thus when the Spanish arrived, most of the Andean area had been politically unified by Inca rule. This unification did not extend to many of the everyday facets of life for the conquered, and many of them felt some resentment toward the Inca leaders. This was a significant factor in the success of the Spaniards during their invasion of the New World. (See p165 for more information on Inca history.)

The Incas in Cuzco ate fresh seafood that was delivered by runners from the coast in under two days.

SPANISH INVASION

After Columbus' first landfall, the Spanish rapidly invaded and conquered the Caribbean islands and the Aztec and Mayan cultures of Mexico and Central America. By the 1520s, the conquistadors were ready to turn their attentions to the South American continent. In 1522 Pascual de Andagoya sailed as far as the Río San Juan in Colombia. Two years later, Francisco Pizarro headed south but was unable to reach even the San Juan. In November 1526, Pizarro again headed south, and by 1528 he had explored as far as the Río Santa in Peru. He noted several coastal Inca settlements, became aware of the richness of the Inca Empire, and returned to Spain to raise money and recruit men. Pizarro's third expedition left Panama late in 1530. He landed on the Ecuadorian coast and began to march overland toward Peru. In September 1532, Pizarro founded the first Spanish town in Peru, naming it San Miguel de Piura. He then marched inland into the heart of the Inca Empire. In November 1532, he reached Cajamarca, captured the Inca emperor, Atahualpa, and effectively put an end to the Incas. (See p333 for more details on Atahualpa's capture.)

European diseases traveled faster than the Spanish conquistadors: the 11th Inca, Huayna Capac, died of smallpox six years before Pizarro arrived in Peru.

COLONIAL PERU

The Inca capital of Cuzco was of little use to the Spaniards, who were a seafaring people and needed a coastal capital to maintain communication with Spain. Accordingly, Pizarro founded Lima in 1535, and this became the capital of the viceroyship of Peru, as the colony was named.

The next 30 years was a period of turmoil, with the Incas fighting against their conquerors, and the conquistadors fighting among themselves for control of the rich colony. The conquistador Diego de Almagro was assassinated in 1538 and Francisco Pizarro suffered the same fate three years later. Manco Inca tried to regain control of the highlands and was almost successful in 1536, but a year later he was forced to retreat to Vilcabamba in the jungle, where he was killed in 1544. Succeeding Incas were less defiant until 1572 when the Inca Tupac Amaru organized a rebellion in which he was defeated and executed by the Spaniards.

If you read only one book about the Incas, make it the lucid and lively The Conquest of the Incas by John Hemming.

The next 200 years were relatively peaceful. Lima became the main political, social and commercial center of the Andean nations. Cuzco became a backwater, its main mark on the colonial period being the development of the Cuzco school of art, the Escuela Cuzqueña, which

1438–1532	1532–33
The Inca Empire is at its peak	Pizarro and 160 Spaniards arrive at Cajamarca, capturing, and later executing, Inca Atahualpa, putting an end to the Inca Empire

blended Spanish and highland Indian influences. Escuela Cuzqueña canvases can be admired now in Lima's museums and in the many colonial churches that were built in Lima and the highlands during the 17th and 18th centuries.

In 1533 Pizarro melted down 6000kg of gold and 12,000kg of silver artefacts, Atahualpa's ransom to him, before he executed Atahualpa and marched toward Cuzco.

The rulers of the colony were the Spanish-born viceroys appointed by the Spanish crown. Immigrants from Spain held the most prestigious positions, while Spaniards born in the colony were generally less important. This is how the Spanish crown was able to control its colonies. *Mestizos* (people of mixed Indian-Spanish descent) were placed still further down the social scale. Lowest of all were the Indians themselves, who were exploited and treated as *peones*, or expendable laborers, under the *encomienda* system. This resulted in the 1780 Indian uprising, led by a self-styled Inca, Tupac Amaru II. The uprising was quelled and its leaders cruelly executed.

INDEPENDENCE

By the early 19th century, the inhabitants of Spain's Latin American colonies were dissatisfied with their lack of freedom and high taxation; South America was ripe for revolt and independence. In Peru's case, two important factors that helped pave the way toward independence were the discovery and exploitation of a variety of rich mineral deposits, beginning with the seemingly inauspicious guano (seabird droppings) used for fertilizer.

Open Veins of Latin America: Five Centuries of the Pillage of a Continent by Eduardo H Galeano, and translated by Cedric Belfrage, puts Peru in a continental setting and provides an often disturbing overview.

For Peru, the change came from two directions. José de San Martín liberated Argentina and Chile, and in 1821 he entered Lima and formally proclaimed independence (in Huacho, north of Lima). Meanwhile, Simón Bolívar had freed Venezuela, Colombia and Ecuador. San Martín and Bolívar met privately in Guayaquil, Ecuador. What transpired during that mysterious meeting is unknown, but as a result San Martín left Latin America to live in France, and Bolívar continued with the liberation of Peru. The two decisive battles for Peruvian independence were fought at Junín on August 6, 1824 and at Ayacucho on December 9.

CONTINUED CONFLICTS

Unfortunately, independence didn't spell the end of warfare for Peru. A brief war broke out with Spain in 1866, which Peru won, and was followed shortly by a longer war with Chile (1879–83), which Chile won. The latter was over the nitrate-rich areas of the northern Atacama Desert and resulted in Chile annexing a large portion of coastal southern Peru. The area around Tacna was returned in 1929.

CONFLICT WITH ECUADOR

Peru went to war with Ecuador over a border dispute in 1941. A treaty drawn up in Rio de Janeiro in 1942 gave Peru jurisdiction over the northern sections of the Departments of Amazonas and Loreto, but Ecuador disputed this border, and deadly skirmishes occurred between the two countries every few years. Finally, in 1998, the border issue was resolved, with Peru granting Ecuador access to the Amazon and leaving a tiny area in Ecuador's control. Essentially, the 1942 border remains almost intact and the two countries are now at peace.

1780	1824
Inca Tupac Amaru II leads Indians against the Spanish colonialists in Cuzco but the uprising is quelled	The battles of Junín and Ayacucho lead to the birth of Peru as an independent state

ALÁN GARCÍA PÉREZ

He was tall, dark and handsome; cultured, charismatic and a gifted speaker. In 1985 Alan García, as he's better known, became Peru's youngest president ever and delighted the passionately proud populace with his weekly *balconazos*, oratory-filled appearances on the balcony of the Presidential Palace. He further pleased Peruvians by cutting taxes and freezing prices. For a while he was Peru's shining star, but the economy could not support García's largesse, and the currency was massively devalued. The last years of his presidency were grim – no more *balconazos*, hyperinflation, Sendero Luminoso (Shining Path) heightening its activities, and a national state of emergency with a nationwide 1am to 5am curfew.

By the end of García's five-year term, the country was in economic and political chaos. García went into exile after being accused of embezzling millions of dollars, and lived in luxurious apartments in Bogotá and Paris. Amazingly, after the statute of limitations had run out, he returned to Peru in 2002 to run for president again. And more amazingly still, the Peruvian population had forgotten the grim 1980s and almost voted the silver-tongued orator back into office. He was beaten, but only by a slim margin, by Alejandro Toledo who is the current president.

DICTATORSHIPS & REVOLUTIONARIES

During the 1960s and 1970s, the governing of Peru was marked by a series of military dictatorships and coups. Civilian rule began in 1980 with President Belaúnde Terry who was replaced in the 1985 elections by Alán García Pérez (see the boxed text).

The Maoist group Sandero Luminoso (Shining Path) waged a terrorist campaign against the central government from 1980 until the early 1990s, and the struggle led to between 40,000 and 60,000 deaths and disappearances. The group was linked to drug cartels and was active mainly in the central part of the country, but the effects were often felt in Lima. Another unrelated and smaller guerrilla group, the Movimiento Revolucionario Tupac Amaru (MRTA), also waged a war against the government, but this conflict was largely localized within the Department of San Martín.

> The world's worst soccer disaster occurred in Lima in 1964 when over 300 fans were killed in a riot following a disputed referee call.

FUJIMORI YEARS

The socioeconomic situation improved after the 1990 elections when Alberto Fujimori, a Japanese-Peruvian, defeated the novelist Mario Vargas Llosa, a right-winger who advocated 'shock treatment' for Peru's ailing economy. Fujimori capitalized on fears that such treatment would mean more poverty and increased unemployment, and he was seen as an alternative to the established parties and policies.

Fujimori's austere program of economic reform resulted in unprecedented rises in the cost of food and other essentials, but it also allowed a liberal reformation of import/export, tax and foreign-investment regulations, leading to international financial support. He favored gradual reforms, deregulation of state monopolies and a new currency pegged to the US dollar.

In 1992 Fujimori suspended the constitution and dissolved congress in an *auto-golpe* (coup from within). This perceived dictatorial, antidemocratic move led to a suspension of foreign aid, as well as outcry within Peruvian government circles. Nevertheless, Fujimori had the backing of the majority of the population and proceeded to catalyze the greatest economic and social improvements Peru had seen in decades.

1879–83	1971
Peru is at war with Chile; Peru loses and concedes a large area of southern coastal land to Chile	A 7.7 magnitude earthquake kills 70,000 people in northern Peru, destroying 90% of Huaraz and burying the town of Yungay

Fortunately for Fujimori, the leaders of both the Sendero Luminoso and the MRTA were captured in 1992, which helped keep his popular support intact following the *auto-golpe*. In 1993 a new constitution was approved. It changed the law stipulating that a president could not run for two successive terms, allowing Fujimori to run for re-election. Other changes included the approval of a new, 120-member unicameral congress (previously bicameral) and the institution of the death penalty for terrorists. In 1994 and 1995 more top-level leaders of the Sendero Luminoso were arrested and the group called for an end of hostilities. Meanwhile, inflation dropped to under 20%, the Peruvian currency stabilized and import taxes were restructured.

In 1995 Fujimori ran for a second term, easily beating opponent Javier Pérez de Cuellar, a former UN secretary general. The most memorable incident during Fujimori's second term was the seizure of a Japanese embassy reception in December 1996 by 14 MRTA members. Hundreds of prominent people were taken hostage; most were soon released, although 71 were held until April 1997 when Peruvian commandos stormed the embassy, killing the captors and releasing all of the hostages except one who died along with two soldiers. This action came under criticism as it was claimed that some of the MRTA members were repeatedly shot, despite attempts to surrender.

In 2000 Fujimori again ran for office, claiming that a third term was possible because his first term predated the 1993 constitutional change. He received 49.9% of the vote, just short of the 50% needed to win outright. His main challenger was Alejandro Toledo, a leftist Indian from the highlands who was trained as an economist but had little political experience. He received 40.2% of the vote but claimed that the elections had been fraudulent, with some departments casting more votes than there were voters. A run-off was scheduled for May 2000. Toledo refused to run, citing electoral fraud. The Organization of American States (OAS) sent a team of investigators, and the international community threatened sanctions against Peru unless the run-off was postponed, irregularities were corrected and the election was held in a democratic manner. Fujimori did not allow the run-off to be postponed and, despite having no opponent, allowed the apparently flawed electoral process to vote him in. The pressure from the OAS diminished as world leaders realized that they had nothing to gain and much to lose by imposing economic sanctions on the country.

Within days of Vladimir Montesinos fleeing the country, about 2700 so-called 'Vladivideos' were discovered, implicating key figures in money laundering and government corruption.

In October 2000, a video was released showing Vladimiro Montesinos, Fujimori's hawkish head of intelligence, bribing a Peruvian congressman, and Fujimori's 10-year presidency spiraled out of control. In early November, Fujimori ordered Montesinos' arrest, but the spymaster fled the country. Fujimori claimed he knew nothing about the money laundering and corruption that Montesinos presided over, and he continued his presidential duties, including a state trip to Asia. While there, the Peruvian government declared him to be morally unfit to govern, and on November 20, 2000 Fujimori sent his resignation, conveniently while visiting Japan. Normally, one of two vice presidents would have taken on the presidency, but both resigned following Fujimori's disgraceful exit. Instead, the opposition head of congress, Valentin Paniagua, was sworn in on November 22. Meanwhile, despite calls to return and face

1980–82	1985–90
The worst years of violence between the Sendero Luminoso and the Peruvian military lead to about 30,000 deaths	Alán García Pérez is elected president; his term is marked by hyperinflation and the resurgence of the Sendero Luminoso

the charges against him, Fujimori claimed his ancestral Japanese citizenship and stayed in Japan.

After several months of flight through Latin America, Montesinos was captured in Venezuela and extradited; he is now jailed in the same high-security prison that he himself designed to hold terrorist leaders.

21ST CENTURY

New elections held in April 2001 eventually resulted in victory for Alejandro Toledo. During the election he made much of his Indian heritage, in a country where the majority of the population is of Indian or mixed-Indian lineage. Toledo took over a country mired in political scandal. Since Fujimori's exit, the economy has been declining as the country struggles to come to terms with lack of strong leadership. Toledo's inexperience swiftly led his popularity ratings to plummet.

An international warrant for the arrest of ex-president Fujimori has been filed with Interpol, stepping up the country's efforts to extradite the former leader from Japan. The arrest warrant, issued by a supreme court judge and based on Fujimori's alleged involvement in two massacres undertaken by the paramilitary death squad La Colina, may convince Japanese authorities to return the exiled Fujimori for trial. At present, no extradition treaty exists between the two countries.

President Toledo, elected in 2001, is the first president of South American Indian descent of any Andean country.

Although Peru quickly joined the 'War on Terrorism' fold, it canceled a joint military exercise with the US in the Amazon basin, saying that foreign military forces were not welcome in Peru.

By 2003, although the currency remained strongly pegged to the US dollar, Peruvians were again facing increased unemployment, stagnant wages and a high cost of living. Toledo's popularity was at an all-time low and, for the first time in almost a decade, the country was plagued by strikes and demonstrations.

1990–2000	2000
Alberto Fujimori is elected president; he changes the constitution in 1993 to allow presidents to run for consecutive terms	Fujimori, disgraced by actions of his head of intelligence, resigns in exile in Japan

The Culture

THE NATIONAL PSYCHE

Peruvians are politically passionate, warm and hospitable, soccer-crazy, unshakably patriotic but highly critical of their political leaders, energetic, never short of a smile, curious, very talkative, entrepreneurial and hard-working. They work on the principles that it only takes a second to make a friend and that you can never have too many! The 40,000 to 60,000 deaths and disappearances during the Sendero Luminoso civil war years (late 1970s to 1982) have left an indelible mark of stoicism, especially on the highland population.

LIFESTYLE

Peru is essentially a bicultural society, with one part containing the mainly white and *mestizo* (people of mixed indigenous and Spanish descent) middle and upper classes, and the other containing mainly the poor Indian *campesinos* (peasants or country people), many of whom live in poverty. Conduct that is appropriate for one group may be not be accepted in the other.

Nonwhite people are sometimes discriminated against, especially in upmarket bars, nightclubs and discos in Lima; less so elsewhere. There is also discrimination against Peruvians in some hotels that prefer to cater to foreign travelers.

Peruvians are all essentially polite, indeed rather formal, in their interactions. Even a brief interchange, such as giving a taxi cab driver your destination, is invariably preceded by a *Buenos días*, which is returned. A handshake is normally given at the beginning and end of even a brief meeting; men may exchange a back-slapping hug known as an *abrazo*, and women may kiss one another on the cheek. Men may give women a decorous kiss on the cheek, except in business settings, where a handshake is appropriate. Indians, on the other hand, don't kiss and their handshakes, when offered, are a light touch rather than a firm grip.

The locals are used to less personal space than many travelers may be accustomed to. Conversations tend to take place face to face, streets and public transport are very crowded, and homes have little individual space.

If you ask someone if they would like to have a drink or a meal with you, you are expected to pay for it. Because of economic constraints, most Peruvians are unable to invite you to their homes or a restaurant for a meal on a casual basis. If you are invited, it is a semiformal occasion, so you should wear nice clothes and bring a small gift (flowers, chocolates, wine).

Many schools offer two sessions, morning and afternoon, in order to accommodate more students.

Noise is part of the Peruvian way of life and radios and TVs in hotel rooms are often turned on early in the morning and late at night.

SOME DOS & DON'TS

- Spitting and urinating in public (especially by the lower socioeconomic classes) is fairly common; however, belching or burping in public is considered the height of bad manners. Don't do it!

- When calling someone over to you, don't beckon by crooking your finger or hand – this is rude. Instead, use a flat, downward swipe of the hand. Body language using hand gestures and facial expressions is hard to describe but an important part of interpersonal communication. Watch to see how the locals do it.

- Litter is a fact of life; trash is often thrown thoughtlessly away. People don't take kindly to having this, or other, cultural differences being pointed out to them. A traveler's best option is to lead by example.

TREATMENT OF ANIMALS

Attitudes towards animals in Peru are fairly pragmatic – animals are used by human beings as needed. Animal-rights activists are generally perceived as lacking in cultural sensitivity and have made little headway with this cause. Bullfighting and cockfighting are accepted and popular sports. In rural areas, especially in southern Peru and Bolivia, animal sacrifice is practiced: llamas are considered auspicious sacrifices. Dogs are generally poorly treated, and vicious, ankle-nipping dogs can be a problem when hiking in the countryside. Do as the locals do: bend down quickly and pick up a rock to throw. Generally, just this action will drive the dogs off – you, hopefully, won't need to throw the rock at the dog.

POPULATION

About half of Peruvians inhabit the highlands – mostly rural Indians or *mestizos* who practice subsistence agriculture. There are few large cities in the highlands but many small towns and villages. The rural highlanders are called *campesinos*. Because of the very poor standard of living in the highlands, many *campesinos* have migrated to the coast, but problems associated with overpopulation in the cities means their lot rarely improves.

Although over half of Peru lies in the Amazon basin, colonization is slow and only 6% of the population lives there.

About 45% of Peru's population is Indian (*indígenas* is an appropriate term; *indios* is insulting). Most *indígenas* are Quechua-speaking and live in the highlands, although a significant number have migrated to the coast following the political unrest caused by terrorism. A few speak Aymara in the Lake Titicaca region, and small Amazon Indian groups speak a plethora of other languages. A further 37% of the population is *mestizo*, 15% is white and the remaining 3% is black, Asian or of other backgrounds. Many black Peruvians live around the southern coastal town of Chincha.

SPORT

Soccer (called *fútbol*) and bullfighting are the best attended of spectator sports. Basketball is also quite popular. Although tennis is not especially popular in Peru, the Peruvian tennis player Jaime Yzaga is one of the country's few athletes whose name might be recognized by non-Peruvians.

The soccer season is late March to November. There are many teams, though their abilities are not exceptional and Peru hasn't qualified to play in the World Cup since 1982. The best teams are from Lima, and the traditional *clásico* is the match between Alianza Lima and Universitario (La U).

The bloody sport of bullfighting is part of the national culture. The traditional season in Lima is October to early December and attracts internationally famous matadors; see Bullfighting (p80) for details. Outside of Lima, bullfights may occur at fiestas, but are rarely of an high standard.

RELIGION

Peru is predominantly Roman Catholic; over 90% of the population at least nominally professes that faith. The Indians, while outwardly Roman Catholic, tend to blend Catholicism with their traditional beliefs.

Although Roman Catholicism is the official religion, the constitution allows citizens to practice any religion they choose. Some churches of other faiths can be found, but these form a small minority.

In remote Andean hamlets, bullfighting still takes the form of tying a condor to the back of the bull – an expression of indigenous solidarity against the Spanish conquerors (as cattle arrived from Europe) – but this spectacle is rarely seen by outsiders.

Cuzco cathedral has a painting of *The Last Supper* featuring a guinea pig as the main course.

RECOMMENDED READING

■ *The Dancer Upstairs*, by Nicolas Shakespeare, is the novel upon which the recent film (see Recommended Viewing on p36) was based. Which is better? Decide for yourself.

■ *Bel Canto*, by Ann Patchett, is a readable novel loosely based on the events of 1996, when the Tupac Amaru guerillas infiltrated the Japanese ambassador's house during a party – and took hundreds of people hostage for four months.

■ *The Feast of the Goat: A Novel*, by Mario Vargas Llosa, is the most recent of his many novels. It's typical of the writer's style, with several timelines and loosely based on history; in this case the ruthless three decades of Rafael Trujillo's dictatorship of the Dominican Republic.

■ *The Bridge of San Luis Rey*, by Thornton Wilder, won the 1928 Pulitzer Prize for literature. It's the philosophical story of a monk who witnesses a rope bridge in rural Peru breaking and killing five people; he wonders who they were and why they died, and decides to learn all he can about them.

■ *Tambo: Life in an Andean Village*, by Julia Myerson, is a highly readable account of this artist who lived in a village for a year, recording a wealth of ethnographical detail about highland Indian culture and lifestyle.

ARTS
Literature

Peru's most famous novelist is the internationally recognized Mario Vargas Llosa (1936–), who ran for president in 1990. His novels often delve deeply into Peruvian society, politics and culture. His first novel, *The Time of the Hero*, was publicly burned because of its exposé of life in a Peruvian military academy. Another one to look out for is *Aunt Julia and the Scriptwriter*. Vargas Llosa's work is very complex, with multiple plots and changing time sequences or flashbacks. The website (www.kirjasto.sci.fi/vargas.htm) provides a biography and detailed bibliography of this writer's works.

> Peru's most famous novelist, Mario Vargas Llosa, ran for president in 1990 but lost against Alberto Fujimori.

Two Peruvian writers are particularly noted for their portrayals of the difficulties facing indigenous communities. José María Arguedas (1911–69) wrote *Deep Rivers* and *Yawar Fiesta*, among others. Ciro Alegría (1909–67) was the author of *The Golden Serpent*, which is about life in a jungle village on the Río Marañón, and *Broad and Alien is the World*, about repression among Andean Indians. Two other important Peruvian writers are Julio Ramón Ribeyro (1929–) and Alfredo Bryce Echenique (1939–).

A recent arrival on the literary scene is Sergio Bambarén (1960–), who was educated in the USA and lived in Australia before returning to Lima. His self-published *The Dolphin – Story of a Dreamer* became a best-seller. The *New Yorker* magazine's 2003 Début Fiction issue included *City of Clowns*, a short story by young Peruvian-American writer Daniel Alarcón. It is set in Lima and weaves together a plot involving Peruvian street clowns and a family. You can read it online on www.newyorker.com/fiction/content/?030616fi_fiction2.

> www.poets.org/poets/poets.cfm?prmID=31 has a biography and bibliography of Peru's greatest poet, César Vallejos.

Women writers can be read in *Fire From the Andes: Short Fiction by Women From Bolivia, Ecuador and Peru*.

Considered as Peru's greatest poet, César Vallejo (1892–1938) wrote *Trilce*, a book of 77 avant-garde poems touted by some critics as one of the best books of poetry ever written in Spanish. Anthologized modern Peruvian poetry is found in *Peru: The New Poetry* and *The Newest Peruvian Poetry in Translation*.

Music

Pre-Columbian Andean music was based on the pentatonic scale and used wind and percussion instruments. String instruments were introduced by the Spanish. Traditional Andean music is popularly called *música folklórica* and is frequently heard at fiestas.

The most representative wind instruments are *quenas* and *zampoñas*. The *quena* (or *kena*) is a bamboo flute of varying lengths, depending on the pitch desired. The *zampoña* is a set of panpipes with two rows of bamboo canes, seven in one and six in the other. *Zampoñas* range from tiny, high-pitched *chulis* to meter-long, bass *toyos*. Also seen are *ocarinas*, small oval clay instruments with up to 12 holes. Occasionally, animal horn or seashell horns are heard as well.

Percussion instruments include drums made from hollowed-out tree trunks and stretched goatskin. Rattles are made of polished goat hooves tied together.

Música folklórica groups use string instruments, the most typical being the *charango*, a tiny 10-stringed guitar with the box traditionally made of an armadillo shell, though most instruments are wooden nowadays. Perhaps the best-known example of Andean music is *El Cóndor Pasa*, adapted by Paul Simon.

More recent additions to the instruments used in the Andes include harps and a variety of brass instruments, which are seen in large outdoor bands strolling around on fiesta days, producing a cacophony of sound and surrounded by masked and elaborately costumed dancers.

On the coast, the different *música criolla* (*criollo* music) has its roots in Spain and Africa. The main instrumentation is guitars and a *cajón*, a wooden box on which the player sits and pounds out a rhythm with his hands. The *cajón* is attributed to black slaves working as produce-loaders in ports who used the fruit crates for entertainment. Afro-Peruvian music is enjoying a comeback, especially in the Chincha area on the south coast. Drawing on Hispanic and Andean influences, Afro-Peruvian music is unique and quite different from Caribbean or Brazilian styles.

> The most representative and popular of many forms of Andean music is *huayno* (traditional Andean music), which has its roots in pre-Columbian times.

RECOMMENDED LISTENING

- *Traditional Music of Peru* (4 vols; Smithsonian Folkways) is organized so that each volume focuses on a different area of Peru, ranging from Cuzco to the northern coast. The expansive liner notes make this a musically educational listen.

- *Huayno Music of Peru* (2 vols; Arhoolie Music) and *Huaynos and Huuylas: The Real Music of Peru* (GlobeStyle) are exceptional compilations of traditional *huaynos*.

- *The Blind Street Musicians of Cusco: Peruvian Harp and Mandolin* (Music of the World) is a compilation of traditional Andean music.

- *Afro-Peruvian Classics: The Soul of Black Peru* (LuakaBop) headlines the incomparable Susan Baca on this 14-track compilation on David Byrne's label. **The authors' pick!**

- *Susana Baca* (LuakaBop) is the self-titled album from one of the only Afro-Peruvian singers to have toured Europe and North America. It's a mix of black and *criollo* music.

- *Chicha* (Tumi), by Belem, is *chicha* music, a fusion of traditional *huayno* with an exciting overlay of salsa and *cumbia*. The band will get your feet going.

- *Music of the Incas* (Lyrichord), by Ayllu Sulca and band, highlights Sulca, a blind harpist known throughout Peru, accompanied by *quena* and mandolin. Despite the title, the tracks wander from traditional Andean to semicontemporary waltzes.

RECOMMENDED VIEWING

■ *The Dancer Upstairs*, based on the search for the leader of the Sendero Luminoso (Shining Path) guerrillas, is a cool, tense political thriller depicting an upstanding police investigator caught between terrorists and a corrupt government. Shot partly in Ecuador, and featuring dialogue in Quechua, the film is a fascinating if grim portrait of the Peruvian psychological landscape.

■ *Aguirre, Wrath of God*, a classic movie (in German with English subtitles) directed by Werner Herzog and starring Klaus Kinski, depicts conquistadors searching for Amazonian gold. The opening scenes, shot at Machu Picchu (but with no ruins visible), are memorable, as is the rest of the film during which conquistador Kinski slowly descends into madness.

■ *Fitzcarraldo* is another Herzog/Kinski classic about a mad rubber baron's attempt to drag a ship between two rivers to monopolize the rubber trade – and fund an opera house in Iquitos.

■ *Full Circle* (Vol 4 of 9), presented by Michael Palin of Monty Python fame, follows Palin as he travels around the Pacific. This episode (available from the BBC or PBS) covers his trip through Peru and shows the country and its people from an independent traveler's perspective.

Modern popular music includes rock, pop, blues, reggae, hip-hop and punk, all usually imported, though there are a few Peruvian rock bands. Chilean-style protest songs also enjoy limited popularity. Especially popular are forms of Latin American dance music, such as the omnipresent salsa, and *cumbia* and *chicha*, both from Colombia. Trance dancing to *techno-cumbia* is the latest rage.

The religious statues and paintings found inside colonial churches were often carved or painted by early Indian artists. This gave rise to the Escuela Cuzqueña art form, which combines Andean and Spanish ideas.

Architecture

The most famous example of Inca architecture is Machu Picchu, Peru's greatest attraction, though many other fine examples can be found in Peru. Also, many other pre-Columbian cultures have left magnificent examples of their architecture (see Visiting Archaeological Sites, p403, for more information).

Colonial architecture is well represented by the many imposing cathedrals, churches, monasteries and convents built during the 16th, 17th and 18th centuries. These are extremely ornate, both outside and inside. The altars are often gold-leafed.

Crafts

Andean crafts are based on pre-Columbian necessities, such as weaving (for clothes), pottery and metallurgy. Today, woven cloth is seen in the traditional ponchos, belts and other clothes worn by Andean Indians. More modern rugs and tapestries are popular souvenirs. The traditionally worked alpaca wool is in great demand for sweaters and other items. Pottery, very important and well developed by many pre-Columbian cultures in Peru, is produced today and often based on ancient designs, shapes and motifs. Jewelry, especially gold and silver pieces with a direct link back to ancient rituals and heritage, is also in demand. (See Shopping under the major cities if you'd like to make some purchases.)

Environment

THE LAND

At 1,285,215 sq km, Peru is the third-largest country in South America, about five times larger than the UK and five times smaller than Australia. It lies in the tropics south of the equator and is divided into three very different geographical regions: the Pacific coastal strip, the Andes mountains and the Amazonian lowlands.

The narrow coastal strip is mainly desert, merging at its southern end into the Atacama Desert, one of the driest places on earth. The coast includes Lima, the capital, and several major cities – oases watered by about 40 rivers that cascade from the Andes. These oases have been developed as agricultural centers where the creation of irrigation chanels over the centuries has utilized the fertile soil deposited as silt by the rivers. It's a strange sight to see green fields morph into sandy or rocky desert at the point where irrigation ends.

The Andes, the world's second-greatest mountain chain, reach over 6000m just 100km inland. Peru's highest peak, Huascarán (6768m), is the world's highest tropical peak and the sixth highest in the Americas. Tropical they may be, but the Andes have year-round glaciers above 5000m. Between 3000m and 4000m lie agricultural lands supporting half of Peru's population. The rugged landscape brims with jagged ranges separated by deep, vertiginous canyons, rewarding travelers with spectacular scenery.

The eastern Andean slopes receive much rainfall and are clothed in green cloud forests as they drop into the fabled Amazon basin. In this low-lying basin, roads are few, and travelers typically venture forth on river voyages – or fly.

The Andes don't stop at the Pacific coast; 100km offshore there is a trench as deep as the Andes are high.

WILDLIFE

With its great variety of ecosystems, resulting from variations in climate, elevation and soils in the tropics, Peru boasts a menagerie of wildlife that is unequalled anywhere else in the world. The only downside is that seeing all these animals takes time and effort. Many of them live in the rainforest, where you can be a scant 20m away from a jaguar and never know it is there. In the highlands, skittish flocks of vicuñas vanish over the horizon as soon as they catch sight of an intruder. What to do? Start with a heavy dose of patience, be prepared for dawn wake-up calls (when the animals are most

---

BOOKS ON NATURAL HISTORY

- *Tropical Nature*, by Adrian Forsyth and Ken Miyata, satisfyingly subtitled 'Life and Death in the Rain Forests of Central and South America', is an eminently readable and often humorous book that introduces the richness of rainforests to everyone.

- *A Parrot Without a Name*, by Don Stap, is the true story of a modern expedition into the remotest reaches of the Peruvian Amazon in search of previously unknown species.

- *A Neotropical Companion*, by John Kricher, provides an introduction to the wildlife and ecosystems of the New World tropics, including coastal and highland regions. It's drier than *Tropical Nature* but aimed at the lay reader.

- *Perú – The Ecotravellers' Wildlife Guide*, by David L Pearson and Les Beletsky, is one of a number of field guides, but it is one that covers the most important and frequently seen birds, mammals, amphibians, reptiles, insects and ecosystems.

active), travel in slow and quiet groups, carry binoculars and hire a local guide. Then you're ready for memorable sightings of tropical wildlife.

Animals

BIRDS

The best field guide for the highlands is *Birds of the High Andes* by Jon Fjeldså and Niels Krabbe. It's heavy and expensive but excellent. Many of the birds are found in the more portable *Field Guide to the Birds of Machu Picchu* by Barry Walker.

Peru has over 1700 bird species – twice as many as found in any one of the continents of North America, Europe or Australia. From the tiniest hummingbirds (see the boxed text) to the 10kg Andean condor with its 3m wing span, the variety is colorful and seemingly endless: a new species is discovered every few years. The best thing about watching birds is that you can do it anywhere – even in the center of Lima you'll see rufous-collared sparrows and Pacific doves, neither of which are found on other continents. If you travel down the coast to the Islas Ballestas (see p93) you'll spot thousands of cormorants and boobies, and a few flamingos and penguins thrown in for good measure. There are gulls as well; how can you visit the coast and not see gulls galore?

An incisive question is; how can you also see gulls galore without visiting the coast? Head into the highlands to see the Andean gull, commonly sighted around lakes and along rivers as high as 4600m. Just don't call it a seagull! Other highland birds include several species of ibis, with their distinctively down-curved bills; the strangely named cinclodes, found only in Andean countries; torrent ducks with a taste for highland whitewater; and a gaggle of Andean geese, Andean flickers, Andean condors, Andean siskins and Andean swallows – you get the picture.

Swoop down towards the Amazon and you'll sight the iconic tropical birds – parrots, macaws, toucans and more. But it's hard to see them for all the trees. The best idea is to take a quiet river trip. This way you can see Amazonian umbrellabirds and toucans gliding across the river, and parrots perched in the river-side trees. Many lodges know a local salt lick where, soon after dawn, flocks of macaws and parakeets come to feed on the mineral-laden clay.

Sloths slowly descend from their trees once a week to defecate on the ground. Scientists don't know why.

MAMMALS

The Amazon is also home to many exciting mammals. Over 20 species of monkeys are found here, many of which are commonly seen, as are sloths and bats. With a guide, you may also see piglike peccaries, three species of anteaters, ambling armadillos, curious coatis and perhaps giant river otters, capybara, river dolphins, tapirs or one of six elusive cats, including the jaguar. The cloud forests rimming the Amazon are home to the endangered spectacled bear, South America's only bear.

HUMMINGBIRDS

For many visitors to Peru, the diminutive hummingbirds are the most delightful birds to observe. About 120 species have been recorded in Peru, and their exquisite beauty is matched by their extravagant names, such as 'green-tailed goldenthroat,' 'spangled coquette,' 'fawn-breasted brilliant' and 'amethyst-throated sunangel.'

Hummingbirds are capable of beating their wings in a figure-eight pattern up to 80 times a second, thus producing the typical hum for which they are named. This exceptionally rapid wing-beat enables them to hover in place when feeding on nectar, or even to fly backward. These tiny birds must feed frequently to gain the energy needed to keep them flying. Species such as the Andean hillstar, living in the *puna* (Andean grassland of the altiplano), have evolved an amazing strategy to survive a cold night. They go into a state of torpor, which is like a nightly hibernation, by lowering their body temperature by about 25°C, thus lowering their metabolism drastically.

LEAF-CUTTER ANTS

One of hundreds of ant species in the Amazon rainforests, leaf-cutter ants live in colonies numbering in the hundreds of thousands. Their homes are huge nests dug deep into the ground. Foraging ants search the vegetation for particular types of leaves, cut out small sections and, holding the leaf segments above their heads like a small umbrella, bring them back to the nest. Travelers frequently come across a long line of them in the jungle, scurrying along carrying leaf sections back to the nest, or returning for another load.

Workers within the nest sort out the leaves that will easily decompose into a type of compost; unsuitable material is ejected from the nest. The composted leaves form a mulch, on which a fungus grows. The ants tend these fungal gardens, for they provide the colony's main diet.

Army ants and other species prey upon this ready and constant supply of foragers. To combat this, leaf-cutter ants are morphologically separated by size and jaw structure into different castes. Some specialize in tending the fungal gardens, others have jaws designed for cutting leaf segments, and yet others are soldier ants armed with huge mandibles, which accompany the foragers and protect them from attackers. Close observation reveals yet another caste – a microscopic ant that rides along on the leaf segments without disturbing the foragers. The riders' function is unclear, but biologists suggest that they act as protection against parasitizing wasps that try to lay eggs on the foragers while they are carrying leaves.

Andean mammals include the domestic llamas and alpacas, and guanacos and vicuñas, their wild relatives. On highland talus slopes, watch out for the vizcacha, which looks like a cross between a rabbit and giant squirrel. Foxes and deer are also highland dwellers, as is the puma (mountain lion). On the coast, huge numbers of sea lions are easily seen on the Islas Ballestas.

Other creatures, especially found in the Amazon, include frogs, reptiles, fish and insects galore. The electric blue morpho butterfly is unmistakable as it flaps along jungle rivers, and tiny but brightly colored poison-dart frogs, once used by Indians to poison the points of their blow-pipe darts, can be found with a careful search. Snakes? Don't worry. Many species live here, but they mostly avoid humans.

Plants

In Peru's highlands, you'll find the distictive *puna*, which is made up of shrublands and grasslands that act as a natural 'sponge' to the Andes. These areas have a fairly limited flora of hard grasses, cushion plants, small herbaceous plants, shrubs and dwarf trees. Many plants in this environment have developed small, thick leaves that are less susceptible to frost, and curved leaves to reflect extreme radiation. In the north of the country there is some *páramo*, which has a harsh climate, is less grassy and the soil more peaty.

As the eastern Andean slopes descend into the western Amazon uplands, the scenery becomes more rugged and remote. Here are the little-known tropical cloud forests, so named because they trap (and help create) clouds that drench the forest in a fine mist, allowing some delicate forms of plant life to survive. Cloud forest trees are adapted to steep slopes, rocky soils and a harsh climate. They are characterized by low, gnarled growth, dense small-leafed canopies and moss-covered branches supporting a host of plants such as orchids, ferns and bromeliads. These aerial plants, which gather their moisture and some nutrients without ground roots, are collectively termed epiphytes.

The dense vegetation at all levels of the cloud forest gives it a mysterious and delicate fairy-tale appearance. It is also important as a source of freshwater and for controlling erosion.

Capybaras are the world's largest rodent and can weigh over 60kg. That's a big rat!

Below the cloud forest is the Amazon rainforest, with its untold wealth of flora and fauna. A short walk into this tropical forest will reveal that it is very different from the temperate forests that many North Americans and Europeans may be used to. Tropical forests have great variety. If you stand in one spot and look around, you see scores of different species of trees, but you often have to walk several hundred meters to find another example of any particular species.

One thing that often astounds visitors is the sheer immensity of some trees. A good example is the ceiba tree (also called the kapok), which has huge flattened supports, or buttresses, around its base and may easily reach five or more meters across. The smooth gray trunk often grows straight up for 50m before the branches are reached. These spread out into a huge crown with a slightly flattened appearance. The shape is distinctive, and the tree is often the last to be logged in a ranching area. When you see a huge, buttressed, and flattened looking tree in a pasture in the Amazon lowlands, it very often is a ceiba.

> Don't pee in jungle rivers. A tiny barbed fish, the *candirú*, swims upstream and can become lodged in your urethra.

Some rainforest trees are supported by strange roots that look like props or stilts. These trees are most frequently found where periodic floods occur – the stilt roots are thought to play a role in keeping the tree upright during the inundation. Rainforest palms are among the trees that have these kinds of roots.

In areas that have been cleared (often naturally, by a flash flood or when a gap is created by an ancient forest giant falling during a storm) various fast-growing pioneer species appear. These may grow several meters a year in areas where abundant sunlight is suddenly available. Some of the most common and easily recognized of these are the genus *Cecropia*, often found on riverbanks. Their gray trunks are often circled by ridges at intervals of a few centimeters, but they are otherwise fairly smooth, and their branches form a canopy at the top of the trunk. The leaves are very large and palmate (like a human hand), with the underside a much lighter green than the top – particularly noticeable when winds make the leaves display alternately light and dark green shades in a chaotic manner.

In stark contrast, the coastal desert is generally barren of vegetation, apart from around water sources. Otherwise, the only forests you'll occasionally glimpse will be those made up of cacti.

NATIONAL PARKS

> Some 30,000 vascular plants have been identified in Peru with over 20,000 of these found in the Amazon basin.

Peru's national parks are administered by Inrena (Instituto Nacional de Recursos Nacionales), a division of the Ministry of Agriculture. In 2003, an impressive 12.7% of the country contained 56 protected areas, including 10 national parks, as well as many reserves, sanctuaries and other areas.

Most protected areas lack tourist infrastructure. Often there is only a park rangers' building with outdated maps at the end of an unpaved road. As such, the amount of protection these parks experience is limited, as outlined following.

ENVIRONMENTAL ISSUES

> Two websites to check out: **Allpa Runa** (www.unii.net/allpa runa/) promotes grass-roots environmental activism with many links, mainly in Spanish.

Major economic activities, which include farming, grazing and logging, cause serious environmental problems in Peru. Deforestation of the highlands for firewood, of the rainforests for valuable hardwoods, and of both to clear land for agricultural use has led to severe erosion.

The problem of rainforest deforestation has caught the attention of the environmentally aware (though fixing the problem remains problematic), but deforestation and overgrazing in the highlands, where many people live, is also a severe problem. The soil needs its protective cover of Andean woodlands and *puna* grasslands. With the ongoing removal of its protective cover, the soil's quality, never good to begin with, is rapidly deteriorating as soil gets blown off the mountains or washed down the rivers. This also leads to decreased water quality, particularly in the Amazon basin, where silt-laden water is unable to support the microorganisms at the base of the food chain.

Other water-related problems include pollution from mine tailings in the highlands and from industrial waste and sewage along the coast. Because of sewage contamination, many beaches around Lima and other coastal cities have been declared unfit for swimming. Coastal pollution, combined with overfishing, is a serious threat to Peru's rich marine resources.

Protected areas lack the fundamental infrastructure needed to conserve them and are subject to illegal hunting, fishing, logging and mining. The government simply doesn't have the money to hire enough rangers and buy necessary equipment to patrol the parks. Nevertheless, the parks do receive some measure of protection, and various international agencies contribute money and resources to help with conservation and local education projects.

**Eco Travels
in Peru** (www
.planeta.com/peru.html)
offers travel information
as well as plenty of environmental information.

Food & Drink

Peruvian cuisine is exceptionally good and surprisingly unknown. Food lovers visiting for the first time are in for a wonderful surprise, and will be thrilled by scrumptious seafood dishes, exciting soups, interesting potato presentations, spicy stuffed peppers, and meats prepared in dozens of innovative ways. Food tends towards the spicy, but chili condiments *(aji)* are often served separately so that diners aren't forced to eat food hotter than they want. At all levels of society, food preparation is done with care, and eating is to be savored, not hurried over. Typical Peruvian cuisine consists mainly of variously prepared meat, chicken or fish served with rice. Potatoes still have a lower-class association with the Andean Indians, but the arrival of the french fry has somewhat alleviated that.

Potatoes originated in Peru.

STAPLES & SPECIALITIES

Peru's most popular dish is ceviche. Originally from the coast, it's made with fresh fish, shrimp or other seafood marinated in lemon juice and chili peppers, and served with corn on the cob or boiled yucca, and perhaps garnished with seaweed – it will win you over. To ensure freshness, this is usually a lunch dish made from the morning's catch.

Throughout Peru, a favored beef dish is *lomo saltado*, grilled strips of beef mixed with fried onions, tomatoes, french fries and a dash of chili (of course), served with white rice. Also popular nationwide, but especially in the highlands, is *sopa a la criolla*, a hearty, mildly spiced noodle soup with beef, milk and peppers that is often topped with a fried egg perched on a toast raft. Soups are popular in the highlands and, in Andean villages, are often served for breakfast, providing a warm start to a cold day.

Most Peruvians' breakfasts, though, consist of white bread rolls with butter and jam, and a hot beverage. American breakfasts, with eggs and ham, are available in restaurants. After a light breakfast, lunch is the main meal of the day. Most lunches include soup, a main course and dessert.

Criollo food is spicy Peruvian fare with Spanish and African influences.

In the highlands, potato lovers can try *papa a la Huancaina* (see the boxed text on p233), a boiled potato topped with a creamy sauce of cheese, oil, chili, lemon and egg yolk. It's eaten as a cold appetizer served with olives and a slice of boiled egg; despite the chili, it is mild. In Lima, cold mashed potatoes are blended with onions and peppers and then mixed with a chicken, tuna or crabmeat salad and served as a *causa* – delicious. Another cold boiled potato salad is *ocopa*, from Arequipa, served with a mildly spicy peanut-flavored sauce and a slice of fried cheese.

Fried cheese? Yes, Peruvian food can be on the fatty side. A national favorite is *chicharrones*, which are deep-fried chunks of pork or pork skins. It's not heart-healthy, but it is tasty. Also a favorite is *lechón* (suckling pig).

BOOKS ON PERUVIAN CUISINE

■ *Peruvian Dishes: Platos Peruanos*, compiled by Brenuil, is a recipe book available in Peru; the New York office of South American Explorers has copies or order through its website (www.saexplorers.org).

■ *The Guinea Pig – Healing, Food, and Ritual in the Andes*, by Edmundo Morales, looks at the guinea pig, once eaten by Inca royalty. Today guinea pig is eaten for important occasions in the Andes, and shamans inspect the entrails in efforts to diagnose disease in humans.

Chicken is served everywhere. The single most ubiquitous kind of restaurant is a *pollería*, with a big rotating grill churning out chickens for the masses. Order a quarter chicken for yourself or a whole chicken for the family. Peru's most unique chicken dish, though, is *aji de gallina*, shredded chicken cooked with a delightful sauce of milk, onions, chilis, garlic and cheese, served on rice.

DRINKS

The usual brands of soft drinks are available, but try the sweet, golden-colored, bubble-gum flavored Inka Kola at least once. Many fruit juices are available, with papaya being particularly popular. *Chicha morada* is a sweet, bland noncarbonated drink made from purple corn. Both carbonated and noncarbonated bottled water is available in restaurants and corner shops everywhere. Don't drink tap water – it will make you sick.

The quality of coffee is inconsistent. Some places just give you hot water and a jar of instant. Others serve a liquid concentrate that is diluted with hot milk or water; it looks like soy sauce, so check before pouring it into your milk (or over your rice!) Cafés serving good espressos and cappuccinos are popping up where tourists and in-the-know locals gather. Tea is served black with lemon and sugar; many varieties of *matés* (herb teas) are available. The iconic highland drink is *maté de coca*, a coca-leaf tea served upon arrival at many highland hotels. It's supposed to help with acclimatization, won't get you 'high' and is completely legal in Peru. Hot chocolate is also popular.

Beer is quite palatable and inexpensive. The best-known brands are Pilsen, Crystal and Cuzqueña, all of which are light lagers. The similar Arequipeña and Trujillana are served in and around those cities. For something different, drink a *malta* or *cerveza negra*, a sweet, dark beer. Microbrews haven't made their way to Peru yet, except for home-made *chicha*. This mild corn beer dates back to pre-Columbian times; it's brewed in huge urns in highland villages and sold in large glasses at Indian markets but not in restaurants. The fermentation process begins with chewing the corn, which puts some visitors off. It tastes sour and is hygienically questionable.

Local wines are quite good, though they come a distinct third after Chilean and Argentine wines, which are imported. The best local labels are Tacama, Ocucaje and Vista Alegre.

The national cocktail, pisco sour, is made from pisco, a locally produced white-grape brandy, blended with lemon juice, ice, egg white, syrup or sugar, and topped with bitters. Salud! See p99 for details on *bodegas* (wineries) that make pisco. Sugar-cane rum is also a local product and a *cuba libre* (rum and coke) is a popular choice. With the exception of pisco and rum, though, locally produced liquors are poor.

WE DARE YOU!

cuy chactado – grilled guinea pig

roccoto relleno – spicy bell pepper stuffed with ground meat; very hot!

cau cau – tripe and potato stew

anticuchos de corazon – shish kebabs of grilled beef hearts

ceviche erótico – mixed ceviche with squid, mussels, oysters, clams and other shellfish; considered an aphrodisiac!

chirimoya – a reptilian-looking custard apple with a sweet interior that looks like frog spawn; tastes better than it looks

The gold-colored Inka Kola is Peru's top-selling soft drink, rivaling the ubiquitous Coca-Cola.

TYPES OF RESTAURANTS

■ *café* – a catch-all phrase; a café may be limited to coffee and desserts, or serve full meals

■ *cevichería (cebichería)* – serves ceviche, of course, but often a variety of seafood also

■ *chifa* – Chinese restaurant, often with some Peruvian dishes

■ *heladería* – ice-cream restaurant; sometimes serves fast food (hamburgers, sandwiches)

■ *marisquería* – seafood restaurant

■ *panadería* – bakery; sells cakes and pastries as well as bread

■ *parrillada* – serves mixed grills

■ *picantería* – a local restaurant serving local food

■ *pollería* – restaurant serving grilled chicken with chips and nothing else

■ *restaurante tipico/turístico* – often designed to showcase regional cuisine to visitors; used by locals as well

WHERE TO EAT & DRINK

Except for in the major travelers' haunts, getting an early breakfast *(desayuno)* can be problematical because restaurants don't open until 8am or later in many towns. If you need to eat earlier, look for the town's best hotels – often they'll be open earlier and will serve breakfasts to nonguests. Otherwise think ahead and buy some bread and cheese the day before.

The Peruvian habit of having lunch as the major meal goes back to ancient times, when Andean Indians found that altitude slowed digestion and so a large lunch and small supper simply felt better.

Be sure of what you're asking for when requesting a menu. Many restaurants serve a *menú*, which is the set meal of the day for lunch *(almuerzo)*. (If you want to look at a menu, ask for *la carta*.) The *menú* consists of a soup, second course and a small dessert, and is designed to get workers and students through lunch quickly and cheaply – the traditional Peruvian equivalent of fast food! It's not always advertised – many restaurants assume that travelers want to eat a la carte. The *menú* is usually a good-value, nutritious option, but it is less available at weekends (when workers and students are at home).

Dinner *(cena)* is eaten late, and restaurants, which may be dead at 7:30pm, come alive at 9pm. In fact, after serving a hearty lunch, many restaurants close in the afternoon. In tiny remote towns, though, everything may be closed by 9pm.

See Eat Your Words (p45) for useful phrases.

VEGETARIANS & VEGANS

Vegetarianism isn't big in Peru, though a few of the main cities and tourist towns now have vegetarian restaurants. Often these places serve popular national meat dishes such as *lomo saltado* made with a soy substitute, so you taste the flavors of Peruvian cuisine without the meat. They also work on some innovative vegetable creations of their own – each place is different. Where they exist, we mention vegetarian restaurants in this book.

Be wary of salads as they might have been washed in contaminated water. Avoid eating watermelon. See p430 of the Health chapter for more details.

If there are no vegetarian restaurants, or you are going out with non-vegetarian friends, there are several good possibilities. *Palta a la jardinera* is a popular appetizer – half an avocado stuffed with a (cooked) vegetable salad. (Make sure it's not *palta a la reyna* – that's a salad with chicken.) *Sopa de verduras* (vegetable soup) is often on the menu as is *tacu tacu* (beans and rice mixed together). The potato dishes mentioned on p46 are also typical Peruvian options. Most towns have *chifas* (Chinese restaurants)

Local man in a wool hat, **Isla Amantaní** (p158)

MARK DAFFEY

ERIC WHEATER

Aymara girls in **Chucuito** (p160), near
Lake Titicaca

Indigenous women in traditional dress, **Pisac** (p196)

GRANT DIXON

Macaws, **Río Tambopata** (p366)

Night courtship for two ocelots, **Amazon basin** (p354)

Brilliant copper-colored orchid, **Amazon basin** (p354)

Green iguana, **Amazon basin** (p354)

where rice or noodle dishes with vegetables are available. Otherwise many restaurants will cook something that isn't on the menu if asked – as long as it isn't too complicated. And, of course, vegetarian pizza, spaghetti and omelets are often available.

Meat usually refers to beef or pork in Peru. Chicken and fish are in a separate class and aren't necessarily considered meat. (It's a linguistic thing.) So vegetarians should ask not only for dishes that contain no meat but also for dishes that don't have chicken or fish.

Vegans may have a harder time of it, because many dishes are cooked with eggs, cheese or milk. Self-catering is an option; markets have great selections of fruits and vegetables.

Alpaca meat tastes like beef but has only half the fat.

WHINING & DINING

Your children may shun seafood ('Squid? Yuk!'), cry off *cuy* and decline discovering new food, but that's no problem. Every town has *pollerías* serving grilled chicken with fries, and most places have Italian restaurants with pizza, or simple restaurants serving hamburgers, cheese sandwiches, scrambled eggs and other recognizable kid-friendly cuisine. Bananas are available everywhere. One thing that is hard to get is peanut butter, so consider bringing a jar.

HABITS & CUSTOMS

Eating in Peruvian restaurants is similar to eating in Miami, Manchester or Melbourne. The only real differences are that nonsmoking sections are rarely found, toilets may lack toilet paper and a free glass of icewater is not provided. It is acceptable to drag a meal out with a leisurely coffee or cocktail, European-style, so don't expect to get moved along for the next diners as in the USA. See Some Do's & Don'ts (p32) for more pointers.

EAT YOUR WORDS

The following is a list of foods, drinks and other useful culinary words and phrases, with their English translations and pronunciations. These should make a good start to your comprehension of Peruvian menus. For pronunciation guidelines see p434 of the Language chapter; for the types of restaurants in Peru, see the boxed text.

Useful Phrases

I would like ...
   Quisiera ...   kee·*sye*·ra ...
I would like the set lunch, please.
   Quisiera el menú por favor.   kee·*sye*·ra el me·*noo* por fa·*vor*
I'm a vegetarian.
   Soy vegetariano/a.   soy ve·he·ta·*rya*·no/a
The menu/bill, please.
   La carta/cuenta, por favor.   la *kar*·ta/*kwen*·ta por fa·*vor*
Is service included in the bill?
   ¿El servicio está incluido en la cuenta?   el ser·*vee*·syo es·*ta* een·*klwee*·do en la *kwen*·ta
Thank you, that was delicious.
   Muchas gracias, estaba buenísimo.   *moo*·chas *gra*·syas es·*ta*·ba bwe·*nee*·see·mo

Basics

breakfast	*desayuno*	de·sa·*yoo*·no
lunch	*almuerzo*	al·*mwer*·so
dinner	*cena*	*se*·na
(cheap) restaurant	*restaurante (barato)*	re·stow·*ran*·te (ba·*ra*·to)

Menu Decoder

aji (a·*hee*) – chili condiments
anticucho (an·tee·*koo*·cho) – shish kebab
cabro, cabrito (*ka*·bro, ka·*bree*·to) – goat
calamares (ka·la·*ma*·res) – squid
camarones (ka·ma·*ro*·nes) – shrimp
cangrejo (kan·*gre*·kho) – crab
carne (*kar*·ne) – meat
cecina (se·*see*·na) – jungle dish of dehydrated pork
cerdo, chancho (*ser*·do, *chan*·cho) – pork
ceviche (se·*vee*·che) – raw seafood marinated in lemon juice
chaufa, chaulafan (*chow*·fa, chow·la·*fan*) – fried rice (Chinese style)
chicharrones (chee·cha·*ro*·nes) – fried chunks of pork or pork skin
choclo (*cho*·klo) – corn on the cob
cordero (kor·*de*·ro) – mutton
cuy (kwee) – guinea pig
empanadas (em·pa·*na*·das) – meat and/or cheese pastries
ensalada (en·sa·*la*·da) – salad
estofado (es·to·*fa*·do) – stew
farína (fa·*ree*·na) – museli-like yucca concoction eaten fried or in lemonade
huevos fritos/revueltos (*we*·vos *free*·tos/re·*vwel*·tos) – fried/scrambled eggs
juane (*khwa*·ne) – jungle dish of steamed rice with fish or chicken, wrapped in a banana leaf
langosta (lan·*gos*·ta) – lobster
lechón (le·*chon*) – suckling pig
locro (*lo*·kro) – meat and vegetable stew
lomo (*lo*·mo) – beef
lomo saltado (*lo*·mo sal·*ta*·do) – grilled strips of beef mixed with fried onions, tomatoes, french fries and a dash of chili (of course); served with white rice
mariscos (ma·*rees*·kos) – seafood
maté (ma·*teh*) – herbal tea
(el) menú (el me·*noo*) – set menu, usually for lunch
ocopa (o·*ko*·pa) – cold boiled potato salad
pachamanca (pa·cha·*man*·ka) – a meat and potato feast cooked in an 'oven' of rocks built impromptu in the countryside
papa a la Huancaina (*pa*·pa a la hwan·*kay*·na) – boiled potato topped with a creamy sauce of fresh cheese, oil, chili, lemon and egg yolk
papas fritas (*pa*·pas *free*·tas) – french fries
parrillada (pa·ree·*ya*·da) – grilled meats
pescado (pes·*ka*·do) – fish
pollo, gallina (*po*·lyo, ga·*lee*·na) – chicken
postre (*pos*·tre) – dessert
quinua (kee·*noo*·a) – a highly nutritious, protein-rich grain of the high Andes
sopa, chupe (*so*·pa, *choo*·pe) – soup
sopa a la criolla (*so*·pa a la cree·*ol*·la) – a hearty, mildly spiced noodle soup with beef, milk and peppers, often topped with a fried egg perched on a toast raft
sudado (soo·*da*·do) – fish (or seafood) soup or stew
tallarines (ta·ya·*ree*·nes) – noodles
tamal (ta·*mal*) – corn dough stuffed with meat, beans, chilies or nothing at all
tortilla (tor·*tee*·ya) – omelet
trucha (*troo*·cha) – trout

Be aware that when you ask for the menu in Peru, you will get the set meal (the *menú*). Ask for *la carta*.

Sesos (cow brains) are a speciality of Cajamarca.

English-Spanish Food Glossary

avocado	palta	pal·ta
beer	cerveza	ser·ve·sa
blackberry	mora	mo·ra
bread	pan	pan
butter	mantequilla	man·te·kee·ya
cake	torta	tor·ta
cheese	queso	ke·so
fruit	frutas	froo·tas
grapefruit	toronja	to·ron·kha
ham	jamón	kha·mon
ice cream	helado	e·la·do
juice	jugo	hoo·go
liquor (strong)	aguardiente, pisco	a·gwar·dyen·te, pees·ko
milk	leche	le·che
orange	naranja	na·ran·kha
passionfruit	maracuya	ma·ra·koo·ya
pineapple	piña	pee·nya
plantain	plátano	pla·ta·no
rice	arroz	a·ros
sugar	azúcar	a·soo·kar
vegetables	verduras	ver·doo·ras
water (carbonated/ noncarbonated)	agua con/sin gas	a·gwa kon/seen gas
water (drinking)	agua potable	a·gwa po·ta·ble
water (mineral)	agua mineral	a·gwa mee·ne·ral
watermelon	sandía	san·dee·a

Lima

CONTENTS

A bustling, fast-moving modern metropolis, Lima is sprawled untidily on the edge of the coastal desert. The capital incredibly now houses almost a third of Peru's 27 million inhabitants, and it's inevitable that the ensuing problems of overpopulation have earned Lima a hardened reputation as a polluted, frenetic and dangerous city hemmed in by impoverished shantytowns.

But don't let such one-sided caricatures put you off. Lima is an ever-evolving city filled with fascinating contrasts and nuances that in no time can transport you from the waning splendor of its colonial architecture to pre-Inca pyramids and ultra-modern shopping malls. In the midst of these, you'll find many of the country's best museums, historic churches and stately mansions.

Lima's climate also echoes its contrasting faces: From April to December, a melancholy *garúa* (coastal fog) blankets the city's skyline, but during the coastal summer the sun breaks through and the high-spirited Limeños make a break for the nearby beaches. Indeed, coastal Lima was once a cluster of laid-back seafront resorts. Although swallowed by the burgeoning city, these resorts have retained their tranquil, flower-scented streets and cliff-top parks, mellowed by the sea breeze. These cosmopolitan areas are brimful with culture and fine dining, not to mention a plentiful nightlife in which to mingle with the hot-blooded and hospitable Limeños.

HIGHLIGHTS

■ **Dining**
Sampling the world-class cuisine scene at Miraflores (p75)

■ **History**
Viewing Peru's rich heritage at the Museo de la Nación in San Borja (p57)

■ **Nightlife**
Losing yourself in a bar-crawl in Barranco (p78)

■ **Archaeology**
Walking around the palaces and pyramids of arid Pachacamac (p85)

■ **Activities**
Paragliding from the cliffs at Miraflores (p65)

■ **Colonial Architecture**
Checking out Iglesia de San Francisco and its fascinating catacombs in Central Lima (p60)

★ Central Lima

★ San Borja

Miraflores ★

★ Barranco

★ Pachacamac

LIMA

HISTORY

Lima was first dubbed the City of Kings when it was founded by Francisco Pizarro in 1535, on the Catholic feast day of Epiphany, or the Day of the Kings. A university opened in 1551, and Lima became the Americas' seat of the Spanish Inquisition in 1569. The city grew quickly and was the continent's richest and most important town during early colonial times, though this all changed in 1746, when a disastrous earthquake wiped out most of the city. However, rebuilding was rapid, and most of the old colonial buildings still to be seen here date from after the earthquake. Following the wars of independence from Spain in the 1820s, other cities were crowned as capitals of the newly independent states, and Lima's importance as a colonial center faded.

For almost 400 years of its history, Lima was a relatively small city. However,

an unprecedented population explosion began in the 1920s with an overwhelming influx of rural poor from throughout Peru, especially the highlands. The urban population of 173,000 in 1919 more than tripled in the next 20 years, and since 1940, there has been a further 13-fold increase. The vast numbers of migrants spawned *pueblos jovenes*, or 'young towns' that surround the capital, many of which still lack electricity, water and adequate sanitation. Jobs are scarce, though entrepreneurial energy is strong; many work as *ambulantes*, or street vendors, selling anything from chocolates to clothespins in the frenetic streets.

ORIENTATION

Lima is a big city to come to terms with, with no less than 50 districts. **Central Lima** (Map p58-9) is where the most interesting colonial buildings are, especially around the Plaza de Armas, Plaza San Martín and Parque de la Cultura. Further south, after passing through the districts of Breña, Santa Beatriz and Jesús María is the fashionably elegant business district of **San Isidro** (Map p53). Below this, removed from the relentless barrage of traffic in central Lima, is the modern suburb of **Miraflores** (Map p66-7), situated on the cliffs overlooking the ocean, and several beaches. Miraflores is packed with excellent hotels, restaurants, shops and clubs, and consequently it is where most travelers now stay.

The main bus route joining downtown with San Isidro and Miraflores is along the congested Tacna, Garcilaso de la Vega and Arequipa, though taxis prefer to take the limited access freeway Vía Expresa, also called the Paseo de la República, which is sunken below ground level and as such, is nicknamed *el zanjón* (the ditch).

Further south of Miraflores is the small cliff-top community of **Barranco** (Map p68). An artists' and poets' colony with up-and-coming accommodations and the liveliest nightlife in town, Barranco also boasts attractive 19th- and early 20th-century architecture around El Puente de los Suspiros (Bridge of Sighs).

Many of Lima's excellent museums are scattered through other suburbs, including **Pueblo Libre** (Map p52) to the west of San Isidro, and San Borja and **Monterrico** (Map p53) to the east of the city centre.

LIMA IN...

Two or three days

Begin your first day with a walking tour around the colonial heart of Lima. Visit the centuries-old catacombs and church of San Francisco, then head down to explore the Plaza de Armas and its stately cathedral and mansions. Continue on through Jirón de la Union to Plaza San Martin, where you can finish your day with a celebratory cocktail in Gran Hotel Bolivar's atmospheric old bar.

On the second day, devote several hours to getting a grip on Peru's multi-layered heritage in the enormous Museo de la Nación then take a peek at the erotic ceramics collection at Museo Larco in the afternoon.

For your third day, take a trip to the arid desert temples at Pachacamac, and if you still have time, barter it away buying handicrafts in Miraflores' huge Mercado del Indios.

Choice lunch options in the center include Barrio Chino (China Town) or the unique L'Eau Vive restaurant, run by nuns. In the evening, take your pick of the top-notch seafood restaurants in Miraflores, then retire to one of the suburb's many street-side cafes or bars for a nightcap. Alternatively, if you're game, head on over to Barranco to sample Lima's nightlife at its busiest, or to San Isidro for its most sophisticated.

The international and domestic airport is in **Callao** (Map p52) – about 12km west of downtown or 16km northwest of Miraflores – but there is no expressway connecting the airport with the rest of the city. Callao also features Lima's port, naval base and an old colonial fort.

Street Names
The Spanish built downtown Lima in the colonial style, with streets in a checkerboard pattern surrounding the central Plaza de Armas. Though street numbers are easy to follow, jumping to the next 100 for each block (ie the '5th block' will be numbered 500 up to 599), street names can be confusing to visitors. Both old and new names are in use; for example Garcilaso de la Vega is often called Avenida Wilson. In addition, some streets have a different name for each block, and these are linked into a *jirón*, such as the lively pedestrianized Jirón de la Unión, which leads southwest from the Plaza de Armas to the Plaza San Martín.

Maps
You are strongly advised to buy a street map of the city to explore outside the principal areas; maps are sold in bookstores or by street vendors around the Plaza San Martín and in Miraflores' central park.

The **South American Explorers' clubhouse** (SAE; Map pp66-7; ☎ 445-3306, Calle Piura 135, Miraflores) has trail maps of Peru's main hiking areas, road maps of Peru and detailed street and bus maps of Lima. If you can't find the maps you want there, the staff will know where you can get them.

For topographical maps, go to the **Instituto Geográfico Nacional** (IGN; Map pp52-3; ☎ 475-9960; ventaign@ignperu.gob.pe; Aramburu 1198, Surquillo; ☻ 9am-4pm Mon-Fri). In January, the IGN closes around lunchtime. Its maps are for sale or for reference on the premises. Its good road map of Peru (1:2,000,000) is US$7, and a four-sheet 1:1,000,000 topographical map of Peru costs US$30. Departmental maps at various scales are US$6.50. High-scale topographic maps for trekking are available, though sheets of border areas might be hard to get. Geological and demographical maps are also sold.

The **Servicio Aerofotográfico Nacional** (Map pp52-3; ☎ 252-3401; ☻ 8am-2pm Mon-Fri), at Las Palmeras Air Force base in Surco, sells aerial photographs. Don't wear shorts when you go there, take a passport and expect a two-week waiting period for prints. Some aerial photos are also available from the IGN. The best way to find it is to take a taxi.

INFORMATION
Bookstores
The best selection of English-language guidebooks is available to members at the South American Explorers' clubhouse (above), which also has a members-only book exchange. For books in Spanish (and a limited number of English books), try the following:

Crisol (Map pp66-7; ☎ 221-1010; Santa Cruz 816, Óvalo Guturierrez, Miraflores; ☻ 10am-11pm daily) Crisol is a big and showy bookshop, with some novels and travel guides in English and French.

El Virrey (Map pp58-9; ☎ 440-0607; Dasso 141, Central Lima; ☻ 10am-6:30pm Mon-Sat) Near the Plaza de Armas, it has a limited selection of glossy travel books.

Zeta (Map pp66-7; ☎ 446-5139; booksell@zetabook .com.pe; ☻ 10am-8pm Mon-Sat); Espinar branch (Espinar 219, Miraflores); Larcomar branch (cnr Miraflores & Larcomar, Miraflores) A small but helpful shop, it has a varied foreign-language selection.

Cultural Centers
All of the following present a variety of plays, film screenings, art shows, lectures and more at irregular intervals. Check the newspapers or the *Peru Guide*, available in hotels and tourist sites, for details.

Alianza Francesa (Map pp66-7; ☎ 241-7014; Arequipa 4598, Miraflores) Has French-language cultural events.

Goethe Institut (☎ 433-3180; Jirón Nazca 722, Jesús María) For German-speakers.

Instituto Cultural Peruano-Norteamericano Miraflores (ICPNA; Map pp66-7; ☎ 241-1940; Arequipa 4798); Central Lima (Map pp58-9; ☎ 428-3530; Cusco 446) Offers US newspapers, a library and Spanish courses, plus visiting art displays. Its Spanish-language website (icpnacultural .perucultural.org.pe) has more information.

Peruvian-British Cultural Association (Map pp52-3; ☎ 221-7550; www.britanico.edu.pe; Arequipa 3495, San Isidro) British newspapers and English-language books are available in the library here. There's also a branch in Miraflores (Map pp66-7; ☎ 447-1135; Jirón Bellavista 531).

Emergency
Fire emergency (☎ 116)

Policía de Turismo (☎ 424-2053; Pasaje Tambo de Belén 106, Pachitea, Central Lima; ☻ 24 hr) Gives advice and assistance on anything from robberies to rabies.

METROPOLITAN LIMA

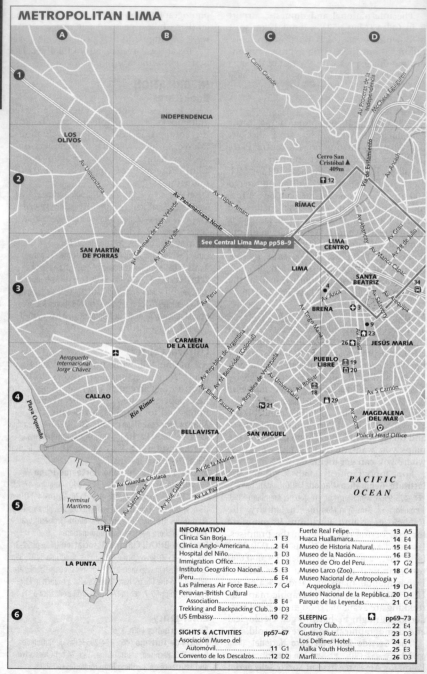

INDEPENDENCIA

LOS OLIVOS

Av Universitaria

Av Panamericana Norte

Av Túpac Amaru

Av Canto Grande

Cerro San Cristóbal ▲ 409m

🚠 12

Via de Evitamiento

MI Chica Esquipuren

Av Procerse de la Independencia

Av Ancash

RÍMAC

SAN MARTÍN DE PORRAS

Av Gammara de León Velarde

Av Torrifs Valle

See Central Lima Map pp58–9

LIMA CENTRO

LIMA

Av Abancay

Av Grau

Av 28 de Julio

Av Manco Cápac

SANTA BEATRIZ

34 🚉

Av Perú

Av Arica

● 4

BREÑA

✚ 3

Av Salaverry

Av Arequipa

● 9

🏠 23

CARMEN DE LA LEGUA

Av República de Argentina

Av Tingo María

26 🏠

JESÚS MARÍA

Aeropuerto Internacional Jorge Chávez

Av Elmer Faucett

Av M Benavides (Colonial)

Av República de Venezuela

Av Bolívar

Av Universitaria

PUEBLO LIBRE

🏛 19

🏛 20

🏛 18

CALLAO

Río Rímac

🚉 21

🏛 29

Av S Carrión

MAGDALENA DEL MAR

Av Sucre

◉

BELLAVISTA

SAN MIGUEL

Policía Head Office

Av de la Marina

Av Guardia Chalaca

LA PERLA

Av Sáenz Peña

Av José Gálvez

Av La Paz

PACIFIC OCEAN

Terminal Marítimo

Playa Oquendo

13 🚉

LA PUNTA

INFORMATION		
Clínica San Borja	1	E3
Clínica Anglo-Americana	2	E4
Hospital del Niño	3	D3
Immigration Office	4	D3
Instituto Geográfico Nacional	5	E3
iPeru	6	E4
Las Palmeras Air Force Base	7	G4
Peruvian-British Cultural Association	8	E4
Trekking and Backpacking Club	9	D3
US Embassy	10	F2

SIGHTS & ACTIVITIES	pp57–67	
Asociación Museo del Automóvil	11	G1
Convento de los Descalzos	12	D2

Fuerte Real Felipe	13	A5
Huaca Huallamarca	14	E4
Museo de Historia Natural	15	E4
Museo de la Nación	16	E3
Museo de Oro del Peru	17	G2
Museo Larco (Zoo)	18	C4
Museo Nacional de Antropología y Arqueología	19	D4
Museo Nacional de la República	20	D4
Parque de las Leyendas	21	C4

SLEEPING	🏠	pp69–73
Country Club	22	E4
Gustavo Ruiz	23	D3
Los Delfines Hotel	24	E4
Malka Youth Hostel	25	E3
Marfil	26	D3

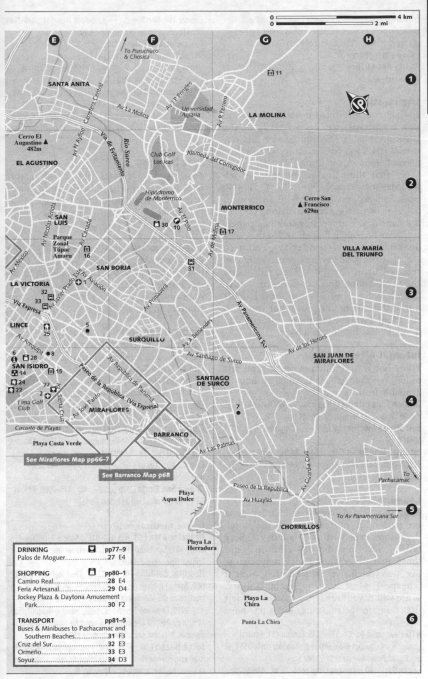

0 — 4 km
0 — 2 mi

E

To Puruchuco
& Chosica

F

G

H

1

SANTA ANITA

Av La Molina

Av J P Pringles

Universidad
Agraria

Av R Ferrero

LA MOLINA

🏛 11

Cerro El
Augustino ▲
482m

Av N Ayllon

Carretera Central

Vía de Evitamiento

Río Surco

Club Golf
Los Icas

Alameda del Corregidor

EL AGUSTINO

2

Hipódromo
de Monterrico

MONTERRICO

Cerro San
▲ Francisco
629m

Av El Polo

🏛 30   🏛 10

🏛 17

Av Nicolás Arriola

Av Canadá

SAN
LUIS

Parque
Zonal
Túpac
Amaru

🏛 16

Av de Molina

VILLA MARÍA
DEL TRIUNFO

3

Av México

Av Javier Prado Este

SAN BORJA

Av Aviación

Av Primavera

Av Panamericana Sur

LA VICTORIA

32

Av Benavides

Av de los Héroes

Vía Expresa

33

🏛 31

LINCE

🏛 25

5 ●

SURQUILLO

Av Santiago de Surco

SAN JUAN DE
MIRAFLORES

Av Arequipa

6 ● 8
ℹ   🏛 28
SAN ISIDRO

🏛 14   🏛 15

🏛 24

Paseo de la República

Av República de Panamá

SANTIAGO
DE SURCO

4

77

🏛 22   2

Lima Golf
Club

Santa Cruz

Av José Pardo

MIRAFLORES

Av República de Panamá (Vía Expresa)

7 ●

Circuito de Playas

Playa Costa Verde

BARRANCO

Av Las Palmas

Av Guardia Civil

To
Pachacamac

See Miraflores Map pp66–7

See Barranco Map p68

Paseo de la República

Av Huaylas

To Av Panamericana Sur

5

Playa
Aqua Dulce

CHORRILLOS

Playa La
Herradura

Playa La
Chira

Punta La Chira

6

English-speaking police are usually available, and will provide reports to make insurance claims or get a traveler's-check refund. It's southwest of Plaza San Martín.
Police emergency (☎ 105)
Policía Head Office (Map pp52-3; ☎ 460-0921; Moore 268, Magdalena del Mar; ⏱ 24 hr)

Immigration

For general information about visas and stay extensions, see Visas (p412) in the Directory chapter. See Embassies & Consulates (p406) in the Directory chapter for a list of embassies in Lima.

Go first thing in the morning to **Migraciónes** (immigration office; Map pp52-3; ☎ 330-4144; España 734, Breña; ⏱ 8am-1pm Mon-Fri) if you want to get your tourist-card extension (US$20) the same day. The specially stamped paperwork can be bought beforehand at the next-door Banco de la Nación (US$7). You need your passport and the immigration slip you received upon entry into Peru (it's more time-consuming and expensive if you've lost it). You may be asked to show a ticket out of the country, or prove that you have sufficient funds – the more affluent you look, the less hassle you'll have.

Internet Access

Many hotels have Internet access, and fast public access for about US$0.60 an hour is available from:
Dragon Fans Internet (Map pp66-7; ☎ 446-6814; Pasaje Tarata 230, Miraflores; ⏱ 24 hr)
Full Screen Internet (Map pp66-7; Angamos Oeste 401, Miraflores)
Internet Mundonet (Map pp58-9; Ancash, Central Lima)
Telefónica del Peru (Map pp66-7; Benavides 4th block, Miraflores; ⏱ 24 hr)

Laundry

Many hotels can have your laundry done for you – the more expensive the hotel, the more expensive the laundry. Many *lavanderías* only do dry cleaning, and those that do wash and dry may charge per item (expensive) rather than by weight (cheaper). Most have overnight laundry; some will have it ready the same day if left first thing in the morning, and a few have self-service.
KTO (Map pp58-9; ☎ 332-9035; España 481, Central Lima; ⏱ 7am-8pm Mon-Sat) Less than 5kg costs US$1.40 per kg, and over five costs US$1 per kg.
Lavandaria 40 minutos (Map pp66-7; ☎ 446-5928;

Espinar 154, Miraflores; ⏱ 8am-8pm Mon-Sat, 9am-1pm Sun) Loads of up to 4kg cost US$4.20.
Lavandería Neptuno (Map p68; ☎ 477-4472; Grau 912, Barranco) Charges US$2 per kg.
Press To (Map pp58-9; ☎ 426-2660; Cusco, Central Lima; ⏱ 9am-10pm Mon-Sat, 9am-9pm Sun) In the Metro supermarket, it charges US$1.40 to US$3 per item.
Servirap (Map pp66-7; ☎ 241-0759; cnr Schell & Grimaldo del Solar, Miraflores; ⏱ 8am-10pm Mon-Sat, 9am-6pm Sun) Charges US$2.30 per kg; there's also self-service.

Left Luggage

Apart from your hotel, you can safely store bags at the airport for US$6 a day. Members of SAE can store their baggage at the clubhouse.

Libraries

The **Biblioteca Nacional** (Map pp58-9; ☎ 428-7690; www.binape.gob.pe; cnr Abancay & Miró Quesada, Central Lima; ⏱ 8am-8pm Mon-Sat) has books in Spanish. For referencing books in English, German and French, check out the Cultural Centers (p51).

Medical Services

The following clinics have emergency service and some English-speaking staff.
Clínica Anglo-Americana (Map pp52-3; ☎ 221-3656; Salazar 3rd block, San Isidro) Charges up to US$60 for a consultation and stocks yellow-fever and tetanus vaccines. There's also a walk-in center in La Molina (☎ 436-9933) near the US embassy.
Clínica Internacional (Map pp58-9; ☎ 433-4306; cnr Washington 1471 & 9 de Diciembre, Central Lima) Charges US$17 to US$35 for consultations.
Clínica Montesur (☎ 436-3630; Av El Polo 505, Monterrico) Specializes in women's issues.
Clínica San Borja (Map pp52-3; ☎ 475-4000, 475-3141; Av Guardia Civil 337, San Borja)

Other medical options:
Dr Victor Aste (☎ /fax 421-9169; Antero Aspillaga 415, office 101, San Isidro) Dr Aste is a well-recommended, English-speaking dentist.
Hospital del Niño (Map pp52-3; ☎ 330-0066; Brasil 600, Breña) It gives tetanus and yellow-fever jabs.
Instituto de Medicina Tropical (☎ 482-3903, 482-3910; Cayetano Heredia Hospital, Honorio Delgado, San Martín de Porres) The institute is good for treating tropical diseases. It is also one of the cheapest places.
Jorge Bazan (☎ 9735-2668; jrbazanj@yahoo.com) He is an English-speaking backpacker medic recommended by readers; he sees travelers at their hotel.

The following pharmacies are modern, well stocked and open 24 hours. They often deliver free of charge:

Botica Fasa (Map pp66-7; ☎ 619-0000; cnr Larco & Palma, Miraflores)
Inka Farma (☎ 314-2020; will deliver)
Superfarma (Map p66-7; ☎ 440-9000; Armendariz 215, Miraflores)

If you have a prescription with you, you can have a spare pair of glasses made cheaply by one of Lima's numerous opticians along Cailloma in the city center or around Schell and Larco in Miraflores.

Money

Most banks have 24-hour ATMs to avoid the long queues in banks, which are at their worst on Monday mornings (although some banks have express windows for foreign-currency transactions). Use caution when making withdrawals from ATMs, especially at night.

Casas de cambio (foreign-exchange houses) usually give similar or slightly better rates than banks for cash (not traveler's checks); they are also quicker and open longer. There are several *casas de cambio* downtown on Ocoña and south of Ocoña on Camaná, as well as along Larco in Miraflores. Street moneychangers hang around the *casas de cambio*. Those around Parque Kennedy in Miraflores have uniforms and badges and are generally the safest option outside of business hours. The following lists some of the most useful options.

American Express (Amex; ☎ 221-8204; amexcard@travex.com.pe; Santa Cruz 621, Miraflores; ☼ 9am-5:30pm Mon-Fri, 9am-1pm Sat) Amex will replace stolen or lost Amex checks, but will not cash its own checks. Somebody is usually there after hours to take telephone reports about lost checks. Most of the banks will cash Amex checks; you get the best rates if you cash them in for nuevos soles.

Banco Continental Miraflores (Map pp58-9; cnr Larco & Tarata; ☼ 9am-6pm Mon-Fri, 9:30am-12:30pm Sat); Central Lima (Cusco 286) It's a representative of Visa and its ATMs also take Cirrus, Plus and MasterCard.

BCP (formerly Banco de Crédito; ☼ 9am-6pm Mon-Fri, 9:30am-12:30pm Sat); Central Lima (Map pp58-9; Lampa 499); Pardo (Map pp66-7; Pardo 491, Miraflores); José Gonzales (Map pp66-7; cnr Larco & José Gonzales, Miraflores); Schell (Map pp66-7; cnr Larco & Schell, Miraflores) All these branches have 24-hour Visa and Plus ATMs, and make cash advances on Visa. It also changes Amex, Citicorp and Visa traveler's checks.

Banco Santander Central Hispano (BSCH; Augusto Tamayo 120, San Isidro; ☼ 9am-6pm Mon-Fri) It has Visa and Plus ATMs and changes Visa and Citicorp traveler's checks.

Banco Wiese (Map pp66-7; Larco 1123, Miraflores; ☼ 9:15am-6pm Mon-Fri, 9:30am-12:30pm Sat) This bank is a MasterCard representative and changes Amex and Citicorp traveler's checks.

Interbanc (☼ 9am-6pm Mon-Fri); Central Lima (Map pp58-9; Jirón de la Unión 600); Larco (Map p66-7; Larco 690, Miraflores) Interbanc has ATMs with Cirrus, Plus, Visa and MasterCard.

LAC Dólar (☼ 9:30am-6:30pm Mon-Sat, 9am-2pm Sun); Central Lima (Map pp58-9; ☎ 428-8127; fax 427-3906; Camaná 779); Miraflores (Map pp66-7; ☎ 242-4069; La Paz 211) LAC Dólar is safe, reliable, and changes cash and traveler's checks at reasonable rates. It will also deliver the money for free if you phone and give the numbers of your traveler's checks.

Moneygram (Map pp66-7; ☎ 0800-15821, 241-2222; moneyexpress@terra.com.pe; Benavides 735, Miraflores; ☼ 10am-6:30pm Mon-Sat)

Photography

Slide- and print-film developing tends to be mediocre in Lima. **Taller de Fotografía Profesional** (Map pp66-7; ☎ 241-1015; Benavides 1171, Miraflores) is the best photo shop in the city, with top-quality processing, camera repairs and sales.

Post

Members of the SAE (see p56) can have mail held at the clubhouse.

Main post office (Map pp58-9; ☎ 427-9370; Pasaje Piura, Central Lima; ☼ 8:15am-8:15pm Mon-Fri, 9am-1:30pm Sat, 8am-4pm Sun) It's inside the city block on the northwest corner of the Plaza de Armas. Mail sent to you at Lista de Correos (ie, General Delivery or Poste Restante), Correos Central, Lima, can be collected here, though it is not 100% reliable; bring some identification.

Miraflores post office (Map pp66-7; ☎ 445-0697; Petit Thouars 5201) Located east of Arequipa, it's open the same hours as the main post office.

For faster, more expensive postal services, try:

DHL (☎ 422-5232, 517-2500; Los Castaños 225, San Isidro)
Federal Express (FedEx; ☎ 242-2280; Pasaje Olaya 260, Surco)

Telephone & Fax

Telefónica del Peru has pay phones on almost every street corner in Lima (many accept only telephone cards). Call ☎ 103 (no charge) for directory inquiries within Lima and ☎ 109 for assistance with provincial numbers. Some offices of **Telefónica del Peru** Central Lima (Map pp58-9; Bolivia 347) Miraflores (Map pp66-7; Benavides 4th block; ◷ 24 hr: and Map pp66-7; Pasaje Tarata 280) also have fax services.

Tourist Information

Intej (Map p68; ☎ 247-3230; intej@intej.org; San Martín 240, Barranco) The official ISIC office; Intej organizes student air fares and changes flight details.

iPeru San Isidro (Map pp52-3; ☎ 421-1627; iperulima@promperu.gob.pe; Jorge Basadre 610; ◷ 8:30am-6:30pm Mon-Fri) The San Isidro office combines services of the tourist protection agency (Indecopi) and the information office PromPeru, dispensing maps and useful advice, as well as dealing with tourist complaints; Aeropuerto Internacional Jorge Chávez (☎ 574-8000; iperulimaapto@promperu.gob.pe);

Miraflores (Map pp66-7; ☎ 445-9400; Larcomar; ◷ noon-8pm daily) The Miraflores office is only tiny but it's useful on weekends.

Tourist office (Map pp58-9; ☎ 427-6080 ex 222-83; Pasaje de los Escribanos 145, Central Lima; ◷ 9am-6pm Mon-Fri, 11am-3pm Sat & Sun) It has limited information that is not always up to date.

Trekking and Backpacking Club (Map pp52-3; ☎ 423-2515; tebac@yahoo.com; Huascar 1152, Jesús María) Provides information in Spanish for independent trekkers and has maps, brochures, equipment rental and guides.

Travel Agencies

For details of companies in Lima offering local tours, including archaeological sites such as Pachacamac as well as tours of Peru, see Tours & Guides (p68). For travel agencies to organize your travel arrangements try the following:

SOUTH AMERICAN EXPLORERS (SAE)

For many long-term travelers, journalists, scientists and expat residents, this club has become almost legendary. Since it was founded by Don Montague and Linda Rojas in 1977, SAE has been involved in activities ranging from the first cleanup of the Inca Trail to medicine drives for local nonprofit organizations. However, it functions primarily as an information center for travelers, adventurers and scientific expeditions, providing excellent advice about Latin American travel, especially in Peru, Ecuador and Bolivia.

The club has an extensive library of books, maps and trip reports of other travelers, indexed by region and date. Various useful books and maps are sold, and there are trail maps for the Inca Trail, Mt Ausangate area, Cordillera Blanca and Cordillera Huayhuash, as well as general maps of South America. You can also get useful current information on travel conditions, currency regulations, weather and so on.

The club is a member-supported, nonprofit organization. Annual membership costs US$50 per person (US$80 for a couple), which covers four issues of their quarterly *South American Explorer* magazine. (Members outside the USA have to add US$10 for postage. Membership dues and donations to the club are tax-deductible in the USA.) Members receive full use of the clubhouse and its facilities, including introductions to other travelers and notification of expedition opportunities; long- or short-term luggage storage; poste restante or forwarding of mail addressed to you at the club; a book exchange; buying and selling of used equipment; and discounts on the books, maps and gear sold at the club. (Note: all imported merchandise is reserved for members only.) It's also a relaxing place to do research or just chat with the friendly staff. Another big advantage for members is that they receive scores of significant discounts (ranging from 5% to 30% off) throughout Peru: Pick up the list of participants from the club. Nonmembers are also welcome to browse for information, and the staff is happy to answer quick questions, but at the end of the day, staff are volunteers and members' needs come first.

If you're in Lima, simply go to the **clubhouse** (Map pp66-7; ☎ 445-3306; limaclub@saexplorers.org; www.saexplorers.org; Calle Piura 135, Miraflores; ◷ 9:30am-5pm Mon-Fri, 9:30am-8pm Wed, 9:30am-1pm Sat) just off Arequipa and sign up.

There's also a clubhouse in **Cuzco** (☎ 24-5484; cuscoclub@saexplorers.org; Choquechaca 188, office 4) and in **Quito** (☎ /fax 593-2-225-228; quitoclub@saexplorers.org; Jorge Washington 311) in Ecuador.

The club's US office in **New York** (☎ 607-277-0488; explorers@saexplorers.org; 126 Indian Creek Rd, Ithaca, NY 14850) publishes the magazine; send them US$6 for a sample copy of the *South American Explorer* and further information. Nonmember subscriptions are US$22 for one year and US$35 for two.

Fertur Peru (Map pp58-9; ☎ 427-1958; fertur@
terra.com.pe; Jirón Junín 211, Central Lima; ☺ 9am-
7pm Mon-Sat) Fertur is a small agency recommended for
countrywide information and good prices on national and
international flights, with discounts for students and SAE
members.

Infotur (Map pp58-9; ☎ 431-0117; Jirón Belén 1066,
Central Lima; ☺ 9:30am-6pm Mon-Fri, 10am-2pm Sat)
Infotur has reliable information about transportation,
hotels and sightseeing.

Lima Tours (Map pp58-9; ☎ 424-5110; fax 330-4488;
www.limatours.com.pe; Jirón Belén 1040, Central Lima;
☺ 8:30am-5:30pm Mon-Fri, 9am-1pm Sat) It is perhaps
the best-known agency in Lima.

Victor Travel Services (Map p58-9; ☎ 431-4195;
victortravel@terra.com.pe; Jirón de la Unión 1068, Central
Lima) Victor Travel is helpful for local information.

DANGERS & ANNOYANCES

With millions of poor and unemployed people, it is inevitable that Lima suffers from
opportunistic crime. While you are unlikely
to be mugged or physically hurt, travelers
do regularly have their belongings stolen.
Reread Dangers & Annoyances (p405) in
the Directory chapter before arriving in
Lima. If you don't take those precautions,
you can expect to have that Rolex ripped
off your wrist.

Downtown Lima and around the bus terminals especially have many pickpockets,
but don't assume that ritzy Miraflores is
free of thieves. Take proper precautions
throughout Lima, especially at night, and
don't parade around with a gold chain or
camera on your neck or a wallet peeking
out of your hip pocket.

SIGHTS

Lima has enough museums, churches
and colonial houses to keep the sight-
seer happy for weeks. The museums are
among the best in the country. The city's
many churches, monasteries and convents
are a welcome break from the city's noisy
traffic and incessant crowds, though they
are often closed for restoration, services or
because the caretaker fancies an extended
lunch. Several of the principal parks and
plazas of central Lima are within easy walking distance of each other. There are several
pre-Inca ruins within the city itself, each
oddly juxtaposed with the modern urban
landscape; the main ones are in San Isidro
and Miraflores.

Museo de la Nación   Map pp52-3
This dominating concrete block houses
the best **museum** (☎ 476-9878; Javier Prado Este
2466, San Borja; adult/student US$2/1, US$3.30 for special
shows; ☺ 9am-5pm Tue-Sun) in the country to
get your head around Peru's myriad prehistoric civilizations. It has excellent models of
Peru's well-known ruins and three levels
of extensive exhibits about all manner of
Peruvian heritage, all at a much more af-
fordable price than at the private collections.
Everything from Chavín stone carvings, to
Nazca ceramics and Paracas weavings is
represented, and there are also exhibits
from the now-defunct Museo de Ciencias
de la Salud describing medical practices in
pre-Columbian and colonial times. Besides
the permanent collections, there are often
special shows, lectures and other events.

French and English guided tours are available (about US$3 per group). A taxi from
Miraflores will cost about US$1.40.

Plaza de Armas   Map pp58-9
Also called Plaza Mayor, this 140-square-
meter plaza was once the heart of Lima.
Though not one original building remains,
the impressive bronze fountain in the
center is its oldest feature, erected in 1650,
and its oldest building is the **cathedral** (see
La Catedral, p60) reconstructed after the
1746 earthquake.

The exquisitely balconied Archbishop's
palace to the left of the cathedral is a relatively modern building, dating to 1924. On
the northeast side, the **Palacio de Gobierno**
(Map pp58-9) was built in 1937 and is the
residence of Peru's president. Here, a hand-
somely uniformed presidential guard is on
duty all day; the ceremonial changing of the
guard takes place at noon. It's a struggle to
get into the palace, which is by guided tour
only (Spanish and English) and has to be
organized 48-hours in advance at the nearby
Office of Public Relations (☎ 311-3908; Jirón de la
Unión, Plaza Pizarro; office 201; admission free). Ask a
guard to point you in the right direction.

On the corner of the plaza, opposite the
cathedral, there is an impressive statue of
Francisco Pizarro on horseback – though
just for the record, he was actually a
mediocre horseman. The statue once sat
in the center of the plaza, but the clergy
apparently took a dim view of the horse's
rear end facing the cathedral, so the statue

LIMA

CENTRAL LIMA

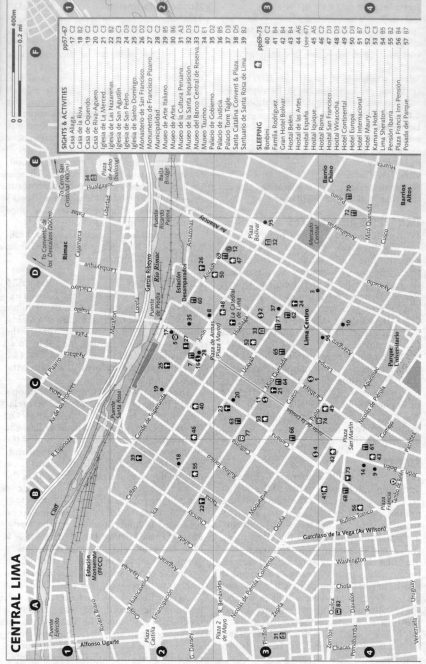

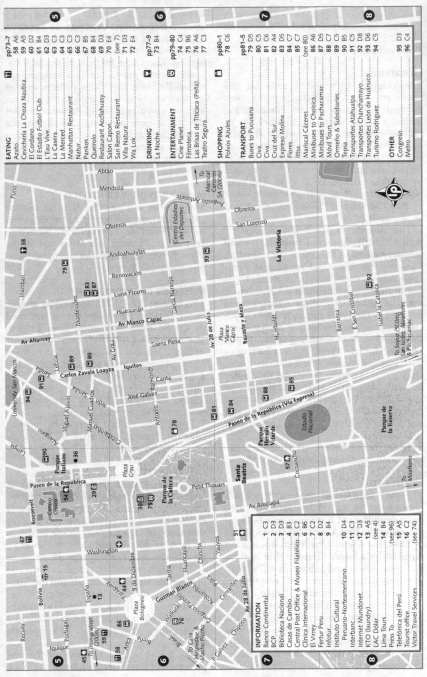

EATING	pp73-7
Azato	58 A6
Cevichería La Choza Náutica	59 A5
El Cordano	60 D2
El Estadio Futbol Club	61 B4
L'Eau Vive	62 D3
La Casera	63 C3
La Merced	64 C3
Manhattan Restaurant	65 C3
Natur	66 C3
Pankos	67 B5
Queirolo	68 B4
Restaurant Acllahuasy	69 D3
Salon Capon	70 E4
San Remo Restaurant	(see 7)
Villa Natura	71 D3
Wa Lok	72 E4

DRINKING	pp77-9
La Noche	73 B4

ENTERTAINMENT	pp79-80
Cine Planet	74 C4
Filmoteca	75 B6
Las Brisas de Titicaca (Peña)	76 A6
Teatro Segura	77 C3

SHOPPING	pp80-1
Polvos Azules	78 C6

TRANSPORT	pp81-5
Buses to Pucusana	79 D5
Civa	80 C5
Civa	81 C6
Cruz del Sur	82 A4
Expreso Molina	83 D5
Flores	84 C7
Ittsa	85 C7
Mariscal Cáceres	(see 80)
Minibuses to Choisica	86 A6
Minibuses to Pachacamac	87 D5
Móvil Tours	88 C7
Ormeño & Subsidiaries	89 C5
Tepsa	90 B5
Transportes Atahualpa	91 C5
Transportes Chanchamayo	92 D8
Transportes León de Huánuco	93 D6
Turismo Rodríguez	94 C5

OTHER	
Congreso	95 D3
Metro	96 C4

INFORMATION	
Banco Continental	1 C3
BCP	2 D3
Biblioteca Nacional	3 D3
Casas de Cambio	4 B3
Central Post Office & Museo Filatélico	5 C2
Clínica Internacional	6 B6
El Virrey	7 C2
Fertur Peru	8 D2
Infotur	9 B4
Instituto Cultural Peruano-Norteamericano	10 D4
Interbanc	11 C3
Internet Mundonet	12 D3
KTO (laundry)	13 A5
LAC Dólar	(see 4)
Lima Tours	14 B4
Press To	(see 96)
Telefónica del Perú	15 A5
Tourist office	16 C2
Victor Travel Services	(see 74)

LIMA

was moved to its present position with its backside safely averted. There is an identical statue in Pizarro's hometown of Trujillo, Spain.

LA CATEDRAL

The original cathedral (1555) on the southeast side of the Plaza de Armas, was deemed too small for its congregation within a single decade, and work on its successor began in 1564, which was still unfinished when it was consecrated in 1625. It was badly damaged in the 1687 earthquake and almost totally destroyed by another earthquake in 1746. The swift **reconstruction** (☎ 427-9647; adult/child US$1.40/1; ☒ 9am-4:30pm Mon-Fri, 10am-4:30pm Sat) is based on the early plans.

The interior is stark but impressive, with a beautifully carved **choir** and a small **religious museum** in the rear of the cathedral. Look for the coffin and remains of Francisco Pizarro in the mosaic-covered chapel just to the right of the main door. A debate over the authenticity of the remains raged for most of the 1980s and early 1990s, especially after several bodies and a mysterious disembodied head were unearthed in the crypt in the late 1970s. After a battery of tests and speculation, the authorities concluded that the body previously on display was an unknown church official and that a brutally stabbed and headless body from the crypt was indeed Pizarro's remains, and was reunited with the head and transferred to the chapel.

Tours in English are available for a tip. Only flashless photography is allowed.

LA MERCED

The **Iglesia de La Merced** (☎ 427-8199; cnr Jirón de la Unión & Miró Quesada; ☒ 8am-noon & 4-8pm daily) has a multilayered history. It was built on the site of the first Mass celebrated in Lima in 1534, but the original church was soon replaced by a larger version. This in turn, was torn down, and rebuilt in 1628, then promptly flattened by the 1687 earthquake, and once again rebuilding began. Work started on a new facade after more damage in the 1746 earthquake, and in 1773, the church was gutted by a fire that destroyed all paintings and vestments in the sacristy. Thus, most of today's church dates to the 18th century.

Around Plaza de Armas   Map pp58-9
MUSEO DEL BANCO CENTRAL DE RESERVA

This **museum** (☎ 427-6250; museo@bcrp.gob.pe; Banco Central de Reserva, cnr Lampa & Ucayali; admission free; ☒ 10am-4:30pm Tue-Fri, 10am-1pm Sat & Sun) specializes in pre-Columbian archaeology, especially from the Vicus culture, as well as housing 19th- and 20th-century Peruvian art and an exhibit of Peruvian monies down the ages. Strolling casually in and out of the bank's old high-security vault also has a certain appeal.

You need to show a passport or national ID card to get in.

MUSEO POSTAL Y FILATELICO

Stamp buffs will want to visit this **museum** (☎ 427-7261; admission free; ☒ 8:30am-6:30pm Mon-Sat, 9am-12:30pm Sun), appropriately housed in central Lima's main post office just off the Plaza de Armas, and allows you to examine, buy and trade Peruvian stamps.

MUSEO DE LA INQUISICIÓN

This **building** (☎ 311-7801; Jirón Junín 548; admission free; ☒ 9am-1pm and 2:30-5pm Mon-Fri) was used by the Spanish Inquisition from 1570 to 1820 and subsequently became the senate building. Visitors can explore the basement where prisoners were tortured, and there's a ghoulish waxwork exhibit of life-size unfortunates on the rack or having their feet roasted. The university library upstairs has a remarkable wooden ceiling.

Entry is by guided tours only, most of which are conducted in Spanish. They leave every half hour.

SAN FRANCISCO

This Franciscan **monastery and church** (cnr Lampa & Ancash; adult/student US$1.40/0.75; ☒ 9:30am-5:30pm daily) is famous for its catacombs and its remarkable library, where you can see thousands of antique texts, some dating as far back as the conquistadors. It also has a very fine museum of religious art.

The underground catacombs are the site of an estimated 70,000 burials and the fainthearted may find the bone-filled crypts unnerving – if only for the conservationists' bizarre decision to rearrange the skulls and femurs into striking rings of concentric circles.

The building, which is one of the best preserved of Lima's early colonial churches, was finished before the earthquake of 1687 and withstood both this and the quake of 1746 better than many others. However, the 1970 earthquake caused considerable damage. Much of the church has been well restored in its original baroque style with Moorish influence. Admission to the monastery includes a 45-minute guided tour. Spanish-speaking tours leave regularly, and there are hourly tours led by English-speaking guides.

OTHER COLONIAL CHURCHES

Santuario de Santa Rosa de Lima (☎ 425-1279; Tacna; admission free; ☼ 9am-12:30pm daily & 5-6:30pm Mon-Sat) venerates the first saint of the Americas in her hometown of Lima. The church and its garden have been built roughly at the site of her birth, and you can find modest adobe sanctuary in the gardens, built in the early 17th century for her prayers and meditation.

Santo Domingo (☎ 427-6793; cnr Camaná & Superunda; admission US$1; ☼ 9am-12:30pm & 3-6pm Mon-Sat, 9am-1pm Sun) is one of Lima's most historic churches, built on land granted by Francisco Pizarro to the Dominican Friar Vicente Valverde, who accompanied Pizarro throughout the conquest and was instrumental in persuading him to execute the captured and ransomed Inca, Atahualpa. Construction began in 1540, though much of the interior was modernized late in the 18th century. The church contains the tombs of Saint Rose and Saint Martín de Porres (one of the few black saints), plus an alabaster statue of Saint Rose presented to the church by Pope Clement in 1669. There is also fine tile work showing the life of Saint Dominic.

San Pedro (☎ 428-3010; cnr Azangaro & Ucayali; admission free; ☼ 10am-noon & 5-6pm Mon-Fri) is a small baroque church considered to be one of the finest examples of early colonial architecture in Lima. It was consecrated by the Jesuits in 1638 and has changed little since. The interior is sumptuously decorated with gilded altars, Moorish-influenced carvings and an abundance of beautiful glazed tile work.

San Agustín (☎ 427-7548; cnr Ica & Camaná) has been significantly altered over the years, though the *churrigueresque* (an elaborate and intricately decorated Spanish style) facade dates from the early 1700s. The church has limited opening times, but the

drab interior is inferior to the elaborate exterior in any case.

COLONIAL MANSIONS

Built in 1735, the famous **Palacio Torre Tagle** (☎ 427-3860; Ucayali 363) is the best surviving colonial mansion in Lima, with striking carved wooden balconies that demonstrate a Moorish influence. It now contains the offices of the Foreign Ministry, so entry on weekdays is prohibited or restricted to the patio. On some Saturdays, a tip to the caretaker may allow you access to the fine rooms and balconies upstairs. More extensive preorganized visits need to be arranged with the **Oficina Cultural** (☎ 311-2400).

Casa Aliaga (☎ 424-5110; Jirón de la Unión 224) is another of Lima's most historic houses, furnished completely in the colonial style. It stands on land given in 1535 to Jerónimo de Aliaga, one of Pizarro's faithful 13 followers and has been occupied by the Aliaga family ever since. The house can be visited only by appointment or through local tour agencies.

The easiest mansion to visit is **Casa Pilatos** (☎ 427-7212; Camaná 390; ☼ 2-6pm Mon-Fri, 9am-5pm Sat & Sun), which houses the National Culture Institute: Simply knock on the door and a guard will usually let you in for a look around. **Casa de la Riva** (Map pp58-9; Ica 426; admission US$1; ☼ 10am-1pm & 2-4pm Mon-Fri) is run by the Entre Nous Society. **Casa de Riva-Aguero** (Map pp58-9; ☎ 427-9275; Camaná 459; ☼ 10am-1pm & 2-8pm Mon-Fri, 9am-1pm Sat & Sun) houses a small folk-art collection. The rest of the house is shown only by appointment. **Casa de Oquendo** (Casa Osambela; ☎ 427-7987; Superunda 298; ☼ 9:30am-4pm Mon-Fri) is a 19th-century house with a lookout tower from whence you can see the port in Callao.

JIRÓN DE LA UNIÓN

As you walk down the five pedestrianized blocks of the jirón from the Plaza de Armas to Plaza San Martín, you'll pass a multitude of fashion and sporting stores, cinemas and fast-food joints, as well as the church of **La Merced** (opposite). The jirón is always very crowded with shoppers, sightseers, street performers, and the inevitable pickpockets, so keep an eye on your valuables.

Plaza San Martín   Map pp58-9

The early-20th-century Plaza San Martín has French-influenced architecture and a

LIMA

bronze equestrian **statue of liberator General San Martín** erected in 1921. But get closer and you'll also discover the overlooked **statue of Madre Patria**, the symbolic mother of Peru. Commissioned in Spain under instruction to give the good lady a crown of flames, nobody thought to iron out the double meaning of the word flame in Spanish (*llama*), and the hapless craftsmen duly placed a delightful little llama on her head.

The **Gran Hotel Bolívar** also presides over the square and it's well worth a stop in its stately bar for a sip or two of its famous pisco sour.

Parque de la Cultura   Map pp58-9

Originally known as Parque de la Exposición, this newly revamped park has a small amphitheatre for outdoor performances and Japanese gardens. It's a welcome relief from the crowds and traffic of Lima's boisterous center. Lima's **Museo de Arte** is in the park.

MUSEO DE ARTE

Lima's **Art Museum** (☎ 423-4732; areaeducativa@ terra.com.pe; Paseo de Colón 125; admission US$2; ☼ 10am-5pm Tue-Sun) is housed in a very handsome building. It exhibits far more than art, and its collection ranges from colonial furniture to pre-Columbian artifacts, as well as canvases spanning 400 years of Peruvian art. Photography is not allowed. Temporary shows cost extra. There is a **café** and cinema **Filmoteca** (see Entertainment on p80).

From Miraflores, catch a combi from Arequipa marked 'Todo Arequipa' to 9 de Diciembre (US$0.30, 10 to 15 minutes).

MUSEO DE ARTE ITALIANO

Located just north from the Museo de Arte, the **Italian Art Museum** (☎ 423-9932; Paseo de la República 250; adult/student/child US$1/0.60/0.30; ☼ 10am-5pm Mon-Fri) is housed in a fairytale, neoclassical building in a park, and exhibits paintings, sculptures and prints mainly from the early 20th century. Italian and other European art is represented, and don't miss the detailed mosaic murals on the outside walls.

Other Sights in
Central Lima   Map pp58-9

MUSEO DE LA CULTURA PERUANA

This small **museum** (Map pp58-9 ☎ 423-5892; A Ugarte 630; adult/student US$1/0.60; ☼ 10am-4:30pm

Tue-Sat) specializes in items closely allied to popular art and handicrafts. Exhibits include ceramics, carved gourds, traditional folk art and costumes from various periods and places. It also runs classes for Peruvian instruments and typical dances.

LAS NAZARENAS

The most passionate of Lima's traditional religious feasts center around the 18th-century **Iglesia de Las Nazarenas** (☎ 423-5718; cnr Huancavelica & Tacna; admission free; ☼ 7am-noon & 5-8:30pm Mon-Sat, 6:30am-1pm & 5-8:30pm Sun). A shantytown inhabited by liberated black slaves once sprawled on this site, and it was here that an ex-slave painted an image of the crucifixion of Christ on a wall that miraculously survived when the area was leveled by the 1655 earthquake. The church of the Nazarene was later built around this wall, and on 18 October of each year, a copy of the mural, known as the Lord of the Miracles, is carried from church to church in a thousands-strong procession lasting two to three days.

Rímac

MUSEO TAURINO

Located just north of the Río Rímac, the **Bullfight Museum** (Map pp58-9; ☎ 481-1467; Hualgayoc 332; admission US$1.40; ☼ 9am-6pm Mon-Sat) is at the Plaza de Acho, Lima's bullring. It boasts all manner of matadors' relics, including a holed and bloodstained costume worn by a Spanish matador who was famously gored and killed in the Lima bullring years ago: Score one for the bulls! There are also paintings and drawings of bullfighting scenes by various artists, notably Picasso.

CERRO SAN CRISTÓBAL

This 409m-high hill to the northeast of central Lima has a *mirador* (lookout) at its crown, with views of Lima stretching off into the *garúa*. A huge **cross**, built in 1928 and illuminated at night, is a Lima landmark and is the object of a pilgrimage every May 1. There is also a small **museum** (Map pp52-3; admission US$0.30; ☼ 8am-6pm Tue-Thu, 8am-10pm Fri & Sat). The route up to the *mirador* is through a poor area, so take a taxi (US$5 to US$6 round-trip) or wait for the erratic tourist bus (US$1.40, 15 minutes) that passes through the Plaza de Armas. It is more frequent at weekends.

CONVENTO DE LOS DESCALZOS

At the end of Alameda de los Descalzos, an attractive if somewhat forgotten avenue is this typical meditation **convent and museum** (Map pp52-3; ☎ 482-3360; museotaurino@hotmail.com; adult/child US$1.40/0.60; ☼ 10am-1pm & 3-6pm Tue-Sat, 11:30am-6pm Sun), run by the Descalzos (or 'the Barefooted,' a reference to the Franciscan friars). Visitors can see old wine-making equipment in the 17th-century kitchen, a refectory, infirmary and the typical cells of the Descalzos. There's also some 300 colonial paintings here of the Quito and Cuzco schools. The convent is in a poor area of Lima, so take a taxi and ask the driver to wait.

Spanish-speaking guides with a little English will show you around. A tour lasts about 45 minutes, and a small tip is appreciated.

East Lima   Map pp52-3
MUSEO DE ORO DEL PERU

This now-notorious **private museum** (☎ 345 1292; Alonso de Molina 1100, Monterrico; adult/child US$8.50/4.20; ☼ 11:30am-7pm) was once at the top of Lima's 'must see' list until 2001, when it was rocked by a scandal that claimed between 10% and an incredible 98% of the museum's collection were fakes. The museum was reopened with an assurance that all pieces now on display in its huge basement are bonafide, but the confusion is yet to be completely cleared up. The thousands of remaining gold pieces range from ponchos embroidered with hundreds of solid-gold plates to huge earrings that make your ears ache just looking at them.

The **Arms Museum**, housed in the top half of the building, is reputedly the largest in the world and even those with no interest in guns can't fail to be fascinated by the mammoth collection of ancient and bizarre firearms. Look for the 2m-long blunderbuss, with a 5cm bore and a flaring, trumpet-like muzzle. Though it looks more suitable for hunting elephants, this 19th century gun was supposedly a mere duck-hunting rifle.

Photography is prohibited. A taxi from Miraflores costs US$2 to US$2.50.

ASOCIACIÓN MUSEO DEL AUTOMÓVIL

The **Automobile Museum** (☎ 368-0373; www.museodelautomovilnicolini.com; cnr La Molina & Totoritas, La Molina; adult/student US$5.60/2.80; ☼ 9am-10pm) has an impressive array of classic cars (mostly imported), collected and restored by millionaire Jorge Nicolini. The collection includes a Cadillac Fleetwood used by no less than four Peruvian presidents.

Pueblo Libre & San Isidro   Map pp52-3
MUSEO LARCO

An 18th-century viceroy mansion built on the site of a pre-Colombian pyramid houses this highly recommended private **museum** (☎ 461-1312; webmaster@museolarco.org; Bolívar 1515, Pueblo Libre; adult/student US$6/3; ☼ 9am-6pm daily) has one of the largest ceramics collections found anywhere. It is said to include over 50,000 pots, many of which were collected in the 1920s by a former vice president of Peru. The first rooms resemble a museum store, stacked right to the ceilings with an overwhelming jumble of ceramics. Further into the museum, the best pieces are displayed in the uncluttered manner they deserve. They include a selection of gold and silver pieces, feathered textiles and an astonishing Paracas weaving that contains 398 threads to the linear inch – a world record. But for all this, many tourists are lured here simply by the famous collection of pre-Colombian erotic pots, illustrating, with remarkable explicitness, the sexual practices of ancient Peruvian men, women, skeletons and animals in all combinations of the above.

Photography is not allowed. Catch a bus from Arequipa in Miraflores marked 'Todo Bolivar' to its 15th block. A taxi costs about US$1.40. A painted blue line should link this building to the Museo Nacional de Antropología, Arqueología y Historia del Peru (see following); a 10- to 15-minute walk away.

MUSEO NACIONAL DE ANTROPOLOGÍA, ARQUEOLOGÍA Y HISTORÍA DEL PERU

This **museum** (☎ 463-5070; Plaza Bolívar, cnr San Martín & Vivanco, Pueblo Libre; adult/student US$3/1; ☼ 9am-5pm Tue-Sat, 9am-4pm Sun) traces the history of Peru from the earliest archaeological sites to the revolution. Some exhibits have been moved to the Museo de la Nación, but a worthwhile collection remains, including scale models of the big archaeological sites, as well as some of the original stelae and obelisks from Chavín. The building was once the home of revolutionary heroes

San Martín (from 1821 to 1822) and Bolívar (from 1823 to 1826) and the museum contains late-colonial and early-republican paintings, furnishings and independence artifacts.

From Miraflores, take a 'Todo Brazil' combi from Arequipa (just up from Óvalo) to the 22nd block on the corner of Vivanco, then walk seven blocks up that street. A blue line connects this museum with Museo Larco (see p63).

MUSEO DE HISTORIA NATURAL

One block west of the 12th block of Arequipa, the **Natural History Museum** (☎ 471-0117; Arenales 1256, San Isidro; adult/student US$1.20/0.60; ☽ 9am-3pm Mon-Fri, 9am-5pm Sat, 9am-1pm Sun) has a modest taxidermy collection that's useful for familiarizing yourself with the fauna of Peru.

HUACA HUALLAMARCA

Also known as Pan de Azúcar (sugar loaf), the **Huaca Huallamarca** (☎ 222-4124; Nicolás de Rivera 201, San Isidro; adult/student/child US$1.70/1/0.30; ☽ 9am-5pm Tue-Sun 9am-5pm) is a highly restored Maranga adobe pyramid dating from AD 200 to 500. Walking up to the ceremonial platform gives you a novel perspective over contemporary San Isidro.

Miraflores & Barranco
MUSEO AMANO

This **museum** (Map pp66-7; ☎ 441-2909; Retiro 160, Miraflores; donation appreciated) has a fine private ceramics collection following the development of pottery through Peru's various pre-Columbian cultures. It specializes in the little-known Chancay culture, of which it has a remarkable collection of textiles. The one-hour tours are free and are available for small groups only (no individuals or large groups) at 3pm, 4pm and 5pm on weekdays; make an appointment in advance. It's best if you understand Spanish or have someone along to translate.

MUSEO PEDRO DE OSMA

This private **art museum** (Map p68; ☎ 467-0141 San Pedro de Osma 423, Barranco; admission US$3; ☽ 10am-6pm Tue-Sun) has an exquisite collection of colonial art and furniture, as well as metalwork and sculpture from all over Peru. It is housed in one of Barranco's older mansions. Take a combi or colectivo from

Tacna/Garcilaso de la Vega in central Lima or Diagonal in Miraflores.

OTHER MUSEUMS

Museo Enrico Poli (Map pp66-7; ☎ 422-2437; Cochrane 400, Miraflores; admission US$10; ☽ 4-6pm Tue-Fri appointments only) has a collection of gold textiles, colonial silver and paintings that was featured in *National Geographic*. Prearranged tours by the owner are given in Spanish only. Also in Miraflores is **Casa de Ricardo Palma** (Map pp66-7; ☎ 445-5836; Gral Suarez 189, Miraflores; adult/student US$1/0.25; ☽ 9:15am-12:45pm & 2:30-5pm Mon-Fri), which was the home of the Peruvian author of that name from 1913 until his death in 1919.

In Barranco, **Museo de la Electricidad** (Map p68; ☎ 477-6577; San Pedro de Osma 105, Barranco; ☽ 9am-1pm & 2-5pm Tue-Sun) has a small exhibit on electricity in Lima, including the electric tramway system that used to link Barranco with Miraflores and Lima. Outside, a restored electric tram runs along rails on a few blocks of San Pedro de Osma on weekends (US$0.60).

HUACA PUCLLANA

Easily accessible is **Huaca Pucllana** (☎ 445-8695; cnr Borgoña & Tarapaca, Miraflores; admission free; ☽ 9am-5pm Wed-Mon), an adobe pyramidal structure of the Lima culture dating back to AD 400 and remodeled over three centuries. Though vigorous excavations continue, the site is open to regular guided tours (in Spanish) and there's a tiny museum with finds and a reconstructed burial.

West Lima   Map pp52-3
ZOO

The Parque de las Leyendas **Zoo** (☎ 451-8696; Parque de las Leyendas, San Miguel; adult/child under 11 US$2.50/1.20; ☽ 9am-5:30pm), between central Lima and Callao, is divided into three areas representing the three major geographical divisions of Peru: the coast, the sierra (or Andes) and the Amazon Basin. Up to 210 native Peruvian animals make up the majority of the exhibits, though there are also typical international zoo animals.

Irregular buses and colectivos (US$0.30 to US$0.60, 25 to 35 minutes) go past the park; catch them from Abancay and Garcilaso de la Vega in central Lima. A taxi from Miraflores will cost about US$2 to US$2.50.

FUERTE REAL FELIPE

This historic **fort** (☎ 429-0532, Plaza Independencia, Callao; foreigner/Peruvian/student US$2/1.20/0.60; ☽ 9am-2pm) was built in 1747 to guard the coast against pirates and corsairs, and is where the Spanish royalists made their last stand during the battles of independence in the 1820s. It still houses a small military contingent complete with assault course and the soldiers' soccer pitch. Visits are by guided tours in Spanish only. Note that the nearby dock area is a rough neighborhood.

ACTIVITIES
Cycling

Popular excursions from Lima include the 31km ride to Pachacamac, where there are several good local circuits open between April and December. Experts can also inquire about the circuit from Olleros to San Bartolo south of Lima. For general information in Spanish on cycling, try **Federación Peruana de Ciclismo** (☎ 340-1850; fpciclo@terra.com.pe).

Dozens of bike shops are listed in Lima's yellow pages under 'Bicicletas.' Check out:
Explore Bicycle Rentals (Map pp66-7; ☎ 241-7494; iexplore@terra.com; Bolognesi 381, Miraflores, no sign; ☽ 9am-7pm Mon-Fri, 9am-2pm Sat) This shop rents out mountain bikes with helmet and lock, charging US$3 per hour, US$8 per day and US$45 per week.
Peru Bike (Map p68; ☎ 467-0757; San Pedro de Osma 560, Barranco; ☽ 9am-1pm & 4-8pm Mon-Sat) Peru Bike is a recommended shop that also does repairs.
Willy Pro (☎ 346-0468; Javier Prado Este 3339, San Borja; ☽ 8am-8pm Mon-Sat)

Diving

There's reasonable deep-sea diving off Peru's southern coast. Contact **Peru Divers** (☎ 251-6231; perudivers@bellnet.com.pe; Huaylas 205, Chorrillos), an excellent dive shop owned by Luis Rodriguez, a PADI-certified instructor who sells gear and has information, arranges certification and diving trips. Also good is **Mundo Submarino** (☎ 441-7604; Conquistadores 791, San Isidro; ☽ 9:30am-1:30pm & 4-8pm Mon-Sat), which has equipment and organizes classes. It is run by Alejandro Pez, who speaks English, German, French, Italian and Portuguese.

Horse Riding

Cabalgatas (☎ 221-4591; www.cabalgatas .com.pe) has Peruvian *paso* (pacing) horses at the Mamacona grounds next to Pachacamac. This company does horseback trips around the ruins and along the beaches. A two-hour tour costs US$35, or three to four hours US$45. Make arrangements in advance.

Paragliding

For paragliding off the cliff-tops of Lima or around the south of Peru, including Lunahuaná, Ica and Paracas, contact **Peru Fly** (Map pp66-7; ☎ 444-5004; www.perufly.com; Jorge Chavez 658, Miraflores). Tandem flights take off near Parque del Amor in Miraflores and cost US$25. Alternatively, intensive six-day courses are offered (US$350). Be sure to wave at the bemused coffee-drinkers in the cliff-side Larcomar shopping mall as you glide past.

Swimming & Surfing

Despite plenty of newspaper warnings of pollution and health hazards, Limeños hit the beaches in their droves during the summer months of January, February and March. If you decide to join them, be aware of local thieves and don't leave anything unattended for a second. **Playa Costa Verde** in Miraflores (also called Waikiki) is a favorite of local surfers and has good breaks year-round. Barranco's beaches have waves better for long boards. There are seven other beaches in Miraflores and four more in Barranco. Serious surfers can also try **La Herradura** in Chorrillos, which has waves up to five meters high. For information on cleaner beaches and good surfing close to the south of Lima, see Beaches in Around Lima (p86).

The following stores sell surfing equipment and provide information:
Big Head (Map pp66-7; ☎ 818-4156; Larcomar; Miraflores; ☽ daily)
Focus (☎ 475-8459; Leonardo da Vinci 208, San Borja)
Waylo Whiler (☎ 247-6343; 28 de Julio 287, Barranco)

Other Activities

You can go tenpin bowling at **Cosmic Bowling** (Map pp66-7; ☎ 445-7776; Larcomar, Miraflores; US$12 per hour; ☽ 10am-midnight daily) in the Larcomar shopping mall. At night, the lanes are illuminated by 'cosmic' lighting. There's also tenpin bowling (US$7 per hour plus drink) and pool (US$1.40 per hour) at the more

MIRAFLORES

INFORMATION
Alianza Francesa	**1** C1
Banco Continental	**2** C3
Banco Latino	**3** C2
Banco Wiese	**4** C4
BCP	**5** C3
BCP	**6** C3
BCP	**7** C4
Botica Fasa	**8** C2
Crisol Books	(see 96)
Dragon Fans Internet	**9** C3
Full Screen Internet	**10** C1
Information Post	**11** C3
Instituto Cultural Peruano-Norteamericano	**12** C1
Interbanc	**13** C3
iPeru	(see 98)
LAC Dólar	**14** D3
Lavandaria 40 minutos	**15** B2
Moneygram	**16** D4
Peruvian-British Cultural Association	**17** C3
Servirap	**18** D3
South American Explorers (SAE)	**19** C2
Superfarma	**20** D5
Taller de Fotografía Profesional	**21** E4
Telefónica del Peru	**22** C3
Telefónica del Peru	**23** D3
Zeta	**24** B2
Zeta	(see 100)

SIGHTS & ACTIVITIES   pp57–67
Big Head	(see 100)
Brunswick Bowl	**25** C3
Casa de Ricardo Palma	**26** D2
Centro Cultural de Miraflores	**27** C3
Cosmic Bowling	(see 98)
El Sol	**28** D4
Explore Bicycle Rentals	**29** B3
Iglesia de La Virgen Milagrosa	**30** C3
Inlingua	**31** A1
Museo Amano	**32** A1
Museo Enrico Poli	**33** A1
Peru Fly	**34** B3

SLEEPING   pp69–73
Albergue Juvenil Internacional	**35** E3
Casa Del Mochilero	**36** A2
Explorer's House	**37** A3
Flying Dog Backpackers	**38** C3
Friend's House	**39** C4
Grand Hotel Miraflores	**40** C4
Hostal El Patio	**41** D3
Hostal Esperanza	**42** D3
Hostal Lucerna	**43** C5
Hostal Señorial	**44** C4
Hostal Torreblanca	**45** A3
Hotel Alemán	**46** C1
Hotel Antigua Miraflores	**47** B3
Hotel Ariosto	**48** D4
Hotel El Doral	**49** C2
Hotel Las Américas	**50** C5
Hotel San Antonio Abad	**51** E4
Inkawasi	**52** A3
La Castellana	**53** D3
La Paz Hotel	**54** D3
Marriott	**55** C5
Miraflores Park Hotel	(see 59)
Olimpus Hostel	**56** C4
Pensión Yolanda	**57** D1
Witches' House	**58** B3

EATING   pp73–7
Ambrosia	**59** D5
Astrid y Gaston	**60** D3
Bircher Benner	**61** D3

Parque Blume
Parque Villena
Parque Correa Elías
To Sachun Peña (500m)
Plaza Centroamérica
Parque Morales Barros
Plaza Manuel Solan
Parque Tahuantinsuyo Huaca Pucllana
Parque Miranda
Parque Central
Parque Kennedy
Plaza Bolognesi
Parque Raimondi
Parque del Amor
Playa Miraflores
PACIFIC OCEAN
Parque Salazar
Parque Melitón Porras

To Palos de Moguer (200m)
Óvalo Gutiérrez
To American Express (100m)
To Sachun Peña (500m)

Av Angamos Oeste
Av Santa Cruz
Av Cordova
Av Mariscal la Mar
Av José Pardo
Av Jorge Chávez
Av Grau
Av Arequipa
Av Ricardo Palma
Óvalo
Av Petit Thouars
General Vidal
Paseo de la República (Vía Expresa)
Mercado del Indios
Av José Larco
Av 28 de Julio
Av Benavides
Av de la Paz
Av Reducto
Circuito de Playas
Malecón de la Reserva

Martinto

run-down **Brunswick Bowl** (Map pp66-7; ☎ 801-5786; Malecón Balta 135, Miraflores; 9am-3pm Mon-Sat).

Daytona Amusement Park (Map pp52-3; ☎ 435-6130; Av El Derby, Monterrico; admission US$2), though lacking the major-league thrills, has laser quest, go-cart racing and you can even do paint-balling.

Lima has several tennis and golf clubs, and the 1st-class hotels and tour agencies can help organize games, but it's extremely pricey for nonmembers. **Lima Cricket and Football Club** (☎ 264-0027 Justo Amadeo Vigil 200, Magdalena) is popular with expats and sometimes allows English-speaking visitors with passports to obtain temporary membership for a small fee.

Sailors can contact the **Yacht Club Peruano** (☎ 429-0775; yachtclubperu@terra.com.pe; Bolognesi 761, La Punta, Callao).

People wishing to visit foreign (English-speaking) **prisoners**, who are mainly in jail on drug charges, can ask the SAE for a list of prisoners, prison addresses and visiting hours.

COURSES
Language
Though Lima has plenty of language schools, most cater to Peruvians learning English and tend to be far more expensive than in other parts of Peru. You can try these:

El Sol (Map pp66-7; ☎ 242-7763; lsol1@terra.com.pe, Grimaldo del Solar 469, Miraflores) El Sol charges US$11/14 per hour for group/individual classes.

Inlingua (Map pp66-7; ☎ 422-0915; www.inlingua.com; Santa Cruz 888, Miraflores) Individual classes are US$25 per hour.

Instituto Cultural Peruano-Norteamericano (Map pp66-7; ☎ 241-1940; Arequipa 4798, Miraflores) It's US$95 per month for five two-hour group classes per week.

Instituto de Idiomas Universidad Católica (☎ 442-8761; Camino Real 1037, San Isidro) Charges US$140 per month for five two-hour group classes per week; Universidad del Pacífico (☎ 421-2969; Prescott 333, San Isidro) It costs US$250 for three months with three 90-minute group classes per week.

You can also try a private teacher for between US$4 and US$8 per hour:

Alex Boris (☎ 423-0697, 9989-2771)

Carol Zuniga (☎ 495-2581)

Lourdes Galvaz (☎ 435-3910) Also teaches Quechua.

Luis Alberto Rivas Valcarcel (☎ 444-3652, 9962-9930)

Sonia (☎ 251-3191 before 10am)

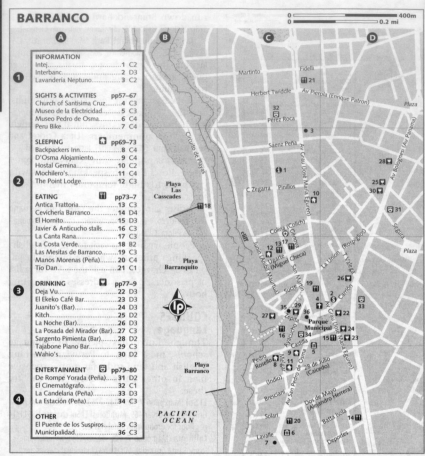

BARRANCO

0 — 400m
0 — 0.2 mi

INFORMATION		
Intej	1	C2
Interbanc	2	D3
Lavandería Neptuno	3	C2

SIGHTS & ACTIVITIES	pp57–67	
Church of Santísima Cruz	4	C3
Museo de la Electricidad	5	C3
Museo Pedro de Osma	6	C4
Peru Bike	7	C4

SLEEPING	pp69–73	
Backpackers Inn	8	C4
D'Osma Alojamiento	9	C4
Hostal Gemina	10	C2
Mochilero's	11	C4
The Point Lodge	12	C3

EATING	pp73–7	
Antica Trattoria	13	C3
Cevichería Barranco	14	D4
El Hornito	15	D3
Javier & Anticucho stalls	16	C3
La Canta Rana	17	C3
La Costa Verde	18	B2
Las Mesitas de Barranco	19	C3
Manos Morenas (Peña)	20	C4
Tío Dan	21	C1

DRINKING	pp77–9	
Deja Vu	22	D3
El Ekeko Café Bar	23	D3
Juanito's (Bar)	24	D3
Kitch	25	D2
La Noche (Bar)	26	D3
La Posada del Mirador (Bar)	27	C3
Sargento Pimienta (Bar)	28	D2
Tajabone Piano Bar	29	C3
Wahio's	30	D2

ENTERTAINMENT	pp79–80	
De Rompe Yorada (Peña)	31	D2
El Cinematógrafo	32	C1
La Candelaria (Peña)	33	D3
La Estación (Peña)	34	C3

OTHER		
El Puente de los Suspiros	35	C3
Municipalidad	36	C3

Other Courses

In Lima, other classes are usually conducted over several months in Spanish, but you may be able to organize flexible schedules if you contact the organizers directly.

Biblioteca Nacional (Map pp58-9; ☎ 428-7690; cafaebnp@binape.gob.pe; cnr Abancay & Miró Quesada, Central Lima) This library sometimes has weekend courses in Quechua and the *zampoña* (Andean panpipes).

Museo de Arte (Map pp58-9; ☎ 423-4732; areaeducativa@terra.com.pe; Paseo de Colón 125, Central Lima) Offers four- to eight-month courses in traditional and modern Peruvian dances including Latin rhythms, Andean folk dances and the Afro-Latino *danzas negras*, as well as typical Andean instruments such as the *zampoña*.

Museo de la Cultura Peruana (Map pp58-9; ☎ 423-5892; A Ugarte 630, Central Lima) It also runs limited classes for Peruvian instruments and typical dances from US$10.

TOURS & GUIDES

For guided tours of Lima and nearby archaeological sites such as Pachacamac as well as to arrange trips around Peru, try the following companies. In addition to these, many travel agencies (see p56), including Fertur Peru, Infotur and Lima Tours, also organize tours. Tours for elsewhere in Peru, though, will be cheaper if organized in the nearest major town to the area you want to visit.

AeroCóndor (☎ 441-1354, 442-5215; reservas@aerocondor.com.pe; Juan de Arona 781, San Isidro) Has flights over the Nazca Lines for around US$300.

It's much cheaper, though, to take a bus to Nazca and fly from there.

Aventours (Map pp66-7; ☎ 444-9060; info@aventours .com; Arequipa 4799, Miraflores) Aventours offer private overland tours or guided trips using public transport, as well as arranging guided treks.

Condor Travel (☎ 442-3000; www.condortravel .com.pe; Blondet 249, San Isidro) This company is recommended for top-end touring.

Ecoaventura Vida (☎ 461-2555; www.ecovida.da.ru) It runs alternative circuits to areas on the coast, such as the Ancon Islands and up to Paramonga.

Explorandes (☎ 445-8683; www.explorandes.com) Explorandes specializes in trekking and adventure sports.

Lima Vision (Map pp66-7; ☎ 9810-2110; limavisi@ limavision.com; Chiclayo 444, Miraflores) Lima Vision has daily city tours from US$20 to US$30.

Peru Expeditions (Map pp66-7; ☎ 445-7874; www .peru-expeditions.com; Arequipa 5241, office 504, Miraflores; ☒ 10am-5:30pm Mon-Fri, 9am-noon Sat) It has trips in 4WDs around Lima and beyond and can also arrange trekking, biking and rafting around Peru.

Servicios Aéreos AQP (☎ 222-3312; www.saaqp .com.pe; Los Castaños 347, San Isidro) This company offers top-end tours throughout Peru.

The following guides are officially registered with **Agotour** (☎ 571-1305), the Peruvian guide organization. The telephone numbers are for Peruvian daytime use only and can't handle calls in the middle of the night.

Gladis Araujo (☎ 463-3642, 9966-4780) Gladis speaks English.

Maria Kralewska de Canchaya (☎ 470-9888, 461-4061; canchaya@terra.com.pe) Speaks Polish.

Monica Velásquez (☎ 9943-0796; vc_monica@ hotmail.com) Speaks English; airport pick-ups offered if you sign for a tour.

Nila Soto (☎ 452-5483, 9965-0951) Speaks English and Italian.

Silvia Rodrich (☎ 446-0391, 446-8185) Speaks English.

Tino Guzman (☎ /fax 429-5779, 9909-5805) Speaks English; member of SAE.

Toshie Matsumura De Irikura (☎ 476-5101) Speaks Japanese.

FESTIVALS & EVENTS

See Festivals & Events (p407) in the Directory chapter for details of national holidays. For other events, see local newspapers and the useful *Peru Guide*. Holidays specific to Lima:

January 18 The anniversary of Lima's founding

August 30 Processions in honor of Saint Rose, the patron saint of Lima and the Americas.

October 18 Huge religious processions celebrating the Lord of the Miracles, with smaller processions occurring on most Sundays in October.

SLEEPING

Apart for the tourist Mecca of Cuzco, hotels are more expensive here than in any other Peruvian city. The cheapest are generally in central Lima, though it's not as safe here as in the more upmarket neighborhoods of Miraflores, Barranco and San Isidro. Wherever you stay, always ask about discounts if you're planning to spend more than a few days in Lima as most places offer good weekly rates. Note that top-end hotels may add a 10% tax onto the rates, but they should not add an additional 18% tax to the rates for foreigners.

It's also worth contacting hotels in advance to find out if they will pick you up from the airport; even budget hostels often arrange for secure taxis for a few dollars less than the official airport taxi service.

Be aware that hostels in Lima face a lot of expensive red tape to put up a sign on the front of their establishment, so many of the following budget options have no sign and can look for all the world like ordinary houses from the outside.

Central Lima   Map pp58-9
BUDGET

Hostal España (☎ 428-5546; hotel_espana@hotmail .com; Azangaro 105; dm US$3, s/d US$6/9) España is in a rambling old mansion full of classical busts, birds and paintings. It's an established gringos-only scene with basic accommodations. There are hot showers in the early morning or late evening, laundry and a rooftop café surrounded by a veritable jungle of trailing plants. The service can be abrupt.

Hostal San Francisco (☎ 426-2735; hostal_san _francisco@terramail.com.pe; Azangaro 127; dm US$5-6; ☐) This is a clean and modern escape from the travelers' scene next door and, though it also has less character, is friendly and has good soft beds.

Hostal Belén (☎ 427-8995; arcobel@terra.com.pe; Jirón Belén 1049; s/d/tr US$6/12/18, with bathroom US$9/ 12) Housed in a characterful, lofty-ceilinged colonial building, Belén has quite basic but good rooms and very hot water, though the popular bar downstairs gets rowdy at weekends.

Familia Rodríguez (☎ 423-6465; jjr-art@mail.cosa pidata.com.pe; Nicolás de Piérola 730, 2nd floor, No 3; dm US$6) This is an informal and very friendly family home in a central position. Rates include breakfast. Recommended.

Pensión Ibarra (☎ /fax 427-8603; pension_ibarra@ ekno.com; Tacna 359, 14th & 15th floors; s/d US$7/10) Situated high above the city in an apartment block, this homely *pensión* is run by the helpful Ibarra sisters, who make a real effort to keep it safe, comfortable and clean. Rooms are simple and there are shared bathrooms and a kitchen. It's good for long-term stays.

Plaza Francia Inn Pensión (☎ 330-6080; franciasquareinn@yahoo.com; Rufino Torrico 1117; dm US$7, s/d US$11/14) This simple budget choice, run by the owners of the excellent mid-range Posada del Parque, has clean dorm rooms with shared hot showers, small personal safes in each room and a lounge with cable TV.

Hostal Iquique (☎ 433-4724 hiquique@terra .com.pe; Iquique 758; s/d US$7/10, with bathroom US$10/ 16) This recommended spot is clean, safe and has warm showers at any time. There is a rooftop terrace, decorative tiling and most rooms have national TV. Kitchen facilities are available – the amiable owner, Fernando, is an excellent cook, and if you're lucky, he might help you with a good meal.

Hostal Roma (☎ 427-7576; resroma@terra.com.pe; Ica 326; s/d US$13/20, with bathroom US$25/36; ☐) This friendly old hostel is clean, central and a little camp with quirky, varied rooms – some are windowless so look at a few first. There is a good choice of breakfasts in the attached restaurant. Off-season discounts are as much as US$5.

Hostal de las Artes (☎ 433-0031; artes@ terra.com.pe; Chota 1469; s/d with bathroom US$8/14-17) This gay-friendly, Dutch/Peruvian-owned hostel has well-maintained rooms that have bathrooms with hot water. It is located on a quiet street in an atmospheric high-ceilinged *casa antigua* with colorful tiling and a glass ceiling.

Others to try are:

Hotel Europa (☎ 427-3351; Ancash 376; s/d US$5/7) Worn budget alternative with flimsy and dark rooms but friendly service.

Hostal Wiracocha (☎ 427-1178; fax 427-4406; Jirón Junín 284; s/d US$6/7, with bathroom US$10/12) Superb location but has some damp rooms. The private showers are hot.

MID-RANGE

Posada del Parque (☎ 433-2412, 9945-4260; posada@ incacountry.com, Parque Hernán Velarde 60; s/d/tr US$27/33/ 48) This well-recommended spot is in a lovely house on a tranquil cul-de-sac just south of central Lima. It is run by a friendly and helpful young English-speaking couple, and boasts spotless rooms with attractive furniture and artwork. All rooms have cable TV, and airport pick-up can be arranged at any time.

Bonbini (☎ 427-6477; hostalbonbini@hotmail.com; Cailloma 209; s/d US$30/40) This central hotel is a comfy, well-manicured spot with spick-and-span bathrooms and cable TV. It's a refreshingly good find in an area short on quality mid-range options.

Kamana Hotel (☎ 426-7204; kamana@amauta.rcp .net.pe; Camaná 547; s/d/tr US$28/35/45) This secure, smart and relatively modern hotel has clean and comfortable rooms. The rates include breakfast, and English is spoken.

Hotel Continental (☎ 427-5890; contihot@terra .com.pe; Puno 196; s/d/tr US$36/45/55) The Continental is a large but faded hotel with spacious rooms decorated by somebody highly enamored of the color beige. Rates include breakfast. The 7th floor and up have newer rooms with cable TV.

Hotel Maury (☎ 428-8188; hotmaury@amauta.rcp .net.pe; Ucayali 201; s/d US$48/59, ste US$108) Newly renovated and looking very well for it, this option borders on the top-end and has been given the thumbs up by readers. The smart rooms boast all the mod cons. Rates include breakfast.

Hotel Internacional (☎ 433-5517; fax 330-4754; 28 de Julio 763; s/d US$20/26) It's a good-value but nondescript choice; breakfast is included.

TOP END

Central Lima has seen its business slipping away in recent years and top-end establishments have been suffering. In response to their plight, many offer periodic promotional rates to woo customers back, so contact them in advance for the latest discounts.

Gran Hotel Bolívar (☎ 428-7672; fax 428-7671; bolivar@terra.com.pe; Jirón de la Unión 958; s/d US$102/115) Nostalgia strikes at this venerable 1920s hotel on Plaza San Martín. The grand old bar is an obligatory stop for aficionados of the Peruvian pisco sour, and a string quartet plays in the domed, stained-glass rotunda during afternoon tea. Sadly, the hotel has had persistent plumbing problems and its rooms, though retaining a rare finesse, are increasingly musty from disuse. At the time of writing, the hotel was offering promotional rates of singles/doubles US$60/70.

Lima Sheraton (☎ 315-5022; reservas@sheraton.com.pe; Paseo de la República 170; s/d US$170/185) Four hundred typically comfortable and spacious Sheraton rooms are housed in this vertigo-inducing, boxy tower overlooking the Palacio de Justicia. There's a Visa ATM, and a casino to spend your freshly withdrawn cash in. At the time of writing, promotional prices were singles/doubles US$86/95.

Breña, Jesús María & Pueblo Libre
Map pp52-3
BUDGET

Casa Hospedaje Machu Picchu (☎ 424-3479; va nessa_new@hotmail.com; Juan Pablo Ferandini 1015, Breña; dm US$3.50) A family homestay, a block off the 10th *cuadra* of Brasil, this place is highly recommended by readers. It is very friendly, secure, has kitchen privileges and a lounge with cable TV. Some English is spoken.

Gustavo Ruiz (☎ 424-6581, cell 949-7054; gus_ribb@hotmail.com; Mello Franco 170, Jesús María; dm US$4) Rooms in this private home are basic but good value. Reservations only.

Marfil (☎ 463-3161; casamarfil@yahoo.com; Parque Ayacucho 126, Pueblo Libre; dm US$6) This hostel is a neatly tended and friendly spot; English is spoken.

San Isidro
Map pp52-3
BUDGET

Malka Youth Hostel (☎ 222-5589; hostelmalka@terra.com.pe; Los Lirios 165; dm nonstudent/student US$6/5) Near to Parque Americas, this hostel has clean, quiet rooms sleeping three to eight people. There are kitchen and laundry facilities, a TV room and a games room, luggage storage and 24-hour hot water.

TOP END

Country Club (☎ 611-9000; country@hotelcountry.com; Los Eucaliptos 590; s/d US$250; 🔊) Built in 1927, this club is housed in one of finest buildings in Lima, which has been superbly renovated with a glorious lobby covered by a stained-glass dome. The hotel manages to meld slick modern class with a carefully nurtured colonial charm. You can arrange a round of golf on the nearby course for US$50.

Los Delfines Hotel (☎ 215-7000; reservas@losdelfineshotel.com.pe; Los Eucaliptos 555; s/d US$141; 🔊)

This hotel is famous as much for its long-term guests Yaku and Wayra – dolphins kept in a cramped pool alongside the hotels lobby bar – as it is for its luxurious rooms and casino. Some travelers have expressed concern over the dolphins' conditions. Rates include a buffet breakfast, and the dolphins perform at regular intervals, including an evening show at 8:30pm Tuesday to Sunday for bar-goers.

Miraflores
Map pp66-7
BUDGET

Albergue Juvenil Internacional (☎ 446-5488; hostell@terra.com.pe; Casimiro Ulloa 328; dm US$11, d with bathroom US$26) This newly renovated hostel is an excellent choice for spotless dorms and private rooms, and also offers a spacious garden, large sociable lounge, travel information and good kitchen facilities (US$0.60 for the gas).

Bed & Breakfast José Luis (☎ 444-1015; hsjluis@terra.com.pe; Paula de Ugarriza 727; r per person US$10) On a quiet residential street off 28 de Julio east of the Vía Expresa, this huge rabbit warren of a place is popular with guests appreciative of the friendly English-speaking host and the characterful old building. All but three of the basic rooms have bathrooms, and rates include breakfast. Reservations only.

Inkawasi (☎ 241-8218; backpackerinkawasi@hotmail.com; Av de la Aviación 210; dm US$10, d with bathroom US$25, with Jacuzzi $30) This small budget newbie is modern, well furnished and close to cliff-top parks. Rates include breakfast and the owner speaks fluent English.

Flying Dog Backpackers (☎ 445-0940; flyingdog@mixmail.com; Diez Canseco 117; dm US$9, d US$25) A neat place right in the heart of Miraflores beside Parque Kennedy, the Flying Dog is run by youthful, laid-back hosts who speak English. There are kitchen facilities, cable TV and a lounge. Prices include breakfast at the nearby El Parquetito café.

Witches' House (☎ 446-7722; gizik@hotmail.com; Bolognesi 364; dm US$5, s/d US$10/20; P) This oddly misplaced, nouveau-Tudor house stands out a mile in a quieter residential area of Miraflores. Popular with Israelis, the hostel has 24-hour hot water, a kitchen, laundry, pool table, DVDs and cable TV, plus the surrounding concrete courtyard boasts basketball and plenty of room to breathe.

Friend's House (☎ 446-6248; Jirón Manco Cápac 368; dm US$6, d US$14) This backpacker-friendly hostel has a highly sociable atmosphere – perhaps inescapable given the cramped nature of the dorms. Kitchen privileges are available, as well as bicycle rental and a small lounge with cable TV.

Casa del Mochilero (☎ 444-9089; pilaryv@hot mail.com; 2nd fl, Chacaltana 130A; r per person US$4) This youthful homestay is so popular the neighbors are having a stab at stealing customers with carefully conceived names such as Hostel Mochileros and the English translation Back Packer's Home. The original is best, but all are welcoming spots with simple rooms, shared hot showers and kitchen privileges.

Pensión Yolanda (☎ 445-7565; pensionyolanda@ hotmail.com; Domingo Elías 230; s/d US$12/24, d with bathroom US$30) Rooms here are plain and a shade overpriced, but the hostel provides very helpful tourist information and the friendly manager speaks fluent English, French and German.

Also well worth a look are:

Explorer's House (☎ 241-5002; explorers.house@ yahoo.es; Alfredo León 158; s/d US$5/10) Homely family pensión with breakfast included.

M Luisa Chávez (☎ 447-3996; Genaro Castro Iglesias 273; s/d US$10/20) Welcoming homestay east of the center of Miraflores.

MID-RANGE

Hostal El Patio (☎ 444-2107; hostalelpatio@qnet.com .pe; Diez Canseco 341a; s/d US$30/35, minisuites US$40, ste US$55) This little gem of a hostel has a cheery, English-speaking owner who takes her role as hostess seriously. The *hostal* has a sunny courtyard with fountain and trailing plants, plus several terraces upon which to sit and ponder. Rates include breakfast, and suites have kitchenettes. It costs an additional US$5 to pay using plastic.

Olimpus Hostel (☎ 242-6077; olimpusperu@terra .com.pe; Diego Ferre 365; r per person US$15, s/d US$30/35) This is another friendly hostel with well-decorated, spotless rooms, welcoming communal areas and a gregarious owner. The rates are flexible and include breakfast.

Hostal Señorial (☎ 445-7306; senorial@viabcp.com; José Gonzalez 567; s/d US$35/45; ▯) Some rooms are better than others at this popular hostel with its tranquil internal lawn and a novel visitor's book scrawled on the walls. The good-sized rooms include cable TV and breakfast, plus there's a solarium.

Hotel San Antonio Abad (☎ 447-6766; hotelsan antonioabad@mail.com; Ramón Ribeyro 301; s/d/tr US$30/

40/50) It's a popular and pleasant hotel set back from the road. It has grassy gardens and comfy rooms with cable TV and phone, and offers free airport pick-up with advance notice. Rates include a tasty breakfast.

La Castellana (☎ 444-4662; hcastelllan@terra.com .pe; Grimaldo del Solar 222; s/d US$48/60) Housed in an attractive colonial-style house, La Castellana offers pleasant, if slightly dark rooms with cable TV, hairdryers and shaving outlets. There's a grassy internal garden and terrace for partaking of some civilized breakfast, which is included in the price.

Hotel Alemán (☎ 445-6999; haleman@terra.com.pe; Arequipa 4704; s/d $32/45) The clean, quiet and secure Hotel Aleman has exceptionally spacious rooms and private bathrooms, with cable TV and minifridge. It gives discounts for long stays or businesses, and rates include an excellent buffet breakfast.

Hostal Torreblanca (☎ 447-0142; hostal@torreblanca peru.com; Pardo 1453; s/d US$45/55, ste US$65) Though the narrow corridors of Torreblanca look initially scruffy, the varied rooms are in very good nick, and a few on the top floor have attractive wood-beamed ceilings, red tiles and fireplaces. Prices are flexible and include a continental breakfast and free airport pick-up.

Hotel El Doral (☎ 242-7799; aparthotel@eldoral.com .pe; Pardo 486; s/d US$65/70; ▯ ▨) Rooms in this high-rise hotel have cable TV, minibars and small sitting rooms plus that all-important double-glazing fronting onto one of Miraflores' busiest streets. There's a very small, open-air swimming pool and bar on a high terrace, and rates include breakfast.

Grand Hotel Miraflores (☎ 241-4647; reservas@ grandhotelmiraflores.com.pe; 28 de Julio 151; s/d US$50/60) This large hotel looks past its best until you see the rooms, which are large, modern and good value. There's a dinky, open-air swimming pool, which can be used by nonguests if they eat in the restaurant. Rates include a welcome cocktail and breakfast.

Hostal Lucerna (☎ 445-7321; hostallucerna@terra .com.pe; Las Dalias 276; s/d US$45/53) Lucerna has a cozy atmosphere and comfortable rooms with TV; some rooms have balconies overlooking a nice little garden. You may get a discount if you show this book.

Hostal Esperanza (☎ 444-2411; htlesperanza@terra .com.pe; Esperanza 350; s/d US$45/60) This place is an externally ugly high-rise that is safe and clean within.

TOP END

Miraflores has numerous top-class establishments, and only a selection of the most noteworthy is given here. All of the following have a restaurant, and bathrooms, phones and cable TV in the rooms.

Hotel Antigua Miraflores (☎ 241-6116; info@peru -hotels-inns.com; Grau 350; s/d traditional US$64/74, colonial US$74/89, senorial US$89/104; 🖳) As its name suggests, the Antigua is in an old converted mansion. Located in a quiet neighborhood, it has elegant lounges decorated with colonial and modern Peruvian art. The rooms, while sporting all the expected modern facilities, also have intriguing antique flourishes. Rooms vary in size and style; the *senorial* suites are most sumptuous with Jacuzzi, kitchen and air-con.

La Paz Hotel (☎ 242-9350; reservas@lapaz.com.pe; Av La Paz 679; s/d US$70/75, ste US$120) This relatively new hotel is clean and modern, if a shade characterless. The suites sleep four and have air-con, kitchenettes and two bathrooms. The rates include breakfast.

Hotel Ariosto (☎ 444-1414; www.hotelariosto .com.pe; La Paz 769; s/d US$80/100, ste US$120; 🖳) This large hotel, which attracts a fair quota of jazz musicians and writers, attempts – and partially pulls off – a woody, country charm. It has a 24-hour restaurant service and a sauna, and rates include a buffet breakfast and free airport pick-up. Discounted rates are frequently arranged for long stays or in the off-season.

Miraflores Park Hotel (☎ 242-3000; bgarcia-rosell@ peruorientexpress.com.pe; Malecón de la Reserva 1035; s/d US$295, ste US$340; 🖳 🖳 Ⓟ) Surely the best of Lima's smaller luxury hotels, the Miraflores Park has glorious ocean views and all the frills expected of a five-star hotel, including gym, sauna, squash court and a small outdoor pool overlooking the ocean. Some rooms have glass walls with stunning views.

Hotel Las Américas (☎ 444-7272; hotel@hote leslasamericas.com; Benavides 415; s or d US$180-330; 🖳 🖳) This standard five-star hotel has all the luxury and services you would expect for the price tag. Businesspeople can often get corporate discounts.

Marriott (☎ 217-7000; www.marriotthotels.com /limdt; Malecón de la Reserva 615; s/d US$175/190, ste US$255; 🖳 🖳 Ⓟ) The newest five-star addition to Miraflores, the enormous Marriott is perhaps the flashiest of them all with a superb seafront location by the Larcomar shopping center. The sparkling rooms seem to have every amenity going, including temperature regulation and no less than three phones in each room, and there's glass-fronted restaurants and bars, a large casino, plus an open-air tennis court and pool. Rates do not include breakfast.

Barranco   Map p68
BUDGET

Once a holiday resort for upper-crust Limeños, Barranco's budget scene is now blossoming, with several top-notch new hostels to rival anything in Miraflores.

The Point Lodge (☎ 247-7997; the_point _barranco@hotmail.com; Junín 300; dm US$7-8; 🖳) This white-washed seafront house hosts a highly recommended hostel run by a couple of laid-back, expat backpackers. It has all the toys – a DVD collection, computer games, ping-pong, modern kitchen and a spacious garden, plus the owners are only too willing to act as guides to the local nightlife.

Backpackers Inn (☎ 247-3709; Backpackersinnperu@ hotmail.com; Malecón Castilla 260; dm US$10) Housed in a newly renovated mansion with sea views, this hostel has rooms with two, four, or six beds, all with bathroom and the price includes breakfast.

Mochileros (☎ 477-4506; backpackers@backpackers peru.com; San Pedro de Osma 135; dm per person US$10) This long-established budget haunt is in an atmospheric, 100-year-old mansion handy for Barranco's nightlife. There is a boisterous bar on the premises.

D'Osma Alojamiento (☎ 251-4178; deosma@ec-red .com; San Pedro de Osma 240; s/d with breakfast US$10/20) Far less of a backpacker scene, this family home has a quiet environment good for long-term stays. There are only a few rooms so book ahead. Some English and German is spoken.

MID-RANGE

Hostal Gemina (☎ 477-0712; hostalgemina@yahoo .com; Grau 620; s/d/tr US$29/42/55) A smart, modern hotel on Barranco's main street, Gemina has been recommended for endless hot water and friendly service. Rates are flexible and include breakfast.

EATING

Lima is arguably the gastronomic capital of its continent, boasting high-quality restaurants of every price range. Seafood is a

LIMA

local specialty, but you'll find restaurants specializing in all types of national and international fare. Don't leave without trying the distinctive sweets *mazmorra morada* (a violet corn dessert), or *suspiro a la Limeña* (rich vanilla meringue with caramel). The traditional drink is *chicha morada*.

People who prefer to see meat only on live animals can check out Vegetarian under Central Lima (p75) and Miraflores (p76).

Note that taxes (*impuestos* or IGV) and service charges on meals can be exorbitant, with fancier restaurants adding up to 28% to your total. Ask if taxes are included before you order.

Central Lima   Map pp58-9
BUDGET

Menús (set lunches) that cost about US$1.50 to US$2 can be found in many of the cheaper restaurants.

Restaurant Accllahuasy (☎ 428-7920; Ancash 400; mains US$2-5) This spot near the backpackers' hotels is popular with gringos and locals alike, with a have-a-go-at-anything menu.

Azato (☎ 423-0278; Arica 298; menú US$1.20-2) It's a recommended spot for fast *criollo* (coastal Peruvian) food.

El Cordano (☎ 427-0181; Ancash 202; snacks US$2-4, mains US$4-7) Though looking a shade rundown these days, El Cordano is a longstanding, downtown restaurant with a 1920s decor serving typical Peruvian snacks and a top selection of Peruvian beers, wines and piscos.

Queirolo (☎ 425-0421; Camaná 900; mains US$3-5; ☒ closed dinnertime Sun) Another atmospheric old restaurant popular for its set lunches and as a drinking-and-gathering spot for Limeños.

La Casera (☎ 427-2380; Huancavelica 244; menú US$2; ☒ closed Sun) This simple and brusque place serves typical Peruvian food for loose change.

La Merced (☎ 427-7933; Miró Quesada 158; mains US$2-6) This restaurant, usually bustling with businesspeople doing lunch, has a bland exterior giving no clue to its spacious interior and intricately carved wooden ceiling within.

Panko's (☎ 424-9079; Garcilaso de la Vega 1296) Panko's is a central-Lima bakery offering a mouth-watering array of sweets, pastries and coffee.

MID-RANGE

San Remo Restaurant (☎ 427-9102; Pasaje de los Escribanos; 2-course menú US$7) Half a block from the Plaza de Armas, tiny de los Escribanos alley has several upscale cafés, including this welcoming outdoor spot.

Manhattan Restaurant (☎ 428-2117; Miró Quesada 253; mains US$4-10; ☒ closed Sat & Sun) This sophisticated, mellow hideaway caters to businesspeople and has good *menús*, as well as a happy hour from 5pm to closing time at 7pm.

El Estadio Futbol Club (☎ 428-8866; Nicolás de Piérola 926; ☒ noon-midnight Mon-Wed, noon-2am Thu-Sat) On Plaza San Martín, this soccer-themed bar serves good food on indoor and outdoor tables, a few of which are already occupied by waxwork soccer stars.

Cevichería La Choza Nautica (☎ 261-5537; Breña 204; mains US$6-10) 'La *choza*' means 'the shack,' in a conscious play of words with the upscale La Rosa Nautica restaurant (see p76). And this popular little *cevichería* (restaurant serving ceviche) doesn't miss the opportunity to play on the aphrodisiacal qualities of seafood either – just look for their 'ceviche erotica' *menú*.

If you can, don't miss a trip to Lima's **Barrio Chino** (China Town), southeast of the Plaza de Armas; Lima houses about 200,000 first-generation Chinese immigrants and its Chinese quarter is thus blessed with numerous authentic restaurants in a lively parade lined with paving slabs inscribed with news of weddings, births and other happy events.

Wa Lok (☎ 427-2656; Paruro 864; mains US$6-12; ☒ closed dinnertime Sun) This is one of the best *chifa* (Chinese) restaurants in China Town, and the friendly owner speaks English.

Salon Capon (☎ 426-9286; Paruro 819; mains US$6-10; ☒ closes 8pm Sun) Much like Wa Lok, Salon Capon has particularly good dim sum.

TOP END

L'Eau Vive (☎ 427-5612; Ucayali 370; lunch/dinner US$10/25; ☒ 12:30-3pm & 7:30-9:30pm Mon-Sat) This unique restaurant has *menús* prepared and served by a French order of nuns; it features dishes from all over the world, as well as some exotic cocktails. It's in a quiet, colonial-style house and is a welcome relief from the Lima madhouse. The profits all go to charity. The nuns sing an 'Ave María' at 9pm.

VEGETARIAN

Villa Natura (☎ 426-3944; Ucayali 326; 3-course menú US$1.50-2; ☯ closed Sun) This is one of a proliferation of no-frills, vegetarian pit-stops in central Lima.

Natur (Moquegua 132; ☯ closed Sun) Another friendly, family-run spot, Natur is also recommended for inexpensive vegetarian fare.

San Isidro

Puerto Perdido (☎ 264-3435; Pezet 1455; mains US$5-7; ☯ lunch only) Two blocks southwest of Lima Golf Club, this seafood restaurant serves excellent ceviche and is popular with a young crowd.

Punta Sal (☎ 441-7431; Conquistadores 958; mains US$9-15) Another great seafood restaurant, Punta Sal is one of the best places for traditional ceviche. Try the Assassin Ceviche with black scallops and sea urchins if you dare.

Al Dente (☎ 221-6845; 2 de Mayo 759; mains US$6-12) A good spot for a romantic tryst, or just to indulge in some choice Italian fare, this restaurant is prettily bedecked in fairy lights and swathes of muslin.

Miraflores   Map pp66-7
BUDGET

Restaurants are more expensive in Miraflores, but if you keep your eyes peeled there's still a few hole-in-the-wall cafés selling cheap set *menús*; check the places on Berlin between Grau and Diagonal. US-style, fast-food joints cluster around Óvalo Gutierrez, at the corner of Santa Cruz and Espinar, in the northwest of Miraflores. Vegetarian options (see p76) are also cheap.

Ima Sumac (☎ 446-2713; Colón 241; 3-course menú US$2; ☯ lunch only) It's a warm and friendly little place with great-value *menús*. Takeaway or delivery (extra US$0.30) is possible if you're in Miraflores.

Santa Isabel (Benavides 487; mains US$2.50-6; ☯ 24 hr) Open all night, this café-restaurant has a varied buffet to peruse.

Chifa Kun Fa (☎ 447-8634; San Martín 459; mains US$3-6) Good Peruvian-style Chinese food is served here.

El Parquetito (☎ 444-0490; Lima 373; mains US$4-8) The El Parquetito has shady outdoor tables on a pedestrian street and good breakfasts.

Pardo's Chicken (☎ 446-4790; Benavides 730; mains US$3-9) An ubiquitous chicken-and-fries restaurant that largely manages to escape the atmosphere of a fast-food restaurant, Pardo's also does ribs and *anticuchos* (kebabs).

Solari (☎ 242-3100; Pardo 216; mains US$4-9) Serving a mix of international dishes in a flashy, modern glass building complete with plants and an artificial waterfall, the atmosphere of this decent restaurant only slightly resembles that of an indoor swimming pool.

MID-RANGE

The trendiest spot to dine in Miraflores is currently in the Larcomar shopping mall, with its spectacular location teetering on the brink of the coastal cliffs. The complex is packed with smart cafés and a young crowd partaking of their pricey beverages, and there's even a sushi bar.

Several British-style pubs in Miraflores offer international pub grub. See Drinking (p77) for details.

Mango's (☎ 242-8110; Larcomar; mains US$6-10) Built into the clifftop and with an attractive patio looking out to sea, Mango's is an elegant, modern restaurant serving a variety of meals and snacks. It does a great breakfast buffet at weekends. Watch for the occasional paraglider floating past along the cliffs.

Vivaldino (☎ 446-3859; Larcomar; mains US$8-14) This sophisticated, glass-walled, new Italian restaurant has good food, if you can forgive the pan-piped Simon and Garfunkel soundtrack.

La Tiendecita Blanca (☎ 445-9797; Larco 111; mains US$9-16) On the main Óvalo by Parque Kennedy, this has been a Miraflores landmark for over half a century and has a superb, if pricey, Swiss-pastry selection.

Vivaldi (☎ 446-1473; Ricardo Palma 258; mains US$6-13) A dark, smoky place near La Tiendecita, Vivaldi has good coffees, meals and an old-world, conspiratorial air.

Sí Señor (☎ 445-3789; Bolognesi 706; mains US$6-10; ☯ evening only). This lively branch serves Tex-Mex food, usually accompanied by Mexican beer and of course, plenty of tequila. There's also a Spanish version at Angamos Oeste 598.

Cebichería Don Beta (☎ 445-8370; José Gálvez 667; 3-course menú US$10-13) Don't be put off by the tiny exterior of this locally popular seafood restaurant; it opens up into an attractive room with a thatched roof and nautical theme. It tends to be quiet in the evenings.

Las Tejas (☎ 444-4360; Diez Canseco 340; mains US$10-15) For a good variety of Peruvian fare, try this small snug place, set below road level near Hostal El Patio. It has live *criollo* music at 8pm Thursday to Saturday.

La Tranquera (☎ 447-5111; Pardo 285; mains US$7-16) An Argentine-influenced recommendation for meat, meat and more meat is this 30-year-old favorite. It serves a US$75 *parrillada* (mixed grill) that supposedly serves five, but looks more fit for 10. There's also a special selection of meats, such as *cuy* (guinea pig; US$14), rabbit and game.

Glorietta (☎ 445-0498; Diagonal 181; mains US$5-10) Parque Kennedy and Diagonal, nicknamed 'Pizza Street,' have numerous open-fronted Italian joints to choose from, including this reasonable choice.

La Trattoria (☎ 446-7002; Manuel Bonilla 106; mains US$7-16) Recommended for tasty, homemade pasta that you can watch them make, La Trattoria is a simple, laid-back Italian restaurant with a quiet ambiance.

Il Postino (☎ 446-8381; Colina 401; mains US$8-13; ☽ closed dinnertime Sun) This is one of Miraflores' best Italian restaurants, with an informal Mediterranean atmosphere and a great collection of reasonably priced international wines.

TOP END

Restaurant Huaca Pucllana (☎ 445-4042; General Borgoño 8th block; mains US$7.50-20) This mellow, sophisticated establishment sits overlooking the pre-Inca pyramidal temple Huaca Pucllana and serves wonderful contemporary Peruvian cuisine. The ruins are floodlit at night, and guided tours can be arranged from here.

La Rosa Nautica (☎ 445-0149; Circuito de Playas; 3-course menú US$17, mains US$11-25) This famous restaurant is in a fabulous building at the end of Playa Costa Verde's historic pier. The location and atmosphere are unique: The ocean is floodlit, surfers sometimes skim through the piling, and you can clearly hear and smell the waves below. Take a taxi to the pier and walk the last 100m.

El Señorio de Sulco (☎ 441-0389; Malecón Cisneros 1470; buffet US$25) A well-known restaurant close to the clifftops of Miraflores, El Señorio is known for its excellent *criollo* seafood and meats.

La Hamaca (☎ 242-7978; Arequipa 4698; mains US$6-18; ☽ closed dinnertime Sun) This high-class restaurant takes its intimate atmosphere to another level with tables in private booths,

each carefully decorated with antique touches. It serves a limited menu of typical Peruvian food.

Las Brujas de Cachiche (☎ 444-5310; alcorta@ brujasdecachiche.com.pe; Bolognesi 460; 3-course menú US$25, mains US$9-15) Las Brujas weaves its image around the tale of the village of Cachiche near Ica, where legendary temptresses and sorcerers meddled with the populace. It's one of the best places in town for quality Peruvian food.

Ambrosia (☎ 242-3000; Malecón de la Reserva 1035; mains US$8-20) Based in Miraflores Park Hotel, this sophisticated, high-brow restaurant gets the culinary thumbs up for its international gourmet meals.

Astrid y Gaston (☎ 242-5387; Cantuarias 175; mains US$9-20) This elegant upper-class Limeño mainstay has Cordon Bleu–trained chefs who create excellent international cuisine with a soupçon of Peruvian flavor.

CAFÉS

Miraflores has by far the best pavement cafés in Lima for people-watching.

Café Café (snacks & sandwiches US$2-3.50, drinks US$1.50-6); Martír Olaya (☎ 445-1165; Martír Olaya 250); Larcomar (☎ 445-9499; ☽ till 3am Fri & Sat) With two branches in Miraflores, this place advertises 120 different drinks, gourmet coffees, sandwiches and desserts. The Larcomar branch is the place to see and be seen, with its great location looking directly out to sea and down to the surfers below: It's not for sufferers of vertigo.

Haiti (☎ 445-0539; Parque Kennedy; mains US$4-8) Located next to Starvision El Pacífico cinema, this is an excellent spot to watch the world go by as its tables spill out onto one of the busiest pedestrian areas in Miraflores. A gay-friendly place, it's equally popular with families, straights and little old ladies. The bow-tied waiters are very suave, but the food receives mixed reviews.

Quattro D (☎ 447-1523; Angamos Oeste 408) Perhaps the best Italian ice cream in town, boasting 36 different flavors, as well as delicious cakes and good coffee.

VEGETARIAN

Govinda (☎ 444-2871; Schell 634, Miraflores; 3-course menús US$2-3; ☽ closed dinnertime Sun) A cheap and cheerful café run by the Hare Krishnas; you'll see Govindas popping up all across Peru.

Decorative ceiling and murals at the **cathedral** (p60), Lima

RICHARD I'ANSON

BRUCE BI

Interior view of the 19th-century **main post office** (p55), Lima

Plaza San Martín (p61) at night, Lima

BRUCE BI

MARK DAFFEY

CHRIS BEALL

Burial ground of the Nazca civilization, south of **Nazca** (p106)

1500-year-old spiral aqueduct, near **Nazca** (p106)

Palm-fringed oasis amid the sand dunes, **Huacachina** (p102)

JANE

Bircher Benner (☎ 444-4250; Diez Canseco 487; mains US$3-7; ✆ closed Sun) Bircher has been established much longer than the other cheaper and cheerful options in town, and it is the place for vegetarians to pamper themselves a little. It has quality food but slow service.

Barranco   Map p68
BUDGET
The passageway under Puente de los Suspiros leads to several *anticucho* stalls and restaurants. The delicious beef-heart shish kebabs (*anticucho de corazon*) served up here are great right off the grill.

Javier (☎ 477-5339; Barjada de los Baños 403; mains US$3.50-6) Recommended for serving a wide range of offerings; a portion of *anticucho* is around US$2.50.

Tío Dan (cnr Grau & Piérola; mains US$2.50-5) Reasonably priced pizza and pasta is served around a circular bar at this popular little spot.

El Hornito (☎ 477-2465; Grau 209; mains US$3-7) This is another, larger pizzeria that's on Barranco's main square.

MID-RANGE
Chain restaurants don't get much of a look-in here, as Barranco strives to maintain its character and hold itself apart from its ritzy international neighbor, Miraflores.

La Canta Rana (☎ 477-8934; Génova 101; mains US$7-10; ✆ lunch only) Literally translated as 'the Singing Frog,' this unpretentious place is a great *cevichería*, serving all manner of seafood. Portions tend to be small, but it has great lunchtime and weekend ambiance.

Cevichería Barranco (☎ 467-4560; Panamá Sur 270; ✆ lunch only; mains US$4-7) This is a cheap seafood restaurant, a short walk from central Barranco; it has a welcoming patio with a thatched roof.

Las Mesitas de Barranco (☎ 477-4199; Grau 341; mains US$3-5) A good but run-of-the-mill choice, Las Mesitas has good service, light meals and an array of tempting Peruvian desserts.

Antica Trattoria (☎ 247-3443; San Martín 201; mains US$6-9) A classy new Italian joint with a nouveau-rustic air gives Barranco the quality pizza it has been waiting for.

Manos Morenas (☎ 467-0421; San Pedro de Osma 409; mains US$5-12; ✆ closed dinnertime Sun) Manos Morenas is an informal *peña* (bar or club featuring live folkloric music) that's highly

recommended locally both for its top-notch *criollo* food and live *criollo* music (after 10pm) Tuesday to Saturday. There's a cover charge of US$10.

TOP END
La Costa Verde (☎ 477-5228; Playa Barranquito; mains US$10-40) Located directly on the Barranco beachfront, this sophisticated restaurant is recommended for its excellent seafood. Take a taxi there and away at night from Miraflores (US$1 to US$1.50). It has a Sunday buffet for about US$43 per person including wine.

Self-catering
There are many supermarkets loaded with both local and imported food, drink, toiletries and medicines. One of the best is **Santa Isabel** (Map pp66-7; Benavides 487, Miraflores; ✆ 24 hr), which rivals any North American mall hang-out. There is also a branch on Pardo in Miraflores, and on Camino Real in San Isidro (both ✆ 8am-10:30pm daily). In central Lima, the best is **Metro** (Map pp58-9; Cuzco; ✆ 8am-10pm daily).

DRINKING
Lima is overflowing with bars of every description – from San Isidro's havens for the modern elite to Barranco's cheap and cheerful stomping grounds. Weekends from January to March also see the fresh-from-the-beach summer crowds heading down to Kilometer 97 on the Panamericana (see p90 of the South Coast chapter) for the nightlife. The clubs in town get going from 11pm or midnight, and continue going strong till dawn. Many have happy hours during the week, but rarely during the crowded weekends, when cover charges can sometimes be as much as US$10.

Unfortunately, several bars and nightclubs discriminate against nonwhites – if this is the case, let us know. As a quick comparison of prices, drinks in Barranco cost between US$2.20 and US$3.50, while in San Isidro they can go as high as US$3.50 to US$5.

Central Lima   Map pp58-9
The nightlife in central Lima is limited.

El Estadio Futbol Club (☎ 428-8866; Nicolás de Piérola 926; ✆ Mon-Sat) This bar, on Plaza San Martín, is a great illustration of soccer fanaticism Peruvian style, where you can literally rub shoulders with the likes of Maradona and Pele (admittedly they're just waxworks) and as much soccer-related paraphernalia as will fit on the walls.

La Noche (☎ 423-0299; cnr Camaná & Quilca; ☽ Mon-Sat) A modern, central-Lima counterpart of Barranco's long popular bar, La Noche has live music after 11pm.

Gran Hotel Bolívar (Jirón de la Unión) Oozing dusty, faded charm and elegance, the bar at this grand old hotel serves up an infamously good pisco sour (the national cocktail).

San Isidro

For the most modern bars (with the most elevated prices), try these in San Isidro:

Tai Lounge (☎ 422-7351; Conquistadores 325; ☽ Mon-Sat) One of Lima's most exclusive spots, Tai Lounge draws the cream of young Limeños who are appreciative of the plush lounging areas, cool outside patios and suave clientele. It also hosts a good Thai restaurant.

Punta G (☎ 440-5237; Conquistadores 510; ☽ Mon-Sat) Another cosmopolitan bar frequented by the in crowd, the intimate Punga G boasts some terrific cocktails. There's no sign: Look for the white doors.

Los Delfines Bar (Map pp52-3; Los Delfines Hotel; Los Eucaliptos 555; ☽ daily) Punters come to this top hotel's elegant bar to watch the resident dolphins do somersaults as they (the patrons) knock back cocktails and try not to think about the conditions the animals are kept in. The show is at 8:30pm Tuesday to Sunday.

Miraflores   Map pp66-7

In Miraflores, there is a proliferation of British-style pubs serving as haunts of upper-class Limeños and expats. The busiest clubs center around Parque Central and the Larcomar shopping center.

Brenchley Arms (☎ 445-9680; Atahualpa 176; ☽ Mon-Sat) An authentic bar serving good English pub grub (US$6 to US$14), the Brenchley Arms also has a dart board and British newspapers.

Palos de Moguer (☎ 221-8363; Cavenecia 129; ☽ Mon-Sat) This international beerhouse boasts by far the best real-ale pints in town, with three choice English varieties alongside Belgian and Peruvian. The tavern-like bar is about 200m north of Óvalo Gutierrez.

Old Pub (☎ 242-8155; San Ramón 295; ☽ daily) Owned by four expats from England, Scot-

land, Australia and the USA, this central pub has darts, cable TV and an international dinner menu specializing in beef.

Treff's (☎ 440-0148; Benavides 571; ☽ daily) This German tavern, tucked away from the street through narrow colonial passageways, is another international favorite. It offers friendly service and a pool table.

Tequila Rocks (Diez Canseco 146; admission US$3; ☽ Mon-Sat) This long-established clubbing haunt, playing all the crowd-pleasing favorites, has a deserved reputation as a travelers pick-up joint.

Señor Frogs (Larcomar; admission US$8-10; ☽ Mon-Sat) A very flashy, electric club, Señor Frogs attracts a young local crowd.

Teatriz (☎ 242-3084; Larcomar; admission US$8-10; ☽ Mon-Sat) Also in Larcomar, the modern Teatriz draws an older clientele who later spill out into the mall's late-night cafés to cool their aching feet.

Other bars to check out in Miraflores include:

O'Murphys (Schell 627; ☽ Mon-Sat) A busy Irish pub.

Media Naranja (☎ 446-6946; Schell 130; ☽ Mon-Sat) An open-air Brazilian bar on Parque Kennedy.

Barranco   Map p68

The tight-knit clubs change on an almost weekly basis around Barranco's Parque Municipal, which throngs with revelers on Friday and Saturday nights. With dozens of bars and clubs, this is by far the simplest place to go club-hopping and the action is so tightly packed that you only need to walk a few steps to find yourself in an entirely different vibe.

Juanito's (Grau 274; ☽ daily) One of the oldest haunts in Barranco, this was a leftist *peña* of the 1960s that retains its traditional decor and is still popular for the quirky antics of its bar staff.

La Noche (☎ 247-2186; Bolognesi 307; admission US$3; ☽ daily) The party crowd is often to be found at this well-known, three-level bar nestling snugly at the end of a busy parade. La Noche prides itself on playing a wide mix of music, with everything from modern Latin pop to the occasional highland tune.

El Ekeko Café Bar (☎ 477-5823; Grau 266; ☽ Mon-Sat) A generally more-sedate option, with free poetry readings on Monday, this faithful old bar comes alive at weekends when the grandfathers of Bohemia play live music (US$5 to US$7 cover), trotting out their lively tango, folklore and cha-cha-chas.

La Posada del Mirador (☎ 477-1120; Ermita 104; ⏲ daily) A *cevichería* by day and a laid-back drinking hole at night, the clifftop Posada has outdoor tables, great for catching the sunset.

Tajabone Piano Bar (☎ 247-7906; Bajada de los Baños 343; admission US$3; ⏲ Wed-Sat) Suitably positioned by the Bridge of Sighs, Tajabone has a romantic, mellow environment with live jazzy and traditional music.

Wahio's (☎ 477-4110; Blvd de los Bomberos; ⏲ Thu-Sat) It's a lively little bar with its fair share of dreadlocks and a classic soundtrack of reggae, ska and dub.

Sargento Pimienta (☎ 477-0308; Bolognesi 755; ⏲ Wed-Sat) The name of this huge barn-like place means Sergeant Pepper in Spanish, and true to form, it plays a mix of international retro from the 1970s to the 1990s plus occasional live rock. Alcohol is cheap, and somehow the enormous dance floor becomes miraculously packed by midnight.

Deja Vu (☎ 247-3742; Grau 294; ⏲ Mon-Sat) A Bohemian club with a dual personality, Deja Vu's upper tier has thumping international music, while below there are usually gutsy live Peruvian performances.

Mochileros (San Pedro de Osma; see Sleeping p73) This budget hostel keeps its guests awake at the weekend with a normally full-to-bursting bar and frequent live rock. Try their knockout 'Pisco Power' cocktail.

ENTERTAINMENT

Cinemas, theaters, art galleries and music shows are listed in *El Comercio* daily newspaper, with the most detailed listings found in Monday's 'Luces' section. Another useful source of general information is the *Peru Guide*, a free booklet published monthly that can be found at hotels and tourist spots in Lima. The free *Lima Night* guide is distributed in nightspots throughout Lima, with scores of addresses for everything from *peñas* to videopubs.

Live Music

Live Peruvian music and dance is performed at *peñas* from Thursday to Saturday, which also double as bars and serve up typical Peruvian food. The programs usually have free sessions for you to strut your own

---

GAY & LESBIAN VENUES

Though still conservative and low key by US and European standards, Lima hosts Peru's most open gay scene and some nightclubs have unofficial gay nights. For the most up-to-date ideas, see the website gaylimape.tripod.com.

Two Sixty Nine (Map pp66-7; ☎ 444-3376; Pasaje Tello 269, Miraflores; ⏲ 8pm-5am Mon-Sat) This intimate little disco-bar is still highly gay-friendly, though it's no longer exclusively gay.

Downtown Vale Todo (Map pp66-7; Pasaje Los Pinos 160, Miraflores; admission US$3 Thu & Fri; ⏲ 10:30pm-late Wed-Sat) This favorite is a mixed straight, gay and Lesbian club with some risqué dancers on the payroll.

Kitch (Map p68; Bolognesi 743, Barranco; ⏲ Thu-Sat) Kitch is a gay-friendly bar.

Oupen Sauna (Map pp66-7; ☎ 242-3094; 28 de Julio 171, Miraflores; ⏲ 2-11pm daily) It's an exclusively gay sauna with massage, grooming, bar and private rest rooms.

---

stuff as well. There are two main types of Peruvian music – *folklórico* and *criollo*. The first is more typical of the Andean highlands while the second is more coastal, and therefore more popular in Lima.

Las Brisas de Titicaca (Map pp58-9; ☎ 332-1901; Wakuski 168, Central Lima; admission US$7; ⏲ 9:30pm-late Wed-Sat) This well-recommended *folklórico peña*, near Plaza Bolognesi, is popular with Limeños.

La Candelaria (Map p68; ☎ 247-2941; www.lacandelariaperu.com; Bolognesi 292, Barranco; admission US$7; ⏲ 9:30-late Fri & Sat) This is a good new *peña*, which has lively *criollo* music and dancing, with plenty of audience participation and dancing.

Sachun Peña (Map pp66-7; ☎ 441-0123; Av del Ejército 657, Miraflores; admission US$10) This recommended place has a variety of acts that get under way in the late evening.

Other rousing *peñas* include:

De Rompe Yorada (Map p68; ☎ 247-3271; cnr Bolognesi & Segura 127, Barranco; ⏲ 9:30-late Thu-Sat) Good-atmospheric place near La Candelaria.

La Estación de Barranco (Map p68; ☎ 247-0344; San Pedro de Osma 112, Barranco; admission US$7-15) A well-known *peña* for *criollo* music.

Manos Morenos (see Eating – Mid-Range for Barranco p77) Also popular for *criollo* music.

Cinemas

The latest international films are usually screened with their original soundtrack and Spanish subtitles, except films for children, which are always dubbed. Some cinemas offer half-price entry midweek. Standard listings, including film festivals and eclectic films are in the newspapers' cultural-events section.

UVK Multicines Larcomar (Map pp66-7; ☎ 446-7336; Larcomar, Miraflores; US$4)

Starvision El Pacífico (Map pp66-7; ☎ 445-6990; Pardo 121, Miraflores; US$3.50)

Cine Planet Miraflores (Map pp66-7; ☎ 452-7000; Santa Cruz 814; US$4); Central Lima (☎ 452-7000; Jirón de la Unión 819; US$2)

Smaller and more esoteric options include:
Filmoteca (Map pp58-9; ☎ 423-4732; Museo de Arte, Paseo Colón 125, Central Lima; US$1.60-4.20)

El Cinematógrafo (Map p68; ☎ 477-1961; Pérez Roca 196, Barranco; US$3.50)

Theater & Music

Unfortunately, the beautiful **Teatro Municipal** (Ica 300, Central Lima) burnt down in 1998, but there is talk of rebuilding what was once the premier venue for symphony, opera, plays and ballet. **Teatro Segura** (Map pp58-9; ☎ 426-7189; Huancavelica 265, Central Lima) has been picking up some of the losses, while others include **Teatro Canut** (☎ 422-5373; Petit Thouars 4550, Miraflores) and **Teatro Britanico** (Map pp66-7; ☎ 447-9760; Bellavista 527; Miraflores), which sometimes has plays in English.

For big-name music concerts, check the Luces section of *El Comercio* on Mondays.

Casinos

Many top-end hotels, including the Lima Sheraton (see p71), Los Delfines (p71) and the Marriot (p73), have casinos and there are slot-machine halls scattered all around Lima, especially in Miraflores. Betting is in US dollars, and rules are similar to Nevada rules. One difference is that Blackjack (21) players must bet in exact multiples of the table minimum, so that on a US$2-minimum table, you can bet US$4 or US$6, but not US$5. Slot machines have a reputation for being very tight here.

Sport

Fútbol (soccer) is the national sport, and Peru's **Estadio Nacional** (Map pp58-9; Central Lima),

off the 7th to 9th blocks of the Paseo de la República, is the venue for the most important soccer matches and other events. Soccer tickets can be purchased at **Farmacia Deza** (☎ 222-3195; corpem@hotmail.com; Conquistadores 1140, San Isidro).

Bullfighting also has a good fan-base in Lima. The bullfighting season is late October to late November (3pm on Sunday), and there is also a short season in March. Matadors, most of whom are Spanish, fight in the **Plaza de Acho bullring** (Map pp58-9; ☎ 481-1467; Hualgayoc 332, Rímac). Rafael Castañeta is the best-known Peruvian matador and, in 1993, Spanish matador Cristina Sanchez was the first woman to fight in Lima. Bullfights are widely advertised in the major newspapers, and tickets are sold well in advance. Prices are expensive, ranging from US$20 to US$100 for one event and up to US$600 for season tickets. Bullfighting tickets are also sold at Farmacia Deza.

Horse racing is popular. The **Jockey Club Of Peru** (Map p52-3; ☎ 435-1035; Hipódromo de Monterrico), at the junction of the Panamericana Sur and Javier Prado, has horse races at 6pm every Tuesday and Thursday, and at 2pm weekends. Betting starts at US$0.70. The members' stand is open to nonmembers for US$3.

Bloodthirsty **cockfighting** is also popular; events are advertised locally.

SHOPPING

Clothing, jewelry and handicrafts from all over Peru are available in Lima. Shop prices tend to be high, but for those with a little less capital, you can haggle your heart out at several good craft markets. Shopping hours are generally 10am to 8pm Monday to Saturday, with variable lunchtime hours. Prices are generally fixed, but it's always worth trying for a discount. US dollars can be used in some of the better stores, and exchange rates are often within 1% of the best rates in town. Traveler's checks and credit cards can also be used, but receive less favorable rates.

On Sundays, your best bets are Lima's US-style malls. The huge Jockey Plaza mall in Monterrico has department stores, a movie theater, food court and specialty stores that will all make you forget you're in Peru. Larcomar, hiding below the Parque Salazar in Miraflores, is a smaller mall with a spectacular location built into the cliffs, and there's also **Camino Real**, a large mall in San Isidro.

Handicrafts

Small art galleries selling work are dotted around downtown: Try Pasaje de los Escribanos in central Lima, Diez Canseco in Miraflores and around Barranco's Parque Municipal.

The enormous **Mercado del Indios** (Map pp66-7; Petit Thouars 5245, Miraflores) is the best place to browse through handicrafts from all over Peru. Prices are varied so shop carefully. Another option is the **Feria Artesanal** (Map pp52-3; Av de la Marina) in Pueblo Libre.

Miraflores also has plenty of good but pricey shops with quality wares. Highly exclusive jewelry and handicrafts stores are to be found in the shady colonial **Centro Comercial El Suche** (Map pp66-7; La Paz) passageway in Miraflores. **Alpaca 111** (Map pp66-7; ☎ 241-3484; Larcomar, Miraflores; ☾ daily) has high-quality alpaca products as does **La Casa de la Alpaca** (Map pp66-7; ☎ 447-6271; La Paz 665, Miraflores; ☾ Mon-Sat), and **Agua y Tierra** (Map pp66-7; ☎ 444-6980; Diez Canseco 298; Miraflores; ☾ Mon-Sat) specializes in Amazonian ornaments.

La Casa de la Mujer Artesana Manuela Ramos (☎ 423-8840; Juan Pablo Fernandini 1550, Pueblo Libre; ☾ 9am-5pm Mon-Fri), at the 15th block of Brasil, is a crafts cooperative with good-quality work from all over Peru. The proceeds support women's programmes that are funded by the Movimiento Manuela Ramos.

A small artists' and artisans' market, with work ranging from garish painting-by-numbers to some good watercolors, functions informally on Parque Kennedy, in the heart of Miraflores most days.

Local Markets

You can buy almost anything at Lima's crowded **Mercado Central** (cnr Ayacucho & Ucayali) to the southeast of Abancay and close to Barrio Chino.

South of Plaza Grau is a black-market area known as **Polvos Azules**; this is the place to find cheap luxuries and consumer goods – even that camera that was stolen from you. The government turns a blind eye to this market, and people from all social strata wander around, but watch your pockets carefully.

At Puente Santa Rosa, where Tacna crosses the Río Rímac, Lima's morning **flower market** is a kaleidoscopic scene of beautiful flowers at bargain prices.

Camping Equipment

For camping gear, try the expensive **Alpamayo** (Map ppp66-7; ☎ 445-1671; Larco 345, Miraflores), or **Todo Camping** (Map pp66-7; ☎ 242-1318; Angamos Oeste 350, Miraflores). **Mountain Worker** (Map pp66-7; ☎ 445-2197; Borgoño 394, Miraflores) has also been recommended.

GETTING THERE & AWAY
Air

Lima's **Aeropuerto Internacional Jorge Chávez** (Map pp52-3; ☎ 595-0606; www.lap.com.pe; Callao) is divided into two sections. Looking at the building from the parking area, the domestic arrivals and departures section is to the right. To the left is the international section.

INTERNATIONAL

There is a bank in the baggage-claim area to change money. After passing through customs, it's only a few meters to taxis and other transportation, so avoid porters in the baggage-claim area, unless you want to have your luggage trundled 20m outside the door and dumped into the most expensive taxi available. When several flights arrive at once, it can be a real zoo, so keep your wits and your luggage about you.

The usual airport facilities are available: local, long-distance, and international phone offices; public phones; banks; snack bars; sundry stores and a post office. A 24-hour, left-luggage room charges about US$6 per item per day. For more general information see p414 in the Transport chapter.

If leaving on an international flight, check in two to three hours early; there is a US$28 international departure tax, payable in US dollars or nuevos soles.

International Airline Offices

The following international airlines have offices in Lima. Call before you go or check the yellow pages under *Lineas Aereas*, as they change addresses frequently:

Aero Continente/Aviandina (see Domestic p82)
Aerolineas Argentinas (☎ 444-0810; Pardo 805, Miraflores)

Air France (☎ 444-9285; Pardo 601, Miraflores)
Air New Zealand (☎ 444-4441; Alijovin 472, Miraflores)
Alitalia (☎ 447-3899; Olaya 129, Miraflores)
American Airlines (☎ 442-8595; Moreyra 380, San Isidro)
Avianca (☎ 446-9902; Pardo 140, Miraflores)
Cathay Pacific (☎ 444-4441; Alijovin 472, Miraflores)
Continental Airlines (Map pp 52-3 ☎ 221-4340; Camino Real, Belaúnde 147, San Isidro)
Delta Airlines (Map pp 52-3 ☎ 440-4328; Camino Real, Belaúnde 147, San Isidro)
Iberia (Map pp52-3 ☎ 411-7800; Camino Real 390, San Isidro)
KLM (☎ 421-9500; Calderón 185, San Isidro)
LanChile (☎ 213-8300; Pardo 513, Miraflores)
Lloyd Aéreo Boliviano (☎ 241-5510; Pardo 231, Miraflores)
Lufthansa (☎ 442-4455; Basadre 1330, San Isidro)
Qantas Airways (☎ 242-6631; Bolognesi 599, Miraflores)
Tame, Linea Aerea del Ecuador (☎ 422-6600; Andalucía 174, Miraflores)
Varig (Map pp52-3; ☎ 422-1449; www.varig.com.br; Camino Real 456, San Isidro)

DOMESTIC

Many domestic airlines have sprung up recently, and at the time of writing competition was fierce, with special offers as low as US$71 to Arequipa and Cuzco. The principle destinations from Lima are Arequipa, Cuzco, Iquitos, Puerto Maldonado, Chiclayo, Trujillo, Juliaca, Pucallpa, Piura, Cajamarca, Ayacucho, Trujillo, Tacna, Tarapoto and Tumbes. Getting flight information, buying tickets and reconfirming flights are best done at the airline offices.

Overbooking is the norm on domestic flights, so check in 90 minutes before your flight. You can reconfirm flights 24 to 72 hours in advance, but it's best to reconfirm upon arrival. This is especially necessary during the busy months of July and August. Members of the SAE (see p56) can have the club reconfirm flights for them. Flights are changed or canceled with depressing frequency, so it's even worth calling the airport or airline before leaving for the airport. For more general information on air travel see p414 in the Transport chapter.

For domestic flights, the departure tax is US$5.

Domestic Airline Offices

Offices of domestic operators include:
AeroCóndor (☎ 441-1354, 442-5215; reservas@aerocondor.com.pe; Juan de Arona 781, San Isidro) Flies to Andahuaylas, Ayacucho, Cajamarca and sometimes Trujillo.
Aero Continente/Aviandina (Map pp66-7; ☎ 242-4260, 242-4113, airport 447-8080; www.aerocontinente.com.pe); Pardo office (Pardo 651, Miraflores); Larco office (Larco 123, Miraflores) Covers Arequipa, Ayacucho, Cajamarca, Chiclayo, Cuzco, Juliaca, Piura, Pucallpa, Puerto Maldonado, Tacna, Tarapoto, Trujillo and Tumbes.
Grupo 8 This military airline has infrequent flights to Cuzco, Puerto Maldonado, Pucallpa and some small jungle towns, but schedules are very erratic and subject to over-booking and cancellation, and so can't be recommended. Check for flights at the airport.
LanPeru (Map pp66-7; ☎ 213-8200; www.lanperu.com; Pardo 513, Miraflores) LanPeru goes to Arequipa, Chiclayo, Cuzco, Juliaca, Puerto Maldonado and Trujillo.
LC Busre (☎ 421-0419; fax 422-6293; www.lcbusre.com.pe; Los Tulipones 218, Lince) Flies to Central and Northern Highlands destinations and Pucallpa.
Star Up (Map pp66-7; ☎ 446-2485; starup@terra.com.pe; Pardo 269, Miraflores) Only flies to Cuzco.
Taca Peru (Map pp66-7; ☎ 213-7000; ventasgt@grupotaca.com.pe; Espinar 331, Miraflores) Cuzco only.
Tans (Map pp66-7; ☎ 213-6000; ventaslima@tans.com.pe; Arequipa 5200, Miraflores) Cuzco, Iquitos, Pucallpa, Puerto Maldonado and Tarapoto.

Bus

The most important road out of Lima is the Carretera Panamericana (Pan-American Highway), which runs northwest and southeast roughly parallel to the coast. Long-distance north- and southbound buses leave Lima every few minutes; it takes about 24 hours to get to either the Ecuadorian or the Chilean border (see p417 in the Transport chapter for more details). Buses also ply the usually rougher roads inland into the Andes and across into the eastern jungles.

There is no central bus terminal; each bus company runs its own offices and terminals. Some major companies have several terminals; always clarify where the bus leaves from when buying tickets. Be aware that Lima's bus terminals are in poor neighborhoods and notorious for theft, so if possible buy your tickets in advance, and take a taxi when carrying luggage.

The busiest times of year are Semana Santa (the week before Easter) and the week before and after Fiestas Patrias (July

28 to 29), when thousands of Limeños make a dash out of the city, and fares double. At these times, book well ahead.

There are scores of long-distance bus companies operating from Lima, though not all are recommended. The best two companies are:

Cruz del Sur (Map pp58-9; ☎ 424-1005/6158; www.cruzdelsur.com.pe); Central Lima (Quilca 531); La Victoria (☎ 225-6163/5748; Javier Prado Este 1109) This is one of the biggest companies and serves the entire coast plus Arequipa, Cuzco, Huancayo, Huaraz and Puno. The old terminal on Quilca is mostly for its cheaper Ideal services, while the terminal on Javier Prado Este offers the more luxurious Imperiale and 1st-class Cruzero services – about twice the cost of normal services. Buses sometimes stop at both terminals: ask when buying your ticket.

Ormeño (Map pp58-9; ☎ 427-5679; www.ascinsa.com /ORMENO); Central Lima (Carlos Zavala Loayza 177); La Victoria (Map pp58-9; ☎ 472-1710; Javier Prado Este 1059) Ormeño is another of the biggest bus companies in Lima, with various subsidiaries at the same address, such as Expreso Ancash (for Huaraz), Expreso Continental (north), Expreso Chinchano (south coast and Arequipa) and San Cristóbal (Juliaca, Puno and Cuzco). It also offers faster, more comfortable business class and Royal Class services to Arequipa, Chiclayo, Ica, Tacna, Trujillo and Tumbes, all of which leave from the international terminal on Javier Prado Este.

Other good and convenient bus companies include:

Civa (Map pp58-9; ☎ 332-5236, 332-5264, 332-0656; www.civa.com.pe); 28 de Julio terminal (cnr 28 de Julio & Paseo de la República 575, Central Lima); Carlos Zavala terminal (Carlos Zavala 211, Central Lima) For Cajamarca, Chiclayo, Piura and Trujillo, plus south coast towns en route to and including Arequipa and Tacna.

Expreso Molina (Map pp58-9; ☎ 428-4852; Ayacucho 1141-1145, Central Lima) Has services to Ayacucho and Cuzco via the newly paved road from Pisco.

Flores (Map pp58-9; ☎ 424-3278; cnr Paseo de la República & 28 de Julio) Flores runs regular buses to Arequipa and all south coast destinations.

Ittsa (Map pp58-9; ☎ 423-5232; Paseo de la República, block 6th) Ittsa is a new company with good service all along the north coast.

Mariscal Cáceres (Map pp58-9; ☎ 427-2844); Carlos Zavala terminal (Carlos Zavala 211, Central Lima); 28 de Julio terminal (☎ 474-7850; 28 de Julio 2195, Central Lima) For the Huancayo area and Jauja.

Móvil Tours (Map pp58-9; ☎ 332-0004, Paseo de la República 749, Central Lima) For Huaraz and Caraz.

Soyuz (Map pp52-3; ☎ 226-1515; cnr Mexico 333 & Paseo de la República, Central Lima) Runs every 20 minutes to Ica.

Tepsa (Map pp58-9; ☎ 427-5642-3; Lampa 1237, Central Lima) Serves coastal destinations and many inland places including Nazca, Arequipa, Piura, Cajamarca and Trujillo.

Transportes Atahualpa (Map pp58-9; ☎ 427-2324; Jirón Sandía 266, Central Lima) For the Cajamarca, Celendín and Chachapoyas areas.

Transportes Chanchamayo (Map pp58-9; ☎ 265-6850; Manco Cápac 1052, La Victoria) Runs services to Tarma and La Merced.

Transportes León de Huánuco (Map pp58-9; ☎ 424-3893; 28 de Julio 1520, La Victoria) For Pucallpa via Huánuco and Tingo María.

Turismo Rodríguez (Map pp58-9; ☎ 428-0506; Roosevelt 354, Central Lima) For Huaraz and Caraz.

BUSES FROM LIMA

Approximate one-way costs and journey times from Lima are shown in the following table. Price ranges are given for normal/luxury class, where available.

destination	cost	duration
Arequipa	US$10/28	16 hours
Ayacucho	US$11.50/14	8½ hours
Cajamarca	US$11.50/28	13 hours
Chachapoyas	US$20	25 hours
Chiclayo	US$10/26	12 hours
Cuzco	US$18.50/28.50	30 hours
Huancayo	US$7/11.50	7 hours
Huaraz	US$5.70/10	8 hours
Ica	US$4.50/13	4½ hours
Nazca	US$5.50/17	8 hours
Pisco	US$3/8.50	3 hours
Piura	US$10/28	14 hours
Puno	US$17/37	21 hours
Tacna	US$12/31	18 hours
Trujillo	US$7/15	9 hours
Tumbes	US$8.50/28	20 hours

Train

A railway line runs from Lima inland to Huancayo, climbing from sea level to 4781m – the highest point for passenger trains in the world – before descending to Huancayo at 3260m. It's an exciting trip, with dozens of tunnels and bridges and interesting views. Though the passenger service was cancelled several years ago, a limited service was reinstated in 2003, running only on festivals and long weekends.

It is essential to check locally for current schedules; for more information, visit Lima's **Desamparados train station** (Map pp58-9; for information ☎ 361-2828 ext 222; Ancash 201). See also Getting There & Away (p237) under Huancayo.

Car Rental

Lima is very congested and parking is difficult, so you're advised to take taxis within the city. However, the following hire companies all have 24-hour desks at the airport. Prices vary between US$28 per day to US$53 per day. Delivery is possible.

Avis (☎ 575-1637)

Budget (☎ 575-1674; budgetperu@tci.net.pe)

Dollar (☎ 575-1719)

Hertz (Inka's Rent a Car; ☎ 575-1390; incasrc@terra.com.pe)

National (☎ 575-1111; national@correo.dnet.com.pe)

GETTING AROUND
To/From the Airport

Regulated (official) taxis parked directly outside the airport-terminal exit charge a whopping US$20 for trips to central Lima and up to US$23 to Miraflores. Walking past these taxis into the parking lot will yield taxis for about US$10 for the same trip. Alternatively, turn left outside the terminal building and walk about 100m to the pedestrian gate, turn right and walk another 100m to the road outside the airport and here, you can get an unregistered taxi for US$4 to US$7 to central Lima or US$5 to US$9 to Miraflores, depending on your bargaining skills and the time of day. Solo travelers might feel safer *not* taking this option. If you book a hotel in advance, the owners will often offer to arrange safe taxi pickup for US$10 to US$15. A travel desk at the airport can arrange taxis and make hotel reservations, but these tend to be expensive.

A good alternative to a taxi is to catch the safe and easy Urbanito bus (US$4.50/6 to the center/Miraflores), which will take you to the hotel you want; organize it at the airport if your hotel is a bit out of the way. Urbanito has a desk near the regulated taxi counter, but someone usually approaches with a sign as travelers come out of customs. There are also a few colectivo taxis available that charge about US$5 per person and drop you off at your chosen hotel. These leave from the same place as the regulated taxis.

The cheapest way to get to the airport from the center is by the buses marked 'Faucett/Aeropuerto' that run south along Alfonso Ugarte and cost US$0.30. Taxis are recommended if you're going to the airport from Miraflores. Getting to the airport by taxi is cheapest if you just flag one down and

bargain (ask them to take off their taxi sign before entering the airport compound, as entrance for taxis costs an extra US$1). For more security, you can call a taxi in advance (see Taxi, opposite) and pay the full US$15 to US$25 fare, which again varies according to your location, company and time of day.

Allow over an hour to the airport if you are traveling during rush hours – the exception is before 6:30am, when traffic is light.

Bus

Taking local buses around Lima is something of an adventure. They're often slow and crowded, but numerous and startlingly cheap (fares are US$0.30 Monday to Saturday and US$0.40 on Sunday). Look for the destination cards placed in the windshield and ignore any signs on the side of the bus. The most useful routes link central Lima with Miraflores along Avenida Arequipa or the Vía Expresa. Buses along Garcilaso de la Vega (also called Wilson) and Arequipa are labeled 'Todo Arequipa' or 'Larco/Schell/Miraflores' when heading to Miraflores and, likewise, 'Todo Arequipa' and 'Wilson/Tacna' when leaving Miraflores for central Lima. Catch these buses along Larco or Arequipa in Miraflores.

From Plaza Grau (there's a stop in front of the Museo de Arte Italiano), buses travel along the Vía Expresa to Avenida Benevides in Miraflores, with regular stops along the way.

A green bus (marked 73A) runs regularly from the center to Barranco via Miraflores, passing through Tacna and Garcilaso de la Vega, then down Arequipa and Larco in Miraflores, and on to Barranco, where it can drop you along San Martín. Alternatively, for Barranco, catch any bus with the sign 'Chorrillos/Huaylas/Metro' from Diagonal in front of the pizza restaurants in Miraflores.

Taxi Colectivo

Colectivos are taxis that drive up and down the same streets all day long. The most useful service goes from central Lima to Miraflores along Avenidas Tacna, Garcilaso de la Vega and Arequipa. Another goes from Plaza San Martín to Callao (passing the airport). A third goes along Paseo de la República onto the Vía Expresa down to Barranco and Chorrillos. These colectivos can be identified by colorful window stickers, and when seats are available, the driver may hold his hand out of the window indicating how many seats are left. You can flag them down and get off anywhere on the route. The fare is about US$0.50.

Taxi

Lima's taxis don't have meters; so negotiate a price with the driver before getting in. As a rough guide for taxis flagged down in the streets, a trip from central Lima to Miraflores costs US$2 to US$2.50, and to the Museo de Oro del Peru or airport US$3 to US$3.50. The trip from Miraflores to the airport costs US$5 to US$9 (the higher price is for night-time travel). Be aware that gringos are often charged more, and that you'll have to haggle harder in rush hour.

The majority of taxis in Lima are unregistered (unofficial). Hawkers sell florescent taxi stickers at busy intersections throughout the city, and anybody who fancies a bit of spare cash can stick one in their windscreen. Indeed, surveys have indicated that no less than one vehicle in seven here is a taxi. It is safer to use registered taxis, which either have a taxi sign or a phone number on the roof and an authorization sticker with the word SETAME on the inner windshield. Registered taxis also usually have a yellow paint job and a licensed number painted on the sides. Flimsy Daewoo Ticos are the most common taxi make.

Taxi companies can be called by phone or you can pick up registered taxis from taxi stands, such as the one outside the Lima Sheraton in central Lima or outside the Larcomar shopping mall in Miraflores. Registered taxis cost about 30% to 50% more than regular street taxis. Taxis can be hired; registered taxis charge about US$6 per hour and street taxis charge between US$3.50 and US$5 per hour.

The following companies all work 24 hours and accept advance reservations.

company	telephone
Moli Taxi	(☎ 479-0030)
Taxi Fono	(☎ 226-0866)
Taxi Lima	(☎ 271-1763)
Taxi Miraflores	(☎ 446-3953)
Taxi Móvil	(☎ 422-6890)
Taxi Real	(☎ 470-6263)
Taxi Seguro	(☎ 241-9292)

AROUND LIMA

PACHACAMAC

Situated about 31km southeast of the city centre, this extensive **archaeological complex** (☎ 01-430-0168; wpro.com/pachacamac; adult/student/child US$1.40/0.60/0.30; ✉ 9am-5pm Mon-Fri); made up of palaces and temple-pyramids is the closest major site to Lima. Although Pachacamac was an important Inca site and a major city when the Spanish arrived, it had been a ceremonial center on the central coast about 1000 years before the the Inca Empire. Begun in AD 200, the site was later expanded by the Wari culture before being conquered and added to by the Incas; each palace and temple thus reflects a different culture. The name Pachacamac, variously translated as 'he who animated the world' or 'he who created land and time,' comes from the Wari god, whose wooden, two-faced image can be seen in the on-site **museum**.

Though most of the buildings are now little more than walls of piled rubble dotted around the desert landscape, the main temples and huge pyramids have been excavated, with their ramps and stepped sides revealed. You can climb the stairs to the top of the impressive **Templo del Sol** (Temple of the Sun), which on clear days offers excellent views of the coast. One Incan complex that has been completely excavated and rebuilt is the **Palacio de Las Mamacuña** (House of the Chosen Women), which can only be entered with a guide (US$3.50 to US$4.50 for the whole site). The complex is surrounded by a garden and the roof beams are home to innumerable swallows.

A visitors center, its small museum and a café are by the site entrance, which is on the road to Lurin, not far from the Panamericana. A simple map can be obtained from the office in the visitors center, and a track leads from here into the complex. Those on foot should allow a leisurely two hours. Those with a vehicle can leave their car in a string of parking spots as they go from site to site. A great way to see the site is from the back of a Peruvian *paso* horse, but you must arrange this in advance (see Horse Riding, p65). Many people cycle to the site, where there are some pleasant tracks to take.

Various tour agencies in Lima offer guided tours to Pachacamac (see p68) including round-trip transport and a guide. Costs depend on the size of the group and the quality of the guide, but start at US$20 per person. Alternatively, catch a minibus signed 'Pachacamac' from the corner of Ayacucho and Grau in central Lima (US$0.60, 45 minutes); minibuses leave every 15 minutes during daylight hours. From Miraflores, catch a taxi to the intersection of Angamos and the Panamericana also known as the Primavera Bridge (US$1.20), then take the bus signed 'Pachacamac/Lurin' (US$0.30, 25 minutes). For both services, tell the driver to let you off near the *ruinas* or you'll end up at Pachacamac village, about 1km beyond the entrance.

To get back to Lima, flag down any bus outside the gate but expect to stand. It's best not to wait until late in the afternoon.

You can hire a taxi from Lima that will wait for you at the ruins for two or three hours. Expect to pay US$5 to US$6 per hour.

BEACHES
☎ 01

Limeños make a beeline for their southern beaches during the January-to-March coastal summer. The exodus peaks at weekends, which are occasionally so congested that the highway becomes temporarily one way, and incoming traffic is diverted to an older stretch of the Panamericana. The beaches south of Lima include El Silencio, Señoritas, Caballeros, Punta Hermosa, Punta Negra, San Bartolo, Santa María, Naplo and Pucusana. Despite their popularity, don't expect the beautiful, tropical beach resorts of other South American countries; many have cold water and strong currents, so inquire locally before swimming as drownings occur annually.

Some beaches have private clubs used by Limeños, but camping is possible outside of the Lima metropolitan area: Go with a large group and watch your belongings closely. **Punta Hermosa** and the popular **San Bartolo** have hostels near the beach at budget to mid-range rates during the busy summer. One good mid-range option sitting above the bay in San Bartolo is **Hostal 110** (☎ 430-7559; Malecón San Martín Norte 110; d Sun-Thu/Fri & Sat US$25/35; ☒) run by an Italian pilot.

For surfers, San Bartolo is great for beginners, but the largest wave in Peru is to be found near Punta Hermosa at **Pico Alto**

(Km43) though it's not for the inexperienced, and requires a long paddle out. **Punta Rocas**, a little further south, is also popular with experienced surfers, and hosts international surfing competitions. At Punta Rocas is the basic **Hostal Hamacas** (☎ 231-5498; surfresortperu@terra.com.pe; Km47; dm US$5) in which to crash. Unfortunately, surfboard rental is almost nonexistent along these beaches so you'll have to buy or rent one in Lima and hire a taxi to transport it (US$10 to US$15 one way).

To get to the southern beaches, take a bus signed 'San Bartolo' from the Panamericana Sur at the Primavera Bridge (taxi from Miraflores US$1.20). You can get off the bus where you want and hike down to the beaches, which are mostly 1km or 2km away from the highway.

CENTRAL HIGHWAY
☎ 01

The Carretera Central heads directly east from Lima, following the Rímac valley into the foothills of the Andes past several places of interest, and on to La Oroya (see p227) in the Central Highlands.

See Getting There & Away (opposite) for transport details to all of the following places.

Puruchuco

The site of **Puruchuco** (☎ 494-2641; admission US$1.70; ☒ 9am-4:30pm Mon-Sat) has been in the news since a huge stash of about 2000 well-preserved mummy bundles was unearthed from its enormous Inca cemetery recently. It's one of the biggest finds of its kind, and the multitude of grave goods buried with the bundles is already revealing fresh insights into the Inca civilization. The site has a highly reconstructed Inca chief's house with one room identified as a guinea-pig ranch. Situated amid the shantytown of Túpac Amaru, Puruchuco is 13km from central Lima. A signpost on the highway marks the turn-off, and from here it is several hundred meters along a road to the right.

Cajamarquilla

The large site of **Cajamarquilla** (admission US$1.40; ☒ 9am-5pm daily) dates to the Wari culture of AD 700 to 1100 and consists mainly of adobe walls, some sections of which have been restored. A road to the left from Lima at about Km10 (18km from central Lima) goes to the Cajamarquilla zinc refinery, almost 5km from the highway. The ruins are located about halfway along the refinery road; you take a turn to the right along a short, rough road. There are some signs, but ask the locals for the Zona Arqueológica if you have trouble finding them.

Chaclacayo
The village of Chaclacayo, at Km27, is about 660m above sea level – just high enough to rise above Lima's coastal *garúa*. You can often bask in sunshine here while 7.5 million people in the capital below languish in the gray fog.

Simple cabins are available at mid-range 'vacation hotels,' such as **Centro Vacacional Huampani** (☎ 497-1188, in Lima 497-1683; Km26; s/d US$14, with bathroom US$24), and there are decent dining, swimming pool and horse-riding facilities. Peruvians usually come to the vacation complexes on day trips.

Chosica
The resort town of Chosica, 860m above sea level and almost 40km along the Carretera Central, was very popular with Limeños early in the 20th century. Today, its popularity has declined, though escapees from Lima's *garúa* will still find it a convenient spot to take advantage of several variously priced hotels in the sun. From Chosica, a minor road leads to the ruins of **Marcahuasi** (see p227 for more details).

Getting There & Away
Buses to Chosica leave frequently from Lima and can be used to get to Puruchuco (US$0.45, 50 minutes), Cajamarquilla (US$0.45, 75 minutes), Chaclacayo (US$0.60, 1½ hours) and Chosica (US$0.75, two hours). Many are minibuses signed 'Chosica,' and they can be picked up at Arica at the Plaza Bolognesi. Recognizing the sites from the road can be difficult, so tell your bus driver where you want to be let off.

South Coast

The coastal lowlands of Peru constitute an extensive sweep of arid desert terrain interspersed with oases clustering around the rivers that flow down the western slopes of the Andes to the ocean. Slicing through these desert lowlands is the Carretera Panamericana, the best highway in the country, stretching all the way from Ecuador to Chile. The section of the highway from Lima to just west of Arequipa is part of the most traveled overland route to Lake Titicaca and Cuzco. But the south coast holds far more depth and diversity than can be seen from kilometer upon kilometer of barren desert and coastline viewed from a bus window.

The parched landscape masks a remarkably rich and intriguing mix of cultural influences, from unique pre-Inca civilizations and Spanish colonial architecture to upbeat African-influenced music and dance. It's a region known for its wine and, of course, the Peruvian national drink, pisco, while the town of Pisco itself is also famous for its rich wildlife reserves and rugged coastline. The nearby town of Ica, noted for its superb museum, is also surrounded by *bodegas* (vineyards and wine cellars) and towering sand dunes, irresistible to sand-boarders and adventure seekers. Meanwhile the region has played host to some of the most highly developed pre-Inca civilizations – not least the Nazca, remembered for its cryptic geometric figures etched across 500 sq km of desolate pampa.

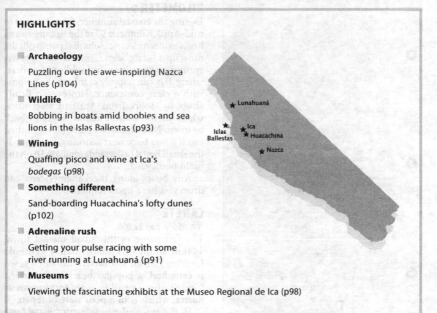

HIGHLIGHTS

■ **Archaeology**

Puzzling over the awe-inspiring Nazca Lines (p104)

■ **Wildlife**

Bobbing in boats amid boobies and sea lions in the Islas Ballestas (p93)

■ **Wining**

Quaffing pisco and wine at Ica's *bodegas* (p98)

■ **Something different**

Sand-boarding Huacachina's lofty dunes (p102)

■ **Adrenaline rush**

Getting your pulse racing with some river running at Lunahuaná (p91)

■ **Museums**

Viewing the fascinating exhibits at the Museo Regional de Ica (p98)

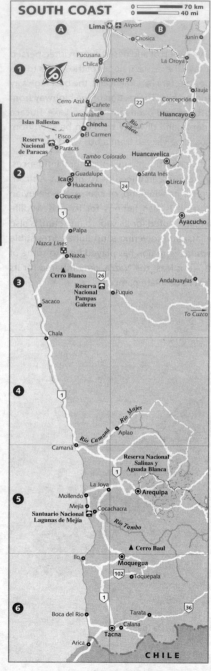

SOUTH COAST

0 ━━━ 70 km
0 ━━━ 40 mi

PUCUSANA

☎ 01 / pop 4000

This small fishing village, 68km south of Lima, is a popular beach resort from January to April. The small Pucusana and Las Ninfas beaches are on the town's seafront and at low tide you can wade to La Isla, which is a beach on the offshore island. The most isolated beach in the area is Naplo, 1km away and reached through a tunnel. A few kilometers south of the Pucusana turn-off from the Panamericana is the village of **Chilca** and a healing, mineral-rich **lagoon** (admission US$0.30).

The best of the simple hotels in Pucusana is **El Mirador de Pucusana** (☎ 430-9228; s/d US$10/ 13), which has a superb location on top of the bay with fantastic views. It's a great place to savor the scenery as you sip on a pisco sour in its restaurant and try to distinguish the various shapes (including Christ's profile and a pig's head) that locals claim can be seen in the surrounding hillsides.

From central Lima, take the Pucusana colectivo (US$1, two hours), which runs every 30 minutes from the corner of Nicolás de Piérola and Montevideo.

KILOMETER 97

During the coastal summer, from January to mid-April, Kilometer 97 of the Panamericana hosts a dozen electric clubs that pump out the most up-to-date beats. This clubbing city has sprung up literally in the middle of nowhere, where DJs can happily crank up the volume with a clear conscience. However, it firmly shuts its doors from April to December, when all the hottest action migrates back to town. Most Limeños party all night then catch a bus back next morning, but there is the small **Hostal La Querencia** (dm US$10-12) on the main boulevard.

Any buses along the Panamericana can drop you here upon request.

CAÑETE

☎ 056 / pop 22,000

The full name of this small market town, 144km south of Lima, is San Vicente de Cañete. Fifteen kilometers north of town is **Cerro Azul**, a popular beach with surfers. There's also a small Inca sea fort known as **Huarco**, which is in a poor state of repair.

In the town, the nondescript **Hostal Costa Azul** (☎ 584-4179; Jose Jordán Torres; d/tr US$4.50/7, with bathroom US$7/8.50) has plain, clean rooms and 24-hour hot water; cable TV can be rented.

In Cerro Azul, the amiable **Señora Blanca Padilla** (☎ 284-6263; Plaza San Martin; r per person US$3-4) has simple rooms for surfers to crash. **Hostal Las Palmeras** (☎ 284-6005; Puerto Viejo, Km132 Panamericana; d US$30-60; ☒) has a gorgeous location looking onto the beach and the pier. Prices vary according to the season and the day of the week.

El Piloto (☎ 284-4114; Panamericana, San Luis suburb; mains US$4.50-12) is a large roadside restaurant and the best in town for seafood.

From Lima, buses for Pisco or Ica can drop you here (US$2, 2½ hours). Buses back to Lima are invariably crowded on Sundays from January to April. There are also combis to Chincha (US$0.70, one hour).

LUNAHUANÁ

From Cañete, a road slopes through the steep-walled Río Cañete valley for 38km to the pleasant village of Lunahuaná, famous for its fine opportunities for river running. It also hosts several wineries that serve free samples year-round: the best time to come is in March, during the **Fiesta de la Vendimia** (harvest festival). One fine rustic pisco- and wine-producing *bodega* is **La Reyna de Lunahuaná**, about 7km from Lunahuaná in Catapalla; it has a restaurant and runs free tours. **Bodega Los Reyes** (☎ 284-1206; ◷ 8am-5pm) is also generous in its measures, and it retains the traditional method of treading the grapes in February and March. Nearby archaeological sites include the large, rough-walled **Incawasi**, and 8km east of Cañete, near Imperial, is **Ungara**.

River Running

The rafting season is December to April, the rainy months in the Andes when the Río Cañete runs high, and in February the rapids reach Class III. This trip is suitable for beginners, and outfitters in Lima often take groups on weekends for about US$25 per person. Contact Javier or José Bello at **Río Cañete Expediciones** (in Lima ☎ 01-9815-7858, 01-9815-0651; expriocanete@terra.com.pe). If you want to organize it in Lunahuaná (see Camping San Jerónimo following), a minimum of four people is required, and trips that last between 40 minutes and one hour cost US$10 to US$15. It also hires out kayaks. Championships are held in February.

Sleeping & Eating

Camping San Jerónimo (☎ 9633-7093; Km33 Carretera Cañete; camping per person US$1.50) This camp site borders the river. It has good facilities and a free artificial climbing wall for guests. Río Cañete Expediciones is run from here.

Hostal Lunahuaná (☎ 284-1089; Malecón; s/d US$6/9, with bathroom US$12/14) The Lunahuaná has simple, serviceable rooms that have hot water; it's located on the outskirts of the village.

Hostal Casuarinas (☎ 581-2627; Jirón Grau 295; s/d US$6/12) It's a central hostel with clean rooms sporting TV and hot showers.

Hostal Río Alto (☎ 284-1125; Km39 Carretera Lunahuaná; s/d US$26/36-42; ☒) Located 1km along the highway beyond Lunahuaná, Río Alto looks down to the river from a shady terrace overrun with plants. Rooms, though plain, are modern and have hot showers.

Hotel Campestre Embassy (☎ 284-1194, in Lima ☎ 01-472-3525; Uchupampa; d US$35-60; ☒) This hotel is quite similar to the Río Alto but also has a restaurant and a disco. The most expensive rooms in the hotel have a balcony overlooking the river.

There are several restaurants which serve seafood and meat in the village; the local specialty is crawfish.

Getting There & Away

From Cañete, catch a combi to the annex of Imperial (US$0.20, 10 minutes); from there, micros run to Lunahuaná (US$0.70, 30 minutes).

CHINCHA

☎ 056 / pop 120,000

The small town of Chincha is the next landmark, some 55km south of Cañete. The small Chincha Empire long flourished here until it was conquered by the Incas in the late 14th century. The best surviving sites are at **Tambo de Mora** on the coast about 10km from Chincha, and at the temple of **La Centinela**. Both can be visited by taxi (US$7).

The area has a large black population and is known for its Afro-Peruvian music, to be heard in the *peñas* (bar featuring live folkloric music) of the district **El Carmen**, a 30-minute minibus ride from the main plaza. The best times are during **Verano Negro** (22 February to 1 March), **Fiestas Patrias** (late July), a local fiesta in late October, and Christmas. During these times, minibuses run from Chincha to

El Carmen all night, and the *peñas* are full of frenzied Limeños and local blacks dancing. One traditional dance not to try at home is El Alcatraz, which features a gyrating male dancer with a candle who attempts to set his partner's skirt on fire. There's usually a cover charge of about US$5.

BCP (formerly Banco de Crédito) and Interbanc have branches with ATMs on Benavides.

Sleeping & Eating

Hotels fill up and double their prices during festivals, though you can always avoid this problem by dancing all night and taking an early morning bus back to Lima.

La Rueda (☎ 9850-7121; Santo Domingo 228; s/d/tr US$7/8.50/10; ☒) This is a friendly cacti-lined place with a mild Wild West theme and a tiny pool. All rooms have bathrooms and hot water from 6am to midnight.

Hotel Sotelo (☎ 26-1681; Benavides 260; s/d US$4.50/7, with bathroom US$6/10) The Sotelo is rudimentary but friendly and serviceable.

Hostal Sausal (☎ 26-2451; sausal@exalmar.com.pe; Km 197.5; s/d/ste US$31/42/53; ☒) A good spot to relax on the Panamericana, the Sausal has a spacious country-club feel with a big pool, sun loungers and lush gardens.

Hostal El Valle (☎ 26-2556; Km195; d US$26; ☒) El Valle is on a smaller scale but has the advantage of hosting Chincha's best seafood restaurant, the Palacio de los Mariscos.

Hotel Princess (☎ 26-1031; fax 261182; Lima 109; s/d US$17/24) Just off the plaza, the Princess is a straight-down-the-line value place with hot showers and cable TV.

Hacienda San José (☎ 22-1458, in Lima 444-5242; hsanjose@terra.com.pe; d full-board US$60; ☒) A slightly ramshackle but grand old country hacienda, the San José is packed with 200 years worth of history, surrounded by orange groves and suffused with the scent of flowers. It has great buffet lunches and also has shows of *criollo* (Afro-Peruvian) dance and music that are open to visitors (US$15/20 for guests/nonguests). There are also dance classes to prime you for the *peñas*. The hacienda, built in 1688, was a sugar and honey plantation worked by black African slaves until a rebellion broke out in 1879, leading to the master being dramatically hacked down by slaves on the main staircase. It also has stables, tennis courts and an atmospheric old chapel with

catacombs. Guided tours are available in Spanish for US$3 per person.

The hacienda is 5km south of Chincha on the Panamericana, then 9km inland. Take a taxi (US$4) or catch one of the frequent colectivos that run back and forth from Chincha (US$0.50, 20 minutes).

Getting There & Away

There are many bus companies based on the Panamericana with buses running between Lima (US$2.50, 2½ hours) and Ica through Chincha. Combis to Cañete leave from Plazuela Bolognesi (US$0.70, one hour). In Pisco, buses for Chincha leave two blocks south of Plaza Belén (US$0.60, one hour).

PISCO–PARACAS AREA
☎ 056 / pop 60,000

Sharing its name with the white-grape brandy produced in this region, Pisco is an important port 235km south of Lima. Generally used as a base to see the abundant wildlife of the nearby Islas Ballestas and Reserva Nacional de Paracas, the area is also of historical and archaeological interest, having hosted one of the most highly developed pre-Inca civilizations – the Paracas culture – and later acting as a base for the revolutionary fever of the 1800s.

DROPPINGS TO DIE FOR

Layers of sun-baked, nitrogen-rich seabird droppings *(guano)* have been diligently deposited over millennia on the Islas Ballestas and Península de Paracas by their large resident bird colonies; in places the guano is as much as 50 meters deep. Guano's recognition as a first-class fertilizer dates back to pre-Inca times, but who would have thought that these filthy riches were to become Peru's principal export during the mid-19th century, being shipped in vast quantities to Europe and America. In fact, the trade was so lucrative that Spain precipitated the so-called Guano War of 1865–66 over possession of the nearby guano-rich Chincha Islands. Nowadays, however, over-exploitation and synthetic fertilizers have taken their toll and the birds are largely left to their steady production process in peace, but for the boatloads of day-trippers from nearby Pisco.

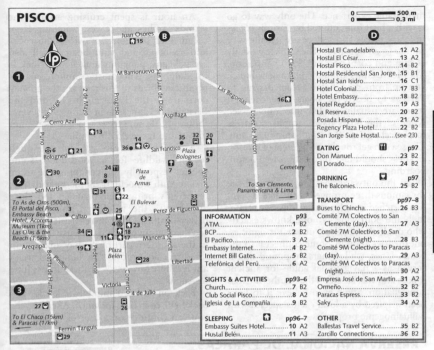

PISCO

Hostal El Candelabro	12 A2
Hostal El César	13 B2
Hostal Pisco	14 B2
Hostal Residencial San Jorge	15 B1
Hostal San Isidro	16 C1
Hotel Colonial	17 B3
Hotel Embassy	18 A3
Hotel Regidor	19 A3
La Reserva	20 B2
Posada Hispana	21 B2
Regency Plaza Hotel	22 B2
San Jorge Suite Hostal	(see 23)

EATING	p97
Don Manuel	23 B2
El Dorado	24 B2

DRINKING	p97
The Balconies	25 B2

TRANSPORT	pp97–8
Buses to Chincha	26 B3
Comité 7M Colectivos to San Clemente (day)	27 A3
Comité 7M Colectivos to San Clemente (night)	28 B3
Comité 9M Colectivos to Paracas (day)	29 A3
Comité 9M Colectivos to Paracas (night)	30 A2
Empresa José de San Martín	31 A2
Ormeño	32 B2
Paracas Espress	33 B2
Saky	34 A2

INFORMATION	p93
ATM	1 B2
BCP	2 B2
El Pacífico	3 A2
Embassy Internet	4 B2
Internet Bill Gates	5 B2
Telefónica del Perú	6 A2

SIGHTS & ACTIVITIES	pp93–6
Church	7 B2
Club Social Pisco	8 B2
Iglesia de La Compañía	9 B2

SLEEPING	pp96–7
Embassy Suites Hotel	10 A2
Hostal Belén	11 A3

OTHER	
Ballestas Travel Service	35 B2
Zarcillo Connections	36 B2

Information

There's no tourist office in Pisco, but tour agencies (see p96) and the **police** (San Francisco; Plaza de Armas) help when they can.

Embassy Internet (Comercio; 9-2am; US$0.60 per hour) is very fast and good, while **Internet Bill Gates** (Plaza Bolognesi; 8am-11pm; US$0.50 per hour) is slower. For snail-mail, there's a **post office** (Callao 176; 8am-9pm Mon-Sat) just west of the Plaza de Armas.

BCP (Figueroa 162) has a Visa ATM and changes cash and US-dollar traveler's checks. For laundry, try **El Pacífico** (Callao 274).

Dangers & Annoyances

The center of Pisco is generally safe, but the market and nearby beaches should be avoided at night and visited only in a group during the day. Tour touts meet incoming buses, and, in the melee, passengers' luggage occasionally disappears, so watch your bags.

Sights & Activities

PISCO

The **Acorema Museum** (53-2046; www.acorema .org; Av San Martín 1471; adult US$1; 10am-1pm &

2-6pm), housed in curious old Swiss-style building, has exhibitions on biodiversity and conservation in Paracas plus a large whale skeleton tucked away to one side.

Pisco was once a revolutionary base for liberator José de San Martín, and his **statue** now peers down on the main plaza. His headquarters, the **Club Social Pisco**, lies nearby at San Martín 132, though it's not officially open to the public.

There is a **Jesuit church** on San Francisco, built with adobe, bamboo and wood in 1729; it is in a sorry state so don't begrudge the US$1 entrance fee. The **cemetery**, to the east of the Plaza de Armas, also has a few hidden secrets: local cab drivers like to tell the story of a 19th-century English witch, Sarah Ellen, whose body was refused by all graveyards until Pisco cemetery was paid handsomely to bury it, prompting a myth that she would arise again after 100 years – though much to everyone's disappointment, she didn't.

ISLAS BALLESTAS

Though all too often referred to as the 'Poor-man's Galapagos,' Islas Ballestas make for a memorable experience. The only way to go is with a boat tour, offered by various places in Pisco; prices and service are usually very similar (see Tours p96). The tours leave daily at 7am and cost US$7 to US$10 per person. They leave either from the plaza or will pick you up from your hotel, before driving to Paracas to board the boats. The cheapest tours are usually pooled into one vessel. None of the boats have a cabin, so dress to protect against the wind, spray and sun. The sea can get rough, so sufferers of motion sickness should take medication well before boarding.

On the outward boat journey, you'll see the famous three-pronged **Candelabra**, a giant figure etched into the coastal hills, over 150m high and 50m wide. No one knows exactly who made the geoglyph or what it signifies, but theories abound. Some connect it to the Nazca Lines, while others propound that it served as a navigational guide for ancient sailors and was based on the Southern Cross constellation. Some even believe it to have been inspired by a local cactus species with hallucinogenic properties.

An hour is spent cruising around the islands' arches and caves, watching large colonies of sea lions sprawl on the rocks and swim around your boat. You'll also see pelicans, penguins and, if your luck is in, dolphins. The most common guano-producing birds in this area are the guanay cormorant, the Peruvian booby and the Peruvian pelican, seen in colonies of several thousand. Be sure to wear a hat, as it's not unusual to receive a direct hit.

Although you can get close enough to the wildlife for a good look, some species, especially the penguins, are more visible with binoculars. Some boat drivers reportedly bring their boats in too close and harass the wildlife: Don't let your driver do this. On your return trip, ask to see the flamingos, which are usually found in the southern part of the bay and not on the direct boat route. The flamingos aren't always there however – the best time is June to August.

Back on shore, a minibus will take you back to Pisco in time for lunch. Alternatively, you can continue on a tour of the Reserva

RESERVA NACIONAL DE PARACAS

INFORMATION	
JC Tello Museum & Information Center	1 B3

SIGHTS & ACTIVITIES	pp93−6
'Graveyard' of Fishing Boats	2 B3
Archaeological Site	(see 1)
Candelabra	3 B2
Fish-Meal Factories	4 B2
Flamingos Often Seen Here	5 B3
Obelisk	6 C3
Paracas Necropolis	7 B2
Playa El Chaco	8 B2

SLEEPING	pp96−7
El Amigo	(see 8)
El Mirador	9 B3
Hotel Paracas	10 B3

TRANSPORT	pp97−8
Boats to Islas Ballestas	(see 10)

OTHER	
Watchtower	11 B3

Nacional de Paracas, or take a combi back to Pisco later.

RESERVA NACIONAL DE PARACAS

Tours to the reserve (US$6 to US$10) from Pisco can be combined with an Islas Ballestas tour to make a full-day excursion, and a discount for combining them can sometimes be arranged. Alternatively, you can hire a taxi in Pisco for US$5 per hour, or take the combi into the village of Paracas and walk – make sure you allow yourself lots of time – and bring food and plenty of water.

Near the entrance to the village of Paracas is an **obelisk** commemorating the landing of the liberator General José de San Martín. The combi continues further in and, if asked, will drop you in front of Hotel Paracas. Continue on foot either along the tarmac road south of Paracas, or the beach, looking out for seashore life.

About 3km south is a park entry point on the road, where a US$1.20 fee is charged (if on a tour, ask if this is included). About 2km beyond the entrance is an **information center** (admission free) that provides insights into conservation and ecology in the area, and the **Museo JC Tello** (☎ 970-3818; adult/student/child US$2/0.60/0.30; ☺ 9am-5pm). Unfortunately, the museum's best pieces were stolen a few years ago, but an interesting collection of weavings, trophy heads and trepanned skulls remains. Chilean flamingos often hang out in the bay in front of the complex, and there's now a walkway down to a *mirador* (watchtower) overlooking them. Try not to step outside the designated route as this can interfere with the flamingos' food supply.

A few hundred meters behind the visitors complex is the 5000-year-old remains of the **Paracas Necropolis**, a late site of the Paracas culture, which predated the Incas by more than a thousand years. A stash of 400 funerary bundles was found here, each wrapped in many layers of the colorful, geometric weavings for which the Paracas culture is famous. There's little to see now though. Visit the Museo de la Nación in Lima or the Museo Regional in Ica to see more exquisite textiles and other finds from the site.

Beyond the park complex the tarmac road continues around the peninsula, past a graveyard of old fishing boats to Puerto

OF FLAGS & FLAMINGOS

Local guides like to tell a fanciful yarn of how the Peruvian flag was born on the beaches of the Península de Paracas. The story goes that Liberator José de San Martín landed here in 1820 and, exhausted after a long journey, he fell into a deep sleep. When he awoke, legend tells that he was dazzled by a flamboyance of flamingos flying overhead, their outstretched wings catching the light of the setting sun, and it was these flashes of red that gave him the inspiration for the scarlet outer panels of what is now the national flag.

San Martín, which has a smelly fish-meal plant and a port on the northern tip of the peninsula. Forget this road and head out on the dirt road that branches off a few hundred meters beyond the museum. After 6km it reaches the tiny fishing village of **Lagunillas**, where you can usually find someone to cook fresh fish for you; it's sometimes possible to catch a ride back to town, squeezed alongside the fresh fish catch.

The road continues a few kilometres to a parking lot, from where you can reach a **clifftop lookout**. Here there are grand views of the ocean, with a **sea-lion colony** on the rocks below and plenty of seabirds gliding by.

Other seashore life includes flotillas of jellyfish (swimmers beware!), some reaching about 70cm in diameter with trailing stinging tentacles of 1m. They are often washed up on the shore, where they quickly dry to form mandala-like patterns on the sand. Beachcombers can also find sea hares, ghost crabs and seashells, and the Andean condor occasionally descends to the coast in search of such rich pickings.

Ask at the visitor center for designated areas to pitch tents, but never camp alone as robberies have been reported. The area is covered by topographic map 28-K from the Instituto Geográfico Nacional in Lima.

TAMBO COLORADO

This early Inca lowland **outpost** (admission US$1.50; ☺ sunrise-sunset), about 46km from Pisco, was named for the red paint that once completely covered its adobe walls. It's one of the best-preserved sites on the south coast and is thought to have served as an administrative base and control point for passing traffic. Look for the distinct hallmarks of Inca architecture, such as trapezoid-shaped niches, windows and doorways. An on-site caretaker will answer your questions and collect the fee. In Pisco, hire a taxi for half a day (US$25) or take a tour (US$10 to US$15, depending on group size). A bus through the village of Humay passes Tambo Colorado 20 minutes beyond the village; it leaves from the Pisco market at about 7:30am (US$1.40, three hours). Once there, ask the locals about when to expect a return bus, as they are infrequent.

Tours

Of the two recommended agencies listed here for local tours, Zarcillo is the best:

Ballestas Travel Service (☎ 53-3095; jpachecot@terra.com.pe; San Francisco 249) It only does tours to the Islas Ballestas and Reserva Nacional de Paracas. Other companies on or near the Plaza de Armas do similar tours.

Zarcillo Connections (☎ 53-6543; zarcillo@terra .com.pe; San Francisco 111) Zarcillo has daily tours to the Islas Ballestas (US$10) and Reserva Nacional de Paracas (US$6 to US$10 depending on the season) with English-speaking guides and some French and Italian too. It also does tours to Tambo Colorado (US$15 per person, 2-person minimum) and will arrange customized trips to Ica/Nazca. Zarcillo rents mountain bikes at US$10 per day and dune buggies at US$10 per person for 40 minutes.

Guests at **Hotel Paracas** (below) can arrange reliable tours in fast boats with the hotel (US$18). **Alas Peruanas** (info@alasperuanas.com), which is affiliated with Alegría Tours (see Nazca p102), has flights from the Pisco area to the Nazca Lines and back for US$130 (three-passenger minimum).

Sleeping

Prices fluctuate according to the season and triple for national holidays such as the Fiestas Patrias (28 July). Many hotels are also noisy; at night with street commotion, and in the morning with tour departees.

PARACAS

El Amigo (☎ 54-5042; El Chaco; s/d US$10/17) The El Amigo is a cheap option for those wanting that extra half an hour in bed before tours. It has clean, cute rooms with TV and it's up to 50% cheaper in the off-season.

El Mirador (☎ 54-5086; fax 54-5085; Carretera Paracas Km20; s/d/tr $30/40/52; 🖭) In the sand

dunes at the entrance to Paracas, the El Mirador is a good get-away-from-it-all option and is often empty in low-season. Rates include breakfast.

Hotel Paracas (☎ 54-5100; hparacas@terra.com.pe; El Chaco; s/d/ste US$70/87/160, bungalow s/d US$117/166; 🖭) Bordering the sea on El Chaco bay 15km south of Pisco, the top-end Hotel Paracas has a swish dining room, neatly trimmed garden, minigolf, table tennis and paddle-boat rental, and its tasteful rooms boast pleasant porches. It's also a good spot to see the amazilia hummingbird. The hotel organizes trips to the Islas Ballestas (US$18) with fast boats and can also organize hire of jet skis or dune buggies. The restaurant and bar are open to nonguests. Prices given are for the high season, but they drop at other times.

PISCO
Budget

Hostal San Isidro (☎ 53-6471; San Clemente 103; hostalsanisidro@hotmail.com; dm US$6, s/d with bathroom US$10/16) A highly recommended spot near the cemetery, San Isidro has a free games room with all the toys (pool, table tennis, table football), plus modern, good-value rooms and plentiful hot water. There's also a kitchen and a bar that closes at 11pm.

Hostal Belén (☎ 53-3046; fax 53-4947; Arequipa 128; r per person US$4, s/d with bathroom US$7/10) This is a faded but very decent, clean hotel with hot electric showers.

La Reserva (☎ 53-5643; lareserva_hostal@hotmail .com; San Francisco 327; s/d/tr US$10/20/30) Housed in a white-washed oval-shaped building, this new place has rooms in sparkling nick. There are private bathrooms, hot water and cable TV.

Hostal El César (☎ 53-2512; 2 de Mayo; s/d US$6/8.50) El César is friendly and in reasonably good shape, though with mostly shared bathrooms. Some English is spoken.

Hostal Pisco (☎ 53-2018; hostalpisco@latinmail .com; San Francisco 120; r per person US$4, s/d with bathroom US$8.50/11) This long-established backpacker place has a laid-back atmosphere and bar, but it's been criticized for having a dodgy water supply, and single women have reportedly been hassled.

Other recommendations are:

Hotel Colonial (☎ 53-2035; Comercio 194; r per person US$3) A friendly but basic and rickety old place with outdoor showers.

Hotel Embassy (☎ 53-2809; Comercio block 1; s/d US$8.50/12) Slightly battered rooms with shower, local TV and erratic hot water.

Mid-Range
All the following have bathrooms and hot water.

Posada Hispana (☎ 53-6363; posahispana@terra .com.pe; Bolognesi 236; s/d US$10/20) A friendly and justifiably popular choice, this hostel has attractive bamboo and wooden fittings, a café and a great terrace for kicking back with a pisco sour. All rooms have spotless bathrooms and some have cable TV. English, French and Italian are spoken.

Hostal Residencial San Jorge (☎ 53-2885; hotel _san_jorgeresidencial@hotmail.com; Juan Osores 267; s/d US$10/16; P) The San Jorge has uniform, standard-issue rooms but is very comfortable and has a café.

San Jorge Suite Hostal (☎ 53-4200; hotel_san _jorge@hotmail.com; Comercio 187; s/d/tr US$15/22/ 30) Run by the same owners as Hostal Residencial San Jorge, this place has smaller, clean rooms with TV and is in a central location.

Las Olas (☎ 53-2315; Miguel Grau 156; www.lasolas peru.com; s/d US$30/35; ☎) Las Olas is a refreshing choice with a games room and terrace fronting the ocean, plus smart rooms with fridge and TV. However, take care in the area around the hostel and catch taxis from the center after dark.

Hostal El Candelabro (☎ 53-2620; in Lima 435-2156; cnr Pedemonte & Callao 198; s/d US$14/20) This is a quiet and cozy hotel with a café complete with piano and collectibles. It has portable fans if the heat strikes you down.

Embassy Suites Hotel (☎ 53-5215; embassyhot eles@terra.com.pe; San Martín 202; s/d/tr US$14/24/28) Professional service, large, smart rooms and an overwhelmingly brown color scheme characterize this choice.

Embassy Beach Hotel (☎ 53-2568; fax 53-2256; San Martín 1119; s/d/tr US$40/60/80; ☎) About 1km west of town but still several hundred meters from the beach, this place has all the expected creature comforts including sparkling rooms with cable TV, telephone and minibar, and a good restaurant and games room.

Other recommendations are:
Hotel Regidor (☎ 53-5220; regidor@terra.com.pe; Arequipa 201; s/d/tr US$20/30/40) Modern rooms with cable TV and bathtubs.

Regency Plaza Hotel (☎ 53-5919; fax 53-5920; Progreso 123; s/d/tr US$14/20/28) A boarding-school atmosphere but with decent rooms and cable TV.

Eating & Drinking
A few cafés are open early enough for simple breakfasts before a Ballestas tour. Unfortunately turtle meat *(motelo)* still winds up on some menus; please don't encourage the catching of this endangered creature by ordering dishes made with its meat.

As de Oros (☎ 53-2010; San Martín 472; mains US$3-12; ☺ opens midday) A few blocks west of the Plaza de Armas, this is a good modern restaurant that hosts the only notable disco in town on Friday and Saturday nights.

Don Manuel (☎ 53-2035; Comercio 179; mains US$3-12) One of Pisco's best options, good for *mariscos* (seafood) and *criollo* dishes.

El Portal del Pisco (☎ 53-2107; Bolívar 135; mains US$4-12; ☺ opens midday) A new place with a grassy garden and nice, sunny courtyard, El Portal serves upmarket Peruvian food and some great homemade pasta. Take a taxi to get here.

El Dorado (Progreso 171; 2-course menús US$1.70; ☺ opens early) On the Plaza de Armas, it has a cheap have-a-go-at-anything menu.

Balconies (2nd fl, Jirón Comercio 108; ☺ 6pm-2am) This is an intimate bar from which to peer down on passing folk below, but take great care negotiating its steep, rickety staircase after a few piscos.

Getting There & Away
Pisco is about 5km west of the Carretera Panamericana, and only buses with Pisco as the final destination stop there. If you're not on a direct bus, you should ask to be left at the San Clemente turn-off where frequent combis to Pisco's market area pass (US$0.30, 10 minutes).

Ormeño (☎ 53-2764) has four daily buses to Lima (US$3.50 to US$10, four hours), two of which go direct with the luxurious Royal Class and do not require a change of bus on the highway. It also has two daily buses to Ica and Nazca (US$4.20 to US$11.20, four hours), and two buses a day on the newly paved road to Arequipa (US$11.20 to US$15.40, 12 to 15 hours). It has three daily buses to Ayacucho (US$7 to US$11.20, seven hours). Most of these buses do not go directly; you will most likely be put on a Lima-bound bus as far as the Panamericana and have to wait there at a 'terminal' (a shack) to connect with southbound buses.

Another bus company offering long-distance services is **Empresa José de San Martín** (☎ 53-2052), with 10 direct buses to Lima (US$3, three hours) daily. **Saky** (☎ 53-4309) has services to Ica every 30 minutes from 5:30am until 7:30pm (US$0.70, one hour).

Buses to Chincha leave two blocks south of Plaza Belén (US$0.60, one hour).

Getting Around

Combis to Paracas leave from near the market about every 30 minutes throughout the day (US$0.50, 20 minutes). Buses for the San Clemente turn-off (for long-distance buses up and down the Panamericana) leave frequently from the market. At night they leave from Libertad near Comercio to avoid the dangerous market area.

A taxi around town costs about US$0.50, to San Clemente about US$1.60 and to Paracas about US$3.

ICA

☎ 056 / pop 190,000 / elevation 420m

The capital of its department, the oasis town of Ica was founded by the Spanish in 1563. It boasts a thriving wine and pisco industry, with grapes irrigated by the river that shares its name, plus attractive colonial churches, an excellent museum and several annual fiestas. Its slightly elevated position means that it sits above the coastal mist and the climate is dry and sunny. Many travelers choose to visit Ica from nearby Huacachina (see p102).

Information

INTERNET ACCESS

Velox Net (Lima 2nd block; ⏰ 8am-11pm; US$0.40 per hour) has about 50 good machines.

MONEY

Moneychangers on the plaza will change cash but your best options are:

BCP (Plaza de Armas) Changes traveler's checks and cash and has a Visa ATM.

Interbanc (2nd block Grau) Has a Visa, Cirrus and Plus ATM.

POST & TELEPHONE

Main post office (San Martín 556; ⏰ 8am-7pm Mon-Sat). It's a block west of the plaza.

Telefónica del Peru (Lima 149, Plaza de Armas; ⏰ 8am-11pm)

TOURIST INFORMATION

At the time of writing, a tourist information office was planned to open on the Plaza de Armas.

Regional Tourist Office (☎ 22-7287; Av Gerónimo de Cabrera 426, Urbanisacion Luren; ⏰ 8am-noon & 2-4pm Mon-Fri)

Tourism Police (☎ 22-7673; JJ Elias 4th block; ⏰ 8am-1pm & 5-8pm) At the southwest end of town.

Dangers & Annoyances

Ica has a reputation for theft. Stay alert, particularly in the bus terminal and market areas.

Sights & Activities

MUSEO REGIONAL DE ICA

Don't miss this gem of a **museum** (☎ 23-4383; Ayabaca; adult/student/child US$2.80/0.60/0.30, cameras US$1.20, video recorders US$1.40; ⏰ 8am-7pm Mon-Fri, 9am-6pm Sat & Sun) in the southwestern suburbs; it's about 1.5km from the city center and can be reached by colectivo (US$0.50, 10 minutes) from the Plaza de Armas. It has an excellent collection of artifacts from the Paracas, Nazca and Inca cultures and some superb examples of Paracas weavings, as well as textiles made from feathers. There are beautiful Nazca ceramics, scarily well-preserved mummies of everything from children to a small macaw, trepanned skulls and shrunken trophy heads, enormous wigs and tresses of hair, plus a fascinating scientific display on what can be discovered from examining the skeletal remains.

MUSEO CABRERA

This **museum** (☎ 23-1933; Bolívar 170, no sign; adult/student US$3/1.50; ⏰ 9:30am-1pm & 4-7pm Mon-Sat), on the Plaza de Armas, has a quirky collection of thousands of carved stones, boulders and totem poles graphically depicting diverse pre-Columbian themes, from astronomy to surgical techniques and sexual practices. The eccentric collector, Dr Cabrera (who died in 2001), claimed the stones are ancient, but they're very likely to be elaborate fakes. If you'd rather not pay, you can get a taster of the stones in the museum entrance.

CHURCHES

The **Iglesia de San Francisco** (Municipalidad) has some fine stained-glass windows. **La Merced** (Bolívar), the cathedral, was rebuilt in 1874 and contains finely carved wooden altars. The **Iglesia de El Señor de Luren** (Cutervo) boasts an image of the Lord that is venerated by pilgrims biannually.

BODEGAS

Local wines and piscos can be bought around Ica's Plaza de Armas, but it's more fun to track them down at their source. *Bodegas* (wineries) can be visited year-round, but the best time is during the grape harvest from late February until early April.

Some of the best of Peru's wine comes from the **Ocucaje winery**, but unfortunately it's fairly isolated, situated 36km south of Ica off the Carretera Panamericana. It runs

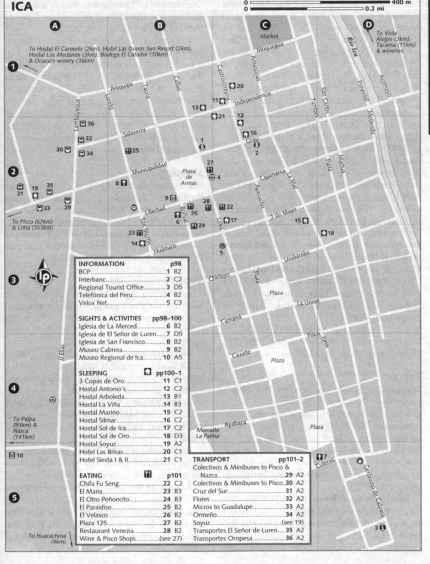

ICA

To Hostal El Carmelo (2km), Hotel Las Dunas Sun Resort (2km), Hostal Los Medanos (2km), Bodega El Catador (10km) & Ocucaje winery (36km)

To Pisco (67km) & Lima (303km)

To Palpa (93km) & Nazca (141km)

To Huacachina (4km)

To Vista Alegre (3km), Tacama (11km) & wineries

Plaza de Armas

Mercado La Palma

tours (US$3, one hour, 11am to 3pm Mon-Fri) and the winery now has an upmarket resort **hotel** (☎ 40-8001; s or d/tr Sun-Thu US$54/65, extra Fri & Sat). Staff can take visitors out on dune buggies and horse rides here. Hiring a taxi to reach the winery costs US$8 one way (40 minutes) or take a tour.

Bodega El Catador (☎ 40-3295; off Km296 Pan-americana) This touristy *bodega*, 10km north of Ica, has wine pressing by foot from February to March, and runs tours and wine-tasting all year. The *bodega* can be reached by catching a combi from the 2nd block of Moquegua before noon (US$0.40, 20 minutes), or from Loreto afterwards, or taxi (US$1.40). Apart from wine and pisco, it has a gift shop and a restaurant with dancing in the evenings during harvest.

Another *bodega* producing the right stuff is the **Tacama**, 11km from Ica, but again you'll have to hire a taxi to get here (US$6). The **Vista Alegre** (☎ 23-2919; ☺ 9am-noon & 1-4pm Mon-Fri, 9am-noon & 2-5pm Sat & Sun), 3km northeast of Ica, is the easiest of the large commercial wineries to visit (US$1 by *taxi-tico*, or a combi from San Martín for US$0.70). It's best to go in the morning, as it occasionally closes in the afternoon.

The simplest to visit of the small family *bodegas* are in the suburb of **Guadalupe**, which is about 3km from Ica on the road to Lima. Here you'll find the **Bodegas Lovera** (☎ 40-6006) and **El Carmen** within a block or two of the plaza. There are many stalls selling huge bottles of various kinds of pisco and wine.

Micros going to Guadalupe (US$0.30, 15 minutes) pass by the Soyuz bus terminal; taxis charge about US$4.20 return.

Tours
It's much cheaper to fly over the Nazca Lines from Nazca (see Nazca p102) but if you're in a hurry, you can do it from Ica. **AeroCóndor** (☎ 25-6230; Hotel Las Dunas Sun Resort; see opposite for contact details) has tourist trips over the Lines for US$142, plus US$5 airport tax. Discounts are available for groups of five or more. A minimum of three people is required per trip.

Roberto Penny Cabrero (☎ 23-3921, 962-4868; icaderttrip@yahoo.es) runs trips into the desert in search of fossilized whales and sharks' teeth for US$50 per day per person. Note that day tours only are recommended here.

Festivals & Events
Ica has more than its share of fiestas. Early March sees the famous wine-harvest **Fiesta de la Vendimia**, with all manner of processions, beauty contests, cockfights and horse shows, music and dancing, and of course, free-flowing pisco and wine. Most of the events are reserved for evenings and weekends at the festival site of Campo Feriado, on the outskirts of town, but during the week, tasting and the buying of wine and honey throughout the town dominates.

In October, Ica holds the religious pilgrim-age of **El Señor de Luren**, which culminates in a traditional procession that goes all night; dates vary. In February the **Carnaval de Yunza** inspires the water-throwing that is typical of any Latin American carnival, plus dancers in beautiful costumes. The founding of the city on 17 June 1563 is also celebrated during **Ica Week**, and late September sees the **Ica Tourist Festival**.

Sleeping
All hotels double or triple their prices during the festivals. The prices following are off-season rates, usually applicable from April to June, September, and also November to December. Other months coincide with the Peruvian coastal summer or northern-hemisphere vacations.

BUDGET
Travelers on tight budgets may consider heading for the oasis town of Huacachina (p102), about 4km west of Ica, which has some good-value and more hospitable options.

Hostal Arboleda (☎ 21-3207; Independencia 165; s/d US$3/4.50, with bathroom US$4.50/9) This is a friendly, bare-bones place and gives straightforward value. Cold-water bathrooms.

Hostal Marino (☎ 21-7201; Av La Mar 330; s/d US$4/8.50) The Marino is new, clean and is pretty good value with cold showers and local TV.

Hostal Antonio's (☎ 21-5565; Castrovirreyna 136; s/d US$4.50/7) Antonio's has neat, well-cared-for rooms with bathroom.

3 Copas de Oro (☎ 80-2920; cnr Independencia & Castrovirreyna 209; s/d US$7/10) This is a new and thoroughly disinfected place that has a central location and is worthy of the price. The small rooms have TV with local channels.

Other recommendations are:

Hostal Sol de Oro (☎ 23-3735; La Mar 371; dm US$3, s/d with bathroom US$6/8.50) A simple, friendly choice with hot water on request.

Hostal La Viña (☎ 21-8188; San Martín 256; s/d/tr US$6/9/10) Simple, basic rooms with TV, bathroom and hot water.

MID-RANGE

Hostal Soyuz (☎ 22-4743; fax 23-3312; Manzanilla 164; s/d US$11/16) Sitting directly over Soyuz bus terminal, this place has exceptionally good-value carpeted rooms with cable TV, but is only for heavy sleepers on account of the rumpus below.

Hotel Las Brisas (☎ 21-8182; Castrovirreyna 246; s/d US$9/13) Las Brisas is a little rough around the edges but secure and run by sweet old ladies. It has rooms with saggy beds but good hot showers for US$11/15.

Hotel Siesta I (☎ 23-4663; Independencia 160; s/d/tr US$10/12/14) This place has clean but characterless rooms with TV; it's similar to its sister Hotel Siesta II next door, which was being renovated at the time of writing.

Hostal Silmar (☎ 23-5089; hsilmar@hotmail.com; Castrovirreyna 106; s/d/tr US$11/14/18) The Silmar has smart carpeted rooms with telephone and cable TV. Overall, it's not a bad choice, even though the corridors can be noisy and service is not overly keen.

Hotel Sol de Ica (☎ 21-8931; soldeicahotel@peru.com; Lima 265; d/tr US$17/26) This central hotel has small rooms with unusual wood paneling, TV and phone. There's hot water between 6am and 10am and 6pm to 10pm.

Hostal Los Medanos (☎ 25-6666; Km301 Panamericana; s/d US$12/24; 🏊) A couple of kilometers out of town, this overgrown and rambling country house has a small pool and spacious grounds.

Hostal El Carmelo (☎ 23-2191; el_carmelo@hotmail.com; Km 301 Panamericana; s/d/tr/ste US$30/38/52/60; 🏊) This hotel, on the Panamericana, is in a 200-year-old hacienda and plays heavily on its undeniable rustic charm. There is a good restaurant plus a winery on the premises.

TOP END

Hotel Las Dunas Sun Resort (☎ 25-6224; dunas@invertur.com.pe; Av La Angostura 400; s/d Sun-Thu US$78/93, Fri & Sat US$94; 🏊) Just off the Panamericana Km300 marker, this is the most luxurious hotel in town, with a wealth of facilities:

water slide, two tennis courts, volleyball court, a small golf course, sand-board rental, sauna, horse riding, Nazca Lines lectures and various excursions. There's also an ATM on the premises. Service can be slow, and prices do not include breakfast.

Another choice is the hotel at the Ocucaje Winery (see p99).

Eating

El Otro Peñoncito (☎ 23-3921; Bolívar 255; mains US$4-10) This is the oldest and most upscale restaurant in the town center; it serves from a varied menu of Peruvian and international fare. It does a mean pisco sour too.

Restaurant Venezia (☎ 23-2241; Lima 230; mains US$4-9) The Venezia is a popular little Italian place.

Plaza 125 (☎ 21-1816; Lima 125; mains US$3-8; ☺ open early and late) Predictably located on the plaza, this café serves good pizzas, hamburgers and chicken.

El Velasco (☎ 21-8582; Libertad 133; 2-course menú US$4, mains US$3-7) Also on the plaza, Velasco serves up lip-smackingly good cakes, desserts and coffee, and is a popular drinking den in the evening.

Chifa Fu Seng (☎ 22-5899; Lima 243; mains US$2.50-5.50) Opposite the Venezia, this is a typical *chifa* place that serves various set meals.

Two no frills vegetarian places are **El Mana** (San Martín; 3-course menú US$1; ☺ closed Sat) and **El Paraidiso** (☎ 22-8308; Loreto; 3-course menú US$1.50; ☺ closed Sat), which both serve up filling *menús* (set lunches) for small change.

Entertainment

There's not much happening in Ica outside of fiesta times, though nearby Huacachina's budget hotels have some friendly watering holes.

Getting There & Away

Ica is a main bus destination on the Carretera Panamericana and is easy to get to from Lima, Nazca and Arequipa. Most of the bus companies are clustered around the west end of Salaverry. For Lima (US$4.20 to US$5, 4½ hours), **Soyuz** (☎ 23-3312) has departures every 15 minutes, while **Flores** (☎ 21-2266) goes every 20 minutes (US$3). A less frequent service is available with **Cruz del Sur** (☎ 22-3333); **Ormeño** (☎ 21-5600), which goes hourly (US$3); **Transportes El Señor** de Luren (☎ 22-3658); and others. If going to Pisco, make sure your bus is entering town and not dropping you on the Panamericana 5km from Pisco (though you can easily get a combi from the junction into Pisco during the day). The easiest way to reach Pisco is to listen for conductors yelling 'Pisco' at the end of Salaverry. Most of the above companies have buses to Nazca (US$1.70, two hours) during the day, but services to Arequipa (US$10 to US$27, 12 hours) are mostly at night. Colectivos and minibuses for Pisco and Nazca leave from Lambayeque at Municipalidad when they are full and charge a bit more than buses.

Transportes Oropesa (☎ 22-3650; by the Flores terminal) has overnight buses to Ayacucho (US$5) at 7:30pm and Huancavelica (US$8, 14 hours) at 5pm.

HUACACHINA

Four kilometers west of Ica, this tiny resort village, dominated by a backdrop of giant sand dunes, nestles next to a small **lagoon** that is featured on the back of the S/50 note. Graceful palm trees, colorful flowers and attractive buildings in pastel shades cluster around the picturesque lagoon. The murky waters supposedly have curative properties, though hotel swimming pools are highly inviting in comparison.

It is possible to rent sand-boards for US$1.50 an hour to slide, surf or ski your way down the irresistible dunes, getting sand lodged into bodily nooks and crannies. Though softer, warmer and safer than snowboarding, don't be lulled into a false sense of security – several people have seriously injured themselves losing control of their sand-boards. A few hotels also rent out *areneros* (dune buggies) for further exploration of the desert.

Sleeping & Eating

Huacachina makes for a much safer and much more welcoming stopping point than neighboring Ica.

Casa de Arena (☎ 21-5439; casadearena@hotmail .com; dm US$3, s/d US$3/4.50, with bathroom US$4.50/6; 🖳 🖳) This is a funky sociable place with clean new rooms, an outdoor bar and a disco: single women can expect attention. It rents sand-boards (US$1.50 per hour) and dune buggies (US$10) and runs tours to another desert oasis as well as to local wineries.

Hostal Rocha (☎ 22-2256; kikerocha@hotmail.com; r per person US$3; 🖳) The Rocha has the same carefree atmosphere as the Casa de Arena, although its rooms are older and all have shared bathrooms. The owner of this place also runs entertaining dune-buggy trips into the desert.

Hosteria Suiza (☎ 23-8762; hostesuiza@yahoo.com; Balneario de Huacachina 264; s/d/tr $15/30/45; 🖳) At far end of the oasis, this is a tranquil alternative: no pumping bars here, just an elegant, characterful building and a restful garden. Breakfast is included.

Hotel Mossone (☎ 21-3630, in Lima 221-7020; fax 23-6137; s/d/ste US$40/55/74-90; 🗶 🖳) The Mossone has simple but stylish rooms centered around a pleasant courtyard. The rooms all have a hot shower and TV. There's also a good restaurant, bar and a games area. Walk-in travelers can get big discounts in the off-season.

Most hotels have a café of sorts and there are several restaurants close to the lagoon.

Getting There & Away

The only way to get to Huacachina from Ica is by taxi (US$1) or *taxi-tico* (US$0.60).

PALPA

From Ica, the Panamericana heads southeast through the small oasis of Palpa, known as 'the land of sun and oranges' for its famous orange groves. Like Nazca, Palpa is surrounded by perplexing **geoglyphs** in the pampa (large, flat area), but the best way to see these lines is on a combined flight from Nazca (below). Guides at the **municipalidad** (☎ 40-4488) may be able to take you around local archaeological sites with advance warning.

NAZCA

☎ 056 / pop 53,000 / elevation 588m

As the Panamericana rises through coastal mountains and stretches across the arid flats to Nazca, you'd be forgiven for thinking that this desolate pampa could hold little of interest. And indeed this sun-bleached expanse was largely ignored by the outside world until 1939, when American scientist Paul Kosok flew across the desert and noticed a series of extensive lines and figures etched below, which he initially took to be an elaborate irrigation system. In fact, what he had stumbled across was

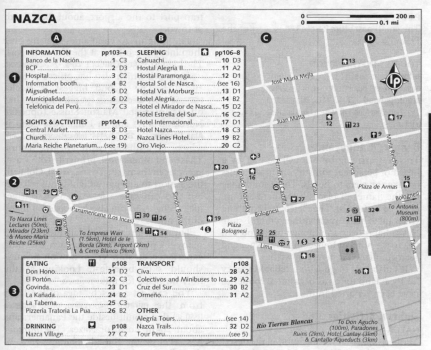

NAZCA

0 — 200 m
0 — 0.1 mi

INFORMATION	pp103–4
Banco de la Nación	1 C3
BCP	2 D3
Hospital	3 C2
Information booth	4 B2
Migsu@net	5 D2
Municipalidad	6 D2
Telefónica del Perú	7 C3

SIGHTS & ACTIVITIES	pp104–6
Central Market	8 D3
Church	9 D2
Maria Reiche Planetarium	(see 19)

SLEEPING	pp106–8
Cahuachi	10 D3
Hostal Alegría II	11 A2
Hostal Paramonga	12 D1
Hostal Sol de Nasca	(see 16)
Hostal Vía Morburg	13 D1
Hotel Alegría	14 D2
Hotel el Mirador de Nasca	15 D2
Hotel Estrella del Sur	16 C2
Hotel Internacional	17 D1
Hotel Nazca	18 C3
Nazca Lines Hotel	19 B2
Oro Viejo	20 C2

EATING	p108
Don Hono	21 D2
El Portón	22 C3
Govinda	23 D1
La Kañada	24 B2
La Taberna	25 C3
Pizzería Tratoria La Pua	26 B2

DRINKING	p108
Nazca Village	27 C2

TRANSPORT	p108
Civa	28 A2
Colectivos and Minibuses to Ica	29 A2
Cruz del Sur	30 B2
Ormeño	31 A2

OTHER	
Alegría Tours	(see 14)
Nazca Trails	32 D2
Tour Peru	(see 5)

To Nazca Lines Lectures (50m), Mirador (23km) & Museo Maria Reiche (25km)

To Empresa Wari (1.5km), Hotel de le Borda (2km), Airport (2km) & Cerro Blanco (9km)

To Antonini Museum (800m)

Río Tierras Blancas

To Don Agucho (100m), Paredones Ruins (2km), Hotel Cantay (3km) & Cantallo Aqueducts (3km)

SOUTH COAST

---

one of ancient Peru's most impressive and enigmatic achievements: the world-famous Nazca Lines. Nowadays the small town of Nazca is continually inundated by travelers who come to marvel and scratch their heads over the purpose of these mysterious lines, now a World Heritage Site.

History

In 1901 the Peruvian archaeologist Max Uhle was the first to realize that the drifting desert sands hid remnants of a culture distinct from other coastal peoples. Thousands of ceramics have since been uncovered, mostly by careless *huaqueros* (grave robbers; see p274) who plundered burial sites and sold their finds to individuals and museums. Archaeologists pieced together the story of this unique culture from the highly distinctive ceramics, from the brightly colored and naturalistic early pottery (AD 200 to 500) to the more stylized and sophisticated designs characterizing the late period (AD 500 to 700), and also the simpler designs of the terminal period (AD 700 to 800), influenced by the Wari people. Invaluable tools for

unraveling Peru's ancient past, the ceramics depict everything from everyday plants and animals to fetishes and divinities; some even echo the Nazca Lines themselves. Even the most casual observer will soon learn to recognize the strikingly different Nazca ceramics, some of which can be seen in the local museum and in Ica, though the best collections are in Lima.

Information
INTERNET ACCESS

La Kañada (Lima 160; US$1.40 per hour) Has only a few machines but they are fast.

Migsu@net (Plaza de Armas; US$0.60 per hour) Offers more machines but they are slower.

MEDICAL SERVICES

Nazca's **hospital** (☎ 52-2586; Callao) is open 24 hours for emergencies.

MONEY

BCP (cnr Lima & Grau) has a Visa ATM and changes traveler's checks. Some hotels geared toward international tourists also change traveler's checks.

POST
The small **post office** (Castillo 379) is west of the Plaza de Armas.

TOURIST INFORMATION
Information Booth (cnr Bolognesi & Lima; ☺ 8am-noon & 2-6pm) Run by enthusiastic students.
Municipalidad (☎ 52-2418; Plaza de Armas; ☺ 7am-2pm Mon-Fri) More useful, but it doesn't have a lot of info.

Dangers & Annoyances
Travelers arriving by bus will be met by a hoard of persistent touts trying to sell tours or take travelers to hotels. These touts may use the names of places listed here but are never to be trusted. They'll tell you anything you want to hear to receive their commission. Never hand over any money until you can talk to the hotel or tour-company owner and get a confirmed itinerary in writing.

It's also best to go with a reliable agency for local land tours, as occasional robberies have been reported in the past.

Sights & Activities
NAZCA LINES
The best-known lines are found in the desert 20km north of Nazca, and by far the best way to appreciate them is to get a bird's-eye view from an overflight. Although you can make reservations in Lima or Ica, it's far cheaper in Nazca.

Flights are taken in light aircraft (three to nine seats) in the morning and early afternoon. The best time is between 8am and 10am, when the sun is low, though flight times inescapably depend on the weather. Planes won't take off without good visibility, and there's often a low mist over the desert until 9am. Strong winds in the late afternoon also make flying impractical. Passengers are usually taken on a first-come, first-served basis, with priority given to those who have made reservations in Lima. The flight lasts 30 minutes.

The standard flight costs US$35 per person, but special low-season deals are sometimes available and prices have been known to climb above US$50 from June to August. In addition, there is an airport tax of US$5. There are also combination flights available that include the Palpa geoglyphs. These cost US$75 per person and last roughly one hour. Packages include transport to the airport, about 2km south of town.

The nine or so companies that fly over the Lines have offices at the Nazca airport. The biggest is **AeroCóndor** (☎ 52-2424; www.aerocondor.com.pe), which also has offices in Lima and Ica. The second biggest is **Aerolca** (☎ 52-2434; areoica@terra.com.pe), which has offices in Hostal Maison Suisse (opposite Nazca airport) and in Lima. Also good is **Alas Peruanas** (☎ 52-2444; info@alasperuanas.com), which is affiliated with Alegría Tours. These and others work primarily with travel agencies in town (see Tours, p106). Going to the airport to arrange a flight is not reliable, but you can save a few dollars if you get lucky. Flights to can also be booked at many of the hotels.

The small aircraft bank left and right and many people find this a stomach-churning experience, so sufferers of motion sickness should skip breakfast. Looking at the horizon helps for mild nausea.

You can get a sketchy idea of the Lines from the **mirador** (observation tower; admission US$0.30) that's built beside the Panamericana about 20km north of Nazca. The *mirador* has a close-up though oblique view of three figures: the lizard, tree and hands (or frog, depending on your angle). It's also a lesson in the damage to which the Lines are vulnerable. The Panamericana runs smack through the middle of the lizard, which from closeby seems all but obliterated. Signs warning of landmines are a humorous reminder that walking on the Lines is strictly forbidden. Walking on them causes damages and you can't see anything at ground level anyway. Take a taxi to get there (and the Museo Marie Reiche nearby) or get a bus or colectivo (US$0.60) from Nazca; a guard will help flag down transport back to Nazca.

NAZCA LINES LECTURES
Maria Reiche Planetarium (☎ 52-2293; Nazca Lines Hotel; adult/student US$6/3; ☺ 7pm & 9:15pm) has fascinating lectures on the Lines lasting 50 minutes and given by Belgian astronomer Barthelemy d'Ans.

Viktoria Nikitzki (☎ 969-9419; Los Espinales 300; US$3; minimum 3 people; ☺ 7pm), an English-speaking Austrian who was a long-time friend of Maria Reiche, also holds one-hour lectures about the Lines. The charmingly eccentric Nikitzki also runs sunset-watching

THE NAZCA LINES

Spread across an incredible 500 sq km of arid, rock-strewn plain in the Pampa Colorada, the Nazca Lines remain one of the world's great archaeological mysteries. Consisting of over 800 straight lines, 300 geometric figures (geoglyphs) and, concentrated in a relatively small area, some 70 spectacular animal and plant drawings (biomorphs), the lines are almost imperceptible at ground level. It's only when viewed from above that they form their striking network of enormous stylized figures and channels, many of which radiate from a central axis.

The Lines were made by the simple process of removing the dark sun-baked stones from the surface of the desert and piling them up on either side of the Lines, thus exposing the lighter, gypsum-laden soil below. The most elaborate designs represent animals, including a 180m-long lizard, a monkey with an extravagantly curled tail, and a condor with a 130m wingspan. There's also a killer whale, hummingbird, spider and an intriguing owl-headed man on the side of a hill, popularly referred to as an astronaut because of its goldfish-bowl shaped head. The figures are mostly etched out in single continuous lines, while the encompassing geoglyphs form perfect triangles, rectangles or straight lines running for several kilometers across the desert.

But the questions remain. Who constructed the Lines and why? And how did they know what they were doing when the Lines can only be properly appreciated from the air? Maria Reiche (1903–98), a German mathematician and long-time researcher of the Lines, theorized that they were made by the Paracas and Nazca cultures between 900 BC to AD 600, with some additions by the Wari settlers from the highlands in the 7th century. She also claimed that the Lines were an astronomical calendar developed for agricultural purposes, and that they were mapped out through the use of sophisticated mathematics (and a long rope). However, the handful of alignments Reiche discovered between the sun, stars and lines were not enough to convince scholars.

Later, English documentary-maker Tony Morrison theorized the Lines were walkways linking huacas, or sites of ceremonial significance. A slightly more surreal suggestion from explorer Jim Woodman was that the Nazca people knew how to construct hot-air balloons and that they did, in fact, observe the Lines from the air. Or, if you believe author George Von Breuniq, the Lines formed a giant running track. Of course, it was inevitable that the Lines would attract the attention of out-there theorists, and author Erich von Daniken – for one – was convinced that the Lines were intended as extraterrestrial landing sites. It's also been suggested that the Lines were linked to the hallucinogenic drugs taken by shamans. Take your pick!

A more down-to-earth theory, given the value of water in the sun-baked desert, was suggested by anthropologist Johann Reinhard, who believed that the Lines were involved in mountain worship and a fertility/water cult. Recent work by the Swiss–Liechtenstein Foundation agrees that they were dedicated to the worship of water, and it is thus ironic that their theory about the demise of the Nazca culture suggests that it was due not to drought but to destructive rainfall caused by a phenomenon such as El Niño!

About the only thing that is certain is that when the Nazca set about turning their barren desert into an elaborate canvas, they also began a debate that will keep archaeologists and documentary-makers happy for many years to come.

trips to Cerrito Mirador in December and June during the equinoxes for US$8.50.

MUSEO DIDACTICO ANTONINI

This excellent little **museum** (☎ 52-3444; cahuachi@terra.com.pe; Av de la Cultura 600; admission US$3, camera fee US$1.50; ☻ 9am-7pm) is highly informative about Nazca culture and various local sites; especially Cahuachi (see p106). It also boasts an original aqueduct running through the back garden, some enlightening replica tombs and a neat scale model of the Lines. Though labels are in Spanish, the front desk lends translation booklets in various languages for you to carry around.

OTHER EXCURSIONS

Many people fly over the Lines then leave, but there's lots more to see around Nazca. If you take one of the many inexpensive tours on offer (see Tours p106 for contact details), they usually include a stop at a potter's and/or gold-miner's workshop for a demonstration of their techniques (tips for those who show you their trade are expected).

The popular **Cemetery of Chauchilla** (admission US$1.20), 30km away, will satisfy any urges you have to see Nazca bones, skulls and mummies. Dating back to between AD 1000 and 1300, the mummies were, until recently, scattered haphazardly across the desert, left by ransacking tomb-robbers. Now they are seen carefully rearranged inside 12 tombs, though cloth fragments and pottery and bone shards still litter the ground outside the demarcated trail. Organized tours last two to three hours and cost US$5 to US$10 per person (two-person minimum).

The **Paredones ruins**, 2km southeast of town via Arica over the river, are not very well preserved, but about 5km further on are the underground **Cantallo aqueducts** (admission US$1), which are still in working order and essential to irrigate the surrounding fields. The Nazca's stonework is fine, and it is possible to enter the aqueducts through the spiraling *ventanas* (windows), which local people use to clean the aqueducts each year – a wet and claustrophobic experience. It's possible to walk there, but don't carry valuables. A taxi round-trip costs US$7. Tours are available from Nazca for about US$5 per person (four-passenger minimum) and may be combined with a guided walk through Buena Fe, where there are some small geoglyphs.

Museo Maria Reiche (☎ 52-2428; Km448; adult/child US$1/0.50; ☽ 8:30am-5:30pm) When Maria Reiche, the German mathematician and long-term researcher of the Nazca Lines, died in 1998, her house, 25km north along the Panamericana, was made into a small museum. Though disappointingly scant on information, you can see where and how she lived, amid the clutter of her tools and obsessive sketches. Maria Reiche's tomb lies in the garden. Buses to Ica can drop you at the gates (US$0.60, 25 minutes).

Though the sun can be punishing, it's possible to walk from here back to the *mirador* (see p104) in a sweaty 30 to 40 minutes, or passing colectivos will take you for US$0.30. See p104 for details on how to get to the museum and *mirador*.

A dirt road also travels 25km west from Nazca town to **Cahuachi**, the most important

known Nazca center, which is still undergoing excavation. It consists of several pyramids, a graveyard and an enigmatic site called El Estaquería, which may have been used as a site of mummification. Tours cost US$8 to US$15, and often include a trip to Pueblo Viejo, a nearby pre-Nazca residential settlement.

Reserva Nacional Pampas Galeras is a vicuña sanctuary high in the mountains 90km east of Nazca and is the best place to these shy animals in Peru, though tourist services are virtually nonexistent. In late May or early June is the annual *chaccu*, when local inhabitants round up the vicuñas for shearing and ceremonies.

Off-the-beaten-track expeditions are also run by several outfitters, including a sand-boarding trip down the nearby **Cerro Blanco**, the highest-known sand dune in the world at 2078m, and a real challenge for budding sand-boarders fresh from Huacachina. There are also local half-day **mountain-bike tours**. Both expeditions cost around US$25.

Tours

See Nazca Lines (p104) for details of flights over this intriguing site.

Alegría Tours (☎ /fax 52-2444; info@alegriatours peru.com; Hotel Alegría) It offers all the usual local tours, plus off-the-beaten-track and mountain-biking options. The tours are expensive for one or two people, so ask to join up with other travelers to receive a group discount if necessary. Alegría provides guides in English and French, and German in some cases.

Nasca Trails (☎ 52-2858; nascatrails@terra.com.pe; Bolognesi 550) Comes well recommended by readers, and is run by the friendly Juan Tohalino Vera, who is an experienced guide who speaks excellent English, as well as German, French and Italian.

Tour Peru (☎ 52-3758; Arica 285) Also does a reasonable job of local tours.

The Fernández family at Hotel Nazca (see Sleeping, following) also organize some of the cheapest tours for budget travelers, but only speak to them directly as travelers have been ripped off by touts at the bus stop using the Hotel Nazca name.

Sleeping

Be aware that prices increase by 25% to 50% in the high season between May and August.

BUDGET

Hotel Estrella del Sur (☎ 52-2106; estrelladelsur hotel@yahoo.com.mx; Callao 568A; s/d/tr US$7/10/13) Estrella has small but very well-cared-for rooms with electric showers and TV. Service is cheerful and there's a sociable outdoor café. Rates include breakfast.

Hotel Alegría (see Mid-Range) This is a mid-range place that keeps 13 basic but clean rooms for budget travelers at US$4 per person. These rooms share two bathrooms that have hot showers.

Hostal Alegría II (☎ 52-2497; alegriatours@hot mail.com; Los Incas 117; r per person US$3, s/d with bathroom US$6/8.50) This sister hotel is run by the younger generation of Alegrías and is friendly and helpful. It has hot water, though the rooms are plain. Prices rise substantially in high season.

Hotel Internacional (☎ 55-2744; Maria Reiche 12; s/d US$7/9, bungalows US$12/14; **P**) The Internacional has basic rooms with hot showers; there are bigger, better bungalows with patios out the back.

Hostal Sol de Nasca (☎ 52-2730; fax 52-2005; Callao 586; s/d US$6/12) Though the rooms are undistinguished, they have hot showers and breakfast is included.

Cahuachi (☎ 52-3786; cahuachi@terra.com.pe; Jirón Arica 115; s/d US$6/9) This option has cramped but well-cared-for rooms with cold-water bathrooms (but there's hot water between March and September).

Hostal Paramonga (☎ 52-2576; Juan Matta 880; s/d US$6/9) A new place with noisy corridors, the Paramonga has well-furnished rooms with bathrooms and hot water. Its prices can double in high season.

Hotel Nazca (☎ 52-2085; Lima 438; r per person US$3) The Nazca has very basic rooms with communal tepid showers. Ticket touts hang around offering cheap tours – don't pay for anything until you have it in writing.

Nido del Condor and **Hostal Maison Suisse** (see Mid-Range and Top End, respectively), by the airport, allow camping on its grassy lawns for about US$3 per person.

MID-RANGE

All the following have bathroom and hot water.

Oro Viejo (☎ 52-2284; Callao 483; oro_viejo@terra .com.pe; s/d/tr US$20/30/40) This recently opened hostel retains a family atmosphere and has well-furnished rooms, a welcoming lounge

and a large, exquisitely tended garden. Breakfast is included.

Don Agucho (☎ 52-2048; donagucho@hotmail.com; Av San Carlos 100; s/d/tr $25/30/40; ☒) The Don Agucho has chatty service, nice rooms and a great terrace for lounging; the terrace is filled with cacti, wickerwork and wagon wheels. It's a short walk over the bridge to central Nazca. Rates include breakfast.

Hotel Alegría (☎ 52-2702; alegriatours@hotmail .com; Lima 168; s US$10-20, d US$20-40) This is a classic travelers' haunt with a restaurant, garden, and a busy travel agency. It has comfortable, carpeted rooms with bathroom, TV and fan; basic budget rooms are also available. English, Italian, Hebrew and German are spoken. Rates double in high season.

Hotel El Mirador de Nasca (☎ 52-3121; fax 52-3741; Tacna 436; s/d US$10/14) On the Plaza de Armas, El Mirador has a glossy entrance but don't expect the rooms to match up. They are, however, comfortable, with TV, phone; the rates include breakfast.

Hostal Vía Morburg (☎ 52-2141; hotelviamorburg@ yahoo.es; José María Mejía at Maria Reiche; s/d US$8.50/14; ☒) This place is clean and secure and has small rooms with cramped showers but lots of hot water. There's a miniature swimming pool – more of a deep bathtub really. It has a decent restaurant on the top floor.

Hotel de la Borda (☎ 52-2750; in Lima 442-6391, Km 447; turmajoro@yahoo.com; s/d/tr US$40/50/67 ☒) Housed in a lovely converted hacienda out in middle of nowhere, this place has simple rooms but tranquil gardens plus a pet peacock and alpaca. It's 3km out of town and beyond the airport, so take a taxi (US$1). Rates include breakfast.

Nido del Condor (☎ 52-3520; contanas@terra .com.pe; Km447; s/d US$25/35; ☒) This place at the airport has decent rooms, and a small pool. It shows films on the Lines and also serves as the AreoCóndor office.

TOP END

Nazca Lines Hotel (☎ 52-2293; fax 52-2112; Jirón Bolognesi; s/d/ste $65/85/101; ☒) This is the best hotel in the center, boasting good rooms, a tennis court, restaurant, quiet lounge and tours. Nonguests can use the pool for US$4.50 (including a sandwich and drink).

Hostal Maison Suisse (☎ 52-2434, in Lima ☎ /fax 01-444-2140; s/d/tr $49/58/79; ☒ ☒) This place, opposite the airport, has a large grassy area with hammocks. The 40 rooms are comfortable, with TV and phone, and suites have air-con, a Jacuzzi and minibar. This hotel is also the AeroIca office, and you receive a discount if you fly over the Lines with them.

Hotel Cantay (☎ 52-2264; hotelcantayo@amauta .rcp.net.pe; Cantayo; s or d US$150; 🛇 🗾) The Cantay is run by Italians, and overrun with monkeys, a family of peacocks, alpacas and horses (which can be hired by nonguests for US$7 per hour). It is 500m from the Cantallo aqueducts. The rooms are top-quality and have various bedroom styles, including four-poster beds and Japanese-style rooms. The hotel also has a top-notch pool area amid extensive lawns.

Eating & Drinking

La Kañada (☎ 52-2917; Lima 160; 3-course menú US$3; 🕑 opens early) This place has tasty Peruvian food and gives a free pisco sour. A decent list of cocktails includes Algarrobina, made with pisco, milk and syrup from the famous *huarango* tree. There's occasional live Andean music. It also has a fast Internet connection (US$1.40 per hour).

Pizzería Tratoria La Pua (☎ 52-2990; Lima 169; mains US$3-9) You may get a free pisco sour with your pizza here. The menu is limited and a little pricey, but good.

La Taberna (☎ 52-1411; Lima 321; mains US$2.50-5) It's an intimate hole-in-the-wall place; the scribbles covering every inch of wall are a testament to its popularity. Try the spicy fish, named challengingly 'Pescado a lo Macho' (US$4.50). There's sometimes live music here on the weekend.

El Portón (☎ 52-3490; cnr Morsesky & Lima; mains US$5-10) A classy option with a nice stone courtyard, El Portón has a varied menu strong on *criollo* and Italian food.

Don Hono (☎ 52-3066; Arica 254; mains US$2-6; 🕑 closed Sat) Just off the plaza, Don Hono serves fresh farm produce and is justifiably proud of its pisco sour.

Govinda (Arica 450; 3-course menú US$1.20) Yes, the ubiquitous Govinda has made it to Nazca. This tiny Hare Krishna–run place serves healthy vegetarian fare.

Nazca Village (☎ 52-1078; Jirón Bolognesi; 🕑 10am-11pm) This is a new open-air bar, swish by local standards, in a town with scant nightlife. Its wildness is measured by the fact that it often shows local history documentaries.

Getting There & Away

AIR

You can fly to Nazca from Lima or Ica with AeroCóndor (sometimes with AeroIca). People who fly into Nazca normally fly over the Nazca Lines and return the same day.

BUS

Nazca is a major destination for buses on the Panamericana and is easy to get to from Lima, Ica or Arequipa. Buses to Arequipa generally originate in Lima, and to get a seat you have to pay the Lima fare. **Ormeño** (☎ 52-2058) has four daily buses to Lima (US$5 to US$20, eight hours), as well as to intermediate points such as Ica and Pisco. **Cruz del Sur** (☎ 52-35000) has five services to Lima daily for the same price range, and **Civa** (☎ 52-3019) has one (US$5).

For Arequipa (nine to 11 hours), most buses leave in the late afternoon or at night. Ormeño has three daily services between 4pm and 4am for US$7 to US$22.50. Civa (US$10 to US$20) also has three buses daily and Cruz del Sur (US$8.50 to US$22.50) has seven daily.

To go direct to Cuzco, several companies take the newly paved road through Puquio and Abancay (US$15.50 to US$22.50, 20 hours). Consider taking the 5pm, 9pm or 11pm service with **Empresa Wari** (☎ 52-3746), which is at El Cruce – the turn-off for the Puquio road about 2km south of town. Cruz del Sur goes to Cuzco (US$20 to US$28) twice daily. The route climbs to 4300m, and gets cold; carry warm clothes.

For those heading to Chile, Civa and Cruz del Sur have twice-daily buses to Tacna (US$12 to US$24, 14 hours).

Frequent combis leave central Nazca for the airport (US$0.30, 10 minutes), 2km away. Taxis cost US$0.60.

COLECTIVO

Fast colectivo taxis (US$4, 1½ hours) and slower minibuses (US$3, 2½ hours) to Ica leave from the Panamericana at Lima when they are full.

CHALA

☎ 054 / pop 2500

The tiny, ramshackle fishing village of Chala, about 170km from Nazca, presents a good opportunity to break the journey to Arequipa and visit the archaeological site of

Puerto Inca (admission free), from whence fresh fish was once sent all the way to Cuzco by runners – no mean effort! The site is 10km north of town. Head up the Panamericana, then turn left near Km603 and follow a dirt road for 4km to the coastal ruins.

Here you'll also find **Hotel Puerto Inca** (☎ 55-1055; puertoinka@terra.com.pe; Km603 Panamericana; s/d/tr US$21/32/44; ☒), a large resort set in the pretty bay. It has a camp site that costs US$2 per person with shower complex, and it also offers horse riding, body-boards, kayaks and jet skis. Alternatively, in Chala itself is the basic **Hostal Grau** (☎ 50-1009; Comercio 701; s/d US$3/6), which is clean and friendly with shared cold showers. Ask for a room in the back with ocean views.

Halfway between Nazca and Chala in the desert is **Sacaco**, where the sand is made of crushed shells; keep your eyes peeled for fossilized crocodile teeth. There is a small site **museum** (admission US$1) with a fossilized whale in the middle of nowhere. The 3km road to Sacaco is marked by a sign on the highway. You can take a taxi from Nazca to Chala with a stop at Sacaco (US$25 to US$30). Alegría Tours in Nazca also brings groups occasionally.

Colectivos from Nazca to Chala leave Óvalo between 6am and 8am only (US$3.50, three hours). Buses to Arequipa leave at 7pm to 8pm (US$6, eight hours).

CAMANÁ
☎ 054 / pop 13,300
From Chala the Panamericana heads south for 220km, clinging tortuously to sand dunes dropping down to the sea, until it reaches Camaná. This coastal town was until recently a summer resort popular with Arequipeños who flocked to its beaches, 5km from the center. Sadly, the earthquake of June 2001 sparked a tidal wave that devastated the beachside community and its tourism industry in one swift strike. Nonetheless, Camaná is still a convenient place to break the journey to Arequipa because its town center is largely unaffected, and its beaches are uncrowded. To get to the coast, take a combi to La Punta beach (US$0.30, 10 minutes), where there are a few sparse restaurants and hotels, many bearing scars of the tsunami.

BCP (9 de Noviembre 139) changes dollars and has a 24-hour Visa ATM.

Sleeping & Eating
Hotels get busier on summer weekends from January to March.

Hostal Lima (☎ 57-2901; Lima 306; s/d US$3.50/US$6, with bathroom US$4.50/7) Hotel Lima is a simple spot for a night's kip, a stone's throw from the bus stops. There's hot water in communal showers while the miniature private bathrooms get cold only.

Hostal Montecarlo (☎ 57-1110; Lima 514; s/d/tr with bathroom US$8.50/11/13) This is a new hotel with immaculate rooms, 24-hour hot water, cable TV and phone. Good value.

Gran Hostal Premier (☎ 57-1008; García Carbajal 117; s/d/tr US$8.50/14/20) Premier has reasonable rooms with bathroom, hot water, phone and cable TV.

Hotel de Turistas (☎ 57-1740; hotelturcamana@terra .com.pe; Lima 138; s/d/tr US$19/25/35; ☒) Housed in a large elegant building in spacious gardens, this place is a cut above the rest. It has a restaurant and rates include breakfast.

Sun Valley (☎ 969-4235; eridv@hotmail.com; Km843, Cerrillos 2; s or d US$14; ☒) This is a clean, new hotel close to the beach, with comfy beds, a sunny terrace and it also has a restaurant that comes highly recommended. Rates include breakfast and off-season discounts are 30% to 40% when your luck is in.

Getting There & Away
Frequent services to Arequipa (US$3 to US$4, 3½ hours) are provided by **Cruz del Sur** (☎ 57-1491; Lima 474), **Flores** (☎ 57-1013; Lima 200) and **Cromotex** (☎ 57-1752; Lima 301). Cruz del Sur and **Civa** (☎ 49-9843) also have daily buses to Lima (US$10, 15 hours) that go via Nazca (US$5, seven hours).

MOLLENDO
☎ 054 / pop 23,400
This small port is a popular beach resort for Arequipeños during the January-to-March summer season but is like a ghost town for the rest of the year. Mollendo is normally reached by road from Arequipa through a scaly desert landscape of delicate pink, brown and grays. Near **La Joya**, large sand dunes resemble half-moons poured in unlikely positions on the pinkish rock. Beyond the dunes the desert becomes very rocky, with tortured-looking cacti eking out an existence in the salt-laden soil.

Mollendo itself is a pleasant town, with hilly streets and a long beach. Once

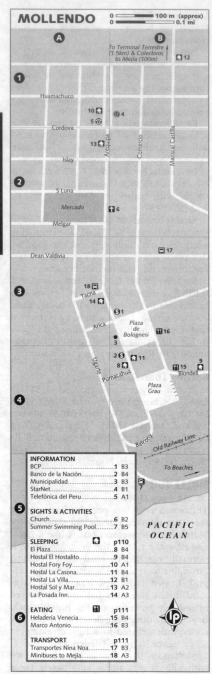

MOLLENDO

0 —— 100 m (approx)
0 —— 0.1 mi

To Terminal Terrestre
(1.5km) & Colectivos
to Mejía (100m)

PACIFIC
OCEAN

To Beaches

To Terminal Terrestre
Old Railway Line

Plaza
de
Bolognesi

Plaza
Grau

Mercado

Huamachuco
Cordova
Islay
S Luna
Melgar
Dean Valdivia
Tacna
Arica
Ugarte
Pumacahua
Balcony

Arequipa
Comercio
Mariscal Castilla

Blondell

INFORMATION	
BCP	1 B3
Banco de la Nación	2 B4
Municipalidad	3 B3
StarNet	4 B1
Telefónica del Perú	5 A1

SIGHTS & ACTIVITIES	
Church	6 B2
Summer Swimming Pool	7 B5

SLEEPING	p110
El Plaza	8 B4
Hostal El Hostalito	9 B4
Hostal Fory Foy	10 A1
Hostal La Casona	11 B4
Hostal La Villa	12 B1
Hostal Sol y Mar	13 A2
La Posada Inn	14 A3

EATING	p111
Heladería Venecia	15 B4
Marco Antonio	16 B3

TRANSPORT	p111
Transportes Nina Noa	17 B3
Minibuses to Mejía	18 A3

a bustling port, most ships now dock in the larger port of Matarani, 15km to the northwest. From January to March, a popular weekend swimming pool opens by the sea (US$1/0.50 per adult/child) and hosts discos in the evening.

BCP (Arequipa 330) changes dollars and has a Visa ATM, and you can find a good Internet connection at **StarNet** (Arequipa 327; 8am-11:30pm; US$0.60 per hour).

One of the best reasons to come to Mollendo is to pay a visit to the nearby nature sanctuary at Mejía (see Mejía & the Río Tambo Valley, opposite).

Sleeping

Single rooms are difficult to find during weekends in the high season, when prices shoot up.

La Posada Inn (☎ 53-4610; Arequipa 337; s/d US$4/8, with bathroom US$7/13) This is an excellent, well-cared-for option run by a welcoming family and scented with honeysuckle in summer. Rates include breakfast. Rooms in the lower area have hot water, and some have local TV.

Hostal Fory Foy (☎ 53-2513; Arequipa 681; r per person US$3, s or d with bathroom US$10) Fory Foy has very basic rooms, some with a bathroom. The hostel was formerly named Hostal 45, which Peruvians pronounce as 'fory foy.'

El Plaza (☎ 53-2460; fax 53-3245; Arequipa 209; s/d/tr US$13/14/15) This large new place has good rooms, hot showers and local TV. Rates are 30% less in midweek and off-season.

Hostal Sol y Mar (☎ 53-2265; Arequipa 569; s/d US$4.50/6, with bathroom US$10/14) This hostel has both bare-bones rooms and better options with bathroom and local TV. Hot water is available.

Hostal El Hostalito (☎ 53-3674; Blondell 169; s/d/tr US$16/19/22) El Hostalito also gets a big thumbs-up, with light, spacious rooms and some views to the busy beach. Some rooms have cable TV and minibar and you can stay in some style without busting the budget here.

Hostal La Casona (☎ 53-3061; Arequipa 188; s/d US$12/14) Very centrally located, La Casona has high-ceilinged, airy rooms with cable TV and hot water.

Hostal La Villa (☎ 53-2700; Mariscal Castilla 366; s/d/tr with bathroom US$20/23/28, ste US$29; P) This is a relaxing place to lie back on a sunlounger with a cold drink and one foot in the pool. It has carpeted rooms with cable TV, plus a garden terrace and restaurant.

Eating

Mollendo's eateries lack pizzazz. **Marco Antonio** (☎ 53-4258; Comercio 254; mains US$2-5.50) is good no-frills place, considered the best in the center. For ice cream and snacks, try **Heladería Venecia** (☎ 53-3600; cnr Blondell & Comercio; ice cream US$0.70-2); it has some intriguing local fruit flavors and often tempts punters with free samples.

Getting There & Away

The Mollendo–Arequipa train is for freight only. The bus terminal is 1.5km west of the center. **Empresa Aragón** (☎ 53-2506), **Santa Ursula** (☎ 53-2008), Carpio and La Joya all have regular departures to Arequipa (US$2 to US$3, 2¾ hours). **Tepsa** (☎ 53-2872) provides a daily service to Lima (US$10, 18 to 20 hours).

There are no direct buses to Moquegua or Tacna. Colectivos from the top end of Castilla, by a gas station, pass through Mejía, the Río Tambo valley, La Curva and Cocachacra to El Fiscal (US$1.50, two hours), another gas station where buses to Moquegua and Tacna regularly stop.

Transportes Nina Noa (Dean Valdivia), northwest of Plaza Bolognesi, has minibuses to Ilo (US$3.50, 3½ hours, four daily). Minibuses to the beach resort of Mejía (US$0.30, 15 minutes) leave from the corner of Tacna and Arequipa.

MEJÍA & THE RÍO TAMBO VALLEY

Mejía is a summer beach resort for Arequipeños, but it's deserted from April to December. About 6km southeast of Mejía along an unbroken line of beaches is **Santuario Nacional Lagunas de Mejía**, a 690-hectare sanctuary protecting coastal lagoons that cover more than 100 hectares. They are the largest permanent lakes in 1500km of desert coastline; hence they attract great numbers of coastal and migratory bird species, best seen in early morning. There is a **visitor center** (☎ 80-0004; admission US$1.50; ☼ sunrise-sunset) with maps. Combis and colectivos pass about once an hour during the day. A round-trip from town by taxi with an hour to explore costs about US$7.

Minibuses marked 'El Valle' leave from the gas station at the roundabout on the upper stretch of Mariscal Castilla and pass the Santuario Nacional Lagunas de Mejía (US$0.40, 25 minutes).

The road continues along the Río Tambo valley, which has been transformed by an important irrigation project into fertile rice paddies, sugarcane plantations and fields of potatoes and corn: a striking juxtaposition with the dusty backdrop of sand dunes and desert. The road joins the Carretera Panamericana at El Fiscal, a fly-blown gas station and the only stop in about 100km of desert road. You can wait here for buses to Moquegua and Tacna.

MOQUEGUA

☎ 053 / pop 49,000 / elevation 1412m

Moquegua is a parched and dusty town lying in the driest point of the Peruvian coastal desert, soon to merge into the Atacama Desert of northern Chile – the driest in the world. Moquegua means 'quiet place' in Quechua, and the region has long been culturally linked with the Andes. It has peaceful cobblestone streets and interesting buildings, many of which are roofed with a type of wattle-and-daub mixture of sugar-cane thatch and clay. Sadly, these structures sustained significant damage during the June 2001 earthquake, which hit Moquegua harder than any other city.

The Río Moquegua manages to provide enough moisture to the surrounding areas to grow avocados and grapes (the basis of Pisco Biondi, one of Peru's best piscos), but as you walk away from the river it becomes harder to believe that any agriculture is possible here.

Information

The **Regional Tourist Offices** (☎ 76-2236; moque gua@mincetur.gob.pe; Ayacucho 1060; ☼ 7:30am-3:30pm Mon-Fri) are primarily administrative, but the staff are willing to answer questions. **Colmeta Internet** (Moquegua 677A; ☼ 8am-11pm; US$0.60 per hour) has a good Internet connection, and the **post office** (Ayacucho 560; ☼ 8am-noon & 3-6:30pm Mon-Sat) is on the plaza.

BCP (Moquegua 861) has an ATM that takes Visa and MasterCard.

Sights & Activities

The small and shady **Plaza de Armas**, with a wrought-iron fountain (thought by some to be designed by Eiffel), flower gardens

and colonial architecture, is a welcome oasis away from the encroaching desert. Readers have written of a tragi-comic scene regularly played out here between an old maintenance man, whose sole duty appears to be chasing the pigeons away from the fountains, and several vendors thoughtfully selling birdseed on the same plaza.

The **Museo Contisuyo** (☎ 76-1844; members .aol.com/contisuyo/museoc.html; Jirón Tacna 294; adult/ student US$0.45/0.20; 🕑 10am-1pm & 3-5:30pm Wed-Mon, 10am-noon & 4-8pm Tue), on the Plaza de Armas, is an excellent little museum of local archaeological atrefacts. The labels are in English and Spanish.

Walk around to see some of the typical **sugar-cane thatching**, especially along Moquegua, and have a peek inside the **cathedral**, which houses the body of 17th-century Saint Fortunata, whose hair and nails are said to still be growing.

A worthwhile excursion outside the city is to the flat-topped and steep-sided hill of **Cerro Baul**, 12km from Moquegua, which was once occupied by the Wari and boasts some fine views. The walk to the top takes

about an hour. A taxi costs US$10 round-trip, or catch a micro for Torata and ask to be let off at Cerro Baul (US$0.60).

Sleeping

Hotel Sparto (☎ 76-2360; Balta 165; s/d US$4.50/8.50, s/d/tr with bathroom US$6/10/14) This is a decent, popular budget choice with sizeable, clean rooms and hot water in the mornings.

Hostal Los Limoneros (☎ 76-1649, Lima 441; s/d US$6/9, with bathroom US$12/15; P) It's the quiet garden, with its shady patios and delicious smells, that makes this traditional hostel the most attractive – if not the most luxurious – in town. Private, and some communal, showers have hot water, and some rooms have cable TV.

Hostel Plaza (☎ 76-1612; Ayacucho 675; s/d/tr US$8/11/16) This is a great spot by the plaza, opposite the cathedral, with spanking new, good-value rooms with bathroom and large-screen cable TV.

Hostal Adrianella (☎ 76-3469; M Grau 239; s/d US$12/16) Adrianella is also clean with private hot showers and cable TV. It's good value if you don't mind the traffic noise outside.

Hostal Carrera (☎ 76-2113; Lima 320; s/d US$3.50/6.50, with bathroom US$4.50/7.50) Carrera is a neat, pastel-colored little hostel with small rooms and a friendly owner. On account of mild earthquake damage, there was only hot water in shared showers at the time of writing.

Hostal Los Angeles (☎ 76-2629; hostalangeles@latinmail.com; Torata 100A off M Grau; s/d US$6/10, with bathroom US$10/14) Los Angeles has some rooms so spacious that they border on emptiness. Cable TV is available for US$2.

Hostal Arequipa (☎ 76-1338; Arequipa 360; s/d US$8/10) Arequipa has clean and cozy rooms with hot showers and cable TV. Service is friendly and helpful.

Hostal Holiday (☎ 76-3163; holiday@peru.com; Manuel de la Torre 221; s/d US$4.50/7; **P**) Atop a flight of stairs looking down on the city and the street vendors below, Hostal Holiday has clean rooms with shared hot showers.

Hotel Alameda (☎ /fax 76-3971; Junín 322; s/d US$19/27) Alameda has quality, spick-and-span rooms with sofa, hot shower, minibar and cable TV. The rates include breakfast. An upstairs salon and terrace have good views.

Hotel El Mirador de Moquegua (☎ 76-1765; fax 76-1895; Alto de la Villa; s/d $32.50/47, bungalow $68; **☒** **P**) Perched on a cliff about 3km from the town center, El Mirador has a pool with a view, children's playground and restaurant. Rooms are a bland '60s style but are comfortable and have cable TV.

Eating

Near the center, **Restaurant Morales** (☎ 76-3084; cnr Lima & Libertad; menú US$1.40; ☾ early closing Sun) and **Restaurant Palermo** (☎ 76-4072; Moquegua 644A; 3-course menú US$1.50) are both not much to look at, but they have good set meals.

For the best restaurants, catch a taxi to nearby Samegua (US$1). Here you'll find the highly popular **Las Glorietas** (☎ 76-1181; Samegua; mains US$3.50-6), which serves typical regional food in an open-air terraced restaurant. It's especially good for duck, *chicharrones* and also avocado dishes, but there's a more varied menu at weekends, when there's also occasional live music.

Getting There & Away

Buses leave from small terminals down a hill west of the center. Buses to Lima (16 to 20 hours) leave with **Ormeño** (☎ 76-1149; Av La Paz 524), with three services daily (US$11

to US$17); **Cruz del Sur** (☎ 76-1405), also with three services (US$27 to US$34); and **Flores** (☎ 76-2647), with two daily (US$20). These buses may make intermediate stops at Nazca (US$8 to US$14, 12 to 14 hours) and Ica.

Buses to Arequipa (four hours) leave with Cruz del Sur (US$4 to US$18, six daily), Ormeño (US$3.50, two daily), Transportes Moquegua and Flores (US$5, 16 daily) about every hour. Buses to Tacna (US$2 to US$3, three hours) depart frequently with the same companies.

Flores also has buses to Ilo (US$1.50, two hours, six daily).

Several companies go on the newly paved route to Puno (US$6 to US$8.50, eight hours) via Desaguadero on the Bolivian border (US$5.50, 5½ hours); most buses leave in the evening, but, if at all possible, travel during the day when you can see the spectacular scenery. The company **San Martín** (☎ 76-3584) offers daytime departures.

A new bus terminal is being built 2km east of the city and may be open by late 2004.

ILO

☎ 053 / pop 50,000

Ilo is the departmental port, about 95km southwest of Moquegua. It's mainly used to ship copper from the mine at Toquepala further south, as well as wine and avocados from Moquegua. Bolivia now also has the right to use the port for importing and exporting goods without paying duty. About 15km inland is **Museo El Algarrobal** (adult/child US$0.60/0.30; ☾ 8am-3:30pm Tue-Fri & 8:30am-2pm Sat & Sun), which hosts a surprisingly interesting collection of exhibits pertaining to the area's archaeology and agriculture, including a collection of feather-topped hats and a mummified llama. A round-trip by taxi costs about US$3.50.

Sleeping & Eating

Hostal Plaza (☎ 78-1633; fax 78-2146; 2 de Mayo 514; s/d US$12/17) Just off the plaza, this is a handy new hostel with good rooms, hot showers and cable TV.

Hotel San Martín (☎ 78-1082; Matará 325; s/d US$7/10) Near the bus companies, this is a good-value hostel with large decent rooms and private hot showers.

VIP Hotel (☎ 78-1492; viphotel@terra.com.pe; 2 de Mayo 608; s/d $24/32; **P** **☒**) A swish, new addition by the plaza, the VIP has spacious rooms with all the frills, from minibar to hairdryer and cable TV, and breakfast is included in the rates. Rooms on higher floors have great views.

Gran Hotel Ilo (☎ 78-2411; granhotelilo@mixmail .com.pe; Cáceres 3007; s/d/ste US$22/29/36; P ⚊) This hotel is situated right on the rocky shoreline and has a big swimming pool and patio with views back toward the port. Rates include breakfast.

Restaurant El Peñon (☎ 78-2929; 2 de Mayo 100; mains US$2-5) has a prime shorefront position, looking down on pelicans and across to the port, but to enjoy the seafood and panoramic views at a safe distance from the port's distinctive smell, **Restaurant Pocoma** (mains US$4-8), in the VIP hotel, is the most refined option.

Getting There & Away

There is a new ship-shaped (literally) bus terminal 1km north of town, but most companies continue to leave from the town center. **Cruz del Sur** (☎ 78-2206; cnr Moquegua & Matará) has daily buses to Lima (US$27, 18 to 22 hours), Arequipa (US$5, five hours) and Moquegua (US$1.50, two hours). **Flores** (☎ 78-1540; cnr Ilo & Matará) goes to the same destinations and has hourly services to Tacna (US$2, 3½ hours).

TACNA

☎ 052 / pop 230,000 / elevation 560m

At 1293km southeast of Lima, Tacna is Peru's southernmost city and the capital of its department. It is situated 36km from the Chilean border and was occupied by Chile in 1880 after the War of the Pacific, until its people voted to return to Peru in 1929. Tacna has some of the best schools and hospitals in Peru; whether this is due to its Chilean ties is a matter of opinion. The city also has British and French influences through its showpiece architecture and train system. Tacna is surprisingly patriotic.

Information

IMMIGRATION

Bolivian Consulate (☎ 71-5792; Bolognesi 1721; ⏱ 9am-2pm Mon-Fri)

Chilean Consulate (☎ 72-3063; www.minrel.cl; ⏱ 8am-1pm Mon-Fri) It's near the train station though most travelers just need a tourist card, which is freely available at the border.

INTERNET ACCESS & POST

Post office (Bolognesi 361; ⏱ 8am-8pm Mon-Sat) It's south of the Plaza de Armas.

Tacna Net (Unanue; ⏱ 10am-9pm; Net surfing US$0.50 per hour)

UPT (Plaza de Armas; ⏱ 8am-11pm Mon-Sat; surfing US$0.60 per hour)

LAUNDRY

Lavandería Latina (Vizcarra 264b; ⏱ 8am-9:30pm Mon-Sat), which charges US$1.40 per kg, is a good option.

MEDICAL SERVICES

For emergencies, try Tacna's fine **hospital** (☎ 72-3361, 74-2121; Blondell).

MONEY

Chilean pesos, nuevo soles and US dollars can all be easily exchanged in Tacna. **BCP** (San Martín 574) has a Visa and MasterCard ATM, changes Amex and Visa traveler's checks and gives cash advances on Visa cards.

TOURIST INFORMATION

Regional Tourist Offices (☎ 74-6944; tacna@ mincetur.com.pe; 4th fl, Blondell 50; ⏱ 7:15am-2:30pm Mon-Fri) Has a mainly administrative function, but can give advice to travelers.

Zesal Tour Agency (☎ 74-2851; zesaltacna@ hotmail.com; international bus terminal) It provides free tourist information.

Dangers & Annoyances

Remember that international-tourist traffic attracts thieves.

Sights & Activities

PLAZA DE ARMAS

Tacna's main plaza, pictured on the front of the S/100 note, features a huge arch – a monument to the heroes of the War of the Pacific. It is flanked by larger-than-life bronze statues of Admiral Grau and Colonel Bolognesi. Nearby, the 6m-high bronze **fountain** was created by the French engineer Alexandre Gustave Eiffel (of Eiffel Tower fame), who also designed the **cathedral**, noted for its fine stained-glass windows and onyx high altar. The plaza, which is studded with palm trees and large pergolas topped by bizarre mushroom-like bushes, is a popular meeting place and has a patriotic flag-raising ceremony at 10am every Sunday.

TACNA

INFORMATION p114
Banco Weise.....................................1 B3
BCP...2 B3
Chilean Consulate............................3 B1
Hospital..4 A2
Interbanc...5 C3
Lavandería Latina.............................6 D3
Regional Tourist Offices....................7 A2
Tacna Net...8 B2
UPT...9 B3

SIGHTS & ACTIVITIES pp114–5
Casa de Cultura...............................10 B3
Museo de Instituto Nacional de
Cultura......................................(see 10)
Museo de Zela................................11 C2
Museo Ferroviario...........................12 A1

SLEEPING pp116–7
Alojamiento Betito......................(see 18)
Gran Hotel Central..........................13 B3
Gran Hotel Tacna............................14 B3
Hospedaje Lido...............................15 D3
Hospedaje Lima..............................16 B3
Hostal Avenida...............................17 C3
Hostal Bon Ami..............................18 C2
Hostal El Mesón.............................19 B2
Hostal HC......................................20 C3
Hostal Hogar..................................21 B2
Hostal Premier...............................22 C3
Hotel Camino Real.........................23 D3
Hotel Copacabana..........................24 C2
Maximo's Hostal.............................25 C2
Plaza Hotel.....................................26 B3
Royal Inn.......................................27 D2
Universo Hostal.........................(see 20)

EATING p117
Café Genova...................................28 C3
Fulin..29 C2
Il Pomodoro...................................30 B3
La Fonda del Cazador.................(see 23)
Sabor Latino...................................31 C3

TRANSPORT pp117–8
Aero Continente.............................32 B3

PARQUE DE LA LOCOMOTORA

A British locomotive built in 1859 and used as a troop train in the War of the Pacific is the centerpiece of this pleasant downtown park.

MUSEO FERROVIARIO

This **museum** (☎ 72-4981; admission US$0.30; ☼ 8am-5:30pm) located in the train station gives the impression of stepping back in time. You can wander amid beautiful though poorly maintained 20th-century steam engines and rolling stock, plus atmospheric salons filled with historic paraphernalia, all to the tune of the lonely tap-tapping of the station master's ancient typewriter.

MUSEO DE INSTITUTO NACIONAL DE CULTURA

This small **museum** (admission free; ☼ 8am-noon Mon-Fri) is in the Casa de Cultura. If it's closed, ask someone in the library below to open it. The main exhibit deals with the War of the Pacific, and features paintings and maps. There is also a small collection of art and archaeological pieces.

MUSEO DE ZELA

This small **museum** (Zela 542; admission free; ☼ 8:30am-12:30pm & 3:30-7pm Mon-Sat) provides a look at the interior of one of Tacna's oldest colonial buildings. It houses a motley collection of 19th-century paintings of stately folk.

Sleeping

There's no shortage of hotels catering to Tacna's cross-border traffic.

BUDGET

Marinas (☎ 74-6014; Circunvalación Sur; s/d US$4/7, with bathroom US$7/10) Positioned by the bus terminals, Marinas is clean, secure and very handy for dropping your stuff when arriving late at night. There's cable TV in rooms with a bathroom.

Hostal Bon Ami (☎ 71-1873; miriiam@hotmail.com; 2 de Mayo 445; s/d US$4/6.50, with bathroom US$6/8) This hostal is shabby but secure. There's hot water, though it's prone to running out when the hostel's full.

Alojamiento Betito (☎ 70-7429; 2 de Mayo 493; s/d US$3.50/7) On the same block as Bon Ami, Betito is in a quirky old high-ceilinged building with a likeably shambolic feel and cold-water communal bathrooms.

Hostal HC (☎ 74-2042; Zela 734; s/d US$7/10) This is a clean place with a familiar atmosphere, cable TV and private hot showers.

Universo Hostal (☎ 71-5441; Zela 724; s/d US$7/10) Next door to Hostal HC, Universo has neat, compact rooms with hot shower, cable TV and phone.

Royal Inn (☎ 72-6094; Patricio Melendez 574; s/d with bathroom US$5/7) This is a clean, bare-bones place with private bathrooms that have hot water from 5:30am to noon and 6pm to midnight.

Hospedaje Lima (☎ 74-4229; San Martín 442; s/d with bathroom US$8/11) Lima is a well-worn-in option with wood paneling and cheerful service. Rooms vary in quality, but it has a decent restaurant. The bathrooms have hot water from 6:30 to 9 every morning and evening.

Hostal Avenida (☎ 72-4582; Bolognesi 699; s/d/tr with bathroom US$10/13/16) This hotel offers clean, business-like rooms with hot water if you request it in advance.

Hospedaje Lido (☎ 74-1598; San Martín 876A; s/d with bathroom US$6/9.50) This is another friendly, decent option with hot water and TV with local channels.

MID-RANGE

Many hotels raise their rates just before Christmas and on weekends, when shoppers from Chile hit the town. All the rooms in this section have bathroom, cable TV, phone and hot water.

Maximo's Hostal (☎ 74-2604; maximos@terra .com.pe; Arias Araguez 281; s/d US$20/24, ste US$27; P) Maximo's has a lobby that's overladen with plants, balconies and candelabra, all suffused by green-tinted light. There's also a snack bar and good clean rooms with fan, and rates that include continental breakfast. And who can resist a place that puts such decorative pleats at the end of your toilet roll every morning?

Hostal El Mesón (☎ 71-4070; mesonhotel@terra .com.pe; Hipolito Unanue 175; s/d US$21/27, ste US$34; P) El Mesón is a clean, modern and friendly option close to the plaza, which also has a cafeteria.

Holiday Suites Hotel (☎ 74-1201; holidaysuites@ terra.com.pe; Alto de Lima 1472; s/d/ste US$20/26/31; P ☎) Away from the center, this hotel offers modern but rather bare rooms with a sitting area. There is a lawn and pool area, bar with occasional dancing and 24-hour cafeteria service. Rates include breakfast.

Hostal Premier (☎ 74-6045; premier@viabcp.com; Bolognesi 804; s/d US$13/16) Premier has comfy and clean rooms, and there's a snack bar below. The busy street outside can be noisy.

Gran Hotel Central (☎ 71-5051; fax 72-6031; Martín 561; s/d US$18/25) Entrance to this hotel is gained past a loudly buzzing neon sign that heralds the slightly seedy, worn-around-the-edges rooms within this once-plush hotel. Rooms are, however, spacious with long sofas.

Plaza Hotel (☎ 72-2101; fax 72-6952; San Martín 421; s/d US$14/20) There's a hushed hospital-like atmosphere to this cool, blocky option by the plaza. The ubiquitous white lino lends the corridors a clinical look, though rooms are more worn in. It has a cafeteria and rates include breakfast.

Hostal Copacabana (☎ 72-1721; copahotel@ terra.com.pe; Araguez 370; s/d US$15/18) The Copacabana has simple, cute rooms with private hot showers, cable TV and good amenities, but may be noisy on weekends because of its disco.

TOP END

Hotel Camino Real (☎ 72-1891; creal-hotel@star.com .pe; San Martín 855; s/d/tr/ste $24/28/34/45) Camino Real has comfy rooms with good amenities that include a minibar, but has disappointing '70s decor. It has a recommended restaurant, a startlingly red bar and a cafeteria. Rates include breakfast.

Gran Hotel Tacna (☎ 72-4193; htacna@derramajae
.org.pe; Bolognesi 300; s/d/ste US$58/77/115; P ⓢ)
This is the best in town, with a choice of
bungalows, suites and many rooms with
a balcony. Rooms are plush, and there's
pleasant grounds and a pool, a restaurant
with 24-hour room service and a bar with
dancing. Rates include breakfast.

Eating & Drinking

Avenida Ayacucho, south of the Plaza
de Armas and at the intersection with
Bolognesi, makes a good hunting ground
for inexpensive restaurants. Popular local
dishes include *patasca a la tacneña*, a thick,
spicy vegetable-and-meat soup, and *picante
de guatita*, hot peppered tripe (it's better
than it sounds).

Café Genova (☎ 74-4809; San Martín 649; mains
US$4-10; ☯ open till late) Brush shoulders
with local socialites at this open-fronted
streetside café with good espressos and a
variety of snacks, desserts and light meals.

Il Pomodoro (☎ 72-6905; San Martín 521; meals
US$4-10) Il Pomodoro is a long-established
place serving popular Italian food.

Sabor Latino (☎ 74-6845; Vigil 68; meals US$1.50-
5) This small café is recommended for
budget travelers, it has good set lunches
and dinners, *criollo*-style.

Fulin (cnr 2 de Mayo & Araguez; 3-course menú US$1;
☯ closed evenings and weekends) This is a cheap
vegetarian *chaufa*.

La Fonda del Cazador (mains US$4-12) Located
at the Hotel Camino Real; it's good.

In the *campiña* (countryside), several
rustic restaurants come alive for weekend
lunches, offering good food and live music.
In Pocollay, 5km northeast of Tacna, there's
La Huerta (☎ 71-3080; Zela 1327), a nice, outdoor
place with uproarious birdsong and a terrace
with vine-covered trellising. There's music
between noon and 2pm.

Restaurant Campestre El Hueco (☎ 74-5909;
mains US$5-12), set back from road, is another
open-air spot on the outskirts of Pocollay,
with good meals (including *cuy*). It has live
music at the weekend. Calana, midway
between Pocollay and Pachía, has several
other rural restaurants.

The small pedestrian streets of Libertad
and Vigil are the center of Tacna's limited
nightlife. Here you'll find a couple of
pubs and clubs, some with live music and
dancing on weekends.

Getting There & Away

AIR

At the time of writing **Aero Continente** (☎ 74-
7300, Apurímac 265) was the only company with
flights to Lima (US$70 to US$80, 1½ hours,
daily). Services sometimes go via Arequipa
(40 minutes). There is a US$3.50 domestic
departure tax charged at the airport, which
is about 5km from town.

BUS & COLECTIVO

There are two bus terminals. Most long-
distance departures leave from Terminal
Terrestre on Hipolito Unanue, at the northeast end of town, while buses and colectivo
taxis for Arica in Chile leave from the
international terminal next door.

International

Numerous colectivo taxis (US$3, one hour)
and infrequent buses (US$2) to Arica in
Chile leave between 7am and 11pm from
the neighboring international terminal.
On Friday and Saturday, you may also
find taxis willing to go outside these times,
but expect to pay over the odds. Taxi drivers usually help you through the border
formalities.

Buses run from Tacna to Desaguadero on
the Bolivian border (see following).

Domestic

Buses to Puno (US$5 to US$8, 12 hours),
as well as to Desaguadero on the Bolivian
border (eight hours), mostly leave from
Avenida Circumvalación, north of the city
and east of the main terminal. There are
about a dozen companies with offices lined
up next to one another here; all buses leave
in the late afternoon or evening.

A US$0.30 terminal use tax is levied at
Terminal Terrestre. **Flores** (☎ 72-6691) has
half-hourly buses to Moquegua (US$2,
three hours) and hourly buses to Arequipa
(US$4.20 to US$7, seven hours) from
5:30am until 10pm, plus 10 buses daily to
Ilo (US$2, 3½ hours). Ormeño also has less-
frequent services to Moquegua (US$1.40)
and Arequipa (US$3.70).

For Lima (18 to 22 hours) there are
services run by **Cruz del Sur** (☎ 72-5729)
for US$11 to US$35, **Ormeño** (☎ 72-3292)
for US$12.50 to US$20, Flores (US$11 to
US$22.50, four daily) and **Civa** (☎ 74-1543)
for US$11 to US$20; the fastest and most

comfortable option being with Cruz del Sur (US$35, two daily). Most Lima-bound buses leave in the afternoon or evening and will drop you off at other south-coast towns, including Nazca (14 hours).

Cruz del Sur has a daily direct bus to Cuzco leaving at 4:30pm (US$20, 14 hours) via Puno (US$17, 11 hours) and Desaguadero (US$16, eight hours).

Note that northbound buses are frequently stopped and searched by immigration and/or customs officials not far north of Tacna. Have your passport handy, and beware of passengers asking you to hold a package for them while they go to the bathroom.

TRAIN
Trains between Tacna **train station** (☎ 72-4981) and Arica in Chile (US$1.50, 1½ to two hours, two to three per day) are the cheapest but slowest way to cross the border. Your passport is stamped at the train station, there is no stop at the actual border and you receive your entry stamp when you arrive near Arica's Plaza de Armas. Services were suspended for several years in 2000, but were due to start again in late 2003. Check at the station for the new schedules.

Getting Around
The airport is 5km south of town. A taxi charges about US$4 to/from Tacna, or you can go direct from the airport to Arica, with the appropriate stop at the border, for US$40. Alternatively, just walk out of the airport parking area and get the same services for under half this price.

A taxi from downtown to the bus terminal costs about US$0.80. Micros from the center go to Pocollay (US$0.30).

Terminal Bolognesi, about 1km away, is the local terminal for buses to the beach at Boca del Río (US$1.50, one hour) and other villages outside of the city but within the Department of Tacna.

AROUND TACNA
The countryside around Tacna is known for its vineyards, olive groves and orchards, and the small *bodegas* produce a few thousand liters of *vino de chacra* – a rough but pleasing table wine. **Pocollay** is a suburb about 5km from Tacna that can be reached by taking a bus along Bolognesi. It is popular with Tacneños for its rural restaurants, which often have live bands on weekends.

Continuing northeast of Tacna are the villages of **Calana, Pachía** and **Calientes**, which are 15km, 17km and 24km from Tacna, respectively. Both Calana and Pachía have many rural restaurants, and Calientes has hot springs.

Tacna's main seaside resort is **Boca del Río**, about 55km southwest of the city. Buses go here from Tacna along a good road.

TO/FROM CHILE
Border-crossing formalities are relatively straightforward in both directions. Colectivo taxis (see p117) are the quickest way of crossing, while trains (see earlier) are the cheapest. The Peruvian border post is open 8am to midnight on weekdays, and 24 hours on Friday and Saturday. Chile is an hour (two hours during daylight-saving time) ahead of Peru. From Arica, you can continue south into Chile by air or bus, or northeast into Bolivia by air. For information about travel in Chile, consult Lonely Planet's *Chile & Easter Island*.

Arequipa & Canyon Country

The beautiful city of Arequipa, known as the 'white city,' is surrounded by some of the wildest terrain in Peru. This is a land of active volcanoes, thermal springs, high-altitude deserts and the world's deepest canyons. The city is frequently used as an overland layover en route to Lake Titicaca and Cuzco and is a valuable intermediate stop for acclimatization to high altitudes. As such, it makes an ideal base for exploring the spectacular landscape that surrounds it – not least, the famous Cañón del Colca, shadowed by snow-topped volcanoes and replete with opportunities for hiking and rafting, and moreover the best place in Peru to marvel at the majestic flight of the condor.

But don't leave town before exploring Arequipa itself. The Monasterio de Santa Catalina just has to be visited; wander around it slowly, exploring its numerous passageways and intricate architecture. The city's fabulous museums will surprise you as well. Nighttime offers some fine dining and, on weekends, a vibrant nightlife.

HIGHLIGHTS

- **Archaeology**
  Mingling with ice mummies in the Museo Santuarios Andinos, Arequipa (p125)

- **History**
  Exploring the delightful passageways of the Monasterio de Santa Catalina, Arequipa (p123)

- **Wildlife**
  Spotting condors in the Cañón del Colca (p137)

- **Climbing**
  Tackling the heights of El Misti volcano (p136)

- **Adrenaline rush**
  Getting thrills river running the Ríos Chile or Majes (p135)

- **People**
  Watching the locals outside Arequipa in their colorful clothing as they go about their daily lives (p137)

AREQUIPA

☎ 054 / pop 750,000 / elevation 2325m

The city of Arequipa nestles in a fertile valley under the perfect cone-shaped volcano of El Misti (5822m). Rising majestically behind the cathedral, El Misti can be viewed from the plaza and is flanked to the left by the higher and more ragged Chachani (6075m) and to the right by the lower peak of Pichu Pichu (5571m).

Locals sometimes say 'When the moon separated from the earth, it forgot to take Arequipa,' waxing lyrical about the city's grand colonial buildings, built from a light-colored volcanic rock called *sillar* that dazzles in the sun. As a result, Arequipa has been baptized 'the white city.' Its distinctive stonework graces the stately Plaza de Armas, flanked by an enormous cathedral, as well as numerous beautiful colonial churches and mansions dotted throughout the city.

The Arequipañs themselves are a proud people fond of intellectual debate, especially about their fervent political beliefs, which find voice through regular demonstrations in the main plaza. In fact, their stubborn intellectual independence from Lima is so strong that at one time they even designed their own passport and flag. The passionate celebration of the founding of Arequipa on August 15 also echoes this regionalist pride.

HISTORY

Evidence of a pre-Inca settlement by Indians from the Lake Titicaca area leads some scholars to think the Aymaras first named the city (*ari* means 'peak' and *quipa* means 'lying behind' in Aymara); hence, Arequipa is 'the place lying behind the peak' of El Misti. However, another oft-heard legend says that the fourth Inca, Mayta Capac, was traveling through the valley and became enchanted by it. He ordered his retinue to stop, saying, '*Ari, quipay*,' which translates as 'Yes, stay.' The Spaniards refounded the city on August 15, 1540, and the date is remembered with a weeklong fair.

Unfortunately, Arequipa is built in an area highly prone to natural disasters; the

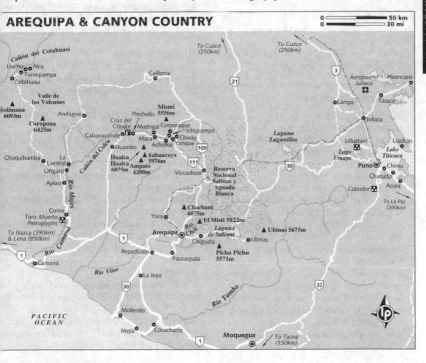

AREQUIPA & CANYON COUNTRY

city was totally destroyed by earthquakes and volcanic eruptions in 1600 and has since been rocked by major earthquakes in 1687, 1868, 1958, 1960 and most recently 2001. For this reason, many of the city's buildings are built low for stability. However, despite these disasters, several 17th- and 18th-century buildings survive.

ORIENTATION

The city center is based on a colonial checkerboard pattern around the Plaza de Armas. Addresses can be confusing, because streets change names every few blocks. Generally, streets have different names north, south, east, and west of the plaza. In addition, they change names again further from the center.

INFORMATION

Bookstores

Colca Trek (see Tours & Guides, p128) The best place for maps of the region.

Librería el Lector (☎ 28-8677; San Francisco 221; ☺ 9am-9pm) There is a book exchange and a wide selection of new titles and guidebooks here.

Cultural Centers

There are several cultural centers with intermittent art shows, concerts and film festivals. They have libraries and cafés and welcome travelers on weekdays.

AREQUIPA IN ONE DAY

Start your day with a coffee at one of the balcony restaurants on the Plaza de Armas, looking down on the cathedral, then head up Santa Catalina to the Museo Santuarios Andinos to shiver at the grisly beauty of frozen sun-bride Juanita and her fellow ice mummies. Afterwards, cross the street and wander the hushed passageways of Monasterio Santa Catalina, wondering at its risqué history. For lunch, catch a cab to one of the traditional restaurants surrounding the city and discuss the hot topics of Peruvian politics over a similarly spicy Arequipeño meal. In the afternoon, perhaps invest in a wooly alpaca sweater from Patio El Ekeko to ward off the chilly Andean night ahead, and in the evening, stroll up to San Francisco to find the city's most popular restaurants and nightlife.

Alianza Francesa (☎ 22-0700; Santa Catalina 208)
Instituto Cultural Peruano-Alemán (☎ 21-8567; Ugarte 207)
Instituto Cultural Peruano-Norteamericano (☎ 21-8567; Melgar 109)

Emergency

The **Policía de Turismo** (☎ 20-1258; Jerusalén 317; ☺ 24hr) is helpful in an emergency.

Immigration

If you need a tourist-card extension, go to **Migraciones** (☎ 42-1759; Parque 2, cnr Bustamente Rivero, Urb Quinta Tristán; ☺ 8-11am & 2-3pm Mon-Fri) A taxi from the center costs US$1.

Internet Access

These two charge about US$0.70 per hour
Chips Internet (☎ 20-3651; San Francisco 202A; ☺ 9am-11pm)
Cibermarket (☎ 22-7055; Santa Catalina 115B; ☺ 9am-9pm) has closed booths, fast computers and Net-to-phone.

Laundry

Jerusalén has many spots for washing you kit. **Magic laundry** (Jerusalén 404; ☺ 8am-7pm Mon-Sat) charges US$1.20 per kg; clothes can b washed, dried and folded in three hours.

Medical Services

Clínica Arequipa (☎ 25-3424, 25-3416; cnr Bolognesi & Av Puente Grau; ☺ 7am-8:30pm Mon-Sat; consultation US$17) This place is considered the best and most expensive.
Clínica San Juan de Dios (☎ 25-2256; Av Ejército 1020, Cayma) This clinic is also recommended.
Hospital Nacional del Sur (☎ 21-4110; cnr Peral & Ayacucho)
Inka Farma (☎ 20-3275; Santa Domingo 103; ☺ 24hr) A branch of one of Peru's biggest pharmacy chains, it's well stocked.
Paz Holandesa Policlinic (☎ 20-6720; info@ pazholandesa.com; Jorge Chavez 527; ☺ 8am-8pm Mon-Sat with appointment only) Doctors here speak English and Dutch. Proceeds go toward providing free medical attention and operations for poor children.

Money

There are moneychangers and ATMs or streets near the BCP (formerly Banco de Crédito.)

BCP (San Juan de Dios 125) Has a Visa ATM and changes traveler's checks; there's also an ATM on the northeast corner of Plaza de Armas.

MONASTERIO MISTERIOSO

The Monasterio de Santa Catalina was founded in 1580 by a rich widow, María de Guzmán, who was very selective in choosing her nuns. They came from the best Spanish families, who naturally had to pay a substantial dowry. Traditionally, the second daughter of upper-class families would enter a nunnery to live in chaste poverty, but in this privileged convent each nun had between one and four servants or slaves (usually black), and the nuns would invite musicians, have parties and generally live it up in the style to which they had always been accustomed.

After about three centuries of these hedonistic goings-on, the pope sent Sister Josefa Cadena, a strict Dominican nun, to straighten things out. She arrived like a hurricane in 1871 and set about sending all the rich dowries back to Europe and freeing the myriad servants and slaves, many of whom stayed on as nuns. From this point, the vast majority of the 450 people who once lived here never ventured outside the convent's imposing high walls and the convent was shrouded in mystery until it opened to the public in 1970, when the mayor of Arequipa forced the convent to modernize, including opening its doors to tourism.

Today, the 30 remaining nuns continue to live a cloistered life in the northern corner of the complex while the rest is open to the public. It's a disorientating place that allows you to step back in time to a forgotten world of narrow twisting streets and tiny fruit-filled plazas, false staircases, beautiful courtyards and simple living quarters. A paradise for photographers, the convent has been excellently restored, and the delicate pastel colors of the buildings are attractively contrasted with bright flowers, period furnishings and religious art.

nterbanc (Mercaderes 217) It has an ATM with Visa, irrus, Plus and MasterCard, and the bank accepts a broad ange of traveler's checks.

Post & Telephone
HL (☎ 22-0045; Santa Catalina 115; ☺ 8:30am-:30pm Mon-Fri, 9am-noon Sat)
Main post office (Moral 118, ☺ 7:30am-8:30pm Mon-at, 7:30am-1pm Sun) Northeast of the Plaza de Armas.
elefónica del Perú (Alvarez Thomas 201)

Tourist Information
There are two offices of **iPeru**: Plaza de Armas ☎ 22-1228; iperuarequipa@promperu.gob.pe; Portal Municipal 112; ☺ 8:30am-7:30pm) and Rodríguez Ballón irport (☎ 44-4564; ☺ 6:30am-6pm). Both iPeru offices combines Prom Peru and Indecopi, which is the tourist-protection agency and leals with complaints against local firms, ncluding tour agencies. Check with them irst if you have doubts about a company.

DANGERS & ANNOYANCES
Petty theft is often reported in Arequipa, and ravelers are urged to hide their valuables. Most crime is opportunistic, so keep your tuff in sight in restaurants and Internet cafés, but also be aware of distraction echniques such as spitting or tapping your houlder. Take great care in the Selva Alegre Park, north of the city center, as muggings have been reported here. Also, only pay for tours in a recognized agency and never trust touts in the street – they bamboozle cash out of a surprisingly high number of tourists.

SIGHTS & ACTIVITIES
Monasterio Santa Catalina
This **monastery** (☎ 22-9798; www.santacatalina.org .pe; Santa Catalina 300; admission US$7; ☺ ticket office 9am-4pm, monastery till 5pm) must be one of the most fascinating colonial religious buildings in Peru, so try to visit even if you've already badly overdosed on churches and colonial architecture. Actually, it's not a monastery but a convent. Nor is it just a religious building; it's a 20,000-sq-m complex and covers an entire block – almost a city within a city. See the boxed text 'Monasterio Misterioso.'

There are two ways of visiting Santa Catalina. One is to wander around at your own pace, discovering the intricate architecture, soaking up the atmosphere and getting slightly lost (there's a mini map on the back of your ticket if things get desperate). Alternatively, guides are available for a tip of US$1.50 to US$2 per person. Among them, they speak a little English, French, German and Italian. The tours last about 90 minutes, after which time you're welcome to wander around by yourself.

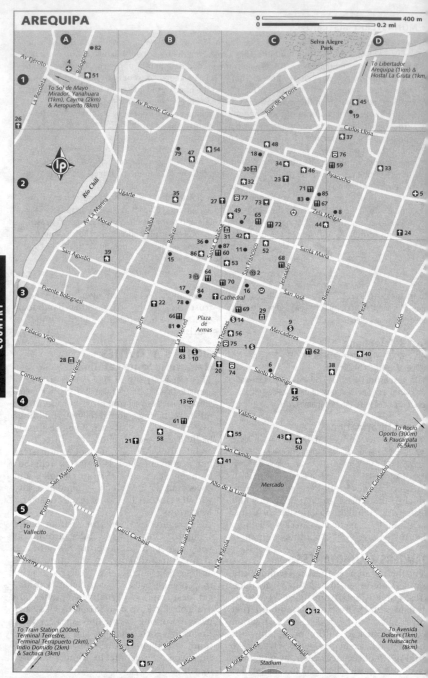

AREQUIPA

0   400 m
0   0.2 mi

AREQUIPA & CANYON COUNTRY

INFORMATION pp122–3
Alianza Francesa.............................(see 60)
BCP...1 C3
Chips Internet....................................2 C3
Cibermarket.......................................3 B3
Clínica Arequipa...............................4 A1
DHL..(see 3)
Hospital Nacional del Sur................5 D2
Inka Farma...6 C4
Instituto Cultural Peruano-Alemán..7 C2
Instituto Cultural
    Peruano-Norteamericano............8 D2
Interbanc...9 C3
iPeru..10 B4
Librería el Lector.............................11 C3
Magic Laundry..............................(see 85)
Paz Holandesa Policlinic................12 C6
Telefónica del Perú.........................13 B4
Visa ATM..14 C3

SIGHTS & ACTIVITIES pp123–8
Casa de Moral...................................15 B3
Casa Ricketts.....................................16 C3
Casona Iriberry.................................17 B3
Claustros de la Compañía...........(see 20)
Craft Shops..18 C3
Giardino...19 D1
Iglesia de La Compañía...................20 B4
Iglesia de La Merced........................21 B4
Iglesia de San Agustín.....................22 B3
Iglesia de San Francisco..................23 C3
Iglesia de Santa Teresa...................24 D2
Iglesia de Santo Domingo..............25 C4
Monasterio de la Recoleta..............26 A1
Monasterio de Santa Catalina........27 C2
Museo Arqueológico.......................28 A4
Museo Arte Textil.............................29 C3
Museo Histórico Municipal.............30 C4
Museo Santuarios Andinos.............31 C2

SLEEPING pp129–31
Casa La Reyna...................................32 C2

Colonial House Inn II........................33 D2
Colonial House Inn...........................34 C2
Hospedaje El Caminante Class....(see 86)
Hostal Las Torres de Ugarte...........35 B2
Hostal Posada de Sancho................36 B3
Hostal Residencial Núñez................37 D2
Hostal Tito...38 D4
Hostal Tumi de Oro..........................39 A3
Hotel Conquistador..........................40 D4
Hotel Miamaka..................................41 B5
Hotel Regis..42 C2
Hotel Tajmahal.................................43 C4
La Casa de Melgar............................44 C2
La Casa de Mi Abuela......................45 D1
La Casona del Puente......................46 C2
La Hostería..47 B2
La Posada del Cacique.....................48 C3
La Posada del Monasterio...............49 C3
La Posada del Parque......................50 C4
La Posada del Puente......................51 A1
Le Foyer..52 C3
Los Balcones de Santa Catalina......53 C3
Piccola Daniela.................................54 B2
Real San Felipe.................................55 C4
Sonesta Posada del Inca.................56 C3
Tambo Viejo......................................57 B6
Tierra Sur Hostal.............................58 B4

EATING pp131–2
Ary Quepay......................................59 D2
Bistrot...60 B3
Cevichería Fory Foy.........................61 B4
El Camaroncito............................(see 65)
El Gaucho Parrilladas..................(see 75)
El Super...62 C4
El Super...63 B4
El Turko..(see 52)
Govinda...64 B3
La Brochetta......................................65 C2
La Serenata & Others......................66 B3
La Truffa.......................................(see 70)
La Viñeda.....................................(see 73)

Lakshimivan......................................67 C2
Mandala...68 C3
Manolo's..69 C3
Mixtos...70 C3
Pizzería Los Leños............................71 C2
Trattoria Gianni...............................72 C2

DRINKING pp132–3
Deja Vu..73 C2
Kibosch..(see 32)
La Casa de Klaus..........................(see 32)

ENTERTAINMENT pp132–3
Cine Felix...74 C4
Cinessur el Portal.............................75 C3
La Quinta...76 D2
La Troica.......................................(see 76)
Las Quenas..77 C2

SHOPPING p133
Incalpaca......................................(see 20)
Patio de Ekeko.............................(see 29)

TRANSPORT pp133–5
Aero Continente...............................78 B3
Andes Bike..79 B2
Aviandina......................................(see 78)
Cruz del Sur (Tickets)......................80 B6
LanPeru...(see 81)
Servicios Aereos AQP...................(see 31)
Tans...81 B3

OTHER
Cepna..(see 8)
Club Internacional...........................82 A1
Colca Trek...83 C2
Colonial Tours..................................84 B3
Cusipata..85 C2
Illary Tours.......................................86 B3
Naturaleza Activa........................(see 36)
Zárate Adventura.............................87 B3

Museo Santuarios Andinos

This museum (☎ 20-0345; www.ucsm.edu.pe/santury; Santa Catalina 210; adult/child US$4.20/1.40; ☉ 9am-6pm Mon-Sat, 9am-3pm Sun) exhibits 'Juanita, the ice princess' – the frozen body of an Inca maiden sacrificed on the summit of Ampato over 500 years ago (see the boxed text on p126). Note that Juanita herself is not on display from January to April each year, but is replaced by other child sacrifices discovered in the mountains. Tours are available in English, Spanish, French, German and Italian, and consist of a video followed by a guided tour of artefacts found at the burial site, culminating with viewing Juanita as well as another frozen mummy preserved in carefully monitored glass-walled freezers. Only guided visits are permitted (expect to tip the guide), and the whole spectacle is done in a respectful, nonghoulish manner. Allow about an hour.

Plaza de Armas

Arequipa's main plaza showcases the city's sillar architecture and the cathedral. The colonnaded balconies overlooking the plaza are a great place to relax over a snack or a coffee.

La Catedral

The history of the cathedral (admission free; ☉ 7-10am & 5-7pm) that dominates Arequipa's Plaza de Armas is one filled with doggedness. The original structure, dating from 1656, was gutted by fire in 1844. It was consequently rebuilt, but was then promptly flattened by the earthquake of 1868, and most of what you now see has been rebuilt since then. The earthquake of June 2001 toppled one enormous tower while the other slumped precariously, yet by late 2002 the cathedral was as good as new once again.

The cathedral is the only one in Peru that stretches the length of a plaza. The interior is simple and airy, with a luminous quality, and the high vaults are uncluttered. The cathedral also has a distinctly international flair; it is one of less than 100 basilicas in the world that are entitled to display the Vatican flag, which is to the right of the altar. Both the altar and the 12 columns (depicting the 12 apostles) are made of Italian marble: the

AREQUIPA & CANYON COUNTRY

HUMAN SACRIFICE IN THE ANDES

In 1992 local climber Miguel Zárate was guiding an expedition on Ampato (6288m) when he found curious wooden remnants suggestive of a burial site exposed near the icy summit. In September 1995 he convinced American mountaineer/archaeologist Johan Reinhard to climb the peak which, following recent eruptions of nearby Sabancaya, had been coated by ash, melting the snow below and exposing the site more fully. Upon arrival, they immediately found a statue and other offerings, but the burial site had collapsed and there was no sign of a body. Ingeniously, the team rolled rocks down the mountainside and by following them, Zárate was able to spot the bundled mummy of an Inca girl who had tumbled down the same path when her icy tomb had crumbled.

Wrapped in finely woven blankets, she had been almost perfectly preserved by the icy temperatures for about 500 years, and it was immediately apparent from the remote location of her tomb and from the care and ceremony surrounding her death (as well as the crushing blow to her right eyebrow) that this 12- to 14-year-old girl had been sacrificed to the gods at the summit. For the Incas, mountains were gods who could kill by volcanic eruption, avalanche or climatic catastrophes. These violent deities could only be appeased by sacrifices from their subjects, and the ultimate sacrifice must surely be that of a human child left on the frozen mountaintop.

It took the men two full days to carry the frozen bundle down to the village of Cabanaconde, from whence she was carried to a princely bed of frozen foodstuffs in Zárate's own domestic freezer, before being taken to the Universidad Católica in Arequipa to undergo a battery of scientific examinations. Quickly dubbed 'Juanita, the ice princess,' the mummy was given her own museum in 1998 (see Museo Santuarios Andinos, p125). In total, over 20 similar Inca sacrifices have been discovered atop various Andean mountains since 1954.

huge Byzantine-style brass lamp hanging in front of the altar is from Spain; and the pulpit was carved in France. In 1870 Belgium provided the impressive organ, said to be the largest in South America, though damage during shipping condemned the devout to wince at its distorted playing for over a century.

La Compañía

Just off the southeastern corner of the Plaza de Armas, this **Jesuit church** (☎ 21-2141; admission free; 🕙 10am-noon & 5-7pm) is one of the oldest in Arequipa and is noted for its ornate main facade and main altar, which is carved in *churrigueresque* style – a Latin American adaptation of Spanish baroque – and completely covered in gold leaf. To the left of the altar is **San Ignacio chapel** (admission US$0.60; 🕙 9am-noon & 3-6pm Sun-Fri, 11am-noon & 3-6pm Sat), with a wonderful polychrome cupola smothered with jungle-like murals, among which mingle warriors and angels.

Attached to the church are two attractive **claustros** (cloisters), now occupied by stores selling alpaca goods, liquors and antiques.

Monasterio de la Recoleta

A short walk from the city center is this **monastery** (☎ 27-0966; La Recoleta 117; adult/student US$1.40/1; 🕙 9am-7pm Mon-Sat), originally constructed on the west side of the Río Chili in 1648 by Franciscan friars, though now completely rebuilt. Scholarship was an integral part of the Franciscans' order, and bibliophiles will delight in their huge library which contains more than 20,000 dusty books and maps; the oldest volume dating to 1494. There is a museum of Amazonian exhibits collected by the missionaries and an extensive collection of preconquest artefacts and also religious art of the Escuela Cuzqueña (Cuzqueño school).

Guides who speak English, French and Italian are available (tip expected).

Other Churches

Visiting hours for churches in Arequipa are erratic, but most are open for worship from 7am to 9am and 6am to 8pm. **San Francisco** (Zela; admission US$1.30), originally built in the 16th century, has been badly damaged by several earthquakes. It still stands, however, and visitors can see a large crack in the cupola – testimony to the power of the quakes. Other colonial churches in the city include San Agustín, Santa Teresa, La Merced (to the south of Plaza de Armas) and Santo Domingo (east of Plaza de Armas).

Museo Histórico Municipal

This small local **museum** (San Francisco 407; adult/student US$0.60/0.30; 7am-3pm Mon-Fri) is housed in a colonial building that once functioned as a prison. There are paintings, historical documents, maps and other paraphernalia pertaining to the city's history here. Most interesting is the hall filled with satirical caricatures of stately 19th-century folk.

Other Museums

Museo Arte Textil (21-5861; www.patiodelekeko.com; El Patio del Ekeko, Mercaderes 141; foreigner/Peruvian/child US$3/1.50/0.30; 10am-8:30pm Mon-Sat, 10am-7:30pm Sun) is only for those who take a keen interest in textiles. Translation booklets are available in several languages. Upstairs is a mini-cinema showing documentaries about Arequipa that last 12 minutes; it's free if you've been to the museum, US$0.60 if not.

Museo Arqueológico (Cruz Verde 303; 9:30am-pm Mon-Fri) has an interesting little display on local sites and artefacts.

Colonial Houses

A few of the stately colonial *sillar* mansions can also be visited. One of the best is **Casa Ricketts** (Casa Tristán del Pozo; 21-5070; San Francisco; admission free; 9.15am-1pm & 4:30-6:30pm Mon-Fri, 9:30am-noon Sun), built in 1738, which has served respectively as a seminary, archbishop's palace, school, home to well-to-do families, and now as a working bank. Look for the puma-headed fountains.

Built in 1730, **Casa de Moral** (22-1084; Moral 318; adult/student US$1.40/1; 9am-5pm Mon-Sat) is named after the 200-year-old mulberry tree in its central courtyard. Owned by BCP, the house is now one of the most accessible for snooping, and bilingual guides are available. It has a fascinating little map collection charting South American development.

Also worth taking a look in is **Casona Iriberry** (Santa Catalina), housing the Universidad San Agustín in its 18th-century colonial halls and patios.

Yanahuara

The suburb of Yanahuara makes a good excursion. It's within walking distance of the town center: go west on Avenida Puente Grau over the bridge, and continue on Avenida Ejército for six or seven blocks. Turn right on Avenida Lima, and walk five blocks to a small plaza, where you'll find the **Iglesia de Yanahuara** (9am-noon & 4-8pm), which dates from 1750. It has housed the highly venerated Virgen de Chapi since the 2001 earthquake brought her small-town church tumbling about her ears. The popular Fiesta de la Virgen de Chapi is held on May 1. At the end of the plaza there's a **mirador** (observation tower) with excellent views of Arequipa and El Misti.

Head back along Avenida Jerusalén, parallel to Avenida Lima, and just before reaching Avenida Ejército you'll see the well-known **Picantería Sol de Mayo**, where you can stop for a tasty lunch of typical Arequipeño food. The round trip should take under two hours, but there are also combis to Yanahuara from Avenida Puente Grau (and returning from Yanahuara Plaza to the city) every few minutes to speed you along.

Cayma

Beyond Yanahuara is Cayma, another suburb, where you'll find the popular 18th-century **Iglesia de San Miguel Arcángel** (9am-4pm). For a tip, the church warden will take you up the small tower, which has panoramic views. From Yanahuara, take San Vicente and then Avenida León Velarde to Cayma, or catch one of the regular combis marked 'Cayma' from Avenida Puente Grau in Arequipa (US$0.30; 10 minutes).

Paucarpata

This suburb, about 7km southeast of town, makes a pleasant country escape. Combis can be caught along Goyeneche, Independencia and Paucarpata – the eastern continuation of Mercaderes (US$0.60, 20 minutes), or take a taxi (US$4 round trip). Paucarpata itself features an attractive colonial church on the main plaza and several good *picanterías*. A 2km walk past notable Inca terracing brings you to **El Molino de Sabandía** (adult/child US$1.40/0.60; 9am-5pm Mon-Sat). This mill was built in 1621, fell into disrepair and was restored in 1973; it now grinds once more for visitors. The neat grounds, shaded with weeping willows and with great views of El Misti, are a favorite of picnickers.

La Mansión del Fundador

This 17th-century **colonial estate** (44-2460; admission US$2; 9am-5pm), once owned by Arequipa's founder Garcí Manuel de

Carbajal, has been restored with its original furnishings and paintings, and even has its own chapel. The mansion is in the village of Huasacache, 9km from Arequipa, and is often included in local tours or can be reached by taxi (US$4.50 round trip).

TOURS & GUIDES

Santa Catalina and Jerusalén host dozens of travel agencies offering daily city tours and excursions to the Cañón del Colca and around; while some are supremely professional, there are also plenty of carpetbaggers muscling in on the action, so shop carefully. Never accept tours from street touts, and, where possible, tours should be paid for in cash as occasional credit card fraud is reported. Most agencies pool their clients into one bus, even though they charge different rates. Minibuses are the norm for trips, and the small vehicles are cramped and overcrowded – tall people should get ready to tuck knees under chins. Guides usually speak some level of English and/or other languages, but some garble a memorized and hard-to-follow script. See p128 for details on what tours are on offer.

Agencies that have a good reputation for trips to the Cañón del Colca include:

Colonial Tours (☎ 28-6868; colonialtours@mixmail .com; Santa Catalina 106)

Giardino (☎ 22-1345; giardino@terra.com.pe; Jerusalén 604)

Illary Tours (☎ 22-0844; Santa Catalina 205)

Trekking, mountaineering and rafting trips are also offered in Arequipa. Make sure that the guide you hire has a guiding card and a booklet listing all the places he or she has guided. The best guides are often away on trips, try to make arrangements in advance, but, failing that, their agencies can put you in touch with other reliable guides. Be aware that, although you can trek year-round, January to March is wet and not recommended. For details of river-running agencies, see Canyon Country (p135).

Colca Trek (☎ 20-6217, 960-0170; colcatrek@ hotmail.com; Jerusalén 401B) Colca Trek is an excellent adventure tour agency and shop run by the knowledgeable and English-speaking Vlado Soto. As well as trekking tours, it rents mountain bikes; organizes rafting; buys, sells and rents equipment; and is one of the few shops selling decent topographical maps of the area as well as a full complement of camping gases.

Naturaleza Activa (☎ 69-5793; naturaleza@yahoo .com; Santa Catalina 211) This new company is making a name for itself for adventure tours, especially those involving climbing and mountain biking. Two popular trips are a five- to six-hour bike tour of Chachani and the *salinas* (US$52 per person for a group of four) and a three- to four-hour bike trip down El Misti (US$33). All prices include transport and bikes, helmet, guide and snacks. It's also possible to hire bikes for US$26 day, or US$2.50 per hour.

Pa`Enrique (☎ 44-3789, 994-8339; tourecuestre@ mixmail.com; Chilina) Pa'Enrique has horse-riding tours for two hours (US$16 to US$18, depending on numbers) or for the day (US$20 to US$25). Staff will pick you up from your hotel and provide all the equipment plus a guide.

Zárate Adventura (☎ 26-3107; www.zarateadven tures.com; Santa Catalina 204) Zárate was founded in 1954 by Carlos Zárate, the great-grandfather of Arequipeño climbing, who, incredibly, is still guiding at over 80 years of age. His son Carlos Zárate Flores (☎ 20-2461) is an experienced guide who speaks French and a little English. The company arranges all manner of treks and also climbs of all the local peaks, charging US$50 plus expenses per day for the guide, plus the vehicle rental to get to base camp (US$50 to US$150, depending on the mountain). Pack mules can also be hired for an extra fee.

For customized Land Rover tours anywhere around Arequipa (except Cañón del Colca) and the beaches and bird sanctuaries of the coast, contact **Anthony Holley** (☎ 25-8459; angocho@terra.com.pe). Anthony is an Englishman who has lived in Arequipa since 1938.

Recommended mountaineering guides includes the energetic **Julver Eguiluz Castro** (☎ 94-4507, 960-1833; julver_mountrekk@hotmail.com) who can also arrange your equipment and transport.

FESTIVALS & EVENTS

Arequipeños claim that their **Semana Santa** (Holy Week; the week before Easter) celebrations are similar to the very solemn and traditional Spanish observances from Seville. Maundy Thursday, Good Friday and Holy Saturday processions are particularly colorful and sometimes end with the burning of an effigy of Judas. Arequipa also fills up for the **Fiesta de la Virgen de Chapi** on May 1 (see Yanahuara on p127).

The founding day of the city, **August 15**, is celebrated with parades, dancing, beauty pageants and other events over the course of several days. The fireworks show in the Plaza de Armas on August 14 is well worth catching.

COURSES

For Spanish-language courses, check out these agencies:

Centro de Intercambio Cultural (☎ 22-1165; cica@terra.com.pe; Urb Universitaria G-9) It charges US$120 for 20 hours of private lessons per week and can arrange family homestays for US$70/40 a week including/excluding meals. Call in advance and they'll pick you up. Recommended.

Cepesma (☎ 40-5927; La Marina 141; cepesma.idi omas@peru.com) Cepesma charges US$6 per hour for private classes.

Ccpna (☎ 89-1020; info@ccpna.edu.pe; Melgar 109) It has flexible private Spanish classes for US$10 per hour.

Rocio Oporto (☎ 28-6929; claro@unas.edu.pe; La Perlita 103) Charges US$6.50 per for an individual class of 60 minutes. Group lessons cost US$65 per person for 20 classes per week.

SLEEPING

Arequipa has long been experiencing a hotel boom, and competition is stiff. It's always worth asking for discounts, especially if you stay put for a few days, though prices rise in July and August.

Budget

Unless otherwise indicated, all hostels listed have hot water. Many are unmarked but recognizable by a sign proclaiming 'Room for Tourist.'

Hospedaje El Caminante Class (☎ 20-3444; 2nd fl, Santa Catalina 207A; s/d US$5.60/9.80, with bathroom US$9.80/14) Central, clean and repeatedly recommended by readers, this place offers spotless rooms and bathrooms, kitchen privileges, friendly English-speaking service and all the *maté de coca* (coca-leaves tea) you can drink. There's a terrace and fine views from the rooftop.

La Posada del Cacique (☎ 20-2170; posadadel cacique@yahoo.es; Av Puente Grau 219; s/d US$4/7, with bathroom US$7/9.80) A very warm and friendly option, the family-run Posada has decent rooms and a tiny central patio good for gazing.

El Indio Dormido (☎ 42-7401; the_sleeping_indian@ yahoo.com; Av Andrés Avelino Cáceres B9; r per person US$4, s/d with bathroom US$5.60/8.40) Near Terminal Terrestre, this new *hostal* is cheap and popular, and has a cute (but noisy) terrace garden on top with hammocks.

Colonial House Inn II (☎ 28-4249; colonialhouse inn@star.com.pe; Rivero 504, no sign; s/d US$7/13, with bathroom US$9/14) This is a top-notch

new budget option that is owned by the English-speaking boss of the local Pizzería Los Leños (p131). Housed in a colonial building, rooms combine a rustic style with cleanliness and convenience.

La Casona del Puente (☎ 28-6243; Av Puente Grau 108; s US$7, d US$14-20) This is a popular homestay with a welcoming family and yapping dogs. Rooms here vary in quality. The characterful colonial building was damaged in the earthquake and may close for restoration in the off-season.

Le Foyer (☎ 28-6473; hostallefoyer@yahoo.com; Ugarte 114; s/d US$5/9, with bathroom US$10/13) Though pervaded with hunger-inducing smells from the Mexican restaurant below, this clean place is good value and a stone's throw from Arequipa's nocturnal action.

Casa La Reyna (☎ 28-6578; Zela 209; r per person US$4, s/d US$5/10) An old favorite, Casa La Reyna has rooftop balconies with pleasant mountain and monastery views; clean shared rooms; and kitchen privileges on request. English is spoken. It's next door to much of Arequipa's nightlife, which can be a plus or minus depending on your sleep requirements.

Tambo Viejo (☎ 28-8195; room@tamboviejo.com; Malecón Socabaya 107; dm US$5, s/d US$9/12, with bathroom US$12/18) This recommended travelers' hang-out has a garden with tiny outdoor bar, book exchange, tourist information and an English-speaking staff. The hotel's terrace has volcano views and raucous pet parrots.

Hostal Residencial Núñez (☎ 21-8648; hostal_nu nez@terra.com.pe; Jerusalén 528; s/d US$10/17) This is a secure, friendly hostel that is popular with gringos. There's a good laundry service and rooms sport frilly decor, bathroom and TV.

Hostal Tumi de Oro (☎ 28-1319; San Agustín 311A; s/d US$8.40/11.20) Run by a chirpy old lady, this informal hostel has a prettily tiled terrace, book exchange and table football. Rooms have bathrooms and there are kitchen and laundry facilities.

Other budget recommendations you can check out include:

Colonial House Inn (☎ 22-3533; colonialhouseinn@ hotmail.com; Av Puente Grau 114; s/d US$7/11.20) Peaceful colonial house with friendly staff and great breakfasts.

Hotel Regis (☎ 22-6111; Ugarte 202; s/d US$5/10, d with bathroom US$14) Clean, safe and close to the action; has a rooftop *mirador*.

La Posada del Parque (☎ 21-2275; Deán Valdivia 238A; s/d US$4/7, with bathroom US$6/8.50) This is a good-value budget choice.

Piccola Daniela (☎ 22-2187; Bolívar 400A; s/d US$4.20/7, with bathroom US$8.40) Recommended by readers; rates include breakfast.

Hostal Tito (☎ 23-4424; Peru 107; s/d US$2.50/3.40, with bathroom US$4.70/7.20) A friendly rock-bottom option.

Mid-Range

All hotels listed here have cable TV, unless otherwise stated.

La Casa de Mi Abuela (☎ 24-1206; lacasa@ terra.com.pe; Jerusalén 606; s/d US$13/17, with bathroom US$26/33; 🖳 🖭) It's worth stretching the budget for this hugely popular and secure choice. The highlight of the hotel is an extensive garden full of birdsong, plus deckchairs, swings, loungers and hammocks for kicking back in any pose you choose. There's also a small pool, games area, library and restaurant. The rooms are a comfortable hodgepodge of differently aged and styled furniture often with quirky touches thrown in. The *abuela* (grandmother) after whom the place is named died in 1994 at the age of 100.

La Casa de Melgar (☎ /fax 22-2459; Melgar 108A; s/d US$18/25) Housed in an authentic 18th-century building made of *sillar* blocks, this hostel is nonetheless fitted with all the expected creature comforts. The ground-floor rooms have high-domed ceilings, and the whole place has a gothic air. Rooms have comfy beds, and there's a good café and several small patios.

Hotel Miamaka (☎ 28-8558; hotel_miamaka@ terra.com.pe; San Juan de Dios 402; s/d US$22/26, family room US$45) A fine choice, this super-clean and friendly hostel has 20 fresh, modern rooms, with phone and, in some, a minibar. There's a small patio and a café. Rates include a continental breakfast.

Real San Felipe (☎ 28-5010; hrealsanfelipe@terra .com.pe; San Juan de Dios 304; s/d US$28/38) Near to Hotel Miamaka, this new hotel makes a good alternative if the other is full. The modern rooms have a minibar, tiny bathtub/shower and phone. Rates include breakfast.

Hostal Las Torres de Ugarte (☎ 28-3532; hostal torresdeugarte@star.com.pe; Ugarte 401A; s/d US$15/25) This is a very clean, friendly new hostel in a quiet location. It has immaculate rooms

and bathrooms. Breakfast is included in the rates.

Tierra Sur Hostal (☎ 22-7132; tierrasur@terra.com .pe; Consuelo 210; s/d US$28/38) Clean, quiet and reminiscent of a good American motel, this place boasts a restaurant, bar, gym and terrace. Rooms come with phone, heating and a continental breakfast.

Hotel Conquistador (☎ 21-2916; fax 21-8987; Mercaderes 409; s/d US$27/35) The fine white-stone courtyard and lobby of this stately colonial house is elegant, though most of the rooms are in a disappointing modern annex. There is a restaurant, and rates include breakfast. Service is friendly and the manager speaks English.

Los Balcones de Santa Catalina (☎ 20-1291; Moral 217; s/d US$18/25) Originally a budget hotel, Los Balcones has gone upmarket with spacious, warmly decorated rooms with wooden floors. Some rooms also have a balcony with a back view of the cathedral. The rates include breakfast. Prices are flexible between October and May.

Hostal Posada de Sancho (☎ 28-7797; posadasan cho@terra.com.pe; Santa Catalina 213 & 223a; s/d US$12/20, with bathroom US$18/25) This hostel is close to the center, has English- and German-speaking owners and a view to El Misti from the rooftop terrace. Rooms could do with sprucing up for the price though.

Other recommendations are:

Hotel Yanahuara (☎ 27-1515; htl-yanahuara@terra .com.pe; Jerusalén 500; s/d US$38/48) A comfortable choice in the suburb of Yanahuara.

Hotel Tajmahal (☎ 28-2221; informes@hoteltaj mahal.com.pe; Valdivia 212, Parque Duhamel; s/d US$30/40) Modern and very roomy.

Top End

Hostal La Gruta (☎ 22-4631; hostal_lagruta@terra .com.pe; La Gruta 304, Selva Alegre; s/d US$45/55, minisuite US$65) Situated 1.5km north of the center, La Gruta (the grotto) is a beautiful small hotel tucked away on a quiet residential street. Rooms are all tastefully furnished and have large windows or glass walls with views of the garden, as well as a refrigerator and bar. Rates include a continental breakfast and airport pick-up on request. The helpful owner speaks English.

La Hostería (☎ 28-9269; lahosteria@terra.com.pe; Bolívar 405; s/d US$45/55, executive US$65) Worth every sol is this picturesque colonial hotel with a flower-bedecked courtyard, light and

uiet rooms with minibar, carefully chosen
ntiques, a sunny terrace and lounge. Some
ooms suffer from street noise; stay in the
ack.

La Posada del Monasterio (☎ 20-6565; fax 24-7353;
anta Catalina 300; s/d US$45/57) In an architecturally
nix-matched building combining old and
ew, this hotel has comfortable and modern
ooms with all the expected facilities. There
re fine views of the Santa Catalina convent
cross the road from the rooftop terrace.
ates include breakfast.

La Posada del Puente (☎ 25-3132; hotel@posada
elpuente.com; cnr Grau & Bolognesi 101; s/d/ste US$60/
0/105) Dipping down to the river, the
xtensive gardens of this hotel make for a
ranquil setting that's surprisingly removed
rom the bustling bridge-traffic above.
he hotel has attractive rooms and a good
estaurant and bar. Staying here gives you
ree access to the swimming pool in the
ountry club next door.

Sonesta Posada del Inca (☎ 21-5530; fax 23-4374;
ortal de Flores 116; s/d US$55/76; ❄ 🖳 🖳) On the
laza itself, this hotel has some front-side
ooms with private terraces and a privileged
iew of the cathedral through the arches.
hose without a view can compensate by
equenting the rooftop pool and terrace,
vhich also boasts a fine panorama of the
laza. The hotel has a restaurant, bar and
ym and rooms have good conveniences
ncluding a minibar and heater. A breakfast
uffet is included. Depending on the season
ou may be charged a 50% surcharge for a
laza view.

Libertador Arequipa (☎ 21-5110; arequipa@liber
dor.com.pe; Plaza Bolívar, Selva Alegre; s or d US$115,
e US$150-185; 🖳 🖳) This is the grande
ame of Arequipa's hotels, situated 1.5km
orth of the center. The stylish building is
icely set in sizable gardens with a pool
nd playground. It has spacious rooms
nd opulent public areas, plus its spa has
sauna, Jacuzzi and gym. There is a sedate
estaurant and a fine Sunday brunch. The
eighboring Selva Alegre park is beautiful,
ut don't wander too far from crowds and
void it after dark.

ATING
afés & Restaurants
istrot (Alianza Francesa; Santa Catalina 208) To get
our caffeine fix, try the espresso and
appuccinos in this cultural café.

Manolo's (☎ 21-9009; Mercaderes 113; mains
US$3.50-7) Although it lacks atmosphere, this
is a good general café that serves coffees,
ice creams, desserts, sandwiches and other
meals.

El Turko (☎ 20-3862; San Francisco 216; mains
US$2.50-6; ☺ open 24 hr Fri & Sat) This funky little
joint serves a hungry crowd its late-night
kebabs, but it also makes a good coffee
stop during the day. Its big brother, in the
thick of things at San Francisco 315, is a
highly recommended Turkish and Italian
restaurant.

La Serenata (☎ 22-1447; 2nd fl, Portal San Agustín
115; mains US$4.50-12) This is one of several
restaurants overlooking the Plaza de Armas
from the surrounding balconies. The food
is so-so for the cost here, but the views are
more than worth the price of an espresso.

El Gaucho Parrilladas (☎ 22-0301; Portal de Flores
112; mains US$6-16; ☺ evenings only, closed Sun) Not
one for vegetarians; these guys are experts
in steak and steak alone. In a lower level
off the Plaza de Armas, the restaurant has
a snug atmosphere, and it doesn't skimp
on portions.

Ary Quepay (☎ 967-2922; Jerusalén 502; mains
US$4-7) This place offers traditional plates
(including alpaca and cuy, or guinea pig) in
a colonial-style building that extends out to
a dimly lit rustic area dripping with plants.
There's enthusiastic *música folklórica* every
evening (7:30pm to 8:30pm).

Pizzería Los Leños (☎ 28-9179, Jerusalén 407;
mains US$1.60-17; ☺ evenings only, closed Sun) One
of the best pizzerías in Arequipa, it bakes
pizza in a wood-burning oven that adds to
the warm and welcoming atmosphere. Rock
music is interspersed with live performances
by Peruvian *folklórica* musicians. If you're
impressed by the food, add your personalized
scribble to the already-covered walls.

El Camaroncito (☎ 20-4342; San Francisco 303;
mains US$4-9) Consistently busy with locals
and travelers alike, this place has typical
Arequipeño and Peruvian food and a
mellow atmosphere.

Cevichería Fory Foy (☎ 24-2400; Thomas 221; mains
US$4-6; ☺ lunch only) This small, to-the-point
place serves good ceviche (and nothing
else). The name is a phonetic spelling of
how Peruvians say 45 in English.

Mixtos (☎ 20-5343; Pasaje Catedral 115; US$4-
7.50) Tucked away in the alley behind the
cathedral on the Plaza de Armas is this

popular and quaint restaurant that serves mainly Italian and *criollo* (spicy Peruvian fare with Spanish and African influences) seafood dishes. It has outdoor balconies and tables.

La Truffa (☎ 40-5290; Pasaje Catedral 111; mains US$3-8) Almost next door to Mixtos is this intimate and dimly lit restaurant also serving good Italian and Peruvian fare.

The 300 block of San Francisco is overrun with good options. Here are three.

La Viñeda (☎ 20-5053; San Francisco 319; mains US$6-10) An intimate spot, this one of the best places to knock back Argentine steaks – try the 'as-thick-as-you-like' T-bone for US$7. It also serves typical Arequipeño and Peruvian food.

Trattoria Gianni (☎ 22-7610; San Francisco 304; mains US$4.50-9; ✆ closed Sun) This place is an old favorite for pizzas and pastas.

La Brochetta (☎ 22-1904; San Francisco 317; mains US$4-8) Italian and typical Peruvian fare are on offer here, plus a free welcome cocktail and live music.

Sambambaia´s (☎ 22-3657; Luna Pizarro 304, Vallecito; mains US$5.60-8.40; ✆ noon-3pm Mon, Wed, Fri-Sun, noon-11pm Tue, Thu) Around 1km out of the center, this restaurant is an elegant, upper-crust alternative with Brazilian specialties and live piano playing in the background.

Also see Entertainment for dinner shows with live music.

Arequipeño Food

The best places for traditional local food are outside the central area, and most open for lunch only. Try the explosively spicy *rocoto relleno* (hot peppers stuffed with meat, rice and vegetables), *ocopa* (potatoes with a spicy sauce and fried cheese), *chupe de camarones* (shrimp soup) or *chancho al horno* (suckling pig) and wash it down with *chicha* (fermented maize beer).

Sol de Mayo (☎ 25-4148; soldemayo@terra.com.pe; Jerusalén 207; 3-course menú US$9, mains US$4-8) Serving good Peruvian food in the Yanahuara district, Sol de Mayo has live *música folklórica* from 1pm to 2pm. Book in advance. You can combine a visit here with a stop-off at the *mirador* in Yanahuara.

Tradición Arequipeña (☎ 42-6467; Av Dolores 111; meals US$4-10; ✆ closes 7pm Sun-Thu, 10pm Fri-Sat) This wonderful restaurant has mazelike gardens with lazing areas and a playground. Live music varies from 'funky bongos' to

criollo. It's 2km southeast of the center; taxi ride here should cost US$1.20.

La Cantarilla (☎ 25-1515; Tahuaycani 106; ✆ lune only) You'll be greeted by an ostrich statu at this locally famous, open-air restaurar in the southwestern suburb of Sachaca. I serves some international fare as well a good-quality Arequipeño food, includin local freshwater shrimp. Take a taxi (US$2

Picantería Los Guisos Arequipeños (☎ 46-515 Lambramani 111; mains US$5-10) This huge, barr like place is in the suburb of Lambraman 2km southeast of the center. It has a garde and play area, plus occasional live music.

Vegetarian

Mandala (☎ 28-7086; mandalaqp@hotmail.com; Jeru salén 207; 3-course menú US$1.20-2; ✆ closed Sun) great vegetarian option with quick, chea and quality offerings. Recommended.

Lakshmivan (☎ 22-8768; Jerusalén 402; mair US$2-3.50) Set in a colorful old building wit a tiny outdoor courtyard, this place ha various set menús and an extensive à l carte selection. Service can be slow.

Govinda (☎ 28-5540; Santa Catalina 120 Cercad 3-course menú US$4.20) Run by the Hare Krishna this large restaurant has a line-up of differer three-course set meals that change daily including Italian, Hindu, and traditiona Arequipeño on Sunday.

Self-Catering

Grocery shopping can be done at the tw branches of **El Super** (cnr Pierola & Portal de Municipalidad, also Plaza de Armas; ✆ 9am-2pm & 4- 30pm Mon-Sat, 9am-2pm Sun).

ENTERTAINMENT
Bars & Nightclubs

The nocturnal scene in Arequipa is prett slow midweek but takes off at weekends. It worth keeping an eye out for free-drink fliers distributed around town.

Deja Vu (☎ 28-3428; San Francisco 319B; ✆ 6pm 2am) With a rooftop terrace overlookin the church of San Francisco, this popula haunt has a long list of cocktails, includin some good specialties – try its cucharach (Kahlua and Tequila, US$3). This bar i good on weekdays and weekends alike.

Forum Rock Cafe (☎ 20-4294; San Francisc 317; admission Fri & Sat US$4; ✆ 10pm-4am Tue-Sa A gutsy Latin rock bar with a thing fo bamboo and waterfalls, this is currentl he most happening club in town. Dancing never gets under way until at least 11pm. Food is sometimes served but the specialties here are bands and booze – burgers are an afterthought.

La Casa de Klaus (☎ 20-3711; Zela 207; ✆ 11am-am Mon-Sat, 11am-5pm Sun) A good and rowdy crowd gathers at this German pub, which has a reasonable choice of international beers, including barrels of Holsten, canned Guinness and Heineken.

Kibosch (Zela 205; ✆ 9pm-late Thu-Sat) This club has no shortage of bars and dance space, and plays a good mix of salsa and rock.

Zero Bar and Pool (✆ 7pm-2am) In the same complex as Forum Rock Cafe, the Zero is a light, bustling international bar with pool tables and spacious booths.

Beyond the tourist haunts, the hottest local action is to be had from numerous nocturnal spots strung along Avenida Dolores, 2km southeast of the center (taxi about US$1).

ive Music
Be aware that some places advertise a nightly *peña* (bar or club featuring folkloric music), but there's rarely anything going on except from Thursday to Saturday nights.

Las Quenas (☎ 28 1115; Santa Catalina 302; admission US$1.40; mains US$3-9; ✆ closed Sun) An exception to the rule, this intimate spot has nightly shows from 9pm Monday to Saturday. The music varies, although *música folklórica* predominates. It also serves decent Arequipeño food starting at 8pm.

La Quinta (☎ 20-0964; Jerusalén 522; mains US$2.80-5.60; ✆ closed Sun) Another good spot for local food and weekend music is this place. There's a US$1.40 cover on Saturday night, but it can be potluck as to whether you get live music on other nights.

La Troica (☎ 22-5690; Jerusalén 522A) Next door to La Quinta, La Troica also has food and music, including Afro-Peruvian and Latin, as well as *folklórica*.

inema
A handful of cinemas show English-language movies dubbed or with Spanish subtitles. Local newspapers have listings, and it's also worth checking at the various cultural centers for film festivals and other events.

Cinessur el Portal (☎ 20-2202; cinesdelsur@cine sur.com; Portal de Flores 112) shows blockbuster movies on the Plaza de Armas.

Cine Felix (☎ 28-2389; Morán 104) has a small screen and regular films, though it was temporarily closed at time of writing.

Deja Vu (see Bars & Nightclubs p132) sometimes shows videos.

Sport
Club Internacional (☎ 25-3384; Bolognesi; admission Mon-Fri US$3, Sat & Sun US$4.50; ✆ 6am-8pm Mon-Sat & 7am-5pm Sun) has two swimming pools, a soccer field, tennis courts and a bowling alley by the river near Puente Grau.

Grand Peleas de Toros Bullfights, conducted Arequipeño style are less bloodthirsty than most; they involve pitting two bulls against each other for the favors of a fertile female until one realizes he's beaten and makes a swift exit. The fights take place on Sundays from April to December, alternating between three stadiums outside the center, so ask locally which stadium to attend. The three most important fights are in April, mid-August and early December (the exact dates vary).

SHOPPING
Good souvenir shopping is to be had in the stores next to the Museo Histórico Municipal, and high-quality alpaca, vicuña, leather and natural cotton goods are sold in the *claustros* of La Compañía by **Incalpaca Grupo Inca** (☎ 20-5931; sales@incalpaca.com; Claustros de la Compañía, local 18, 2nd patio). The new **Patio de Ekeko** (Mercaderes 141) also has plenty of expensive but good alpaca stores, and a museum on textiles to educate you a little on what you're buying.

GETTING THERE & AWAY
Air
Arequipa's **airport** (☎ 44-3464) is about 9km northwest of the center of town. There are several daily flights to Lima (US$72 to US$80) and Cuzco (US$43 to US$70), and less-frequent flights to Puerto Maldonado (US$41 to US$50) and Iquitos (US$70 to US$83). A US$3.50 airport departure tax applies.

Aero Continente/Aviandina (☎ 20-3294, 20-1887; Portal San Agustín 113, Plaza de Armas; ✆ 8am-7:30pm Mon-Sat, 9am-12:30pm Sun) has flights to Lima and Cuzco daily, while **Tans** (☎ 20-5231; Portal de San Agustín 143A; ✆ 9am-4pm Mon-Sat) has services to Iquitos and Puerto Maldonado via Cuzco and Lima. **LanPeru** (☎ 20-1100; Portal de San

Agustín 118; ☻ 8am-7:30pm Mon-Sat, 9am-12:30pm Sun) also goes to Cuzco and Lima daily.

Servicios Aéreos AQP (☎ 28-1800; mbegazo@saaqp .com; Santa Catalina 210) flies nine-passenger, Piper Comanches anywhere you want to go, including local sightseeing spots.

Bus

INTERNATIONAL

Ormeño also has two international buses a week to Santiago in Chile (US$80, 2¼ days) and three a week to Buenos Aires in Argentina (US$130, three days).

DOMESTIC

The Terminal Terrestre and Terrapuerto bus terminals are together on Avenida A Avelino Cáceres, about 3km south of the center of town. The terminals are well organized, with shops, restaurants, ATM and also an **information office** (☎ 24-1735). Check which terminal your bus leaves from in advance and keep a close watch on your belongings. There's a US$0.30 departure tax.

Lima is about 16 hours away. Several buses a day ply this route including **Ormeño** (☎ 42-41870), which charges US$9 to US$25; **Cruz del Sur** (☎ 42-7375) charges US$9 to US$32; **Flores** (☎ 23-8741) US$20; and **Civa** (☎ 42-6563) US$10 to US$14. Most buses leave in the afternoon. Cruz del Sur still maintains a ticket office at San Juan de Dios and Socabaya, but it's often as convenient to get tickets a day before at the terminal. For intermediate south-coast points, most buses stop in Camaná (3½ hours), Nazca (US$6 to US$25, 10 to 12 hours) and Ica (13 to 14 hours), but Pisco is about 5km off the Panamericana, and few buses go directly.

The same companies also have buses to Cuzco (US$12 to US$15, 12 to 16 hours) on a direct but only partially paved road or on the asphalted roads via Puno.

If you're going inland to Lake Titicaca, the bus lines Ormeño (US$10), Cruz del Sur (US$6) and Civa (US$4.50) have several buses a day to Juliaca (five hours) and Puno (5½ hours). Flores and **Señor de los Milagros** (☎ 42-3260) has buses through Puno all the way to Desaguadero (US$7, nine hours) on the Bolivian border. Services to La Paz, Bolivia, are occasionally offered, but these usually involve a bus change at the border.

Flores and Cruz del Sur have many buses via Moquegua (US$4, four hours) to Tacna

(US$4 to US$7, seven hours). **Transporte Carpio** (☎ 42-7049) has hourly departure during the day for Mollendo (US$5, tw hours). For Ilo, Flores (US$3 to US$7, fiv hours) has several departures a day.

Regional Services

Travel times and costs can vary depending on road conditions. Many buses useful for sightseeing in the region also leave from Terminal Terrestre and Terrapuerto.

For Chivay (US$3, three hours), con tinuing through Yanque, Achoma and Maca to Cabanaconde (US$4, seven hours) on the upper Cañón del Colca, try **La Reyna** (☎ 43 0612), with three services daily, Transporte Andalucía, **Transportes Colca** (☎ 42-6357; US$3 or **Turismo Pluma** (☎ 28-4721). Buses leave around 1am, 11am and 2pm daily.

For buses to Corire (US$2, three hours to visit the Toro Muerto petroglyphs (se p140), **Transportes Trebol** (☎ 82-9319) has one service at 5:30am daily, while **Transportes de Carpio** (☎ 42-7049) has hourly services. Carpio also goes hourly to Valle de Majes (US$2.50 four hours) for river running, as do othe companies. The Transportes Trebol servic continues through Corire to Andagua (US$7, 10 hours), leaving at 4pm, to visi the Valle de los Volcanes. For Cotahuas (US$7 to US$9, 12 hours), La Reyna has 5pm departure, and **Transportes Alex** (☎ 42 4605) has a 3:45pm departure.

Train

The train station is about 1.2km south of the Plaza de Armas. Services between Arequipa and Juliaca/Puno were suspended in 2002, though PerúRail will run trains for private charter for groups of 40 or over The Arequipa–Juliaca part of the route i bleak, but the views of the altiplano are appealing and you'll see vicuñas, alpacas and llamas, plus flamingos along the way if you're lucky.

GETTING AROUND
To/From the Airport

There are no airport buses, although buse and combis marked Río Seco, Cono–Norte or Zamacola go along Avenida Puente Gra and Ejército and pass within 700m of the airport – ask the driver where to get off. A taxi from downtown costs about US$3.50 From the airport, shared colectivo taxis

harge US$2 per person to take you to
our hotel.

ocal Bus

Combis and minibuses go south along
Bolívar and Sucre to the Terminal Terrestre
US$0.30, 10 minutes). A taxi ride will cost
about US$1.

ar & Taxi

vis (☎ 95-3780) rents cars at the airport. You
eed to be at least 25 years old and have a
major credit card and driver's license. You
an often hire a taxi with a driver for less.
Two local taxi companies to call are **Ideal
axi** (☎ 28-8888) and **Gino Taxi** (☎ 27-2828).

Bicycle

ndes Bike (☎ 20-5078; Villalba 414) sells spare
arts and bicycles.

CANYON COUNTRY

A tour of Cañón del Colca is the most
popular adventurous excursion from Are-
uipa, but climbing the city's guardian
olcano El Misti, visiting the Majes Canyon
nd the petroglyphs at Toro Muerto, hiking
n the Valle de los Volcanes and exploring
he world's deepest canyon in Cotahuasi
re also worthwhile. Most of these places
an be visited by a combination of bus and
iking. Alternatively, friends can split the
ost of a taxi and driver; two-days hire will
et you back US$100 to US$120.

TREKKING

The spectacular canyons around Arequipa
ffer many excellent hiking options. Trek
ing agencies can arrange a whole array
f off-the-beaten-track routes to suit your
imescale and fitness level. The best time
o trek is from May to November; be aware
here is an increased danger of rock falls in
he canyons between January and March.

Unless you are an experienced hiker,
o with a guide. There are dozens of tour
ompanies based in Arequipa offering
rekking excursions; see Tours & Guides
p128). Be sure you book with a reputable
ompany, never exchange money with
outs on the street and always ask to see
our guide's guiding card and booklet
isting all the places he or she has guided.

Hiking from village to village is another
simple option in this scenic region. The
main road from Chivay to Yanque and
then on to Anchoma, Maca and Pinchollo
is a possible, less-strenuous route. It's a
great way to experience village life at a
slower pace.

Details on short hikes and tours appear
throughout this section.

RIVER RUNNING

After Cuzco, Arequipa is one of Peru's
premier bases for white-water rafting and
kayaking. The **Río Chile**, about 7km from
Arequipa, is the most frequently run local
river, with a half-day trip suitable for
beginners leaving almost daily from April
to December (US$25 to US$30). Further
afield, you can also do relatively easy trips
on the **Río Majes**, into which the Colca
flows. The commonly run stretches pass
Grade II and III rapids. Another more off-
the-beaten-track possibility is the remote
Río Cotahuasi, a relatively new white-water
discovery reaching into the deepest sections
of the world's deepest known canyon.
Expeditions here are infrequent and only
for the experienced, taking nine to 12 days
and passing through numerous Grade IV
and V rapids.

The river of the **Cañón del Colca** was first
run back in 1981, but this is a dangerous,
difficult trip and not to be undertaken
lightly. However, a few outfitters will do
infrequent and expensive rafting trips, and
easier sections can be found upriver from
the canyon.

Many trips are unavailable during the
January-to-March rainy season, when water
levels can be dangerously high.

The **Casa de Mauro** (no tel; camping per person
US$2; dm US$3), in the village of Ongoro,
190km by road west of Arequipa, is the
most convenient base for rafting the Río
Majes. A one-hour Class III white-water
run in inflatable rafts costs about US$16.
Experienced river runners can take a 25km,
Class-IV run lasting three hours for US$29.
The lodge can be contacted in advance
through Colca Trek (see Tours & Guides
p128) or Cusipata in Arequipa. Toro
Muerto and Valle de los Volcanes (p140)
can also be visited from here. It is cheapest
to take a bus from Arequipa's Terminal
Terrestre with Trebol to Aplao (US$2, three

hours) and then take a minibus to Ongoro (or a taxi for US$3.50).

Cusipata (☎ 20-3966, 931-1576, 999-5995; gvellutino@terra.com.pe; Jerusalén 408; ☯ closed Dec-Feb) is currently the best river-running company in Arequipa. It leads recommended white-water and kayaking trips to all the major destinations with the English-speaking Vellutino brothers, Jean Marco and Piero. They also organize courses in kayaking.

Amazonas Explorer (☎ in Cuzco 084-20-3966, sales@amazonas-explorer.com) is a British company that does an annual 14-day rafting and hiking trip to the Río Cotahuasi in June; it includes six days of Class IV and V rapids. This is only for the experienced.

You can also try asking in Pizzería Los Leños (p131) in Arequipa, whose owner sometimes does kayaking trips.

MOUNTAIN CLIMBING

Superb mountains for climbing surround Arequipa. Adequate acclimatization for this area is essential and its best to have spent some time in Cuzco or Puno immediately before a high-altitude expedition. Lack of water can also be a problem, as can the icy temperatures, which sometimes drop to -29°C at the highest camps. Though many climbs in the area are not technically difficult, they should never be undertaken lightly. Watch for the symptoms of altitude sickness and if in doubt, go back down.

Maps of the area can be obtained from Colca Trek (see Tours & Guides p128) in Arequipa or the Instituto Geográfico Nacional (p52) in Lima.

Guides

Always check the ID of guides carefully and ask to see the little black book that identifies trained and registered guides. Colca Trek and Zárate Expediciones (see Tours & Guides p128) rent tents, ice axes and crampons, but climbers should bring their own sleeping bags, climbing boots and warm clothes. The standard official rate for hiring a mountain guide is US$50 per day, plus the cost of food and transport. One guide can take a group of up to four climbers for this price.

El Misti

Looming 5822m above Arequipa, the city's guardian volcano El Misti is the most popular climb in the area. It is technically one of the easiest ascents of any mountain of this size in the world, but it's hard work nonetheless and you normally need an ice axe and, sometimes, crampons. The mountain is best climbed from July to November, and October and November are the least cold. At the top is a 10m-high iron cross, which was erected in 1901. Below the summit is a sulfurous, yellow crater with volcanic fumaroles hissing gas, and there are spectacular views down to the *salina* (see p141) and back to the city.

There are several routes, but none are clearly marked and at least one is notorious for robberies, so taking a guide is highly recommended. A two-day trip costs about US$75. Public transport to the mountain base is scarce. You can hire a 4WD vehicle for US$50 to take you up to about 3300m and pick you up on your return. Another route, on the back of the mountain, allows you to get up to 4000m by 4WD, but it costs US$120 to US$150 for the vehicle.

Other Mountains

One of the easiest 6000m peaks in the world is **Chachani** (6075m), which is as close to Arequipa as El Misti. You need crampons, an ice axe and good equipment. There are various routes, one of which involves going by 4WD (US$120) to Campamento de Azufrera at 4950m. From here you can reach the summit in about nine hours and return in under four. Alternatively, for a two-day trip, there is a good spot to camp at 5200m. Other routes take three days but are easier to get to by 4WD (US$50).

Sabancaya (5976m) is part of a massif on the south rim of the Cañón del Colca, which includes **Hualca Hualca** (6025m) and **Ampato** (6288m). Sabancaya is currently the most active of the region's volcanoes and has erupted in recent years. The crater can be approached between eruptions if you have an experienced guide, but neighboring Ampato (see the boxed text 'Human Sacrifice in the Andes' p126) is a fairly straightforward three-day ascent, and you get safer views of the active Sabancaya from here.

Other nearby mountains of interest include **Ubinas** (5675m), a two-day climb with a lot of geothermal activity. **Mismi** (5556m) is a fairly easy three- or four-day climb on the north side of the Cañón del Colca. You can approach it from the village of Cailloma and, with a guide, find the lake that is reputedly the **source of the Amazon**. The highest mountain in southern Peru is the difficult **Coropuna** (around 6425m).

AREQUIPA TO CAÑÓN DEL COLCA

The road from Arequipa climbs northwest past the **Chachani** volcano and following the route of the railway, to **Reserva Nacional Salinas y Aguada Blanca**, which covers 367,000 hectares at an average elevation of 3850m. Here, vicuñas – the delicate wild cousins of llamas and alpacas – are often sighted. Later in the trip, domesticated alpacas and llamas are frequently seen, so it is possible to see three of the four members of the South American Camelid family in one day. Seeing the fourth member, the guanaco, is very hard, as they have almost disappeared from this area. The road continues through bleak altiplano and over the highest point of 4800m, from where the snowcaps of **Ampato** (6388m) are seen. Flamingos may also be seen around here between January and April. From here, the road drops spectacularly to Chivay (see later).

CAÑÓN DEL COLCA

For years there was raging controversy over whether or not this was the world's deepest canyon at about 3191m, but it has recently drawn in a close second to the neighboring Cañón del Cotahuasi, which is all of 163m deeper. The sections seen on a standard guided tour are impressive in themselves but to witness the deepest sections you have to make an overnight trip and put in some serious hiking.

The local people are known for their painstakingly decorated traditional clothing, especially the women's clothes. Their dresses and jackets are intricately embroidered, and their hats are distinctive. In the Chivay area at the east end of the canyon, the white hats are usually woven from straw and are embellished with lace, sequins and badges. At the west end of the canyon, the hats are of cotton and are heavily embroidered. The women don't particularly enjoy being photographed; always ask permission.

Tours

Guided tours of one and two days follow the same route around the canyon (see Tours & Guides on p128). The cost of a day trip is about US$20, but it sets off painfully early, rushes around the sites in just 15 hours (arriving back in the evening), and is not recommended if you are not acclimatized to altitude. The two-day trip is far more relaxed and costs US$18 to US$70 per person depending on the season, group-size and the comfort of the hotel. The standard two-day tour leaves Arequipa at 7am to 9am, passing through the Reserva Nacional Salinas y Aguada Blanca. Breakfast is taken at **Cañahaus** (4000m) and a stop is made to take in the views at the highest point and before descending to Chivay, where lunch is taken. Some agencies then take their groups on a short hike, and the thermal hot springs of Chivay are almost always visited so bring swimsuits and towels. There is usually a visit to a lively *peña* in the evening. Note that the cost includes lodging with breakfast in Chivay, but other meals are paid for from your own pocket. The following morning the group leaves at 6am to reach Cruz del Cóndor by 8:30am for an hour of condor spotting, before returning to Arequipa with a brief stop at the church in Yanque. During their tour, many groups are approached by locals with birds of prey in the hope that tourists will pay a tip to have their picture taken with the bird. Please do not encourage the capture and endangerment of these wild birds.

Chivay

☎ 054 / pop 4000 / elevation 3700m

Chivay, at the head of the Cañón de Colca, is the capital of the province of Cailloma. The police station next to Hostal Municipal on the plaza offers tourist information. Limited help with trekking can be gleaned from a semiprofessional office at the front of the market on Salaverry. There are no money-changing facilities in the canyon, so bring plenty of cash. Internet access is available at **Albicsa Hotel** (Jose Galvez 109; ☺ 8am-10pm) for a whopping US$2.30 per hour.

SIGHTS & ACTIVITIES

Don't miss the **hot springs** (foreigner/Peruvian US$1.40/0.30, plus locker deposit US$1.40; ☺ 4am-7pm) that are 4km to the northeast of the village by road. There is a large, clean pool, showers, changing rooms and a tiny cafeteria. The mineral-laden water is said to have curative properties; one traveler writes that it does a good job of boiling eggs for a picnic lunch. It's also handy when the hot-water supply in Chivay packs up. There are occasional colectivos (US$0.30) to the springs, or you can easily walk.

Mountain bikes can be hired at **Bici** (Zaramilla 112; 9am-6pm) behind the market for US$10 per day.

Several short treks can be made around Chivay. The road to the villages of **Corporaque** and **Ichupampa** sees few vehicles and makes a scenic walk of three to four hours. In Corporaque is the excellent mid-range **La Casa de Mamayacchi** (in Arequipa ☎ 24-1206; reserv as@lacasademamayacchi.com; s/d US$32/38). There are some small ruins below the village and a few cliff tombs above. It's also possible to cross the river to Yanque and return to Chivay to make a full day. Travel about 17km further up the northern side of the canyon and you'll reach the rarely visited town of **Madrigal**, which is a good spot from which to trek into the deepest parts of the canyon. Combis also run from Chivay.

SLEEPING

Hospedaje Rumi Wasi (☎ 53-1101; Sucre 714; s/d/tr US$6/9/12) This family-run, quiet and secure hostel has a central garden and decent rooms with bathroom. Bikes can be hired for US$14 per day or US$1.50 per hour.

Hospedaje Estrella de David (☎ 48-8625; Siglo xx 209; s/d/tr US$4.20/5.60/9) A simple and clean spot with bathrooms, this *hospedaje* is just a few steps from the plaza.

Ricardito's (☎ 53-1051; Salaverry 121; s/d US$6/12) This simple place has decent rooms with bathrooms complete with heart-shaped mirrors. Tariffs are half price in the low season.

Hostal Municipal (☎ 53-1093; Plaza de Armas; s/d US$7/12) Though unexciting this place is fine for an exhausted traveler.

Hostal Plaza (Plaza de Armas; s/d US$3/6) It's a very basic place in a shaky wooden building with only shared cold-water bathrooms.

Hostal Anita (☎ 52-1114; Plaza de Armas 607; s/d US$6/12) Half price in low season, this friendly place has rooms around a small courtyard, with bathroom and hot water.

Hostal La Pascana (☎ 53-1019; gromup@latin mail.com; cnr Siglo xx & Puente Inca; s/d/tr US$10/20/35) La Pascana is a very good new option with carpeted, well-decorated rooms and firm mattresses.

Hostal Kolping (☎ 53-1076; fax 25-3744; s/d/tr US$30/40/50) This seven-bungalow hostel is set in spacious grounds on the outskirts of town, a minute's walk from the bus terminal. Rates include breakfast.

Colca Inn (☎ 53-1088; hotelcolcainn@planet.com.pe, Salaverry 307; s/d/tr US$24/34/45) The Colca Inn is a modern place that's very comfortable, with local TV and decent bathrooms. There's a good restaurant and pool table downstairs.

Hostal Posada Chivay (☎ 53-1032; posadachivay@ latinmail.com; Salaverry 325; s/d/tr US$10/25/30) Two or three blocks west of the plaza, this *hostal* is favored by tour groups and is solid value, though there are occasional problems with hot water and the restaurant is overpriced. Rates include breakfast.

Rumi Llaqti Hotel (☎ 53-1020; fax 53-1098; Huayna Cápac; s/d/tr/ste US$50/64/79/94) The name of this hotel means 'stone town' in Quechua and, sure enough, the complex recreates a rustic idyll with quaint stone-and-thatch cottages, neatly sculptured bushes, and garden views to the snow-capped peaks. It has a good restaurant with live music in the evening.

EATING & DRINKING

Calamarcito's (☎ 53-1102; José Gálvez 232; 3-course menú US$4) serves recommended typical Andean food, as does **Wayra Punko** (☎ 25-5698 Siglo xx 215; pizzas US$5-40, 3-course menú US$4). **Lobo's** (☎ 53-1081; Plaza de Armas; pizza US$2-7) has good fast food.

The nightlife in this tiny village revolves around the tourists. And yes, it's official **M´elroys** (Plaza de Armas; 4pm-1am) proves that Irish pubs really are everywhere. For some dancing, there's **Latigo's** (cnr Puente Inca & Bolognesi; 8:30pm-6am) and, within 15m stumbling distance, is **Rolo´s** (Bolognesi 705 9pm-4am).

GETTING THERE & AWAY

Bus offices are found near the plaza and at the new terminal, 400m east of the plaza Buses to Arequipa leave at 12:30pm, 3pm and 10:30pm (US$3, 3½ hours) and onward buses for Cabanaconde via Cruz del Condor leave four to five times daily, with the earliest at 6am (US$1, 2¾ hours). Combis run to the surrounding villages from the plaza. Traveling on to Cuzco from Chivay is complicated and not recommended although some travelers have managed catch combis to Puente Callalli and flag down a bus there. It's much safer to return to Arequipa.

Chivay to Cabanaconde

The road following the south bank of the upper Cañón del Colca leads past several villages that still use the Inca terracing that surrounds them. One of these villages, **Yanque**, has a small museum on the plaza and an attractive 18th-century church. A 30-minute walk down to the river also brings you to some hot springs (US$0.30). Across the river from here is the upmarket **Colca Lodge** (in Arequipa ☎ 20-2587; info@colca-lodge .com; s/d/tr/4-bed room US$53/60/75/85), a large and attractive stone-and-thatch hotel tucked into the bend of the river amid Inca terracing. Activities including fishing and horse riding can be arranged here.

Further up the canyon, the landscape is remarkable for its Inca and pre-Inca terracing, which goes on for many kilometers and is some of the most extensive in Peru; some tours also stop at a small carved boulder that is supposed to represent a pre-Columbian map of the terracing. **Pinchollo** is the next big village. From here, a trail climbs south toward **Nevado Hualca Hualca** (a snowcapped volcano of 6025m) to an active geothermal area set amid wild and interesting scenery. There is a clearly marked four-hour trail up to a bubbling geyser that used to erupt dramatically before a recent earthquake contained it. In Pinchollo, there is the very basic **El Refugio** (dm US$1.50) near the plaza, and the owner is also a local guide. A sleeping bag and flashlight are recommended.

You can continue from Pinchollo to **Cruz del Cóndor** (admission US$2) on foot, which takes about two hours. This viewpoint, also known locally as Chaglla, is for many the highlight of their trip to the Colca. A large family of Andean condors nests by the rocky outcrop and can be seen gliding effortlessly on thermal air currents rising from the canyon, often swooping low over its onlookers' heads. It's a mesmerizing scene, heightened by the spectacular 1200m drop to the river below and the sight of **Mismi** reaching 3200m above the canyon floor on the other side of the ravine. Early morning (8am to 9:30am) or late afternoon (4pm to 6pm) are the best times too see the birds, though they can appear at various hours during the day. The condors are less likely to appear on rainy days so it's best to visit during the dry season. You can walk from the cruz to Cabanconde (see p140).

Cabanaconde

☎ 054 / pop 3000 / elevation 3290m

The quiet rural town of Cabanaconde makes an ideal base for some spectacular hikes on into the canyon.

SLEEPING & EATING

La Posada del Conde (☎ 44-0197; main street; s/d US$7/14) Highly recommended, this hostel has only double rooms but they are modern and well-cared for with clean bathrooms. Prices include a welcome *maté* or pisco sour, as well as breakfast. Prices can rise to US$15 in July to August, but likewise drop in low season.

Hostal Valle del Fuego (☎ 28-0367; r per person US$3) This budget hostel is an established travelers' scene, with DVDs, a full bar, solar-powered showers and knowledgeable owners. Rooms are very basic and share bathrooms. There's also a newer annex with singles/doubles for US$5/9.

Hotel Kuntur Wassi (☎ 25-2989; kunturwassi@ terra.com.pe; Calle Cruz Blanca; s/d/tr/ste $25/35/45/80) This is a new upmarket option built into the hillside, with stone bathrooms and a nouveau-rustic feel. In low season prices drop to US$10 per person. Suites boast enormous bathtubs.

There are also basic family-run pensions that charge about US$2.50 per person.

GETTING THERE & AWAY

Buses for Chivay and Arequipa leave Cabanaconde from the plaza at 5am, 8am, 10:30am and 8pm. They stop at Cruz del Condor en route if you ask. Times change frequently though, so check locally.

Around Cabanaconde

A wealth of rewarding treks surround Cabanaconde. Hiring a local guide costs US$4 to US$10 per day depending on their experience; Henry López is a highly recommended young guide; ask for him in Cabanaconde. Horses or mules are also easily arranged for about US$7 per day.

The most popular short trek is one that involves a steep two-hour hike down to **Sangalle** (also popularly known as the Oasis) in the bottom of the canyon, where several sets of basic bungalows and camp sites have sprung up, all costing US$2.50 to US$3 per person. There are two natural pools for **swimming**, the larger of which is claimed by Oasis Bungalows, which charges US$3 (or US$1.40 if you are staying in its bungalows) to swim. Paradaíso Bungalows don't charge for the smaller swimming pool, and there is a local dispute over whether travelers should be charged to use the pools at all. Do not light campfires as almost half of the trees in the area have been destroyed in this manner, and take all trash away with you. The return trek to Cabanaconde is a stiff climb and thirsty work; allow about three to four hours.

A five- to seven-days trek goes down to the canyon bottom, passes through the village of Tapay, then goes up the other side of the canyon by the village of Choco and over a 5500m pass, before descending through the town of Chacas and the **Valle de los Volcanes** (see later). Another pass brings you to Andagua, where there are buses back to Arequipa.

Less-demanding day-hike destinations around Cabanaconde include the Inca ruins at **La Casa del Inca** and **La Muraya**, and some short strolls to *miradors* at **Achachigua** and **San Miguel**. Local guides can suggest a wealth of other treks to waterfalls, geysers and archaeological sites.

The hike to **Cruz del Cóndor** (see p139) from Cabanaconde takes about 2½ to 3½ hours.

TORO MUERTO PETROGLYPHS

This is a magnificent and quite unusual archaeological site in the high desert. It consists of thousands of black volcanic boulders carved with stylized animals, people and birds. The rocks are spread over about 2 sq km of desert. Archaeologists are uncertain of the cultural origins of this site, but it is thought that it was made by the Wari culture about 1200 years ago.

To reach the site by public transport, take a bus to **Corire** (see Getting There & Away p133) and then walk for about 1½ hours or catch a taxi (US$6 to US$7 round trip). In Corire there is the basic **Hostal Willy** (☎ 47-2046; s/d US$3/5, with bathroom US$5.50/7), which can provide information on reaching the site. Bring plenty of water, sunblock and insect repellent (as there are plenty of

mosquitoes en route). If you don't want to sleep in Corire, take an early bus (they start at 5:30am) from Arequipa and get off at a small church 2km before the town of Corire where you'll see a sign for Toro Muerto. From here, a dirt track goes up a valley to the petroglyphs. Buses return from Corire to Arequipa once an hour, usually leaving at 30 minutes past the hour.

The Toro Muerto petroglyphs can also be visited more conveniently but expensively on full-day tours from Arequipa.

VALLE DE LOS VOLCANES

This unusual valley is covered with scores of small and medium-sized volcanic cones and craters creating a veritable moonscape. The 65km-long valley surrounds the village of **Andagua** near the snowcapped mountain of Coropuna. It is a weird and remote area that is seldom visited by travelers. There are some *chullpas* (pre-Columbian funerary towers) at **Soporo**, a two-hour hike or half-hour drive from Andagua. En route to Soporo is a pre-Columbian city named **Antaymarca**. Northeast of Andagua, at a place called **Izanquillay**, the Río Andahua runs through a lava canyon 50m deep but only 5m wide, forming a spectacular 40m-high waterfall.

There are several cheap and basic hostels and restaurants. To get here from Arequipa take a bus to Andagua (see Getting There & Away p133). Return buses leave Andagua around 4pm and arrive in Arequipa at around 4am.

CAÑÓN DEL COTAHUASI

☎ 054

While the Cañón del Colca has stolen the limelight for many years, it is actually this remote canyon 200km northwest of Arequipa as the condor flies that is the deepest known canyon in the world. It is around twice the depth of the Grand Canyon, with stretches dropping down to below 3300m. While the depths of the ravine are only accessible to experienced river runners, the rest of the fertile valley is also rich in striking scenery and trekking opportunities. The canyon also shelters several traditional, rural settlements that currently see only a handful of adventurous travelers.

The main-access town is appropriately named **Cotahuasi** (pop 3200) and is at 2680m

Hardy strands of grass of the *puna* (high Andean grasslands), en route to **El Misti** (p136)

Cobbled pathway in the grounds of the **Monasterio Santa Catalina** (p123), Arequipa

Colonnaded municipal offices on the **Plaza de Armas** (p125), Arequipa

Brooding volcano rising above the *puna*, **El Misti** (p136)

Reed boat on Lake Titicaca, **Islas Flotantes** (p156)

Bow of a reed boat, **Islas Flotantes** (p156)

Cool mountain stream of the *puna*, near **Juliaca** (p147)

above sea level on the southeast side of the canyon. Northeast of Cotahuasi and further up the canyon are the villages of **Tomepampa** (10km away, 2700m), **Liucho** (17.5km away) and **Alca** (20km, 2750m), which also have accommodations; Liucho has hot springs (US$0.30).

Trails lead into the canyon, and **waterfalls** and **hot springs** can be visited. One can allegedly hike from Cotahuasi to the coast along the canyon in about two weeks, but more popular short treks include the waterfall of **Sipia** and the rock forest and salt mines near **Pampamarca**, north of Cotahuasi.

Backpacking and trekking trips of several days' duration can be arranged in Arequipa; some can be combined with the Toro Muerto Petroglyphs, and, if you ask, they may return via a collection of dinosaur footprints on the west edge of the canyon.

Sleeping & Eating

Unless stated otherwise, accommodation is in shared rooms of up to four beds.

Hostal Villa (☎ 58-1018; Independencia 118; r per person US$3) The Villa has a flowery stone courtyard and basic rooms sharing one bathroom, which has hot water.

Hostal Fany Luz (☎ 58-1002; Independencia 117; r per person US$3, s/d with bathroom US$6/7) Opposite Hostal Villa is this friendly place with 11 rooms (some with an ancient black-and-white TV) and two shared bathrooms. Private bathrooms have cold water only.

Alojamiento Chávez (☎ 58-1028; Cabildo 125; r per person US$3) Señor Chávez has a colonial house with a muddy central patio. Ask for hot water in the two shared bathrooms.

Hostal Don Lucho (Centenario 303; r per person US$3) Don Lucho is friendly and has plenty of rooms, sharing two bathrooms. There's a good little restaurant with *menús* for US$1. There is warm water during the day.

In Lucha, **Hostal Wasi Punko** (r per person US$5) is a rustic building with shared bathrooms

with hot showers. In Alca, there's the new **Alcalá** (☎ 28-0455; Plaza de Armas; dm US$3-4, s or d US$5.50, with bathroom US$7), which has a good mix of clean rooms and prices – including some the most comfortable rooms in the whole valley. There is 24-hour hot water here. In Pampamarca, there is only the basic **Casa Albergue** (dm US$3).

Getting There & Away

The 385km bus journey from Arequipa, half of which is on unpaved roads, takes 12 hours if the going is good (US$7). Over three-quarters of the way there, the road summits a 4650m pass between the huge glacier-capped mountains of **Coropuna** (6425m) and **Solimana** (6093m) before dropping down to Cotahuasi. Buses return to Arequipa at 4:30pm and 5pm.

There are hourly combis from Cotahuasi plaza up to Alca (US$0.80, 50 minutes) via Tomepampa and Liucho. For Pampamarca, there is one daily bus at 2pm (US$1.20, one hour).

LAGUNA DE SALINAS

This lake (4300m), east of Arequipa below Pichu Pichu and El Misti, is a salt lake that becomes a white salt flat during the dry months of May to December. Its size and the amount of water in it vary from year to year depending on the weather. During the rainy season it is a good place to see all three flamingo species, as well as other Andean water birds.

Buses to Ubinas (US$4, 3½ hours) pass the lake, but catching a bus from the lake back to Arequipa is difficult because the bus begins at the village of Ubinas and is very full by the time it passes the lake. You can hike around the lake, which can take about two days, then return on the packed daily bus at around 3pm (expect to stand) or catch a lift with workers from the nearby Borax mine. One-day tours from Arequipa cost US$35 per person.

Lake Titicaca Area

The immense Lake Titicaca (3820m above sea level) is accredited with all manner of memorable trivia. Generations of schoolchildren have been taught that this is the highest lake with passenger boat services in the world, while it is also South America's largest lake and the largest lake in the world above 2000m at over 170km in length and 60km in breadth. But it is not the statistics that make this lake such a magical place to visit.

At this altitude, the air is unusually clear, and the luminescent quality of the sunlight suffuses the highland altiplano and sparkles on the deep waters of the lake. Horizons here seem limitless, and the earthy tones of the scenery are reflected in the crumbling colonial churches and ancient funeral towers scattered around the lake's shores.

The port of Puno is a convenient base from which to visit far-flung islands dotted across Titicaca, from the artificial reed islands constructed by the Uros culture to more isolated communities where islanders live their lives much as they have done for centuries.

And there are many other reasons to linger in the area, especially the opportunity to explore the unique intermingling of ancient and colonial cultures. This can be seen in remote and peaceful lakeshore communities where Aymara and Quechua are still the first languages, and to witness their traditions celebrated through wild and colorful folkloric festivals for which the region is world famous.

HIGHLIGHTS

■ **Cultural Encounter**
  Hanging out with islanders on Amantaní (p157) or Taquile (p158)

■ **Archaeology**
  Wandering the windswept Inca funerary towers of Sillustani (p155) and Cutimbo (p156)

■ **History**
  Marveling at the history of the steamboat *Yavari* (p151)

■ **Special Events**
  Catching Candlemas, just one of the region's myriad folkloric festivals, in Puno or Juliaca (p148)

■ **Tourist Pilgrimage**
  Walking on nothing but reeds on the Islas Flotantes (floating islands) of the Uros (p156)

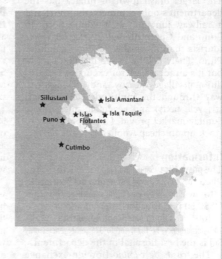

LAKE TITICACA AREA

LAKE TITICACA AREA

0 — 50 km
0 — 30 mi

Pucara · To Cuzco
Lago de Arapa
Huancané
3
Lampa
Cueva de los Toros
Taraco
Moho
108
Aeropuerto Juliaca
Juliaca
Isla Suasi
Tilali
111
To Arequipa
Conima
Puerto Acosta
Isla Soto
B O L I V I A
Sillustani
Llachón
Isla Amantani
Lago Umayo
Isla Taquile
Isla Campanario
112
To Arequipa
Puno
Chimú
Chucuito
Lake Titicaca
Platería
Molleko
Cutimbo
Isla del Sol
Ilave
Isla de la Luna (Koati)
32
Coparabana
Juli
3
Yunguyo
Isla Taquiri
Pomata
Punta Hermosa
Anapia
P E R U
113
Laguna de Huiñaimarca
Zepita
La Paz
Desaguadero
Tiahuanaco
36
To Tacna

JULIACA

☎ 051 / pop 178,500 / elevation 3822m

The large, brash town of Juliaca has the department's only commercial airport and a railway junction with connections to Puno and Cuzco, though it sees far fewer tourists than its smaller lakeside neighbor Puno. There is little to see in Juliaca itself, but it's an ideal base for excursions to traditional villages nearby, and picking your way through the multitude of *trici-taxis* (tricycle taxis) and vegetable piles in the Sunday market provides an opportunity to stock up on cheap woolies.

Information

The **post office** (Sandía 3rd block) is north of the Plaza de Armas and **Telefónica del Peru** (Nuñez) is to the east. **Wayr@net** (Nuñez 5th block) charges US$0.50 per hour for Internet access.

Juliaca's **Clínica Americana Adventista** (☎ 32-1001, emergency 32-1071; Loreto 315; emergencies only Sat) is the best hospital in the department.

The *casas de cambio* (foreign-exchange offices) cluster around the intersection of Bolívar and M Nuñez. There are branches of **BCP** (formerly Banco de Crédito; Nuñez 1st block) and **Interbanc** (Nuñez 2nd block).

Dangers & Annoyances

If you arrive from the coast, especially by air, take it easy for a few days to help avoid problems with the altitude.

Sleeping

Most of the following will give discounts if you ask for their best price.

Hostal Luquini (☎ 32-1510; Bracesco 409; s/d US$4.50/7.50, with bathroom US$7.50/12.50) The recommended Luquini has simple, clean rooms around a courtyard and is run by a charmingly absent-minded family. There is hot water from 5pm till morning.

Hostal San Antonio (☎ 32-1803; San Martín 347; s/d US$3/5, with bathroom US$8/11.50) San Antonio has a large array of basic but clean rooms; the better options are in the new wing with hot showers and national TV. For those without a bathroom, hot showers are an extra US$0.80 for 20 minutes. It also has an attached sauna for US$3, open 9am to 6pm (women only Thursday and Saturday).

Hostal Sakura (☎ 32-2072; San Roman 133; s/d US$6.50/10) Sakura also has a warm family environment, and most rooms have hot showers.

Hostal San Martin (☎ 32-5317; Nuñez 233; s/d US$10/14) This is a fairly new option with plain homey rooms, good showers and cable TV.

La Maison Hotel (☎ 32-1444; fax 32-1763; 7 de Junio 535; s/d/tr US$17/26/35) La Maison has very comfortable if classless rooms with cable TV, plastic chairs and a restaurant open for breakfast.

Hotel Royal Inn (☎ 32-1561; hotel_royal_inn@ latinmail.com; San Román 158; s/d/tr US$20/28/38) An excellent choice for the price, the centrally located Royal Inn boasts newly revamped modern rooms with hot showers and cable TV, plus one of the best restaurants in Juliaca.

Hostal Don Carlos (☎ 32-3600; fax 32-2120; 9 de Diciembre 124; s/d US$32.50/42.50) Though the building isn't ageing as gracefully as it could, Don Carlos has very clean and pleasant rooms with a surprising number of accessories including hairdryer, heating, cable TV and minibar. There is a restaurant and breakfast is included.

Don Carlos Suites Hotel (☎ 32-1571, in Lima 224-0263; dcarloslima@terra.com.pe; Manuel Prado 335; s/d/ste US$65/78/100) Easily the best hotel in town, the large Don Carlos Suites has spacious, new-and-improved rooms in its freshly built extension. The old wing is less plush, but

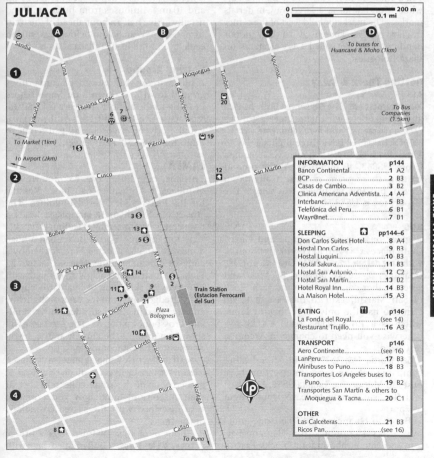

JULIACA

INFORMATION	p144
Banco Continental	**1** A2
BCP	**2** B3
Casas de Cambio	**3** B2
Clinica Americana Adventista	**4** A4
Interbanc	**5** B3
Telefónica del Peru	**6** B1
Wayr@net	**7** B1

SLEEPING	pp144–6
Don Carlos Suites Hotel	**8** A4
Hostal Don Carlos	**9** B3
Hostal Luquini	**10** B3
Hostal Sakura	**11** B3
Hostal San Antonio	**12** C2
Hostal San Martín	**13** D2
Hotel Royal Inn	**14** B3
La Maison Hotel	**15** A3

EATING	p146
La Fonda del Royal	(see 14)
Restaurant Trujillo	**16** A3

TRANSPORT	p146
Aero Continente	(see 16)
LanPeru	**17** B3
Minibuses to Puno	**18** B3
Transportes Los Angeles buses to Puno	**19** B2
Transportes San Martín & others to Moquegua & Tacna	**20** C1

OTHER	
Las Calceteras	**21** B3
Ricos Pan	(see 16)

all rooms boast cable TV, hairdryer and minibar.

Eating & Drinking

Ricos Pan (cnr Unión & Chávez; ☾ closed lunchtime Sun) is the best place for coffee and cake, while **Restaurant Trujillo** (☎ 32-1945; San Roman 163; mains US$3-4.50) is good for more substantial meals and boasts a decent drinks list. However, the restaurant at **La Fonda del Royal** (Hotel Royal Inn; mains US$3-5) is the best in town. There is a paucity of *peñas* here, though discos come and go in the center.

Shopping

If you're hot for some haggling, Juliaca has some of the cheapest prices for alpaca goods you'll find. Sunday is the best market day, while Monday hosts a large, raw-materials market. The market is held west of the center in Plaza Melgar. There is also a daily indoor handicrafts market called 'Las Calceteras' on Plaza Bolognesi.

Getting There & Away

AIR

Juliaca airport (☎ 32-1391) serves both Juliaca and Puno. Between them, **LanPeru** (☎ 32-2228; San Roman 125) and **Aero Continente** (☎ 33-3004; San Roman 154) have three flights a day to Lima (from US$74, 1½ hours) via Arequipa (from US$43, 40 minutes). At the time of writing there were no direct flights to Cuzco, but this is subject to change. The airport tax is US$3.50.

BUS

Regular buses go to Arequipa and Cuzco (both places US$4.20 to US$10, five hours), with **Cruz del Sur** (☎ 32-2011), **Civa** (☎ 32-6229), **Cromotex** (☎ 33-2733), **Ormeño** (☎ 54-5057) and several other companies on the 12th block of San Martín, 1km to the east of town. Ormeño has the only direct bus to Lima, which is a Royal Class service (US$34); otherwise you need to change in Arequipa or Cuzco.

San Martín (☎ 32-7501) and several other companies at the same intersection have buses to Moquegua, Tacna (US$6, 11 hours) and Ilo, which tend to leave around 6pm to 7pm.

Buses to Huancané (US$0.60, one hour) leave every 15 minutes from Benigno Ballón and Sucre, about four blocks east of Apurímac and 1½ blocks north of Lambayeque.

To get to Puno, minibuses (US$0.60, 50 minutes) leave when they are full from the southeast corner of Plaza Bolognesi. Colectivo taxis also leave from here. Larger buses that cost the same depart from 8 de Noviembre at Piérola.

TRAIN

The **train station** (☎ 32-2701) in Juliaca was once at the busiest railway crossroad in Peru, serving Puno, Cuzco and Arequipa. However, improved roads have led to a suspension of services to Arequipa. Trains still run from Puno to Cuzco but can be erratic out of high season. See Puno (p155) for schedules; trains reach Juliaca between 9am and 10am. Minibuses from Juliaca to Puno usually arrive half an hour ahead of the train from Cuzco. Watch your belongings with an eagle eye in the ill-lit Juliaca station.

Getting Around

A bus with an 'Aeropuerto' placard cruises around town and down 2 de Mayo before heading to the airport. The fare is US$0.30. Taxis cost US$1.25 to US$2. At the airport, you'll find colectivos heading directly to Puno for US$1.50 a passenger.

LAMPA

This charming little town, 23km northwest of Juliaca, is known as 'La Ciudad Rosada' for its dusty, pink-colored buildings. The attractive church of **La Inmaculada** holds a few secrets worth seeing: Leading local citizen Don Enrique Torres Belón had a huge domed tomb constructed here, topped by a copy of Michelangelo's famous statue La Pieta. The structure below it is lined with hundreds of skeletons of Spaniards apparently dredged up from the catacombs below and arranged in ghoulishly decorative, skull-and-crossbones patterns. The caretaker will show you around the church and take you down into the catacombs for a tip.

Staff at the tiny **Kamping museum** (Ugarte 462; voluntary admission) will give you an enthusiastic guided tour of the small collection and, at their discretion, may show you a unique vase inscribed with the sacred cosmology of the Incas.

About 6km west of town over a bridge is **Cueva de los Toros**, a bull-shaped cave with prehistoric carvings of llamas and other animals. The cave is in some rocks on the right side of the road and en route, you'll see several *chullpas* (funerary towers) not unlike the ones at Sillustani (p155).

Most visitors come on day trips, but you could overnight at the friendly **Hospedaje Milam** (Juan José 513; dm US$1.50). Combis leave when full from Avenida Huáscar in Juliaca (US$0.80, 45 minutes), near the market. They return from Lampa to Juliaca to 2 de Mayo, again near the market area.

NORTHWEST OF JULIACA

Almost 56km northwest of Juliaca, the sleepy village of **Pucara** (pop 2500) is famous for its earthy colored ceramics – not least the *toritos* (bulls) often seen perched on the roofs of Andean houses for good luck. Asking around on weekdays will lead you to several workshops. There is also the **Museo Litico Pucara** (adult/student US$1.40/1; 8am-5pm) displaying a surprisingly good little selection of anthropomorphic monoliths from the town's pre-Inca site, which was connected to the ancient Tiahuanaco culture. **Hostal Turistico** (051-68 0065; s or d with bathroom US$6) is a new hostel with a restaurant looking somewhat lonesome on the highway by the bus stop.

Almost 100km northwest of Juliaca is **Ayaviri**, the first sizable town on the route to Cuzco. At 3928m above sea level, it is a bustling, chilly market town with a colonial church, and a few kilometers away are the hot springs of **Poypoy Kella**. There are several simple hotels, including the friendly **Hotel Paraíso** (86-3024; Prado 254; s/d US$3.50/7) with bathrooms and hot water.

From here, the route climbs for 70km through bleak altiplano to **Abra La Raya**, a pass at 4319m and the highest point on the trip to Cuzco. Buses often stop here, to allow passengers to take advantage of the cluster of handicrafts sellers and the view of snowcapped mountains. The pass also marks the departmental line between Puno and Cuzco, and places beyond here are described in Southeast of Cuzco (p216) in the following chapter.

SOUTHWEST OF JULIACA

The pretty little village community of **Llachón** is found on the Peninsula of Capachica, which offers some fantastic views and short hikes to surrounding pre-Inca sites. It's an area that sees very few tourists, but families here will happily welcome visitors into their rudimentary homes and cook all their meals for around US$4. A boat from Puno runs at 9am every Wednesday and Saturday (US$3 one way, 2½ hours).

TO/FROM BOLIVIA VIA THE NORTH SHORE

This little-traveled route into Bolivia is recommended only for hardy off-the-beaten-track travelers with little concern for time or comfort. First get an exit stamp from Peruvian migracions and ask them to predate the stamp by three days. Then catch a regular combi from Juliaca to the small town of **Huancané** (see Getting There & Away p146) where you can stay at **Hostal Samana Wasi** (Puno 1127; s/d US$5.50/9), near to where the buses from Juliaca stop, or at the very basic **Hostal Huancané** (Lima 309; r per person US$3) on the Plaza de Armas.

Several buses and trucks leave daily from Juliaca and Huancané on the unpaved road to the friendly little villages of **Moho** (US$1.50, two hours) and **Conima**, though they get crowded so you may have to stand. There are a couple of unsigned and basic *alojamientos* (lodging houses) for around US$1.40 per person on the cobbled streets just off the main plaza in Moho. The town's electricity is limited, so bring spare batteries for your flashlight.

A truck runs from Moho to Bolivia most mornings, leaving well before dawn but you can walk about five hours to Conima, on the shores of Lake Titicaca, then follow the shore for another two hours to **Tilali** near the Bolivian border. From there, it's about four more hours to the nearest Bolivian town of **Puerto Acosta**. There are very few vehicles, so don't count on hitchhiking. It's possible to stay on Isla Suasi (see p159), near Conima.

A night bus goes from Juliaca to Tilali via Huancané, Moho and Conima leaving Juliaca from the 10th block of Lambayeque, at the corner with the Colegio Encinas, on Tuesday, Friday and Sunday. From Tilali, buses/trucks head to Puerto Acosta in Bolivia. There is a big weekend market in Tilali, and it becomes easier to find transport to Puerto Acosta, but you might get stuck midweek. There are no hotels, but local families have rooms to stay in.

LAKE TITICACA AREA

The police on the border can be unhelpful, so make sure your documents are in order. Ask them where the Bolivian migraciónes currently is to get your passport stamped. Transportation out of nearby Puerto Acosta does not leave regularly, so take the first vehicle you can, be it truck or bus, heading toward La Paz.

The nearest Bolivian consulate is in Puno. Also see p161 for information about entering Bolivia via simpler, more popular routes.

PUNO

☎ 051 / pop 102,800 / elevation 3830m

The small port of Puno is by far the most convenient departure point to make forays to Lake Titicaca's various islands or to surrounding archaeological sites. Also the capital of its department, the town was founded on November 4, 1668, near the site of the now-defunct silver mine called Laykakota. Few colonial buildings remain, but the claustrophobic streets are busy with *trici-taxis* and the markets filled with local women garbed in many-layered dresses and bowler hats, lending them a charming resemblance to pepperpots.

Puno's high altitude gives it extreme weather conditions. Nights here get especially cold, particularly during the winter months of June to August, when temperatures can drop well below freezing. But luckily, Puno stocks plenty of thick alpaca

---

FIESTAS & FOLKLORE AROUND LAKE TITICACA

Puno is oft said to be the folklore capital of Peru, boasting as many as 300 traditional dances and celebrating numerous fiestas throughout the year. Although they often occur during celebrations of Catholic feast days, many dances usually have their roots in preconquest celebrations usually tied in with the agricultural calendar. The dazzlingly ornate and imaginative costumes worn on these occasions are often worth more than an entire household's everyday clothes, and range from strikingly grotesque masks or animal costumes to glittering sequined uniforms.

Accompanying musicians play a host of traditional instruments from Spanish-influenced brass and string to percussion and wind instruments that have changed little since Inca times. The ancient instruments include *tinyas* (hand drums) and *wankaras* (larger drums), and of course there has to be a chorus of panpipes, which range from tiny, high-pitched instruments to huge base panpipes almost as tall as the musician. Also, keep an eye out for the *flautas* (flutes), ranging from simple bamboo pennywhistles called *quenas*, to large blocks that look as though they've been hollowed out of a plank of wood. The most esoteric is the *piruru*, which is carved from the wing bone of an Andean condor.

Seeing street fiestas can be planned, or can simply be a matter of luck. Some celebrations are held in one town and not in another or, at other times, the whole region lets loose. Ask at the tourist office in Puno about any fiestas in the surrounding area.

The following are fiestas that are particularly important in the Lake Titicaca region, but many country-wide celebrations are used as an excuse for a party. Candlemas is one of the most spectacular and is spread out for several days around the actual date, depending upon which day of the week Candlemas falls. If it falls on a Sunday to Tuesday, things get under way the previous Saturday; if it falls on a Wednesday to Friday, things get going the following Saturday. Puno Week is also celebrated in style, marking the legendary birth of Manco Capac, the first Inca.

This list of holidays and fiestas is not exhaustive. Most are celebrated for several days before and after the actual day:

special event	date
Epiphany	6 January
Candlemas (or Virgen de la Candelaria)	2 February
Saint John	7-8 March
Alacitas (Puno miniature handicrafts fair), Holy Cross (Huancané, Taquile)	2-4 May
Saint James (Taquile)	25 July
Our Lady of Mercy	24 September
Puno Week	1-7 November

PUNO

0 _____ 0.2 mi
0 _____ 0.4 km

Lake Titicaca

LAKE TITICACA AREA

sweaters in its markets. Despite the cold, the sun is very strong at this altitude and sunburn is a common problem, so remember your hat and sunblock.

Information

IMMIGRATION

Migraciónes (☎ 35-7103; Ayacucho 240; ⏱ 8am-2pm Mon-Fri) will extend Peruvian visas and tourist cards, though it can be quicker and easier to go to Bolivia and return.

INTERNET ACCESS

Choza@net (2nd fl, Lima 339; ⏱ 8am-11pm; US$0.60 per hr)

Puno Line (Lima 288; ⏱ 8am-11pm; US$0.50 per hr) Slower but has more machines.

LAUNDRY

Lavaclin (Valcárcel 1st block; ⏱ 8am-noon & 2-7pm Mon-Sat; US$1.40 per kg) A wash and a dry takes eight hours.

Lavandería Don Manuel (☎ 35-2444; Lima 4th block; ⏱ 7am-6pm Mon-Sat; US$1.40 per kg) Staff can get clothes back to you by the following day.

MEDICAL SERVICES

Botica Fasa (☎ 36-5543; Arequipa 314) A good 24-hour pharmacy.

Regional Hospital (☎ 35-2931; El Sol 1022) OK but the best regional hospital is in Juliaca (see p144).

MONEY

Bolivian pesos can be exchanged in Puno or at the border near Yunguyo; rates vary so ask travelers coming from Bolivia which is currently the best choice. Moneychangers hang outside the banks, but check your change carefully.

BCP (cnr Lima & Grau) Has a Visa ATM and gives cash advances from Visa cards.

Interbanc (Lima 4th block) ATM for Plus, Visa and Cirrus networks, and changes traveler's checks.

POST & TELEPHONE

Post office (☎ 35-1141; Moquegua 267; ⏱ 8am-6pm Mon-Sat, 8am-1pm Sun) About 200m east of Plaza de Armas.

Telefónica del Peru (cnr Moquegua & El Puerto)

TOURIST INFORMATION

The website www.titicacaalmundo.com has good general information on the area.

Indecopi (☎ 36-6138; cnr Lima & Arbulu) The place to register serious complaints against agencies or hotels.

iPeru (☎ 36-5088; Lima 549; iperupuno@promperu.gob .pe; ⏱ 8:30am-7:30pm) Puno's very helpful and friendly main tourist office.

Policía de Turismo (Deustua 588; ⏱ 24hr) By Plaza de Armas, it provides help in cases of emergency.

Dangers & Annoyances

The elevation means that travelers run a real risk of getting *soroche* (altitude sickness) if arriving directly from the coast. Rather than flying in from Lima, plan on spending time in Arequipa (2325m) or Cuzco (3326m) to acclimatize.

Sights & Activities

The **Plaza de Armas** sports neatly trimmed and shaped bushes in various suggestive shapes; on its western flank is the baroque **cathedral** (⏱ 8am-noon & 3-5pm), completed in 1757. The interior is more spartan than you'd expect after seeing the well-sculpted facade, though there is a silver-plated altar that, following a 1964 visit by Pope Paul VI, has a Vatican flag to its right.

Just off the plaza is the 17th-century **Casa del Corregidor** (☎ 35-1921; www.casadelcorregidor.com.pe; Deustua 576; admission free; ⏱ 10am-10pm Tue-Fri, 10am-2:30pm & 5-10pm Sat), one of Puno's oldest houses, which has been converted into a cultural center and café/bar. Around the corner from here is the small **Museo Carlos Dreyer** (Conde de Lemos 289; adult/student US$0.80/0.20; ⏱ 7:30am-3:30pm Mon-Fri), which houses a collection of assorted archaeology that was bequeathed to the city upon the owner's death.

The **Museo Naval** (☎ 35-3192; cnr El Puerto & El Sol; ⏱ 9am-5pm Mon-Fri, 9am-1pm Sat-Sun), near the port, has a fascinating if tiny exhibit on navigating the lake, from rudimentary reed boats up to the 19th-century steamers.

A 10-minute walk southwest of town brings you to **Huajsapata Park** atop a little hill crowned by a larger-than-life white statue of the first Inca Manco Capac looking out over the legendary site of his birth. The view is excellent but do not walk here alone; several robberies have been reported. The same applies with the walk to **Arco Deusta**, an arch built to commemorate war heroes, which has good views.

Although the frothy green waters of the lake make going for a swim unappealing, the **Bahia Club** has a pool (admission US$1.40) 2km outside town towards Chimú.

THE YAVARI PROJECT

The much-loved *Yavari* (☎ 36-9329, 962-2215; yavaricondor@terra.com.pe; admission free; ✆ 8am-10pm) is the oldest steamship on Lake Titicaca. In 1862, the *Yavari* and its sister ship, the *Yapura*, were built in England of iron parts – a total of 2766 for the two vessels. These were shipped around Cape Horn to Arica, from where they were moved by train to Tacna, before incredibly being hauled by mule over the Andes to Puno – an undertaking that took six years to complete.

The ships were assembled in Puno and the *Yavari* was launched on Christmas Day 1870, followed by the *Yapura* 17 months later. (The *Yapura* was later renamed the *BAP Puno* and became a Peruvian Navy medical ship; it can still be seen in Puno.) Both had coal-powered steam engines, but due to a shortage of coal, the engines were powered by dried llama dung! To make room for the fuel, the *Yavari* was cut in half, and an extra 12m of length was added to the hull, and in 1914, it was further modified with a unique Bolinder four-cylinder, hot-bulb, semi-diesel engine.

After long years of service, the ship was decommissioned by the Peruvian Navy and the hull was left to rust on the lakeshore, but in 1982, Englishwoman Meriel Larken visited the forgotten boat and decided it was a piece of history that could and should be saved. She formed the Yavari Project to buy and restore the vessel, and was fortunate in gaining the royal support of Britain's Prince Philip as well as finding the perfect captain in the enthusiastic Carlos Saavedra, formerly of the Peruvian Navy.

Now open as a museum, the *Yavari* is moored by the Sonesta Posada Hotel del Inca. The captain happily gives guided tours of the ship and, with prior notice, enthusiasts can see the engine fired up. In 1999 to mark the restoration of the engine, the *Yavari* left port under her own power for the first time in nearly half a century, and in the foreseeable future the vessel should be ready for passage across Lake Titicaca.

The Yavari Project is looking for support both in the way of finance and volunteers. To send donations and receive information, contact the **Yavari Project** (☎ /fax 44-20-8874-0583; yavari.larken@virgin.net; 61 Mexfield Rd, London, SW15 2RG, UK) or call direct to the captain in Puno.

Tours

It pays to shop around agencies in Puno. Several of the cheaper tour agencies have reputations for ripping off the islanders of Amantaní and Taquile so ask how your money will be distributed. Also beware of street touts hanging around the popular gringo hotels and on the train from Cuzco. Never part with your money until you are in a hotel or travel agency or you may never see the guide again.

Agencies with good reputations include:

All Ways Travel (☎ 35-5552; awtperu@terra.com.pe; Tacna 234) This is an excellent agency run by helpful multilingual staff and has a more responsible attitude to the islanders than most. This agency is also good for more off-the-beaten track options and sometimes organizes posts for volunteers.

Edgar Adventures (☎ 35-3444; edgaradventures@terra.com.pe; Lima 328) An agency that receives positive recommendations, it's run by the enthusiastic and knowledgeable Edgar and Norka, who both speak English and use good guides.

Inka Travel (☎ 36-9877; inkatravel@terra.com.pe; Ugarte 156) This company is also fairly efficient with the standard tours.

Kollasuyo Tours (☎ 36-8642; kollasuyos@terra.com; Valcárcel 155) A newer agency, Kollasuyo is recommended for organizing slightly more flexible tours.

For water-borne trips to Bolivia, see p161.

Sleeping

The prices given here are for the June to August high season and fiestas. Prices drop to as much as half during other months, and bargaining can almost always reap rewards.

BUDGET

Some barest-bones hostels in Puno have only cold showers, which can be painful at this altitude. If you want to economize yet avoid freezing off any appendages, use the public hot showers dotted around town, which charge US$1 for a 30-minute shower between 7am and 7pm. Most of these budget haunts drop their prices especially low in the low season; take full advantage.

Hostal Los Uros (☎ 35-2141; Valcárcel 135; s/d/tr US$5/8/12, with bathroom US$6/10/14) This clean, quiet and decent choice, which is often full, has hot water in the evenings and mornings plus a cafeteria open for early simple breakfasts. There are few single rooms.

Hospedaje Virgen de Copacabana (☎ 36-3766; llave 228; r per person US$4) This friendly YHA-affiliated hostel has clean homely rooms with shared bathrooms, tucked off the road on a narrow passageway. It's good value for the price tag.

Hostal Q'oñi Wasi (☎ 36-5784; qoniwasi@mundo mail.net; Av La Torre 119; s/d US$4/7, with bathroom US$7/10) The small and quirky Q'oñi Wasi has snug, older rooms, electric showers and smiley service.

Hostal Europa (☎ 35-3026; heuropa@punoalmundo .com; Ugarte 112; s/d US$4/6, with bathroom US$7/12) Surrounded by local flower sellers, the Europa has standard, good-value rooms and hot water all day. Those rooms with bathrooms also have thick, cozy duvets and national TV.

Hostal Los Pinos (☎ 36-7398; hostalpinos@hot mail.com; Tarapacá 182; s/d US$10/15) A highly recommended budget hostel, Los Pinos has large, spotless rooms and an exceptionally warm welcome.

Don Julio (☎ 36-3358; hostaldonjulio@hotmail .com; Tacna 336; s/d/tr US$10/15/20) Run by a very friendly family, Don Julio has a relaxed atmosphere, and is set back from the road in a quiet courtyard. Rooms have cable TV and heating on request. Breakfast is included.

Hospedaje Margarita (☎ 35-2820; hostalmargarita@ terra.com.pe; Tarapaca 130; s/d US$10/15) This long-established choice has cozy rooms with national TV, and hot showers are available between 5:30am and 10pm. Breakfast is included in the price.

Pachacutec (☎ 36-4827; Arbulu 235; s/d US$11/ 15.50) A popular, neat little place, Pachacutec has well-cared-for rooms with hot showers, and accommodating hosts. Rates include breakfast.

Santa Maria (☎ 36-8608; hssantamaria@terra.com; Ugarte 171; s/d US$4/6, with bathroom US$10/13/18) Another friendly and personable choice, the Santa Maria has smart if spartan rooms and 24-hour hot water. The rooms without bathrooms are uncarpeted and more basic.

Hostal Monterrey (☎ 35-1691; servicios@hostal monterrey.com; Lima 441; s/d US$3/4, with bathroom US$5.50/9) The Monterrey is right in the thick of things on the main pedestrianized boulevard. The hot showers have erratic hours, and rooms without bathrooms are basic

compared to those with, which are very comfortable and boast cable TV.

Other recommendations are:

Hotel Internacional (☎ 35-2109; Libertad 161; s/d/tr US$10/15/20) Well-worn-in rooms with cable TV and reliable hot water.

Hotel Arequipa (☎ 36-3303; Arequipa 153; r per person with shared bathroom US$5, s/d/tr with bathroom US$10/12/20) Comfortable with good bathrooms.

Hostal Imperial (☎ 35-2386; Valcárcel 145; s/d US$12/20) Clean though colorless, with hot showers.

Hostal Inti (☎ 35-1594; Torre 137; r per person US$3, s/d with bathroom US$7/11) Very varied rooms and electric showers.

Hostal Rosario (☎ 35-2272; Moquegua 325; r per person US$3) Cold shared showers but consistently cheap.

MID-RANGE

Totorani (☎ 36-4535; totoranihostal@hotmail.com; Av La Torre 463; s/d/tr US$15/20/25) A short walk from the center is this small, new, family-run place in sparkling nick, with good, firm beds, quality furnishings and heating.

Ollanta Inn (☎ 36-6743; ollanta_inn@latinmail.com; Ilo E-1; s/d US$15/25) Just off Los Incas by a military center, this hostel has cramped but cozy rooms with flowery decoration and cable TV in a narrow, elongated building.

Posada Don Giorgio (☎ 36-3648; dongiorgio@ titicacalake.com; Tarapacá 238; s/d/tr US$24/33/45) An excellent choice with a classic, mellow interior and exceptionally comfy rooms, Don Giorgio is still small enough to have personal service. The rooms have a phone, cable TV and deep armchairs. Rates include breakfast.

Hostal Pukara (☎ 36-8448; pukara@terra.com.pe; Libertad 328; s/d US$25/40) The Pukara is a quirky hostel that strives to leave no corner undecorated. It has an eye-catching four-story-high relief in the entrance, plus murals, unusual tiling and other touches throughout the hallways. Rooms are heated, have cable TV and phone, and rates include breakfast in a glass-covered rooftop café.

Tikarani Misthycal (☎ 36-5501; fax 36-8448; Independencia 143, no sign; s/d US$25/40) This funky, new choice is run by the owners of Pukara and is decorated with the same eye for detail. Walls are decked out in bold, primary colors, stars hang from the ceiling and stone, tiling and modern furnishings are harmoniously combined. There are also lofty, open-plan public areas for lounging and a restaurant below. Breakfast is included. The hostel is set back from the road and can be hard to distinguish.

Hotel Ferrocarril (☎ 35-1752; mail@hotelferrocarril .com; Avenida La Torre 185; s/d/tr US$33/44/55) Though it has seen grander days, this large railway hotel retains old-fashioned, attentive service and has comfortable rooms with cable TV, phone and heating. Rates include breakfast in the restaurant below it.

Maria Angola Hostal (☎ 36-4596; mariaangola@ punored.com; Bolognesi 190; s/d/tr US$36/53/65) Situated away from the hustle of the center, the Maria Angola has a fixation with intricately carved, wood paneling and doors. It offers big reductions in low season.

Hostal Italia (☎ 36-3639; hitalia@hotelesonline .net; Valcárcel 122; s/d/tr US$33/44/55) Rooms vary in quality at this large, bland but well-established mid-range choice. It is generally good value, however, with cable TV and heating. Rates include a buffet breakfast.

Joya del Titicaca (☎ 35-1823; joyadeltiticaca_hotel@ hotmail.com; Arequipa 522; s/d/tr US$15/20/30, with bathroom US$36/46/60) Highly recommended by readers, Joya has quality rooms with alpaca furnishings and cable TV. French, Italian and some English are spoken.

Hostal Hacienda (☎ 35-6109; Deustua 297; s/d/tr US$40/53/69) This excellent, little, colonial-style hotel has an intimate patio covered in trailing plants and warm-colored rooms boasting cable TV, heating and phone. Rates include breakfast.

Qelqatani Hotel (☎ 36-6172; qelqatani@punonet .com; Tarapata 355; s/d/ste US$43/56/85) Qelqatani is a large, modern hotel with helpful staff and spacious rooms with heaters, cable TV and radio alarms. It has first-class, spotless bathrooms with a tub and shower. A full buffet breakfast is included.

Best Western Colón Inn (☎ 35-1432; colon@ titicaca-peru.com; Tacna 290; s/d/tr US$45/53/69) This central, colonial-style hotel is well known for promoting responsible tourism in the area. It has classy rooms with all the modern facilities, a restaurant and room service as well as a tiny indoor patio dripping with plants.

Plaza Mayor (☎ 36-6089; reservas@plazamayorhostal .com; Deusta 342; s/d US$43/56) The Plaza Mayor is a high-class, newly renovated hotel right by the Plaza de Armas with a glamorous entrance and very comfy rooms. Service here can be almost ridiculously attentive. Rates include a breakfast buffet.

TOP END

Eco Inn (☎ 36-5525; ecoinn@terra.com.pe; Chulluni 195; s/d US$60/65; **P**) The small, new Eco Inn has exceptionally light and airy rooms, with large windows and a glass-walled restaurant looking out to its three pet alpacas in the attached enclosure. Rates include breakfast.

Sonesta Posada del Inca (☎ 36-4111; posada@so nestaperu.com; Sequicentenario 610; s/d US$77/90; **P**) This recent addition to the Posada chain is 5km from Puno on the shores of Lake Titicaca. Half of the pleasantly decorated 62 rooms (two are designed for wheelchairs) have lake views, and all have cable TV, telephone and heating. A good restaurant and bar offer lake-view dining and the hotel's extensive lawn runs down to where the steamship Yavari is moored.

Hotel Libertador Isla Esteves (☎ 36-7780, in Lima 442-0166; hpuno@libertador.com.pe; Isla Esteves; r/ste US$150/215; **P** **⊠**) This local landmark dominates its own private island in the western part of Lake Titicaca. The island is connected to Puno by a 6km road over a causeway. Taxis charge about US$2.50 for the trip or you can hop on one of the frequent combis from the northeastern edge of Puno (US$0.20). Half of the 126 luxurious rooms and all the five suites have fabulous views out over the lake plus there are beautiful gardens on the islands slopes, and a collection of 34 pet llamas. There is also a good restaurant, bar and gift shop.

Eating

Tourist haunts huddle together on the glitzy pedestrian street of Calle Lima. Note that many don't advertise their set meals (el menú), which are cheaper than à la carte. All serve the requisite banana pancakes and during the evening, many welcome visitors with a flaming cauldron in the doorway to warm your hands by.

CAFÉS

Ricos Pan (☎ 35-4179; Lima 424 and Moquegua 330; ☺ open early, closed Sun) This cool, calm and modern café is an invaluable escape from the heaving masses on Calle Lima; the larger branch on Moquegua is the best bakery in town with great coffees and melt-in-the-mouth cakes.

Casa del Corregidor (see Sights & Activities p150; ☺ closed Mon) This café, housed within the Casa del Corregidor, a 17th-century place, is a great place to hobnob with the local well-to-do over a cappuccino and pastry. It also has a decent book exchange and newspapers to browse.

RESTAURANTS

IncAbar (☎ 36-8031; Lima 348; mains US$5-7; ✆ closed lunch Sat) This stylish restaurant has creative international food with a local twist, such as alpaca with whisky and curried chicken with papaya.

La Casona (☎ 35-1108; Lima 517; mains US$2-6) La Casona, which calls itself a 'restaurant-museum', retains an old-fashioned 1920s air with its collection of antique irons lining the walls. It serves typical local food and a lovingly prepared *pejerrey* (kingfish).

La Estancia (☎ 36-5469; Libertad 137; mains US$3-6) This curvy, country-style building houses a mellow restaurant with a wide range of dishes. Try its spicy 'chicken in fire.'

Restaurant Don Piero (☎ 36-5943; Lima 364; mains US$3-5) Don Piero doesn't match the other restaurants on Calle Lima for glitz, but has excellent local food and an elegant simplicity; the number of locals dining here is testament to its quality. There's music at 7pm daily.

Apu Salkantay (☎ 36-3955; Lima 425; mains US$3-6) This rustic, popular place serves up local dishes as well as good pizza, and has live *música folklórica* every night. Try its mixed *flambre salkantay*, which includes alpaca, trout and sweet potato.

La Hostería (☎ 35-1424; Lima 501; mains US$3.50-5, 3-course menú US$4; ✆ closed lunch Sun) Popular for pizzas, La Hostería also has great apple pie and chocolate cake. The space around its low, semi-circular bar is also well heated; a good asset in Puno.

Keros (☎ 36-4602; Lambayeque 131; 3-course menú US$4-5.50; ✆ closed lunch Sun) The low-key Keros has some nice variations on typical local dishes, such as its excellent trout served with wine and almond sauce.

Plaza Restaurant (☎ 35-1424; Puno 425; mains US$4.50-7) This large restaurant on the plaza has a surreptitiously jazzy feel with subtle, leopard-print cloths and mirrored walls. It serves great fish dishes.

Ukuku's (☎ 36-7373; Lima 332; mains US$2.50-6; ✆ closed Sat) Crowds of travelers and locals thaw out in this balmy restaurant based in the heart of gringo central and serving both good local and Andean food typical of the area, and pizza.

Porton Colonial (☎ 36-4989; Lima 345; mains US$3-6) This tiny, backpacker-friendly place has a low, curvaceous ceiling woven with bamboo, and seating insulated with llama skins. The food can be so-so here, but it has a good atmosphere.

VEGETARIAN

Vida Natural (☎ 36-6386; Libertad 449; 3-course menú US$1.40-3; ✆ closed Sat) This friendly, little vegetarian place is run by a certified nutritionist and has an excellent, wide-ranging menu.

Govinda (Deusta 312; 3-course menú US$1-2; ✆ closes 8pm) True to form, Govinda serves up its usual hearty *menús* without burning a hole in your pocket.

Entertainment

Musicians do the rounds of all the restaurants, playing a half-hour set of *música folklórica*, passing the hat, and then moving on. Though central Puno's nightlife is geared toward the tourists, plenty of lively local bars are scattered around beyond the bright lights on Lima.

Ekeko's (Lima 355; ✆ 7pm-late) Travelers tend to gravitate to Ekeko's tiny, ultraviolet dancefloor splashed with psychedelic murals and moving to a thumping mixture of modern beats and the old favorites that can be heard several blocks away.

Kamizaraky Rock Pub (Pasaje Grau 148; ✆ 5pm-late) This intimate, laid-back bar hands out free *cuba libres* to lure its punters in and plays a classic travelers' soundtrack to keep them there.

Shopping

Puno is a good town to get quality, woolen and alpaca sweaters at a fair price. These items are sold at the open-air **handicrafts market** on the corner of Cahuide and Duesta and near the railway station. The lively **Mercado Central** is also a great place to explore but watch for pickpockets.

Getting There & Away

AIR

The nearest airport is in Juliaca, about 44km away. Several travel agents in Puno will sell tickets and provide shuttle service direct to the airport for about US$2.50 per person, though this service can be painfully slow. **Tans** (☎ 36-7227; Tacna 299) is currently the only airline with an office in Puno.

See Juliaca (p146) for further information about flights.

BOAT
There are no boats from Puno to Bolivia, but bus services can connect with pricey hydrofoil and catamaran services in Bolivia (see p161). Boats from the Puno dock leave for various islands in the lake. Tickets bought directly from the boats at the dock are invariably cheaper than those bought from agencies in town.

In the future, the *Yavari* (see the boxed text p151) will provide services on the lake.

BUS
Terminal Terrestre, 2km southeast of the town center, now houses all of Puno's long-distance bus companies. There is a departure tax of US$0.30 for all passengers. The roads to Arequipa and Cuzco are now paved and fast efficient services run to Lima (21 to 25 hours), Arequipa (five hours) and Cuzco (six hours), as well as to the Bolivian border.

For information on buses to south-shore towns and the Bolivian border see South-shore Towns (p159) and To/From Bolivia via Puno (p161)

Ormeño (☎ 962-2155) has the most luxurious buses that go daily to Lima (US$35), Arequipa (US$9) and Cuzco (US$7) with its Royal Class service, while **Cruz del Sur** (☎ 35-2451) has cheaper buses to Arequipa (US$4.20, five hours, three daily) and Cuzco (US$3.70, six hours, daily). **Civa** (☎ 36-5882), **Julsa** (☎ 36-4080) and several others also have buses to Cuzco, Arequipa and Lima for similar prices.

To get to Tacna (10 hours), try **San Martín** (☎ 36-3631), which has four daily departures for US$6 to US$7.

Buses for Arequipa and Cuzco go via Juliaca (US$0.60, 50 minutes), and minibuses also run there from Terminal Zonal, the new local terminal just a few blocks before Terminal Terrestre.

First Class (☎ 36-5192; firstclass@terra.com.pe; Lima 177) and **Inka Express** (☎ 36-5654; Tacna 2nd block) run comfortable tour buses to Cuzco every morning. The US$25 fare includes beverages and an English-speaking tour guide, who talks about sites that are briefly visited en route, including Pucara (p147), Abra La Raya Pass (p147), Sicuani (p217),

Raqchi (p217), Andahuayillas (p216) and Pikillacta (p216).

TRAIN
Puno's **train station** (☎ 36-9179; puno@perurail.com; ☉ 7am-noon & 2-5pm Mon-Fri, 7-11am Sat-Sun) is on Avenida La Torre. It currently only has trains to Cuzco following the suspension of the service to Arequipa.

First-class fares to Cuzco have also tripled in recent years – they are now US$83 for Inca class (or US$71 during promotions), which includes lunch and a bar, and US$14 in the more basic Turismo class where meals are not included. This line has a 50% reduction on Inca-class tickets if you purchase them 24 hours in advance.

The train leaves at 8am on Monday, Wednesday and Thursday from June to August, supposedly arriving at 6pm though it's often hours late. During other months, the service officially runs on Monday, Wednesday and Saturday, though this is subject to whether there are enough passengers and the line suffers routine cancellations. Trains also occasionally run on other days for group bookings made by travel agents; it is therefore essential to check at the station.

The first few kilometers of the journey to Cuzco have great views along the shores of Lake Titicaca, but note that even in the best class, seats are not very comfortable, and the ride is known for being a bit of a bone-shaker. Most travelers now take the faster bus service to Cuzco.

Getting Around
A short taxi ride anywhere in town should cost about US$1. One taxi-cab company to call is **Movil** (☎ 36-8000). Tricycle taxis are a fun way of getting around Puno and are cheaper than ordinary taxis. A short ride in town will cost US$0.35 to US$0.70.

SILLUSTANI
The Colla people that once dominated the Lake Titicaca area were a warlike, Aymara-speaking tribe, which later became the southeastern arm of the Incas. The Colla, along with their sparring partners, the rival Lupaca tribe, buried their nobility in funerary towers called *chullpas* that can be seen scattered widely around the hilltops of the region. The most impressive of these are those at **Sillustani** (admission US$1.40), where the

tallest reaches a height of 12m. Sitting on rolling hills in the Lake Umayo peninsula, the towers of Sillustani stand out for miles against the bleak landscape.

The cylindrical structures once housed the remains of complete family groups, along with plenty of food and belongings for their journey into the next world. Their only opening was a small hole facing east, just large enough for a person to crawl through, which would be sealed immediately after a burial.

The outside walls of the towers are made from massive coursed blocks reminiscent of Inca stonework, but considered even more complicated (perhaps because conservationists are struggling to rebuild some of them). Carved but unplaced blocks and a ramp used to raise them are among the points of interest at the site, and you can also see the site of their makeshift quarry. A few of the blocks are also decorated, including the well-known carving of a lizard on one of the *chullpas* closest to the car park.

Sillustani is partially encircled by the sparkling Lago Umayo (3890m), which is home to a wide variety of plants and Andean waterbirds, plus a small island with vicuña. There is a small on-site museum and gift shop. Dress warmly and bring sunblock.

Getting There & Away

Agencies run tours that usually leave Puno at 2:30pm and cost at least US$6, including the entrance fee. The round trip takes about 3½ hours and allows you about 1½ hours at the ruins plus a stop at a specially built 'traditional' homestead nearby. The afternoon light is the best for photography, though the site can get crowded in the afternoon. If you prefer more time at the site, you could hire a taxi for US$12 with waiting time or catch any bus to Juliaca and ask to be let off at where the road splits. From there, occasional combis run to the village of Atuncolla (US$0.60, 10 minutes), 4km from the ruins. In high-season they will occasionally continue to the ruins but don't bank on this.

CUTIMBO

This dramatic windswept **site** (admission US$1) has an extraordinary position atop a table-topped volcanic hill surrounded by a plain, 22km from Puno. Its modest number of well-preserved *chullpas*, built by the Colla,

Lupaca and Inca cultures, are concentrated in a small area and come in both square and cylindrical shapes. You can still see the ramps used to build them. Look closely and you'll find several monkeys, pumas and snakes carved into the structures.

Combis en route to Laraqueri leave the cemetery by Parque Amista, 1km from Puno center (US$0.50, 25 minutes). You can't miss the site, which is a steep 500m climb up from the road. A taxi to both Sillustani and Cutimbo will cost US$20 with waiting time.

ISLAS FLOTANTES

The unique **Islas Flotantes** (Floating Islands; admission US$0.60) of the Uros people (and often referred to as the Uros Islands) are Lake Titicaca's top tourist attraction, and though in some areas their popularity has led to shocking over-commercialization, there is still nothing quite like them to be found anywhere else.

Intermarriage with the Aymara-speaking Indians has seen the demise of the pure-blooded Uros, who nowadays all speak Aymara. Always a small tribe, they began their unusual floating existence centuries ago in an effort to isolate themselves from the aggressive Collas and the Incas. Today, several hundred people still live on the islands and eke out a living with fishing and tourism.

The biggest of the islands contains several buildings, including a school, post office and of course, an overabundance of souvenir shops. The inhabitants of some islands have also built rickety observation platforms from which to survey the surroundings. There used to be a problem with begging and, while this has abated somewhat, you are asked not to give candy to the kids.

The Uros usually have an elaborately designed version of their tightly bundled reed boats on hand to offer tourists a ride to another island (US$0.60 to US$1). When they are made well, these unmistakable canoe-shaped boats can carry a whole family for several months before beginning to rot.

It's worth noting that more authentic reed islands do still exist; these are located further from Puno through a maze of small channels and can only be visited with a private boat. The islanders here continue to live in a relatively traditional fashion, and prefer not to be photographed.

Getting There & Away

Getting to the Floating Islands is easy; just go down to the docks and within minutes, you'll be asked to take a trip to the islands. You can hire a private boat (US$20) or go with the next group (US$3). Boats leave regularly from 7am until early afternoon according to passenger demand, but it's best to leave early to avoid being surrounded by tour groups. Pay on the boat rather than the pier as you may be overcharged there.

The standard trip, visiting the main island and one or two others, takes around two hours. Boats leave when they have 15 to 20 passengers. Many agencies in Puno will sell tickets and provide a guide from about US$6 per person, which often includes transport to the dock. Trips to other islands on the lake sometimes stop at the Islas Flotantes on the way out.

ISLA TAQUILE

Inhabited for many thousands of years, **Taquile** (admission US$1) is a real, 6km-long island with a population of around 2000. The Quechua-speaking islanders here are distinct from most of the surrounding Aymara-speaking island communities and maintain a strong sense of group identity. They rarely marry non-Taquile people, and their lives are largely untrammeled by the modernities of the mainland.

The island has a particularly fascinating tradition of weaving, and the islanders' creations are made according to a system of deeply ingrained social customs. The menfolk wear tightly woven, woolen hats resembling cute, floppy nightcaps, which they take great pride in knitting themselves. It's a common sight to see them wandering about the island with knitting in hand. These hats are closely bound with social symbolism: Men wear red hats if they are married and red-and-white hats if they are single, while different colors can denote the man's current or past social position. The women also weave thick colorful waistbands for their husbands, which when worn with their knitted caps, roughly spun white shirts and thick, calf-length, black pants, give them an altogether raffish air. The women also look eye-catching in their multilayered skirts and delicately embroidered blouses. These fine garments are

> **MAKING ISLANDS**
>
> The islands are built using the buoyant *totora* reeds that grow abundantly in the shallows of Lake Titicaca. Indeed, the lives of the Uros are interwoven with these reeds, which are partially edible and are also used to make their homes, their boats and the crafts they currently churn out for tourists. The islands are constructed from many layers of the *totora*, which are constantly replenished from the top as they rot from the bottom, so the ground is always soft and springy. Be careful not to put your foot through any rotten sections.

among the best-made traditional clothes in Peru, and can be bought in the island's cooperative store on the main plaza.

Taquile often feels like its own little world, completely detached from the rest of the earth. Its scenery is beautiful with deep, red-colored soil that, in the strong highland sunlight, contrasts with the intense blue of the lake and the glistening backdrop of Bolivia's snowcapped Cordillera Real on the far side of the lake. Several hills boast **Inca terracing** on their sides and small **ruins** on top. Visitors are free to wander, exploring the ruins and enjoying the tranquility, but you can't do this on a day trip without skipping lunch or missing the returning boat, so stay overnight if you can. It's a wonderful place to watch the sunset and see the moon, looking twice as bright in the crystalline air, rising over the peaks of the Cordillera Real.

When enterprising individuals from Puno first began bringing tourists to visit this remote island, the islanders fought the invasion. It wasn't the tourists they objected to but the Puno entrepreneurs. Now, many passenger boats to Taquile are owned and operated by the islanders, enabling them to keep tourism at reasonable levels, but the mild antipathy towards tour agencies remains. Unfortunately, there are also rare instances of thieving and begging, as tourism begins to have negative effects.

San Diego (Saint James Day; 25 July) is a big feast day on Taquile. Dancing, music and general carousing go on for several days until the beginning of August, when the Indians traditionally make offerings to Mother Earth, Pachamama. New Year's Day

LAKE TITICACA AREA

is also festive and rowdy. Many islanders go to Puno for La Virgen de la Candelaria and Puno Week, when the island becomes somewhat deserted.

Sleeping & Eating

Staying overnight on Taquile is worthwhile because tours tend to inundate the island with day-trippers from noon to 2pm and it can be difficult to appreciate the island in its normal serene state. A steep stairway of over 500 steps leads from the dock to the center of the island. The climb takes a breathless 20 minutes or more if you're not acclimatized, though local porters are on hand to help carry your luggage for around US$2.

Independent travelers will be met by a group of inhabitants next to the arch at the top of the stairs; these islanders can arrange accommodation in familial guesthouses that sleep up to 10 people. There is a standard charge of about US$3 per person, and gifts of fresh food are appreciated. Beds are basic but clean, and facilities are minimal. You will be given some blankets, but if possible bring a sleeping bag too, as it gets very cold at night. Bathing here means doing what the locals do; washing in cold water from a bucket. Toilets are basic, outdoor affairs. Campers are charged about half of the cost of a bed in someone's house.

A limited electricity supply was introduced to the island in the 1990s, but is still not widely available so remember to bring a flashlight, and take in the lay of the land while it's still light as travelers have been known to get so lost in the dark that they had to end up roughing it for the night.

Several simple restaurants in the center of the island sell fresh trout, potatoes, rice and fried eggs. The San Santiago, on the main plaza, is the only communally owned restaurant, the profits of which benefit the entire community. However, increasing numbers of islanders are opening their own small eateries. You can buy bottled drinks, and boiled tea is usually safe to drink, though it's worth bringing purifying tablets or a filter as backup. Make sure you have small bills, because change is limited and there's nowhere to change dollars. And bring extra money to buy the exquisite crafts sold in the island's cooperative store.

Getting There & Away

A passenger boat for the 24km trip to Taquile leaves the Puno dock every day by 7:30am (US$6/8.50 one way/round trip, four to five hours), and tour boats leave around 8am. Boats sometimes include a brief stop at the floating islands en route. Get to the dock early and pay the captain of the passenger boat directly. The return trip leaves at 2pm, arriving in Puno around nightfall. Remember to bring sunblock for the journey – the intensity of the tropical sun bouncing off the lake at almost 4000m can cause severe sunburn.

Tour agencies offer this trip for about US$10 with a guide, or US$14 with an overnight stay including accommodation and meals, though the islanders benefit much more directly from travelers who go independently.

ISLA AMANTANÍ

Less-frequently visited, **Isla Amantaní** (admission US$1.50) is similar to and a few kilometers north of the smaller Taquile. Almost all trips to Amantaní (pop 4000) involve an overnight stay with islanders where basic food and accommodations are available (see p158 for a description of what to expect) and the villagers often organize rousing traditional dances, letting travelers dress in their traditional partying gear to dance the night away. (Women might note that hiking boots may look a mite comical with the island skirts.)

The island is very quiet, and there are great views, and no roads or vehicles. Several hills are topped by ruins, among the highest and best-known of which are **Pachamama and Pachatata** (Mother Earth and Father Earth), which date to the Tiahuanaco culture. This was a largely Bolivian culture that appeared around Lake Titicaca and expanded rapidly between 500 BC and AD 900. There are eight village communities on the island, each housing a cluster of adobe dwellings. As with Taquile, the islanders speak Quechua, but their culture is more heavily influenced by the Aymaras.

Boats to Amantaní leave the Puno dock between 7:30am and 8:30am most mornings, and return fares are US$5.50 if you pay the captain directly (islanders pay US$3.50). Though many people in the dock will tell you they are from Amantaní, the only regular boat service genuinely run by the islanders at the time of writing was named *Virgen de la Candelaria*. To ensure you catch the islanders' boat (thereby directly helping the islanders), write to the island's collective email address at pachatata_isla@yahoo.com in advance (in Spanish) so somebody can meet you at the dock in Puno.

Boat connections make it is easiest to travel from Puno to the Islas Flotantes then to Amantaní and on to Taquile, rather than in reverse as boats often stop at the floating islands on the way out, but not on the return trip. A daily boat from Amantaní runs to Taquile for US$1.50 one way.

Upon arrival, the islanders will find you accommodation according to a rotating system. A bed and full board costs around US$3 per night.

Puno travel agencies charge US$12 and up for a two-day tour to Amantaní, with a quick visit to Taquile and the floating islands. Three-day, two-night tours are also available, with the first night at Amantaní and the second at Taquile. Generally, tours are fair value for money; though remember that the islanders see less of the money this way.

ISLA SUASI

This idyllic five-acre island is near the north shore of Lake Titicaca. In the late 1990s, a small hotel – the only building on the island – was built here using local resources and minimizing the ecological impact. The hotel runs on solar power and provides modern services such as bathrooms, hot showers and heating in a rustic, stone-and-thatch structure that blends harmoniously with its surroundings. It can be used as a base to visit other islands or the tiny north-shore towns of Moho and Conima (see p147). There are rowboats, a sauna and a garden of native plants, herbs and vegetables. The island also hosts a few flocks of Camelids.

You must book in advance to stay here. Programmes of two days/one night, or three days/two nights, are offered, with either land or lake transport or a combination of the two. Rates include a full breakfast but other meals cost US$12 to US$15. Reservations can be made at any of the major travel agencies in Puno. Information is available from the friendly owner of the hotel, **Martha Giraldo Alayza** (☎ 35-1417, 962-2709; albergue@islasuasi.com; s/d/tr US$55/77/99) or see its website at www.islasuasi.com.

ISLA DEL SOL & ISLA DE LA LUNA

The most famous island on Lake Titicaca is Isla del Sol (Island of the Sun), the legendary birthplace of Manco Capac (the first Inca), and the sun itself. Both Isla del Sol and Isla de la Luna (Island of the Moon) have **Inca ruins**, which can be reached by delightful **walking trails** across the islands that often pass traditional villages. Isla del Sol has some fine sandy **beaches** and an interesting **museum**. It also is the best of the two islands for acccommodations options, though you can camp on both islands.

The islands can be visited by hopping over the Bolivian border to the port of Copacabana, about 12km beyond the border town of Yunguyo. Allow at least two days for this trip.

ANAPIA

Well off the beaten track, this pristine island is in Laguna de Huiñaimarca near the border with Bolivia. It sees very few tourists so can be visited as an alternative to the popular islands of Amantaní and Taquile. Families will take in travelers and prepare their meals for around US$4 per night. A tiny island nearby also hosts a vicuña reserve. All Ways Travel in Puno (p151) can organize trips here or you can catch a boat from Punta Hermosa near Yunguyo between noon and 3pm on Sunday when the islanders return after visiting Yunguyo's market (US$2 one way).

SOUTH-SHORE TOWNS

If you start early enough, you can visit all of the following south-shore towns in a day and either be back in Puno by nightfall or continue on to Bolivia.

The road to Bolivia via Lake Titicaca's southern shores passes through several traditional, bucolic villages, notable for their myriad colonial churches, busy market days and, in Chucuito, the bizarre Templo de la Fertilidad.

For public transport to any of the south-shore towns, go to Terminal Zonal, 1.5km from the center of Puno on Simón Bolívar. Cheap, slow minibuses and faster combis leave from here for Chimú (US$0.50, 10 minutes), Chucuito (US$0.60, 35 minutes), Juli (US$1, 1½ hours), Pomata (US$1.20, 1¾ hours) and the Bolivian border (US$1.20, 2½ hours). Buses to the nearer towns, such as Ilave, are more frequent, but if you're patient, you should be able to leave for the town of your choice within an hour.

Chimú

The road east of Puno closely follows the margins of the lake on what hikers might find a pleasant lakeshore stroll. After about 8km, you reach the village of Chimú, whose inhabitants have close ties with the Uros and are famous for their *totora* industry. Bundles of reeds are piled up to dry, and there are usually a few reed boats in various stages of construction.

Chucuito

The principal attraction in the village of Chucuito (pop 1500), 18km southeast of Puno, is the fascinatingly outlandish **Templo de la Fertilidad** (Inca Uyu; admission free; ☼ 6am-8pm), which consists of dozens of large, stone phalluses, some up to 1.2m in length. Local guides tell various entertaining stories about the carvings, including tales of maidens sitting atop the stony joysticks to increase their fertility. Whether you buy into their theories or believe another suggestion that the temple may in fact be a fake is up to you.

The town also has a trout hatchery and two attractive colonial churches, Santo Domingo and La Asunción, though you'll have to track down the elusive caretaker to get a glimpse inside.

SLEEPING

The only restaurants in town are those at the hotels. Of these, Taypikala has the best.

Hostal Cabañas (in Puno ☎ 35-2176; leave a message for Alfredo Sanchez; lodgecabanas@chucuito.com; dm US$7-10, s US$14-20, d US$28-32) This is a large, rambling, YHA-affiliated site on the outskirts of Chucuito with a spacious, overgrown garden and a superb view of the lake. Rooms are in rustic, stone cabins and familial bungalows complete with log fires. Prices here are extremely flexible and only estimations are given.

Taypikala Hotel (☎ 35-6042, 62-3307; taypikala@punonet.com; Km18; s/d/ste US$51/67/95) This unmissable, New-Age hotel is buried under a confusion of model condors and jagged, artificial rocks by the road. Its main entrance is at the back near the temple, but the rooms have lake and garden views and are decorated with copies of local rock art. It also has all the modern amenities expected of the price range. The owner is reputedly an Aymara shaman.

Chucuito to Juli

Near Chucuito, the road turns southeast away from the lake and soon reaches **Platería**, a village once famous for its silverware. About 40km from Puno, the road passes through the straggling community of **Molleko**, noted for the great number of mortarless stone walls that snake eerily across the bleak altiplano. The road continues inland to the crossroad town of **Ilave**, before returning to the lake near the bay of Juli, where flamingos are sometimes seen.

Juli itself (pop 7000), 80km from Puno, is called Peru's Pequeña Roma (Little Rome) on account of its four colonial churches dating from the 16th and 17th century, which are slowly being restored. The Church of **San Juan de Letran** (admission US$1; ☼ 7:30am-4pm) contains richly framed, colonial paintings depicting the lives of Saint John the Baptist and Saint Teresa. The Church of **La Asunción** (same hours) offers excellent vistas of Lake Titicaca from its large courtyard. Its belfry was struck by lightning several years ago. The Church of **Santa Cruz** has lost half of its roof and is closed for the foreseeable future, while the Church of **San Pedro** (☎ 85-4070; ☼ 7am-noon & 2-4pm Wed-Mon), on the main plaza, is in the best condition.

Market days in Juli are Wednesday and Saturday. The very basic but friendly **Alojamiento El Rosal** (Puno 128; s/d US$3/6), just off the main plaza, has rooms. **Señora Angelica** (☎ 85-4123; Tacna 209; s/d US$5/10) will also take in visitors sometimes with advance warning; she has shared hot-water showers.

Pomata

Beyond Juli, the road continues east to Pomata (pop 1600), 106km from Puno. As you arrive, you'll see the Dominican **church**, dramatically located on top of a small hill. It was founded in 1700 and is known for its windows made of translucent alabaster and its intricately carved, baroque, sandstone facade. Look for the puma carvings; the name 'Pomata' means 'place of the puma' in Aymara. The only accommodation is the **Hostal Rosario** (Plaza de Armas; s/d with shared showers US$3/6), which has some hot water.

Just out of Pomata, the road forks. The main road continues southeast through Zepita to the border town of **Desaguadero**, where there is another crumbling colonial church. A side road, leading to the other border crossing at Yunguyo, hugs the shore of Lake Titicaca.

If you're going to Bolivia via Yunguyo, consider stopping off at the **Mirador Natural de Asiru Patjata,** 4km from Yunguyo. Here a 5000m-long rock formation resembles a snake *(culebra)*, whose head is a viewpoint looking over to the Isla del Sol. The area around here is known for its isolated villages and shamans.

TO/FROM BOLIVIA VIA PUNO

For many travelers, Puno and Lake Titicaca are stepping-stones to Bolivia, which borders the lake to the south. The **Bolivian Consulate** (☎ 35-1251; Arequipa 120; ⏲ 8:30am-2pm Mon-Fri) is located in Puno. Visa regulations change frequently, but citizens of the USA and most European countries can stay 90 days without a visa while citizens of the Canada, Australia and New Zealand can stay 30 days without a visa. A few other nationalities require a visa in advance – usually issued for a 30-day stay. These include Russia and the Benelux countries.

If you indicate you'll be returning to Peru the same day, they will put your documents in a separate box at the border to pick up when you return. Remember that Bolivian time is one hour ahead of Peruvian time.

Exit taxes are sometimes asked for but these are not legal and the money only lines the official's pocket. There have also been unconfirmed reports of a scam in which border police search travelers' luggage for 'fake dollars' that are then confiscated.

Over Lake Titicaca

Transturin (☎ 35-2771; leontours@terra.com.pe; Ayacucho 1st block) offers catamaran trips to Bolivia costing about US$167. Groups leave Puno by bus at 6:30am and go to Copacabana, Bolivia, from where a catamaran sails to the Isla del Sol for a quick but interesting visit before continuing to the Bolivian port of Huatajata and on to La Paz by bus, arriving at 6:30pm. This service includes hotel transfers, lunch and a guide. It also offers longer trips including an overnight stay on a catamaran in comfortable private cabins

for US$217. The trips can also be done in reverse; Transturin has an **office** (☎ 591-2-310442; sales@turismo_bolivia.com; Camacho 1321s) in La Paz.

Arcobaleno (☎ 36-4068; arcobaleno@titicacalake .com; Lambayeque 175) is the Puno agent for Crillon tours, which also has daily waterborne tours to Bolivia, this time on hydrofoils. Timings are roughly the same as Transturin and cost US$165. The two-day tour (US$230) overnights in a hotel.

Overland

There are two overland routes from Puno to La Paz, Bolivia; via Yunguyo or via Desaguadero. The rarely used third route from Juliaca is described earlier in this chapter (p147). The Yunguyo route is the more attractive and some travelers like to break the trip in the chilled Bolivian resort of Copacabana, from where the Isla del Sol (see p159) can easily be visited. The Desaguadero route is faster, slightly cheaper and more direct than Yunguyo, however, and can be combined with a visit to the Bolivian ruins at Tiahuanaco.

VIA YUNGUYO

By far the most convenient option to get from Puno to La Paz is with a company such as **Colectur** (☎ 35-2302; colectur@latinmail.com; Tacna 221), which has daily departures at 1:30pm to Yunguyo, and will stop at a reliable *casa de cambio* , show you exactly where to go for exit and entrance formalities and then drive you to Copacabana (US$3 to US$4; three hours), where you are met by a Bolivian bus for the trip to La Paz (US$6 to US$7 five hours, from Copacabana). Alternatively, **Tour Peru** (☎ 36-5517), at Puno's Terminal Terrestre, has similarly priced departures at 8am daily.

To go independently, buses leave from Terminal Zonal, 1.5km from central Puno on Simón Bolívar for the border town of Yunguyo (US$1.20, 2½ hours), which has a couple of basic hotels. Try the basic **Hostal Isabel** (☎ 85-6019; San Francisco 110; r per person US$3), which has hot water and will change money, or **San Andres** (☎ 85-6009; Grau 516, Plaza 2 de Mayo; s/d US$4.20/5.50), which is also good.

You will find moneychangers in Yunguyo's plaza and by the border, which is about 2km away in Casani (combis US$0.30); count your money carefully. The border is open from 8am to 6pm and formalities are fairly straightforward.

From the border, it's 10km more to Copacabana (combis US$0.50). Transportation is more frequent on Sunday, which is market day in Yunguyo. On weekdays you may have to wait up to an hour. Copacabana has better hotels than Yunguyo, as well as a port from where inexpensive tours to Isla del Sol are available.

There are several buses a day for the trip from Copacabana to La Paz (US$2.50, five hours), which includes a boat crossing over the Estrecho de Tiquina. If you leave Puno early, you can reach La Paz in a day.

VIA DESAGUADERO

Buses and minibuses leave Puno's Terminal Zonal and Terminal Terrestre regularly for Desaguadero (US$2, 2½ hours). Basic hotels here include **Hostal Panamericano** (☎ 85-1021; Panamericana 151; s/d/tr US$3/6/9), near the border, with basic but clean little rooms and shared cold showers. A better choice is **Hostal San Carlos** (☎ 85-1171; 28 de Julio 322; s/d US$4.20/5.50,

with bathroom US$7/10), which is very large and has shared warm showers. A sauna costs an extra US$2.50, and a games room is planned in the near future. **Hostal Corona** (☎ 85-1120; Panamericana 248; s/d US$3/6, with bathroom US$7/9) is also decent with hot water.

Border hours are 7:30am to 8pm, though you can cross back and forth outside these hours if you stay within the border area. Remember that Bolivia is an hour ahead of Peru, so you can't enter Bolivia after 7pm Peru time. Moneychangers at the border and a *casa de cambio* have exchange rates comparable to La Paz or Puno.

There are many buses from Desaguadero to La Paz (US$1.80, 3½ hours). If you leave Puno at dawn, you can be in Bolivia early enough for a quick stop at the archaeological site of Tiahuanaco before continuing on to La Paz (the bus passes the turn-off to the ruins and connecting combis run to the site).

The best bus from Puno to La Paz is with Ormeño's Royal Class service (US$14, six hours), but there are plenty of cheaper options.

Cuzco & the Sacred Valley

As the heart of the once-mighty Inca Empire, the magnetic city of Cuzco heads the list of many a traveler's itinerary. Each year it draws hundreds of thousands of tourists to its cobbled streets, lured by the city's unique combination of colonial and religious splendors built on the hefty stone foundations of the Incas. And lying within easy hopping distance of the city is the country's biggest draw card of all, the lost city of the Incas, Machu Picchu. Admired by one and all, no trip to Peru is complete without visiting this lofty Inca citadel perched high on its isolated mountain top.

But the far-reaching Department of Cuzco encompasses much more than its historic capital and the must-see ruins of Machu Picchu. The city lies in exceptionally beautiful Andean surroundings filled with some of the most fascinating and accessible archaeological sites on the continent, not least those to be found in the Inca's ancestral homeland in the Sacred Valley of the Río Urubamba. The department also offers some of the best and most varied opportunities for rafting, mountain biking and trekking in the country, as well as hosting a long list of flamboyant fiestas and carnivals in which Peru's pagan past collides colorfully with solemn Catholic ritual and modern Latin American mayhem.

HIGHLIGHTS

■ **Archaeology**

Machu Picchu: discovering for yourself Peru's most celebrated Inca citadel (p207)

■ **Hiking**

Making the awe-inspiring Inca Trail pilgrimage (p212)

■ **Adrenaline Rush**

River running in the Río Urubamba (p177)

■ **Shopping**

Trawling through the craft workshops of San Blas (p191)

■ **Short Walks**

Doing the ruin crawl from Tambo Machay to Sacsayhuamán (p195-6)

■ **Festivals**

Witnessing the colorful Festival del Carmen (p220) in Paucartambo or Inti Rymi (p196) at Sacsayhuamán

■ **History**

Exploring centuries of colonial treasures in Cuzco cathedral (p172) as well as some Inca stonework (p173) and impressive religious buildings buildings (p172-6)

Machu ★★ Inca Trail
Picchu   ★ Río Urubamba
      Sacsayhuamán ★
              ★ Cuzco

CUZCO

☎ 084 / pop 350,000 / elevation 3326m

The beautiful city of Cuzco (Qosq'o in Quechua) is an uneasy bearer of many grand titles. It was once the foremost city of the Inca Empire, and is now the undisputed archaeological capital of the Americas as well as the continent's oldest continuously inhabited city. And while the city has rapidly developed an infrastructure to cope with the massive influx of tourism it has seen over the last few decades, its past still retains a powerful grip on the present.

Massive Inca-built walls line the city's central streets and form the foundations of both colonial and modern buildings, and the cobbled streets are often stepped, narrow and thronged with Quechua-speaking descendants of the Incas. Plus a wealth of colonial treasures can be found in the churches and mansions of the conquistadors.

But while Cuzco was long ruled by Inca or conquistador, there's no question of who rules the roost now: the city's economy is almost totally at the whim of the international tourist, and every second building is a tourist restaurant, shop or hotel.

Travelers regularly report seeing the gay pride flag in Cuzco; actually, it's the city's own well-loved flag.

Take care not to overexert yourself during your first few days if you've flown in from low altitude (see Altitude Sickness p429 for more details).

HISTORY

Cuzco is a city so steeped in history, tradition and legend that it can be difficult to know where fact ends and myth begins. Legend tells that in the 12th century, the first Inca, Manco Capac the son of the sun, was charged by Inti the sun god to find 'qosq'o' or the navel of the earth – a spot where he could plunge a golden rod into the ground until it disappeared. When at last Manco discovered such a point, he founded the city that was to become the thriving capital of the Americas' greatest empire.

Of course, the area was also occupied by other cultures for several centuries before the rise of the Incas, some of which were involved in the Wari expansion of the 8th and 9th centuries.

According to oral history passed down through the generations, the empire's main expansion occurred in the hundred years prior to the arrival of the conquistadors in 1533. When the Spanish, led by Francisco Pizarro, reached Cuzco, they began keeping chronicles, including Inca history as related by the Incas themselves. The most famous of these accounts was *The Royal Commentaries of the Incas*, written by Garcilaso de la Vega, the son of an Inca princess and a Spanish conquistador, who lived in Cuzco until the age of 21 before moving to Spain.

The reigns of the first eight Incas spanned the period from the 12th century to the early 15th century (originally the term Inca meant king, although subsequently it came to apply to the people as well). These Incas left few signs of their existence, though the remains of some of their palaces can still be seen in Cuzco. In chronological order, they were:

Manco Capac – The Palace of Colcampata is traditionally attributed to Manco Capac, though some sources claim that Atahualpa's brother built it shortly before the Spaniards arrived. The massive retaining walls can be seen next to the Church of San Cristóbal, on Cuzco's northwestern outskirts.

Sinchi Roca – Some of the walls of his Palace of Cora Cora can be seen in the courtyards of houses to the right of Calle Suecia as you walk uphill from the Plaza de Armas.

Lloque Yupanqui

Mayta Capac

Capac Yupanqui – Named the 'Unforgettable King,' though nobody knows very much about him.

Inca Roca – The huge blocks of this Inca's palace now form the foundations of the Museo de Arte Religioso and include the famous 12-sided stone of Hatunrumiyoc.

Yahuar Huacac

Viracocha Inca – His palace was demolished to make way for the present cathedral on the Plaza de Armas.

The ninth Inca, **Pachacutec**, gave the empire its first bloody taste of conquest. Until his time, the Incas had dominated but a modest area close to Cuzco, though frequently skirmishing with other highland tribes. However, one such tribe was the Chanka, whose growing thirst for expansion led them to Cuzco's doorstep in 1438. Viracocha Inca fled in the belief that his small empire was lost, but his third son refused to give up the fight. With the help of some of the older generals, he rallied the Inca army and, in a desperate final battle, in which legend claims that the very boulders transformed themselves into warriors to fight

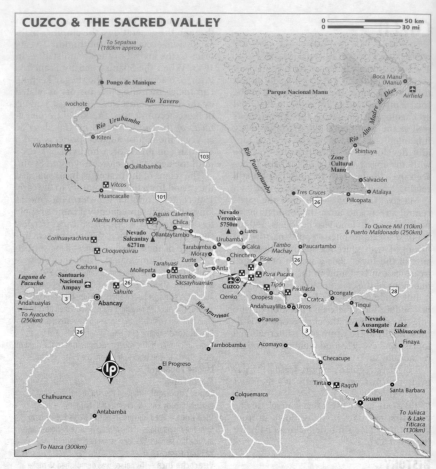

CUZCO & THE SACRED VALLEY

0 [____] 50 km
0 [____] 30 mi

alongside the Inca, he famously managed to rout the Chanka.

The victorious younger son changed his name to Pachacutec, proclaimed himself Inca and, buoyed by his victory over the Chanka, embarked upon the first wave of Incan expansion that was eventually to create the Inca Empire. During the next 25 years, he bagged much of the central Andes, including the region between the two great lakes of Titicaca and Junín.

But Pachacutec the mighty military figure also proved himself a sophisticated urban developer, devising Cuzco's famous puma shape and diverting rivers to cross the city. He also built some fine buildings, including the famous Coricancha temple

and his palace on what is now the western corner of the Plaza de Armas.

There was, of course, no Plaza de Armas before the arrival of the Spanish. In its place was an even greater square, divided by the Sapphi Canal and encompassing the area now called the Plaza Regocijo. Together, they formed a huge central plaza that was the focus of the city's social life.

Pachacutec's successor, **Tupac Yupanqui**, was every bit his father's son. During the 1460s, he helped his father subdue a great area to the north, including the northern Peruvian and southern Ecuadorian Andes of today, as well as the northern Peruvian coast. And as the 10th Inca, his empire continued to expand dramatically, extending from Quito in Ecuador to south of Santiago in Chile by his death.

Huayna Capac, the 11th Inca, was the last to rule over a united empire, an empire so big that it seemed to have little left to conquer. Nevertheless, Huayna Capac marched to the northernmost limits of his empire, along the present-day Ecuador–Colombia border and fought a long series of campaigns during which he sired his son, **Atahualpa**, who was born of a Quitan mother.

But then something totally unexpected happened: Europeans discovered the New World and brought with them various Old World diseases. Epidemics, including smallpox and the common cold, swept down from Central America and the Caribbean. Huayna Capac died in such an epidemic around 1525. Shortly before his death, he divided his empire, giving the northern part to Atahualpa and the southern Cuzco area to another son, **Huascar**.

Both sons were well suited to ruling an empire – so well suited that neither wished to share power and civil war ensued. As a pure-blooded native Cuzqueño, it was Huascar who had the people's support, but Atahualpa had the backing of the northern army and in 1532, his battle-hardened troops won a key battle, capturing Huascar outside Cuzco, before retiring to Cajamarca.

Meanwhile, **Francisco Pizarro** landed in northern Ecuador and marched southward in the wake of Atahualpa's conquests. Atahualpa himself had been too busy fighting the civil war to worry about a small band of foreigners, but by the autumn of 1532, a fateful meeting was arranged with the Spaniard in Cajamarca. This meeting was to radically change the course of South American history, as Atahualpa was ambushed by a few dozen armed conquistadors, who succeeded in capturing him, killing thousands of unarmed Indians and routing tens of thousands more.

In an attempt to regain his freedom, the Inca offered a ransom of a roomful of gold and two rooms of silver from Cuzco, including that stripped from the temple walls of Coricancha, or the 'Golden Courtyard.' But after holding Atahualpa prisoner for a number of months, and teasing the Incas with his ransom requests, Pizarro murdered him anyway, and soon marched on Cuzco.

Mounted on horseback, protected by armor and swinging steel swords, at the time the Spanish cavalry was virtually unstoppable. Furthermore, the Indians were initially terrified of the Spaniards' horses and primitive firearms, neither of which the Andes had ever seen before.

Pizarro himself entered Cuzco on November 8, 1533, by which time Pizarro had appointed Manco, a half-brother of Huascar, as a new puppet Inca. But after a few years of keeping to heel, the puppet rebelled. In 1536 **Manco Inca** set out to drive the Spaniards from his empire, laying siege to Cuzco with an army estimated at well over a hundred thousand. Indeed, it was only a desperate, last-ditch breakout and violent battle at Sacsayhuamán that saved the Spanish from complete annihilation. Manco was forced to retreat to Ollantaytambo and then into the jungle at Vilcabamba.

But once Cuzco had been safely captured, looted and settled, the seafaring Spaniards turned their attentions to their newly founded capital Lima, and Cuzco's importance waned, becoming just another quiet colonial town. All the gold and silver was gone, and many Inca buildings were pulled down to accommodate churches and colonial houses.

Few events of historical significance have rocked Cuzco since the Spanish conquest, but for two earthquakes in 1650 and 1950, and an infamous Indian uprising led by **Tupac Amaru II** in 1780. His was the only late Indian revolt that came close to succeeding, but eventually he too was defeated by the Spaniards. The battles for Peruvian independence in the 1820s achieved what the Inca armies never had, but it was the descendants of the conquistadors who wrested power from Spain, and life in Cuzco continued much as before.

Indeed, it was the rediscovery of **Machu Picchu** in 1911 that has affected Cuzco far more than any event since the arrival of the Spanish, changing the city from provincial backwater to Peru's foremost tourist center.

ORIENTATION

The heart of the city is the Plaza de Armas, while nearby Avenida Sol is the main business thoroughfare. Walking just a few blocks north or east of the plaza, however, will take you to twisting, cobbled streets

CUZCO

To Sacsayhuamán, Qenko, Puca Pucara & Tambo Machay

To Sacsayhuamán

To trucks for Mollepata, Abancay & Ayacucho

To Hospedaje Inka (200m)

Tandapata

Tres Cruces

Choquechaca

Pumacurco

Atoc

Atocsaycuchi

Carichipampa

Angelitos

Carmen Alto

Ladrillos

Suecia

Resbalosa

Koskacalle

Teteccocha

Coricalle

Anahuarca

Saphi

Saphi

Saphi

Kiskapata

Iris

Plazoleta de las Nazarenas

Plaza del Tricentenario

Plaza de Armas

Cathedral

Steps

Plaza Regocijo

Plaza San Francisco

Plaza San Blas

Huaynapata

Purgatorio

7 Culebras

Palacio

Hatunrumiyoc

Choquechaca

Carmen Bajo

Cuesta San Blas

Calle Triunfo

Herrajes

Santa Catalina

Ruinas

San Agustín

Av Tullumayo

Maruri

Loreto

Av Sol

Arequipa

Maruri

Pampa del Castillo

Puente Rosario

Pardo

Culchipunco

Centenario

Grau

Lechugal

Beldín

Kancharina

3 Cruces de Oro

Trinitarias

Peta

Calle Nueva

Tecte

Matará

Ayacucho

San Andrés

Cruz Verde

Quera

Mesón de la Estrella

Márquez

San Bernardo

Nueva Baja

Conevidayoc

Santa Clara

Túpac Amaru

Cascaparo

Mercado Central

San Pedro

To Santiago Terminal (1km), Action Valley (10km) & Poroy (12km)

San Pedro Train Station (Machu Picchu)

Chaparro

Av Baja

Unión

Desamparados

Ceniza

Nueva Alta

Granada

San Juan de Dios

Arones

Siete Cuartones

Teatro

Meloc

Tambo de Montero

Tigre

Santa Teresa

Plateros

Medio

Espinar

Mantas

Heladeros

Calle Garcilaso

Hospital

Calle Nueva

San Andrés

Afligidos

Tandapata

Plaza San Blas

Ese

Ataud

Amargura

Tecsecocha

Frontispicio

Suecia

Tucumán

Procuradores

Plateros

0 — 0.5 km
0 — 0.3 mi

Museo de Historia Regional	**36**	B4
Museo de Santa Catalina	**37**	C4
Museo Inka	**38**	C3
Museo Palacio Municpal	**39**	B4
Pre-columbian Art Museum	**40**	C3
San Blas Spanish School	(see 125)	
Siluet Sauna and Spa	**41**	C5
Waterfall Monument	**42**	F6

SLEEPING 🏠 pp182–6
Albergue Municipal	**43**	B3
Amaru Hostal	**44**	D3
Andenes de Saphi	**45**	A3
Casa de Campo	**46**	C2
Casa Grande	**47**	C4
Del Prado Inn	**48**	B3
El Dorado Inn	**49**	D5
El Mirador de la Ñusta	(see 125)	
Gran Hostal Machu Picchu	**50**	C5
Hospedaje Cassana	**51**	A3
Hospedaje Iquique	**52**	E3
Hospedaje Kiswarcancha	**53**	C3
Hospedaje Rumi Punku	**54**	C3
Hostal Centenario	**55**	D6
Hostal Corihuasi	**56**	B3
Hostal El Arcano	**57**	C2
Hostal El Arqueólogo	**58**	C3
Hostal El Balcón	**59**	A3
Hostal El Grial	**60**	C2

Hostal El Solar	**61**	B5
Hostal Familiar	**62**	A3
Hostal Incawasi	**63**	B4
Hostal Kuntur Wasi	**64**	C2
Hostal La Casona de San Agustín	**65**	D4
Hostal Loreto	**66**	C4
Hostal Los Ninos	**67**	A4
Hostal Mirador del Inka	**68**	D2
Hostal Pascana	**69**	E5
Hostal Plaza de Armas	**70**	C4
Hostal Qorichaska	**71**	A4
Hostal Resbalosa	**72**	B3
Hostal Rikch arty	**73**	A4
Hostal Royal Qosco	**74**	B3
Hostal Saphi	**75**	A3
Hostal Suecia II	**76**	B3
Hotel Cristina	**77**	C5
Hotel Cuzco	**78**	B4
Hotel Don Carlos	**79**	D6
Hotel Garcilaso I	**80**	B4
Hotel Imperio	**81**	A6
Hotel Internacional San Agustín	**82**	D4
Hotel Libertador	**83**	D4
Hotel Monasterio del Cusco	**84**	C3
Hotel Royal Inka I	**85**	B4
Hotel Royal Inka II	**86**	B4
Hotel Ruinas	**87**	D3
Hotel Virrey	**88**	C4
Hotel Wiracocha	**89**	B5
Los Apus	**90**	C2
Los Aticos II	(see 158)	
Los Aticos	**91**	C5
Novotel Accor	**92**	D4
Pensión Aleman	**93**	D2
Posada del Inca	**94**	C4
Residencia de la Solidaridad	**95**	A6
Residencial Madres Dominicanas	**96**	E5
San Agustín Plaza	**97**	D5
Suecia I	**98**	B3
Tupac Yupanqui Palace	**99**	D4

EATING 🍴 pp186–9
Al Grano	**100**	D4
Ama Lur	(see 122)	
Blueberry Lounge	(see 105)	
Café Bagdad	(see 105)	
Café Cultural Ritual	**101**	D3
Café Varayoc	(see 110)	
Chez Maggy	**102**	B3
Coco Loco	(see 107)	
Dimart	**103**	C5
Don Antonio	**104**	B4
El Ayllu Café	**105**	C3
El Buen Pastor	**106**	D3
El Mesón de los Espaderos	**107**	B4
El Truco	**108**	B4
Fallen Angel	**109**	C3
Govinda	**110**	B4
Granja Heidi	**111**	D3
Greens	**112**	D2
I Due Mondi	(see 140)	
Inka Grill	**113**	B4
Inkanato	**114**	D5

Kin Taro	**115**	B4
La Tertulia	**116**	B3
La Yunta	(see 105)	
Los Cuates	**117**	B3
Macondo	**118**	D3
Market	**119**	C4
Moni	**120**	D4
Naturaleza	**121**	E6
Pucará	**122**	B4
Quinta Eulalia	**123**	C2
Restaurant El Paititi	**124**	C4
The Muse	**125**	D3
The Pi Shop	**126**	C2
Tiziano Trattoria	**127**	B3
Trattoria Adriano	**128**	C4
Trotamundos	**129**	C4
Tunupa	(see 134)	
Ukuku's Restaurant	**130**	B3
Victor Victoria	**131**	B3
Witches Garden	**132**	D3

DRINKING 🍸 pp189–90
Azucar	**133**	C5
Cross Keys	**134**	B4
El Muki (Disco)	**135**	C4
Kamikaze (Bar)	**136**	B4
Los Perros	**137**	B3
Mama Africa Pub	**138**	C4
Mystique	(see 98)	
Norton Rat's (Bar)	(see 66)	
Paddy O'Flaherty's (Bar)	**139**	C4
Rosie O Grady's	**140**	D4
Ukuku's Bar	**141**	B4
X'ss	**142**	C3

SHOPPING 🛍 p191
Center for Traditional Textiles of Cusco	**143**	E5
Galeria Latina Cuzco	**144**	C4
Inca Craft Market	**145**	C5

TRANSPORT pp191–5
Aero Continente	**146**	C3
Buses to Chinchero, Urubamba & Ollantaytambo	**147**	D6
Buses to Pisac, Calca and Urubamba	**148**	E5
Cruz del Sur (ticket office)	**149**	G6
First Class Buses to Puno	**150**	E5
First Class	**151**	F6
Inka Express	**152**	C5
Lloyd Aereo Boliviano	**153**	C4
Taca	(see 161)	
Tans	(see 120)	

OTHER
Aventours	**154**	D5
Fric Adventures	**155**	B4
InkaNatura	**156**	D4
Manu Expeditions	**157**	E6
Milla Turismo	**158**	D6
Municipalidad	(see 39)	
Peruvian Andean Treks	**159**	E6
Q'ente	**160**	B4
Qosqo Center of Native Dance	**161**	E6
SAS	(see 63)	
Sunset	(see 74)	
Tatoo Outdoors & Travel	(see 109)	
Teatro Municipal	**162**	B5
United Mice	(see 156)	

To Quinta
Zárate
(300m)

Recoleta

Chihuampata

To Hospital Regional (2km),
Clínica Centro Medico Pardo (2km),
Albergue San Juan de
Dios Luxemburgo (2km),
Casa de la Gringa (2.5km)
& La Perez (3km)

Av de la Cultura

Av Huáscar

Intihuatorina

Ahuacplta

Av Garcilaso

Av Sol

Av Tullumayo

M Cápac

Manco Inca

Huayna Cápac

Tacna

Pachacutec

San Miguel

Av Pardo

To Manu Nature Tours
& Lima Tours (20km)

Park

Centro
Artesanal
Cuzco

**Huanchac Train
Station (Puno
& Arequipa)**

To Torredorado (1km), Torre de
Pachacutes (1km) & Airport (2km)

little changed for centuries. The pedestrian street between Plaza del Tricentenario and Huaynapata gives great views over the Plaza de Armas. The central street leading from the northwest side of the plaza is officially named Procuradores (tax-collectors street), but has long been nicknamed Gringo Alley thanks to its huddle of budget haunts, cafés and predatory street-sellers. Recently, the city has had a resurgence of Quechua pride, and the official names of many streets have changed from Spanish to Quechua spellings. Cuzco has officially become Qosq'o, Cuichipunco is K'uychipunko, and so on. Maps usually retain the old spellings, however, and most people still use them.

INFORMATION
Books & Bookstores

There are plenty of books on Cuzco to choose from. The best source of general information about the city and the surrounding area is the excellent *Exploring Cuzco* by Peter Frost. For some historical background try *The Lost City of the Incas* by Hiram Bingham, a dated but interesting account of his 'discovery' of Machu Picchu, and *Monuments of the Incas* by John Hemming and Edward Ranney, with its fabulous photographs in black-and-white. Book-exchanges abound throughout Cuzco. A few places to try include: South American Explorers Club (SAE: members only, see contact details p171); Norton Rat's tavern (see p190); and Granja Heidi (see p187).

Bookstores include the following:

Jerusalen (☎ 23-5428; Heladeros 143; ☯ 9am-9pm Mon-Sat) Has an extensive book exchange in several languages, as well as new titles and music.

Los Andes (☎ 23-4231; Portal Comercio 125; ☯ 10am-2pm & 5-9pm Mon-Sat)

SBS Bookshop (☎ 24-8106; Av Sol 781; ☯ 8am-1pm & 3:30-7pm Mon-Fri, 8am-1pm Sat) Though small, specializes in foreign-language books, especially in English.

Emergency

The **Policía de Turismo** (☎ 24-9654; Saphi 510; ☯ 24 hr) are trained to deal with most problems pertaining to tourists. If you have something stolen, they'll help with the official police reports needed for insurance claims and will also tell you how to place a radio announcement offering a reward for the return of stolen property of no commercial value. Some English is spoken.

Internet Access

Internet access is fast and cheap in Cuzco.
MundoNet (☎ 26-0285; Santa Teresa 344; ☯ 8am-10pm Mon-Sat 5-10pm Sun; US$0.60 per hr) Has good, fast machines.

Telser (☎ 24-2424; Calle del Medio 117; ☯ 7am-midnight; US$0.60 per hr) It's also good.

Trotamundos (see Eating later) Also has a few machines and cheap net-to-phone facilities.

Immigration

At **migraciónes** (☎ 22-2741; Av Sol 612; ☯ 8am-noon Mon-Fri) you can renew your tourist card for US$27 per 30 days but consider going to Bolivia for a day – those of most nationalities get 90 days on their return and save the renewal cost.

There are representatives of many foreign consulates, including:
Belgium (Federico Alarco Suarez; ☎ 22-1098)
France (Jorge Escobar Medrano; ☎ 23-3610)
Germany (Maria Sophia Jurgens; ☎ 23-5459)
Ireland (Charlie Donovan; ☎ 24-3514)
Italy (Fedos Rubatto; ☎ 22-4398)
Spain (Juana Maria Lambarri; ☎ 65-0106)
UK (Barry Walker; ☎ 23-9974)
USA (Olga Villa Garcia; ☎ 22-4112)

Laundry

There's a high concentration of lavandarías on Suecia, Procuradores, Plateros and Espaderos (just off the Plaza de Armas) that will wash, dry and fold your clothes for just US$1 to US$2 per kilogram. However, during the busiest months, it's best not to stake your last pair of socks on their promise of 'in by 10am, ready by 6pm.'

Medical Services

Cuzco's facilities are good but limited and a transfer to Lima is recommended for the most complicated procedures. The best medical services available include:

Clínica Centro Medico Pardo (☎ 24-0387; Av de la Cultura 710; consultation US$14)

Clínica Paredes (☎ 22-5265; clinica@terra.com.pe; Lechugal 405; consultation US$30)

Dr Oscar Tejada (☎ 23-3836, 965-0336; consultation from US$25) Speaks English and is OK for straightforward problems such as altitude sickness.

Hospital Regional (☎ 23-1131; emergencies 22-3691; Av de la Cultura) Cheaper than the other three places, but not as consistently good.

Inka Farma (☎ 24-2601; Av Sol 174) A well-stocked, 24-hour pharmacy.

Money

Several banks on Avenida Sol have foreign-card-friendly ATMs and you'll find several more strategically positioned in shops around the Plaza de Armas and in Huanchac train station. *Casas de cambio* (exchange offices) all give similar exchange rates and are scattered around the Plaza de Armas and along Avenida Sol. Expect a loss of several percent for traveler's checks. Street money-changers can also be found outside the banks and *casas de cambio*, but their rates equal what you'll get at the *casas de cambio* and rip-offs are not uncommon.

BCP (formerly Banco de Crédito; Av Sol 189) Has a Visa ATM, gives cash advances on Visa and changes traveler's checks to soles for no commission.

Interbanc (Av Sol 380) Interbanc has ATM machines that accept Cirrus, MasterCard, Plus and Visa.

LAC Dolar (☎ 25-7969; lacdolar@terra.com.pe; Av Sol 150; 🕑 9am-7pm Mon-Sat) This is a respected money-changer that will deliver direct to your hotel if you ring to tell them your traveler's check numbers.

Post & Telephone

International calls can be made from any callbox with a Telefónica phonecard, available widely. Mail addressed to you at c/o Lista de Correo, Correos Central, Cuzco, can be held for collection at the main **post office** (☎ 22-4212; Av Sol 800; 🕑 7:30am-8pm Mon-Sat, 8am-2pm Sun) about 800m southeast of the Plaza de Armas. Bring proof of identity.

Tourist Information

Websites with tourist information include www.portalcuzco.com and www.cuscoperu.com. Local tour operators all help out with travel arrangements; see p179.

iPeru Plaza de Armas (☎ 25-2974, 23-4498; iperucusco@promperu.gob.pe; Portal Carrizos 250; 🕑 8:30am-7:30pm); Aeropuerto Alejandro Velasco Astete (☎ 23-7364; iperucuscoapto@promperu.gob.pe; 🕑 6am-2pm) Apart from providing information iPeru runs Indecopi, the tourist protection office, through its offices. It can help with problems and complaints. English is spoken.

Regional Tourist Office (☎ 26-3176; cusco@mincetur.gob.pe; Mantas 117-A; 🕑 8am-7pm Mon-Fri, 8am-2pm Sat) is good and also has fortnightly leaflets with a cultural programme.

South American Explorers Club (SAE; ☎ 24-5484; cuscoclub@saexplorers.org; office 4, Choquechaca 188; 🕑 9:30am-5pm Mon-Fri & 9:30am-1pm Sat) has a huge stock of traveler's information, plus good-quality maps for sale, a huge book exchange (members only) and a long

BOLETO TURÍSTICO

You can't easily buy individual entrance tickets to many of the major sights in and around Cuzco. Instead, you have to buy a *Boleto Turístico* (Tourism Ticket), which costs US$10, US$5 for students under 26, or is free for children under 10. The ticket gives access to 16 different sites and can be purchased from **Oficina Ejecutiva del Comité** (OFEC; ☎ 22-6919, 22-7037; 🕑 8am-6pm Mon-Fri & 8:30am-1pm Sat), in the back of the Municipalidad at Avenida Sol 103 or on Garcilaso at Heladeros. *Boletos Turísticos* may also be purchased from the tourist office, a travel agent or at some of the sites and should be valid for 10 days. Students will need to show their ID card along with the *Boleto Turístico* when entering sights.

A cost of US$10 represents good value if you visit most of the sights. Within Cuzco, it's valid for La Catedral, the church of San Blas, the Santa Catalina convent, the Museo de Historia Regional, the Museo de Arte Religioso, the Museo Palacio Municipal and the Museo Arqueológico Coricancha (but not Coricancha itself). The ticket also covers Sacsayhuamán, Qenko, Puca Pucara, Tambo Machay, Pisac, Chinchero, Ollantaytambo, Pikillacta and Tipón – all outside Cuzco. The biggest drawback to the *Boleto Turístico* is that each sight can only be visited once. Other museums, churches and colonial buildings in and around Cuzco can be visited free or for a modest admission charge.

It's also possible to buy three partial *Boletos Turísticos*: One covering the sites of Sacsayhuamán, Qenko, Pukapukara and Tambo Machay; one granting access to central Cuzco's churches and museums; and the other valid for Sacred Valley sites. These tickets all cost US$6 but are valid for one day only and have no student discount

list of discounts available to members in Cuzco. From May to September, the club is also open until 5pm on Saturday and from 9:30am to 1pm on Sunday. For more information about the club, see the boxed text on p56.

DANGERS & ANNOYANCES

While most travelers will experience few problems in Cuzco, it's a sad fact that more tourists are robbed here than any other Peruvian city. Avoid displays of wealth and leave valuables in a hotel safe. Take special care going to and from the Machu Picchu train station and central market, as these are prime areas for pickpockets and bag-slashers. Distraction tricks include spitting and tapping on your shoulder.

When taking cabs, use only official taxi firms – look for the company's lit number on top of the taxi. Lock your doors from the inside and never allow the driver to admit a second passenger. Ruthless robberies in taxis have been increasing.

Try also to avoid walking by yourself late at night or very early in the morning. Revelers returning late from bars or travelers setting off solo for the Inca Trail before sunrise are particularly vulnerable to a spate of strangle muggings.

Don't buy drugs. Dealers and police often work together, and Procuradores is one of several areas in which you can make a drug deal and get busted, all within a couple of minutes. Women especially should try not to let go of their glass or accept drinks from strangers as spiking has been reported.

Also, beware of altitude sickness if you're flying in from sea level. It's worth reread-ing Altitude Sickness (p429) in the Health chapter for more information.

SIGHTS

There are four things to remember when sightseeing: buy your *Boleto Turístico* (see the boxed text on p171); carry a student card if you have one; don't get so excited by what you're seeing that you forget to keep an eye on your pockets; and opening hours are er-ratic and can change for any reason – from feast days to the caretaker slipping off for a beer with his mates. A good time to visit Cuzco's well-preserved colonial churches is in the early morning from 6:30am to 8am, when the churches are open for services. Officially, they are closed to tourists at this time, but if you go in quietly as one of the congregation, you can see the church as it should be seen – as a place of worship, not just a tourist attraction. Flash photography is normally not allowed in churches. Most ruins in Cuzco have been converted into colonial or modern buildings, but their walls remain visible.

Most of the sights listed here have local guides available, some of whom speak Eng-lish, but you should always agree to a fair

price in advance. A respectable minimum is usually US$1 per person in a small group or a little more for individuals.

Plaza de Armas

In Inca times, the plaza, called Huacaypata or Aucaypata, was twice as large as it is today. It was the heart of Inca Cuzco and remains the heart of the modern city. Two flags usually fly here – the red-and-white Peruvian flag and the rainbow-colored flag of Tahuantinsuyo (representing the four quarters of the Inca Empire). Colo-nial arcades surround the plaza. On the northeastern side is the cathedral, fronted by a large flight of stairs and flanked by the churches of Jesús María and El Tri-unfo. On the southeastern side is the very ornate church of La Compañía. The quiet pedestrian alleyway of Loreto, both sides of which have Inca walls, is a historic means of access to the plaza.

LA CATEDRAL

Started in 1559 and taking almost a hundred years to build, the cathedral (🕑 10-11:30am & 2-5:30pm Mon-Wed & Fri-Sat, 2-5:30pm Thu, 2-5pm Sun; entry with Boleto Turístico) is combined with the church of **El Triunfo** (1536) to its right – the oldest church in Cuzco, and the church of **Jesús María** (1733) positioned to the cathe-dral's left. The main structure is positioned on the site of Inca Viracocha's palace and was built using blocks pilfered from the nearby Inca site of Sacsayhuamán.

The cathedral is one of the city's greatest repositories of colonial art, especially from the Escuela Cuzqueña (Cuzco school) of painting, which produced striking combi-nations of 16th- and 17th-century European style with the imagination and customs of the Andean Indian artists. The most striking example is perhaps *The Last Supper* by Mar-cos Zapata, which depicts one of the most solemn occasions in the Christian faith, but graces it with a small feast of Andean special-ties: Look for the plump and juicy-looking roast *cuy* (guinea pig) stealing the show with its feet held plaintively in the air.

The **sacristy** itself is covered with paintings of Cuzco's bishops, starting with Vicente de Valverde, the friar who accompanied Pizarro during the conquest. The crucifix-ion at the back of the sacristy is attributed to the Flemish painter Van Dyck, though some

Calle Lima in the morning light, **Puno** (p148)

RYAN FOX

SUNA KANGA

Funerary towers, called *chullpas*,
Sillustani (p155)

Stone archway and path to the dock, **Isla Taquile** (p157)

MARK DAFFFY

WOODS WHEATCROFT

Final descent of the **Inca Trail** (p212),
Machu Picchu

View descending into the Urubamba valley,
Machu Picchu (p207)

WES WALKER

Visitors on **Huayna Picchu** (p211) look across to the road leading to the ruins, Machu Picchu

MA

PAUL HELLANDER

Ruins in the mist, **Machu Picchu** (p207)

Peru's best-known icons, llamas and **Machu Picchu** (p207)

ERIC L WHEATER.

ANDREW PETERS

Inca doorway and stonework, **Machu Picchu** (p207)

DONALD C. & PRISCILLA ALEXANDER EASTMAN

Temple of the Sun (p210) overlooking the Urubamba valley, Machu Picchu

Inca terraces, the **Sacred Valley**
(p196)

BRUCE BI

Monolithic Inca fortress of **Sacsayhuamán**,
(p195), near Cuzco

Relaxing at the **hot springs** (p205), Aguas Calientes

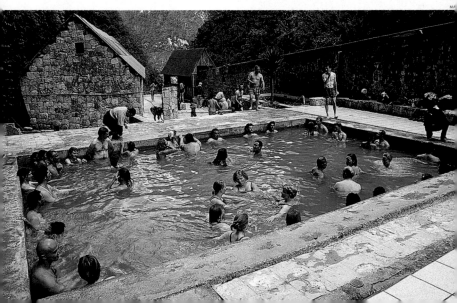

guides claim it to be the work of the 17th-century Spaniard Alonso Cano.

Also look for the **oldest surviving painting** in Cuzco, showing the entire city during the great earthquake of 1650. The inhabitants can be seen parading around the plaza with a crucifix, praying for the earthquake to stop, which miraculously it did (don't they all?). This precious crucifix, called **El Señor de los Temblores**, or 'The Lord of the Earthquakes,' can still be seen in the alcove to the right of the door leading into El Triunfo, blackened by the countless votive candles that have been lit beneath it.

El Triunfo also houses a vault containing the remains of the famous Inca historian, **Garcilaso de la Vega** whose remains were returned to Cuzco several years ago by the king and queen of Spain.

The original wooden **altar** is at the very back of the cathedral, behind the present silver altar, and opposite both is the magnificently carved **choir**, dating from the 17th century. There are also many glitzy silver and gold **side chapels** with elaborate platforms and altars that contrast with the austerity of the cathedral's stonework. The last side chapel to the left of the altar has a painting of Pope John Paul II during his visit to Sacsayhuamán in 1985.

The huge main doors are also open for genuine worshippers between 6am and 10am. Religious festivals are a superb time to see the cathedral. At Corpus Christi it is filled with pedestals supporting larger-than-life statues of saints, surrounded by thousands of candles and bands of musicians honoring them with mournful Andean tunes.

LA COMPAÑÍA
This **church** (admission free) is often lit up at night and can be seen from the train as you come in from Machu Picchu after dark. Its foundations are built from the palace of Huayna Capac – the last Inca to rule an undivided, unconquered empire.

The church was built by the Jesuits in 1571, and was reconstructed after the 1650 earthquake. The Jesuits planned to make it the most magnificent of Cuzco's churches. However, the bishop of Cuzco complained that its splendor should not rival that of the cathedral, and the squabble grew to a point where Pope Paul III was called upon

to arbitrate. His decision was in favor of the cathedral, but by the time word had reached Cuzco, La Compañía was just about finished, complete with an incredible baroque facade that makes it one of Cuzco's most ornate churches.

Two large canvases near the main door show early marriages in Cuzco and are worth taking note of for their wealth of period detail.

Opening hours are erratic.

MUSEO DE HISTORIA NATURAL
This **museum** (🕑 9:30am-noon & 3-6pm Mon-Fri; foreigner/national US$0.30/0.20) is run by the Universidad Nacional, and the entrance is to the right of La Compañía on the Plaza de Armas. It houses a motley collection of stuffed local animals and birds and a few other items.

INCA WALLS
If you walk southeast away from the Plaza de Armas along the narrow alley of **Loreto**, there are Inca walls on both sides. The wall on the right-hand side belongs to Amarucancha, or the 'Courtyard of the Serpents.' Its name may be derived from the pair of snakes carved on the lintel of the doorway near the end of the enclosure. Amarucancha was the site of the palace of the 11th Inca, Huayna Capac. The church of La Compañía was built here after the conquest, and there is now a school and tourist market behind the church. On the other side of Loreto is one of the best and the oldest Inca walls in Cuzco. The wall belonged to the Acllahuasi, or the 'House of the Chosen Women.' Following the conquest, the building became part of the closed convent of Santa Catalina and so went from housing the Virgins of the Sun to housing pious Catholic nuns.

Heading northeast away from the Plaza de Armas along Calle Triunfo, you soon come to the street of Hatunrumiyoc, named after the well-known **12-sided stone**. The stone is on the right, about halfway along the second city block, and can usually be recognized by the small knot of Indians selling souvenirs next to it. This excellently fitted stone belongs to a wall of the palace of the 6th Inca, Inca Roca. It is technically brilliant but by no means an unusual example of polygonal masonry. In Machu Picchu there are stones with more than 30 angles (though these are corner stones and are therefore counted in three dimensions) and a block with 44 angles in one plane has been found at Torontoy, a minor ruin roughly halfway between Machu Picchu and Ollantaytambo.

There is a great difference between the wall of Hatunrumiyoc and that of the Aclla-huasi. The first is made of polygonal stone blocks in no regular pattern, while the other is made from carefully shaped rectangular blocks that are coursed, or layered, in the manner of modern-day bricks. In general, the polygonal masonry was thought to be stronger and was therefore used for retaining walls in terraces. The coursed masonry, which was considered more aesthetically appealing, was used for the walls of Inca temples and palaces.

North & East of Plaza de Armas
SANTA CATALINA
This **convent** (☎ 22-8613; entry with Boleto Turístico; ☒ 9am-5:30pm Sat-Thu, 8am-4pm Fri) has a colonial and religious-art **museum**, with many religious paintings of the Escuela Cuzqueña and a dramatically friezed baroque side chapel, with the convent's main altar.

MUSEO DE ARTE RELIGIOSO
Originally the palace of the Inca Roca, the foundations of this **museum** (Archbishop's Palace, Hatunrumiyoc; entry with the Boleto Turístico; ☒ 8-11:30am & 3-5:30pm Mon-Sat) were converted into the residence of the Marquis of Buenavista and later into the archbishop's palace. The beautiful mansion is now home to a fascinating religious-art collection, notable for the accuracy of its period detail and especially its insight into the interaction of the conquistadors and the Indians. There are some impressive ceilings and the curious Sala de Arzobispos (Room of Archbishops) filled with jovially grinning life-size models of the great men. The colonial-style tile work of the interior is not original and was replaced in the 1940s.

PRE-COLUMBIAN ART MUSEUM
This **museum** (☎ 23-3210; Plaza de las Nazarenas; adult/student/child US$4.20/2.50/1.40; ☒ 9am-10pm) was founded in June 2003 to showcase a varied collection of 450 archaeological pieces that were previously buried in the vast storerooms of Lima's Largo Museum.

SAN BLAS
A simple adobe church, **San Blas** (Plaza San Blas; entry with Boleto Turístico; ☒ 10-11:30am & 2-5:30pm Mon-Wed & Fri-Sat, 2-5:30pm Thu, 2-5pm Sun) is comparatively small, but its exquisitely carved pulpit has been called the finest example of colonial woodcarving in the Americas. Legend claims that its creator was an Indian who miraculously recovered from a deadly disease and subsequently dedicated his life to carving this pulpit for the church. Supposedly, his skull is nestled in the topmost part of the carving. In reality, no one is certain of the identity of either the skull or the woodcarver. Also note the very ornate, baroque, gold-leafed principal altar.

MUSEO INKA
This **museum** (☎ 23-7380; cnr Ataúd & Tucumán; adult/under-15 US$1.40/free; ☒ 9am-5pm Mon-Fri, 9am-4pm Sat), a steep block northeast of the Plaza de Armas, rests on Inca foundations; it's also known as the Admiral's House, after the first owner, Admiral Francisco Aldrete Maldonado. It was badly damaged in the 1650 earthquake and rebuilt by Pedro Peralta de los Ríos, the Count of Laguna, whose crest is above the porch. Further damage from the 1950 earthquake has now been fully repaired, restoring the building to its position among Cuzco's finest colonial houses.

Look for the massive stairway guarded by sculptures of mythical creatures, as well as a corner window column that from the inside looks like a statue of a bearded man but from the outside appears to be a naked woman. The facade is plateresque – an elaborately ornamented 16th-century Spanish style suggestive of silver plate. The ceilings are ornate, and the views from the windows are good.

This is also the best museum for those interested in the Incas. The building's restored interior is filled with a fine collection of metal and gold work, jewelry, pottery, textiles, mummies and more. The museum has 450 *queros* (Inca wooden drinking vessels), which is the largest *quero* collection in the world; some are in storage.

SANTO DOMINGO
The church of Santo Domingo is famous as the site of Coricancha (see p175 for details), which was Cuzco's major Inca temple. The church has twice been destroyed by

earthquakes, first in 1650 and again in 1950, as well as being damaged in the 1986 earthquake. Photographs in the entrance show the extent of the 1950 damage – compare the state of the colonial building with that of the Inca walls, which sustained minimal damage in these earthquakes. Also in the entrance is a doorway carved in the Arabic style – a reminder of the centuries of Moorish domination in Spain. Remains of the Inca temple are inside the cloister. Colonial paintings around the outside of the courtyard depict the life of Santo Domingo (Saint Dominic). The paintings contain several representations of dogs holding torches in their jaws. These are God's guard dogs, or *dominicanus* in Latin, hence the name of this religious order.

CORICANCHA

This **Inca site** (☎ 24-9176; Plazoleta Santo Domingo; adult/student US$1.60/1; ☽ 8:30am-5:30pm Mon-Sat, 2-5pm Sun) forms the base of the colonial church of Santo Domingo. Today, all that remains of Coricancha (once the Inca Empire's richest temple) is the stonework – the precious stones and metals were looted by the conquistadors.

In Inca times, Coricancha (or Q'orikancha, which is Quechua for 'golden courtyard') was literally covered with gold. The temple walls were lined with some 700 solid-gold sheets, each weighing about 2kg. There were life-size gold and silver replicas of corn that were ceremonially 'planted' in agricultural rituals. Also reported were solid-gold treasures such as altars, llamas and babies, as well as a replica of the sun, which was lost. But within months of the arrival of the first conquistadors, this incredible wealth had all been looted and melted down.

Various religious rites took place in the temple. The mummified bodies of several previous Incas were kept here, brought out into the sunlight each day and offered food and drink, which was then ritually burnt. Coricancha was also an observatory from which priests monitored major celestial activities.

Most of this is left to the imagination of the modern visitor, but the remaining stonework ranks with the finest Inca architecture in Peru. A curved, perfectly fitted, 6m-high wall can be seen from both inside and outside the site. This wall has withstood

the violent earthquakes that leveled most of Cuzco's colonial buildings.

Once inside the site, the visitor enters a courtyard. The octagonal font in the middle was originally covered with 55kg of solid gold. Inca side chambers lie to either side of the courtyard. The largest, to the right, were said to be temples to the moon and stars and were covered with sheets of solid silver. The walls are perfectly tapered upward and, with their niches and doorways, are excellent examples of Inca trapezoidal architecture. The fitting of the individual blocks is so precise that, in some places, you can't tell where one block ends and the next begins as you glide your finger over them.

Opposite these chambers, on the other side of the courtyard, are smaller temples dedicated to thunder and the rainbow. Three holes have been carved through the walls of this section to the street outside, which scholars think were drains, either for the sacrificial *chicha* drink, for blood or, more mundanely, for rainwater. Alternatively, they may have been speaking tubes connecting the inner temple with the outside. Another noteworthy feature of this side of the complex is the floor in front of the chambers. It dates from Inca times and is carefully cobbled with pebbles.

After the conquest, Coricancha was given to Juan Pizarro. He was not able to enjoy it for long, because he died in the battle at Sacsayhuamán in 1536. In his will, he bequeathed Coricancha to the Dominicans, and it has remained in their possession ever since. Today's site is a rather bizarre combination of Inca and colonial architecture, topped with a modern protective roof of glass and metal.

MUSEO ARQUEOLÓGICO CORICANCHA

This small modern underground **museum** (entry with the Boleto Turístico; ☽ 9:30am-5:30pm) is in front of the church of Santo Domingo and is entered from Avenida Sol. There are various archaeological displays that interpret both Inca and pre-Inca cultures.

South & West of Plaza de Armas
LA MERCED

Just off Plaza de Armas, **La Merced** (☎ 23-1821; Mantas; adult/student US$1/0.60; ☽ 9am-noon & 2-5pm Mon-Sat) is considered to be Cuzco's third most important colonial church. It was destroyed in the 1650 earthquake and rebuilt; the present structure, consisting of two sections, dates from 1654.

The church itself is open for worship from 7am to 9am and 5pm to 7:30pm. To the left of the church, at the back of a small courtyard, is the entrance to the monastery and museum.

The Order of La Merced was founded in Barcelona in 1218 by San Pedro Nolasco. Paintings based on his life hang around the walls of the beautiful colonial cloister. The church on the far side of the cloister contains the tombs of two of the most famous conquistadors, Diego de Almagro and Gonzalo Pizarro. Also on the far side of the cloister is a small religious museum that houses vestments that are said to have belonged to the conquistador/friar Vicente de Valverde. The museum's most famous exhibit is a priceless, solid-gold monstrance, 1.3m high and covered with precious stones, including no less than 1500 diamonds and 1600 pearls.

MUSEO DE HISTORIA REGIONAL

This **museum** (☎ 22-3245; entry with the Boleto Turístico; ☯ 8am-5pm Mon-Sat) is in the colonial Casa Garcilaso de la Vega, the house of the Inca historian who is buried in the cathedral. The chronologically arranged collection begins with arrowheads from the Preceramic Period and continues with a few pots of the Chavín, Vicus, Mochica, Chimu, Chancay and Inca cultures. There is also a Nazca mummy, a few Inca weavings and some small gold ornaments excavated from Coricancha between 1972 and 1979, and from the Plaza de Armas in 1996 while the fountain was being renovated. Also on display are a few dozen paintings from the Cuzco school, as well as some more recent Mestizo art (mainly with religious themes) and pieces of colonial furniture. There are some changing local craft shows.

MUSEO PALACIO MUNICIPAL

There's a small collection of modern, local art on display at this **museum** (☎ 24-0006; entry with the Boleto Turístico; ☯ 9am-6pm Mon-Sat) on the Plaza Regocijo in the municipality building.

SAN FRANCISCO

This **church and monastery** (☎ 22-1361; Plaza San Francisco; admission including guide US$1; ☯ 9am-4pm Mon-Fri), dating from the 16th and 17th centuries, is more austere than many of Cuzco's other churches, but it does have a large collection of colonial religious paintings and a well-carved, cedar choir. One of the paintings measures 9m x 12m (supposedly the largest painting in South America) and shows the family tree of St Francis of Assisi, the founder of the order. His life is celebrated in the paintings hung around the colonial cloister.

Also of interest are the two crypts, which are not totally underground. Inside are plenty of human bones, some of which have been carefully arranged into phrases designed to remind visitors of the transitory nature of life.

SANTA CLARA

This 16th-century **church** (Santa Clara), part of a strict convent, is difficult to visit but it's worth making the effort to go at Mass around 6am to 7am, because this is one of the more bizarre churches in Cuzco. Mirrors cover almost the entire interior; apparently, the early clergy used them to entice local Indians into church for worship. The nuns provide the choir during Mass, sitting at the very back of the church and separated from both the priest and the rest of the congregation by an ominous grille of heavy metal bars stretching wall to wall and floor to ceiling.

ACTIVITIES

For information about companies that organize the following activities, see Tours & Guides (p179).

Bird-watching

Serious birders should definitely get hold of *Birds of the High Andes*, by Jon Fjeldså and Niels Krabbe. One of the best birding trips is from Ollantaytambo to Quillabamba, over the Abra de Malaga. This gives a fine cross section of habitats from 4600m down to 950m, but you need to rent a truck or jeep to do it. Barry Walker, owner of Manu Expeditions and the Cross Keys Pub in Cuzco, is a self-confessed 'birding bum' and the best resident ornithologist who can give serious birders plenty of enthusiastic advice.

Horse Riding

Most agencies can arrange a morning or afternoon's riding for about US$10, or you can walk to Sacsayhuamán where many of the ranches are and negotiate your own terms. However, choose carefully as many horses are in a sorry state. Other horseback options require more legwork. Select agencies will offer two-day trips to the area around Limatambo, and there are some first-rate ranches with Peruvian *paso* horses in Urubamba (see p200).

Kayaking

This activity is becoming increasingly popular in the Cuzco area. Some of the river-running trips mentioned later can be accompanied by experienced kayakers, many of whom bring their own kayaks. A few outfitters have kayaks available (see Tours & Guides on p179).

Mountain Biking

This is another growing industry in the Cuzco area. The rental bikes available are not always up to speed, so serious bikers may prefer to bring their own. However, the selection is ever improving. The cheapest bikes can be rented for about US$8 a day, but aren't really up to the rigors of unpaved roads on the wilder rides. Better bikes are available for US$15 to US$20 a day, but check them carefully as well. Make sure you get a helmet, puncture-repair kit, pump and tool kit.

There are several excellent one- or two-day biking trips around Cuzco, especially from Moray to Lares and Calca. Longer trips are possible, but a guide and a support vehicle are recommended. From Ollantaytambo, you can go by bike, bus or truck to the **Abra de Malaga** (4600m) and then downhill to the jungle in three or four days. If heading to Manu, you can break up the long bus journey by biking from Tres Cruces to La Unión – a beautiful, breathtaking downhill ride – or you could go all the way down by bike. The outfitters of Manu trips can arrange bicycle rental and guides. The descent to the Río Apurímac makes a great burn as would the journey to the Tambopata, which boasts a descent of 3500m in five hours. Beat that if you can. A few bikers attempt the over-500km trip all the way to Puerto Maldonado, which gets hot and sweaty near the end but is a great challenge.

Loreto Tours is a recommended agency for bikers to contact in Cuzco. It runs good three- and four-day biking trips around Lares and down to Paucartambo and has decent bikes to rent for US$15 per day including helmet, puncture kit, pump and gloves. See p181 for contact details of this and other companies offering biking tours.

Mountaineering & Skiing

Peruvian Andean Treks (see Tours & Guides on p179) is your best source for information and guides for scaling any of the high peaks in the Cuzco area. There are no skiing areas, but adventurous and expert mountain skiers have been known to carry their skis to a mountain summit and ski back down.

Relaxation

For some pampering or a well-deserved post-Inca-Trail splurge, the following offer massage, aromatherapy and reflexology:
Luz Marina Usca (☎ 22-5159, 968-2233)
Olga Huaman (☎ 25-4254)
Romina Medrano Calderón (☎ 994-3670)
Siluet Sauna and Spa (☎ 23-1504; Quera 253;
🕙 10am-10pm)

River Running

The most popular rafting trip is down the Urubamba. Trips typically last half a day (three hours of rafting plus a couple of hours for transportation at either end) and start at US$25. Full-day tours, combining a raft trip with a lunch and a visit to the Pisac or Ollantaytambo ruins, are also offered for a little more. Two-day trips offer two half days of rafting on different sections of the river, and ruin visits and overnights in the Urubamba valley are possible at extra cost.

The Urubamba is not very wild and offers a great introduction to white-water rafting, some spectacular scenery and a chance to visit some of the best Inca ruins near Cuzco. Three sections are regularly run. The popular Huambutiyo to-Pisac section is the easiest and includes three or four hours of fun rafting, as well as a chance to explore the Pisac ruins or market. This section can be run year-round, although during the dry season, it is far from wild. The Ollantaytambo-to-Chilca run is also very popular – it combines the ruins of Ollantaytambo with some exciting rapids and reaches Class III level of difficulty. The most exciting nearby section is the short but action-packed Cañón Huaran, with Class

CUZCO & THE SACRED VALLEY

III+ rapids; this is not a frequently offered trip, however. Further downstream, the river becomes unraftable as it approaches Machu Picchu. Beyond Machu Picchu the Urubamba offers more possibilities, but access is limited.

Other rivers that can be run are further from Cuzco. For these, you definitely need to book with a top-quality outfit that have highly experienced guides who know first-aid as well as rafting, because you will be days away from help in the event of illness or accident. The Río Apurímac has three- to 10-day options but can only be run from May to November. The rapids are exhilarating (Classes IV and V), and the river goes through remote and wild scenery with deep gorges. Rafters camp on sandy beaches (where sand flies can be a nuisance), and sightings of deer, otters, condors and even pumas have been recorded. The end of the run enters the recently declared Zona Reservada Apurímac – a huge protected area of rainforest with no tourist services. Three- or four-day trips are most often offered, but this stretch of river has limited camping places, and those that exist are becoming increasingly trashed. Make sure your outfitter removes everything and leaves a clean camp site.

An even wilder expedition is the 10- to 12-day possibility on the Río Tambopata, starting in the area of the Andes north of Lake Titicaca and ending at the Reserva Nacional Tambopata in the Amazon. It takes two days just to drive to the put-in point from Cuzco. The first days on the river are full of technically demanding rapids in wild Andean scenery, and the trip finishes with a couple of gentle floating days in the rainforest. Tapirs, capybara, caiman, giant otters and jaguars have all been seen by keen-eyed boaters. Rapids are Class III and IV, but can be run only from June to October.

For recommendations of river running outfits, see Tours & Guides (p181).

Trekking

The best time to go trekking is during the May-to-September dry season. At other times, trails have a tendency to turn into muddy slogs, and views disappear under a blanket of clouds. The country's most celebrated hike, the Inca Trail, can be done using a number of routes. See Machu Picchu & The Inca Trail (p213) for details. See p180 for a list of companies offering trekking.

For those going it alone or on a private guided trek, tents, sleeping bags, backpacks and stoves can all be rented in Cuzco, usually for around US$2 per item per day. Check the equipment carefully before you rent it, as some is pretty shoddy. Maps are available from the SAE club. Eric Adventures (see Tours & Guides p181) has been recommended for cheap rental gear; check all rental equipment carefully. To buy new, **Tatoo Outdoors & Travel** (☎ 26-3099; Plazoleta Las Nazarenas 211; ✆ 10am-9pm Mon-Sat & 1-9pm Sun) has a quality selection of packs, tents, sleeping bags and other gear.

The recently rediscovered ridge-top Inca site of **Choquequirau** (admission US$3) is a remote ruin at the end of an Inca road, fast becoming a popular and cheaper alternative to the crowded Inca Trail. The site can currently only be reached on foot, a great attraction for some people. Get to it quickly before tourist authorities, funded by Unesco, make the site more accessible to the masses.

The site has an incredible location at the junction of three valleys, and though much of the ruins are still covered by cloud forest, they display clear religious and agricultural elements. The most common route begins from Cachora, a village off the road to Abancay – the turn-off is shortly after Saihuite, about four hours from Cuzco. A bus sometimes runs from Abancay, or it's a matter of hitchhiking the final stretch. Most tour agencies follow the route from Cachora, bypassing a road currently under construction to Choquequirau.

The trek can be combined with other routes, including a further five-day hike to Machu Picchu itself. Other, longer routes to Choquequirau also exist, including the spectacular eight-day trek from Huancacalle, which reaches ranges between altitudes of 2400m and 5000m. To trek with an agency, the five-day trip costs an average of US$195 per person, and the combined 10-day Machu Picchu trip costs about US$350.

The newly discovered site of **Corihuayrachina,** located on Cerro Victoria towards the Vilcabamba region, can also be reached in two days of fairly tough trekking from Choquequirau. The site was featured in the *National Geographic* in March 2002, and consists of more than a hundred dispersed structures, including some circular homes, funeral towers, terraces and a truncated pyramid, though the site is now presumed to be less significant than first thought. Also see Vilcabamba (p219) for details of the trek to this site, which the Spanish called Espíritu Pampa.

Another popular trek is the five- to seven-day circuit around the area's highest peak, **Ausangate** (6384m), which takes two spectacular passes higher than 5000m. See p220 for details.

COURSES

Cuzco is one of the best places in the country to study Spanish.

Excel Language Center (☎ 23-5298; contact@excelinspanish.com; Cruz Verde 336) Recommended. It charges US$7 an hour for private lessons, US$5 in a group of two or US$4 in a group of three to four. It also arranges homestays with local families. Rates are US$215 per week, including 20 hours of classes, family homestay with meals, and other activities.

Cusco Spanish School (☎ 22-6928; info@cuscospanishschool.com; 2nd fl, Garcilaso 265) Costs US$255 per week for individual classes, or US$205 in a small group. Prices include a family homestay and meals, plus a city tour and salsa classes. It can also arrange further classes in salsa (US$5 to US$6 per hour), Andean cookery (US$15 daily in a minimum group of four), Andean instruments (US$8 per hour) or ceramics.

Centro Cultural Andino (☎ 23-1710; andinos@wayna.rcp.net.pe; Pardo 689) Associated with Milla Turismo, it has a variety of courses. Classes range from Spanish to Quechua and many aspects of Andean culture, including agriculture, archaeology, architecture, ecology, geography, folklore, arts and anthropology. Seminars can be combined into tailored academic programmes.

Academia Latinoamericana (☎ 24-3364; info@latinoschools.com; Av Sol 580) Opposite Coricancha, it charges US$125 per week in a mini group or US$170 for private classes. Volunteer work and some free dance classes can be organized here.

Don Quijote (☎ 24-1422; www.donquijote.org; Calle Suecia 480) Previously known as Amauta, this popular Spanish school offers 20 classes per week for US$98 in a small group or US$184 individually. Prices include a welcome dinner, Internet access and complimentary courses. It can also arrange accommodation or family stays. It also runs programmes at a site in the Sacred Valley at Urubamba.

La Casona de la Esquina (☎ 23-5903; spanishlessonscusco@yahoo.es; Calle Purgatorio 395) This is a cheaper, more informal option, which has individual programmes for US$5 per hour.

San Blas Spanish School (☎ 24-7898; sbspanishschool@hotmail.com; Tandapata 688) Has private lessons for US$7 per hour or US$140 per week.

Andrea (☎ 25-2515) Charges just US$3 per hour for Spanish classes.

TOURS & GUIDES

Cuzco suffers from no dearth of tour companies, many of which cluster around Procuradores, Plateros and the Plaza de Armas. The agencies fall roughly into two groups: those that provide standard tours of Cuzco and its immediate environs and outfitters offering adventure tours such as trekking, river running and mountain biking. Many jungle lodges and outfitters are also based in Cuzco and visit the Puerto Maldonado and Manu area; they are listed in appropriate parts of the Amazon Basin chapter.

Ask fellow travelers about their experiences, then approach the agency forearmed with questions. Is there an English-speaking guide? Where will we stop for lunch and is it expensive? How big will the group be? What kind of transport is used? How long will everything take? Can you check the equipment (for a trek or rafting trip)? Can you meet the guide or explain a special diet to the cook? If you're unsure, get guarantees in writing, as some agencies will say literally anything to get your business. Also be aware that agencies may be selling you a trip run by someone else, just to secure a commission.

Periodic price wars can lead to local bad feeling, with underpaid guides and overcrowded vehicles. The cheaper tours are liable to be crowded, multilingual affairs. Due to tax exemptions for young agencies, cheaper outfits also regularly change names and offices, so budgeteers should compare notes with other travelers for up-to-the-minute recommendations.

No particular agent can be 100% recommended, but those described here are, however, reputable outfits that receive mostly positive feedback.

Local Tours

The standard tours include a half-day city tour (US$5 to US$10), a half-day tour of the nearby ruins of Sacsayhuamán, Qenko, Puca Pucara and Tambo Machay (US$6 to US$7), a half-day tour to the south of Cuzco including Pikillacta and Tipón and Andahuaylillas (US$6 to US$7) and a full-day trip to the Sacred Valley including Pisac, Ollantaytambo and Chinchero (US$5.50 to US$13). Agents also offer the one-day trip to Machu Picchu costing US$95 to US$130, and US$135 to US$160 for the two-day trip, including the bus from the Aguas Calientes station up to the ruins, admission, a guide and accommodation for those staying the night.

The city tours on offer can often be rushed, and make too much time for visiting the obligatory craft factory.

Destinos Turisticos (☎ 22-8168; destinos@telser .com.pe; office 101, Portal de Panes 123) Owned by a helpful Dutchman.

Elim Travel (☎ 24-1470; elimtravelperu@hotmail.com; Garcilaso 265) Elim is a new start-up company good for travel connections.

Inca Explorers (☎ 24-1070; info@incaexplorers.com; Suecia 339) This company is helpful and economical.

Kantu Tours (☎ 24-3673; kantuperu@wayna.rcp.net. pe; Portal Carrizos 258) Also specializes in motorbike and 4WD tours, as well as rafting on the Urubamba.

Lima Tours (☎ 24-5110 ext 409; me@limatours .com.pe; Av Machu Picchu D-24, Urb Mañuel Prado) Caters to 1st-class travelers and international tour groups.

Milla Turismo (☎ 23-1710; info@millaturismo.com; Avenida Pardo 675 & Portal Comercio 195) Milla is also geared to providing 1st-class services to international tour groups. It also arranges courses on Andean culture (see Courses earlier p179).

Naty's Travel (☎ 23-9437; natystravel@terra.com.pe; Triunfo 338) It's an economical choice.

Peruvian Travel y Turismo (☎ 23-5529; peruvian travel@terra.com.pe; San Agustín 307) This is a well-established company with all the standard tours.

Hiking

All of the previously mentioned companies also offer hiking trips, but the following specialize in trekking. Inca Trail prices are given as a benchmark only and are not fixed. Shop around and ask a lot of questions. Some agencies ask that you carry 'a small day pack,' which ends up being your regular backpack, so clarify this. Find out how many people sleep in tents, how many porters each group has, what the arrangements for special diets are, and whether trekkers will be collected from their hotel if the tour leaves very early (early starters can be caught off-guard by street thieves). Make your wishes clear and get them in writing. Be aware that the cheapest agencies change names regularly in order to retain tax benefits afforded to new companies so ask around if you're on a very tight budget. Of the following list, the two most highly recommended agencies are United Mice and SAS.

Andean World (☎ 22-1491; andeanlife01@terra.com .pe; Plateros 341) It is recommended by readers for good service, charging US$260 for the trail.

Apu Expeditions (☎ /fax 24-6377; www.geocities .com/apuexpeditions) This is a similar all-round outfitter catering to foreign reservations.

Aventours (☎ 22-4050; info@aventours.com; Pardo 545) Also known as EcoInka, it has top-of-the-line guides, equipment, food and services specializing in the Cuzco-area highlands and also offers a llama trek. It operates the private Veronica Km82 camp at the Inca Trail entrance. Expensive but worth it; its tours and Inca Trail entrance camp are unique.

Emperadores Tours (☎ 23-1183; emperadoresto20@ hotmail.com; Procuradores 366) Emperadores is one of the very cheapest offering the Inca Trail for US$170/150 adult/student, but note that it changes its name often and gets very mixed reports.

Enigma (☎ 22-2155; info@enigmaperu.com; Garcilaso 132) Enigma is a new company offering several alternative treks as well as conventional, mid-range, hiking trips. The Inca Trail costs US$265/40 per adult/student.

Liz's Explorer (☎ 24-6619; lizarenas@hotmail.com; Calle del Medio 114) Rents camping equipment and runs Inca Trail trips for approximately US$230/215 per adult/student.

Peruvian Andean Treks (☎ 22-5701; postmast@patc usco.com.pe; Pardo 705) Run by Tom Hendrickson, who has pioneered local mountaineering. It has some of the best guides and equipment for climbing the local snowpeaks, as well as trekking and jungle trips. It can send you a list of representatives in the USA, Canada, UK, Australia and New Zealand that charge the same rates as in Cuzco. The Inca Trail costs over US$400.

Q'ente (☎ /fax 22-2535; qente@terra.com.pe; Garcilaso 210) Has good service and charges US$300/275 per adult/student for the trail.

SAS (☎ 23-7292; sastravel@planet.com.pe; Portal de Panes 143 & Calle del Medio 123) A well-established company with few detractors. The trail costs US$260/235 per adult/student, and English, French, German and even some Dutch are spoken.

United Mice (☎ 22-1139; unitedmi@terra.com.pe; Plateros 351) Gets consistently good recommendations. Italian and Portuguese are spoken as well as English. The trail costs around US$250/215 per adult/student.

Tours into the Jungle

The following companies in Cuzco provide tours to the Manu area. For more details on what the tours cover, see Tours in the Manu Area (p369).

Expediciones Vilca (☎ 24-4751; manuvilca@terra.com.pe; Plateros 363)

InkaNatura (☎ 25-1173; Plateros 361) Also has lodges in the Puerto Maldonado area.

Manu Ecological Adventures (☎ 26-1640; www.manuadventures.com; Plateros 356)

Manu Expeditions (☎ 22-6671, 23-9974; www.manuexpeditions.com; Pardo 895)

Manu Nature Tours (☎ 25-2721; www.manuperu.com; Pardo 1046)

Pantiacolla Tours (☎ 23-8323; www.pantiacolla.com; Plateros 360)

River Running & Mountain Biking

The basic, one-day Río Urubamba trip with lunch costs US$15 to US$35 (minimum four passengers) depending on the season and stretch covered.

Amazonas Explorer (☎ 22-7137; sales@amazonas-explorer.com; Jose Gabriel Cosio 400, Urb Magisterial) You could make reservations for a Tambopata or Apurímac trip with this professional international company, which has top-quality equipment and guides. It also does other river trips, as well as mountain biking and hiking.

Apumayo Expeditions (☎ 24-6018; contact@apumayo.com; Garcilaso 265) Another professional outfitter which takes advance international bookings for Tambopata trips. It's also equipped to take disabled travelers to Machu Picchu.

Eric Adventures (☎ /fax 22-8475; cusco@ericadventures.com; Plateros 324) Offers inexpensive one- and two-day trips on the Urubamba and four-day trips on the Apurímac (US$200). Eric Arenas is a Peruvian kayaking champion who represented Peru in the 1992 Olympics. He also offers kayaking tours and classes on the Apurímac, where he uses a hot spring to comfortably teach the Eskimo roll! A three-day course is US$120. It also runs economical hiking and mountain-bike tours.

Instinct (☎ 23-3451; instinct@chavin.rcp.net.pe; Procuradores 50) Has a range of rafting, hiking and mountain-biking tours.

Loreto Tours (☎ 22-8264; loretotours@planet.com.pe; Calle del Medio 111) Loreto runs cheap one-day river trips and is particularly recommended for its motorbike and mountain biking tours.

Mayuc (☎ 23-2666; chando@mayuc.com; Portal Confiturias 211) Does excellent four-day rafting trips on the Apurímac, including transportation, food and camping. It also runs cheap, 10-day trips (seven days of rafting) on the Tambopata.

Peru Discovery (☎ 24-7007; www.perudiscovery.com; office 214, Triunfo 392) This outfit runs recommended mountain-bike tours.

Other Activities

See Urubamba (p200) for information on **paragliding** in the Sacred Valley. PeruFly (see Activities p176) also arranges trips. There is a lot more you can do:

Action Valley (☎ 24-0835; www.actionvalley.com; 🕙 10am-4pm Sun-Fri Apr-Nov) This adventure park has a climbing pole ($19), free rappel (US$24), climbing wall (US$9), 120m bungee jump (US$59) and a bungee sling shot (US$59) at the ready. The park is 11km outside Cuzco on the road to Poroy (taxi US$2 one way). It's closed in the wet season.

Another Planet (☎ 22-9379; another.planet@terra.com.pe; Triunfo 120) For those interested in local shamans, or who are curious to try the curative properties of the notorious San Pedro and Ayahuasca plants, contact Lesley Myburgh here. Never buy these plants in the street or try to prepare them yourself, as they can be highly toxic in the wrong hands.

Globos de los Andes (☎ 23-2352; www.globosperu.com; Calle Arequipa 271) Runs hot-air ballooning trips over the Sacred Valley, which can be combined with 4WD tours to the Salinas and Maras. It costs US$300 per person for an extended trip, or US$55 for a short ride with a moored balloon, which requires a minimum of 15 people per day.

Private Guides

Independent licensed guides registered with Inrena can be contacted through agencies or the following organizations:

Agotur (Asociación de Guías Oficiales de Turismo; ☎ 24-9758; agotur_cusco@hotmail.com; Calle Nueva Baja 424, Office 02)

Colitur (Colegio de Licenciados en Turismo; ☎ 24-2065; colitur_cusco@yahoo.es; Urb. Zarumilla Bloque 5-B Dpto 102)

Guides recommended by travelers include:

Raul Castelo (☎ 24-3234, 969-2270; raulcastelo10@mlxmail.com)

Roger Valencia Espinoza (☎ 25-1278; vroger@qenqo.rcp.net.pe)

FESTIVALS & EVENTS

The area celebrates many fiestas and holidays. Apart from the national holidays, the following dates mark crowded, lively occasions that are particularly important in Cuzco:

Monday before Easter The procession of the Lord of the Earthquakes dates from the earthquake of 1650 (see La Catedral p172).

May 2-3 A hilltop Crucifix Vigil is held on all hillsides with crosses atop them.

CUZCO & THE SACRED VALLEY

First Thursday after Trinity Sunday Corpus Cristi is a movable feast that usually occurs in early June and features fantastic religious processions and celebrations in the cathedral.

June 24 Cuzco's most important festival is Inti Raymi, or 'Festival of the Sun.' It attracts tourists from all over the world, and the whole city celebrates in the streets. The festival culminates in a reenactment of the Inca winter-solstice festival at Sacsayhuamán.

December 24 This date marks the Santuranticuy or 'Christmas Eve' shopping festival.

Other festivals are important in particular villages and towns outside Cuzco; they are mentioned in the appropriate sections.

SLEEPING

Cuzco has over 250 hotels of all types and prices tend to be some of the highest in the country. It's important to note that the high-season prices given here should not be taken as gospel – tariffs are market driven and vary dramatically according to the season. It gets crowded here from June to August, when accommodations can be tight, especially in the 10 days before Inti Raymi on June 24 and around July 28, during the national Fiestas Patrias. At these times, the best hotels are often fully booked and prices skyrocket. During the rest of the year, it is well worth bargaining for better rates.

Most hotels in Cuzco will store excess luggage so you don't have to lug it around with you. Always securely lock and clearly label all pieces of luggage to prevent light fingers dipping into unlocked luggage and get a receipt – especially for any valuables left in the hotel safe.

Watch out for early check-out times. A surprising number of hotels require you to leave your room between 8:30am and 10am.

Budget

Budgeteers are at a distinct advantage in the off season, when room prices automatically drop and even mid-range accommodations can be reduced to upper-range budget prices with a little haggling. Cuzco also sees new, cheap places mushrooming every season. The cheapest hotels are not always in safe areas, however, so be ready to take official taxis after dark or walk back in a group. Budget hotels abound in the San Blas neighborhood, particularly and also on streets leading to San Pedro Station.

Casas de Hospedaje (☎ 24-2710) is an association that provides lodging in small, family-run hostels with prices ranging from US$5 to US$12 per person depending on the season and the facilities.

Albergue Municipal (☎ /fax 25-2506; albergue@municusco.gob.pe; Kiskapata 240; dm US$6-7) The Albergue, up a steep hill, affords great city views from the balcony. The rooms are spotless and have bunk beds for four to eight people, and there is hot water, a large common room, a small café, laundry facilities and safe luggage storage.

Hostal Resbalosa (☎ 22-4839; Resbalosa 494; s/d/tr US$4.20/7/10) Round the corner from the Albergue, Resbalosa's main attraction is a fabulous terrace overlooking the plaza. It also has shared warm showers and decent rooms, plus a friendly and helpful owner and safe luggage storage. It is in a steep pedestrian-only street, and cabs can only reach within 100m of the hostel.

Hospedaje Inka (☎ 23-1995; americopacheco@hotmail.com; Suytuccato 848; s/d US$3.50-6/7-12) This is a scruffy but charming, converted, hillside farmhouse above San Blas, popular with backpackers and affording some great views. There's erratic hot water, private bathrooms, and a large farm kitchen available for cooking your own meals. Taxis can't climb the final stretch, so be prepared for an uphill walk.

Hostal El Arcano (☎ /fax 23-2703; Carmen Alto 288; s/d US$4.20/8.40, with bathroom US$7/8.50) El Arcano is an intimate, friendly little place, though rooms are nothing to write home about. There is hot water during the day.

Hostal Kuntur Wasi (☎ 22-7570; Tandapata 352A; s/d US$5/10, with bathroom US$10/15) Kuntur Wasi has a warm and friendly environment, with limited views over downtown, warm showers and kitchen privileges.

El Mirador de la Ñusta (☎ 24-8039; elmiradordelanusta@hotmail.com; Calle Tandapata 682; s/d/tr US$10/20/30) This hostel has light, little rooms with bathrooms, and it takes approximately 30 seconds to be seated on Plaza San Blas for your morning mate.

Hostal El Grial (☎ 22-3012; grial_celta@yahoo.com; Atoqsayk'uchi 594; s/d/tr US$7/12/15, with bathroom s/d/tr US$12/20/25) This is a relaxed spot in a rickety old wooden-floored building run by accommodating folks.

Hospedaje Iquique (☎ 22-5880; hicuzco@terra.com.pe; Recoleta; s/d US$4.20/8.40, with bathroom US$8.40/

16.80) This newly opened, friendly, budget place is a brisk walk up from the plaza through winding, cobbled streets and has plain rooms set around a courtyard. The price includes breakfast. Rooms with bathrooms usually go for half price between November and April.

Casa Grande (☎ 26-4156; fax 24-3784; Santa Catalina Ancha 353; s/d/tr US$4.20/8.40/12.60, s/d with bathroom US$8.40/11.20) Though a little ragged round the edges, Casa Grande is friendly, popular and very central.

Hostal Rikch'arty (☎ 23-6606; Tambo de Montero 219; s/d US$5/10) Rikch'arty is a relaxed, family-run hostel with kids usually scampering around the small garden. Rooms are basic and share small bathrooms with hot showers. Rates include breakfast and tourist information is available.

Hostal Qorichaska (☎ 22-8974; h-qorichaska@hotmail.com; Nueva Alta 458; s/d US$5/10, with bathroom s/d US$8/11.50) Qorichaska, which feels a bit like entering a secret society hidden behind several gates, is basic but friendly and safe. Guests have use of a small kitchen. The prices include breakfast and there's hot water from 5am to 11pm.

Hostal Royal Qosco (☎ /fax 22-6221; royalqos@hotmail.com; lecsecocha 2; s/d/tr US$5/9/12, with bathroom s/d US$10/20) Hostal Royal Qosco is popular largely for its position just a stone's throw from Gringo Alley and the plaza. Rooms are basic and dark, and there is hot water in the morning.

Residencial Madres Dominicanas (☎ 22-5484; Ahuacpinta 600; s/d/tr/quad US$7/14/21/28) An excellent alternative option run by Dominican nuns on the grounds of the busy Colegio Martín de Porres, Residencial Madres Dominicanas is clean, safe and friendly and overlooks frequent games lessons on the courtyard. There's hot water and many rooms have bathrooms.

Hotel Imperio (☎ 22-8981; Chaparro 121; s/d/tr US$4.20/6.50/8.50, with bathroom US$5.60/8/10) Hotel Imperio, across from the Mercado Central, has an unintentionally 1950s atmosphere, basic rooms and reliable hot water in the morning. It has a hard-core support group of budget travelers who like the staff.

Hotel Wiracocha (☎ 22-1014; Cruz Verde 364; s/d US$15/25) Back towards the center, this is a good new option set in a colonial house and courtyard, freshly renovated with a great deal of care and carved wooden doors and

trellises. All rooms have bathrooms. Rates include breakfast.

Hostal Pascana (☎ /fax 22-5771; hpascana@terra.com.pe; Ahuacpinta 539; s/d US$15/30) Tucked away on the quiet street to the back of the coricancha complex, Pascana is small, friendly and well run. Rates include breakfast.

Gran Hostal Machu Picchu (☎ 23-1111; Quera 282; s/d/tr US$10/20/30) This friendly spot, set around two pretty courtyards with intricate old wooden balconies, has hot water most of the time.

Hospedaje Cassana (☎ 26-1177; Don Bosco A-7; s/d US$15/25) Situated opposite Colegio Salesiano all the way up Suecia and outside the center, Cassana is a very clean, new, family bed and breakfast.

Hostal Familiar (☎ 23-9353; hostalfamiliar@hotmail.com; Saphi 661; s/d US$8.50/13, with bathroom US$11.50/18.50) Hostal Familiar has a well-kept, colonial courtyard and clean, spartan rooms. It's often full. Prices are flexible and English is spoken. Prices for rooms with bathrooms include breakfast.

Hostal Suecia II (☎ 23-9757; Tecsecocha 465; s/d US$5.60/8.40, with bathroom US$8.40/14) This safe, popular colonial-style place has friendly staff, a central position (no huffing and puffing to get here) and is often full. There is reliable hot water and a glassed-in courtyard for snacks and hanging out. However, rooms are slightly stuffy and there are very few singles.

Suecia I (☎ 23-3282; hsuecia1@hotmail.com; Suecia 332; s/d US$6/10, with bathroom US$10/15) A short walk from the plaza, the Suecia has nondescript rooms around a sociable indoor courtyard.

Hostal Incawasi (☎ 22-3992; Portal de Panes 147; s/d/tr US$10/16/21, with bathroom US$15/23/30) Incawasi has a great (if noisy) location smack on the Plaza de Armas and fairly reliable hot water. The staff is friendly enough, but it's the position you're paying for.

Hospedaje Rumi Punku (☎ 22-1101; Choquechaca 339; s/d US$12/24, with bathroom US$25/30) Recognizable by the Inca stonework around the entrance, the Rumi Punku is in an attractive, older house with rooms that have been steadily rising in quality and cost in recent years.

Albergue San Juan de Dios Luxemburgo (☎ 24-0135; albergue@sanjuandedioscusco.com; Av Manzanares s/n, Urb. Manuel Prado; s/d/tr US$12.50/25/37.50) This hostel is a quiet, spotless, new place outside the center and behind the regional hospital, run as part of a nonprofit enterprise funding the clinic for handicapped children. Prices include breakfast. A taxi from the center is US$1.

Casa de la Gringa (☎ 24-1168; another.planet@terra .com.pe; Calle Pensamiento E-3, Urb Miravalle; r per person with bathroom US$8-12) This laid-back hostel is a spiritual, New Age retreat and an interesting alternative for budget travelers. The quiet garden has a mini sweat lodge and hammocks, and the rooms are wildly colorful. It's 3km east of the center, though, so you'll have to catch a taxi (US$1).

Amaru Hostal (☎ /fax 22-5933; amaru@telser .com.pe; Cuesta San Blas 541; s/d US$14/16, with bathroom US$17/25) Taller travelers mind to duck through the colonial doorframes of this exceptionally friendly choice in a characterful old building. Rates include breakfast and national TV.

Other recommendations:

Hostal Mirador del Inka (☎ 26-1384; miradorde linka@latinmail.com; Tandapata 160; s/d US$4/8, with bathroom US$7/14) Basic, musty place but many rooms have Inca walls.

Hospedaje Kiswarcancha (☎ 25-3831; kiswarcan cha@hotmail.com; Palacio 135; per person with shared bathroom US$12) Tiny, down-to-earth spot with a handful of rooms in a family home.

Hostal Saphi (☎ 26-1623; hostalsaphi@yahoo.es; Calle Saphi 107; s/d US$15/25) Plain rooms but excellent water pressure in the hot private showers, and cable TV.

Mid-Range

Hostal Los Niños (☎ 23-1424; ninoshotel@terra.com.pe; Meloc 442; s/d US$12/24, with bathroom US$30; 🖳) This well-recommended hostel comes with a story to tell. The Dutch-run hotel is dedicated to helping local street children. A dozen formerly homeless children live on the premises and are afforded a caring home, education and a chance to earn money in the hotel, and the project has expanded to help feed and get medical care to a further 250 kids. Much of the funding relies on guests' staying at the hotel. The traditional colonial house has a café with a book exchange, a courtyard surrounded by a traditional-style balcony and large, spotless, carefully decorated rooms with decent beds. Several languages are spoken. A second hostel is nearby on Fierra 476.

Residencia de la Solidaridad (☎ 23-1118; hspedro@hotmail.com; Ccascaparo 116; s/d/tr US$15/20/ 30) You'll be greeted with dozens of smiling faces at this delightful new option situated in the Hogar San Pedro for girls by the Machu Picchu train station. The hostel is run by missionaries to help fund the home. The building has several courtyard gardens, surprisingly comfortable rooms for the price and a convenient wake-up call from church bells.

Hostal Corihuasi (☎ /fax 23-2233; corihausi@amauta .rcp.net.pe; Suecia 561; s/d/tr US$30/40/50) Corihuasi is in a maze-like, colonial-style building on the hillside with some fantastic views. It's often recommended for good service, homely atmosphere and reliable hot water. Prices include breakfast and English is spoken.

Casa de Campo (☎ 24-4404; amautaa@mail.cosapidat a.com.pe; Tandapata 296; s/d/tr US$25/40/55) Though it's a bit of a trek to get here, this large hillside hostel is friendly and has a garden, good views and a traditional cottage feel. It's not a bad idea to get a taxi back at night.

Hostal El Arqueólogo (☎ 23-2569; reservation@ hotelarqueologo.com; Ladrillos 425; s/d/tr US$35/55/75) Named for the Inca stonework in the narrow street fronting the hostel, El Arqueólogo is clean and has hot water, a pleasant garden complete with deck chairs and a cafeteria with a city view. It gets mixed reader reports, however, and is a shade overpriced. Rates include breakfast.

Los Aticos (☎ 38-0414; info@millaturismo.com; Quera 253; s/d/apt US$30/35/50; 🖳) This is an excellent mid-range option in a side alley. It has a very welcoming atmosphere, 12 good doubles and an apartment with fully equipped kitchenette – great for longer stays. Prices include breakfast and free drinking water. Once a week the hosts cook up a free typical meal and guests are welcome to learn preparation techniques in the large open kitchen (which guests are welcome to use). Internet access is free, as is the tea and coffee. **Los Aticos II** (Pardo 689; s/d/ste US$25/30/45) is also informal and has cable TV in every room.

Hotel Virrey (☎ /fax 22-1771; hvirrey@amauta.rep .net.pe; Portal Comercio 165; s/d US$30/45) Right on the Plaza de Armas, Virrey has just two rooms with unbeatable plaza views, but for the most part you're paying for location rather than value. Rooms have cable TV and rather sad little bathrooms.

Hostal Loreto (☎ 22-6352; hloreto@terra.com.pe; Loreto 115; s/d/tr US$25/40/50) Loreto, just off the

Plaza de Armas, has four rooms with Inca walls, which make them rather dark, but how often do you get to sleep next to an Inca wall? It has hot water in the morning and evening, and some rooms sleep up to five. The hostel has a curious mix of old and new furnishings and has a helter-skelter-like staircase in the center.

Tupac Yupanqui Palace (☎ 25-4523; tyupanquihotel@terra.com.pe; Calle San Agustin 236; s/d/tr US$40/50/65) This new place is built in a grand colonial mansion set around a courtyard, and has authentic, high-ceilinged rooms that are sparsely decorated. Prices given are confidential rates dependent on reservation.

Del Prado Inn (☎ 22-4442; admin@delpradoinn.com; Suecia 310; s/d US$57/98, ste with Jacuzzi US$109) Del Prado is a very welcome addition to midrange hotels around the Plaza de Armas. The snug rooms are in good nick, and a few have reconstructed Inca walls.

Andenes de Saphi (☎ 22-7561; andenes-saphi@telser.com.pe; Calle Saphi 848; s/d/tr US$41.50/48.50/55.50) This is a very attractive, new, option with a rustic, wooden construction and fantastic, colorful murals in every room. Prices include breakfast.

Los Apus (☎ 26-4243; info@losapushotel.com; Atocsaycuchi 515; s/d US$59/89) Los Apus is a neat, classy little hotel under Swiss management with an attractive courtyard restaurant and quality rooms with wooden furnishings.

Hotel Cristina (☎ 22-7251; hcristina@terra.com.pe; Av Sol 341; s/d/tr US$40/55/65) Cristina has cozy, curvy little rooms and very friendly service, plus cable TV. Rates include continental breakfast. Recommended.

Hotel Garcilaso I (☎ 23-3031; hotelesgarcilaso@hotmail.com; s/d/tr US$40/55/69) Though some rooms are a little drab, staying here will give you the thrill of staying in part of Garcilaso de la Vega's own mansion, which extends into the next-door Museo de Historia Regional.

Hostal El Balcón (☎ 23-6738; balcon1@terra.com.pe; Tambo de Montero 222; s/d/tr US$30/55/64) El Balcón is in an attractively renovated building dating from 1630. It has a beautiful little garden filled with curiosities and some great views over Cuzco. Rooms have cable TV. It may offer a 20% discount in the off season. Rates include continental breakfast and a sauna is on the premises.

Hostal La Casona de San Agustín (☎ 25-2633; lcsanagustin@wayna.rcp.net.pe; San Agustín 371; s/d/tr US$55/80/90) This is another renovated colonial house but on a grander scale. Rooms have cable TV, minibar and telephone and rates include a buffet breakfast. There is also a Jacuzzi and sauna (an extra US$10). However, readers have complained of their doors being tried during the night here.

Hostal Plaza de Armas (☎ 22-2351; peruhotel@peruhotel.com; cnr Mantas & Portal Comercio; s/d US$55/77) This place appears to have prime position on the corner of the Plaza de Armas, though none of the rooms have plaza views or are particularly well cared for. They are, however, comfortable enough and have cable TV. Rates include breakfast.

Torredorada (☎ 24-1698; peggyk@terra.com.pe; Calle los Cipreses N-5, Residencial Huancaro; s/d/tr with reservation US$40/50/60) Torredorada is a modern, family-run hotel in a quiet residential district close to the bus terminal. It's recommended for the high quality of the service, including free pick-up from and drop off to the airport and train stations. Fluent English is spoken and prices include breakfast.

Other recommendations are:

Pensión Aleman (☎ 22-6861; www.cuzco-stay.de; Calle Tandapata 260; s/d/tr US$33/45/57) Homely pension with well-kept rooms and a dinky garden.

Hostal El Solar (☎ 23-2451; Plaza San Francisco 162; s/d US$15/25) Run-down exterior but with colorful rooms and low, arched ceilings.

Hostal Centenario (☎ 24-4235; centenario@planet.com.pe; Centenario 689; s/d/tr US$40/55/70) Small, personable place with modern rooms, cable TV and heating.

Top End

Cuzco's swanky, top-end hotels tend to be full during the high season and advance reservations are recommended. Reserving through an agency can result in a better price than booking directly. Unless otherwise stated, all the following have heating, telephone, cable TV and include breakfast. Prices given here don't include taxes.

Hotel Royal Inka I (☎ 22-2284) and **Hotel Royal Inka II** (☎ 23-1067; royalinka@terra.com.pe; s/d US$68/90) The Royal Incas are sister hotels practically joined at the hip on Plaza Regocijo 299 and Santa Teresa 335, respectively. Both are in interesting buildings dating from the early 19th century, and Royal Inka II has a sauna, Jacuzzi, massage therapist and beauty salon (all at extra charge). Rooms surround a central atrium dominated by a huge mosaic of Cusqueño history. This is also where you'll find the restaurant and bar, which form a constant hive of activity from early break-fasters to late revelers. The slightly thriftier Royal Inka I was undergoing renovation at the time of writing, but was set to reopen by 2004.

Incatambo Hacienda Hotel (☎ 22-1918; inca tambohotel@terra.com.pe; Km2 Carretera Cuzco-Sacsay huamán; s/d/tr US$65/70/80, ste US$85-115) This is a good place to stay in the countryside yet be within minutes of Cuzco and a short walk from the site of Sacsayhuamán. Part of the colonial hacienda was once Francisco Pizarro's home, and now houses faded but comfortable rooms. Fields and woodlands surround the hotel and horse rides can be arranged for visitors.

Hotel Cuzco (☎ 22-4821; Heladeros 150) This is the oldest of Cuzco's 1st-class hotels and has been operating for over half a century. However, at the time of writing, Hotel Cuzco was closed for extensive restoration work. When it reopens rates are likely to be in excess of US$65/75.

Hotel Ruinas (☎ 26-0644; ruinas@mail.interplace .com.pe; Calle Ruinas 472; s/d/tr US$95/125/155) Hotel Ruinas is a large, new place with smart, spacious rooms, though its a shade on the characterless side.

El Dorado Inn (☎ 23-1232; doratur@telser.com.pe; Av Sol 395; s/d US$80) El Dorado has a swish restaurant/bar with musicians and dancers in the evening. The 54 rooms are smart, comfortable, and come complete with cable TV and heaters; some have balconies with street views. Rooms overlooking the elevator/restaurant area tend to be noisy with early morning departees.

San Agustín Plaza (☎ 23-8121; inter@terra.com.pe; Av Sol 594; s/d US$76/89) San Agustín is helpful, friendly and has wooden-ceilinged rooms with castle-like doors and intricate iron-work and there's a cafeteria with a view of Coricancha.

Hotel Internacional San Agustín (☎ 22-1169; inter@terra.com.pe; Maruri 390; s/d/tr US$89/102/120) This hotel has cavern-like corridors and rooms, with curving walls and curious lighting fixtures resembling noses lit from within. It has good facilities, including new bathrooms, as well as a restaurant and bar.

Sonesta Posada del Inca (☎ 22-7061; posada@sonestaperu.com; Portal Espinar 142; s/d/ste US$85/99/115) The most central of Cuzco's top-end hotels, the Posada lies unobtrusively

between the Plaza de Armas and Plaza Re-gocijo. It has comfortable but slightly bland uniform rooms (two are fully wheelchair accessible), a restaurant with a view of the plaza and good service.

Novotel Accor (☎ 22-8282; reservations@novotelcusco .com.pe; San Agustín 239; s/d US$179/230) The latest top-range addition to Cuzco, Novotel separates its tariffs according to whether the room is in the contemporary wing or the more expensive but vastly more characterful, colonial rooms, each of which is different from the rest. There's a huge covered colonial courtyard as you enter. Prices include a buffet breakfast.

Hotel Monasterio del Cusco (☎ 24-1777; reser vas@peruorientexpress.com.pe; Palacio 136; s/d/tr US$265/ 275/305, ste US$360-815) The minute you walk into this hotel, you know it's in a different league. Set in a restored convent, the Monasterio is indisputably Cuzco's most beautiful hotel, with stunning public areas and over 100 exquisitely decorated rooms surrounding two colonial courtyards. It has an excellent restaurant and everything expected of the staggering price tag.

Hotel Libertador (☎ 23-1961; hotel@libertador .com.pe; Plazoleta Santo Domingo 259; s/d US$236, ste US$275-332) This is another contender for the title of Cuzco's best hotel. Set in a huge, opulently furnished, old, colonial mansion with a fine courtyard, it also boasts Inca foundations, and parts of the building date back to the 16th century, when Francisco Pizarro was the occupant for a time. Rooms sport all the comforts you would expect, and some you wouldn't (free slippers to take away). There's also a Jacuzzi, sauna, gym, gift shop and good restaurants.

EATING

As you'd expect in a city with such a cosmo-politan range of visitors, Cuzco is packed with a vast variety of restaurants catering to every taste and budget. Book ahead for the better restaurants in high season.

Andean

A few inexpensive restaurants serve up a limited menu of tasty, authentic Andean specialties – no opt-out hamburgers clauses here for the suddenly faint of heart. Called *quintas*, these spots are usually open only for lunch or afternoon snacks so expect to be out by early evening.

If you don't treasure childhood memories of pet guinea pigs and you want to try something distinctively Andean, roast *cuy*, is an Inca delicacy. Other typical dishes include *anticucho de corazon* (shish kebab made from beef hearts), *adobo* (spicy pork stew), *chicharrones* (deep-fried chunks of pork ribs, *chancho*, or of chicken, *gallina*), *lechón* (suckling pig), *tamales* (boiled corn dumplings filled with cheese or meat and wrapped in a banana leaf) and various *locros* (hearty soups and stews). The meal is often washed down with the infamous Inca chicha, a fermented, mildly alcoholic corn beer, sometimes mixed with fruits.

Quinta Eulalia (☎ 24-1380; Choquechaca 384; mains US$2-6; ⊗ noon-6pm) This is a no-nonsense spot close to the central city area, with a rustic, open-air courtyard. It also sells cuy cheaper than most city-center places (US$6).

Quinta Zárate (☎ 24-5114; Totora Paqcha 763; mains US$1.50-4.50; ⊗ noon-5pm Tue-Sun) Further afield in San Blas up above the city through a maze of twisting streets, is this quiet spot with a shady garden and good views. It isn't the easiest spot to find, so hire a taxi (US$0.70) or walk to the end of Tandapata and ask directions.

There are also several funky hole-in-the-wall places along Pampa del Castillo that serve chicharrones hot from the grill, which is often placed in the door. Get them *para llevar* (to go) at lunchtime, when they're fresh.

You can also get local Andean food in many of the more mainstream Peruvian and international restaurants that follow.

Cafés

El Buen Pastor (☎ 24-0586; Cuesta San Blas 575; ⊗ closed Sun) You won't get much better than El Buen Pastor for a morning bakery, which has a great selection of breads and cakes for US$0.50 to US$1. The warm glow isn't just from supping a hot chocolate with your pastries, but also from the knowledge that the profits all go towards a charity-run home for teenage girls.

La Tertulia (☎ 24-3062; Procuradores 44; breakfast US$2.50-4.50, mains US$2.50-6; ⊗ year-round, Oct-Mar morning only) Another excellent and popular breakfast choice, La Tertulia makes homemade bread, good strong coffee and you won't leave hungry after its 'eat-as-much-as-you-want' breakfast.

El Ayllu Café (☎ 23-2357; Portal Carnes 208; snacks US$1.50-3; ⊗ closes at noon Sun) El Ayllu is a simple and reasonably priced spot next to the cathedral. It plays classical music and offers a good selection of juices, coffee, tea, yogurt, cakes and other snacks.

La Yunta (☎ 23-5103; Portal de Carnes 214; 3-course menú US$4.50) Next to El Ayllu, La Yunta offers a huge variety of juices, as well as cakes, coffee and inexpensive meals.

Café Bagdad (☎ 23-9949; Portal de Carnes 216; mains US$6-9) Upstairs from La Yunta is this good budget choice with an open-fronted balcony overlooking the plaza.

Café Varayoc (Calle Espaderos 142; mains US$4-6) Varayoc makes a good pit stop conducive to reading (magazines are on hand), writing or conversing. Its coffee and cakes are good.

I Due Mondi (☎ 24-7677; Santa Catalina Ancha 366) If it's ice cream you want, you'll find 15 seductive flavors (including *chicha*!) to choose from in this chic, Italian-style café.

The Muse (☎ 974-4669; Calle Tandapata 684; snacks US$1.50-3, coffee US$1.50) Several enticing cafés and bars have tables spilling out onto and around Plaza San Blas, including this one, just above the plaza. It's a popular spot for taking in the sun, and often has live music from 10pm.

Trotamundos (☎ 23-2387; Portal Comercio 177; snacks US$1.50-4; 🖵) The Trotamundos has a great view of the cathedral and sells a bit of everything, with especially good coffees and snacks. It's also a popular late-night bar/café.

International

Greens (☎ 24-3820; Tandapata 700; mains US$4.50-7.50) This is a cheery den hidden away behind the church of San Blas. It serves some lip-smacking, international food, especially with a British influence, such as traditional Sunday roasts (by reservation, US$5.50 to US$7), as well as curries, steaks and fettuccine. Cable TV, plus a stack of magazines, books and board games also make this a great place to hang. Another branch, known as the **Blueberry Lounge** (Portal de Carnes 236) has also opened on the Plaza de Armas.

Granja Heidi (☎ 23-8383; 2nd fl, Cuesta San Blas 525; ⊗ closed Sun) Follow the pictures of cows to this light, Alpine-feel café with terrific fresh produce, yogurts, cakes and other light snacks on offer. It also has a reasonable book exchange.

HOW TO PLAY SAPO

Ever wondered what Cuzqueños do to relax instead of whiling away the hours over a game of darts or pool in the local bar? Well, next time you're in a local *picanteria* (literally 'spicy place') or *quinta* (country houses serving typical Andean food) look out for a strange metal *sapo* (toad) mounted on a large box and surrounded by various other holes and slots. Men will often spend the whole afternoon drinking *chicha* and beer while competing at this old test of skill in which players toss metal disks as close to the toad as possible. Top points are scored for landing it smack in the mouth.

The Pi Shop (☎ 24-7006; Atoqsaykuchi 599; ☻ Tue-Sun) Travelers looking for a few home comforts can find everything from apple pies to vegemite in this welcoming, informal spot. It's also a good meeting point, and the young, English-speaking owners are fountains of local knowledge.

Chez Maggy (☎ 23-4861; Procuradores 344, 365, 374; 3-course menú US$4) Chez Maggy has virtually taken over Gringo Alley with three deja-vu-inducing branches and another on Plateros 348, all serving up reasonable pizza and pasta. Many have live music (a hat is passed for tips) in the evenings.

Tiziano Trattoria (Tecsecocha 418; 3-course menú US$4) Tiziano is a tiny corner pizza place recommended by budget travelers.

Trattoria Adriano (cnr Av Sol & Mantas; mains US$3-10) This place has been serving decent Italian food at the northwest end of Avenida Sol for over two decades.

Al Grano (☎ 22-8032; Santa Catalina Ancha 398; closed Sun) Al Grano has a selective menu of delicious plates from nine Asian countries including Thailand, India, Vietnam and Indonesia. Prices are modest, and it's popular with travelers looking to treat their tastebuds to a change.

Kin Taro (☎ 22-6181; Heladeros 149; mains US$2-4.50; ☻ closed Sun) Another excellent choice, Kin Taro serves as authentic a Japanese menu as you'll find anywhere outside of Lima, including trout sushi and saki.

Los Cuates (☎ 23-4298; Procuradores 386; 3-course menú US$3-7) One of a few Mexican-style hang-outs on Gringo Alley, Los Cuates offers free drinks with its set meals.

Coco Loco (☎ 24-3707; Calle Espaderos 135; snacks US$1.50-2.50; ☻ open till 5am Mon-Sat) This is a fast-food joint serving international- and Peruvian-style morsels all into the small hours. It's just the place to get your post-clubbing burger fix.

Peruvian

A multitude of touristic restaurants litter Cuzco's center, each with its own pastiche of Peruvian and international dishes. Good hunting grounds include the upscale venues on the Plaza de Armas, most of which are visited by bands who wander in and out during the evening, and the first block of Plateros, just off the plaza. A new breed of trendy eatery is also taking over the San Blas area up the hill from the center, where backpackers tend to congregate.

Fallen Angel (☎ 25-8184; Plazoleta Nazarenas 221; mains US$4.50-7) Fallen Angel is an ultra funky restaurant and bar almost falling over itself in the rush to cram in as much kitsch as possible: glitter balls, silver angels, plush cushions of all sizes and varieties of fake fur, even bathtub-cum-aquarium tables complete with goldfish. The cocktails (US$2.50 to US$5), though distinctly unangelic, are recommended.

Macondo (☎ 22-9415; Cuesta San Blas 571; mains US$2.80-5.60; ☻ closed lunchtime Sun) Another trendy spot, Macondo gets busy with backpackers in the evening and you'll eat the nuevo-Andean and jungle dishes with dozens of grinning faces staring up at you from the photo-bedecked tables.

Witches Garden (☎ 962-3866; Carmen Bajo 169; mains US$2.20-7) This is a stylish, small and dimly lit spot to shelter from the summer hoards. It serves up some wickedly indulgent food: witness the 'Black Hole' giant cookie, smothered in ice cream, brandy and fudge (US$2.80).

Pucará (☎ 22-2027; Plateros 309; ☻ closed Sun) Back in the center of town, this Japanese-run place has good food and menus with handy photographs, so even the linguistically challenged can order a chicken and not get eggdrop soup.

Ama Lur (☎ 22-4203; Plateros 327; 3-course lunch menú US$1.80, mains US$3-7; ☻ closed Sun) A small, dimly lit spot that also serves good, moderately priced food, including Bourguignon, Chinoise or a wicked rum-and-chocolate fondue (US$8 to US$14 for two).

Victor Victoria (☎ 25-2854; Calle Tigre 130; mains US$2.50-6) Around the corner on Calle Tigre is this recommended budget restaurant, which slips a few French and Israeli dishes into its primarily Peruvian menu.

Ukuku's Restaurant (☎ 22-7867; Procuradores 398; mains US$3.40-7) One of the better budget options on Gringo Alley, this place has walls decked with striking works of art and a mellow atmosphere enjoyed by locals and travelers. Do not confuse it with Ukuku's nightclub on Plateros.

Restaurant El Paititi (☎ 25-2686; Portal Carrizos 270) El Paititi is an elegant, exclusive spot with Inca walls once part of the House of the Chosen Women. It often has musicians in the evening.

Inka Grill (☎ 26-2992; Portal de Panes 115; mains US$7-14) This place is deservedly popular and recommended for both food and service; reservations are a good idea and try to order cuy dishes a day in advance.

La Retama (☎ 22-6372; Portal de Panes 123) La Retama is a restaurant and lounge bar with innovative versions of some favorite Peruvian dishes and live music (often international jazz) at 8:30pm. Again, cuy should be ordered in advance if possible. You may also score a complimentary pisco sour.

Tunupa (☎ 23-5370; 2nd fl, Portal Confitura 233; mains US$8-12) Tunupa, an elegant new restaurant in the same building as the Cross Keys pub, has good food and a panoramic view of the plaza.

El Mesón de los Espaderos (☎ 23-5307; 2nd fl, Espaderos 105; mains US$9-12) The huge photo of a juicy steak on entry to this place is a large clue for what is to come: They serve *parrilladas* (mixed grills), steaks, cuy or chicken. Get there early or make a reservation to sit in the intricately carved balcony overlooking the plaza.

El Truco (☎ 23-5295; Plaza Regocijo 262; buffet US$10, mains US$7-15) This restaurant combines a mix of lofty architecture with murals, an original ceiling and excellent food. It has a nightly dinner and show from 8:30pm to 10:30pm. Make reservations in the high season, because it's popular with tour groups.

Don Antonio (☎ 24-1364; Santa Teresa 356; lunch buffet US$12, dinner buffet US$16) Don Antonio is another top-notch dinner-and-show restaurant in a huge barn of a venue.

Inkanato (☎ 22-2926; reservas@inkanato.com; Plazoleta Santo Domingo 279 -2A; 3-course menú US$10-15,

mains US$7-10; ☯ closed lunchtime Sun) Somewhat incongruously positioned above a scruffy courtyard opposite Santo Domingo, is this new top-range dinery, which takes the cultural experience of eating seriously. Set in a barn-like hall with long tables and a clutter of rustic paraphernalia, it serves up a mix of traditional Andean and jungle dishes.

Self-Catering

The best supermarket in the center is **Dimart** (Ayacucho 248; ☯ 7am-10pm). Far smaller is the originally titled **Market** (Mantas 119; ☯ 8am-11pm) just off the plaza.

Vegetarian

Whether you're vegetarian or simply economizing, Cuzco has some surprisingly good options:

Naturaleza (☎ 976-0187; Av El Sol 765-A; 3-course menú US$1; ☯ closed Sun) A vegetarian's paradise, Naturaleza is a fair-sized, bustling restaurant with an open feel and startlingly cheap menus.

Café Cultural Ritual (☎ 968-2223; Choquechaca 140; 3-course menú US$1.40, mains US$1.40-4.20) This is a bright, cute little vegetarian option with gaudy decoration and a mild, stuffed-toy fixation, near the South American Explorers. There is also a carnivorous branch on Plaza San Blas.

Moni (☎ 23-1029; www.moni-cusco.com; San Agustin 311; mains US$3-4.50; ☯ closed Sun) Moni is run by a Peruvian-English couple and is highly recommended for it's à la carte vegetarian fare, including a mean veg curry and adapted Peruvian dishes. There's a laid-back, coffee-bar ambiance and guidebooks are on-hand for browsing.

Govinda (☎ 962-4588; Espaderos 128; 3-course menú US$2.50-4.50) This vegetarian institution, run by Hare Krishnas, serves good, filling set meals in an incense-infused atmosphere. Service can be slow.

DRINKING

Savvy travelers will soon twig to the fact that competition is intense between Cuzco's nocturnal establishments, and that they can count on enough free drinks and happy hours to forget those aching feet fresh from the Inca Trail and set out on a lengthy bar crawl of the city. Of course, the free drinks in question are almost exclusively *cuba libre*, cheap wine and the ubiquitous pisco sour, so beer-lovers may prefer more sedentary tactics. Meanwhile, the clubs of Cuzco open early but crank up a few notches after 11pm.

The first four bars listed here are good places to track down those all-important soccer matches, with TVs more or less permanently tuned into sports.

Cross Keys (Portal Confiturías 233; 🕑 11am-late) Cross Keys is the most established watering hole in town, housed in a rickety old building on the plaza and smothered in the trappings of a typical British pub. You can talk without having to scream over the music here, or, if you're pressed for conversation, there's cable TV, a dartboard and the most challenging pool table in town – its banana-like trajectory is as yet unparalleled. Happy hours run from 6pm to 7pm and 9pm to 9:30pm (excluding beer).

Paddy O'Flaherty's (☎ 24-7719; Triunfo 124; 🕑 11am-late) Paddy's is a cramped, little Irish bar, filled with high stools, games and a sizable foam leprechaun.

Rosie O'Grady's Irish Pub (☎ 24-3514; Santa Catalina Ancha 360; 🕑 11am-late) Rosie's is also a great spot for a Guinness with far more room to breathe than its smaller, older compatriot Paddy's, though a touch less authentic. Happy hour is 7pm to 8pm and 10pm to 10:30pm.

Norton Rat's (Calle Loreto 115; 🕑 9am-late) This is a down-to-earth, US-run, biker bar with reputedly the best burgers in town. It can be reached through the entrance of Hostal Loreto. It has cable TV, darts and a pool table to help you work up a thirst. It's also considered gay friendly in a conservative town.

Los Perros (☎ 24-1447; Tecsecocha 436; 🕑 11am-1am) Los Perros is one of Cuzco's best drinking dens with a funky, laid-back couch bar and a top-notch music collection. So sink back into the plush sofas and soak up the atmosphere, or make use of the book-exchange, magazines or board games.

Mystique (☎ 22-2610; Suecia 320; 🕑 5pm-midnight) Built on Inca foundations with a back wall of enormous Inca blocks, Mystique is a relaxed place with chatty bar staff and a good happy hour from 5pm to 10pm.

ENTERTAINMENT
Dancing
Ukuku's Bar (☎ 24-2951; Plateros 316; 🕑 8pm-late) The most consistently popular spot in

town, Ukuku's plays a winning combination of crowd-pleasers and Latin pop, and hosts live local bands nightly. Usually full to bursting after midnight, it's good, sweaty dance fun with as many locals as tourists. There's a US$1.50 cover charge after 9:30pm, though it's often ignored, and happy hour is from 8pm to 10pm.

X'ss (Portal de Carnes 298; 🕑 8:30pm-6am) X'ss has the most up-to-the-minute music collection, with techno, trance and hip-hop mixed with the mainstream. There are chill-out sofas upstairs but this isn't the place for chat. Free drinks are offered on entry and there's plenty of cheap booze during happy hour from 9pm to 11pm.

Kamikase (☎ 23-3865; 274 Plaza Regocijo; admission US$2.50; 🕑 8pm-late) Kamikase is an older, more intimate option that doesn't offer free drinks, but has a disarmingly large variety of music, that can switch from foot-stomping rock to live *folklórica* in an instant. Happy hour is from 8pm to 10pm, and there's often a live show at 10:30pm. Try its appropriately named 'Camino a la Ruina' cocktail.

Mama Africa Pub (Portal de Belén 115; 🕑 7pm-late) Mama Africa is the city's classic backpackers' hang-out, usually packed with people sprawled across cushions or swaying to rock and reggae rhythms. It has a happy hour from 3pm to 9pm and also a 'very happy hour' between 11pm and midnight. It often offers a free drink on entry.

El Muki (Santa Catalina 114; 🕑 9pm-late) Just off the plaza, El Muki is a dark, intimate club with plenty of barely lit alcoves and a couples-only rule at the door (though they rarely count when a group goes in).

Azucar (Quera 251; 🕑 8pm-late Mon-Sat) For those looking to show off their newly acquired salsa and merengue moves, this tiny new Cuban-owned club will oblige with a great mixture of Latin beats. It also offers dance classes.

Live Music
Several places have evening *folklórica* music and dance shows; cover charges vary from US$3 to US$6. **Qosqo Center of Native Dance** (☎ 22-7901; Av Sol 604; admission US$4.20) is the best-known place with daily shows at 7pm. **Teatro Municipal** (☎ 22-7321; Mesón de la Estrella 149) has a range of shows, plays and dancing at weekends.

Cinema

Sunset (☎ 80-7434; Calle Tecsecocha 2; admission US$0.90) is a small video bar above Hotel Royal Qosqo showing three different up-to-date movies daily at 4pm, 7pm and 9:30pm. Several nightclubs also show movies during the day: Check at Mama Africa, Ukuku's and X'ss for their current times and listings.

SHOPPING

Cuzco offers a tremendous variety of woolens, textiles, pottery, jewelry and art. A good starting point is the sizeable, new, covered **Centro Artesanal Cuzco** (☻ 8am-10pm) just south of town on the intersection of Avenida Sol with Tullumayo, where you can literally shop till you drop. Other craft markets include one on the corner of Quera and San Bernardo and another off Loreto (☻ both roughly 9am-8pm).

The area surrounding Plaza San Blas is Cuzco's artisan quarter, packed with the workshops and showrooms of local craftspeople. It offers the chance to watch artisans at work and to sneak a look into the interiors of the colonial buildings while hunting down that perfect souvenir. Prices and quality vary greatly, so shop around and expect to bargain (except in the most expensive stores, where prices are often fixed). Quality workshops include: **Taller Olave** (☎ 23-1835; Plaza San Blas 651; ☻ 9am-7pm), to the left of the church, a treasure trove of exceptional reproductions of colonial sculptures and precolonial ceramics; **Taller Mérida** (☎ 22-1714; Carmen Alto 133) for striking earthenware statues; and the nationally famous **Taller Mendivil** (☎ 23-3247; ☻ 8am-8pm Mon Sat), on the plaza, for its hallmark, giraffe-necked, religious figures. For silver jewelry and ornaments, check the workshop of the **Camero family** (☎ 995-7705; Palacio 122; ☻ 9am-8pm Mon-Sat) where bargaining is acceptable. There are also many stores along Hatunrumiyoc and Cuesta San Blas down to the Plaza de Armas that sell most souvenirs imaginable.

For high-quality fabrics and jewelry in the center, visit **Arte Perú** (☎ 23-5530; Portal Confituria 295; ☻ 9am-10pm) on the corner of Plateros and Espaderos, or the more arty **Galeria Latina Cusco** (☎ 24-6588; Calle Triunfo 350; ☻ 9:30am-9pm Mon-Sat & 4:30-8:30pm Sun), which is reputed to be one of the best art and crafts galleries. Also around the plaza, look for

watercolors by local artists, especially those by Irma Valdivia and her husband.

An insight into Andean textiles can be gained at the **Center for Traditional Textiles of Cusco** (☎ 22-8117; Av Sol 603A), a commendable, nonprofit organization promoting the survival of traditional weaving. The store has constant shop-floor demonstrations to illustrate the techniques in all their finger-twisting complexity.

La Pérez (☎ 23-2515; Urb Mateo Pumacahua 598, Tienda 1, Wanchaq; ☻ 7am-8pm Mon-Sat & 1-8pm Sun) offers the chance to shop from a variety of regional *artesanias* away from the crowds and with minimal pressure. It's in a warehouse outside town, so you'll either need to catch a cab (US$1 each way) or serious shoppers can call in advance and they'll pick you up from your hotel.

The Mercado Central near the San Pedro railway station isn't the place for crafts, but can be a good spot to pick up fruit or that vital spare pair of socks. Go in a group and don't take any valuables, as the thieves here are extremely professional and persistent.

Tourists inevitably equal targets for the innumerable street-sellers of Cuzco. Though it can be wearisome the only thing to do is smile, say a firm 'No, gracias' and be careful not to show the slightest spark of curiosity in their wares, which would inevitably result in five minutes of hard-sell.

GETTING THERE & AWAY

Cuzco is a hub in the South American travel network, catering for several thousand travelers every week.

Air

Almost all departures and arrivals from Cuzco's **Aeropuerto Alejandro Velasco Astete** (☎ 22-2611) are in the morning, because climatic conditions make landing and take off difficult in the afternoon. Airport departure tax is US$10 for international flights and US$3.50 for internal flights. There are regular daily flights to and from Lima (from US$73, one hour). Be aware that many of these get canceled or lumped together with other flights during quiet periods. Your best bet is to get the earliest flight available, as later ones are the most likely to be delayed or canceled. A few companies also have flights to Puerto Maldonado (from US$43, 30 minutes),

Juliaca (from US$89, 30 minutes) and Arequipa (from US$43, 30 minutes). Flights to Ayacucho have been available in the past, but no companies offered them at the time of writing.

Companies include:

Aero Continente/Aviandina (☎ 24-3031, 24-3032, airport 23-5696, toll-free 0800-42420; www.aerocontinente.com; Portal de Carnes 254, Plaza de Armas) It flies several times a day to Lima, and also has daily services to Arequipa and Puerto Maldonado.

LanPeru (☎ 25-5552, airport 25-5550; Av Sol 627-B) Has regular services to Lima, Puerto Maldonado, Juliaca and Arequipa.

Lloyd Aereo Boliviano (LAB; ☎ 22-2990; Santa Catalina Angosta 160) Goes to La Paz, Bolivia. Flights cost US$106 and leave on Tuesday and Saturday mornings, with more services in the high season.

Taca (☎ 24-9921, airport 24-6858; www.taca.com; Av Sol 602-B) Has only three services weekly to Lima.

Tans (☎ 24-2727; San Agustín 315) Goes to Lima and Puerto Maldonado.

The military airline **Grupo 8** (☎ 22-1206) sells tickets at the airport for its flights (US$55, usually on Wednesday) to Lima, but these flights don't always go, are usually full and normally cannot be booked in advance. Go to the airport before 6am on the day of the flight, packed and ready to go, get your name on the waiting list and hope. Grupo 8 also flies twice-monthly via Puerto Maldonado to Iberia or Iñapari near the Brazilian border.

Flights tend to be overbooked, especially in high season, so confirm your flight when you arrive in Cuzco, then reconfirm 72 hours in advance and again 24 hours before departure. If you buy your ticket from a reputable travel agent in Cuzco, they'll reconfirm for you.

Check-in procedures are often chaotic, and even people with confirmed seats and boarding passes have occasionally been denied boarding because of overbooking errors. Check in is two hours early. During the rainy season, flights can be postponed for 24 hours because of bad weather. Bring valuables and essentials with you on the plane, and securely lock baggage.

When flying from Cuzco to Lima, check in as early as possible to get a seat on the right-hand side of the plane for the best views of Salcantay's 6271m peak. Some pilots like to fly quite close to the mountain, and the views are sometimes stupendous. (Sit on the left from Lima to Cuzco.) Very occasionally a different route is taken over Machu Picchu.

Bus

All the journey times given are approximate and apply only during good conditions. In the wettest months of the rainy season, especially January to April, long delays are possible.

INTERNATIONAL

Several companies offer through buses to Copacabana (US$10, 13 hours) and La Paz (US$12 to US$15, 18 hours) in Bolivia. Many will swear blind that the service is direct, though the evening buses (except Ormeño) usually stop in Puno for several hours until the Bolivian border opens. Try **Transportes Zela** (☎ 24-9977) and **Litoral** (☎ 24-8989), which both leave at 10pm and **Imexso** at 9pm. **Ormeño** Royal Class has the only direct service to La Paz leaving at 10pm (US$25, 15 hours), but it goes via the border post at Desaguadero and does not pass through Copacabana.

To get down to Tacna, by the Chilean border, **Cruz del Sur** has a 4.30pm service daily (US$17, 16 hours).

LONG DISTANCE

Cuzco has a long-distance bus terminal 2km from the center in Ttio, on the way to the airport. Buses to most major cities leave from this terminal, though buses for towns around Cuzco still leave from elsewhere, so check carefully in advance. Agencies on and near the Plaza de Armas also sell tickets for a commission. There is a platform tax of US$0.30 payable in the terminal.

Companies with bus services to Juliaca (US$5 to US$7, five hours) and Puno (US$6 to US$7, six hours) include **Ormeño** Royal Class (☎ 22-7501), **Cromotex** (☎ 24-9573) and **Imexso** (☎ 22-9126). Two similar companies called **First Class** (☎ 22-3102; firstclass@terra.com.pe; Av Sol 930) and **Inka Express** (Calle Matará 274) have comfortable tour buses to Puno that stop at significant sites en route (see Getting There & Away p216).

Frequent buses also run to Arequipa (US$6 to US$14, 11 hours). Companies include **Ormeño** Royal Class, **Cruz del Sur** (☎ 22-1909) and **Civa** (☎ 24-9961).

CUZCO & THE SACRED VALLEY

There are two options to get to Lima. Most direct buses now plough the quicker route via Abancay, Puquio and Nazca (US$17 to US$25, 22 to 26 hours), but this can be a rough ride and is prone to crippling delays during the rainy season (November to April). Companies include the most luxurious **Cruz del Sur**, the cheapest **Palomino** (☎ 22-2694), and the most frequent **Expreso Molino** (☎ 24-9512). In the dry season, Ormeño also has services on this route.

The alternative is to go via Arequipa, a longer but more comfortable route (US$17 to US$40, 30 to 34 hours). **Ormeño** Royal Class has a daily departure at 9am and a cheaper option at 7pm.

Trucks, combis and colectivos for Limatambo (US$1 to US$2, 1½ to two hours) and some on to Abancay leave from various places on Arcopata. Alternatively, take a long-distance bus to Abancay from one of several companies in the new bus terminal. For example, **Transportes San Jeronimo** (☎ 20-1142) goes to Abancay (US$4, six hours) and Andahuaylas (US$7, 10 hours) at 11am and 6pm; there are several other companies at the terminal. To continue on to Ayacucho, you have to change at Andahuaylas. The road to these towns is rough and cold at night.

There are no buses to the southeastern jungles except for those to Quillabamba (US$4.20 to US$5, nine hours); several companies leave from the Santiago terminal in eastern Cuzco (take a taxi US$0.90; terminal tax US$0.30), including **Ampay** (☎ 22-7541), which has three departures daily. Daytime departures have the advantage of the spectacular scenery while climbing the 4600m Abra de Malaga pass and then dropping down into the jungle. For other jungle destinations, you have to fly, go by truck or on an expedition. There are daily trucks to Puerto Maldonado during the dry season along a wild and difficult road, and the trip from Cuzco takes anything from two days to over a week in the wet season. Trucks leave from near Plaza Túpac Amaru, two blocks east of Tacna along Avenida Garcilaso. You could also get a bus to Urcos or Ocongate and wait for a truck there.

Getting to Manu is just as problematic. **Expreso Virgen del Carmen** (☎ 27-7755 or 22-6895) has buses to Paucartambo (US$2, five hours) leaving from Diagonal Angamos 1952 behind the Coliseo Cerrado daily at 3am, 11am and 3pm. Trucks also do the journey from the Coliseo Cerrado area – ask around. Continuing from Paucartambo to Manu, there are only passing trucks or expedition buses, though **Gallito de las Rocas** (Av Angamos) has buses from Cuzco to Pillcopata at 10am on Monday, Wednesday and Friday (US$5.60, 12 hours). Trucks from the Coliseo Cerrado also go to Pillcopata (12 hours), Atalaya (16 hours) and Shintuya (20 hours).

Buses to Oropesa (US$0.50), Urcos and Sicuani (US$2) leave from near the Coliseo Cerrado on Manco Capac, about five blocks east of Tacna. Buses for Urcos (US$1) also leave from Avenida de la Cultura opposite the Regional Hospital. Take these buses to visit the ruins of Tipón, Pikillacta, Rumicolca and Raqchi. For Ausangate, **Transportes Huayna Ausangate** (☎ 965-0922; Av Tomasa Tito Condemayta) has buses to Ocongate and Tinqui (US$3.40, seven hours) at 10am from Monday to Saturday.

SACRED VALLEY

Buses to Pisac (US$0.90, one hour), Calca and Urubamba (US$0.80, two hours) leave frequently from Tullumayo 800 between Aropunco and Garcilaso from 5:30am until 8pm. There are also micros and colectivos to Pisac from Calle Puputi off Avenida de la Cultura. Buses for Urubamba via Chinchero (US$0.50, 50 minutes) leave from the 300 block of Grau near Puente Grau every 15 minutes from 5am to 8pm.

The Pisac buses will drop you off at the nearby Inca site of Tambo Machay. To get to Ollantaytambo, change at Urubamba or you can catch the 7:45am or 7:45pm buses direct from Puente Grau. Buses to Quillabamba (see Bus – Long Distance p192) stop in Ollantaytambo too, but you'll have to pay the full fare (US$4.20).

Car Rental

Avis (☎ 24-8800; avis-cusco@terra.com.pe; Av Sol 808 & Aeropuerto Alejandro Velasco Astete) hires a good selection of cars.

Helicopter

The helicopter service to Aguas Calientes was stopped in 2001 due to the damage that was being inflicted on the ruins and ecology of the valley by the vibration of the choppers.

Train

Cuzco has two train stations. Estación Huanchac, near the end of Avenida Sol, serves Urcos, Sicuani, Juliaca and Puno. Estación San Pedro next to the Mercado Central, serves Ollantaytambo and Machu Picchu. The two stations are unconnected so it's impossible to travel directly from Puno to Machu Picchu. For the most up-to-date schedules, check the website www.perurail.com.

Estación Huanchac (Estación Wanchaq; ☎ 23-8722; reservas@perurail.com; ☀ 7am-5pm Mon-Fri, 7am-noon Sat-Sun) has trains for Puno that leave at 8am Monday, Wednesday and Saturday (or Thursday from June to August) and take about 10 hours (though they are often late). Catching a bus from Juliaca station to Puno can lessen the journey by half an hour. The connecting train for Arequipa now only runs for group bookings. See Train under Puno (p155) for details.

Tickets for the Machu Picchu train to Aguas Calientes are also sold from the Huanchac station (bring ID to buy tickets) but leave from **Estación San Pedro** (☎ 22-1992) near the central market. It is the most frequently used train station in Peru, with services departing several times a day. The station is a prime target for thieves, and though security around the station has been tightened it's best to remain vigilant.

There are three tourist trains a day, with more during the high season. It is no longer possible for foreigners to use the cheaper local train, or *tren local*. The tourist trains, or *trenes de turismo*, leave Cuzco between 6am and 6:35am and stop at Poroy (6:40am to 7:25am), Ollantaytambo (8am to 9am) and Aguas Calientes for Machu Picchu (9:40am to 10:40am). Services return between 3:30pm and 4:20pm, arriving back between 7:20pm and 8:45pm. You can cut the return journey short by up to 45 minutes by getting off at Poroy and catching one of the comfortable AATC buses (US$1.40) back to Cuzco center.

Single/round-trip tickets cost US$41.30/ 53.10 on backpacker trains, or US$59/ 88.50 in the 1st-class Vistadome (formally *autovagón*) train, which is the earliest and fastest service and includes snacks and drinks. Children younger than 12 travel for 50% less. These prices have skyrocketed in recent years, though, and it's likely they will rise again. At the time of writing, a second train company was bidding to break Perúrail's monopoly on the line, which may make for more competitive prices. Travelers visiting the Sacred Valley should note that they can travel for less from Ollantaytambo to Machu Picchu, and the cheapest backpacker train service is available from here (see p204). Also note that last minute 50% reductions are available when you book one-way fares within 48 hours of the date you want to leave, though these are difficult to obtain in high season.

The journey begins with a steep climb out of Cuzco. Too steep for normal railroad curves, this is accomplished in four back-and-forth switchbacks. It takes about 30 minutes before the train starts leaving Cuzco proper, and late-risers who miss it can often make a dash for the station at Poroy (US$5 in taxi) to catch up. The tracks then drop gently through agricultural countryside to Ollantaytambo station. As the train draws out of the station, you may be able to catch a glimpse of the Ollantaytambo ruins as well as Nevado Veronica (5750m) to your right. The train descends down the narrow gorge, affording superb views of the white water of the lower Urubamba. Km82 is where hikers begin the Inca Trail and the stop at Km104 is for the shorter two-day Inca Trail. The last station on the line is at Aguas Calientes, also known as Machu Picchu Pueblo. It is 8km from here to Machu Picchu itself, which can be reached by bus from the station. The tracks beyond Aguas Calientes used to continue into the jungle at Quillabamba, but catastrophic damage during the 1998 El Niño closed the line.

On the return to Cuzco, the view of the city is enhanced by the beautifully floodlit church and cathedral on the Plaza de Armas, but unfortunately, the slow-moving trains on the switchbacks have become the target for water and even rock-throwers: don't stick any expensive cameras out of the window here.

GETTING AROUND
To/From the Airport

The airport is 2km from the center; frequent colectivo taxis run to and from Plaza San Francisco/Avenida Sol (US$0.30) to just outside the airport precinct. A trip to just outside the airport to the airport terminal itself costs US$2.50 or US$3.50 (drivers have to pay an extra fee to enter the precinct).

Bus

Rides around Cuzco cost about US$0.30.

Taxi

There is a standard fare for taxi rides within the central area, currently US$0.60 in the daytime and US$0.90 after 10pm. You can hire a taxi for a whole day for about US$40 to US$50 to visit sites around Cuzco. Taxis belonging to an official company, identified by a roof light and company phone number, are safer than 'pirate' taxis, which simply have a sticker in the window. It's a good idea to take note of the registration plate before getting in. A recommended taxi company to call is **Aló Taxi** (☎ 22-2222), whose drivers are all licensed and should carry photo ID.

Tranvia

The Tranvia (☎ 22-4377; tinticusco@hotmail.coms) is a free-rolling tourist tram service that conducts a two-hour tour of Cuzco for US$2, including the Plaza de Armas, Sacsayhuamán and San Blas. It leaves from Portal Comercio on the Plaza de Armas at 10am and 1pm daily.

AROUND CUZCO

The four ruins closest to Cuzco are Sacsayhuamán, Qenko, Puca Pucara and Tambo Machay. They can all be visited in a day, or far less if you're whisked through on a guided trip. Entry to each is with the *Boleto Turístico*, and they're officially open from 7am to 6pm though there's little to stop you visiting outside these times. The cheapest way to visit is to take a bus to Pisac and get off at Tambo Machay, the furthest site from Cuzco and, at 3700m, the highest. From there, you can walk the 8km back to Cuzco, visiting all four ruins along the way: go in a group and give yourself plenty of time to return before nightfall. Alternatively, a taxi will charge roughly US$20 to all four sites giving you enough time to explore. Locals in their traditional finery with their most photogenic llamas wait near each site, hoping to be photographed for a tip (US$0.30 to US$60). Local guides also offer their services: agree a price before beginning the tour.

Tambo Machay

In a sheltered spot about 300m from the main road, this site consists of a beautifully wrought, ceremonial stone bath channeling crystalline spring water through fountains that still function today. It is thus popularly known as El Baño del Inca, and theories connect the site to an Inca water cult. Puca Pucara, the next ruin, can be seen from the small signaling post opposite.

Puca Pucara

Just across the main road from Tambo Machay is this commanding structure looking down on the Cuzco Valley. In some lights, the rock looks pink and the name literally means 'red fort,' though it is more likely to have been a hunting lodge, guard post and stopping point for travelers. It is composed of several lower residential chambers, storerooms and an upper esplanade with great views.

Qenko

The name of this small but fascinating shrine means 'zigzag.' It consists of a large limestone rock riddled with niches, steps and extraordinary symbolic carvings, including the zigzagging channels that gave the site its name. These channels were probably used for the ritual sacrifice of *chicha* or, perhaps, blood. Scrambling up to the top you'll find a flat surface used for ceremonies, and if you look carefully, some laboriously etched representations of a puma, condor and a llama. Back below you can explore the tunnels carved into the rock and a mysterious subterranean cave with altars hewn into the rock.

Qenko is about 4km before Cuzco, on the left of the road as you descend from Tambo Machay. The site of **Salapunco** (Temple of the Moon) is about 1.5km from Qenko: head back uphill, turn right and head out into the fields. Ask locals for directions as you go.

Sacsayhuamán

This immense ruin of both religious and military significance is the most impressive in the immediate Cuzco area. The long Quechua name means 'satisfied falcon,' though most tourists inevitably remember it by the mnemonic 'sexy woman.'

To reach the site from Cuzco, you can climb the steep street of Resbalosa, turn right past the Church of San Cristóbal and continue to a hairpin bend in the road. Here, you'll join the old Inca road between Cuzco and Sacsayhuamán to the top and left. The climb is steep and takes between 20 and 40 minutes so make sure you're acclimatized before attempting it. Guards are particularly active in demanding to see your *Boleto Turístico* here. Arriving at dawn will give you the site almost to yourself, though a few opportunistic robberies have been reported early and late in the day, so go with friends or a group.

Although Sacsayhuamán seems huge, what today's visitor sees is only about 20% of the original structure. Soon after the conquest, the Spaniards tore down many walls and used the blocks to build their own houses in Cuzco, leaving the largest and most impressive rocks, especially those forming the main battlements.

The site is composed of three different areas, the most striking being the magnificent, three-tiered, zigzag fortifications. One stone incredibly weighs over 300 tonnes.

The Incas envisioned Cuzco in the shape of a puma, with Sacsayhuamán as the head, and these 22 zigzagged walls form the teeth of the puma. They also form an extremely effective defensive mechanism that forced attackers to expose their flanks when attacking the wall.

Opposite is the hill called **Rodadero**, with its retaining walls, curiously polished rocks and a finely carved series of stone benches known as the throne of the Inca. Between the zigzag ramparts and Rodadero Hill lies a large, flat parade ground that is used for the colorful tourist spectacle of **Inti Raymi**, (see p182) held every June 24.

Three towers once stood above these walls. Only the foundations remain, but the 22m diameter of the largest, Muyuc Marca, gives an indication of how big they must have been. With its perfectly fitted stone conduits, this tower was probably used as a huge water tank for the garrison. Other buildings within the ramparts provided food and shelter for an estimated 5000 warriors. Most of these structures were torn down by the Spaniards and later inhabitants of Cuzco.

The fort was the site of one of the most bitter battles of the Spanish conquest. About 2½ years after Pizarro's entry into Cuzco, the rebellious Manco Inca recaptured the lightly guarded Sacsayhuamán and used it as a base to lay siege to the conquistadors in Cuzco. Manco was on the brink of defeating the Spaniards when a desperate last-ditch attack by 50 Spanish cavalry led by Juan Pizarro succeeded in retaking Sacsayhuamán and putting an end to the rebellion. Manco Inca survived and retreated to the fortress of Ollantaytambo, but most of his forces were killed. Thousands of dead littered the site and attracted swarms of carrion-eating Andean condors, leading to the inclusion of eight condors in Cuzco's coat of arms.

SACRED VALLEY

☎ 084

The beautiful Vilcanota/Urubamba valley, popularly called El Valle Sagrado, or the Sacred Valley, of the Incas, can be reached about 15km north of Cuzco as the condor flies. Situated 600m lower than Cuzco, the valley enjoys a pleasant, sheltered climate and fertile land that the Incas took full advantage of, scattering towns and agricultural centers throughout its length. The valley's star attractions are the lofty Inca citadels of Pisac and Ollantaytambo, which proudly preside over its undulating twists and turns, but the valley is also packed with other Inca sites, as well as bustling Indian markets and charming Andean villages. It is also famous for its high-adrenalin activities, from rafting the Urubamba (see p177) to soaring down mountains on a paraglider or drifting off in a hot-air balloon organized in Cuzco (see p181) or Urubamba (p200).

A multitude of tour companies in Cuzco offer whirlwind tours of the Sacred Valley, stopping at numerous craft markets and some of the most significant archaeological sites, but if you have a few days it's more rewarding to explore this peaceful rural corner of the Andes at your own leisure. Note that entrance to the sites of Pisac, Ollantaytambo and Chinchero requires either the US$10 or one-day US$6 Boleto Turístico.

PISAC
pop 2000

Pisac is 32km from Cuzco by paved road and is the most convenient starting point for a visit to the Sacred Valley. There are two distinct parts to Pisac: the colonial village lying beside the river and the Inca

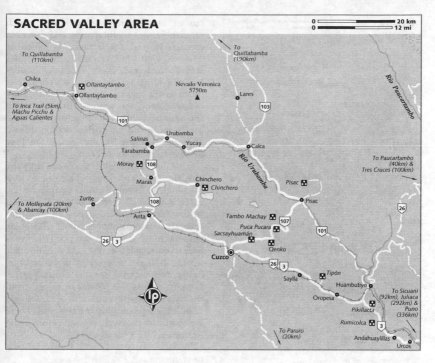

SACRED VALLEY AREA

0 _____ 20 km
0 _____ 12 mi

fortress perched dramatically on a mountain spur 600m above.

Colonial Pisac & Market

For most of the week, colonial Pisac is a quiet, rural Andean village. The village comes alive on Sunday, however, when the famous weekly **market** takes over. This bustling spectacle attracts traditionally dressed locals from miles around, and, despite also drawing tourists from the world over, still retains a traditional side. The selling and bartering of everyday produce goes on alongside the hordes of colorful craft stalls. Nonetheless, the market is a professional affair and, even after hard bargaining, prices are comparable to those in Cuzco.

The main square becomes thronged with people early and becomes even more crowded after the Mass (given in Quechua), at 11am when the congregation leaves the church in a colorful procession, led by the mayor holding his silver staff of office. Things start winding down after lunch, and by evening the village has returned to its normal somnolent state. There's a smaller craft market on Thursday and one smaller still on Tuesday, and a few stallholders also sell souvenirs daily during the height of the season.

When the markets have gone, Calle Bolognesi still has several craft workshops and you can visit the clay-oven bakery on Mariscal Castilla for the hot-out-of-the-oven flatbread rolls typical of the area; take a look at their elaborate *castillo de cuyes* (a miniature castle inhabited by guinea pigs). A small museum on the plaza is also set to open in 2004.

There's a payphone on the plaza, and a small **cyber café** (US$0.90 per hour; ⏰ 3-11pm Mon-Sat, noon-11pm Sun) can be found on Bolognesi, opposite the mini-market. Pisac has a fiesta in mid-July around the 15th to the 18th.

Inca Pisac

The hilltop Inca citadel lies high above the village on a triangular plateau with a plunging gorge on either side. Though it's a truly spectacular site, you'll see relatively few tourists here, except mid-morning on Sunday, Tuesday and Thursday when

PISAC

0 —————— 100 m (approx)
0 —————— 0.1 mi

Path to Pisac
Ruins (5km)

Residencial
Beho

Church

Bakery
Mariscal Castilla

Parador
de Pisag

Plaza
Constitución

Samana
Wasi

To Road
to Ruins
(10km)

Ulrike's Café

Museum

Hostal Pisaq

Kisay
Cchocha
Hostal

Mullo Café

Bolognesi

Grau

Cyber Café

Minimarket

To Intihuasi Hotel (1km),
Urubamba (40km) &
Ollantaytambo (58km)

To Paz y Luz
(1km), Hotel Royal
Inka Pisac (1.5km) &
Road to Ruins (10km)

Buses &
Police Post

Río Urubamba

To Cuzco
(32km)

curves, almost unbroken by steps, which require greater maintenance and promote erosion. Instead, the terracing is joined by diagonal flights of stairs made of flagstones set into the terrace walls. Above the terraces are cliff-hugging footpaths, watched over by caracara hawks and well defended by massive stone doorways, steep stairs and a short tunnel carved out of the rock. Vendors meet you at the top with welcome drinks; and after carrying the bottles this far, they deserve to make a few cents.

This dominating site guards not only the Urubamba valley below, but also a pass into the jungle to the northeast. Topping the terraces is the site's **ceremonial center**, with an Intihuatana (or hitching post of the sun), several working water channels and some painstakingly neat masonry in the well-preserved **temples**. From here a path leads up the hillside to a series of ceremonial baths and around to the military area. Looking across the Kitamayo Gorge from the back of the site, you'll also see hundreds of holes honeycombing the cliff wall. These are **Inca tombs** that were robbed before being examined by archaeologists.

The site is large and warrants several hours of your time.

Sleeping & Eating

Pisac has only limited accommodations, so get there early on market days in high season.

Hostal Pisaq (☎ /fax 20-3062; hotelpisaq@terra.com .pe; Plaza Constitución; s/d US$10/20, with bathroom US$26) Hostal Pisaq, which is recognizable by its funky geometric designs, has a small, pretty courtyard, good rooms and an underground sauna (US$10 shared between four). Breakfast is available for US$3 in the connected café. German, English and French are spoken.

Paz y Luz (☎ 20-3204; dianedunn@terra.com.pe; s/d US$10/20, with bathroom US$15/30, apt per night/ week/month US$15/50/150) This is a newly built bed and breakfast, a 1km walk east along the river. It's a spiritual spot surrounded by fields and run by a North American who also organizes mystical tours.

Parador de Pisaq (☎ 20-3061; Plaza Constitución; s or d US$7) The Parador is a familiar spot with five clean rooms with shared bathroom and views.

Residencial Beho (☎ 20-3001; Intihuatana 642; s/d US$5/8.50, with bathroom US$7/14) On the path

it becomes flooded with tour groups. To get there, either hire a cab in Pisac to drive along the 10km, paved road up the Chongo valley (US$3/$5 one way/round trip) or walk up the steep 5km footpath from the plaza. You can sometimes catch a truck carrying workers up from Pisac at 7am and occasional minibuses run to within a kilometer of the ruins. On market day, combis also make the trip from the eastern edge of the village (US$0.60). Entry is by *Boleto Turístico*, but the guards often knock off around 4pm.

The footpath to the site starts from the west side of the church. Allow 90 minutes to two hours for this stiff but spectacular climb. There are many criss-crossing trails, but if you keep heading upward toward the terracing, you won't get lost. The western gorge (to the left of the hill as you climb up on the footpath) is the Río Kitamayo gorge; to the right, or east, is the Río Chongo valley, where the road ascends.

Pisac is famous for its agricultural **terracing**, which sweeps around the south and east flanks of the mountain in huge and graceful

to the ruins and easily hidden by stalls on market day, Beho has basic rooms and warm showers. The owners also run a shop selling handicrafts.

Samana Wasi (☎ 20-3018; Plaza Constitución; dm US$4-5) This place has plain but clean rooms and shared baths with hot water. There's a cheap restaurant serving good trout below.

Kisay Cchocha (☎ 20-3101; Plaza Constitución & Arequipa; s/d US$5/10) This hostel provides simple lodging, with another building on Calle Arequipa. Rates are only US$3 if you can make do with cold water.

Hotel Royal Inka Pisac (☎ 20-3064/5; fax 20-3067; s/d US$54/78) The Royal Inka, which is about 1.5km from the plaza on the road to the ruins, is a large converted hacienda operated by the Royal Inka group in Cuzco (royalin@terra.com.pe). Though many of the rooms lack character, the hotel does boast an impressive list of amenities: restaurant, bar, sauna, massage, indoor swimming pool, tennis court, games room, horseback rides and local tours. Rates include a buffet breakfast. It also has a **camp site** (per person US$3 (with own tent), tent hire 1-person/2-person/4-person US$10/12/15, bungalows US$20) with good facilities and sports pitches.

Ulrike's Café (☎ 20-3195; Plaza Constitución; 3-course menu US$3) Ulrike's serves up a great vegetarian menu, home-made pasta and melt-in-the-mouth muffins and brownies (US$0.60). There's a book exchange, DVD collection and the owner also rents two rooms above the café.

Mullo (Plaza Constitución; ☽ closed Mon) It has a prime position looking down on the plaza, and has a long list of juices and smoothies (US$1.50 to US$3) plus a small art gallery.

Getting There & Away

Minibuses (US$0.50, one hour) leave frequently from the bridge to Cuzco between 5:30am and 8pm to Avenida Tullumayo and Calle Putupi in Cuzco. Buses in the opposite direction continue down the valley to Calca and Urubamba. Many agencies in Cuzco operate tourist buses, especially on market day, or you can hire a cab for about US$20.

CALCA

pop 8500 / elevation 3000m
About 18km beyond Pisac, Calca is a key town in the valley and a pleasant stop though it has few facilities for tourists.

There are some small Inca sites in the vicinity.

The clean **Villa María** (☎ 20-2110; Los Santos 388; s/d/tr/4-bed room US$3/6/9/12; s/d/tr with bathroom US$6/10/13) is the best choice in town with friendly service and a small orchard. Bathrooms have hot water. **El Carmen** (☎ 20-2208; Vilcanota 848; 3-course menu US$1.20; ☽ closes 7pm) is a tourist restaurant with plain rooms for rent, charging US$6 per person with cold-water bath. Good food is served at **Quinta Jacaranda** (☎ 20-2026; mains US$3-7; closes 6pm) 1km west on the highway. Also 10km west on the road to Yucay, is the small and modern **Bellavista Inn** (☎ 962-6447; Km61.5; s/d US$20/30; P ☲), which has a restaurant, games room and swimming pool.

YUCAY

The pretty little village of Yucay (pop 3000) is approximately 4km before Urubamba from Calca and has three good hotels surrounding a grassy plaza.

Hostal Y'llary (☎ 20-1112; fax 22-6607; s/d US$25/30, camping per person US$6) Y'llary, which means dawn in Quechua, is run by a charming old gent and has clean, pleasant rooms with private hot showers. Rates include breakfast. There's also a large garden and camping area with separate hot shower and bathroom.

La Casona de Yucay (☎ 20-1116; casonayucay@terra.com.pe; s/d US$60/80) La Casona is a colonial house built in 1810, in which the liberator Simón Bolívar stayed in 1825. Indeed, if you book ahead you may even be allowed to stay in his antique-filled room. The 20 large rooms surround a traditional stone courtyard, and there is a restaurant and bar. Rates include a buffet breakfast.

Posada del Inca (☎ 20-1107; posada@sonestaperu.com; Plaza Manco II 123; s/d US$85/99, mini-suite US$115) The entrance to this hotel is through a beautiful 300-year-old building, which was formerly a monastery and then a hacienda, behind which are flower-filled gardens, a restaurant, a chapel and a little museum. Most of the 69 rooms are in modern buildings, but a few in the original part are more creaky and characterful; one is supposedly haunted. Some rooms are wheelchair accessible. Rates include buffet breakfast, and there's a handy ATM accepting Visa, Cirrus, Plus and MasterCard in the lobby. The hotel also arranges local activities, including mountain-bike rental (US$10 an hour or US$50 a day, including helmet), river rafting (US$35 a half-day), horse riding, hiking and hot-air ballooning.

URUBAMBA

pop 8000 / elevation 2871m

Urubamba is 4km beyond Yucay at the junction of the valley road with the Chinchero road. Although it has little of historical interest, it's surrounded by beautiful countryside and makes a convenient and serene base from which to explore the extraordinary Salinas and terracing of Moray (see p201) as well as to enjoy some of the valley's best outdoor activities.

There's a Visa ATM on the main road by Quinta Los Geranios and **Banco de la Nación** (Mariscal Castilla) changes US dollars. The post office is on the plaza and Internet access is available at **Academia de Internet Urubamba** (cnr Grau & Belén; ☼ 8am-10pm; US$0.70 per hour).

Pottery

Pablo Seminario (☎ 20-1002; www.ceramicaseminario.com; Berriozabal 111) is a prolific and well-known local potter who creates attractive, original work with a preconquest influence that is different from anything else you'll see in Cuzco. He speaks English and is happy to explain his art to visitors. The workshop is in western Urubamba just off the main highway near the Hotel Valle Sagrado de los Inkas.

Activities

Many outdoor activities that are organized from Cuzco take place from Urubamba (see Activities p200), including horse riding, hot-air ballooning as well as paragliding.

Perol Chicho (☎ 20-1694, 962-4475; info@perolchico.com), run by Dutch–Peruvian Eduard van Brunschot Vega, has an excellent ranch outside Urubamba with Peruvian *paso* horses. He organizes horse riding tours of one to 10 days; during the dry season only, a one-day trip to Moray and the Salinas costs roughly US$60.

Viento Sur (☎ 20-1620; www.aventurasvientosur.com; Hotel Sol y Luna) organizes numerous activities from horse-riding tours on Peruvian *paso* horses (half day/full day/two day for US$50/85/250) to paragliding (in high season only, tandem US$100), mountain biking (one hour/half day/one day for US$15/50/85) and guided walks.

Sleeping & Eating

BUDGET

Hotel Urubamba (☎ 20-1062; Bolognesi 605; s/d US$3/6, with bathroom US$6/9) Hotel Urubamba, a couple of blocks from the central plaza, is a basic but friendly choice in the town center. The shared showers on the 2nd floor have hot water if you ask.

Señor de Torrechero (☎ 20-1033; Mariscal Castilla 114; s/d/tr US$6/9/12) This place offers fair value and unexciting rooms with bathrooms.

Quinta Los Geranios (☎ 20-1093; Cabo Conchatupa; s/d/tr US$10/20/30) Los Geranios, opposite top-end eatery El Maizal, has spotless new rooms with bathrooms, and a garden running down to the river. It's also a popular open-air restaurant (mains US$3-7; ☼ noon-6pm).

Posada Las 3 Marias (☎ 20-1006; posada3marias@yahoo.com; Zavala 307; s/d US$15/30) Las 3 Marias, several streets above the plaza, is a modern, welcoming new place with a garden and decent rooms, though with shared bathroom. Rates include breakfast.

Las Chullpas (☎ 969-5030; Pumahuanca; r per person US$10) Hidden 5km above the town, these woodland cottages make the perfect getaway. The site is nestled beneath a mountain and thick eucalyptus trees surround the homely cabins. There is an open kitchen and vegetarian food is available.

Camping Los Cedros (☎ 20-1416; r per person US$4-6) This camp site, run by Cesár Bera, is about 4km above the town on winding country roads.

Che Mary (☎ 20-1003; cnr Comercio & Grau; 3-course menu US$2.50) Che Mary is a cozy little restaurant back on the plaza with a bar and a friendly, English-speaking hostess.

MID-RANGE TO TOP END

San Agustín Monasterio de la Recoleta (☎ 22-1025; inter@terra.com.pe; Jirón de la Recoleta; s/d US$25/30) This old building is a hauntingly beautiful mission on the outskirts of town. It has a chapel, cloistered courtyards and 26 colonial-style rooms with bathrooms. Prices are set to rise after renovations are completed.

Inkaland Hotel & Conference Center (☎ 20-1126/27; rec-incaland@terra.com.pe; Cabo Conchatupa; s/d US$60/80; **P** **⚤**) Close to Terminal Terrestre, this is a huge, rambling complex with two swimming pools, a restaurant, a few pet llamas and 65 comfortable suites and wooden-floored bungalows.

Hostal El Maizal (☎ /fax 20-1054; maizal@planet
.com.pe; s/d US$45) El Maizal, a short walk west
of the bus terminal at Km73, is a quiet
place with a large grassy garden. German
and English are spoken and rates include a
continental breakfast.

Quinta Patawasi (☎ 20-1386; quinta-patawasi@
telser.com.pe; s/d US$45/59) On a small street
right behind Hostal El Maizal, the Quinta
is a characterful spot recommended for extremely cheerful, attentive service. English
is spoken

Willka T'ika (☎ 20-1508; wtika@terra.com.pe;
Castilla Postal 70; s/d US$44/88) This place is at
Km75, 3km west of town, and has attractive rooms set in riotously colorful gardens.
The guesthouse features yoga, massage and
meditation rooms, healing and shamanism
workshops and vegetarian meals. It is essential to make advance reservations here,
and it sometimes closes at weekends. Willka
T'ika is run by tour operator **Magical Journeys**
(☎ in the USA 415-665-4645; info@magicaljourney.org).

Hotel Sol y Luna (☎ 20-1620; reservas@hotelsol
yluna.com; s/d/tr/quad US$105/120/150/180; P ☎)
Around 2km west of town is this swish
new top-end complex with a restaurant,
spacious gardens, beautiful self-contained
cottages and a stable; it also hosts the activity specialists Viento Sur (see Activities
p200). Rates include buffet breakfast and
taxes.

Hotel San Agustín (☎ 22-1025; inter@terra.com.pe;
s/d/tr US$77/90/106; ☎) Part of the Cuzco-based
chain, Hotel San Agustín is a spacious option about a kilometer east of town. Rooms
all have TV and minibar, and there's also
a sauna (US$20 for two to four people),
Jacuzzi and masseur (US$30). Rates include
buffet breakfast. The garden has an outdoor
buffet-style restaurant often filled with tour
groups. Confidential rates are as much as
half the given prices.

Restaurant El Maizal (☎ 20-1054; Cabo Conchatupa; lunch only) El Maizal has excellent
buffet lunches with traditional Andean
food (US$9).

Alhambra (☎ 20-1200; reservas@alhambrarestaurant
.com; meals US$5-10) Alhambra is a smart new
restaurant set away from the highway 2km
towards Ollantaytambo amid serene green-
ery and birdcalls. The tranquility is broken
at lunchtime on Tuesday, Thursday and Sunday, when tour groups descend on the restaurant to enjoy its buffet lunches (US$8).

Getting There & Away

Urubamba serves as the valley's principle
transport hub. Buses to Cuzco (US$0.90,
two hours) go via Calca (US$0.20, 30 min-
utes) and Pisac (US$0.60, one hour), or via
Chinchero (US$0.50, 30 minutes) every
20 minutes and combis to Ollantaytambo
(US$0.30, 25 minutes) all leave from the
new terminal on the main road. Buses to
Cuzco finish up either at Puente Grau or
Avenida Tullumayo. You can buy tickets
to Quillabamba (US$4.20, 10:30am daily)
from a small shop opposite the *grifo* (gas
station) 1km east on the main road.

SALINAS

About 6km further down the valley from
Urubamba is the village of Tarabamba.
Cross the Río Urubamba here by footbridge,
turn right and follow a footpath along the
south bank of the river to a small cemetery,
where you turn left and climb roughly
southward up a valley to the **salt pans** of
Salinas. It's about a 3km uphill hike.

Thousands of salt pans have been used
for salt extraction since Inca times. A hot
spring at the top of the valley discharges
a small stream of heavily salt-laden water,
which is diverted into salt pans and evapor-
ated to produce a salt used for cattle licks.
The local salt-extracting cooperative
charges US$0.60 for entry to this incredible
site, but there's rarely anyone to collect the
money if you enter from the path climbing
up from the river.

A rough dirt road enters Salinas from
above, giving spectacular views. Tour groups
visit via this route most days.

MORAY

The deep amphitheatre-like terracing of
Moray (adult/student US$1.50/0.90) is both a fas-
cinating and impressive spectacle. Different
levels of concentric terraces are carved into
a huge bowl, each layer of which apparently
has its own microclimate, according to how
deep into the bowl it is. For this reason, the
Incas are thought to have used them as a
kind of crop-laboratory to determine the
optimal conditions of each species. There
are two large bowls and one small, the first
of which has once again been planted with
various crops as a kind of living museum.

This site is challenging to reach. First,
catch one of the frequent buses or combis

(US$0.60) from Urubamba's bus terminal toward Chincheros. Ask the driver to drop you at the road to Maras. In high season taxis sometimes wait at this turn-off (US$0.30/3/6 to Maras/Moray/Salinas), but be prepared to tackle the 3km walk to the village of Maras yourself. From there, follow the trail another 7km to Moray, asking locals for directions. From Moray it is possible to continue walking to Salinas about 6km away and on down to Urubamba, which fills a long but satisfying day. Ask the guard in Moray to point out the trail as it can be hard to find.

Alternatively, take a taxi trip direct from Urubamba (US$12 round trip or US$16 including Salinas). The road is extremely rough and goes for about 13km from the paved Urubamba–Chinchero highway to Moray.

OLLANTAYTAMBO

pop 2000 / elevation 2800m

The village of Ollantaytambo, dominated by the massive Inca fortress above, is also the best surviving example of Inca city planning with narrow cobblestone streets that have been constantly inhabited since the 13th century. The village was divided into blocks called *canchas*, and each *cancha* had just one entrance, which led into a courtyard.

The spectacular, huge, steep **terraces** that guard the **Inca complex** (entry by Boleto Turístico; ⏰ 7am-6pm) mark one of the few places where the conquistadors lost a major battle. It was to this fortress that Manco Inca retreated after his defeat at Sacsayhuamán and in 1536, Hernando Pizarro (Francisco Pizarro's younger half-brother) led a force of 70 cavalrymen here, supported by large numbers of native and Spanish foot soldiers, in an attempt to capture Manco Inca. Pizarro's men were showered with arrows, spears and boulders from atop the steep terracing and were unable to climb to the fortress. They were further hampered when Manco Inca, in a brilliant move, flooded the plain below the fortress through previously prepared channels. The Spaniards' horses were bogged down in the water and Pizarro ordered a hasty retreat – which almost became a rout when the conquistadors were followed down the valley

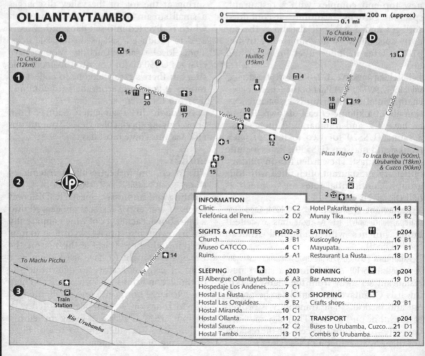

OLLANTAYTAMBO

0 — 200 m (approx)
0 — 0.1 mi

To Chilca (12km)

To Chaska Wasi (100m)

To Huilloc (15km)

Convención

Ventiderio

Chapicalle

Costado

To Machu Picchu

Av Ferrocarril

Train Station

Río Urubamba

Plaza Mayor

To Inca Bridge (500m), Urubamba (18km) & Cuzco (90km)

INFORMATION		
Clinic	1	C2
Telefónica del Peru	2	D2

SIGHTS & ACTIVITIES	pp202–3	
Church	3	B1
Museo CATCCO	4	C1
Ruins	5	A1

SLEEPING		p203
El Albergue Ollantaytambo	6	A3
Hospedaje Los Andenes	7	C1
Hostal La Ñusta	8	C1
Hostal Las Orquídeas	9	B2
Hostal Miranda	10	C1
Hostal Ollanta	11	D2
Hostal Sauce	12	C2
Hostal Tambo	13	D1

Hotel Pakaritampu	14	B3
Munay Tika	15	B2

EATING		p204
Kusicoylloy	16	B1
Mayupata	17	B1
Restaurant La Ñusta	18	D1

DRINKING		p204
Bar Amazonica	19	D1

SHOPPING		
Crafts shops	20	B1

TRANSPORT		p204
Buses to Urubamba, Cuzco....	21	D1
Combis to Urubamba	22	D2

by thousands of Manco Inca's victorious soldiers.

However, the Inca's victory was short lived; soon after, strengthened Spanish forces returned with a quadrupled cavalry force and Manco fled to his jungle stronghold in Vilcabamba (see p219).

Though Ollantaytambo was a highly effective fortress, it was as much a temple as a fort to the Incas. The **temple area** is at the top of the terracing. Some extremely well-built walls were under construction at the time of the conquest and have never been completed. The stone was quarried from the mountainside 6km away, high above the opposite bank of the Río Urubamba. Transporting the huge stone blocks to the site was a stupendous feat that must have involved the sweat and blood of thousands of Indian workers. Their crafty technique to move the massive blocks across the river was to leave the blocks by its side then divert the entire river channel around them!

A good walk from Ollantaytambo is the 6km trail to the Inca quarry on the opposite side of the river. The trail starts from the Inca bridge by the entrance to the village and takes three to four hours to reach the site, passing several abandoned blocks known as the tired stones. Looking back towards Ollantaytambo, you can see the enigmatic optical illusion of a pyramid in the fields and walls in front of the fortress, which a few scholars believe marks the legendary place where the original Incas first emerged from the earth.

Local community history and ethnography are the main focus of the **Museo CATCCO** (☎ 20-4024; rao@apu.cbc.org.pe; Casa Horno, Patacalle; admission US$1.50; ⏰ 10am-1pm & 2-4pm Tue-Sun). It is connected with the Ollantaytambo Pilot Project (www.cbc.org.pe/rao), working to develop the town. There is also Internet access available for a whopping US$3 per hour.

Ollantaytambo is a great place to be when the locals are having a fiesta.

Sleeping

Hostal Miranda (☎ 20-4091; miranda_ollanta@hotmail .com; s/d/tr US$4.50/9/13.50) Miranda is a rickety, old place with a cheap restaurant below.

Hostal Tambo (☎ 20-4003; Costado; s/d/tr US$3/6/9) This decidedly run-down but friendly place housed in a characterful old building has shared cold-water showers.

Hostal La Ñusta (☎ 20-4035; s/d/tr US$4.50/9/13.50, with breakfast US$8/16/24) La Ñusta has a dozen rooms with shared showers and serves breakfast at the connected Restaurant La Ñusta on the plaza. Though slightly rundown and chaotic, the hostel has a miniature terrace overlooking the river with ruin views.

Chaska Wasi (☎ 20-3061; chaskawasihostal@hot mail.com; Chaupicalle; s/d US$5-6/10-12) The Chaska Wasi is a cheap and cheerful new spot with shared bathrooms and electric showers.

Hostal Ollanta (☎ 20-4116; Plaza de Armas; s/d US$6/12) Situated behind a village shop, the Ollanta has clean rooms and shared showers with 24-hour hot water.

Hospedaje Los Andenes (☎ 20-4095; Ventiderio; s/d US$4.50/9, with bathroom s/d US$7/14) This recommended spot has hot water and is connected with a cute hole-in-the wall café called Puka Rumi outside.

Munay Tika (☎ 20-4111; tika@latinmail.com; Av Ferrocarril; s/d US$15/20, with bathroom US$20/25) Munay Tika, meaning jungle flower, is a good, youthful hostel with a pretty garden, kitchen privileges and sauna (US$5). Rates include breakfast.

Hostal Las Orquídeas (☎ 20-4032; Av Ferrocarril; s/d US$12/24) Next door to Munay Tika, Las Orquídeas has a small, grassy courtyard with deck chairs, and seven good rooms, some with shared bathrooms.

El Albergue Ollantaytambo (☎ /fax 20-4014; albergue@rumbosperu.com; s/d US$15/30) On the train platform 800m from the center, El Albergue is run by Wendy Weeks, a North American who has been a local resident for almost three decades. It's a characterful old hostel with a lovely garden and tiny sauna (US$5), and there's certainly no fear of missing your train. Rates include a sturdy breakfast. Do not confuse it with Albergue Kapuly, which is next door outside the platform gates.

Hostal Sauce (☎ 20-4044; hostalsauce@viabcp.com; Ventiderio 248; s/d/tr US$69/79/105; P) This is a smart new building constructed on high ground so that some rooms have a great view to the ruins. There are reductions of 30% when it's quiet.

Hotel Pakaritampu (☎ 20-4020; hotel@pakari tampu.com; Av Ferrocarril; s/d/tr US$99/104/134) Pakaritampu, a 200m walk from the train station, is a peaceful hotel with nouveau-rustic rooms in spacious gardens. Rates include a buffet breakfast.

Eating & Drinking

Mayupata (☎ 20-4000; Convención; 3-course menú US$7) This is a new riverside restaurant serving good Peruvian food by the bridge, with a garden and an open fireplace for those cold Andean nights.

Kusicoylloy (☎ 20-4114; Plaza Araccama; mains US$4-7) Kusicoylloy is a stylish new café-bar with a wide-ranging menu and an ice-cream store for the sweet-toothed next door.

Bar Amazonica, near Restaurant La Ñusta, is the only nightlife in Ollantaytambo, serving up some colorful jungle cocktails.

Getting There & Away

BUS

Frequent combis and occasional minibuses leave from Urubamba's bus terminal to Ollantaytambo's plaza (US$0.30, 25 minutes); services peter out in late afternoon. To get to Cuzco it's easiest to change in Urubamba, where minibuses leave every 15 minutes or you can catch the 7:45am or 7:45pm buses to Puente Grau (US$1, 2½ hours) in Cuzco. Buses to Quillabamba (see Bus – Long Distance p192) stop in Ollantaytambo too, but you'll have to pay the full fare (US$4.20).

TRAIN

Ollantaytambo is an important half-way station between Cuzco and Machu Picchu; all trains stop here about two hours after leaving Cuzco (see Train p194) or Machu Picchu. These trains usually charge the same expensive fare to Machu Picchu as from Cuzco. However, there are also two daily, Vistadome services (one way/round trip US$35/69) and a high-season backpacker train (one way/round trip US$29.50/41.30) that leave from Ollantaytambo itself, plus a local train with two coaches for backpackers that leaves at 7:45pm daily (one way/round trip US$11.80/23.60). This limited service is currently the cheapest option to get to Machu Picchu. Vistadome one-way tickets also receive a 50% discount when purchased within 48 hours of departure. See Aguas Calientes (p207) for details of return trains to Ollantaytambo.

The ticket office at the station is open from 6:30am to noon in the daytime and 5pm to 8pm in the evening. It can save hassle on the platform to ask the ticket seller to put your name on the ticket.

CHINCHERO

pop 2000 / elevation 3762m

This village, known as the 'birthplace of the rainbow' to the Incas, is almost 400m higher than Cuzco, so take it easy if you aren't acclimatized. The site combines **Inca ruins** with a typical Andean village, a colonial church, some wonderful mountain views and a colorful Sunday market. Access to the Chinchero site requires a Boleto Turístico.

Steep steps run up to the main village square, which features a massive **Inca wall** with 10 huge, trapezoidal niches. The colonial church just above the square is built on Inca foundations and the interior is decked in elaborate floral and religious designs. It's opened for tour groups on Tuesday and Thursday and open for worship on Sunday. There's also a small **museum** focussed on local archaeology opposite the church.

The most extensive Inca ruins, however, consist of terracing, and walking away from the village through the terraces on the right-hand side of the valley, you'll find various rocks carved into seats and staircases. On the opposite side of the valley, a clear trail climbs upward before heading north and down to the Río Urubamba valley about four hours away. At the river, the trail turns left and continues to a bridge at **Huayllabamba**, where you can cross. From here, the Sacred Valley road will take you to Calca (turn right, about 13km) or Urubamba (turn left, about 9km). You can flag down a bus until midafternoon.

The Sunday **markets** are marginally less touristy than those in Pisac. One in front of the old church sells crafts with prices similar to Pisac and Cuzco, but it's good to see local people still dressed in traditional garb, a habit that isn't just for the tourists. A local produce market is also held at the bottom of the village. Both markets are held to a smaller extent on Tuesday and especially Thursday.

Hospedaje Mi Piuray (☎ 30-6029; Garcilaso 187; s/d US$3/4.50, with bathroom US$7/10) is a welcoming family hostel set around an open courtyard. Though some rooms have bathrooms, the hot showers are communal.

Buses leave Cuzco from near Puente Grau in Cuzco, some continuing to Urubamba. Buses also go from Urubamba (US$0.50, 50 minutes).

Textiles for sale, **Ollantaytambo** (p202)

JEFF CANTARUTTI

RICHARD I'ANSON

Interior of the church of **La Compañía** (p173), Cuzco

Glacial lake, **Ausangate** (p220)

GRANT DIXON

PAUL KENNEDY

Adobe walls, **Chan Chan** (p269)

Abandoned cinema in a deserted oil town, near **Piura** (p286)

PAUL KENNEDY

Detail of wall friezes, **Chan Chan** (p269)

TOM

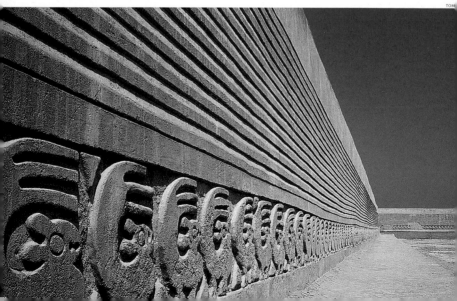

MACHU PICCHU & THE INCA TRAIL

AGUAS CALIENTES

☎ 084 / pop 2000

Also known as Machu Picchu Pueblo, this village is nestled in the deep valley below Machu Picchu (8km away) enclosed by towering walls of stone and cloud forest. All travelers to and from Cuzco pass through the town on their way to Machu Picchu, and many choose to stick around and indulge in a spot of serious rest and recuperation after the Inca Trail.

Information

A small information office is in the municipality. Internet is available at several places, including **Ink@net** (Imperio de los Incas; US$1.50 per hour). There's a **medical center** near the station and a **police station** (☎ 21-1178) on Imperio de los Incas. Small amounts of money and traveler's checks can be changed in hotels and tourist shops. The telephone office

doubles as an office for **Rikuni Sacred Experience** (☎ 21-1036; Imperio de los Incas 119) travel agency, which organizes local trips.

Sights & Activities

Trekkers completing the Inca Trail may want to soak away their aches in the **hot springs** (admission US$1.50; ⏰ 5am-8:30pm), which are tiny, natural thermal springs from which the village of Aguas Calientes derives its name. Head up Avenida Pachacutec for about 10 minutes to reach the gates. Bathing suits can be rented outside (US$1.50).

Footsore trekkers may also be interested in the **massage-to-your-door services** (☎ 974-5617 or through your hotel; US$10-20).

And for those who still have energy for trekking, there's some good walks in the vicinity, including one up the steep **Putucusi** mountain directly opposite Machu Picchu; follow the railway track 250m west of the station and you'll see a steeply ascending pathway. Parts of the walk are up ladder rungs, which get slippery in the wet season, but the view across to Machu Picchu is worth the trek.

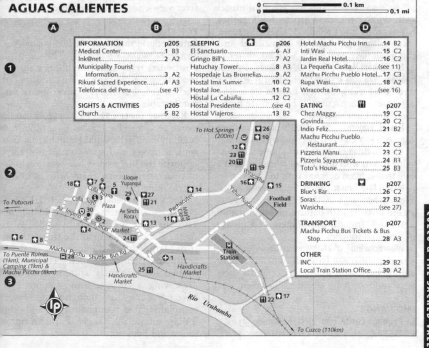

AGUAS CALIENTES

0 — 0.1 km
0 — 0.1 mi

INFORMATION	p205
Medical Center	1 B3
Ink@net	2 A2
Municipality Tourist Information	3 A2
Rikuni Sacred Experience	4 A3
Telefónica del Perú	(see 4)

| SIGHTS & ACTIVITIES | p205 |
| Church | 5 B2 |

SLEEPING	p206
El Sanctuario	6 A3
Gringo Bill's	7 A2
Hatuchay Tower	8 A3
Hospedaje Las Bromelias	9 A2
Hostal Ima Sumac	10 C2
Hostal Joe	11 B2
Hostal La Cabaña	12 C2
Hostal Presidente	(see 4)
Hostal Viajeros	13 B2

Hotel Machu Picchu Inn	14 B2
Inti Wasi	15 C2
Jardin Real Hotel	16 C2
La Pequeña Casita	(see 11)
Machu Picchu Pueblo Hotel	17 C3
Rupa Wasi	18 A2
Wiracocha Inn	(see 16)

EATING	p207
Chez Maggy	19 C2
Govinda	20 C2
Indio Feliz	21 B2
Machu Picchu Pueblo Restaurant	22 C3
Pizzeria Manu	23 C2
Pizzeria Sayacmarca	24 B3
Toto's House	25 B3

DRINKING	p207
Blue's Bar	26 C2
Soras	27 B2
Wasicha	(see 27)

| TRANSPORT | p207 |
| Machu Picchu Bus Tickets & Bus Stop | 28 A3 |

OTHER	
INC	29 B2
Local Train Station Office	30 A2

To Hot Springs (200m)

To Putucusi
Lloque Yupanqui
Colla Suyo
Colla Raymi
Av Imperio de los Incas
Pachacutec
Av Sinchi Roca
Maita Cápac
Wiracocha
Yahur Huaca
Football Field
Plaza
Market

To Puente Ruinas (1km), Municipal Camping (1km) & Machu Picchu (8km)
Machu Picchu Shuttle Bus Rd
Handicrafts Market
Train Station
Handicrafts Market
Río Urubamba

To Cuzco (110km)

Sleeping

Prices given here are for high season, and you should expect to pay 20% to 40% less for the rest of the year. Check out times between 8:30am and 10am are the norm.

BUDGET

Municipal Camping (r per person US$1.40) This is a small camp site with basic facilities a 1km walk west of the center by the bridge over the Río Urubamba.

Inti Wasi (☎ 21-1151; hanan65@latinmail.com; dm US$6) Inti Wasi has a wood-cabin feel and bunk beds in four- to six-bedded dorms, but does not have private bathrooms. It plans to offer camping space in the future.

Hostal Joe (☎ 21-1190; trasoc@latinmail.com; Mayta Cápac 103; s/d US$5/10, s/d with bathroom US$10/15) Up the hill from the plaza, Joe's has clean rooms and hot water, though some of the communal showers are a mite exposed for the cold Andean nights.

Hospedaje Las Bromelias (☎ 21-1145; Colla Raymi; s/d US$4/6) On the plaza, Las Bromelias has plain rooms but good value with hot-water bathrooms.

Rupa Wasi (☎ 21-1101; rupawasi@hotmail.com; dm with bathroom US$10-15) This is a youthful hostel with rooms in wood-cabins built rather haphazardly into the hillside above the town center. It's often been recommended and rooms all have bathrooms with hot water.

Jardin Real Hotel (☎ 21-1234; jardinrealhotel@hotmail.com; Wiracocha 7; s/d US$15/30) Jardin Real is one of several good new hostels springing up close to Pachacutec. It has private bathrooms and hot water.

Hostal Viajeros (☎ 21-1237; info@sastravelperu.com; Sinchi Roca 4; s/d US$15/30) Run by SAS tours in Cuzco, this new hostel has spotless, good-value rooms with hot-water bathrooms and a café that is often overrun with trekkers.

Hostal Ima Sumac (☎ 21-1021; imasumac@hostal.net; Pachacutec; s/d/tr US$15/20/30) Ima Sumac is an old favorite with bathrooms and reliable hot water, friendly atmosphere and plenty of personal touches.

Wiracocha Inn (☎ 21-1088; wiracocha-inn@peru.com; Wiracocha; s/d US$15/20) This new option is simple and friendly, with smiley service and a sheltered outdoor patio area near the river.

MID-RANGE

La Pequeña Casita (☎ 21-1153; Hermanos Ayar 13; s/d US$20/30) This is an excellent new place with very chirpy service, where you can be lulled to sleep by the rushing river beside the hotel. Rates include breakfast brought to your room.

Hostal La Cabaña (☎ 21-1048; lacabana_mapi@latinmail.com; Pachacutec; s/d/tr US$25/35/45) Further up the hill is this popular spot with warm woody rooms and a rustic feel, plus 24-hour hot water.

Gringo Bill's (☎ 21-1046; gringobill@yahoo.com Colla Raymi; s/d/tr US$25/35/50) Bill's attracts a laid-back crowd that enjoys the informal atmosphere and spacey wall murals, though the hostel was recently suffering from persistent plumbing problems. Discounts of 50% are available in the off season.

El Sanctuario (☎ 21-1094; sanctuario@mixmail.com s/d/tr US$35/50/65) El Sanctuario is a somewhat bland, modern hotel opposite the bus stop to Machu Picchu, but it has quality fittings and down-to-earth service, as well as balconies overlooking the river.

Hostal Presidente (☎ 21-1034, in Cuzco 084-24-4598; presidente@terra.com.pe; Imperio de los Incas, s/d/ste US$50/60/70) Situated by the railway tracks, the Presidente is very clean, relaxed and often full. The good-sized rooms have river views, some with balconies.

TOP END

Hotel Machu Picchu Inn (☎ 21-1011; mapiinn@terra.com.pe; Pachacutec; s & d US$92) This hotel is positioned right amid the budget accommodations and gringo restaurants on Pachacutec, but has 75 very smart and comfortable rooms.

Hatuchay Tower (☎ 21-1200; mapi@hatuchaytower.com.pe; Carretera Puente Ruinas 4; s or d US$178, deluxe US$195, ste US$218) What Hatuchay lacks in soul, it makes up for in comfort. Situated opposite the bus stop, it has several stories of smart, new rooms, many with balconies overlooking the river.

Machu Picchu Pueblo Hotel (☎ 21-1032, in Cuzco 24-5314, reservas@inkaterra.com.pe; s & d US$173; ▣) This first-rate hotel is 100m walk east of Aguas Calientes through the train station. It has large, thatched bungalows scattered around lush, tropical gardens. The spacious rooms are extremely comfortable while preserving a rustic charm – some even have open fireplaces, though some readers complain that in-room hairdryers and cable TV are unavailable. There is also an onsite sauna and masseur.

Eating

Cheap restaurants cluster along the railway tracks and on Pachacutec on the way to the hot springs.

Indio Feliz (☎ 21-1090; Lloque Yupanqui Lote; 3-course menú US$10-14) Indio Feliz is owned by a friendly French-Peruvian couple and the French cook whips up some fantastic meals. The restaurant itself is very cozy, with friendly staff and walls plastered with the business cards of happy customers.

Toto's House (☎ 21-1020; Imperio de los Incas; lunch buffet US$10; ☒ closed dinnertime Sun) This upmarket option with traditional buffets is in a large, glass-roofed building which overlooks the river.

Machu Picchu Pueblo Hotel (see Sleeping p206; buffet US$15) A high-class spot for a filling lunch or dinner buffet, this restaurant is at the back of the train station.

Pizzería Manu (Pachacutec; mains US$4-8, 3-course menú US$5.50) This recommended, open-fronted, budget restaurant has an international flavor to its food and also to its atmosphere.

Govinda (Pachacutec; 3-course menú US$2.50-7) Govinda's is a rustic, stone-floored place with good-value vegetarian fare.

Chez Maggy (Pachacutec; mains US$4-8; ☒ closed lunchtime Sun) Chez Maggy has stained-glass walls, sociable long tables and board games. Service can be unenthusiastic.

Pizzería Sayacmarca (☎ 21-1165; Hermanos Ayar; mains US$3.50-7; ☒ lunch only) Sayacmarca is a convenient place for a snack near the station and a popular meeting point for weary trekkers before their train departs.

Entertainment

Blue's Bar (Pachacutec; ☒ 9am-11:30pm) is a funky gringo bar playing predictable but good music near the springs. Happy hours are from 6pm to 7pm and 9:30pm to 10pm. Or for dance floors open till the wee hours, try **Wasicha** or **Soras**, both on Lloque Yupanqui Lote.

Getting There & Away

BUS

Buses to Machu Picchu (US$4.50 one way, 20 minutes) leave from the Río Urubamba bridge for the tightly winding 8km up to the site. Departures are hourly between 6:30am and 12:30pm, plus a service at 1pm and enough extra buses to handle the crowds

when trains arrive. Buses return when full, the last departure being at 5:30pm. For people on a guided tour, the return bus ticket to the ruins is usually included.

TRAIN

The tourist trains from Cuzco (see Getting There & Away p194) arrive in Aguas Calientes after about four hours. Trains from Ollantaytambo (see Getting There & Away p204) take two hours. Except for a nearby hydroelectric plant, Aguas Calientes is the end of the line from Cuzco. Tourist trains arrive at the new station close to the Machu Picchu Pueblo Hotel, and you can buy tickets here or in the old station in the town center. The path from the station to the bus stop is short and stepped, and passes through a scrum of handicraft sellers. Wheelchairs should be directed across the small bridge and through the center of town.

The Vistadome service leaves at 3:30pm daily and is usually full with returning day-trippers. It passes Ollantaytambo at 4:55pm and arrives in Cuzco at 7:20pm. The other Cuzco-bound backpacker services leave at 3:55pm and 4:20pm, arriving in Cuzco at 8:20pm and 8:45pm. Catch a bus back to the city center from Poroy station if you want to speed things along a little (see Train under Cuzco p194).

The Urubamba train service to Ollantaytambo (see Ollantaytambo p202) has three Vistadome services that return at 8:35am, 1:20pm and 4:45pm. There's also a high-season backpacker train at 5pm, and the local service with two cheap backpacker carriages attached leaves at 5:45am.

MACHU PICCHU

For many visitors to Peru and even South America itself, a visit to the lost Inca city of Machu Picchu is the whole purpose of their trip. With its spectacular and awe-inspiring location, it is the best-known and most spectacular archaeological site on the continent. From June to September, around a thousand people arrive daily. Despite this great tourist influx, the site manages to retain its air of grandeur and mystery, and is a must for all visitors to Peru.

History

Machu Picchu is both the best and the least known of the Inca sites. It is not mentioned

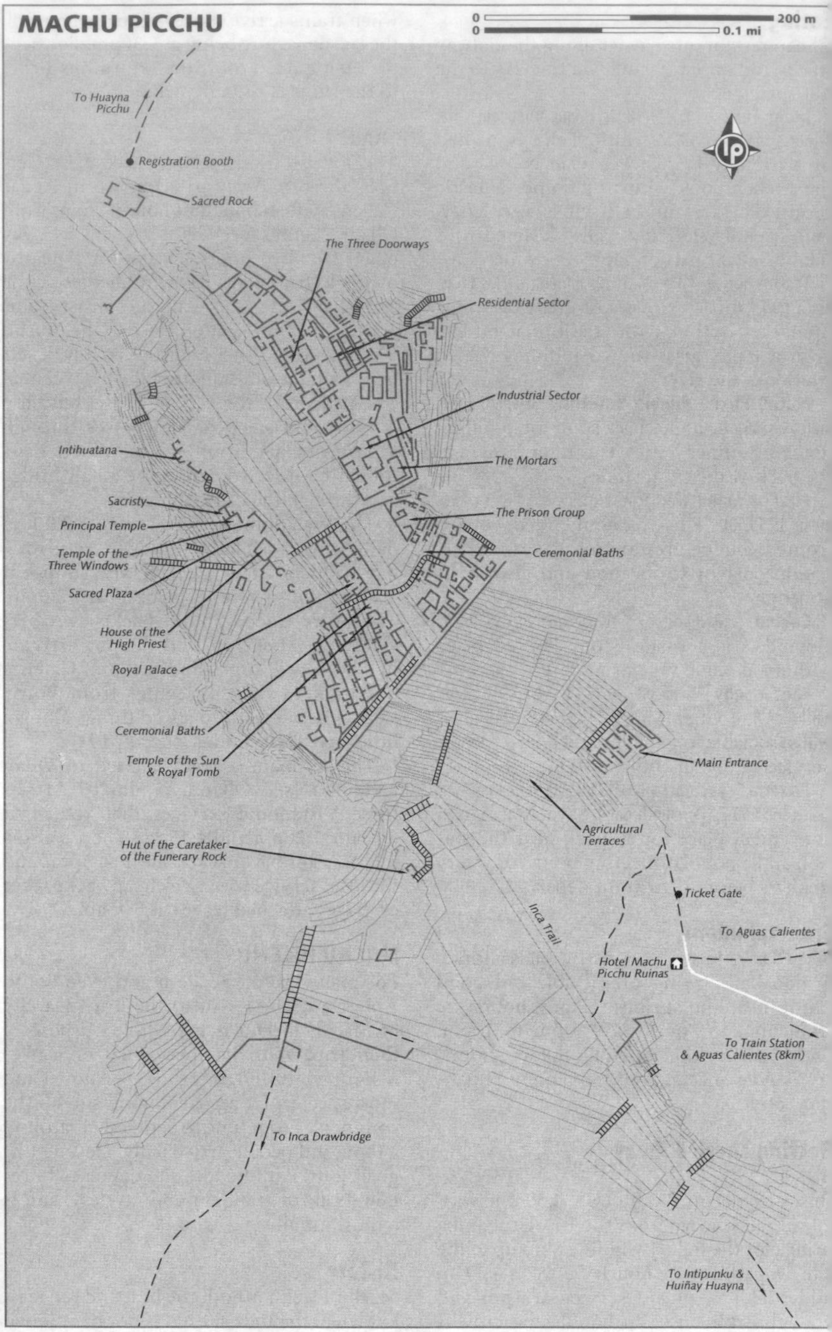

MACHU PICCHU

0 _____ 200 m
0 _____ 0.1 mi

To Huayna Picchu

Registration Booth

Sacred Rock

The Three Doorways

Residential Sector

Industrial Sector

Intihuatana

The Mortars

Sacristy

Principal Temple

The Prison Group

Temple of the Three Windows

Ceremonial Baths

Sacred Plaza

House of the High Priest

Royal Palace

Ceremonial Baths

Temple of the Sun & Royal Tomb

Main Entrance

Hut of the Caretaker of the Funerary Rock

Agricultural Terraces

Ticket Gate

To Aguas Calientes

Inca Trail

Hotel Machu Picchu Ruinas

To Train Station & Aguas Calientes (8km)

To Inca Drawbridge

To Intipunku & Huiñay Huayna

in any of the chronicles of the Spanish conquistadors, and archaeologists today are
forced to rely heavily on speculation and
educated guesswork as to its function.

Apart from a few indigenous Quechuas,
nobody knew of Machu Picchu's existence
until American historian Hiram Bingham
stumbled upon it in 1911. Bingham's search
was for the lost city of Vilcabamba, the last
stronghold of the Incas, and he thought he
had found it at Machu Picchu. We now
know that the remote ruins at Espíritu
Pampa, much deeper in the jungle, are actually the remains of Vilcabamba. Machu
Picchu remains a mysterious site, never
revealed to the conquering Spaniards and
virtually forgotten until the early part of
the 20th century.

The site was initially overgrown with
thick vegetation, forcing Bingham's team
to be content with roughly mapping the
site. Bingham returned in 1912 and 1915
to carry out the difficult task of clearing the
thick forest, when he also discovered some
of the ruins on the Inca Trail. Peruvian
archaeologist Luis E Valcárcel undertook
further studies in 1934, as did a Peruvian–
American expedition under Paul Fejos in
1940–41. Despite these and other, more
recent studies, knowledge of Machu Picchu
remains sketchy.

Over 50 burial sites, containing more
than 100 skeletal remains were discovered
over the course of excavations. The remains
were first though to be 80% female, leading to an early theory that it was a city of
chosen women, but this theory quickly lost
support when it emerged that the male/
female ration was actually fifty-fifty.

Some believe the citadel was founded in
the waning years of the last Incas as an attempt to preserve Inca culture or rekindle
their predominance, while others think it
may have already become an uninhabited,
forgotten city at the time of the conquest.
A recent suggestion holds that the site was
a royal retreat or country palace that was
abandoned when the Spanish invasion took
hold of Cuzco. But what is obvious from the
exceptionally high quality of the stonework
and the abundance of ornamental works is
that Machu Picchu must once have been
an important ceremonial center. Indeed, to
some extent, it still is: Toledo, who is the
country's first native Quechua-speaking

president, staged his colorful inauguration
here in July 2001.

Admission

Machu Picchu (foreigner/national/student under 26 US$20/
10/10; ☺ 6am-9:30pm) is Peru's showpiece site,
and entrance fees are correspondingly high.
You are not allowed to bring large packs or
food into the ruins, and packs have to be
checked at the gate. Do not walk on any of
the walls as this loosens the stonework and
prompts an angry cacophony of whistle-
blowing from the guards. Trying to spend
the night here is also illegal; don't try it as
guards do a thorough check of the site before
it closes.

You can buy a so-called *Boleto Nocturno*
for another US$10 to get into the ruins at
night, which is popular during full moons.
Tickets are only sold during the day, however, and may not be offered during the
wet season.

Many visitors buy a combined-ticket
book for Machu Picchu from agencies in
Cuzco (see Tours & Guides p180). This
ticket includes round-trip tickets for the
train, the bus to and from the ruins, admission to the ruins, an English-speaking guide
and lunch at the Machu Picchu Sanctuary
Lodge. However, it is valid for just one day,
and you only get to spend two or three
hours in the ruins before it's time to return
to the train station.

When to Go

The ruins are most heavily visited between
about 10am and 2pm. Many tours combine
visits of Machu Picchu with the Sunday
markets at either Pisac or Chinchero, so
Sunday is fairly quiet, but Friday, Saturday
and Monday are busy. June to August are
the busiest months. Plan your visit early
or late in the day and you should avoid
the worst of the crowds. Plus the changes
in light as the sun comes up over or goes
down behind the surrounding mountains
are mesmerizing. An early, wet, midweek
morning in the rainy season will guarantee
you room to breathe.

Inside the Ruins

Unless you arrive via the Inca Trail, you'll
officially enter the ruins through a ticket
gate on the south side of Machu Picchu.
About 100m of footpath brings you to the

ON A SLIPPERY SLOPE?

While visitors marvel at the seemingly untouchable beauty of Machu Picchu, the popularity of this age-old site has placed it under the shadow of significant environmental threats. Japanese scientists from the University of Kyoto caused a scare in early 2001 when they announced that the steep slopes on the western side of Machu Picchu were slipping downwards at the rate of 1cm per month, prefacing a possible catastrophic landslide in the not-too-distant future. While the scientists conceded that their results were exaggerated by excessive rainfall and construction work at the time, the area has seen many landslides in the past, and the fear is that constant busloads of tourists are further unsettling the subsoil of the sacred mountain. Unesco also warned that the site could not support the more than 200 to 500 visitors per day without sustaining damage – a number dwarfed by current visitor numbers in the high season. But their exhortations have not found an echo in Lima.

While a long-mooted plan to build a cable car to the summit has been put firmly on the backburner following condemnation from the national and international community (see www.mpicchu.org), the threat of private interests encroaching on the site has also long simmered in the background, periodically rearing its head with worrying new plans. One unbelievable accident even saw a crew filming a beer commercial smash a crane into the site's showpiece, the Intihuatana, breaking a large chip off the principal granite block!

carved rock behind the hut may have been used to mummify the nobility, hence the hut's name.

If you continue straight into the ruins instead of climbing to the hut, you pass through extensive terracing to a beautiful series of 16 connected **ceremonial baths** that cascade across the ruins, accompanied by a flight of stairs. Just above and to the left of the baths is Machu Picchu's only round building, the **Temple of the Sun**. This curved and tapering tower contains some of Machu Picchu's finest stonework and appears to have been used for astronomical purposes. Inside are an altar and a curiously drilled trapezoidal window that looks out onto the site. This window is popularly named the **Serpent Window**, though the holes were probably used to suspend a ceremonial, gold, sun disk. The Temple of the Sun is cordoned off to visitors, but you can see into it from above.

Below the towering temple is an almost hidden, natural rock cave that has been carefully carved, with a step-like altar and sacred niches, by the Inca's stonemasons. It is known as the **Royal Tomb**, though no mummies were actually ever found here.

Climbing the stairs above the ceremonial baths, you reach a flat area of jumbled rocks, once used as a quarry. Turn right at the top of the stairs and walk across the quarry on a short path leading to the four-sided **Sacred Plaza**. The far side contains a small viewing platform (with a curved wall) that offers a view of the snowcapped Cordillera Vilcabamba in the far distance and the Río Urubamba below. Important buildings flank the remaining three sides of the Sacred Plaza. The **Temple of the Three Windows** commands an impressive view of the plaza below through the huge, trapezoidal windows that give the building its name. With this temple behind you, the **Principal Temple** is to your right. Its name derives from the massive solidity and perfection of its construction. The damage to the rear right corner of the temple is the result of the ground settling below this corner rather than any inherent weakness in the masonry itself. Opposite the Principal Temple is what is known as the **House of the High Priest**.

Behind and connected to the Principal Temple lies a famous small building called the **Sacristy**. It has many well-carved niches,

mazelike entrance of Machu Picchu proper, where the ruins lie stretched out before you, roughly divided into two areas separated by a series of plazas.

About 100m into the complex, a zigzagging path climbs up to your left to a hut on the southeast spur. This vantage point affords the most complete overview of the site for the classic photograph. The hut, known as the **Hut of the Caretaker of the Funerary Rock**, is one of a few buildings that has been restored with a thatched roof, making it a good shelter in the case of rain. The Inca Trail enters the city just below this hut. The

perhaps used for the storage of ceremonial objects, as well as a carved, stone bench. The Sacristy is especially known for the two rocks flanking its entrance; each is said to contain 32 angles, but it's easy to come up with a different number whenever you count them.

A staircase behind the Sacristy climbs a small hill to the major shrine in Machu Picchu, the **Intihuatana**. This Quechua word loosely translates as the 'hitching post of the sun' and refers to the carved rock pillar, often mistakenly called a sundial, which stands at the top of the Intihuatana hill. The Inca's astronomers were able to predict the solstices using the angles of this pillar. Thus, they were able to claim control over the return of the lengthening summer days. Exactly how the pillar was used for these astronomical purposes remains unclear, but its elegant simplicity and high craftwork make it a highlight of the complex. It is recorded that there were several of these Intihuatanas in various important Inca sites, but the Spaniards smashed most in an attempt to wipe out the pagan blasphemy of sun worship.

At the back of the Intihuatana is another staircase. It descends to the **Central Plaza**, which separates the important sites of the Intihuatana, Sacred Plaza and Temple of the Sun from the more functional areas opposite. At the lower end of this opposite area is the **Prison Group**, a labyrinthian complex of cells, niches and passageways both under and above the ground. The centerpiece of the group is a carving of the **head of a condor**, the natural rocks behind it resembling the bird's outstretched wings. Behind the condor is a well-like hole and, at the bottom of this, the door to a tiny underground cell that can only be entered by bending double.

Above the Prison Group is the largest section of the ruins – the **Industrial & Residential Sectors**. These buildings are not as well constructed and had more mundane purposes than those across the plaza.

Walks near Machu Picchu

HUAYNA PICCHU
The most famous of several short walks around Machu Picchu is the climb up the steep mountain of Huayna Picchu at the back of the ruins. Huayna Picchu is normally translated as 'young peak,' but 'picchu,' with the correct glottal pronunciation, refers to the wad in the cheek of a coca-chewer. At first glance, it would appear that Huayna Picchu is a difficult climb but, although the ascent is steep, it's not technically difficult. Beyond the Central Plaza and right between two open-fronted buildings is a registration booth, where you have to sign in; it's only open from 7am until about 2pm and you must be back by 4pm. The 45-minute to 1½-hour climb takes you through a short section of Inca tunnel, and for all the puffing it takes to get there, the view from the top is well worth the effort.

Another walk begins part way up Huayna Picchu, where a marked path plunges down to your left, continuing down the rear of Huayna Picchu to the small **Temple of the Moon**. The trail is easy to follow, but involves steep up-and-down sections, a ladder and an overhanging cave, where you have to bend over to get by. The descent takes about an hour, and the ascent back to the main Huayna Picchu trail longer. The spectacular trail drops and climbs steeply as it hugs the sides of Huayna Picchu before plunging into the cloud forest. Suddenly, you reach a cleared area where the small, very-well-made ruins are found. Unfortunately, they are marred by graffiti.

From the Temple of the Moon, a newly cleared path leads up behind the ruin and steeply on up the back side of Huayna Picchu.

INCA DRAWBRIDGE
On the other side of the ruins, a scenic but level walk from the Hut of the Caretaker of the Funerary Rock takes you right past the top of the terraces and out along a narrow, cliff-clinging trail to the Inca drawbridge. The 20-minute walk gives you a good look at the vegetation of the high cloudforest and a different view of Machu Picchu. You'll have to be content viewing the bridge from behind a barrier about 100m away, however, as someone crossed the bridge some years ago and tragically fell to their death.

INTIPUNKU
The Inca Trail ends after its final descent from the notch in the horizon called Intipunku, or the 'Sun Gate.' Looking at the hill behind you as you enter the ruins, you

can see both the trail and Intipunku. This hill, called Machu Picchu, or 'old peak,' gives the site its name. It takes about an hour to reach Intipunku, and if you can spare about a full half day for the round trip, it's possible to continue as far as Huiñay Huayna (see the Inca Trail later). Expect to pay US$3 and be sure to return before 3pm when the checkpoint closes.

Sleeping & Eating
Most people choose to stay at nearby Aguas Calientes or come here on day trips from Cuzco.

Machu Picchu Sanctuary Lodge (☎ 21-1038, c/o Hotel Monasterio in Cuzco; www.monasterio.orient -express.com; s/d/ste US$455/547/646, with view US$575) The Sanctuary Lodge is the only place to stay at Machu Picchu itself. Rates have skyrocketed recently and are overpriced for what you get, though it's still often full so book as far ahead as possible in the high season (reserve at the website www.peru orientexpress.com.pe). Only two rooms have views of the ruins, but all rooms are equipped with every luxury, and there's a new terrace with a partial view of the site.

The hotel restaurant serves a good but expensive buffet lunch and supper (US$22.50), and there is a cafeteria serving pricey snacks and light meals on a patio by the ruins. Bring a packed lunch and water bottle if possible, though you'll have to leave food in the cloakroom outside the site.

Getting There & Away
There are only two options to get to Machu Picchu: trek it or catch the train to Aguas Calientes, from where buses go directly to the ruins or you can walk – but be aware that it's all uphill.

THE INCA TRAIL
The most famous hike in South America, the four-day Inca Trail, is walked by many thousands of people every year. Although the total distance is only 33km, the ancient trail laid by the Incas from the Sacred Valley to Machu Picchu winds its way up and down and around the mountains, taking three high passes en route, that have collectively led to the route being fondly dubbed 'The Inca Trial.' The views of snowcapped mountains and high cloud forest can be stupendous and walking from one cliff-

hugging ruin to the next is a mystical and unforgettable experience.

When to Go
Groups leave all year-round, except for February when the annual clean up of the trail takes place (though the two-day trail remains open). However, in the wettest months from December to April, trails can be slippery and camp sites muddy, and views are often obscured behind a thick bank of rolling clouds. In contrast, the dry season from June to September is the most popular time, as well as the most crowded. Temperatures can drop below freezing year-round, however, and it occasionally rains even in the May to September dry season.

Regulations & Tours
The Peruvian government has introduced a string of reforms to the Inca Trail since 2001 in an attempt to reduce the number of hikers and prevent further damage to the trail caused by overcrowding. The new regulations state that all Inca Trail hikers must now go with a licensed guide, and that groups should not exceed 16, with one guide per 10 hikers. (No more than 500 hikers are allowed to start the trail per day.) Registered tour agencies also now have to pay huge annual fees and taxes and their trail prices have consequently shot up.

Trail fees, at the time of writing, had reached US$50 per person (or US$25 for students with a valid ISIC card), which includes the US$20 one-day entrance to Machu Picchu. This all adds up to the four-day Inca Trail costing the barest minimum of US$170/145 for adults/students, but to be sure of a reliable tour company, it is necessary to pay over US$220. This price includes a tent, food, porters, a cook, admission price to the ruins and the train fare back to Cuzco. For details of outfitters to choose from, see Tours & Guides (p179).

Tickets must be bought at the Instituto Nacional del Cultura (INC) office at least 72 hours before the trek, but tour agents will mostly handle this for you (note that the office is closed Saturday afternoon and Sunday so plan on having to wait four to five days if you book at the weekend). There are also many benefits from booking ahead and reconfirming four to five days in advance. This primarily avoids the delays caused by

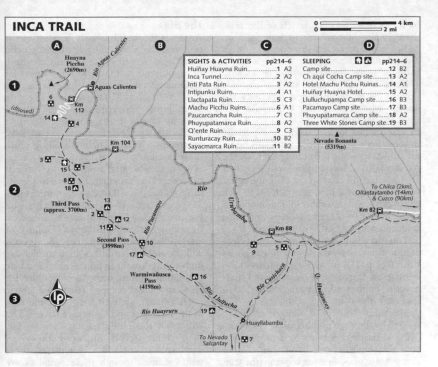

INCA TRAIL

SIGHTS & ACTIVITIES	pp214–6
Huiñay Huayna Ruin	1 A2
Inca Tunnel	2 A2
Inti Pata Ruin	3 A2
Intipunku Ruins	4 A1
Llactapata Ruin	5 C3
Machu Picchu Ruins	6 A1
Paucarcancha Ruin	7 C3
Phuyupatamarca Ruin	8 A2
Q'ente Ruin	9 C3
Runturacay Ruin	10 B2
Sayacmarca Ruin	11 B2

SLEEPING	⌂ ⌂ pp214–6
Camp site	12 B2
Ch aqui Cocha Camp site	13 A2
Hotel Machu Picchu Ruinas	14 A1
Huiñay Huayna Hotel	15 A2
Llulluchupampa Camp site	16 B3
Pacamayo Camp site	17 B3
Phuyupatamarca Camp site	18 A2
Three White Stones Camp site	19 B3

bottlenecks in high season. Second, camp sites are allotted according to a first-come, first-served basis, and late-comers are more likely to spend the night at a site three to four hours short of the final camp site at Huiñay Huayna. This is inconvenient the following morning as it necessitates getting up at 3am and hiking down a perilously steep trail in the pitch black in order to catch the sunrise at the Sun Gate (you also miss fantastic views on the way down, and there's little time to visit the ruins at Huiñay Huayna). Beware of agencies claiming late-comers will be staying in Huiñay Huayna simply to get them signed up.

Another recent change has been to order all tourists to carry their passport (a copy will not do) and student card where appropriate, as these are checked at regular points throughout the trail.

For those who do not want to do the hike in a big group, it's possible to organize trips with an independent licensed guide registered with the governing body Inrena (Instituto Nacional de Recursos Nacionales). This option allows hikers some degree of flexibility, but can be expensive. Also, the new regulations state that such groups (which can be no more than seven persons including a guide) cannot take porters with them, so you must be prepared to carry all the necessary equipment yourself. See Private Guides on p181 for details.

Budget travelers intent on saving pennies, can ask to organize their own train fare home, catching the train to Ollantaytambo (see Getting There & Away p207) or they may be able to work out a deal with the tour operator to carry their own gear and do their own cooking to save on porter costs.

Preparation & Conservation

Sleeping bags and other gear can be found at travel agencies in Cuzco. The trail gets extremely cold at night so make sure the sleeping bag you rent is warm enough (down is preferable) and bring plenty of layers. Also remember sturdy shoes, rain gear, insect repellent, sunblock, a flashlight (with fresh batteries), water-purification tablets and basic first-aid supplies. Apart from high-energy snacks and drinks sold by locals over the first stretch of the trail, there is almost nowhere to buy food en route. You'll be served three square meals a day but stocking up on snacks is not a bad idea as the digestive system slows with altitude. Also take a small stash of cash for tipping the guide, cook and especially the porters who are woefully underpaid and work the hardest of all. It's also a good idea to take money for emergencies, especially in the rainy season when it's not unknown for landslides along the railway to delay the return to Cuzco. Metal-tipped walking sticks are no longer allowed on the trail, though if you'd like some added support, locals sell cheap canes with an embroidered handle en route to the start of the trail. Bring water in a canteen as plastic bottles are banned.

You can obtain detailed maps and information from the South American Explorers Club (see p171), as well as from trekking agencies in Cuzco (p180). Occasional theft happens on the trail, and you are advised to take gear into your tents at night.

The Inca Trail is in danger of being spoiled by the large number of hikers it sees daily, so please remember to clean up after yourself. Don't defecate in the ruins, leave garbage, use wood fires for cooking (the trail has been badly deforested over the past decade) or pick orchids and other plants in this national park. Also remember that it is illegal to graffiti any trees or stones en route.

When choosing your tour group, check that each agency works actively to preserve the trail. The cheaper guided tours have less idea about ecologically sensitive camping, while more expensive trips make some effort to camp cleanly and provide adequate facilities for porters. The best local outfitters work hard to keep the trail clean and help to fund an annual clean up that occurs throughout February (collecting over 400kg of unburnable garbage!).

Warning

There are very few staffed park stations along the Inca Trail. Although the rangers have radios, these don't always work because of mountain interference. Medical facilities are almost nonexistent. If you have an accident on the trail, it could be days before evacuation can be arranged (the standard procedure, though, is to carry people out).

The Hike

Agencies run minibuses to the start of the trail near the village of Chilca at Piscacucho (Km82 on the railway to Aguas Calientes), or, upon request, may take the train as far as **Corihuayrachina (Km88)**. After crossing the Río Urubamba (2200m) and taking care of trail fees and registration formalities, the trail climbs gently alongside the river to the first archaeological site of **Llactapata**, or 'town on hillside,' before heading south down a side valley of the Río Cusichaca. (For those who start from Km88, you can turn west after crossing the river to see the little-visited site of **Q'ente**, or 'hummingbird,' 1km away, then return east to Llactapata on the main trail.) The trail south leads 6km to the hamlet of **Huayllabamba** (2750m), or 'grassy plain,' near which many tour groups will camp. You can buy bottled drinks and high-calorie snacks in houses here, and take a breather to look over your shoulder for views of the snowcapped **Veronica** (5750m).

Huayllabamba is situated near the fork of the Llullucha and Cusichaca Rivers. You will cross Río Llullucha on a log bridge, then climb steeply up along the river. This area is known as **Llulluchayoc** 'three white stones', though these boulders are no longer visible. From here it is a long, very steep climb, through humid Polylepis woodlands for about 1½ hours. At some points, the trail and streambed become one, but stone stairs keep hikers above the water. The trail eventually emerges on the high, bare mountainside of **Llulluchupampa**, where water is available and the flats are dotted with good camp sites (these sites get very cold at night). This is as far as you can reasonably expect to get on your first day, though many groups will actually spend their second night here.

From Llulluchupampa, a good path up the left-hand side of the valley climbs for a two- to three-hour ascent to the pass of **Warmiwañusca**, also colorfully known as 'dead woman's pass.' At 4198m above sea level, this is the highest point of the trek, and leaves many a seasoned hiker gasping. From Warmiwañusca, you can see the Río Pacamayo, or 'sunrise river,' far below, as well as the ruin of Runturacay halfway up the hill, above the river.

The trail continues down a long and knee-jarringly steep descent to the river, where there are large camp sites with toilets. At an altitude of about 3600m, the trail crosses the river over a small footbridge and climbs to toward **Runturacay**, or 'basket-shaped building,' a round ruin with superb views about an hour's walk away.

Above Runturacay, the trail climbs to a false summit before continuing past two small lakes to the top of the second pass at 3998m, which has views of the snowcapped Cordillera Vilcabamba. The clear trail descends past an uninvitingly green lake to the ruin of **Sayacmarca**, or 'dominant town,' a tightly constructed complex perched on a small mountain spur, and offering incredible views. The trail continues downward and crosses an upper tributary of the Río Aobamba, or 'wavy plain,' 3600m above sea level. There are camp sites and a shower block here, though the ground gets too boggy for camping in the wet season.

The trail leads on across an Inca causeway and up a gentle climb through some beautiful cloud forest to the third pass at 3700m. Along the way, you'll pass through an Inca tunnel carved from the rock. There are great views of the Urubamba valley from the pass. Soon afterwards, you'll reach the beautiful and well-restored ruin of **Phuyupatamarca**, or 'town above the clouds,' about 3650m above sea level and approximately two or three hours beyond Sayacmarca. The site contains a beautiful series of ceremonial baths with water running through them. A ridge here offers camp sites where some groups spend their final night, with the advantage of watching the sun set over a truly spectacular view, but with the disadvantage of having to leave at 3am in the race to reach the Sun Gate in time for the sunrise (which leaves no time to visit the ruins of Huiñay Huayna).

From Phuyupatamarca, the trail makes a dizzying dive into the cloud forest below, following an incredibly well-engineered flight of many hundreds of Inca steps (which can be nerve-racking in the early hours – take extra batteries for your flashlight). After two to three hours, the trail eventually zigzags its way down to a red-roofed, white building that provides last-night youth-hostel facilities for those who want to pay a bit extra. It offers hot showers, meals and bottled drinks. The hostel is usually quite full, but there are some areas for camping nearby.

A 500m trail behind the hostel leads to the exquisite little Inca site of **Huiñay Huayna** (also spelled Wiñay Wayna), which is variously translated as 'forever young,' 'to plant the earth young' and 'growing young,' (as opposed to 'growing old'). Peter Frost, meanwhile, writes that the name is Quechua for an orchid that blooms here year-round. A rough trail also leads from this site to another newly uncovered, terraced ruin called **Inti Pata**.

From the Huiñay Huayna guard post, the trail contours around through the cliff-hanging cloud forest for about two hours to reach **Intipunku**, or 'Sun Gate' – the penultimate site on the trail, where you can catch your first glimpse of majestic Machu Picchu itself and wait for the sun to rise over the encompassing mountain tops.

The final triumphant descent takes almost an hour. Backpacks are not allowed into the ruins and park guards will pounce on you to check in your pack and have your trail permit stamped. Though it is rather a brusque return to rules and regulations, trekkers generally arrive long before the morning trainloads of tourists, and can enjoy the exhausted exhilaration of reaching their goal without having to push past sweet-smelling tour parties fresh from Cuzco.

Alternative Inca Trails

There are many other less-publicized approaches that can be made to Machu Picchu. These are not a method of avoiding the sky-high agency prices, however, as treks link up with the principal trail and the guidelines regarding licensed guides still apply. The trail fee also applies but is slightly less for the two-day hike (adult/student US$25/15) and the Salcantay trek (adult/student US$25/15, but note that this particular fee does not include entrance to Machu Picchu).

THE SHORT HIKE

A shorter version of the Inca Trail leaves from Km104, and gives a good flavor of what hiking the Inca Trail is like. You'll be let off the train shortly before Aguas Calientes where the signed trail crosses the river on a footbridge before climbing steeply to Huiñay Huayna. Alternatively, a fork in the trail follows the river down past the ruins of Choquesuysuy and then climbs up the right-hand side of the ravine to Hui-ñay Huayna, but this is much steeper and not normally used. Even the usual climb is steeper than most sections of the Inca Trail proper, and takes about three hours. An overnight at the hostel near Huiñay Huayna is usual (two-day trail hikers cannot camp here) but not always possible, especially when trips are organized at short notice as the hostel needs to be paid for and a place authorized prior to the trek. The alternative is to carry on to Machu Picchu and down to Aguas Calientes – a long, tiring hike better attempted by those who are fit and acclimatized. The average price for the all-inclusive two-day trek is around US$150 to US$160.

SALCANTAY
The village of **Mollepata**, a few kilometers off the main Cuzco–Abancay road beyond Limatambo, is the starting point for a longer and more spectacular approach to the Inca Trail, climbing over 4800m-high passes near the magnificent, glacier-clad peak of Salcantay (6271m), the second-highest peak in the Cuzco area. The scenic drive to Mollepata takes three to four hours: Sit on the right if the weather is clear for views of the snowcaps. From Mollepata, the trek descends to the pampa below the peak itself, before climbing a steep trail over a high pass and down to Sisaypampa and **Pampacahuana**, a stunning Inca site that sees few visitors. From here, the trail continues to the ruins of **Paucarchancha** and eventually to Huayl-labamba on the Inca Trail. It takes three to four days to reach this point, after which trekking follows the Inca Trail as outlined earlier. There is a checkpoint at Huaylla-bamba to make sure you paid the fees and have a licensed guide.

ALTERNATE ROUTE
Another variation on the four-day Inca Trail follows the Río Urubamba closely from Km82 to Km104, where it picks up the trail of the short hike mentioned earlier.

SOUTHEAST OF CUZCO

Most of the places described here can be reached on day-trips from Cuzco. First Class and Inka Express buses between Cuzco and Puno also make stops at some of these places, including Raqchi (see p217) and Andahuaylillas (see later).

TIPÓN
A demonstration of the Incas' mastery over their environment, this extensive **Inca site** (entry only with the Boleto Turístico – see p171; 7am-6pm) consists of some excellent terracing at the head of a small valley and boasts an ingenious irrigation system. To get there, take an Urcos bus from Cuzco and ask to be let off at the Tipón turn-off, a few kilometers before Oropesa. A steep dirt road from the turn-off (which is an excellent spot for cheap *cuyerías* – guinea pig – to build up your strength) climbs the 4km to the ruins. A taxi to Tipón and Pikillacta (see following) costs about US$20 with waiting time.

PIKILLACTA & RUMICOLCA
Literally translated as 'the place of the flea,' **Pikillacta** (entry only with the Boleto Turístico; 7am-6pm) is the only major pre-Inca ruin in the area, and it can be reached on an Urcos bus from Cuzco. The site is just past a lake on the left-hand side of the road, about 32km east of Cuzco. Pikillacta was built around AD 1100 by the Wari culture. It's a large city of crumbling, two-story buildings, all with entrances that are strategically located on the upper floor. The city is surrounded by a defensive wall. The stonework here is much cruder than that of the Incas, and the floors and walls were paved with slabs of white gypsum, and you can still see traces of this.

Across the road from Pikillacta and about 1km east is the huge Inca gate of **Rumicolca**, built on Wari foundations. The cruder Wari stonework contrasts with the Inca blocks.

The area's swampy lakes are also interesting. You can see Indians making roof tiles from the mud that surrounds the lakes. The **Centro Recreacional Huacarpay** (74-6652; dm US$3) has budget accommodation, a bar and a games pitch by the Laguna de Nukré not far below Pikillacta.

ANDAHUAYLILLAS
Don't confuse this place with Andahuaylas, west of Cuzco. Andahuaylillas (pop 2500) is about 40km southeast of Cuzco and 7km before Urcos. This pretty Andean village is famous for its lavishly decorated **Jesuit**

church (admission US$1; ☼ 8:30am-noon & 2-5pm Mon-Sat, 8:30-10am & 3-5pm Sun), almost oppressive in its heavy, baroque embellishments. The church dates from the 17th century and houses many carvings and paintings, including a canvas of the Immaculate Conception by Esteban Murillo. There are reportedly many gold and silver treasures locked in the church, and the villagers are all involved in taking turns guarding it 24 hours a day.

Hospedaje El Sol (in Cuzco ☎ 22-7264; Garcilaso 514; r per person US$10-12) has good accommodation in a colonial house, and **El Casona** (Cuzco 410; s/d US$10/15) is a spa hotel set around a cool, tree-filled courtyard.

You can reach Andahuaylillas on the Urcos bus.

URCOS TO SICUANI

The road splits at **Urcos**, 47km southeast of Cuzco, where one road heads northeast to Puerto Maldonado in the jungle (see From Cuzco to the Jungle, p217), while another continues southeast toward Lake Titicaca. About 60km southeast of Urcos is the village of **Tinta**, which has another fine colonial church and a basic place to stay. About 25km further is **Sicuani**, a market town of about 40,000 people, which can be used as a base for the pretty highland **Lago Sibinacocha**. To get to the lake, take the early Wednesday combi to Santa Barbara (two hours) then catch any available ongoing transport. You won't be able to make it back in one day so plan on spending the night. One economical place to stay in Sicuani is **Hostal Samariy** (☎ 35-2518; Centenario 138; s/d with bathroom US$4/6), which has hot water.

A few kilometers before Sicuani is the little village of San Pedro and the ruins of **Raqchi** (adult/student US$1.40/1; ☼ 7am-6pm), which look like a huge aqueduct from the road. These are the remains of the Temple of Viracocha, which once supported the largest known Inca roof. Twenty-two circular columns made of stone blocks helped support the roof; most were destroyed by the Spanish, but their foundations are clearly seen. This was once one of the holiest shrines of the Inca Empire. The remains of many houses and storage buildings are also visible and reconstruction is an ongoing process. In early June, Raqchi is the site of a very colorful **fiesta** with much traditional dancing and other events.

The trip from Cuzco to Raqchi (US$1.75, 2½ hours) or Sicuani (US$2, three hours) can be done in any Puno-bound bus. The Cuzco–Puno train also passes by the site but far less frequently and reliably. There are also combis to Raqchi from Sicuani (US$0.30, 30 minutes).

FROM CUZCO TO THE JUNGLE

There are three overland routes from Cuzco to the jungle, all by unpaved roads that frequently get bogged down in the wet months. One road goes northwest to Quillabamba; another through Paucartambo, Tres Cruces and Shintuya for Parque Nacional Manu; and the other east through Ocongate and Quince Mil to Puerto Maldonado.

QUILLABAMBA

☎ 084 / pop 16,300 / elevation 1050m

Lying on the Río Urubamba at the end of a spectacular route high over the spectacular pass of **Abra de Malaga**, Quillabamba is one of Peru's most important tea-producing regions. The narrow road from Ollantaytambo with its stomach-testing twists and turns passes through several ecological zones, from subglacial plunging down to subtropical. Quillabamba itself is a hot and humid town of the high jungle, known as the city of the eternal summer. It's quiet and pleasant if not particularly interesting, and can be used as a base for trips deeper into the jungle.

Information

BCP (Libertad) has a Visa ATM and changes US dollars. There's Internet access at **Cybermaster** (Espinar 229; ☼ 7am-11pm) for US$0.60 per hour. **Kiteni Tours** (☎ 28-2477; Libertad 577) offers a limited selection of tours to the Pongo de Manique (see p219), Vilcabamba (see p219) and also a one-day tour of local waterfalls.

Sleeping

Hostal Urusayhua (☎ 28-1426; Lima 114; s/d/tr US$3/ 4.50/6) This is a friendly, basic place with a cold-water, communal bathroom.

Hostal Pineda (☎ 28-1447; Libertad 530; s/d US$4/7; ☼ Jun-Nov) Pineda is also welcoming

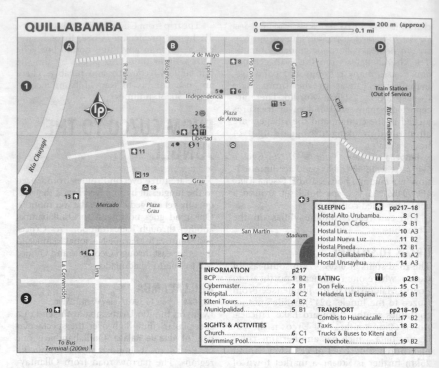

QUILLABAMBA

and has pokey rooms with bathrooms (cold water) above the owner's grocery store. Some English is spoken.

Hostal Alto Urubamba (☎ 28-2616; 2 de Mayo 333; s/d/tr US$5/7/10, with bathroom US$10/13/18) Alto Urubamba is clean, economical and recommended. There are 68 comfortable rooms, some with fans, circling a sunny courtyard. Rooms with national TV cost US$1.50 more.

Hostal Nueva Luz (☎ 28-1801; Palma 400; s/d US$3/6, with bathroom US$5/8) This *hostal* has smart clean rooms available to travelers and a plant-filled roof terrace, though it's not the friendliest in town.

Hostal Lira (☎ 28-1324; La Convención 200; s/d US$6/14) Lira is large and impersonal but comfortable; it has bathrooms that have hot water in the morning and evening.

Hostal Quillabamba (☎ 28-1369; chisaluna@ hotmail.com; Grau 590; s/d/tr US$13/18/24; 🏊) This is a large, professionally run place recommended for clean rooms with hot showers and TV, a rooftop restaurant and garden.

Hostal Don Carlos (☎ 28-1150; doncarlos@viabcp .com; Libertad 556; US$15/20) Don Carlos is the

best place in town, with a neatly trimmed garden in the pretty courtyard; the rooms have a TV and 24-hour hot shower.

Eating

The rooftop restaurant at **Hostal Quillabamba** (mains US$2-4) has good views and offers adequate meals, but the service is slow. **Don Felix** (☎ 28-2234; Independencia 247; mains US$1.50-3) has a range of good-value food.

Heladería La Esquina (cnr Espinar & Libertad; closed lunchtime Sun) is a modern café with good-value juices and snacks.

Getting There & Away
BUS

Buses for Cuzco leave at 8am, 2pm and 7pm daily (US$4.20, nine hours) traveling through Ollantaytambo and Urubamba. A good company is **Ampay** (☎ 28-2576), though many similarly priced companies leave from the terminal, six blocks south of Plaza Grau.

Pickup trucks leave every morning from the market area to the village of Ivochote, further into the jungle. Slower buses also run, leaving at 10:30am and 6:30pm (US$4.20, 12 to 16 hours). Trip times vary wildly in the wet season.

Combis make long, bumpy trips from Plaza Grau to Huancacalle at 9am and 11am (US$3, eight hours); from here you can proceed to Vilcabamba.

TRAIN
Quillabamba lies at the end of the Cuzco–Aguas Calientes–Quillabamba railway line, but services beyond Aguas Calientes have been suspended since 1998.

VILCABAMBA
The beleaguered Manco Inca and his followers fled to this jungle retreat after being defeated by the Spaniards at Ollantaytambo in 1536. They lived here until Spanish outlaws killed Manco in 1544. After this Vilcabamba, also called Espíritu Pampa, slowly fell into disrepair and was forgotten for centuries until it was rediscovered by American explorer, Gene Savoy, during expeditions in the mid-1960s. Although the site, about 70km due west of Quillabamba, is of great importance, it has not yet been properly excavated and is still largely overgrown. An interesting book you can read on the site is Vincent R Lee's *Sixpac Manco: travels among the Incas*, available in Cuzco.

To get there, you have to hike for several days. The most frequent starting point is the village of **Huancacalle**, which can be reached by trucks from Quillabamba (see earlier). In Huancacalle, there's one basic hostel called Manco Sixpac, which is run by Señor Cobos, a local guide. The old palace of **Vitcos** is an hour's walk away, and from there you can continue to the sacred white rock of **Yurac Rumi**.

You can hire pack mules and guides (each US$7 per day) to Vilcabamba in Huancacalle. Also bring mosquito repellent. The hike, which takes five to seven days on the round trip, is over rugged mountains and passes through several small villages and ruins along the way. Take note that it is rough going, with many steep ascents and descents before reaching Vilcabamba at about 1000m above sea level.

An expedition to a recently rediscovered site called **Corihuayrachina** atop Cerro Victoria, also in Vilcabamba, was led by Peter Frost

and featured in the *National Geographic* in March 2002.

IVOCHOTE & BEYOND
A long bus journey from Quillabamba takes you through the oil town of Kiteni and on to the more remote **Ivochote**, a small jungle village with a few basic accommodations. This marks the end of the road into the jungle, and the only way to continue is by river. The route from here on in is little traveled and adventurous, but it's possible for experienced and self-sufficient travelers. Take a means to purify water.

The first major landmark is the **Pongo de Manique**, a steep-walled canyon carved by cascading waterfalls on the lower Río Urubamba. Boats as far as the *pongo* (canyon) can occasionally be found in Ivochote; trips take the best part of a day. The canyon is too dangerous to navigate, and from December to April, the river runs so high that boat owners are reluctant to go through it.

During the dry season, a few boats continue through the *pongo*; but for a few rapids, the river after the canyon is relatively calm. You can build (or have someone else build) a balsa raft once past the *pongo*. Tours can be arranged in Cuzco or Quillabamba, or you can sometimes find local guides in Kiteni and Ivochote. There are a few communities after Timpia (just beyond the *pongo*), where you can have a raft built. Basic food and accommodations can be obtained from friendly locals in these villages. In return, they often prefer useful gifts to money – for example flashlights and batteries, fishhooks and lines or basic medicines.

InkaNatura (see Tours into the Jungle p180) has a jungle lodge near the *pongo*, and close to the **Sabeti clay lick** (providing a rare chance to see all three types of large macaws together), though the lodge was temporarily closed at the time of writing.

There are occasional settlements until you reach the oil town of **Sepahua**, two to four days away, where there are three basic hostels and the oil workers are often interested in a new face. From Sepahua, there are flights to Satipo (see p376 in the Amazon Basin chapter) with light aircraft and also some flights to Lima for the oil workers. These are not cheap and can be very unreliable.

Sometimes, it's possible to continue down the Urubamba to the village of **Atalaya** and beyond (see p377 in the Amazon Basin chapter).

A nonprofit organization, the **Cabeceras Aid Project** (www.onr.com/cabeceras), provides humanitarian aid to the indigenous peoples of the Amazon Basin, knows about this area. You can find out more on its website.

PAUCARTAMBO

This small village (pop 3000) lies on the eastern slopes of the Andes, about 115km northeast of Cuzco along a narrow dirt road with exhilarating views of the Andes and the high Amazon Basin beyond. Paucartambo is famous for its riotously colorful celebration of the **Fiesta de la Virgen del Carmen**, held annually around July 15 to 17, with hypnotic street dancing, processions and all manner of weird and wonderful costumes. The highly symbolic dances are inspired by everything from fever-ridden malaria sufferers to the homosexual practices of the Spanish conquistadors. Few tourists make it here, simply because it's so difficult to reach and because you either have to camp, find a room in one of three extremely basic hotels or hope a local will give you floor space. Many tourist agencies in Cuzco (see Tours & Guides p179) run buses specifically for the fiesta and can help arrange accommodation with families.

Expreso Virgen del Carmen (☎ 27-7755 or 22-6895; Diagonal Angamos 1952, Cuzco) has three daily services from Cuzco (US$2, five hours). Alternatively, trucks leave Cuzco early in the morning from near the Urcos bus stop.

The Inca ruins of **Macha Cruz** and **Pijchu** are within walking distance of Paucartambo; ask for directions in the village.

TRES CRUCES

About 45km beyond Paucartambo is the extraordinary jungle view at Tres Cruces, about 15km off the Paucartambo–Shintuya road. The sight of the mountains dropping away into the Amazon Basin is gorgeous in itself, but is made all the more magical by the sunrise phenomenon that occurs from May to July (other months are cloudy), especially around the time of the winter solstice on June 21. The sunrise here gets optically distorted causing double images, halos and an incredible multi-colored light show. At this time of year, many adventure

tour agencies (see Tours & Guides p179) run sunrise-watching trips to Tres Cruces.

You can also take a truck en route to Pillcopata and ask to be let off at the turn-off to Tres Cruces (a further 13km walk). There are buses from Cuzco to Pillcopata at 10am on Monday, Wednesday and Friday (see Getting There & Away under Cuzco p82). During Paucartambo's Fiesta de la Virgen del Carmen, minibuses run to and forth between Paucartambo and Tres Cruces all night long. Alternatively, ask around to hire a truck for about US$45 round trip. Make sure you leave in the middle of the night to catch the dawn.

For details of the trip from here to the Manu area, see p370 in the Amazon Basin chapter.

CUZCO TO PUERTO MALDONADO

According to Peruvian road engineers, this is Peru's worst road between two major towns. It's almost 500km long and takes about 2½ days to travel in the dry season, and much longer in the wet. Trucks leave daily from the Coliseo Cerrado or near the Plaza Túpac Amaru in Cuzco. Fares to Puerto Maldonado are about US$15; the cheapest places are in the back, and more expensive ones are in the cab with the driver. The least comfortable but fastest trucks are *cisternas* (gasoline trucks), with a narrow ledge on top upon which to crouch. The trucks stop about three times daily to let the driver eat, and once more so he can sleep (never for long though). If you want to split the journey, the best place to stop is Quince Mil (see p221), which has basic accommodations. Most tourists travel from Cuzco to Puerto Maldonado by air, but the difficult, adventurous trip by road is a chance to see the impressive scenery of the Andes' eastern slopes.

The route heads toward Puno until Urcos, where the dirt road to Puerto Maldonado begins. (You could bus to Urcos and wait there for a truck.) About 125km and seven or eight hours from Cuzco, you come to the highland town of **Ocongate**, which has a couple of basic hotels around the plaza. From here, trucks go to the village of **Tinqui**, under an hour's drive beyond Ocongate, which is the starting point for a five- to seven-day hike encircling **Ausangate** – at 6384m, the highest mountain in southern Peru. The trek begins in the *puna* (the

Andean grasslands of the altiplano) and crosses four high passes (two over 5000m) en route. Consequently, it features quite varied scenery, including fluted icy peaks, tumbling glaciers and turquoise lakes, rolling brown *puna* and green marshy valleys. There are warm **mineral springs** near Tinqui, at the start and finish of the walk. Along the way you'll find huge herds of alpacas and tiny hamlets unchanged in centuries.

Ausangate is the site of the traditional festival of **Q'oyoriti**, held in early June. Thousands of locals converge on the mountain's icy slopes to celebrate the 'star of the snow' with a night trek to the top of a glacier. Tinqui is the gathering point for this. Outfitters in Cuzco can arrange guided trips to this little-known festival.

There is a basic hotel in Tinqui, and the locals rent pack mules (about US$6 per day plus US$7 for an *arriero*, or mule driver) to do the trek. Apart from trucks, a daily bus also goes to Tinqui (US$3.40, seven hours) from Cuzco at 10am from Condemayta near the Coliseo Cerrado.

After Tinqui, the road drops steadily to **Quince Mil**, 240km from Cuzco, less than 1000m above sea level, and the halfway point. The area is a gold-mining center, and the hotel here is often full. After another 100km, the road into the jungle reaches the flatlands, where it levels out for the last 140km into Puerto Maldonado (see p361 of the Amazon Basin chapter).

WEST OF CUZCO

Traveling by bus from Cuzco to Lima via Abancay, and down through to Nazca takes you along a remote route closed from the late 1980s until the late 1990s by guerilla activity and banditry, but now is safe and largely paved. Going west through Abancay, Andahuaylas and on to Ayacucho is a tough ride on a rough road often used by independent travelers.

LIMATAMBO

This pretty village (pop 1000), set in mountainous countryside 80km west of Cuzco by road, is at the upper end of the valley of a headwater tributary of the Río Apurímac. It's named after the Inca site of Rimactambo or 'speaker's inn,' more popularly known as

Tarahuasi (adult/student US$1.40/0.85), which is beside the road 2km east of Limatambo. Its painstakingly constructed stonework suggests that it was used as a ceremonial center as well as a resting place for the Inca *chasquis* (Inca runners, used mostly for delivering messages). The exceptional polygonal retaining wall, with its 28 human-sized niches, is in itself worth the trip and the guard will happily point out half a dozen flower shapes and a nine-sided heart shape amid the patchwork of perfectly interlocking stones.

You can reach Limatambo from Cuzco (US$1.50, two hours) on buses to Abancay. If you leave early in the morning, you can visit the ruins and return to Cuzco on an afternoon bus (passing between 2pm and 3:30pm), although there's also the basic **Hostal Rivero** (dm US$3) in a farmhouse just off the highway.

SAIHUITE

The Inca site of **Saihuite** (adult/student/child US$3/1/0.30), 45km east of Abancay and near the main road, has a sizeable, intricately carved boulder called the Stone of Saihuite, which is similar to the famous sculpted rock at Qenko, near Cuzco, though it's smaller and more elaborate. The carvings of animals are particularly intricate.

To get to Saihuite, either catch a bus between Cuzco and Abancay (US$2, 1¼ hours) and ask to be let off at the turn-off, from where its a 1km walk downhill.

ABANCAY

☎ 083 / pop 95,000 / elevation 2378m

This sleepy rural town is the capital of the Andean Department of Apurímac, one of the least-explored departments in the Peruvian Andes. Despite its status as a departmental capital, Abancay has no scheduled air service, and the place has a forlorn, forgotten air. Travelers use it as a resting place on the long, tiring bus journey between Cuzco and Ayacucho.

The **BCP** changes money and has a Visa ATM. Several **Internet cafés** cluster together opposite the bus companies and charge US$0.60 per hour.

Sights & Activities

During the dry season (late May to September), hikers and climbers may want to take advantage of the best weather to head for the sometimes snowcapped peak of **Ampay** (5228m), about 10km north-northwest of the town. For the rest of the year, the weather tends to be wet, especially during the first four months of the year. The mountain is the center of the 3635-hectare **Santuario Nacional Ampay** where camping and birding are good.

Festivals & Events

Abancay has a particularly colorful **Carnival** held in the week before Lent, which is a chance to see Andean festival celebrations uncluttered by the trappings of tourism and includes a nationally acclaimed folk-dancing competition: book ahead or arrive before the festivities get under way. The **Abancay Day festival** is held on November 3.

Sleeping & Eating

Hostal Gran Hotel (☎ 32-1144; Arenas 196; s/d US$3/ 5, with bathroom US$4/6) This large, noisy hostel is adequate but old; only a few rooms have hot water.

Hostal El Dorado (☎ 32-2005; Arenas 131; s/d US$7/10) El Dorado has decent, white-washed rooms, some with hot showers and TV.

Hostal Victoria (☎ 32-1301; Arequipa 305; s/d US$4.50/7, with bathroom US$6/8.50) This is an excellent and very clean, little hostel roughly opposite the BCP. Rooms that come with cable TV cost an additional US$2.50.

Hostal Imperial (☎ 32-1578; Díaz Bárcenas 517; s/d US$6/10, with bathroom US$13/20; **P**) The Imperial has an unprepossessing entrance, but opens up to a light courtyard, and has decent rooms with 24-hour hot water and TV. Rates for rooms with a bathroom include breakfast.

Hoturs Hotel de Turistas (☎ 32-1017; fax 32-1628; Díaz Bárcenas 500; s/d 2nd level US$22/37/47, 3rd level US$30/45/55, ste US$70) Located opposite Hostal Imperial, this is the best hotel in town. Housed in an old-fashioned country mansion. The third floor rooms have cable TV, minibar and phone. This hotel also has the best restaurant in town.

Restaurant La Delicia (☎ 32-1702; Elias 217; 2-course menú US$2; ☯ closed Sat) This tiny health-food joint has vegetarian food.

There are also plenty of cheap cafés near the bus companies.

Getting There & Away

Most bus companies leave from Arenas near Nuñez. There are several companies going to

Lima (US$12 to US$22, 18 to 20 hours) via the Nazca road; book a day in advance to ensure a seat. All the companies leaving for Cuzco (US$3, five hours) or Andahuaylas (US$4, five hours) depart at the same times: 6am, 1pm and 8pm. The journeys from Cuzco may take longer in the wet season. Change in Andahuaylas for Ayacucho.

ANDAHUAYLAS

☎ 083 / pop 26,000 / elevation 2980m
Andahuaylas, 135km west of Abancay on the way to Ayacucho, is the second most important town in the Department of Apurímac, and a convenient half-way stop on the rough but scenic route between Cuzco and Ayacucho. The **BCP** (Ramon Castilla) has a Visa ATM and changes dollars. The best Internet connection is in the back of the **Telefónica del Peru office** (JF Ramos 317).

Sights & Activities

The colonial **Catedral** on the Plaza de Armas is worth a look, though it's more sober than its counterparts elsewhere in Peru. Andahuaylas' main attraction, though, the beautiful **Laguna de Pacucha**, is 17km from town and accessible by bus or car. There are meals, fishing and rowboat rental available there. A one-hour hike from the lake brings you to the imposing hilltop site of **Sondor**, built by the Chanka culture, traditional enemies of the Incas. The site is accessible by taxi from town (US$15 return), and has good mountain views.

There is a new town **swimming pool** (Lázaro Carrillo; adult/child US$0.30/0.15; ☯ 9am-4pm Tue-Sun).

Both Andahuaylas and Pacucha have a Sunday **market**, and there's a small **cinema** (Casafranca) in Andahuaylas with daily films.

Festivals & Events

The annual **fiesta** is on June 28, when traditional dances and music are performed. In the village of **Pacucha** near the laguna, the fiesta includes the gory spectacle of lashing a condor to the back of a bull and allowing the two to fight in a representation of the Indians' struggle with the Spanish conquistadors. This event is appropriately called the Fiesta de Yahuar, or 'blood feast.'

Sleeping

Hostal Los Libertadores Wari (☎ 72-1434; JF Ramos 424; s/d US$3.50/5, with bathroom US$4.50/7) This

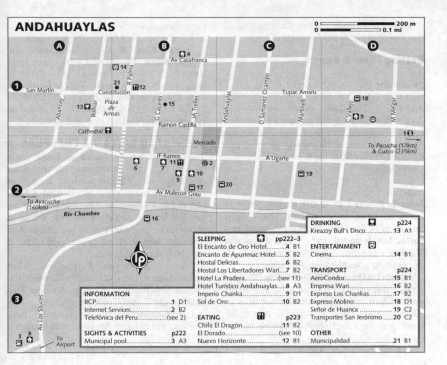

ANDAHUAYLAS

INFORMATION	
BCP...1 D1	
Internet Services.........................2 B2	
Telefónica del Peru................(see 2)	

SIGHTS & ACTIVITIES	p222
Municipal pool...........................3 A3	

SLEEPING	pp222–3
El Encanto de Oro Hotel..........4 B1	
Encanto de Apurimac Hotel.....5 B2	
Hostal Delicias.........................6 B2	
Hostal Los Libertadores Wari...7 B2	
Hotel La Pradera................(see 11)	
Hotel Turístico Andahuaylas....8 A3	
Imperio Chanka........................9 D1	
Sol de Oro................................10 B2	

EATING	p223
Chifa El Dragón........................11 B2	
El Dorado...........................(see 10)	
Nuevo Horizonte.....................12 B1	

DRINKING	p224
Kreazzy Bull's Disco..................13 A1	

ENTERTAINMENT	
Cinema....................................14 B1	

TRANSPORT	p224
AeroCondor.............................15 B1	
Empresa Wari...........................16 B2	
Expreso Los Chankas................17 B2	
Expreso Molino........................18 D1	
Señor de Huanca.....................19 C2	
Transportes San Jerónimo......20 C2	

OTHER	
Municipalidad..........................21 B1	

bare-bones hostel is clean and safe and has hot water, but closes its doors at 11pm.

Hotel La Pradera (JF Ramos 409; s/d with bathroom US$4.50/6) La Pradera is a small new budget place next to Libertadores Wari. The rooms have thin walls and hot water is provided in the morning and on request thereafter.

Hostal Delicias (☎ 72-1104; JF Ramos 525; s/d US$6/10) Delicias is a light well-kept place run by welcoming folks and rooms have private hot showers.

Encanto de Apurimac Hotel (☎ 72-3527; JF Ramos 401; s/d/tr with bathroom US$6/8.50/13) This hotel, which faces onto JF Ramos but has its door on JA Trelles, has modern, shiny rooms with hot water.

Hotel Turístico Andahuaylas (☎ 72-1014; www.hotelturisanda.com; Lázaro Carrillo 620; s/d/tr with bathroom US$12/14/20; P) The Turístico Anda-huaylas has boxy rooms with cable TV, and has the advantage of being next door to the swimming pool. There's also a sauna in the hostel, open weekends only (US$1.50).

El Encanto de Oro Hotel (☎/fax 72-3066; elencant orohotel@hotmail.com; Casafranca 424; s/d/tr US$13/17/21; P) El Encanto has good rooms with private

hot showers (some rooms even have two bathrooms), cable TV and telephone.

Imperio Chanka (☎ 72-3065; C Vallejo 384; s/d US$13/17) This new hostel is by the Expresa Molino bus station and has very good clean rooms and cable TV, though it lacks character.

Sol de Oro (☎ 72-1152; JA Trelles 164; s/d/tr with bathroom US$13/17/20) Sol de Oro is the best hotel in town, boasting extremely smart modern rooms with 24-hour hot water, cable TV and attentive service.

Eating & Drinking

Chifa El Dragón (☎ 72-1956; cnr JF Ramos & JA Trelles; 3-course menú US$1.70) El Dragón is a smart res-taurant serving Chinese meals with a touch of *criollo* (traditional Peruvian).

El Dorado (3-course menú US$1.40, mains US$1.40-5) Located at the Sol de Oro hotel, this res-taurant is surprisingly elegant considering the low prices.

Nuevo Horizonte (☎ 80-1870; Constitución 572; 2-course menú US$1.50; ✆ closed Sat) Nuevo Hori-zonte, just off the plaza, is a simple place with cheap, tasty vegetarian fare.

CUZCO & THE SACRED VALLEY

Kreazzy Bull's Disco, on the plaza, is one of the few spots in town for nightlife.

Getting There & Away
AIR
AeroCóndor (☎ 72-2877; Cáceres 326) has Lima flights at 7:45am Sunday to Friday (US$59, one hour). The flight sometimes goes via Ayacucho (US$25), but not on a scheduled basis. Minibuses run from its office to the regional airport, a 20-minute drive south of town (US$1.70). Taxis are available for about US$3.

BUS
Señor de Huanca (☎ 72-1218; Martinelli 170) has buses to Abancay at 6:30am, 10am, 1pm and 8pm (US$4, five hours). **Empresa Transportes San Jeronimo** (☎ 72-1400; Andahuaylas 116) has a 6:30pm bus to Cuzco (US$7, 10 hours) that goes through Abancay.

Expreso Los Chankas (☎ 72-2441; Grau 232) runs a twice-daily service to Ayacucho at 6:30am and 6:30pm, as well as running services to Abancay and Cuzco. The road to Ayacucho goes over very high *puna*, may be snow-covered and is very cold at night. Make sure to bring a sleeping bag or thick clothes.

Empresa Wari (☎ 72-1936; Av Los Sauces) and **Expreso Molino** (☎ 72-1248; C Vallejo) each have three daily buses to Lima (US$14, 22 to 24 hours) that go through Nazca. Both also have a daily service to Ayacucho (US$6).

Combis to Pacucha (US$1, 20 minutes) run along the eastern end of R Castilla.

ABANCAY TO NAZCA VIA CHALHUANCA
The road down to Nazca and the coast passes through **Chalhuanca** 120km from Abancay, then 189km further, it reaches **Puquio**, which has the basic **Hostal Los Andes** (☎ 45-2103; s/d US$4/8) and simple restaurants. For the last 50km before Puquio, the road traverses an incredibly wild-looking area of desolate, lake-studded countryside that is worth staying awake for.

About 65km beyond Puquio and 90km before Nazca, the road passes through the vicuña sanctuary of Pampas Galeras (see p106 in the South Coast chapter).

For transport details, see Getting There & Away (p191) and Andahuaylas (earlier).

Central Highlands

The central Peruvian Andes is one of the least-visited areas of Peru and is ripe for exploration. This region has several delightful, friendly colonial towns that are among the least spoiled in the entire Andean chain. Improving infrastructure over the past decade, especially in bus services and road quality, are making travelers' lives easier. However, travel to and within the region is exciting, with memorable mountain views and ear-popping passes. Added to this are some colourful markets and festivals to experience.

The Central Highlands have historically been one of the most neglected areas of Peru. A combination of harsh mountain terrain and terrorist discontent (the Sendero Luminoso – the Shining Path guerrillas – began in Ayacucho) has made ground communications difficult, and the region suffers from a lack of air services. If you want to travel to a lesser-known part of Peru read on.

HIGHLIGHTS

Shopping
- Shopping for handicrafts from the Mantaro valley in Huancayo (p237)

Festivals
- Celebrating the country's finest Semana Santa fiesta in Ayacucho (p244)

Bird-watching
- Watching the highest and finest birds at Lago de Junín (p249)

Studying
- Gazing at 20,000 colonial-era books at Concepción's colonial library (p232)

Chilling out
- Being the only gringo in forgotten, colonial Huancavelica (p238)

★ Lago de Junín

★ Jauja

Huancayo ★

★ Huancavelica

Ayacucho ★

LIMA TO LA OROYA

SAN PEDRO DE CASTA & MARCAHUASI

San Pedro de Casta (pop 500, elevation 3180m) is a small village only 40km from Chosica (80km from Lima). About 3km from San Pedro, on foot, is **Marcahuasi**, a 4-sq-km plateau at 4100m. Marcahuasi is famed for its weirdly eroded rocks shaped into animals such as camels, turtles and seals. These have a mystical significance for some people, who claim they are signs of a pre-Inca culture or energy vortices. Locals have fiestas here periodically but usually it's empty.

Because of the altitude, it's not advisable to go there from Lima in one day; acclimatize for at least a night in San Pedro. It takes three hours to hike up to the site. A **Centro de Información** (☎ 01-571-2087), on the Plaza de Armas in San Pedro, has some information and maps; staff can arrange guides for US$3. Mules and horses can also be hired for a few dollars.

You can camp at Marcahuasi, but carry water, as the water of the few lakes there isn't fit to drink. In San Pedro **Hostal Marcahuasi** (s/d US$3/6), a block from the plaza, has hot showers and a restaurant. Local families also have beds for US$1 (ask at the information center). There are a couple of simple restaurants.

Take a bus from Lima to Chosica. Then ask for Transportes Municipal San Pedro, which leaves from Parque Echenique in Chosica at 9am and 3pm (US$1.50, four hours).

LA OROYA

☎ 064 / pop 32,000 / elevation 3731m

This highland, industrial town proudly calls itself 'the metallurgical capital of Peru.' Unless you're interested in metallurgy, which, in La Oroya, means a huge smelter and refinery with its attendant slag heaps, you'll not want to linger in this cold, unattractive place. However, because La Oroya is a major junction, most travelers to Peru's central interior at least pass through the town.

From La Oroya, roads lead in all directions: east to Tarma (and into the central jungle); south to Huancayo, Huancavelica and Ayacucho (and on to Cuzco); and north to Cerro de Pasco, Huánuco and Tingo María (and then into the northern jungle). All these towns are described in this chapter.

There is a **BCP** (formerly Banco de Crédito; ☎ 39-1191) and **Banco Continental** (☎ 39-1174).

Sleeping & Eating

Few travelers stop here. If you are stranded, try the basic **Hostal Inti** (☎ 39-1098; Arequipa 117; d US$4.50), which has shared hot showers, or **Hostal Chavín** (☎ 39-1185; Tarma 281; s/d US$3/6) with shared hot showers and a restaurant. Better hotels are away from the center. About 2km or 3km from the center towards Lima, near the prison on the edge of town, the **Hostal San Juan** (☎ 39-2566; fax 39-1539; RH Rubio 114; s US$7, s/d with bathroom US$10/16; P) is clean and has hot showers. **Hostal San Martín** (☎ 39-1278, 39-1963; RH Rubio 134; s/d US$13/20; P) is the best. Rooms have hot showers, cable TV and heaters.

EAST OF LA OROYA

The area to the east of La Oroya covers the historic town of Tarma and several pleasant nearby villages.

TARMA

☎ 064 / pop 80,000 / elevation 3050m

This pleasant city on the eastern slopes of the Andes, 60km east of La Oroya, is known locally as 'the pearl of the Andes.' It has a long history. The overgrown Inca and pre-Inca ruins that are found in the hills and on the mountains surrounding the town are not well known, and there's plenty of scope for adventurous travelers to go and discover ruins on the nearby peaks.

The town itself was founded by the Spanish soon after the conquest (althought the exact date is uncertain). Nothing remains of the early colonial era, but the town has quite a number of attractive, 19th- and early 20th-century houses that have white walls and red-tiled roofs.

Information

The **tourist office** (☎ 32-1010 ext 20; fax 32-1374; turistarma@hotmail.com; 2 de Mayo 775; 8am-1pm & 3-6pm Mon-Fri) is on the Plaza de Armas and has brochures and information about local tours, in Spanish. Internet access is available at Paucartambo 567.

You can change money at the **BCP** (☎ 32-2149; Lima at Paucartambo), which also has an ATM. *Casas de cambio* (foreign-exchange offices) are on Lima nearby.

CENTRAL HIGHLANDS

CENTRAL HIGHLANDS

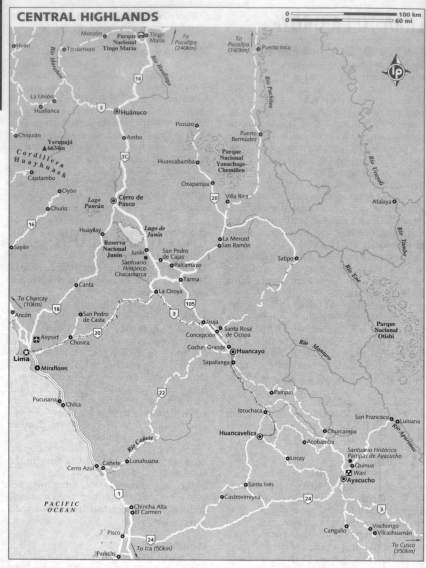

Sights & Activities

Tarma is high in the mountains and the clear nights of June, July and August provide some ideal opportunities for stargazing. There is a small **astronomical observatory** run by the owners of Hostal Central (see Sleeping opposite). The owners are usually away in Lima, but public use is permitted 8pm to 10pm every Friday. Admission is US$0.30.

The **cathedral** is modern (1965) and it contains the remains of Peruvian president Manuel A Odría (1897–1974). He was born in Tarma and organized the construction of the cathedral during his presidency. The clock in the tower dates to 1862.

Several nearby excursions include visits to the religious shrine of El Señor de Muruhuay in Acobamba (9km from Tarma, see p231), the Gruta de Guagapo (33km; see the boxed text 'The Gruta's Bottomless Depths' p231) and the weaving village of San Pedro de Cajas (50km, p231).

Festivals & Events

The big annual attraction is undoubtedly Easter. Many processions are held during **Semana Santa** (Holy Week), including several by candlelight after dark. They culminate on the morning of Easter Sunday with a marvelous procession to the cathedral along an 11-block route entirely carpeted with flower petals. This attracts thousands of Peruvian visitors, and the hotels are usually full, with prices increasing by up to 50%.

The annual fiesta of **El Señor de los Milagros**, or 'the Lord of the Miracles,' takes place in late October; the main feast days are the 18th, 28th and 29th. This is another good opportunity to see processions over beautiful, flower-petal carpets.

Another fiesta is **Tarma Tourism Week** near the end of July.

Sleeping

BUDGET

The following hotels have hot water, usually in the morning, though they may claim all day. Tarma's hotel selection is unexciting.

Hostal Vargas (☎ 32-1460; fax 32-1721; 2 de Mayo 627; s US$5.80, s/d with bathroom US$7.30/11.50) This clean hotel has spacious rooms and hard beds if you're fed up with sagging mattresses. The friendly staff are upfront with the hot water hours: 5am to 10am only. TV rental is US$1.50. The hotel is popular with Peruvians who know a good place when they see it.

Hostal Aruba (☎ 32-2057; Moquegua 452; s/d US$10/14.50) A very secure hotel; ring the bell for admittance. Rooms are clean, showers are hot and cable TV is provided.

Hotel El Dorado (☎ 32-1598, 32-1914; Huánuco 488; s/d US$3/5.80, s/d with bathroom US$5.80/8.80) Rooms can be noisy, but otherwise are quite good and clean. A central courtyard invites relaxation. TV watchers can rent one for US$1.50.

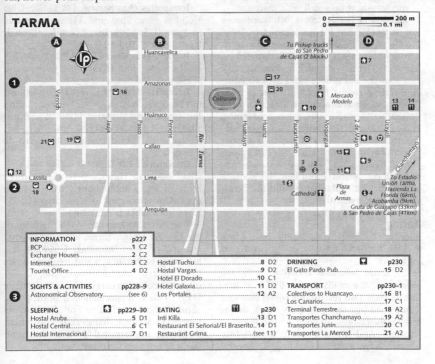

Hostal Central (☎ 32-3134; Huánuco 614; s/d US$4.50/5.80, s/d with bathroom US$6.80/8.80) This old but adequate hotel has the observatory mentioned in Sights & Activities (p228). The rooms are a bit dark but the staff are friendly.

Other recommendations include:

Hostal Tuchu (☎ 32-3483; 2 de Mayo 561; s/d US$7.30/10) Hot showers when requested, TV for US$1.50 and cheap laundry.

Hotel Galaxia (☎ 32-1449; Lima 262; s/d US$10/15) Clean, hot showers but slightly overpriced because of its plaza location.

Hostal Internacional (☎ 32-1830; 2 de Mayo 307; s/d US$11.50/14.50) Rooms with cable TV, hot showers and worn carpets.

MID-RANGE

Los Portales (☎ 32-1411; fax 32-1410; Castilla 512; s/d US$44/62; P). Set in pleasant gardens at the west end of town, the hotel features a children's playground and 45 standard hotel rooms with cable TV. Rates include continental breakfast and the restaurant provides room service. Apart from holidays, however, the hotel is usually half empty, and if you just show up you'll get a discount.

Hacienda La Florida (☎ 34-1041; laflorida@terra .com.pe; s/d US$25/50; P) Six kilometres from Tarma on the road to Acobamba, this 18th-century hacienda is now a B&B owned by a Peruvian-German couple. Rooms all have hot showers and groups can rent two communicating rooms for US$20 per person. Visitors who want to do the hacienda thing can gather firewood, collect eggs, feed lambs, milk cattle and ride horses. Rates include homemade breakfast, and lunch or dinner is available on request (US$5). Secure camping on the grounds, with use of bathrooms, is US$5 per person. From here, it's about a one-hour hike to Acobamba and the Señor de Muruhuay sanctuary.

Eating

Plenty of cheap restaurants line Lima (which becomes Castilla in the west end of town).

Restaurant Señorial/El Braserito (☎ 32-3334; Huánuco 138/140; menú US$1.20, mains US$2-5; ☼ 8am-3pm & 6-11pm) Two restaurants rolled into one (they open just one side if it's slow), this is the locals' favorite, judging by the nonstop crowds. And wouldn't it be? Sprightly service, huge portions and bright, cheerful

surroundings with mirrored walls and neon signs lure diners in. They aren't disappointed by the menu of Peruvian standards, plus traditional dishes such as *cuy* (guinea pig).

Restaurant Grima (☎ 32-1892; Lima 270; meals US$1-2; ☼ 7am-7pm). On the Plaza de Armas, this is a good budget option for breakfasts and set lunches.

Inti Killa (☎ 32-1020; Huánuco 190; menús from US$1, mains US$2-5; ☼ 7am-10pm) Formerly the highly-respected El Mejorcito de Tarma, this new restaurant in the same huge locale boasts a large menu of Peruvian coastal, highland and jungle dishes. Worth a try.

Entertainment

El Gato Pardo Pub (Callao 227) is a club with recorded and live Latin music.

Getting There & Away

The forlorn Terminal Terrestre has buses leaving for Lima (US$3, six hours) when they are full. There's usually just one bus, waiting for passengers. By the gas station next to the terminal, colectivo cars take four passengers to Lima (US$8.50 each).

Transportes Chanchamayo (☎ 32-1882; Callao 1002) has 9am, 2pm and 11pm departures to Lima (US$4.50). Buses coming through from Lima go to La Merced.

Transportes La Merced (☎ 32-2937; Vienrich 420) has buses to Lima at 11:30am, 1:30pm and 9:45pm (US$4.50).

Transportes Junín (☎ 32-1234, 32-2972; Amazonas 667) has five daily buses to Lima including *bus-camas* (bed buses) at 11:30am and also 11:45pm (US$4.50 to US$7.30). It also has 5:30am and 1pm departures for Cerro de Pasco.

Los Canarios (☎ 32-3357; Amazonas 694) has small buses to Huancayo (US$2.50, three hours) leaving about hourly from 5am to 6pm. Colectivo cars to Huancayo (US$5) leave from Jauja at Amazonas.

Transportes San Juan (☎ 32-3139), in front of the Estadio Unión Tarma at the northeastern end of town (mototaxi US$0.20), has big buses to Huancayo and frequent buses to La Merced (US$1.50, two hours). Almost opposite, colectivo cars to La Merced charge US$3. This is a spectacular trip, dropping about 2.5km vertically. For destinations beyond La Merced, change at the convenient La Merced bus terminal (p375). Ask around the stadium area for other destinations.

A bus stop next to Empresa de Transportes San Juan has minibuses going to Acobamba and Palcamayo. Pickup trucks and cars for San Pedro de Cajas leave from the northern end of Moquegua. The tourist office can advise on getting to other villages.

ACOBAMBA
☎ 064

The village of Acobamba, about 9km from Tarma, is famous for the religious sanctuary of **El Señor de Muruhuay**, which is visible on a small hill about 1.5km away.

The sanctuary is built around a rock etching of Christ crucified. Historians claim that it was carved with a sword by a royalist officer who was one of the few survivors after losing the Battle of Junín (a major battle of independence fought on August 6, 1824). Despite this, legends relating to the image's miraculous appearance persist. The first building erected around the image was a roughly thatched hut, which was replaced in 1835 by a small chapel. The present sanctuary, inaugurated in 1972, is a modern building with an electronically controlled bell tower and is decorated with huge weavings from San Pedro de Cajas (see later).

The colorful feast of El Señor de Muruhuay, held throughout May, has been celebrated annually since 1835. Apart from the religious services and processions, there are ample opportunities to sample local produce and to see people dressed in traditional clothes. There are dances, fireworks and even a few gringos. Stalls sell *chicha* (corn beer) and *cuy*, but be wary unless your stomach is used to local food. Visitors usually stay in nearby Tarma.

PALCAMAYO
☎ 064

This attractive village, 28km from Tarma, is serviced by several colectivo taxis a day. From Palcamayo, you can visit the Gruta de Guagapo, a huge limestone cave in the hills about 4km away. The cave has been the subject of various international expeditions and is one of Peru's largest and best-known caves, officially protected as a National Speleological Area. Several other, lesser-known caves in the area would also be of interest to speleologists.

THE GRUTA'S BOTTOMLESS DEPTHS

About 1500m into the Gruta de Guagapo is an underwater section, named 'The Siphon,' which was first penetrated in 1976. Peruvian teams reached 2000m and 2400m into the cave during two 1988 expeditions. In 1994 Carlos Morales Bermúdez and local Ramiro Castro Barga, accompanied by US and German cavers, reached 2745m into the cave. No one knows how much further it goes.

To get to the cave, ask in Palcamayo. You'll be shown a dirt road winding off into the hills – it's a pleasant 4km walk. The cave is accessed through a large opening in the side of the mountain to the right of the road; Señor Castro's house is on the left. Bottled drinks are available, and members of prospective expeditions can camp here.

A descent into the **Gruta de Guagapo** requires caving equipment and experience (see the boxed text). The cave contains waterfalls, squeezes and underwater sections (scuba equipment required), and although it is possible to enter the cave for a short distance, you soon need technical gear. A local guide, Señor Modesto Castro, has explored the cave on numerous occasions and can provide you with ropes and lanterns to enter the first sections. He lives in one of the two houses below the mouth of the cave and has a collection of photographs and newspaper clippings describing the exploration of the cave. He doesn't do much caving himself any more, but his son, Ramiro, can be of assistance.

SAN PEDRO DE CAJAS
☎ 064 / elevation 4040m

This large town is known throughout Peru for the excellence of its unique and often exported tapestries. Made out of stuffed rolls of wool (it's difficult to visualize until you actually see one), the tapestries can be bought from the weavers for less than you'd pay in Lima. However, as the village is not oriented toward tourists, facilities here are limited, and you'll need some elementary Spanish to communicate, although the weavers are usually delighted to show you their work.

The basic **Hostal Comercio** (s/d US$2/4) lacks hot showers, but the owners are friendly.

A couple of simple restaurants are available. There are no money-changing facilities.

Colectivos from Tarma and Junín are available several times a day.

SOUTHEAST OF LA OROYA

The main road to Huancayo, the largest city in the Central Highlands, heads southeast from La Oroya, passing several small towns of note. Beyond Huancayo, a rough unpaved road makes a long scenic route to Ayacucho.

JAUJA
☎ 064 / pop 20,000 / elevation 3352m
The first place you pass along this route is Jauja, a friendly and historic town located about 80km southeast of La Oroya, 60km south of Tarma and 40km north of Huancayo. You can change money at **BCP** (☎ 36-1614; Junín 785).

Before the Incas, this area was the home of an important Huanca Indian community, and **Huanca ruins** can be seen on a hill about 3km southeast of town. An adventurous walk will get you there. Jauja was Pizarro's first capital in Peru, though this honor was short lived. Some finely carved wooden altars in the main church are all that remain of the early colonial days.

About 4km from Jauja is **Laguna de Paca**, a small resort offering restaurants, rowing boats and fishing. A boat ride around the lake will cost about US$1 per passenger, five minimum. There are ducks and gulls to look at, and you can stop at the **Isla del Amor** – a tiny artificial island not much bigger than the boat you're on.

There is a colorful **market** every Wednesday morning.

Sleeping & Eating
Many visitors stay in Huancayo and travel to Jauja on one of the frequent buses. If you choose to stay in Jauja, try the simple **Hotel Ganso de Oro** (☎ 36-2165; R Palma 217; s/d US$5/7), two blocks from the train station. Rooms have sinks and toilets, but the hot showers are shared. **Hotel Santa Rosa** (☎ 36-2225; Ayacucho 792; s/d US$5/10), on the corner of the main plaza, has a restaurant, hot water and rooms

with showers. **Cabezon's** (☎ 36-2206; Ayacucho 1025; s US$4.50, d with shower US$11.50; P) has hot water and rooms with TV. **Hostal Maria Nieves** (☎ 36-2543; Gálvez 491; s/d US$11.50/14.50; P) is good, with breakfast included and TVs in the rooms.

Out by the lake, a row of lakeshore restaurants attempts to entice diners with loud music; the lakeside tables are quieter and pleasanter than the noisy entrances.

Jauja has several cheap, basic restaurants near the Plaza de Armas. **Hotel Ganso de Oro** has a good restaurant. Trout and (during the rainy season) frog are local specialties.

Getting There & Away
During the day, frequent, inexpensive minibuses leave for Jauja from the Plaza Amazonas in Huancayo as soon as they are full. Jauja has the regional airport, but there are no scheduled flights.

CONCEPCIÓN
☎ 064 / elevation 3250m
South of Jauja, the road branches to follow both the west and east sides of the Río Mantara valley to Huancayo. Local bus drivers refer to these as *derecha* (right) and *izquierda* (left). Concepción, a village halfway between Jauja and Huancayo on the east (*izquierda*) side, is the entry point for the famous convent of **Santa Rosa de Ocopa** (admission US$1.50; ☿ 9am-noon & 3-6pm Wed-Mon). Admission is by guided tour every hour. The tours take around 45 minutes. There is a student discount.

Set in a pleasant garden, this beautiful building was built by the Franciscans in the early 18th century as a center for missionaries heading into the jungle to convert the Ashaninka and other tribes. During the years of missionary work, the friars built up an impressive collection that is displayed in the convent's museum. Exhibits include stuffed jungle wildlife, Indian artefacts, photographs of early missionary work, old maps, a fantastic library of some 20,000 volumes (many are centuries old), a large collection of colonial religious art (mainly of the Escuela Cuzqueña style) and many other objects. Frequent colectivos to the convent leave from Concepción for Ocopa, about 5km away.

Concepción is easily visited by taking a Huancayo–Jauja *izquierda* bus.

HUANCAYO

☎ 064 / pop 400,000 / elevation 3260m

This modern city lies in the flat and fertile Río Mantaro valley, which supports a large rural population. About 300km from Lima, Huancayo is the Junín departmental capital and the major commercial center and market for people living in the nearby villages.

The city has some excellent Spanish classes and fun nightlife, and makes a convenient base from which to visit the many interesting villages of the Río Mantaro valley. Huancayo's Sunday market, where both crafts and produce from the Río Mantaro valley are sold, is famous among locals and travelers (see Shopping later in this section).

Information

The **Policía de Turismo** (☎ 23-4714; Ferrocarril 580) can help with tourist information as well as with emergencies. **Incas del Peru** (see Tours below) is a recommended source for information on just about anything in the area. The **tourist office** (☎ 23-8480, 23-3251; Real 481; ☺ 8am-1:30pm & 4-6pm Mon-Fri) is located in the Casa del Artesano (indoor crafts market) and has information about sightseeing in the Río Mantaro valley and how to get around on public transport.

The main post office is on the Centro Civico. Many places offering Internet access are found along Giráldez and other central streets.

Lavandería Chic (☎ 23-1107; Breña 154; ☺ 8am-10pm Mon-Sat, 10am-6pm Sun) offers both self-service (US$3 per load, wash and dry, soap included) and drop-off laundry.

English is spoken at **Clínica Ortega** (☎ 23-2921; Carrión 1124; ☺ 24hr), and, for a dentist, try **Dr Luis Mendoza** (☎ 23-9133; Real 968).

BCP, Interbanc, Banco Continental, Banco Wiese and other banks and *casas de cambio* are on Real. Most banks have ATMs and open on Saturday morning.

Sights

Museo Salesiano (☎ 24-7763; admission US$0.60; ☺ vary) can be entered from the Salesian School, and has Amazon fauna, pottery and archaeology exhibits.

Head northeast on Avenida Giráldez for a great view of the city. About 2km from the town center is **Cerro de la Libertad**, where, apart from the city view, there are snack bars and a playground. About 2km further

---

PAPA A LA HUANCAINA

Visitors to Huancayo should try the local speciality, *papa a la huancaina*, which consists of a boiled potato topped with a creamy white sauce of fresh cheese, oil, hot pepper, lemon and egg yolk. The whole concoction is served with an olive and sliced boiled egg, and is eaten as a cold potato salad. Despite the hot pepper, its flavor is pleasantly mild.

(there is a sign and an obvious path), you will come to the eroded geological formations known as **Torre Torre**.

In the city itself, the church of **La Merced**, on the 1st block of Real, is the most interesting; this is where the Peruvian Constitution was approved in 1839. In the suburb of San Antonio, the **Parque de la Identidad Wanka** is a fanciful park full of stone statues and miniature buildings representing the area's culture.

Tours

Incas del Peru (☎ 22-3303; fax 22-2395l; www.incas delperu.org; Giráldez 652), in the same building as the restaurant La Cabaña, offers tours arranged by Lucho Hurtado, a local who speaks English and knows the surrounding area well. He guides adventure treks down the eastern slopes of the Andes and into high jungle on foot, horseback or public transport. It isn't luxurious, but it's a good chance to experience something of the 'real' rural Peru. Lucho's father has a ranch in the middle of nowhere. You can stay there and meet all kinds of local people. Several people have recommended his trips. If you are unable to get a group together, you may be able to join up with another group. The trips last anywhere from four to eight days and cost about US$35 per person per day including simple food. Accommodations are rustic and trips may involve some camping.

Guided day hikes can be arranged for about US$25 per person including lunch. Mountain bikes are US$15 per day, or US$35 including a guide and lunch. Guided days on horseback are US$35.

Courses

Incas del Peru also arranges Spanish lessons, which include meals and accommodations

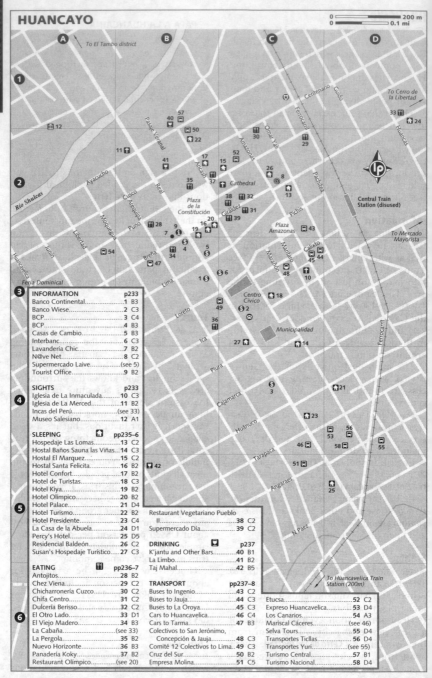

HUANCAYO

0 —————— 200 m
0 —————— 0.1 mi

with a local family (if you wish) for about US$200 a week. Lessons can be modified or extended to fit your interests: learn to cook local dishes, play the panpipes or make weavings and other local crafts.

Festivals & Events

There are hundreds of fiestas in Huancayo and surrounding villages – supposedly almost every day somewhere in the Río Mantaro valley. Ask at the tourist office. One of the biggest events in Huancayo is **Semana Santa** (Holy Week), with big religious processions attracting people from all over Peru. **Fiestas Patrias** (28 and 29 July) is also very busy. Hotels fill up and raise their prices during these times.

Sleeping

BUDGET

La Casa de la Abuela (Giráldez 691; dm US$5.50, d US$14, d with shower US$17; ☒) Incas del Peru runs this clean and friendly hostal in an older house with a garden, hot water, laundry facilities, games and cable TV. It's popular with backpackers who are mothered by *la Abuela* (Lucho's mom). Ten basic rooms sleep two to six people; rates include continental breakfast with homemade bread and jam and killer coffee.

Peru Andino (☎ 22-3956; www.geocities.com /peruandino_1; Pasaje San Antonio 113; dm US$3, s/d US$5/ 10, with shower US$6/12) Another backpacker's favorite, this place is a few blocks northwest of the map and offers hot showers, kitchen and laundry facilities, book exchange, bike rental, tour information and Spanish lessons. Rates include breakfast.

Hospedaje Las Lomas (☎ 23-7587; Giráldez 327; s/ d US$7/10) Spotless, hot-water bathrooms and excellent mattresses make this a fine choice. Rooms vary in size; some are quite large. The friendly owners are on the premises to answer questions or rent a TV (US$1.50).

Hotel Confort (☎ 23-3601; Ancash 237; s/d US$6/9; P) This huge barn of a hotel echoes with institutional corridors leading to scores of stark, faded rooms. But the rooms are clean, larger than average, have hot showers, good mattresses, writing desks and cable TV (US$1.50). It's good value if you don't mind characterless convenience.

Residencial Baldeón (☎ 23-1634; Amazonas 543; s/d US$3/6) In a friendly family house, teeny rooms line a small courtyard. Shared hot

showers with advance notice, kitchen and laundry privileges and a secure entrance make this basic place fair value. A US$1 breakfast is offered.

Percy's Hotel (☎ 21-2749; Real 1339; s/d US$4.50/ 7.30) Rooms are clean, good-sized and have showers; TV is available for US$1.50 extra. Friendly staff will provide hot water with 30-minutes' notice.

Hotel Palace (☎ 23-8501; Ancash 1127; s/d US$3/6, with bathroom from US$6/9) Rooms are reasonably sized and have decent mattresses and TV on request; the bathrooms vary in size so check out a few rooms. Hot water is available in the early morning only.

Hostal y Baños Sauna Las Viñas (☎ 23-1294; Piura 415; s/d US$10/13) Rooms are small but squeeze in hot baths, cable TV and phone. Its sauna (US$2) is open 6am to 9pm. The building offers lovely views from the upper floors.

Hotel Plaza (☎ 23-6858; Ancash 171; s/d US$8.50/ 11.50) All rooms have 24-hour hot water and cable TV.

MID-RANGE

Hostal El Marquez (☎ 21-9026, 21-9292, 20-0777; caslazjo@ec-red.com; Puno 294; s/d/ste US$22/27/40; P)

CALIENTES

Calientes, or 'hot ones,' are drinks sold on cold Andean nights. All through the night, you will find people on street corners selling these drinks from little stoves on wheels. Here's a recipe to warm the cockles of your heart.

½ cup of black tea leaves
1 stick of cinnamon
1 teaspoon aniseed
Add a generous pinch of each of the following:
lemon grass
lemon balm
chamomile
fennel
fig leaves

Put all of these ingredients into a kettle and boil for 10 minutes. In a cup, put the juice of one lime, two teaspoons of sugar or honey and one measure of pisco or rum, then fill the cup with the hot tea mixture. Drink it while it's hot.

- recipe courtesy of Beverly Stuart

An elegant sitting room off the lobby suggests that this hotel is better than most. Rooms are sweetly furnished with direct-dial phones, cable TV and restful beds. Three suites feature a large bathroom with Jacuzzi tub, king-sized bed and minibar. A small café offers room service, breakfast is included and the staff are pleasingly professional.

Susan's Hospedaje Turístico (☎ 20-2251; Real 851; s/d US$18/24) Multinational flags over the entrance welcome visitors to this spotless and cheerful hotel. Rooms have good-sized bathrooms, cable TV, writing desks, quality mattresses and dazzlingly bright bedspreads. An elevator takes you up to the 5th floor where there are some good views of the civic center. There is a café, and breakfast is included. The hotel also has a sauna.

Hotel Kiya (☎ 21-4955, 21-4957; hotelkiya@terra.com.pe; Giráldez 107; s/d US$17/20) This six-story hotel boasts an elevator and has rooms painted in pink stencil to look like wallpaper. If you can live with that, you'll get comfy beds and hot showers (some rooms have large bathrooms with tubs), telephone and optional cable TV. The staff strive to please. Some rooms have plaza views (but also plaza noise). A restaurant is on the premises with breakfast available.

Hotel Turismo (☎/fax 23-1072; luisbrena@terra.com.pe; Ancash 729; s/d US$26/35; P) This pleasant-looking, old building with wooden balconies and public areas has a certain faded grandeur. Rooms vary in size and quality but have bathrooms. The hotel has a restaurant and bar and works with Hotel Presidente.

Hotel Presidente (☎/fax 23-1275, 23-1736; Real 1138; s/d US$34/48; P) This good modern hotel includes breakfast in the price, has nicely carpeted rooms and larger-than-average bathrooms.

Hostal América (☎/fax 24-2005; hostalamerica@mixmail.com; Trujillo 358; s/d US$30/50; P) In the El Tambo suburb, about seven blocks north of Río Shulcas, this comfortable hotel has modern, carpeted rooms with cable and phones. A 24-hour café is on the premises.

Other recommendations are:

Hotel Olímpico (☎ 21-4555; fax 21-5700; Ancash 408; s/d US$23/28) Eclectic art in every corner; rooms with cable TV; low season discounts.

Hostal Santa Felicita (☎ 23-5476, ☎/fax 23-5285; Giráldez 145; s/d US$14.50/20) Plaza views, hot water, solid mattresses, cable TV and phone.

Eating

La Cabaña (☎ 22-3303; Giráldez 652; mains average US$4.50; 5-11pm) Large pizzas are US$10, hamburgers are US$2 and grills, trout, pastas etc are in between. Local folklórica bands perform at 9pm Thursday to Saturday. The house drink is *sangría*, which fuels a party crowd of locals and travelers. It's connected to **El Otro Lado** (Giráldez 658), which is also open for lunch, does cuy on request and has an art gallery.

Restaurant Olímpico (☎ 23-4181; Giráldez 199; breakfasts, set lunch US$2, mains US$4-8) Here for over six decades, this is Huancayo's oldest (though modernized) restaurant. It features a large open kitchen where you can see the traditional Peruvian dishes prepared and a popular Sunday buffet lunch (US$5).

Antojitos (☎ 23-7950; Puno 599; meals US$1.50-8; 5pm-late Mon-Sat) This restaurant-cum-bar, housed in an antique-filled, wood-beamed, two-story building with the obligatory Lennon and Santana posters, brings in friendly crowds of upscale locals bent on having roaring conversations over the sounds of anything from *cumbia* to Pink Floyd. Local bands perform most nights from 9pm. The food is well-prepared bar food – burgers, pizzas and grills.

La Pergola (Puno 444; set lunch US$2) Upstairs with a plaza view and courtly atmosphere, La Pergola offers inexpensive sandwiches, snacks and light meals.

Panadería Koky (☎ 23-4707; Puno 298; snacks from US$1; 7am-9pm) This modern bakery/coffee shop serves tasty sandwiches, pastries, empanadas, real espresso and other coffees.

Nuevo Horizonte (Ica 578; meals US$1-1.50; 7:30am-10pm Sun-Fri) Inside an atmospheric older house with attractive ceilings, this place has an excellent vegetarian menu using soy and tofu to recreate Peruvian plates such as *lomo saltado*, as well as straightforward veggie meals. Vegetarian products are for sale.

Chicharronería Cuzco (Cuzco 173; meals US$2) This hole-in-the-wall is run by Doña Juana Curo Ychpas, who makes excellent traditional plates of *chicharrones* (fried pork ribs) – for dedicated carnivores only – for about US$2.

La Estancia (☎ 22-3279; M Castilla 2815; meals US$7) Northwest of town, Real becomes Avenida Mariscal Castilla in the El Tambo district. La Estancia does a great lunchtime *pachamanca*, containing *cuy*, pork, lamb, potatoes, beans and tamales, among other possible ingredients, wrapped in leaves and cooked in an underground earth oven (basically, a hole in the ground). Go early and watch them disinter it. Cheaper plates also available.

Other recommendations include:

Recreo Huancahuasi (☎ 24-4826; M Castilla 2222, El Tambo; meals US$5) Another recommended place for *pachamanca* lunches, with live music on weekends.

Restaurant Vegetariano Pueblo II (Giráldez 224; meals US$1-2; ⌚ 10am-8pm) Tiny place with good vegetarian plates.

Chifa Centro (☎ 22-4154; Giráldez 245; mains average US$2) Good Chinese food.

Chez Viena (☎ 23-4385; Puno 125; snacks US$1) Nice coffee/pastry shop with an ornate interior.

El Viejo Madero (☎ 21-7788; Breña 125; meals US$2) The best chicken restaurant, with juicier and bigger pieces than other places.

Dulcería Berisso (Giráldez 258) Great chocolate cakes.

Self-caterers can try **Supermercado Dia** (Giráldez near Ancash) or **Supermercado Laive** (Real at Lima).

Entertainment

Good restaurants for entertainment include **La Cabaña** and **Antojitos** (see Eating p236). **K'jantu** (Ayacucho 308) is a nightclub with live *folklórica* music and dancing; **Chucclla** and a couple of other places on the same block are worth checking out. **La Limbo** (Cuzco 374) offers live local rock bands. **Taj Mahal** (Huancavelica 1052) is a club with video karaoke and dancing.

Shopping

Huancayo has two main markets: **Mercado Mayorista** (daily produce market) and the **Feria Dominical** (Sunday craft market). The colorful produce market spills out from Mercado Mayorista (which is covered) east along the railway tracks. In the meat section, you can buy Andean delicacies such as fresh and dried frogs, guinea pigs, rabbits and chickens. Although it's a daily market, the most important day is Sunday, coinciding with the weekly craft market.

The Feria Dominical occupies numerous blocks along Huancavelica to the northwest of Piura. Noncraft items range from cassette tapes to frilly underwear. Weavings, sweaters, textiles, embroidered items, ceramics and wood carvings are also sold here, as well as *mates burilados* (carved gourds). These

are made in the nearby villages of Cochas Grande and Cochas Chico. This is definitely a place to keep an eye on your valuables.

Getting There & Away

BUS

Bus services change often depending on season and demand. Lima (US$5 to US$10, six to seven hours) is served by **Mariscal Cáceres** (☎ 21-6633; Real 1241), **Etucsa** (☎ 23-6524; Puno 220), with the most departures, and **Cruz del Sur** (☎ 23-5650; Ayacucho 251), with the most expensive and comfortable service. **Comité 12** (☎ 23-3281; Loreto 421) has colectivo taxis to Lima (US$14, five hours).

For Ayacucho (US$7.30, 10 to 12 hours) the best service is **Empresa Molina** (☎ 22-4501; Angaraes 334) with morning and night departures on a rough road.

Huancavelica (US$3, five hours) is served most frequently by **Transportes Ticllas** (Ancash at Angaraes) with 10 daily buses. Others include the nearby Turismo Nacional, Expreso Huancavelica and Transportes Yuri, with late night buses only.

Empresa de Transportes San Juan (☎ 21-4558; Ferrocarril 131) has minibuses almost every hour to Tarma (US$2.50, 3½ hours) and can drop you off at Concepción or Jauja. **Los Canarios** (Puno 739) also serves Tarma.

For Satipo (US$4.50, eight to nine hours) the best service is **Selva Tours** (Ferrocarril at Ancash) with four daily buses.

Turismo Central (☎ 22-3128, Ayacucho 274) has buses north to Cerro de Pasco, Huánuco (US$5, eight hours), Tingo María and Pucallpa (US$11.50, 20 hours).

Local buses to nearby villages leave from the street intersections shown on the map. Just show up and wait until a bus is ready to leave. Ask other passengers for more details. The tourist office is a good source of local bus information.

TRAIN

Huancayo has two unlinked train stations in different parts of town. Passenger trains run up from Lima a few times a year, usually on holiday weekends for US$30 round trip. It's a fabulous run, passing through La Galera (4781m) the world's highest station on single-gauge track. Very occasionally, the train will also go to Cerro de Pasco. The train station is closed, but Incas del Peru knows the schedule, or you can check at the

Lima train station (p83). Train enthusiasts are fighting to keep this service operating, though the private company that owns it doesn't have much interest.

The **train station** (☎ 23-2581) for Huancavelica is at the south end of town. From here Expreso services depart for Huancavelica at 6:30am Monday to Sunday (five hours) and Ordinario services depart at 12:30pm Monday to Saturday (6¼ hours). Tickets are about US$2/3/4 in 2nd/1st/buffet class. The buffet class is reasonably comfortable and has guaranteed seating and the quickest meal service; 2nd class is crowded and allows standing; 1st is in between. Tickets are sold from noon to 6pm on the day before travel and at 6am on the day of travel.

On Sunday and Monday, there's a faster *autovagón* (electric train) that takes 4¾ hours and leaves at 6pm. The fare is US$6.

Trains leave Huancavelica at the same times as from Huancayo.

RÍO MANTARO VALLEY

Two main road systems link Huancayo with the villages of the Río Mantaro valley and are known simply as the left and right of the river. Left *(izquierda)* is the east and right *(derecha)* is the west side of the river, as you head into Huancayo from the north. It is best to confine your sightseeing on any given day to one side or the other because there are few bridges.

Perhaps the most interesting excursion is on the east side of the valley, where you can visit the twin villages of **Cochas Grande** and **Cochas Chico**, about 11km from Huancayo. These villages are the major production centers for the incised gourds that have

---

MARKET DAYS AROUND HUANCAYO

Each little village and town in the Río Mantaro valley has its own *feria*, or market day. If you enjoy these, you'll find one on every day of the week.

Monday San Agustín de Cajas, Huayucachi
Tuesday Hualhuas, Pucara
Wednesday San Jerónimo, Jauja
Thursday El Tambo, Sapallanga
Friday Cochas
Saturday Matahuasi, Chupaca, Marco
Sunday Huancayo, Jauja, Mito, Comas

---

made the area famous. Oddly enough, the gourds are grown mainly on the coast and are imported into the highlands from the Chiclayo and Ica areas. Once they are transported into the highlands, they are dried and scorched, then decorated using woodworking tools.

Other villages of interest for their handicrafts include **San Agustín de Cajas**, **Hualhuas** and **San Jerónimo de Tunán**. Cajas is known for the manufacture of wicker furniture. Hualhuas is a center for the manufacture of wool products – ponchos, weavings, sweaters and other items. San Jerónimo is known for its filigree silverwork and also has a 17th-century church with fine wooden altars. While the villages can be visited easily from Huancayo, most buying and selling is done in Huancayo, and the villages have few facilities. The key here is the ability to speak Spanish and make friends with the locals.

HUANCAVELICA

☎ 067 / pop 36,000 / elevation 3690m
Huancavelica, 147km south of Huancayo, is the capital of its department. High and remote, most of the department lies above 3500m and has a cold climate, though it can get 'T-shirt' hot during the sunny days of the dry season (May to October). The rest of the year tends to be wet, and during the rainiest months (between February and April), the roads are sometimes in such bad shape that Huancavelica can be virtually cut off from the rest of Peru. It's a beautiful but forgotten and remote area; the telephone directory's yellow pages for the entire department take up just over half a page, which gives an idea of Huancavelica's isolation.

This historic city was a strategic Inca center, and shortly after the conquest, the Spanish discovered its mineral wealth. By 1564 the Spaniards were sending Indian slaves to Huancavelica to work in the mercury and silver mines. The present town was founded in 1571 under the name of Villa Rica de Oropesa and retains a very pleasant colonial atmosphere and many interesting churches. It's a small but attractive town visited by few tourists; it's tough to reach but worth the effort.

Information
Dirección de Turismo (☎ 75-2938; 2nd fl, V Garma 444; ⏰ 8am-1pm & 2-5pm Mon-Fri) provides good

HUANCAVELICA

directions (in Spanish) for local hikes. A dozen central places provide Internet access, including **@Internet** (Segura 166), on the Plaza de Armas. The main **post office** (Pasaje Ferrua 105) is near Iglesia de Santa Ana. **BCP** (☎ 75-2831; V Toledo 384) has a Visa ATM and changes money. **Multired** is a stand-alone ATM next to the Municipalidad.

Instituto Nacional de Cultura

The **INC** (☎ 75-2544; Raimondi 205; admission free; ☯ 10am-1pm & 3-6pm Tue-Sun), in a colonial building on Plaza San Juan de Dios, has information and displays about the area; don't hesitate to ask the helpful director if you have any questions. A small **museum** features the usual Inca artefacts plus a display

of local costumes. You can even take a class in folklórica dances or music!

Churches

Huancavelican churches are noted for their silver-plated altars, unlike the rest of Peru's colonial churches, which are usually gold-plated. There are several churches of note, although they are generally closed to tourism. You can go as a member of the congregation when they are open for services, usually early in the morning on weekdays, with longer morning hours on Sunday.

The oldest is **Santa Ana**, founded in the 16th century. The **cathedral**, built in the 17th century, has been restored and contains what some say is the best colonial altar in

Peru. Other 17th-century churches include **San Francisco,** famous for its 11 intricately worked altars, **Santo Domingo**, with famous statues of Santo Domingo and La Virgen del Rosario, which were made in Italy, **San Sebastián**, which has been well-restored, **San Cristóbal** and **La Ascensión**.

San Cristóbal Mineral Springs

The **mineral springs** (pool US$0.30, private shower US$0.50; 5:30am-4pm Sat-Thu, 5:30am-noon Fri) are fed into two large, slightly murky swimming pools. The water is lukewarm, and supposedly has curative properties. There is a café, and it's reasonably pleasant. You can rent a towel, soap and a bathing suit if you've forgotten yours (though their selection is limited and unlovely). Reach the springs via a steep flight of stairs and enjoy the city view as you climb.

Market

Market day in Huancavelica is Sunday, and although there are smaller daily markets, Sunday is the best day to see the locals in traditional dress (see Lircay, opposite, for a description). The main Sunday market area is along Torre Tagle behind the cathedral.

Handicrafts are sold almost every day on the north side of the Plaza de Armas and also by the Municipalidad. Colorful wool leggings are especially popular.

Mercury Mine Hike

An interesting hike of about three hours (round trip) leads to the old mercury mines. Leave town from near the train station, heading south. It's a bit difficult to find the right path at first, but after a few hundred meters, it becomes an obvious pack-animal trail. It is a steep ascent, going to over 4000m above sea level, and brings you to the village of Santa Barbara, with its now-deserted colonial church. Nearby are the abandoned modern mining installations, which were finally closed in 1976. Between the village and the mining installations, you can find the old entrance to the original 16th-century mine, carved into the rock and with a coat of arms beside it. If you have a good flashlight, it's possible to enter it a little way, but do so at your own risk. A few villagers still extract mercury as a cottage industry, and if you speak Spanish, you might be able to find someone to

show you the process. Note that the mine is locally known as Mina de la Muerte (death mine), which refers to the deadly effects of mercury.

Apart from the deserted church and mine, the walk is of interest because of the many llama and alpaca herds in the mountain landscape. Huancavelica has many other little-known areas that may be of interest to the adventurous traveler.

Festivals & Events

Colorful traditional fiestas occur on major Peruvian holidays, such as Carnaval, Semana Santa, Todos Santos and Christmas and others held throughout the year. Check with the INC for upcoming festivals. Huancavelica's **Semana Turística** (Tourism Week) is held in late September and early October.

Sleeping

Most hotels are cheap and only have cold water, but with the natural mineral baths in town, this is not a great hardship.

Hotel Presidente Huancavelica (/fax 75-2760; s/d US$26/34; P) In a nice old building on the Plaza de Armas, this is the only nonbudget hotel in town, and a bit pricey for what you get. The rooms are very plain, though they do have hot showers and a TV. It has a restaurant.

Hostal Camacho (/fax 75-3298; Carabaya 481; s/d US$2.50/4, s/d with shower US$4/6.50). This clean, well-run budget choice has small rooms but good mattresses with piles of blankets. Showers are hot in the mornings only.

Hotel Ascensión (75-3103; Manco Capac 481; s/d US$3/4.50, s/d with shower US$4.50/6.50) In a good location on the Plaza de Armas, this hotel has larger rooms. It claims 24-hour hot water but don't bet your skin on it.

Hotel Tahuantinsuyo (75-2968; Carabaya 399; s/d US$4/5.80) Basic rooms with bathrooms have hot water in the morning.

Eating

There are no particularly good restaurants in Huancavelica, though there are plenty of cheap chicken places and *chifas*. The best is **Restaurant Joy** (75-2826; V Toledo 216; menú US$2, mains US$2.50-6; 9am-2pm & 5-10pm). Its three-course set lunches are tasty, and it does cheap snacks and sandwiches as well as other Peruvian plates. Nearby, the similarly-priced **Mochica Sachun** (V Toledo 303) is another good choice.

Getting There & Away
The train from Huancayo is faster than the buses, but the road goes higher than the train and has better views.

BUS
Almost all major buses depart from near Parque Santa Ana. Companies serving Huancayo (US$3, almost five hours) include **Transportes Ticllas** (☎ 75-1562; O'Donavan 505) with six daily departures. Other companies go less often or may go via Huancayo en route to Lima. Colectivo taxis (US$6, four hours) leave when full (four passengers) from the Plaza Santa Ana.

For Lima (about US$10, 12 to 15 hours) some companies go via Huancayo while others go via Pisco. Via Huancayo is usually a little faster but it depends on road conditions. The Pisco route goes over a 4850m pass and is freezing at night, bring warm clothes. **Transportes Oropesa** (☎ 75-3181; O'Donavan 599) goes via Pisco at 6pm and also has an overnight bus to Ica. **Expreso Lobato** (☎ 75-2964; M Muñoz 489) has comfortable overnight buses via Huancayo. Also try **Expreso Huancavelica** (☎ 75-2964; M Muñoz 516).

For Ayacucho, there may be a direct service with Transportes Ticllas leaving at dawn. Most Peruvian travelers take local buses to Santa Inés, which is on the paved road from Pisco to Ayacucho. Here, wait for any Ayacucho-bound bus. Ask locally about the best, current route, as it changes depending on road conditions.

Minibuses go to Lircay and other nearby towns from Torre Tagle at Barranca.

TRAIN
Trains leave from **Huancavelica station** (☎ 75-2898) for Huancayo at 6:30am daily and 12:30pm Monday to Saturday. A faster *autovagón* leaves at 5:30pm on Friday. Buy tickets in advance if possible (see Train, p237, for more information).

LIRCAY
☎ 067
The small, colonial town of Lircay is almost 80km southeast of Huancavelica (US$2, 3½ hours). Its main claim to fame is as the center for the department's

traditional clothing, which can be seen at Huancavelica's Sunday market. The predominant color is black, but the men wear rainbow-colored pompoms on their hats and at their waists (supposedly love tokens from women), and the women wear multicolored shawls over their otherwise somber clothing. Stay at **Hostal Rosario** (s/d US$2.50/4) on Jirón Puno. Beds are OK and shared showers are sometimes hot.

IZCUCHACA
☎ 067
Izcuchaca, the main village between Huancayo and Huancavelica, has a basic hotel, a pottery center, hot springs and archaeological ruins, which are accessible only on foot. There is also a **historic bridge**, which, as legend has it, was built by the Incas and was defended bitterly by Huascar against the advance of Atahualpa's troops during the civil war that was raging in the Inca Empire when the Spaniards arrived.

AYACUCHO
☎ 066 / pop 126,000 / elevation 2750m
Arguably Peru's most fascinating Andean city after Cuzco, Ayacucho is well worth a visit. It has retained its colonial atmosphere more than most Peruvian cities, and colonial buildings and churches dominate the skyline. The city overflows during the Semana Santa celebrations, which are easily the most colorful yet most devout in Peru.

As mentioned at the beginning of this chapter, the central Andes is one of Peru's least-visited areas. Ayacucho is no exception to this. Its first road link with the Peruvian coast was not finished until 1924, and in 1960, there were only two buses and a few dozen vehicles in the city. Departmental statistics show that as late as 1981, there were still only 44km of paved roads in the department, only 7% of the population had running water in their houses and only 14% had electricity. The paving of the road to Lima, completed in 1999, has turned Ayacucho to face the 21st century, but not without forgetting its storied past.

History
The first signs of human habitation in Peru were discovered in the Pikimachay caves, near Ayacucho. (There is nothing of interest to be seen there.)

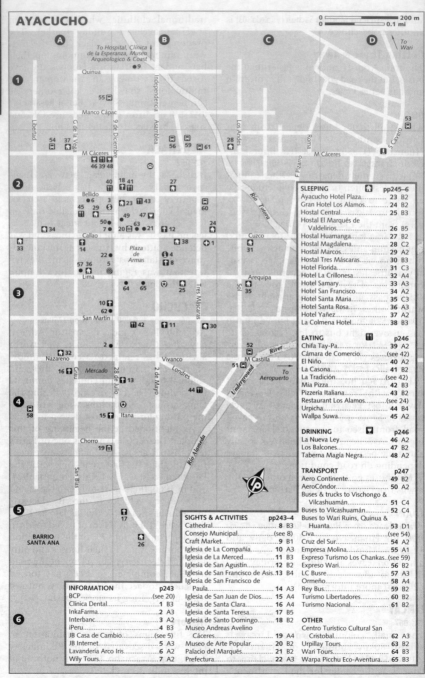

AYACUCHO

CENTRAL HIGHLANDS

Five hundred years before the Inca Empire, the Wari Empire dominated the Peruvian highlands. The Wari's ruined capital (see p247), 22km northeast of Ayacucho, is reached along a paved road. The city played a major part in the battles for independence, and a huge nearby monument marks the site of the important Battle of Ayacucho, fought in 1824. And it was here, in a rural university campus, that Professor Abimael Guzmán nurtured the Sendero Luminoso (Shining Path) Maoist revolutionary movement in the 1970s, which became an armed guerrilla organization bent on overthrowing the government.

The Sendero's activities in the 1980s focused on deadly political, economic and social upheaval. In remote towns and villages, mayors were murdered, community leaders assassinated, uncooperative villagers massacred, police stations and power plants bombed, and government and church-sponsored aid projects destroyed. The government responded by sending in the armed forces who were often equally brutal and, in the ensuing civil war, between 40,000 and 60,000 people died or disappeared, most of them in the Central Andes. Ayacucho was almost completely off-limits to travelers during most of the 1980s. Things finally changed when Guzmán was captured and imprisoned for life in 1992, followed quickly by his top lieutenants, leading to a halt in hostilities.

Today, Ayacucho is a safe place to visit. The populace doesn't discuss the dark days of the 1980s much, and welcomes travelers with enthusiasm and good cheer.

Orientation

Plaza de Armas is also known as Plaza Mayor de Huamanga. The street names of the four sides of the plaza, clockwise from the east (with the cathedral), are Portal Municipal, Portal Independencia, Portal Constitución and Portal Unión.

Information

EMERGENCY
Police (☎ 81-2332; 28 de Julio 325; ☼ 24hr)
Policía de Turismo (☎ 81-2179; 2 de Mayo 100; ☼ 7:30am-8pm)

INTERNET ACCESS
There are many options; you can try **JB Internet** (Portal Constitución 3).

LAUNDRY
Lavandería Arco Iris (Bellido 322) provides both wash and dry and dry cleaning service.

MEDICAL SERVICES
Hospital Central (☎ 81-2180/1; Independencia 335; ☼ 24hr) Provides basic services.
Clínica de La Esperanza (☎ 81-7436; Independencia 355; ☼ 8am-8pm) English spoken.
Clínica Dental García Tresierra (☎ 964-1763; Cuzco 200)
Inka Farma (☎ 81-8240, 83-6273; 28 de Julio 250; ☼ 7am-10:30pm)

MONEY
BCP (☎ 81-4102; Portal Unión 28) Visa ATM
Interbanc (☎ 81-2480; 9 de Diciembre 183)
JB Casa de Cambio (Portal Constitución 3)

POST
The **post office** (☎ 81-2224; Asamblea 293; ☼ 8am-8pm Mon-Sat) is 150m from the Plaza Armas.

TOURIST INFORMATION
iPeru (☎ 81-8305; iperuayacucho@promperu.gob.pe; Portal Municipal 48; ☼ 8:30am-7:30pm)
Wily Tours (☎ 81-4075; 9 de Diciembre 107) Good for flights and bus reservations.

Sights & Activities

In the past a US$3 tourist ticket covered entrance into major churches, museums and colonial buildings. This system was discontinued in 2003 but may be revamped in the future. Note that opening hours for all of Ayacucho's attractions are erratic and changeable.

The 17th-century **cathedral**, on the Plaza de Armas, has a religious-art museum. The cathedral and a dozen other colonial churches from the 16th, 17th and 18th centuries are well worth a visit for their incredibly ornate facades and interiors, mainly Spanish baroque but often with Andean influences evinced by the plants and animals depicted. Ayacucho claims to have 33 churches (one for each year of Christ's life) but there are in fact several more. The most important of Ayacucho's churches are marked on the map. Except for during Semana Santa (when churches are open for most of the day), opening hours are erratic; ask at the tourist office.

Most of the **old mansions** are now mainly political offices and can be visited, usually during business hours. The offices of the Department of Ayacucho (the **Prefectura**) on the Plaza de Armas are a good example. The mansion was constructed between 1740 and 1755 and sold to the state in 1937. On the ground floor is a pretty courtyard where visitors can see the cell of the local heroine of independence, María Parado de Bellido. Go upstairs to see some excellent tile work.

Also worth a look is the Salon de Actas in the **Consejo Municipal**, next to the cathedral, with its excellent view of the plaza. On the north side of the plaza are several more fine colonial houses, including the **Palacio del Marqués**, at Portal Unión 37, which is the oldest and dates from 1550. There are various others scattered around the town center, many housing professional offices; the tourist office can suggest which ones to visit.

The **Museo de Arte Popular** (Portal Unión 28; admission free; ☺ 10am-1pm & 3-5pm Thu-Fri, 10am-12: 30pm Sat) is in the 18th-century Casa Chacón, owned by and adjoining the Banco de Crédito. The popular art covers the Ayacucheño spectrum – silverwork, rug and tapestry weaving, stone and wood carvings, ceramics (model churches are especially popular) and the famous **retablos**. These are colorful wooden boxes ranging from the size of a matchbox to a meter or more in height, containing intricate papier-mâché models; Peruvian rural scenes or the nativity are particularly popular, but some interesting ones with political or social commentary can be seen here. Old and new photographs show how Ayacucho changed during the 20th century.

The **Museo Andres Avelino Cáceres** (28 de Julio 512; admission US$0.60; ☺ 10am-1pm & 3-5pm Mon-Sat) is housed in the Casona Vivanco, a mansion dating from the 16th century. Cáceres was a local man who commanded Peruvian troops during the War of the Pacific (1879–83) against Chile. Accordingly, the museum houses maps and military paraphernalia from that period, as well as some colonial art.

The **Museo Arqueológico Hipolito Unanue** (Museo INC; ☎ 81-2056; admission US$0.60; ☺ 9am-1pm & 3-5pm Mon-Sat, 9am-1pm Sun) is in the Centro Cultural Simón Bolívar at the university, a little over a kilometer from the town center along Independencia – you can't miss it. Wari ceramics make up most of the small exhibit. While there, check the university library for a free exhibit of mummies, skulls and other niceties. The buildings are set in a botanical garden in which cacti are the main exhibits.

The best time to visit is in the morning as, sometimes, afternoon hours aren't adhered to.

Tours

Several agencies arrange local tours; they cater mainly to Peruvian tourists and their guides mainly speak Spanish. Ask about tours in other languages.

Urpillay Tours (☎ 81-5074; Portal Unión 33-D)
Wari Tours (☎ 81-3115; Portal Independencia 70)
Warpa Picchu Eco-Aventura (☎ 81-5191; Portal Independencia 66)

Festivals & Events

Ayacucho's **Semana Santa** celebration, held the week before Easter, has long been considered Peru's finest religious festival, and it attracts visitors – though relatively few foreigners – from all over the country. Rooms in the better hotels are booked well in advance, and even the cheapest places fill completely. The tourist office has lists of local families who provide accommodations for the overflow.

Each year, iPeru prints a free brochure describing the Semana Santa events with street maps showing the main processions. Visitors are advised to use this detailed information. The celebrations begin on the Friday before Palm Sunday and continue for 10 days until Easter Sunday. The Friday before Palm Sunday is marked by a procession in honor of La Virgen de los Dolores, or 'Our Lady of Sorrows,' during which it is customary to inflict 'sorrows' on bystanders by firing pebbles out of slingshots. Gringos have been recent targets, so be warned.

Each succeeding day is marked with solemn yet colorful processions and religious rites, which reach a fever pitch of Catholic faith and tradition. They culminate on the Saturday before Easter Sunday with a huge all-night party leading up to dawn fireworks to celebrate the resurrection of Christ.

In addition to the religious services, Ayacucho's Semana Santa celebrations include numerous secular activities – art shows, folk-dancing competitions and demonstrations, local music concerts, street events, sporting events (especially equestrian ones), agricultural fairs and also the preparation of traditional meals.

The tourist office here is a good source of information about the large number of minor fiestas held throughout the department (there seems to be one almost every week).

Sleeping

The revival of tourism in the late 1990s has resulted in a hotel boom with over 50 hotels and hospedajes listed by the tourist office. Most hotels are quite basic but new hotels continue to open. The budget hotels have limited hot water; talk to the staff about the best time to take a shower. Prices here will rise by 25% to 75% over Semana Santa.

BUDGET

Hotel Yañez (☎ /fax 81-4918; M Cáceres 1210; s/d US$8/ 12) Spacious rooms, comfortable mattresses, large mirrors, maroon bedspreads, kitsch wall art, cable TV and hot showers are the hallmarks of this well-run hotel. The large rooms tend to echo and are noisy, but the hotel is clean and the roof has nice views. A cafeteria serves breakfasts, included in the rates.

Hostal Marcos (☎ 81-6867; 9 de Diciembre 143; s/d US$13/21) Twelve spotless rooms in a little place at the end of an alley; hard to find and often full. Rooms offer 24-hour hot water and cable TV, and a light breakfast is included.

Hotel La Crillonesa (☎ 81-2350; hotelcrillonesa@ latinmail.com; Nazareno 165; s/d US$5/8, with shower US$8/11.50) A small but popular and helpful hotel, it offers a rooftop terrace with photogenic church-tower views, a café, TV room with cable, tour information and 24 hour hot water. Rooms have comfy beds; those with shower may have a cable TV. Recommended.

Hostal Tres Máscaras (☎ 81-2921, 81-4107; Tres Máscaras 194; s/d US$12/15; P) The pleasing walled garden and friendly staff make this an enjoyable place to stay. Hot water is on in the morning and later on request; rooms have bathrooms and TV. Breakfast is available for US$2.

Hostal Huamanga (☎ 81-3527, 81-1871; Bellido 535; s/d US$3/6, with shower US$6/12) These folks manage to crank out the hot water all day and have a café and a garden, eh? Rooms are basic but OK.

La Colmena Hotel (☎ 81-2146, 81-1318; Cuzco 140; s US$4.50, s/d with bathroom US$7/9) This popular hotel is often full by early afternoon, partly because it's one of the longest-standing places in town and partly because it's steps from the plaza. It's a great building, but has rather been resting on its laurels – the shared bathrooms are run down and rates are lower than in recent years. Still, it has a locally popular restaurant, a courtyard with balconies, and a great location, so check it out.

Hotel Samary (☎ 81-2442, 81-3562; Callao 329; s/d US$5.80/7.30, with bathroom US$8/10; P) A simple but clean hotel with great rooftop views and hot water in the early morning and evening.

Hotel Florida (☎ 81-2565; fax 81-6029; Cuzco 310; s/d US$10/16) This traveler-recommended hotel has a nice garden and clean rooms with bathrooms and TV. Hot water in the morning and later on request.

Gran Hotel Los Alamos (☎ /fax 81-2782; Cuzco 215; s/d US$6/11.50) This hotel is over one of the town's most favored restaurants. The decent-sized rooms overlook the restaurant action (not very noisy) and supposedly have hot showers all day, but, as with most budget hotels, ask.

Other recommendations are:

Hostal Central (☎ 81 2144, 81-9652; Arequipa 188; s/d US$3.50/7, with shower US$7.30/11.50) Spacious rooms but limited hot water hours.

Hostal Magdalena (☎ 81-8969; M Cáceres 816; s/d US$4.50/8, d with shower US$12) Clean, rooms vary, hot water in the morning and on request.

MID-RANGE

Hotel Santa Rosa (☎ 81-4614; ☎ /fax 81-2083; Lima 166; s/d US$16/26; P) Less than a block from the Plaza de Armas, this quiet hotel has a nice patio with a decent restaurant (good breakfast US$2.50) and a roof terrace. Large rooms all boast cable TV, telephone and hot showers. Management is friendly.

Hotel San Francisco (☎ 81-2353, ☎ /fax 81-4501; Callao 290; s/d US$14/18) The hotel has a restaurant and bar and will serve meals on its attractive patio. Rooms feature cable TV and hot water; some have a minibar. Rates include continental breakfast.

Hostal El Marqués de Valdelirios (☎ 81-8944; fax 81-4014; Bolognesi 720; s/d US$13/18, P) This lovely colonial building is about 700m from the center. There is a restaurant, bar and a grassy garden where food can be served. Rooms vary in size and in amenities (views, balconies, telephone) but all have beautiful furniture, cable TV and hot showers.

Ayacucho Hotel Plaza (☎ 81-2202, 81-4467, 81-4461; fax 81-2314; 9 de Diciembre 184; s/d US$46/62) Considered the best in town, it's a nice-looking colonial building, but the rooms are plain and no more than adequate; the nicest have balconies, some with plaza views. The restaurant is just OK.

Other recommendations are:

Hotel Santa María (☎ /fax 81-4988; Arequipa 320; s/d US$14.50/17.50) This comfortable new hotel provides the usual amenities.

Ciudadela Warpa Picchu (☎ 81-5191, 81-9483; verbist@terra.com.pe; s/d US$30/40; P ♨) Five rooms, 6km out of town, with city views, breakfast included.

Eating

Restaurants within two blocks of the Plaza de Armas tend to be aimed at tourists and are slightly pricey, though not exorbitant (there are no fancy or expensive restaurants in Ayacucho). Regional specialities include *puca picante*, a potato and beef stew in a spicy red peanut and pepper sauce, served over rice, *patachi* a wheat soup with various beans, dehydrated potatoes and lamb or beef, and *mondongo*, a corn soup cooked with pork or beef, red peppers and fresh mint. Chicharrones and cuy are also popular; vegetarianism isn't big here.

El Niño (☎ 81-4537, 81-9030; 9 de Diciembre 205; mains US$2.80-6; ☾ 11am-2pm & 5-11pm) In a colonial mansion with a nice patio containing tables overlooking a garden, El Niño specializes in grills and has a variety of Peruvian food. Service is good. A local tip is that seafood arrives from the coast on Saturday, so take advantage of its fish dishes during the weekend.

Urpicha (☎ 81-3905; Londres 272; mains average US$4; ☾ 11am-8pm) This is a homey place, with tables in a flower-filled patio, familial attention, and an authentic menu of traditional dishes, including cuy and the ones listed earlier. The neighborhood isn't great, so take a cab after dark.

Wallpa Suwa (☎ 81-2006; G de la Vega 240; mains US$2-5; ☾ 6-11pm Mon-Sat) This is an upscale and locally popular chicken restaurant, with a quarter chicken and fries starting at US$2, and various other meat plates available. *Wallpa Suwa* is Quechua for 'chicken thief' – this might lead to some interesting conversations with the locals.

Restaurant Los Alamos (☎ 81-2782; Cuzco 215; mains average US$3; ☾ 7am-10pm) In an attractive patio within the hotel of the same name, though operated as a separate entity, this restaurant has good service and a long menu of Peruvian selections and a few vegetarian plates; it may have musicians in the evening.

La Casona (☎ 81-2733; Bellido 463; mains US$2-6; ☾ 7am-10:30pm) This popular restaurant has been recommended by several travelers for its big portions. It focuses on Peruvian food and occasionally has regional specialities. This place also may have musicians, especially on weekend nights.

Pizzería Italiana (☎ 81-7574; Bellido 490; pizzas US$4-8; ☾ 4:30pm-11:30pm) The wood-burning oven makes this a very cozy place on cold nights; musicians may wander in and the pizza is excellent.

Chifa Tay-Pa (☎ 81-5134; M Cáceres 1131; mains average US$2; ☾ 5-11pm) Good-value Chinese food with some vegetarian options.

The 400 block of San Martín has several decent inexpensive places, including:

Cámara de Comercio (☎ 81-4191; San Martín 432; mains US$2-4; ☾ 9am-10pm) Serves Peruvian food.

La Tradición (☎ 81-2595; San Martín 406; menús US$1.50; ☾ 8am-3pm Mon-Sat) Locals flock here for good cheap set lunches.

Mia Pizza (☎ 81-5407; San Martín 420; pizzas US$2.50-7; ☾ 5-11pm) Another good pizzería with pasta as well.

Entertainment

Outside of Semana Santa, this is a quiet town, but there is a university, so you'll find a few bars to dance or hang out in, mostly favored by students. The popular **Los Balcones** (2nd fl, Asamblea 187) has occasional live Andean bands (US$1 cover) and a variety of recorded Andean, Latin, reggae and Western rock music to dance to. Its balconies offer a less-loud environment for conversation. **Taberna Magía Negra** (9 de Diciembre 293) is a bar/gallery with good local art, beer and pizza. **La Nueva Ley** (Cáceres 1147) does disco and salsa dancing.

Centro Turístico Cultural San Cristobal (28 de Julio 178) is a remodeled colonial building transformed into a hip little mall. Here, you'll find bars, restaurants and coffee shops, along with art galleries, craft stores and flower stands. A nice place to hang during the day.

There are a few *peñas* on weekends (as usual, they start late, go until the wee hours and feature Peruvian music). It's best to ask locally about these.

Shopping

Ayacucho is famous as a craft center, and a visit to the Museo de Arte Popular will give you an idea of local products. The tourist office can recommend local artisans who will welcome you to their workshops. The Santa Ana barrio is particularly well known. The area around the Plazuela Santa Ana has various workshops, including that of the Sulca family, who has been weaving here for three generations. There is also a craft market on Independencia and Quinua, open during the day.

Getting There & Away

AIR

The airport is 4km from the town center. Taxis charge under US$2.

Aero Continente (☎ 81-3177; fax 81-7504; 9 de Diciembre 160) has a 5:50am flight from Lima on Monday, Wednesday, Friday and Saturday, returning to Lima at 6:45am.

AeroCóndor (☎ 81-2418; ☎ /fax 81-3060; 9 de Diciembre 123) has a 6am flight from Lima on Tuesday, Wednesday, Thursday and Sunday, continuing to Andahuaylas at 7:20am and returning to Lima at 8:45am. The Andahuaylas leg may be canceled if there are not enough passengers.

LC Busre (Lima 178) has a daily 6:15am flight from Lima, returning at 7:35am.

Flight times and airlines change often. There is no flight between Ayacucho and Cuzco.

BUS

At the time of writing, a new Terminal Terrestre was being constructed next to the airport. The offices listed here may all move there.

If you travel by the poor, unpaved roads from Abancay or Huancayo, be prepared for long delays, especially during the rainy season (the worst months for this are February to April). The route from Lima via Pisco to Ayacucho is paved and fast. All routes are spectacular, but unfortunately, many buses travel overnight.

Coming up from the coast, the road climbs an incredible series of hairpin bends to Castrovirreyna, a small mountain town with basic restaurants where buses may stop for meals. Beyond Castrovirreyna, the road reaches an altitude of about 4750m at Abra Apacheta as it passes blue, green and turquoise Andean lakes. The road flirts with the snowline for over an hour and offers dramatic views of high Andean scenery and snowcaps. Bring warm clothes if traveling at night. Finally, the road begins its descent toward Ayacucho, and the countryside becomes greener as forests of the dwarf *Polylepis* trees appear.

For Lima (US$6 to US$18, nine hours), **Cruz del Sur** (☎ 81-2813; M Cáceres 1264) has the most expensive departure at 9:30pm. Cheaper buses leave with **Ormeño** (☎ 81-2495; Libertad 257) at 7:30am and 9:30pm; Ormeño also goes to Ica at 9pm. **Empresa Molina** (☎ 81-2984; 9 de Diciembre 459) has five daily buses to Lima and 7am, 8pm departures to Huancayo (US$7.30, 10 hours). **Turismo Libertadores** (☎ 81-3614; Tres Mascaras 493) has two night buses to Lima. Other companies to try for Lima are **Civa** (☎ 81-9948; M Cáceres 1242), **Rey Bus** (☎ 81-9413; Pje Cáceres 166) and **Expreso Wari** (☎ 89-1686; Pje Cáceres 171).

Expreso Wari also goes to Cuzco (US$14, 24 hours) at 4:30am. Other Cuzco departures are with **Expreso Turismo Los Chancas** (☎ 81-2391; Pje Cáceres 150) at 6:30am and 7pm. It's a rough trip and the journey can be broken at Andahuaylas (US$6, about 10 hours).

For Huancavelica, try **Turismo Nacional** (☎ 81-5405; M Cáceres 884).

Note that these companies change their routes and services frequently. There are other possibilities if you ask around, especially during times of high demand.

Buses to Cangallo and Vischongo (US$2.50, four hours) leave from the Puente Nuevo area, which is the bridge on Castilla over the Río Alameda. Departures are normally in the morning. Buses leave for Vilcashuamán (five hours) at 5am, 6am, 7am, 8am and 9am.

Pickup trucks and buses go to many local villages, including Quinua (US$0.80, one hour), and to the Wari ruins, departing from the Paradero Magdalena at the traffic circle at the east end of M Cáceres.

WARI RUINS & QUINUA

An attractive 37km road climbs about 550m to Quinua, 3300m above sea level. After about 20km, you will pass the extensive **Wari ruins** (admission including small museum US$0.60;

(⊗ 8am-5:30pm) sprawling for several kilometers along the roadside. The five main sectors of the ruins are marked by road signs; the upper sites are in rather bizarre forests of *Opuntia* cacti. If you visit, don't leave the site too late to look for onward or return transport – vehicles can get hopelessly full in the afternoon. Note that you have to pay the full fare to Quinua and remind the driver to drop you off at the ruins.

The ruins have not been well restored and the most interesting visits are with a guide from Ayacucho. Agencies charge about US$8 per person for a one-day tour combined with Quinua (you need to speak Spanish).

Wari is built on a hill, and as the road from Ayacucho climbs through it, there are reasonable views. The road climbs beyond Wari until it reaches the pretty village of **Quinua**; buses usually stop at the plaza. Steps from the left-hand side of the plaza, as you arrive from Ayacucho, lead up to the village church. The church is on an old-fashioned cobblestone plaza, and a small **museum** (admission US$1; ⊗ 10am-4:30pm) nearby displays various relics from the major independence battle fought in this area. It's of little interest however, unless you are particularly fascinated by the battle fought here. Beside the museum, you can see the room where the Spanish Royalist troops signed their surrender, leading to the end of colonialism in Peru.

To reach the battlefield, turn left behind the church and head out of the village along Jirón Sucre, which, after a walk of about 10 minutes, rejoins the main road. As you walk, notice the red-tiled roofs elaborately decorated with ceramic model churches. Quinua is famous as a handicraft center and these model churches are especially typical of the area. Local stores sell these and other crafts.

The **white obelisk**, which is intermittently visible for several kilometers as you approach Quinua, now lies a few minutes' walk in front of you (bus drivers may drive here if there is enough demand). The impressive monument is 40m high and features carvings commemorating the Battle of Ayacucho, fought here on 9 December 1824. The walk and views from Quinua are pleasant. The whole area is protected as the 300-hectare **Santuario Histórico Pampas de Ayacucho**.

There are no accommodations in Quinua, but simple local meals are available. There is a small market on Sunday.

VILCASHUAMÁN & VISCHONGO

Vilcashuamán ('sacred falcon') was considered the geographical center of the Inca Empire. Here, the Inca road between Cuzco and the coast crossed the road running the length of the Andes. Little remains of the city's earlier magnificence; Vilcashuamán has fallen prey to looters, and many of its blocks have been used to build more modern buildings. The once-magnificent Temple of the Sun now has a church on top of it! The only structure still in a reasonable state of repair is a five-tiered pyramid, called an *usnu*, topped by a huge double throne carved from stone and used by the Incas.

To get there, take a vehicle from Ayacucho to Vischongo (about 110km by rough but scenic road). From here, it's about 45 minutes by car, or almost two hours uphill on foot, to Vilcashuamán, where there are basic accommodations, such as **Hostal El Pirámide** and **Hostal Fortaleza** (both s/d US$2/4).

From Vischongo, you can also walk about an hour to an **Intihuatana ruin** (US$0.80), where there are reportedly **thermal baths**. If coming from Ayacucho, the turn-off to Intihuatana is about 2km before the village, and then another 2km on a trail. You can also walk to a *Puya raimondii* **forest** (see the Huaraz & the Cordillera Blanca chapter for a description of this plant p326), which is about an hour away by foot.

If you don't want to spend the night, you can do a day tour with an agency from Ayacucho for about US$20 per person. Independent travelers will find buses returning to Ayacucho in the afternoon; ask for times.

NORTH OF LA OROYA

The road north of La Oroya passes through the highland towns of Junín, Cerro de Pasco, Huánuco and Tingo María, ending up at the important jungle town of Pucallpa.

JUNÍN AREA

☎ 064 / elevation 4125m

An important independence battle was fought at the nearby Pampa of Junín, just south of Junín, 55km due north of La Oroya. This is now preserved as the 2500-hectare **Santuario Histórico Chacamarca**, where there is a monument, 2km off the main road.

At the south end of Junín village is a modern **Villa Artesanal** (craft market). Stay at the cold-water **Hostal San Cristobal** (☎ 34-4215; Manuel Prado 255; s/d US$2.80/4) and eat at restaurants around the **Plaza de Libertad**.

About 10km beyond the village is the interesting **Lago de Junín**, which, at about 30km long and 14km wide, is Peru's largest lake after Titicaca. Over 4000m above sea level, it is the highest lake of its size in the Americas. Lago de Junín is known for its birdlife, and some authorities claim that 1 million birds live on the lake or its shores at any one time. It is a little-visited area and a potential destination for anyone interested in seeing a variety of the water and shore birds of the high Andes. The lake and its immediate surroundings are part of the 53,000-hectare **Reserva Nacional Junín**. Visit by taking a colectivo 5km north to the hamlet of **Huayre**, from where a 1.5km path leads to the lake.

A further 5km from Huayre brings you to the village of **Carhuamayo**, where there are basic restaurants and the cold-water **Residencial Patricia** (Tarapacá 862; s/d US$2/4).

The wide, high plain in this area is bleak, windswept and very cold, so be prepared with warm, windproof clothing. There are several villages along the road and buses stop quite often. Between these settlements, herds of llama, alpaca and sheep are seen.

CERRO DE PASCO

☎ 063 / pop 62,000 / elevation 4333m
Cerro de Pasco is the highest city of its size in the world, the capital of the Department of Pasco and rather a miserable place, though the inhabitants are friendly. The altitude makes the town bitterly cold at night, and its main reason for existence is mining.

Change your money at **BCP** (☎ 72-2123; Daniel Carrión 12). Emergency health care is available at **Clínica Gonzales** (☎ 72-1515; Daniel Carrión 99).

Southwest of Cerro de Pasco

A poor and infrequently used road goes southwest of Cerro de Pasco to Lima. West of Lago de Junín, the road goes close to the village of Huayllay and nearby the 6815-hectare **Santuario Nacional Huayllay**, known for its strange geological formations. Several hours further southwest is the small town of **Canta**, which has a basic hotel and restaurant and is a few kilometers away from the pre-Columbian ruins of **Cantamarca**, which can be visited on foot.

Sleeping

The friendly **Hotel El Viajero** (☎ 72-2172; s/d US$3.50/5), on the Plaza de Armas, has clean rooms and shared bathrooms with hot water in the mornings. Nearby, the basic **Hotel Santa Rosa** (☎ 72-2120) is similar.

Hostal Arenales (☎ 72-3088; Arenales 162; s/d US$4/6) is near the bus terminal. Clean rooms have hot showers and TV. **Villa Minera** (☎ 72-3073; Angamos at Parque Universitario; s/d US$7.25/10; **P**), in the suburbs, has rooms with hot water showers, heating and cable TV. Similar facilities are offered at **Hostal Rubi** (☎ 72-1011; Antonio Martínez 306; s/d US$6/13; **P**)

Getting There & Away

The bus terminal, five blocks south of the Plaza de Armas, has buses to Huánuco (US$2, three hours), Huancayo (US$3.50, five hours), Lima (US$5, eight hours) and La Oroya (US$2, 2½ hours). Faster colectivos from the plaza or bus terminal charge US$4.50 to both Huánuco and Tarma.

In 2003 three holiday trains were scheduled to arrive from Lima (see Lima p83 and Huancayo p237 for details).

HUÁNUCO

☎ 062 / pop 153,000 / elevation 1894m
Huánuco is 105km north of Cerro de Pasco and provides welcome relief for *soroche* sufferers. It lies on the upper reaches of the Río Huallaga, the major tributary of the Río Marañón before it becomes the Amazon. Huánuco is the capital of its department and the site of one of Peru's oldest Andean archaeological sites: the Temple of Kotosh (also known as the Temple of the Crossed Hands). The town has a museum and a pleasant, shady Plaza de Armas. Although Huánuco dates from 1541, little is left of its colonial buildings. Inhabitants boast that the perfect elevation and location gives Huánuco the best climate in Peru.

About 25km south of Huánuco the road goes through the village of **Ambo**, noted for its *aguardiente* distilleries. This locally

CENTRAL HIGHLANDS

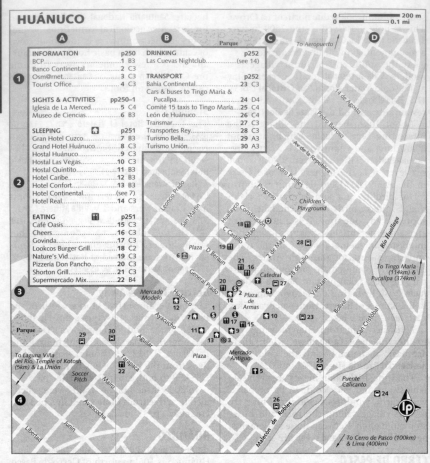

HUÁNUCO

0 ————— 200 m
0 ————— 0.1 mi

To Aeropuerto

To Tingo María (114km) & Pucallpa (374km)

To Laguna Viña del Río, Temple of Kotosh (5km) & La Unión

Soccer Pitch

To Cerro de Pasco (100km) & Lima (400km)

---

popular liquor is made from sugar cane, which can be seen growing nearby. Sometimes the bus stops and passengers can buy a couple of liters.

Information

The **tourist office** (☎ 51-2980; General Prado 718; ⏲ 8am-1:30pm & 4-6pm Mon-Fri) has brochures. **Osm@arnet** (Huánuco 740) has Internet access. There's a **BCP** (☎ 51-2213; 2 de Mayo 1005) with a Visa ATM and a **Banco Continental** (☎ 51-3348; 2 de Mayo 1137).

Museo de Ciencias

Small but well organized, with labeled exhibits, this **museum** (☎ 51-8104; General Prado 495; admission US$0.30; ⏲ 9am-noon & 3-6pm Mon-Sat,

10am-1pm Sun) is worth a peek. The museum director, Señor Néstor Wenzel, is dedicated and enthusiastic, and delights in showing visitors around. He loves to talk to foreigners and has flags and 'welcome' signs in many languages decorating the entrance lobby. Exhibits are mainly stuffed Peruvian animals, but there are also a few ceramic and archaeological pieces.

The Temple of Kotosh

This archaeological **site** (adult/student including guide US$0.90/0.50; ⏲ 9am-3pm) is also known as the Temple of the Crossed Hands because of the lifesize, mud molding of a pair of crossed hands, which is the site's highlight. The molding dates to about 2000 BC and is now at Lima's Archaeological Museum; a replica remains.

Little is known about Kotosh, one of the most ancient of Andean cultures. The temple site is not in great shape, but is easily visited by taxi (US$4.50, including a 30-minute wait and return) or the bus to La Unión. The site is about 5km west of town off the road to La Unión.

Sleeping

BUDGET

Hostal Huánuco (☎ 51-2050; Huánuco 777; s US$5.80; s/d with shower US$7.30/8.80) This traditional mansion with old-fashioned, tiled floors, a 2nd-floor terrace overlooking a lush garden, and hall walls covered with art and old newspaper clippings, simply exudes character. Rooms are worn and contain old furniture, but the beds are comfortable. Showers are hot but can take up to an hour to warm up, so ask in advance. The door is usually locked for security; ring that bell and travel back a century.

Gran Hotel Cuzco (☎ 51-3578; fax 51-4360; Huánuco 616; s/d US$5.80/11.50; P) This five-story old hotel isn't bad and has clean, bare but good-sized rooms with hot showers and cable TV. Some of the upper-story rooms don't have hot water and TV; they go for half the price. The hotel has a cafeteria, laundry service and is popular with Peruvian businesspeople.

Hotel Caribe (☎ 51-3645; fax 51-3753; Huánuco 546; s/d US$2/3, with shower US$3/4.50) Showers are cold, cable TV costs an extra US$1.50 and there's a karaoke café downstairs. This is among the best-run of several basic, budget hotels near the market.

Hostal Las Vegas (☎ /fax 51-2315; 28 de Julio 934; s/d US$7.30/10.30) This basic but clean and popular hotel is on the plaza. Although rooms don't have plaza views, they do have a TV. Hot water in the showers is available morning and evening.

Other recommendations:

Hotel Confort (☎ 51-7880; Huánuco 736; s/d US$5.80/ 11.50) Bland, small but spotless rooms with electric showers and cable TV.

Hostal Quintito (☎ 51-2691; 2 de Mayo 987; s/d US$7.30/10) Secure hotel with spacious rooms but tiny bathrooms.

Hotel Continental (☎ 51-9898; Huánuco 602; s/d US$7.30/11.50) Spartan rooms have electric showers and firm mattresses.

MID-RANGE

Hotel Real (☎ 51-2973, 51-1777; fax 51-2765; realhotel@terra.com.pe; 2 de Mayo 1125; s/d US$20/26; P) On the Plaza de Armas, this fairly comfortable, modern hotel has unattractive scuffed, bare hallways leading to large rooms with good beds, cable TV and phone. It has a sauna, restaurant and a good 24-hour café.

Grand Hotel Huánuco (☎ 51-4222, ☎ /fax 51-2410; hotel.huanuco@terra.com.pe; D Beraún 775; s/d US$32/43; P) Also on the Plaza de Armas, this is the grand dame of Huánuco hotels. Its public areas are pleasant and the hotel has character. A sauna, Jacuzzi, restaurant and bar are on the premises. Rooms have phones and cable TV.

Eating

The 24-hour restaurant at Hotel Real is an excellent choice for midnight munchies or pre-dawn breakfasts.

Cheers (☎ 51-4666; 2 de Mayo 1201; mains US$2-3; 11am-midnight) On the plaza, neon-bright, cheaply chic, this place draws the crowds for its inexpensive chicken and Peruvian dishes.

Shorton Grill (☎ 51-2829; D Beraún 685; mains US$2-3; 11am-midnight) Just off the plaza, this grilled chicken restaurant is thinly disguised as a grill; chicken, chips and beer is where this place is at, and it's good.

Govinda (☎ 52-5683; 2 de Mayo 1044; plates US$1-2; 7am-9:30pm Mon-Sat, 7am-3pm Sun) This Hare Krishna–run restaurant serves excellent vegetarian meals.

Pizzeria Don Pancho (☎ 51-6906; Prado 645; meals US$3; 6-11pm Mon-Sat) The town's best pizza and pasta joint is hopping with Huanúqueños.

Lookcos Burger Grill (☎ 51-2460; Abtao 1021; meals US$1-2; 6pm-midnight) It's a squeaky-clean, white restaurant (with B&W photos on the wall) that serves burgers and sandwiches. Popular with a young student crowd.

Other recommendations:

Nature's Vid (☎ 51-6053; Abtao 951; meals US$1-2; 7am-9pm) Soya burgers and local art on the wall.

Cafe Oasis (28 de Julio; mains US$1-2.50; 9am-7pm) Near Prado, this place serves good, cheap, Peruvian food.

Supermercado Mix (☎ 51-1114; Tarapacá 550) For self-catering.

Entertainment

Cheers Karaoke (see Eating earlier) If you're cool with karaoke, stop by this restaurant on a Friday or Saturday night to catch a budding Peruvian star – or not!

Las Cuevas (see Hotel Real; ☺ 8am-4pm) A small door at the side of the hotel leads down into a largish dance club with fairly standard Latin and top 40 recorded music. The name is for the pseudo caves where couples kiss and friends raise a glass – a bit loud to talk. Locals troop in at weekends.

La Granja Also known as La Nueva Granja, this nightclub on the outskirts of town advertises local bands. Cab drivers know it.

Getting There & Away

AIR

Flight service is irregular and subject to change. Currently, LC Busre flies from Lima on Tuesday, Thursday and Saturday mornings only. The airport is 8km from town.

BUS

Buses go to Lima (US$6 to US$10, eight hours), Pucallpa (US$6, nine hours), La Merced (US$5.50, six hours), Huancayo (US$5, six hours), La Unión (US$3, five hours) and Tantamayo (US$6, eight hours) with companies all over town. Among the best are:

León de Huánuco (☎ 51-1489, 51-2996; Robles 821) To Lima at 10am, 8:30pm and 9:30pm; La Merced at 8pm; Pucallpa 7:30pm.

Bahía Continental (☎ 51-9999; Valdizán 718) Buscama to Lima at 10pm for US$10.

Transportes Rey (☎ 51-3623; 28 de Julio 1215) Lima 8:30am, 9pm and 9:30pm; Huancayo 10:15pm.

Transmar (28 de Julio 1067) Pucallpa aty 6am.

Turismo Unión (☎ 52-6308; Tarapaca 449) La Unión at 7am.

Turismo Bella (San Martín 571) Tantamayo at 6:30am.

Other companies near Turismo Unión and Turismo Bella also go west towards villages on the eastern side of the Cordillera Blanca; rough roads, poor buses.

For Tingo María (US$2, 3½ hours), take a Pucallpa–bound bus or a colectivo taxi (US$3.50) with **Comite 15** (☎ 51-8346) at General Prado near the river. There are more colectivo taxis for Tingo María on the other side of the river, or wait here for a passing bus.

For Cerro de Pasco, minibuses (US$2, three hours) or colectivo taxis (US$4.50) leave from a bus stop about 3km southwest of town. *Mototaxis* charge US$0.30.

LA UNIÓN

This remote village is between Huánuco and Huaraz via rough roads. About a three-hour walk (one way) from La Unión are the extensive and impressive Inca ruins of **Huánuco Viejo** (admission US$1.50; ☺ 7am-5pm). Take the path from behind the market heading toward a cross up on a hill. Vehicles can also be found to take you almost to the site, which is worth a visit.

La Unión lacks banks, has a few public but no listed phones, several simple eateries and two or three basic hotels. **Hostal Picaflor** (2 de Mayo 840; s/d US$5.50/9) has shared hot showers.

Buses leaves the plaza early in the day for Lima via Chiquián.

TANTAMAYO

This small, remote village, in the mountains north of La Unión, has several ruins within a few hours' walk. Guides can be hired. Ask at one of the simple hotels.

TINGO MARÍA

☎ 062 / pop 15,000 / elevation 649m

The 129km road north from Huánuco climbs over a 3000m pass before dropping steadily to the town of Tingo María, which lies in the *ceja de la selva* (eyebrow of the jungle) as the lush, tropical slopes of the eastern Andes are called. It is surrounded by mountains, waterfalls and caves, and is hot and humid most of the year.

Tingo María is a thriving market town, though it includes coca (for the production of cocaine) and, to a lesser extent, marijuana among its local products, so the town has developed a rather unsavory atmosphere. It is definitely not a good place to buy drugs!

Nevertheless, the town center is no more dangerous than any other city. The dangerous area is the Río Huallaga valley north of Tingo María and should be avoided. Remember that growing coca is not necessarily illegal, and coca leaves are legally sold for chewing or making *maté* in most highland towns. It is the mashing of coca into *pasta básica* for use in cocaine production that is illegal. Local authorities are encouraging the production of other tropical crops, notably cocoa. Bus travel on the Huánuco–Tingo María–Pucallpa route is safe, particularly during the day.

TINGO MARÍA

INFORMATION	p253
BCP...1 B3	
Banco Continental..........................2 B1	
Hospital..3 C3	
Rock@s Internet..............................4 B3	
Tourist Office...................................5 B1	

SIGHTS & ACTIVITIES	p253
Jardín Botánico...............................6 C4	
Municipalidad..................................7 B1	

SLEEPING	p254
Hospedaje La Cabaña......................8 B1	
Hostal Cuzco....................................9 B1	
Hostal Viena..................................10 B2	
Hotel Las Palmeras.......................11 B3	
Hotel Marco Antonio....................12 B2	
Hotel Nueva York..........................13 B1	
Hotel Palacio.................................14 B3	
Hotel Royal....................................15 B3	

EATING	p254
El Mango.......................................16 B1	
Simon's..17 B2	
Trijalo..18 B1	

TRANSPORT	p255
León de Huánuco..........................19 B4	
Star Up...20 B3	
Tocache Express............................21 B3	
TransInter...............................(see 19)	
Transmar.......................................22 B4	
Transportes Cueva del Pavo.........23 B3	
Transportes Rey............................24 B3	
Turismo Ucayali............................25 B3	

Information

The **tourist office** (☎ 56-2351; Alameda Perú 525) is on Plaza Leoncido Prado.

The main post office is on Plaza Leoncido Prado. **Rock@as Internet** (Tito Jaime 101) is open til late.

There's a **hospital** (☎ 56-2017/8/9; Ucayali 114) a block east of Alameda Perú.

US cash can be changed at **Banco Continental** (☎ 56-2141; A Raimondi 543) and **BCP** (☎ 56-2111; A Raimondi 249), which has a Visa ATM and may change traveler's checks.

For a tour guide, try **Segundo Cordova** (☎ 56-2030, 969-5383) who has a booth next to the León de Huánuco bus terminal, or ask at the tourist office. He knows the waterfalls, lakes and caves of the area well.

Universidad Nacional Agraria de la Selva (UNAS)

The university (☎ 56-2341) runs a **jardín botánico** (botanical garden; admission free; ⏰ 8am-2pm Mon-Fri, 8-11am Sat), which, though rather run-down and overgrown, has labels on some of the plants with useful information. The garden is at the south end of Alameda Perú and you may need to yell for the gatekeeper.

The university itself, 4km south of town, has a small **Museo Zoológico** (Zoological Museum) with a collection of living and mounted animals from around the region.

Parque Nacional Tingo María

This 18,000-hectare park lies on the south side of town around the mouth of the Río

Monzón, a tributary of the Río Huallaga. Within the park is the **Bella Dormiente** (Sleeping Beauty), a hill overlooking the town. From some angles, the hill looks like a reclining woman.

Also in the park is **La Cueva de las Lechuzas** (the Cave of the Owls), which, despite its name, is known for the colony of oilbirds that lives inside. In addition, there are stalactites and stalagmites, bats, parrots and other birds around the cave entrance, but the oilbirds are the main attraction.

The caves are about 6km away near the village of Monzón; taxis can take you. There is a US$1.50 national-park fee and guides to show you around. Locals say the best time to visit is in the morning, when sunlight shines into the mouth of the cave, though dusk, when the oilbirds emerge, may also be good. Bring a flashlight and wear shoes you don't mind getting covered in bat and bird droppings.

Sleeping

Hotels are of a generally low standard with little to recommend them except their price. Showers are cold unless stated otherwise.

BUDGET

Hotel Royal (☎ 56-2166; fax 56-2167; Tito Jaime 214; s/d from US$4.50/7.30; P) All rooms have showers; an extra US$3 buys you hot water and cable TV. This well-kept property with clean blue walls, small courtyard and plenty of plants is a good budget choice.

Hotel Palacio (☎ 56-2319, 56-2055; www.surf.to /palacio; A Raimondi 158; s/d US$4.50/7.30, with shower US$7.30/12) It looks well run and clean, with rooms surrounding a plant-filled courtyard with caged parrots. Although the rooms are a bit spartan, they have fans and TV; the staff claim to be installing air-conditioning soon. A café is on the premises. Check out its hilariously garbled retro website.

Hotel Nueva York (☎ /fax 56-2406; Alameda Perú 553; s/d from US$7/10) Spacious rooms have fans and showers hooked up to rooftop tanks so water gets a bit warmer in the afternoon. For an extra US$3 per room, cable TV and breakfast are included. The rooms are set back from the road and quiet.

Other recommendations:

Hostal Cuzco (☎ 56-2095; A Raimondi 671; s/d US$2/3.50). Shared showers; popular with Peruvians and often full.

Hospedaje La Cabaña (☎ 56-2178; A Raimondi 634; s/d US$2/3.50) Family run and reasonably clean.

Hostal Viena (☎ 56-2194; Lamas 254; s/d US$2.75/ 4.59, with shower US$4.50/5.75) Large, clean and reasonable value though rooms vary in quality.

Hotel Marco Antonio (☎ 56-2201; Monzón 364; s/d US$5/7) Rooms are clean, quiet, have showers but lack fans.

Hotel Las Palmeras (☎ 56-1338; Callao 283; s/d US$3.50/5, with shower US$5.80/7.30) Tiled, cool, clean and with fans, cable TV US$1.50.

MID-RANGE

Villa Jennifer (☎ 969-5059; villajennifer53@hotmail .com; Km 3.4 Castillo Grande; s/d US$14/22; P 🖳) North of the airport, this farm and lodge is run by a Danish/Peruvian couple. Rooms have fans and comfortable beds; hot showers are shared. Rates include a country-style breakfast; lunch and dinner is available on request. The farm has hammocks, barbecue area and games; the surrounding rainforest can be explored and the helpful owners can arrange tours.

Madera Verde Hotel (☎ /fax 56-1800, 56-2047; maverde@terra.com.pe; s/d US$50/60; P 🖳) Just over 1km south of town. Walk-in rates can be discounted, and continental breakfast is included. The rooms are good sized, have bathrooms and hot water, TV and minibar. Quadruple bungalows are also available. The hotel is set in pleasant gardens with a playground and simple but adequate restaurant and bar.

Eating

Hotel Nueva York and Hotel Marco Antonio have OK restaurants.

El Mango (☎ 56-1671, 56-3454; Lamas 232; 🕥 8am-3pm, Mon-Sat, 7-11pm daily; sandwiches and breakfasts US$1-2; mains US$2.50-5.50) A surprising garden restaurant; good food, friendly service and a place to linger.

Simon's (🕥 7am-3pm & 6-10pm; mains US$2-3) On Tito Jaime, between José Prado and Lamas, this hot restaurant has few fans and little breeze. Still, if you can sweat it, the food is good and varied. Locals say it's the best value in town. You can get most Peruvian dishes here, and the staff are helpful. Order a big beer, and it'll be a 1L bottle.

Trijalo (☎ 56-1638; Tito Jaime 540; mains US$2.25-4.25; 🕥 6-11pm) Tingo María's best pizza and pasta restaurant will deliver if you can't tear yourself away from your hotel room.

Getting There & Away

AIR
The airport is 1.5km from town on the west side of the Río Huallaga. Carriers and schedules change frequently. **Star Up** (☎ 56-2250; Raimondi 210) flies to Lima on Saturday. At the airport you can find light aircraft flying to other nearby towns.

BUS
Schedules change frequently. As a general rule, avoid night travel and be careful in the Río Huallaga region due north of Tingo María.

Buses to Lima (US$7 to US$12, 12 hours) are operated by **León de Huánuco** (☎ 56-2030),

Transmar (☎ 56-3076), **Transportes Rey** (☎ 56-2565) and TransInter. Buses usually leave at 7am or 7pm. Some of these go to Pucallpa (US$5, eight hours). Faster service to Pucallpa is with Turismo Ucayali, which has colectivo cars (US$12). The journey from Tingo María to Pucallpa is described under Pucallpa (p378) in the Amazon Basin chapter.

Tocache Express (☎ 56-3324) has cars to Tocache (US$8.50, four hours) from where trucks continue another five hours on to Juanjui.

Transportes Cueva del Pavos is a signed stop with *mototaxis* to the cueva.

North Coast

Few travelers get to appreciate this area of Peru, because most choose to visit the Inca sites and Lake Titicaca to the south. They don't know what they are missing! The North Coast is home to huge and awe-inspiring pre-Inca sites; vast adobe cities and towering pyramids will introduce you to Chimu and Moche cultures, among many others, and the sites are uncrowded and fascinating.

This area is part of the great South American coastal desert. On the drive north from Lima, you pass huge, rolling sand dunes, dizzying cliffs, some oases of farmland and busy fishing villages, as well as some of Peru's largest and most historic cities. The coast is constantly caressed by surf, including some classic waves that international surfers seek out. And the further north you go, the better the weather gets, as Lima's *garúa* (coastal fog) gives way to increasingly longer months of sunshine, which means more beach time. Slowly traveling the north coast gets you away from the gringo scene and allows greater involvement with the friendly local people who wonder 'How come it took you so long to find us?'

HIGHLIGHTS

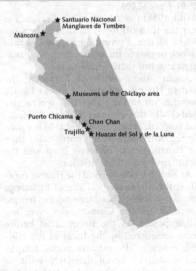

■ **Archaeological Adventures**

Admiring mind-boggling Chan Chan (p269) and the pyramids of Huacas del Sol y de la Luna (p274)

■ **Colonial Architecture & Culture**

Checking out the mansions, pacing horses and costumed *marinera* dancers of Trujillo (p262)

■ **Marvelous Museums**

Delighting in the world-class museums of the Chiclayo area (p284–5)

■ **Beach Bumming**

Chilling out at the year-round international scene at Máncora (p294) or watching the locals on *totora* (reed) canoes in Huanchaco (p275)

■ **Wildlife Watching**

Touring around the mangroves and crocs near Tumbes (p301)

■ **Supreme Surfing**

Gliding along the world's longest left at Puerto Chicama (p277)

RESERVA NACIONAL LOMAS DE LACHAY

Off the Panamericana north of Lima between Km105 and Km106, a marked dirt road heads 4km east to Lomas de Lachay, a 5070-hectare natural reserve. Lomas de Lachay is a hill that seems to gain most of its moisture from the coastal mists, creating a unique microenvironment of dwarf forest and small animals and birds. There are camping and picnicking areas, pit toilets and trails. Admission is US$1.50. There are no buses, so you have to hire a vehicle or walk from the Panamericana.

HUACHO & HUAURA

The small town of Huacho is almost 150km north of Lima at the mouth of the Río Huaura. Across the river is the village of Huaura, where San Martín proclaimed Peru's independence. Anyone can show you the building, where there is an inconsequential **museum** (admission US$0.90) with a Spanish-speaking guide who'll show you the balcony, or you can see it from outside for free.

BARRANCA & PARAMONGA

☎ 01 / pop 46,000

About 195km north of Lima, Barranca is near the turn-off for Huaraz and the Cordillera Blanca. Everything happens within a block or two of the main street, the Panamericana, but there's little to see.

About 10km north of Barranca, the road to Huaraz and the Cordillera Blanca branches off to the right. This spectacular road climbs through cactus-laden cliff faces and is worth seeing in daylight. Many people see little more of the north coast than the Panamericana between Lima and the mountain turn-off at Pativilca.

At Km210, 4km beyond the Huaraz turn-off, is the archaeological site of **Paramonga** (admission US$0.90). This huge adobe temple was built by the Chimu, who were the ruling power on the north coast before being conquered by the Incas in the mid-15th century. The massive adobe temple, surrounded by seven defensive walls, is clearly visible on the right-hand side of the Panamericana coming from Lima and is worth a visit. (For more details on the Chimu see the boxed text on p270.) Local buses traveling between Barranca and the

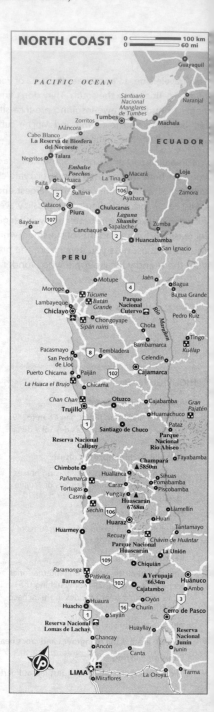

port of Paramonga will drop you off 3km from the entrance, or you can take a taxi from Barranca for a few dollars.

Sleeping & Eating

Most hotels are along Barranca's main street. The best is **Hotel Chavín** (☎ 235-2358, 235-2253; fax 235-2480; Gálvez 222; s/d US$15/25), for clean rooms with warm showers. There's a decent restaurant below it. Other places include **Hostal Residencial Continental** (☎ 235-2458; A Ugarte 190), which is clean, secure and a bit cheaper.

CASMA

☎ 043 / pop 35,000

The small town of Casma is 370km north of Lima. The archaeological site of Sechín is about 5km away and is easily reached from Casma. Once an important colonial port that was sacked by various pirates during the 17th century, Casma's importance has declined greatly, and the town was largely destroyed by the earthquake of May 31, 1970. There's not much to do in either the port (11km from town) or the town itself, and most people only come here to visit the Sechín ruins or to travel to Huaraz via the Punta Callán road – a route offering excellent panoramic views of the Cordillera Blanca. Yungay Express occasionally takes this route between Chimbote (via Casma) to Huaraz, but there is no office in Casma.

Information

There's no tourist office, but **Sechín Tours** (☎/fax 71-1421, ☎ 71-2065, 961-9821; Centro Comercial Montecarlo, office 7) gives tourist information and travelers' assistance, as well as arranging local tours. There's a branch of **BCP** (formerly Banco de Crédito; ☎ 71-1314, 71-1471; Bolívar 111) here and an Internet café on the Plaza.

Sechín

This **site** (admission US$1.50; 🕒 8am-5pm) is one of the oldest in Peru (about 1600 BC) and is among the more important and well preserved of the coastal ruins. First excavated in 1937 by the renowned Peruvian archaeologist JC Tello, it has suffered some damage from grave-robbers and natural disasters. The site is 5km southeast of Casma and is easily reached on foot or by taxi; there are good road signs.

The site at Sechín, part of which is thought to have been buried by a landslide, is still being excavated, and only some of the area is open to visitors. This consists of three outside walls of the main temple that are completely covered with bas-relief carvings of warriors and captives being eviscerated. The gruesomely realistic carvings are up to 4m high. The warlike people who built this temple remain a mystery. Inside the main temple are earlier mud structures still being excavated; you can't go in, but there is a model in the small on-site **museum**. The Sechín ruins and museum have a small shady garden and picnic area.

To get to Sechín, head south of Casma on the Panamericana for 3km, then turn left and follow the paved road to Huaraz for an additional 2km to the site. If you're coming from Huaraz, and don't have too much gear, you can visit the ruins en route to Casma.

There are several other early sites in the Sechín area; most of them have not been excavated because of a lack of funds. From the museum, you can see the large, flat-topped hill of **Sechín Alto** in the distance. The nearby fortress of **Chanquillo**, consisting of several towers surrounded by concentric walls, can be visited, but is best appreciated from the air. Aerial photographs are on display at the museum. If you wish to explore more than just Sechín, the museum attendant or the people at Sechín Tours can give directions, and there is a detailed area map in the museum.

The entry ticket to Sechín also allows you to visit the Mochica ruins of **Pañamarca**, 10km inland from the Panamericana on the road to Nepeña (the turn-off is about halfway between Casma and Chimbote). These ruins are badly weathered, but some murals can be seen if you ask the guard. The murals are normally covered up for protection.

Tortugas

This is a small beach resort about 22km northwest of Casma; drivers leave the Panamericana at Km392. There's a decent beach with clean water and pleasant swimming in a bay; high season is January to March.

Tours

Sechín Tours (see earlier) takes groups to Sechín for about US$10 per person (four-person minimum) with an English-speaking guide, or less with a Spanish-speaking guide. Ask about visiting other local sites. The company also rents sand boards (US$2) for sliding down the nearby Manchan dunes (10 minutes away by a mototaxi).

Sleeping & Eating

The best place to stay in Casma is the pleasant **Hotel El Farol** (☎ /fax 71-1064, in Lima 424-0517; Túpac Amaru 450; s/d US$18/26; 🖵 **P**). It's set in a garden, has a simple restaurant and bar, and helpful, friendly staff. There's a useful map in the lobby if you plan to explore some of the ruins in the area. The rooms boast hot showers and cable TV. The hotel also has similarly priced bungalows with hot showers and an ocean view at Tortugas in **Hotel Farol Beach Inn** (☎ 961-9732).

Hotel Los Poncianos (☎ 71-1599, ☎ /fax 71-2123; Panamericana Norte Km376; s/d US$18/30, d with bathtub US$45; 🖵 **P**) Just a block off the main highway and six blocks from the Plaza de Armas, this place is in a quiet spot and has both an Olympic-sized and children's pool in its grounds. There is a restaurant and all rooms boast hot showers, minifridge, cable TV and ceiling fan. The larger doubles with bathtubs have upgraded furnishings.

A popular budget choice is the clean and friendly **Hostal Gregori** (☎ 71-1073, 71-1173; L Ormeño 579; s/d US$4.50/5.75, d with shower US$7.25), which has hot water and TVs on request. A café is attached. **Hostal Selene** (☎ 71-1065; L Ormeño 595; s/d US$4.50/8.50; s/d with shower US$5.75/10; **P**) has friendly management and its large rooms with hot water and cable TV attracts travelers. **Hostal Indoamericano** (☎ 71-1395; Huarmey 132; s/d US$4.50/5.75, d with shower US$7.25) is also clean but the showers are usually tepid unless you request hot water. **Hostal Rebeca** (☎ 71-1143, Huarmey 368; s/d with shower US$7.25/11.50) has hot water and TV in the rooms.

There are no fancy restaurants, but the **Chifa Tío Sam** (☎ 71-1447; Huarmey 138; mains average US$3.50; 🕐 7am-9pm) is one of the better ones.

Getting There & Away

Many bus companies run buses north and south along the Panamericana, but few have offices in Casma. For Trujillo (US$2.50, three hours) or Lima (US$4.50,

five hours), ask where you can flag down a bus as it comes through, and hope for a seat. Buses often stop by the gas station on the Panamericana at the Lima end of town. Small offices along the Panamericana sell a few tickets.

Near the plaza are frequent colectivos taxis to Chimbote (US$1.10, one hour), 50km to the north, where there are better connections.

CHIMBOTE

☎ 043 / pop 300,000

This is the first major town along the north coast from Lima, about 420km north of the capital. Chimbote is Peru's largest fishing port, and millions of tons of fish were caught here in the 1960s. Since then, the industry has declined because of overfishing. Despite this and the 1970 earthquake (which destroyed much of the city), the population has continued to grow dramatically. The town is not a tourist destination, and there's little to do, but Chimbote is a good place to stay overnight if you're heading to Huaraz via the spectacular Cañón del Pato route.

There is no tourist office. The post office is east of the market and several banks can be found on Bolognesi. Internet access is on Aguirre to the south of Pardo.

The modern **Plaza de Armas** is a nice place to sit. The local fiesta of **San Pedro**, patron of fishers, is on June 29, so hotel rooms may be much more expensive around then.

Sleeping

BUDGET

Chimbote offers a large selection of hotels; a few are described here.

Hostal Residencial El Parque (☎ 34-1552, 34-5572; Palacios 309; s/d US$7/11.50) Right on the Plaza de Armas, this secure, small, clean and popular hotel has simple rooms with hot showers and cable TV.

Hostal Antonios (☎ 33-3026; fax 32-5783; Bolognesi 745; s/d 11.50/17.50; **P**) It's a safe place with slightly scruffy, mid-sized rooms, fans, cable TV and reliably hot showers. Some rooms have minifridges. There's a café here.

Hotel Felic (☎ 32-5901, J Pardo 552; s/d US$4.50/7.25, with shower US$6/9.50) This old and funky three-story building is enlivened by a tiny courtyard overflowing with trees. Showers

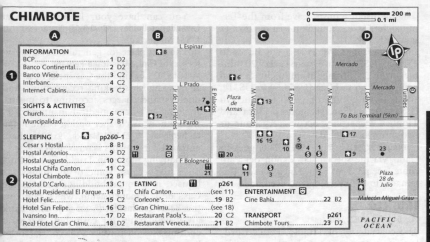

CHIMBOTE

INFORMATION	
BCP....................................	1 D2
Banco Continental.............	2 D2
Banco Wiese......................	3 C2
Interbanc..........................	4 C2
Internet Cabins.................	5 C2

SIGHTS & ACTIVITIES	
Church..............................	6 C1
Muncipalidad....................	7 B1

SLEEPING	pp260–1
Cesar s Hostal..................	8 B1
Hostal Antonios................	9 D2
Hostal Augusto.................	10 C2
Hostal Chifa Canton..........	11 C2
Hostal Chimbote...............	12 B1
Hostal D'Carlo..................	13 C1
Hostal Residencial El Parque..	14 B1
Hotel Felic.......................	15 C2
Hotel San Felipe...............	16 C2
Ivansino Inn.....................	17 D2
Real Hotel Gran Chimu.......	18 D2

EATING	p261
Chifa Canton...................	(see 11)
Corleone's.......................	19 B2
Gran Chimu.....................	(see 18)
Restaurant Paola's............	20 C2
Restaurant Venecia...........	21 B2

ENTERTAINMENT	
Cine Bahía......................	22 B2

TRANSPORT	p261
Chimbote Tours................	23 D2

are electric and the rooms are satisfactorily clean.

Also consider:

Cesar's Hostal (☎ 32-4946; Espinar 286; s/d US$6/10) Rooms come with electric showers.

Hostal Chimbote (☎ 34-4721; Pardo 205; s/d US$3.50/ 6; with showers US$6/9) There's cold water only, rooms with showers have cable TV.

Hostal Augusto (☎ 32-4431; Aguirre 265; s/d US$4.25/ 5, with showers US$6/9) Clean cold-water place.

MID-RANGE

Hotel San Felipe (☎ 32-3401; J Pardo 514; s/d US$14.50/ 21) Rates include a continental breakfast on the 5th-floor terrace with plaza views. The clean rooms have good hot showers and cable TV and are reached by elevator.

Hostal D'Carlo (☎ 34-4044, ☎ /fax 32-1047; Villavicencio 376; s/d US$25/31; P) Cheerfully painted walls, nice bedspreads, fans and cable TV welcome guests. Rooms are spacious but the bathrooms (with hot water) are on the small side. Rates include a continental breakfast and the hotel café offers room service from 7am to 10pm. Some rooms overlook the plaza.

Hostal Chifa Canton (☎ 34-4388; hotelcanton@ usa.net; Bolognesi 498; s/d US$28/35) The town's best hotel, it has large, attractive rooms with modern amenities and breakfast is included in the rates. Some rooms have ocean views. It has a good *chifa* (Chinese restaurant) and a pool hall on the premises.

Real Hotel Gran Chimu (☎ 32-3721, 32-8104; Gálvez 109; s/d US$29/38; ste to US$60; P 🛜) The

grand dame of Chimbote's hotels has a faded charm with a relaxed public area, comfortable couches and an aquarium. Upstairs, 76 rooms and three suites mostly offer fans (a few have air-con), cable TV and phone, and some come with a sea view. It has a decent restaurant and bar.

Ivansino Inn (☎ 33-1811; ivansino@perumix.com; J Pardo 738; US$28/40) The Ivansimo has modern rooms with minifridges.

Eating

Restaurant Venecia (☎ 32-5490; Bolognesi 386; mains average US$5) is recommended for seafood and has good breakfasts. **Restaurant Paola's** (☎ 34-5428; Bolognesi 401; US$2-4) makes good sandwiches, ice cream and snacks. **Corleone's** (☎ 32-8932; Bolognesi 175; pasta US$3, large pizza US$8-11) is decorated with Beatles posters and attracts a young crowd.

The restaurants at the hotels Chifa Canton and Gran Chimu (see Sleeping earlier) are both good. There are also cheap *chifas* and chicken restaurants (about US$1.50) on Pardo to the south and east of the Plaza de Armas.

Getting There & Away
AIR

There are flights (subject to change!) from Lima with LC Busre on Monday and Friday mornings, returning in the evenings, but there's no office in Chimbote. **Chimbote Tours** (☎ 32-4982, 32-3200; chimbotetours@hotmail .com; Bolognesi 801) sells airline tickets.

Long-distance buses leave from the Terminal Terrestre, about 5km east of town (a taxi costs US$1).

America Express (☎ 35-3468) has buses to Trujillo (US$1.50, two hours) every 20 minutes from 5am to about midnight. Several companies go to Lima (US$4.50 to US$14, six to seven hours), or north to Chiclayo (US$4.50 to US$6, six hours), Piura and Tumbes. Departures occur every hour or two throughout the day.

Yungay Express (☎ 35-1304, 35-2850) goes to Caraz via the spectacular Cañón del Pato route (see p323) at 8am. Linea goes to Cajamarca in the morning and evening.

TRUJILLO

☎ 044 / pop 621,000

The coastal city of Trujillo, Peru's third-largest, is the capital and only important city of the strangely H-shaped Department of La Libertad. Trujillo is about 560km north of Lima and the area warrants a visit of several days. Founded in 1535 by Pizarro, it is an attractive colonial city and retains much of its traditional flavor.

Nearby is the ancient Chimu capital of Chan Chan (see p269), which was conquered by the Incas (local guides say that the Chimu surrendered to the Incas, rather than were conquered). Also in the area are several other Chimu sites and the immense Moche pyramids of the Temples of the Sun and Moon (Huacas del Sol y de la Luna; see p274), which date back about 1500 years. If so much ancient culture wears you out, you can relax at the beach village of Huanchaco.

During the 1998 El Niño, central Trujillo was briefly flooded to a depth of a few inches, but suffered less than many other coastal towns.

Information

Both **iPeru** (☎ 29-4561; Pizarro 412; ✆ 9am-1pm & 2-5pm Mon-Fri) and the **Policía de Turismo** (Tourist Police; ☎ 29-1705, 20-4025; Independencia 630) can provide tourist information, as can the many useful local tour companies and guides (see p265). The Tourist Police may also be helpful in an emergency.

The **post office** (Independencia 286) is southwest of the Plaza de Armas. For Internet access, **DeltaNet** (Orbegoso 641) and many others open late.

You can have your laundry done at **Lavanderías Unidas** (☎ 20-0505; Pizarro 683) for US$1.80 per kg.

The best place for general medical services is the **Clínica Americano-Peruano** (☎ 23-1261, Mansiche 702), behind the Cassinelli Museum. It has English-speaking receptionists and doctors, and charges according to means. If you don't have medical insurance, let them know. A cheaper option is the **Hospital Regional** (☎ 23-1581, Mansiche 795); the main entrance for patients is on Napoles.

Changing money in Trujillo is a distinct pleasure, because some of the banks are housed in colonial buildings such as the Casa de la Emancipación, which contains the **Banco Continental** (Pizarro 620). This bank gives good rates for cash, but charges a commission on traveler's checks. **Interbanc** (Gamarra at Pizarro) offers fast service and good rates for travelers' checks; it has Visa and MasterCard ATMs. **Banco Wiese** (Pizarro 314) has a MasterCard ATM, while **BCP** (Gamarra 562) has a Visa ATM. You can also change traveler's checks with other banks – shop around for the best rate. Bank lines are long, so go around the opening time of 9:30am. *Casas de cambio* (foreign-exchange offices), near Gamarra and Bolívar, give good rates for cash.

Dangers & Annoyances

Single women tend to receive a lot of attention from males in Trujillo bars – to exasperating, even harassing levels. Locals say that Trujillo is one of the more conservative cities in Peru, and women are not expected to be out alone in the evenings. One woman told us that this was the only place in Ecuador and Peru where she was 'hit on' by numerous men, some of whom were very persistent and all of whom were a nuisance.

Sights & Activities

The colonial mansions and churches, most of which are near the Plaza de Armas, are worth seeing, though they don't have regular opening hours and the listed times may change without notice. Some are closed for days on end and many are closed Sunday. Hiring a local guide (see p265) is recommended if you are seriously interested in visiting as many of them as possible. The churches often are open for early morning mass, as well as evening masses, but visitors at those times should respect the worshippers and not wander around.

The single feature that makes Trujillo's colonial center especially distinctive is the beautiful wrought-iron grillwork fronting almost every colonial building in the city. This, combined with the buildings' pastel shades, results in a distinct Trujillano ambiance not found in Peru's other colonial cities. Several buildings have changing **art shows** at various times and are best visited then. Admission is normally free or nominal. Hours vary, so check locally. Some of the best-known are described following.

PLAZA DE ARMAS

Trujillo's very spacious and attractive main square has an impressive central statue dedicated to work, the arts and liberty. The plaza is fronted by the **cathedral**, begun in 1647, destroyed in 1759 and rebuilt soon afterward. The cathedral has a famous basilica and often opens around 6pm. The cathedral has a museum of religious and colonial art.

Elegant colonial mansions surround the plaza. One is now the **Hotel Libertador**. Another, **Casa de Urquiaga** (Pizarro 446; admission free; 9am-3pm Mon-Fri), now belongs to the Banco Central de la Reserva del Peru.

At 10 am on Sunday there is a **flag-raising ceremony** on the Plaza de Armas, complete with a parade. On a few Sundays, there are also *caballos de paso*, or pacing horses (see the boxed text, p265), and *marinera* dances.

SOUTH & EAST OF PLAZA DE ARMAS

The following places can be seen on a walking tour starting from the Plaza de Armas.

The church of **La Merced**, on the corner of Pizarro and Gamarra, has a dome with noteworthy carvings under a balcony.

Now the Banco Continental building, the **Casa de la Emancipación** (Pizarro 610) is where Trujillo's independence from colonial rule was formally declared on December 29, 1820. This is a reliable place to see changing art and cultural exhibits.

The early 19th-century mansion, **Palacio Iturregui** (Pizarro 688; 11am-6pm Mon-Fri), is unmistakable and impossible to ignore – it is painted bright yellow. Built in neoclassical style, it has beautiful window gratings and slender, interior columns and gold moldings on the ceilings. Its main claim to fame

is that General Iturregui lived here after he proclaimed Lambayeque's and Trujillo's independence from Spain in 1820. The building is now used by the private Club Central, and the mansion is open later if there's an art exhibition.

The Carmelite Museum in the church of **El Carmen** (cnr Colón & Bolívar; US$0.90; 9am-1pm Mon-Sat) has reputedly Trujillo's best collection of colonial art.

The university-run **Museo de Arqueología** (24-9322; Junín 682; adult/student US$1.50/0.30; 9:30am-2pm Mon; 9:15am-1pm & 3-7pm Tue-Fri, 9:30am-4pm Sat & Sun) has a small but interesting collection of artefacts from the Huaca de la Luna (Temple of the Moon; see p275), as well as reproductions of some of the murals found there and an explanation of the ongoing excavations, signed in Spanish. The museum is housed in the 17th-century La Casa Risco, a restored colonial house. A gift shop has a small selection of archaeology books, a few of which are in English.

Casa Aranda (Bolívar 621) is another interesting mansion. **Casona Orbegoso** (Orbegoso 553), named after a former president of Peru, is a beautiful 18th-century mansion with a collection of art and furnishings of that period. On the opposite side of Bolívar, **San Agustín**, with its finely gilded high altar, dates from 1558 and is usually open. Further southwest is the church of El Belén and, north of here, is another mansion, **Casa de Mayorazgo de Facala** (Pizarro 314), which houses Banco Weise.

NORTH & WEST OF PLAZA DE ARMAS

The following places can also be visited on a walking tour from the Plaza de Armas.

Northeast of the cathedral is **Casa Ganoza Chopitea** (Independencia 630), also known as Casa de los Léones, which is considered to be the best mansion of the colonial period; the Tourist Police are housed here. Good, modern Peruvian art is sometimes shown, as are some rather arcane pieces that you may never have a chance to see elsewhere, thus offering relief from the interminable religious and colonial art that is the stock of most museums. Hours vary. Further east of the mansion is the church of Santa Clara.

The **Museo Cassinelli** (US$2; 9:30am-1pm & 3-6pm Mon-Sat, 9am-1pm Sun), about 900m northwest of the Plaza de Armas, is a private archaeological collection at N de Piérola

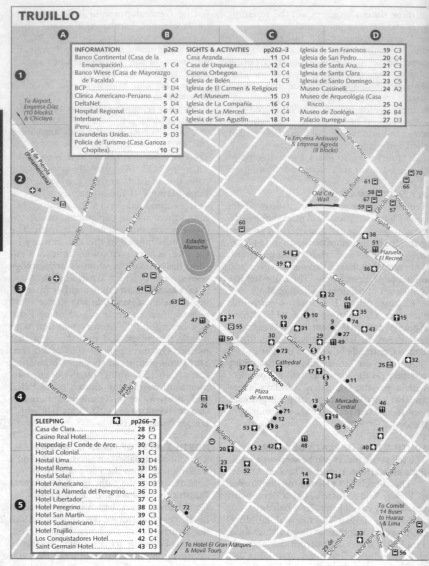

TRUJILLO

INFORMATION	p262
Banco Continental (Casa de la Emancipación)	1 C4
Banco Wiese (Casa de Mayorazgo de Facalda)	2 C4
BCP	3 D4
Clínica Americano-Peruano	4 A2
DeltaNet	5 D4
Hospital Regional	6 A3
Interbanc	7 C4
iPeru	8 C4
Lavanderías Unidas	9 D3
Policía de Turismo (Casa Ganoza Chopitea)	10 C3

SIGHTS & ACTIVITIES	pp262–3
Casa Aranda	11 D4
Casa de Urquiaga	12 C4
Casona Orbegoso	13 C4
Iglesia de Belén	14 C5
Iglesia de El Carmen & Religious Art Museum	15 D3
Iglesia de La Compañía	16 C4
Iglesia de La Merced	17 C4
Iglesia de San Agustín	18 D4

Iglesia de San Francisco	19 C3
Iglesia de San Pedro	20 C4
Iglesia de Santa Ana	21 C3
Iglesia de Santa Clara	22 C3
Iglesia de Santo Domingo	23 C5
Museo Cassinelli	24 A2
Museo de Arqueología (Casa Risco)	25 D4
Museo de Zoología	26 B4
Palacio Iturregui	27 D3

SLEEPING	pp266–7
Casa de Clara	28 E5
Casino Real Hotel	29 C3
Hospedaje El Conde de Arce	30 C3
Hostal Colonial	31 C3
Hostal Lima	32 D4
Hostal Roma	33 D5
Hostal Solari	34 D5
Hotel Americano	35 D3
Hotel La Alameda del Peregrino	36 D3
Hotel Libertador	37 C4
Hotel Peregrino	38 D3
Hotel San Martín	39 C3
Hotel Sudamericano	40 D4
Hotel Trujillo	41 D4
Los Conquistadores Hotel	42 C4
Saint Germain Hotel	43 D3

601, in the basement of a Mobil gas station. (Ask to gain admittance; hours may vary.) The museum is fascinating, with hundreds of pieces. It's amazing to see them under a gas station!

Among the most interesting pieces are the whistling pots, which produce clear notes when air is blown into them (ask

the curator to show you). One pair of pots represents a pair of birds (probably tinamous). Superficially, the pots are very similar, but when they are blown, each produces a completely different note. These notes corresponded to the distinctively different calls of the male and female birds.

The university-run **Museo de Zoología** (San Martín 368; US$0.30; 9am-5pm Mon-Fri), just west of the Plaza de Armas, is mainly a taxidermic collection of Peruvian animals.

There are three interesting churches around the southwest of the Plaza de Armas; **La Compañia** (Independencia), **San Pedro** (Bolognesi) and **Santo Domingo** (Larco).

CABALLOS DE PASO

Breeding, training and watching the *caballos de paso* (pacing horses) is a favorite Peruvian activity. The idea is to breed and train horses that pace more elegantly than others. Trujillo and Lima are both centers of this upper-class pastime. Trujilleños will tell you that the activity originated in the Department of La Libertad.

Tours & Guides

There are dozens of tour agencies. Some agencies, though, have been criticized for supplying guides who speak English but don't know much about the area, or vice versa. **Chacón Tours** (/fax 25-5212; España 106) run tours to the nearby sites and can book flights. **Guía Tours** (24-5170; Independencia 580) organizes tours that last 2½ to four hours and go to several of the local archaeological sites for US$12 to US$18 per person (two-person minimum). Its guides speak some English.

If you prefer your own guide, it's best to go with a **certified official guide** who knows the area well and will take you to wherever you want to go, as well as suggest places you may not have thought of. Guiding here is a competitive profession, and you shouldn't believe everything you hear from one guide about the other guides.

Official guides charge about US$6 to US$8 an hour, but will take several people for the same price as one. **Clara Luz Bravo D** and her English husband, **Michael White** (29-9997, 66-2710; microbewhite@yahoo.com; Cahuide 495), lead tours to all the local sites of interest. Both are knowledgeable, educated, enthusiastic and recommended. Travelers can stay at their house (see Sleeping, p266).

Readers have recommended **Edith Taçanga de Rodas** (24-1669) and **Laura Duran** (959-5935) for local tours.

Special Events

Trujillo's major festival is **El Festival Internacional de la Primavera** (International Spring Festival), which has been held annually for about 50 years. Its attractions include parades, national dancing competitions (including, of course, the *marinera*), *caballos de paso* displays, sports, international beauty contests and various other cultural activities. It all happens in the last week in September, and better hotels are fully booked well in advance.

The last week in January is also busy, with the national **Fiesta de la Marinera** contest. The *marinera* is a typical coastal Peruvian dance involving much romantic waving of handkerchiefs. Students of folk dance should not miss this one. Again, hotels are booked up at this time.

Sleeping

Travelers often enjoy staying in the nearby village of Huanchaco (see p275).

Mid-range and top-end hotels often give substantial discounts to walk-in guests.

BUDGET

Hostal Colonial (☎ 25-8261; hostcolonialtruji@hotmail .com; Independencia 618; s/d US$11.50/17.25) A great location just a block from the Plaza de Armas, helpful staff, a pleasant courtyard and a garden attract travelers. Cozy rooms have private hot shower and a TV showing local channels. A popular restaurant is conveniently adjacent.

Casa de Clara (☎ 29-9997; www.xanga.com/Casa deClara; Cahuide 495; s/d US$6/10; P ☐) A small hotel in a private house on a quiet park 10 minutes walk from the center, Casa de Clara offers hot showers, kitchen and laundry privileges, a garden, cable TV, videos and all kinds of help. The owners are English-speaking tour guides who can set you up with other, similarly priced private-house accommodations. Inexpensive meals are available on request.

Hotel Americano (☎ 24-1361; Pizarro 792; s/d US$4.50/7.50, with cold shower US$6/9, with hot shower US$9/11.50) This perennially popular hotel is in a rambling and dilapidated old mansion with lots of character. Travelers either love it or hate it. Basic but fairly clean rooms have bathrooms; somewhat grungier rooms with shared bathrooms are a bit cheaper.

Hotel Trujillo (☎ 24-3921; fax 24-4241; Grau 581; s/ d US$6/10) The floral floor tiles add a welcome touch of brightness to this simple, older but well-run and decent hotel. Rooms have a private hot shower, a towel and soap is laid out for you, and an extra US$1.50 hires you a TV.

Hospedaje El Conde de Arce (☎ 94-3236; Inde-pendencia 577; dm US$4.50, d US$11.50) It's a simple, small, safe and friendly budget lodging right in the center. Hot electric showers

are in each room, and a quiet patio is good for relaxing.

Hotel San Martín (☎ /fax 25-2311; San Martín 745; s/d US$12/20) The hotel has over 150 rooms and is rarely full. It is characterless, but is fair value for rooms with cable TV and phone. It has a restaurant and bar.

Other choices are:

Hostal Lima (☎ 23-2499; Ayacucho 718; s/d US$3/4) Basic dive used by gringos on shoestring budgets. It looks like a jail but is secure.

Hostal Roma (☎ 25-9064; Nicaragua 238; s/d US$11.50/ 16) Clean and secure, the rooms have hot showers and cable TV.

Hotel Sudamericano (☎ 24-3751; M Grau 515; s/d US$6/9) The friendly owners often give discounts. It has clean rooms with cramped cold showers.

MID-RANGE

Most of these hotels can be pretty noisy if you get street-side rooms, so ask for an interior room for more quiet. All hotels here have private hot showers.

Hostal Solari (☎ 24-3909; hsolari@hostalsolari.com .pe; Almagro 715; s/d US$25/35; P) Large, sensibly decorated 'executive' rooms feature a separate sitting area, excellent mattresses, cable TV, minifridge and phone. A café has room service available, and the helpful front-desk staff will arrange tours, confirm airline tickets and try and do whatever you need.

Hotel La Alameda del Peregrino (☎ 47-0512, 47-0517; alamedaperegrina@hotmail.com; Pizarro 879; s/d US$33/43; P ☐) This hotel is on a pedestrian street near the Plazuela El Recreo and, therefore, doesn't suffer from street noise (though taxis can pull up to within 10m of the hotel entrance and valet parking is available). There is a reasonably priced restaurant here with room service during the day, a patio and bar. Neat and spotless, parquet-floored rooms feature a minibar, cable TV and phone with Internet connection. Rates include a continental breakfast. When the going is slow, walk-in clients can negotiate a substantial discount.

Hotel Peregrino (☎ 20-3988; elperegrino@viabcp .com; Independencia 978; s/d US$30/40, ste US$100; P ☐) This hotel is clean, pleasant and quiet. Carpeted, comfortably furnished rooms have minibar, cable TV, phone and writing desk. Suites have Jacuzzis and a sitting area. Rates include a continental breakfast. A restaurant provides room service, and the front desk strives to please.

Los Conquistadores Hotel (☎ 24-4505; losconq uistadores@viabcp.com; Almagro 586; s/d US$50/62; ste US$100; 🕸 P 🖵) A modern hotel a few steps away from the Plaza de Armas, it has comfortable, carpeted rooms with cable TV, phone, minibar and 24-hour room service. Suites have Jacuzzis. Rates include a full breakfast and airport transfer A business center, travel service and exercise room are available.

Casino Real Hotel (☎ /fax 25-7416; crealh@viabcp .com; Pizarro 651; s/d US$23/35; P 🕸) It has good rooms with all conveniences over a casino and disco, so it's not for a quiet night. An American breakfast is included in the rates.

Saint Germain Hotel (☎ 25-0574; saintgermainhot el@terra.com.pe; Junín 585; d US$50) The Saint Germain has pretty rooms with usual services in a boutique hotel. It has a bar and café.

TOP END

Hotel Libertador (☎ 23-2741; trujillo@libertador.com; Independencia 485; s or d US$90, ste US$135-180; 🐾 P) The grand dame of the city's hotels, the Libertador is in a beautiful, old building right on the Plaza de Armas. It is one of two four-star hotels in Trujillo. There is a sauna, good restaurant, pleasant bar, 24-hour coffee shop and comfortable rooms with the usual conveniences. Try to avoid the street-side rooms unless you want to watch the goings-on, as they are apt to be noisy. Breakfast is included.

Hotel El Gran Marques (☎ 24-9161, 24-9366; Diaz de Cienfuegos 145; s/d US$56//0, ste US$125-155; 🕸 P 🐾) A couple of kilometers southwest of the city center, this hotel offers a sauna, exercise room, restaurant and bar and is Trujillo's other top-end choice.

Eating

The 700 block of Pizarro has several trendy cafés and restaurants, popular both with locals and tourists, and they serve a variety of good food at moderate prices. This is a fine place to start your culinary adventures.

Restaurant Romano (☎ 25-2251; Pizarro 747; mains US$3-6; 🕑 8am-11pm) The Romano has good espresso and cappuccino, as well as breakfast and light or full meals all day. Meaty and meatless sandwiches, desserts, and a mainly Peruvian menu are offered.

Restaurant De Marco (☎ 23-4251; Pizarro 725; breakfast US$2, mains US$3-7.50; 🕑 7:30am-11pm)

This small bistro specializes in Italian food – if you read Italian, so much the better for deciphering the extensive menu. It has good desserts and ice cream as well as good coffees.

Asturias (Pizarro 741; breakfast & sandwiches US$1.50-3.50, mains US$3.50-6.50; 🕑 7:30am-10pm) This café has a little bit of everything. A long menu of Peruvian and international plates will yield something good.

El Sol Restaurante Vegetariano (Pizarro 660; meals US$1-2; 🕑 8am-6pm) A limited menu attests to experience; the cooks know what you want and have been here a long time to serve it. A few nonvegetarian items sneak into the menu.

Chelsea Restaurant & Pub (☎ 25-7032; Estete 675; mains average US$5.50) This lovely English pub plus restaurant has several different dining rooms to meet your tastes – elegant or simple, stone or wooden–plus a live music venue at the back. The menu is varied with grills, seafood and pasta. This is a great place for a special date.

Le Valentino (☎ 24-6643, 29-5339; Orbegoso 224; mains US$5-7.50, large pizza US$9; 🕑 5pm-1am) This place is currently enjoying popularity as the best Italian restaurant in town. Pasta and meat dishes are on the menu.

Chifa Ah Chau (24-3351; Gamarra 769; mains average US$5). This is a funky, faded but fun place, with individual private curtained booths and genuine Chinese food. Portions are huge; a main dish with rice will easily feed two or even three.

Also try:

Restaurant Vegetariano Vida Sana (Pizarro 917; meals US$1-2) Good for lunch.

Chifa El Dragón (Orbegoso at Zepita; set menú US$1-1.50) A clean, locally popular Chinese cheapie. Good value.

El Mochica (Bolívar 462; mains US$2.50-6) Has a variety of mid-priced steaks and seafood, as well as cheaper local dishes.

Supermercado Merpisa (Pizarro 700; 🕑 9:15am-1:15pm & 4:30-9pm) For self catering.

Entertainment

The local newspaper *La Industria* is the best source for local entertainment, cultural exhibitions and other events.

Restaurante Turístico Canana (☎ 23-2503, 23-1482; San Martín 791; cover averages US$3, mains US$4-9; 🕑 5pm-late) Although this place is open every night and serves good Peruvian coastal food, late Thursday to Saturday is the time to go when local musicians and dancers perform starting at 11pm, and the audience joins in (or watches, if they are chowing down *chicharrones* – fried chunks of pork or pork skins).

La Luna Rota (☎ 22-8877, 24-2182; América Sur 2119; cover free–US$3) The 'shattered moon', around 2km southeast of the Plaza de Armas, has a restaurant, live music and dancing, disco, slot machines – a little bit of everything.

Las Tinajas (☎ 29-6272; Pizarro at Almagro; 🕑 9pm-late; cover varies) This pleasant bar on the corner of the plaza is very quiet during the week, but attracts a younger, more lively crowd on weekends, when there is live music or a hot DJ.

Haizea Pub (Bolognesi 420; 🕑 7pm-late, closed Sun) The Hazy Pub can be dead boring or super lively later on weekend nights. Rock music and videos play, and local live bands occasionally strut their stuff.

Cine Primavera (☎ 24-1277; Orbegoso 239) With four screens, this is the best of Trujillo's several cinemas and offers the best choice for an evening out midweek, when about everything else is closed or dead.

Getting There & Away
AIR
The **airport** (☎ 46-4013) is 10km northwest of town. **Aero Continente** (☎ 24-4042; Pizarro 470) has flights to/from Lima daily in the morning and afternoon. The morning flight continues to/from Tumbes. Other airlines, including AeroCóndor and LC Busre have served Trujillo in the past and may do so in future but had suspended services at the time of research. Schedules and destinations change often; check with a local travel agent. The usual US$3.50 airport tax applies.

BUS & COLECTIVO
Buses often leave Trujillo full, so booking ahead, even if only by a few hours, is advised. Companies offer a huge variety of services; the eight-hour ride to Lima can cost from US$7 to US$27! Several companies that go to southern destinations also have terminals on the Panamericana Sur, the southern extension of Avenida Moche; they may stop there briefly to pick up passengers on the way out of town. Check where your bus actually leaves from when buying a ticket.

Linea (☎ 23-5847, 26-1482; Carrión 142) goes to Lima (US$8 to US$17, eight hours) six times daily, mostly overnight; to Piura (US$6, six hours) at 11pm; to Cajamarca (US$6 to US$9, six hours) at 10:30am, 10pm, 10:30pm; to Chiclayo (US$3, three hours) hourly from 6am to 6pm, stopping at Pacasmayo and Guadalupe; to Chimbote (US$1.50, two hours) eight times a day; and to Huaraz (US$9, nine hours) at 9pm. For an extra US$0.60, Linea will deliver a ticket booked by phone at ☎ 29-9666, between 8am and 8pm Monday to Saturday.

Cruz del Sur (☎ 26-1801; Amazonas 237) only goes to Lima five times a day for US$10 to a whopping US$27 for their bus-cama. **Civa** (☎ 25-1402; Ejército 285) goes to Lima (US$7 to US$9) at 6am, 7am and 9pm. **Ormeño** (☎ 25-9782; Ejército 233) has several a day to Lima and night buses to Tumbes (US$9 to US$14, 10 hours). **Cial** (☎ 20-1760; Amazonas 393); **Transportes Flores** (☎ 20-8250; Ejército 350); **Oltursa** (☎ 26-3055; Ejercito 342); and **Ittsa** (☎ 25-1415; Mansiche 171) also go to Lima.

El Dorado (☎ 29-1778; Mansiche at Carrión) goes to Piura and Tumbes (US$10, 11 hours) at 7pm, 8pm and 8:30pm, and to Piura and Sullana at 12:45pm and 10:20pm.

Transportes El Sol (☎ 29-0328; Lloque Yupanqui 282) and **Americas Bus** (☎ 26-1906; Lloque Yupanqui 162) have frequent buses to Chimbote. **Comité 14** (☎ 26-1008; Moche 544) has an 8pm bus to Huaraz (US$7.50, nine hours). **Movil Tours** (☎ 28-6538; América Sur 3955) also has an overnight bus to Huaraz. If you want to travel to Huaraz by day, go to Chimbote and catch a bus from there.

Empresa Antisuyo (☎ 23-4726; Túpac Amaru 760) goes to Huamachuco (see p275) for the back route into Cajamarca. **Empresa Agreda** (☎ 22-1960; Farfan 647) also goes to Huamachuco. **Empresa Díaz** (☎ 20-1237; N de Piérola 1079), on the Panamericana about 1km northwest of the town center, goes to Cajamarca. Connections from Chiclayo to Cajamarca are better than those from Trujillo.

For buses to Moyobamba, Tarapoto and Chachapoyas, go from Chiclayo.

Getting Around
TO/FROM THE AIRPORT
The **airport** (☎ 46-4013), 10km northwest of Trujillo, is reached cheaply on the Huanchaco bus (see following), though you'll

have to walk the last kilometer. A taxi to or from the city center costs about US$3.50.

TO/FROM ARCHAEOLOGICAL SITES
White-yellow-and-orange B combi colectivos to La Huaca Esmeralda, Chan Chan and Huanchaco pass the corners of España and Ejército, España and Industrial, and other places every few minutes. Minibuses (red, blue and white) or buses (green and white) for La Esperanza go northwest along Mansiche and can drop you off at La Huaca Arco Iris. Minibuses leave every half hour from Suarez for the Huacas del Sol y de la Luna. Fares are roughly US$0.25 on these routes. Note that these buses are worked by professional thieves looking for cameras and money – keep valuables hidden, and watch your bags carefully.

Taking a taxi or joining a tour isn't a bad idea, even for budget travelers. The ruins certainly will be more interesting and meaningful with a good guide – some recommended ones are listed on p265. Guides can arrange a taxi or their own vehicle. Alternatively, a taxi to most of these sites will cost US$3 to US$4, then you can hire an on-site guide.

La Huaca Prieta and La Huaca El Brujo, about 60km northwest of Trujillo, near the coast on the north side of the Chicama valley, are harder to reach. Start at the Provincial Bus Terminal Interurbano off Atahualpa to Chocope. Ask here for combis towards the site.

TAXI
A taxi ride within the circular Avenida España shouldn't cost more than US$1. For sightseeing, taxis charge about US$6 per hour, depending on how far you expect them to go.

AROUND TRUJILLO
The main reason to travel around Trujillo is to see the archaeological sites. These are all described here. For transport details, see To/From Archaeological Sites earlier.

The Moche and Chimu cultures left the greatest marks on the Trujillo area, but are by no means the only ones. In a March 1973 *National Geographic* article, Drs ME Moseley and CJ Mackey claimed knowledge of over 2000 sites in the Río Moche valley, and many more have been discovered since then.

Most of these sites are small and well-nigh forgotten, but one is the largest pre-Columbian city in the Americas (Chan Chan), as well as pyramids that required about 140 million adobe bricks to construct.

Five major archaeological sites can be easily reached from Trujillo by local bus or taxi. Two of these are principally Moche, dating from about 200 BC to AD 850. The other three, from the Chimu culture, date from about AD 850 to 1500. The recently excavated Moche ruin of La Huaca El Brujo (60km from Trujillo) can also be visited, but not as conveniently.

The entrance ticket for Chan Chan is also valid for the Chimu sites of La Huaca Esmeralda and La Huaca Arco Iris, as well as the Chan Chan museum (by the Panamericana), but it must be used within two days. All sites are open from 9am to 4:30pm, except 1 January, 1 May and 25 December. The ticket is sold at each site except La Huaca Esmeralda.

Chan Chan
Most visitors to the north coast see **Chan Chan** (adult/student US$2.80/1.40), the huge ruined capital of the Chimu Empire. Built around AD 1300 and covering about 28 sq km, it is the largest pre-Columbian city in the Americas and the largest adobe city in the world. At the height of the Chimu Empire, it housed an estimated 60,000 inhabitants and contained a vast wealth of gold, silver and ceramics. After Chan Chan's conquest by the Incas, the wealth remained more or less undisturbed. The Incas were interested in expanding their imperial control, not in amassing treasure. As soon as the Spaniards arrived, however, the looting began, and within a few decades, there was little left of the treasures of Chan Chan. The remainder has been pillaged through the centuries by *huaqueros* (grave robbers; see the boxed text p274), though remnants can be seen in museums. Chan Chan must have been a dazzling sight at one time. Today, only the mud walls and a few molded decorations remain, and the visitor is amazed by the huge expanse of the site as much as anything else.

The damage at Chan Chan has not only been caused by the *huaqueros*. Occasional devastating floods and heavy rainfall have severely eroded the mud walls of the city. Several decades can pass with almost no rain, but occasionally, the climatic phenomenon of El Niño causes rainstorms and floods in the coastal desert.

The Chimu capital consisted of nine major subcities, each built by a succeeding ruler – hence the nine areas are often referred to as the Royal Compounds. Each contains a royal burial mound, where the ruler was buried with an appropriately vast quantity of funerary offerings, including dozens of sacrificed young women and chambers full of ceramics, weavings and jewelry. The Tschudi compound (see p272), named after a Swiss naturalist who visited

---

PRE-COLUMBIAN PEOPLES OF THE TRUJILLO AREA

Huaca Prieta

One of the earliest groups in Peru to be studied were the Huaca Prieta people, who lived at the site of that name around 3500 BC to 2300 BC. These hunters and gatherers began simple agriculture, growing cotton and varieties of bean and pepper, but corn, now a national staple, was unheard of. Finds of simple nets and hooks indicate that they primarily ate seafood. Homes were single-room shacks half buried in the ground, and most of what is known about these folks has been deduced from their middens, or garbage piles. It seems that they were a Stone Age people who didn't use jewelry, but had developed netting and weaving. At their most artistic, they decorated dried gourds with simple carvings; similarly decorated gourds are produced today as a Peruvian handicraft. Hot stones may have been dropped into these gourds to cook food.

Chavín

About 850 BC, a major new cultural influence, that of the Chavín, began to leave its mark on the area. This period was named after the Andean site of Chavín de Huántar (p327), where a feline-worshipping cult had its main center. The Chavín influence swept over the northern mountains and the northern and central coasts of Peru. At its most simple, the Chavín influence consisted of a highly stylized art form based especially on jaguar motifs. Formerly called the Chavín Horizon (many archaeologists now prefer the term Early Horizon), this was the first major culture in Peru, as well as one of the most artistically developed. The various areas and groups it encompassed were typified by the rapid development of ceramic ware and a common art form. In the Trujillo area, the Chavín influence was represented by the Cupisnique culture. Examples of Cupisnique pottery can be seen in the museums of Lima and Trujillo, though there are no especially noteworthy ruins from the Cupisnique culture open to visitors.

In the Trujillo area, archaeologists have identified other geographically smaller and less-important cultures that followed the Cupisnique period. These include the Salinar, Vicus and Gallinazo.

Moche

With the decline of the Cupisnique period came the beginnings of the fascinating Moche period, which is defined by the Moche culture's impressive archaeological sites and some of the most outstanding pottery to be seen in Peru's museums.

The Moche culture is named after the river that flows into the ocean just south of Trujillo. The word 'Mochica' has been used interchangeably with Moche and refers to a dialect spoken in the Trujillo area at the time of the Spanish conquest, though not necessarily spoken by the Moche people. Moche is now the preferred usage.

The Moche culture evolved from around 200 BC to AD 850. The Moche didn't conquer the Cupisnique; rather, there was a slow transition characterized by a number of developments. Ceramics, textiles and metalwork improved greatly under the Moche, architectural skills allowed the construction of huge pyramids and other structures, and there was enough leisure time for art and a highly organized religion.

As with the Nazca culture, which developed on the south coast at about the same time, the Moche period is especially known for its ceramics, which are considered the most artistically sensitive and technically developed of any found in Peru. The thousands of Moche pots preserved in museums are realistically decorated with figures and scenes that give us a very descriptive look at life during the

Peru in the 19th century and published *Peruvian Antiquities* in Vienna in 1851, is partially restored and open to visitors. Most of the other compounds have also been named after archaeologists and explorers.

Chan Chan is about 5km west of Trujillo (see p269 for transport details). Tschudi lies to the left of the main road almost 1km north of the Chan Chan site museum on the Panamericana; it's a 2km walk along a dusty dirt road. (Sometimes taxis are waiting at the site museum, or at the turn-off, or you can take a taxi from Trujillo.) As you walk, you'll see the crumbling ruins of the other compounds

Moche period. As there was no written language, most of what we know about the Moche comes from this wealth of pottery. Pots were modeled into lifelike representations of people, crops, domestic or wild animals, marine life and monumental architecture. Other pots were painted with scenes of both ceremonial activities and everyday objects. From these pots, archaeologists have deduced that Moche society was very class conscious. The most important people, especially the priests and warriors, were members of the urban classes and lived closest to the large ceremonial pyramids and other temples. They were surrounded by a middle class of artisans and then, in descending order, farmers and fishers, servants, prisoners and beggars.

Moche ceramics usually depicted priests and warriors being carried in litters wearing particularly fine jewelry or clothing. Further evidence of the authority of priests and warriors is given by pots showing scenes of punishment, including the mutilation and death of those who dared to disobey. Other facets of Moche life illustrated on the pots include surgical procedures, such as amputation and the setting of broken limbs. Sex is realistically shown; one room in Museo Larco (in Lima; p63) is entirely devoted to erotic pots (mainly Moche) depicting most sexual practices, some rather imaginative. Museo Cassinelli in Trujillo (see p263) also has a fine collection. Clothing, musical instruments, tools and jewelry are all frequent subjects for ceramics.

The ceramics also show us that the Moche had well-developed weaving techniques. But rare rainstorms, which occurred every few decades, destroyed most of their textiles. Their metalwork, on the other hand, has survived. The Moche used gold, silver and copper mainly for ornaments, but some heavy copper implements have also been found.

Two main Moche sites have survived, side by side, a few kilometers south of Trujillo and are easily visited. They are the Huacas del Sol y de la Luna (see p274 for more details).

The Moche period declined around AD 700, and the next few centuries are somewhat confusing. The Wari culture, based in the Ayacucho area of the central Peruvian Andes, began to expand, and its influence was felt as far north as the Chicama valley.

Chimu

The next important period in the Trujillo area, the Chimu, lasted from about AD 850 to 1470. The Chimu built a huge capital at Chan Chan, just north of Trujillo. The Chimu was a highly organized society – it must have been to have built and supported a city such as Chan Chan. Its art work was less exciting than that of the Moche, tending more to functional mass production than artistic achievement. Gone, for the most part, was the technique of painting pots. Instead, they were fired by a simpler method than that used by the Moche, producing the typical blackware seen in many Chimu pottery collections. Despite its poorer quality, this pottery still shows us life in the Chimu kingdom. But, while the quality of the ceramics declined, metallurgy developed, and various alloys (including bronze) were worked. The Chimu were also exceptionally fine goldsmiths.

It is as an urban society that the Chimu are best remembered. Their huge capital contained about 10,000 dwellings of varying quality and importance. Buildings were decorated with friezes, the designs molded into mud walls, and important areas were layered with precious metals. There were storage bins for food and other products from across the empire, which stretched along the coast from Chancay to the Gulf of Guayaquil (southern Ecuador). There were huge walk-in wells, canals, workshops and temples. The royal dead were buried in mounds with a wealth of offerings.

The Chimu were conquered by the Incas in 1471, but the city was not looted until the arrival of the Spanish. Heavy rainfall has severely damaged the mud moldings, though a few survived, and others have been restored.

all around you. Stick to the footpath, and do not be tempted to stroll off into the ruins on either side. Not only are these ruins dilapidated, but they are also the haunt of muggers who hope some unsuspecting, camera-toting tourist will enter alone. Stay on the path, and go with a friend or guide if possible.

At the Tschudi complex, you'll find an entrance area where tickets, snacks, souvenirs, bathrooms, a small unsigned introductory **museum** (free with entry ticket to Chan Chan; see p273) and guides are available. If you haven't already hired a guide in Trujillo, you can hire a local guide for about US$5.75 an hour to make sure you don't miss anything and to be shown the original (not the restored) friezes and decorations. (A guide will accompany up to four people for this price. You'll be charged US$17.25 for a tour of all fours sites, plus taxi fare. Some speak English.) The complex is well marked by fish-shaped pointers, so you can see everything without a guide if you prefer. During the disastrous El Niño rains of 1998, metal roofs were built over the walls to protect them.

Note that your entry ticket for Chan Chan is also valid for the Chimu sites of La Huaca Esmeralda and La Huaca Arco Iris.

TSCHUDI COMPLEX
Entry is through a 4m-thick defensive wall. Inside, you turn right and almost immediately enter the huge and largely restored **Ceremonial Courtyard**. All four interior walls

are decorated with geometric designs, most of which are recreations. Just to the right of the massive doorway as you enter, you'll see a few designs at ground level. We're told those closest to the door, representing three or four sea otters, are unrestored. They're slightly rougher looking than the modern work. The design is repeated all the way around the Ceremonial Courtyard and is topped by a series of lines representing waves. A ramp at the far side of the plaza accesses the second level (stairways are not a frequent feature of the major Chimu structures). Note also the great restored height of the walls in this plaza. Though all the Chan Chan walls have crumbled with time, the highest of Tschudi's walls once stood over 10m high.

Follow the pointers out of the Ceremonial Courtyard through a door to the right and make a sharp left turn to walk along the **outside wall** of the courtyard. This is one of the most highly decorated and best restored of Tschudi's walls. The adobe friezes show waves of fish rippling along the entire length of the wall above a line of seabirds. See if you can tell where the original moldings end and the restored ones begin. As with the sea-otter designs, the rougher-looking fish are the originals. Despite their time-worn appearance, they retain a fluidity and character somehow lacking in the modern version. Nevertheless, the modern work has been done with care and succeeds in restoring the entire wall.

TRUJILLO AREA

0 _____ 6 km
0 _____ 4 mi

To Chiclayo (200km)
La Huaca Arco Iris
To Otuzco (60km)
Huanchaco
Airport
La Esperanza
Laredo
Museo de Sitio Chan Chan
Mansiche
La Huaca Esmeralda
Río Moche
Chan Chan
Trujillo
See Trujillo Map pp264–5
PACIFIC OCEAN
1
La Huaca del Sol
La Huaca de la Luna
Carretera
Panamericana
Moche
Las Delicias
To Chimbote (130km)

At the end of this wall, the marked path goes through a labyrinthine section known as the **Audience Rooms**. Their function is unclear, but their importance is evident in both the quantity and quality of the decorations. Though less restored than the wall, they are the most interesting section of friezes in Tschudi. Their square- and diamond-shaped designs represent, quite simply, fishing nets. Being so close to the ocean, the Chimu based much of their diet on seafood, and the importance of the sea reached venerable proportions. Fish, waves, seabirds and sea mammals are represented throughout the city, and here, in the Audience Rooms, you will find all of them interspersed with the fishing nets. The moon was also very important, and there are several series of full-moon symbols here. For the Chimu, the moon and the sea were of religious importance (unlike the Incas, who worshipped the sun and venerated the earth).

From the Audience Rooms, pointers lead into a **Second Ceremonial Courtyard**, smaller in size than the main Ceremonial Courtyard but similar in shape. It also has a ramp to the second level. From behind this plaza, you can see a huge rectangular depression resembling a drained swimming pool. In fact, it was once a **walk-in well** that supplied the daily water needs of the Tschudi Royal Compound. The water level was reached by a series of ramps from the surface and each compound had its own cistern. The Tschudi cistern is the largest in Chan Chan and measures 130m x 45m.

To the left of the cistern is an area of several dozen small cells that have been called the **military sector**. Perhaps soldiers lived here, or the cells may have been used for storage. These constructions are not very well preserved. Next is the **Mausoleum** where a king was buried along with various (sacrificed) people and ceremonial objects. To the left of the main tomb, a pyramid containing the bodies of dozens of young women was found.

A straight path leads you from the military sector almost back to the main entrance, passing a series of storage bins. The final area visited is the **Assembly Room**. This large rectangular room has 24 seats set into niches in the walls, and its acoustic properties are such that speakers sitting in any one of the niches can be clearly heard all over the room.

You are now back by the main entrance, free to wander around again to inspect more thoroughly those areas of particular interest to you.

SITE MUSEUM

The site museum contains exhibits explaining Chan Chan and the Chimu culture. It is on the main road to the Chan Chan turn-off, about 500m before the turn-off. The museum has a few signs in Spanish but none in English so a guide is useful. A sound-and-light show plays every 30 minutes, in Spanish. What's interesting are the aerial photos and maps showing the huge extension of Chan Chan; we can only visit a tiny portion of it. Also see some fine ceramics and metalwork. Taxis wait outside.

It is possible that other areas will open in the future, but until they are properly policed and signed, you run the risk of being mugged if you visit them.

La Huaca Esmeralda

This **temple** (entry free with Chan Chan ticket) was built by the Chimu at about the same time as Chan Chan. La Huaca Esmeralda lies at Mansiche village, halfway between Trujillo and Chan Chan. Returning from Chan Chan to Trujillo, the *huaca* is to the right of the main road, four blocks behind the Mansiche Church. Thieves reportedly prey on unwary tourists wandering around, so go with friends or a guide, and keep your eyes open.

The site was buried by sand and was accidentally discovered by a local landowner in 1923. He attempted to uncover the ruins, but El Niño of 1925 began the process of erosion, which was exacerbated by the floods and rains of 1983. Little restoration work has been done on the adobe friezes, but it is still possible to make out the characteristic designs of fish, seabirds, waves and fishing nets. The temple consists of two stepped platforms; an on-site guard will take you around for a tip.

See p269 for details on getting here.

La Huaca Arco Iris

Also known locally as Huaca del Dragón, **La Huaca Arco Iris** (the Rainbow Temple; entry free with Chan Chan ticket) is just to the left as you head

HUAQUEROS

The word *huaquero* is heard frequently on the north coast of Peru and literally means 'robber of *huacas.' Huacas* are temples, shrines and burial sites of special significance. They are often decorated with sheets of precious metals and other treasures that accompanied a royal burial.

Since the Spanish conquest, *huaqueros* have worked the ancient graves of Peru. They make their living by finding and opening these graves, then removing the valuables and selling them to anybody prepared to pay for an archaeological artefact. Some of these artefacts find their way into some of Peru's museums. To a certain extent, one can sympathize with a poor *campesino* grubbing around in the desert, hoping to strike it rich; but the *huaquero* is one of the archaeologist's greatest enemies. The *huaqueros'* ransacking has been so thorough that an unplundered grave is almost never found by archaeologists.

These days, visitors to Trujillo and the surrounding sites are sometimes offered a 'genuine' archaeological artefact. These are not always genuine – but if they are, it is illegal to export them from Peru. And you'll be plundering the country's heritage.

up the Panamericana, in the suburb of La Esperanza about 4km northwest of Trujillo (see p269 for details on getting here).

La Huaca Arco Iris is one of the best preserved of the Chimu temples simply because it was covered by sand until the 1960s. Its location was known to a handful of archaeologists and *huaqueros*, but excavation did not begin until 1963. Unfortunately, the 1983 El Niño caused damage to the friezes.

The excavation of the temple took about five years, and the upper parts were rebuilt. It used to be painted, but these days only faint traces of yellow paint can be seen. The temple consists of a defensive wall over 2m thick enclosing an area of about 3000 sq meters. Through the single entrance in this rectangular wall is one large structure, the temple itself. The building covers about 800 sq meters in two levels, with a combined height of about 7.5m. The walls are slightly pyramidal and covered with repeated rainbow designs, most of which have been restored. Some of the decorations are said to show Recuay, Tiahuanaco or Wari influence. Ramps lead the visitor to the very top of the temple from where a series of large storage bins can be appreciated. These almost surround the structure and have openings only at the top. There are also good views from the top level of the temple.

There is a tiny on-site **museum**, and local guides are available to show you around. You can buy inexpensive, well-made reproductions of Chimu ceramics from the souvenir stand near the entrance.

Huacas del Sol y de la Luna

The **Temples of the Sun and the Moon** (admission US$2.75 including guide; ☾ 9am-4pm) are over 700 years older than Chan Chan and are attributed to the Moche period. They are on the south bank of the Río Moche, about 10km southeast of Trujillo by rough road (see p269 for transport information).

The **Huaca del Sol** is the largest single pre-Columbian structure in Peru, although about a third of it has been washed away. Estimates of its size do vary, but recent measurements suggest a maximum length of 342m, breadth of 159m and height of 45m. The structure was built with an estimated 140 million adobe bricks, many of them marked with symbols. These are not evidence of writing or hieroglyphics; they are merely the hallmarks of the workers who made them. Over 100 symbols have been identified and one theory holds that groups or communities of workers were taxed a certain number of adobe bricks and marked their contributions with distinctive hallmarks to keep track of how many bricks they had provided.

At one time, the pyramid consisted of several different levels connected by steep flights of stairs, huge ramps and walls sloping at 77° to the horizon. Around 1500 years have wrought their inevitable damage, and today the pyramid looks like a giant pile of crude bricks partially covered with sand. Despite this, the brickwork remains very impressive from some angles. It appears that there are a few graves or rooms within the structure, and it must have been used primarily as a huge ceremonial site. Certainly, its size alone makes the pyramid an awesome structure, and the views from the top are excellent.

The smaller but more interesting **Huaca de la Luna** is about 500m away across the open desert. The entrance to the site is actually here, and restrooms, souvenirs and snacks are available. Guides accompany visitors into this *huaca* to explain the ongoing archaeological research that is happening there. The structure is riddled with rooms that contain ceramics, precious metals and some of the beautiful polychrome friezes for which the Moche were famous. The *huaca* was built over six centuries to AD 600, with succeeding generations expanding it. By about AD 550, six different levels had been built, each one completely covering the previous one. Archaeologists are currently peeling away selected parts of the *huaca* to discover what lies beneath each layer. At every level, there are friezes of stylized figures, some of which have been well protected by the later levels built around them. Parts being excavated, restored and conserved, and a number of the friezes are now open to the public, with more being stabilized each year. It's well worth a visit; you'll see newly excavated friezes every year. Reproductions of some of the murals are displayed in the Museo de Arqueología in Trujillo (see p263).

As you leave, check out the souvenir stands. One of the men selling pots here makes them using original molds, so you can buy a modern-day replica of ancient pots for just a few dollars. They are very good, and are stamped 'replica' to avoid any possible problems with customs authorities. Also look around for one of the unique Peruvian hairless dogs that hangs out here. Their body temperature is higher than the normal dog, and they have traditionally been used as body warmers for people with arthritis.

Complejo Arqueológico La Huaca El Brujo

This **archaeological complex** (admission US$2.75; ☼ 9am-5pm) consists of the Huaca Prieta site, the newly excavated Moche site of Huaca Cao Viejo with its brilliant mural reliefs, and Huaca El Brujo, which has yet to be excavated. The complex is 60km from Trujillo on the coast and is hard to find without a guide. Clara Luz Bravo D and Michael White (see p265) have both been there more times than most guides.

HUACA CAO VIEJO

The main section of **Huaca Cao Viejo** is a 27m-truncated pyramid with some of the best friezes in the area. They show multicolored reliefs with stylized life-sized warriors, prisoners, priests and human sacrifices. There are also many burial sites from the Lambayeque culture, which followed the Moche. Many other ruins are in the area, few of which have been properly studied.

HUACA PRIETA

Huaca Prieta, on the other hand, has been one of the most intensively studied early Peruvian sites. However, for nonarchaeologists, it's generally more interesting to read about than to tour. Although it's simply a prehistoric pile of garbage, it does afford extensive views over the coastal area and can be visited along with the nearby *huacas* at El Brujo.

HUANCHACO

☎ 044

The fishing village of Huanchaco, a 12km bus ride northwest of Trujillo, is the best beach resort in the Trujillo area, though you won't find expensive, high-rise buildings. Huanchaco is still very low key and retains its fishing village ambiance. It's too cold for swimming, except in the late-December to April summer, though surfing is OK year-round, and is especially good January to April, and July.

Of particular interest are the *totora* (reed) boats, which look superficially like those found on Lake Titicaca in the southern highlands. However, unlike the ones on Lake Titicaca, these boats are hollow. Because the fishers ride on them rather than in them, these high-ended, cigar-shaped boats are called *cabullitos*, or 'little horses.' The *caballitos* are similar to the boats depicted on 2500 year-old ceramics.

The inhabitants of Huanchaco are among the few remaining people on the coast who still remember how to construct and use these precarious-looking craft, and you can always see some stacked up at the north end of the beach.

The reed itself grows at the north end of the village. When the surf is good, the fishers paddle the boats beyond the breakers to fish and then surf back to the beach with their catch. It's worth seeing. If the surf is too strong, they might not be able to work for weeks.

Apart from walking on the beach and waiting for the *caballitos* to go into action, there's not much to do in Huanchaco, and that's one of its attractions. It's a quiet, easygoing place. You can climb up to the massive **church** at the north end of the village for extensive views of the surrounding area. The church is Peru's second oldest (built 1535–40) and has been restored.

Information

The Municipalidad changed all the house numbers in 2003; where we know the new ones we give them thus: old/new. Most places still use the old ones.

See www.huanchaco.com for useful tourist information. Internet access is at **La Casa Suiza** (Los Pinos 451/310). There's a Banco Continental ATM next to the Municipalidad (but no bank).

Dangers & Annoyances

Use the bus to get to Trujillo. There are dangerous slum areas on the beach between Huanchaco and Trujillo, though Huanchaco itself is safe.

Surfing

Surfboards can be rented for about US$5 per day from **La Casa Suiza** (Los Pinos 451/310). If there are no boards there, the staff know who will have some. To try surfing the 2000-year-old way, ask the fishers on the beach to show you how to use their *totora* craft. US$1.50 will get you paddled out and surfed back in – a wet rush!

Festivals & Special Events

Huanchaco is host to the **Festival del Mar**, held every other year (even years) during the first week in May. This festival re-enacts the legendary arrival of Takaynamo, founder of Chan Chan. There are various events, such as surfing and dance competitions, cultural conferences, food and music. **Carnaval** in February is also a big event.

Sleeping

BUDGET

La Casa Suiza (☎ 46-1825; www.casasuiza.com; Los Pinos 451/310; r per person US$4, d with bathroom US$9.30; P ⌨) The friendly German- and English-speaking owners pride themselves on their quiet, clean, well-run *hostal*. It provides guests with a book exchange, cable TV room, laundry facilities, a rooftop barbecue area, hot showers, free boogie-board use, and surfboard and wet-suit rental. Cheap breakfasts are available as well. Two single, two double and a quad room share two bathrooms, and four double rooms have private showers. This place is popular and often full!

Naylamp (☎ 46-1022; naylamp@terra.com.pe; Victor Larco 3; camping US$2, dm US$3, d with bathroom US$9) On the beach at the north end of town, Naylamp provides kitchen and laundry facilities, hot showers, a garden with hammocks and a café. The camp site has a shower and beach view – nice sunsets!

Hospedaje Los Ficus de Huanchaco (☎ 46-1719; losficus@huanchaco.org; Los Ficus 516/215; r per person US$3.50; P) This spotless, family house provides guests with shared hot showers, breakfast on request and kitchen privileges.

Huanchaco's Garden (☎ 46-1194; Av Circunvalación Mz U, Lote 3; huanchacosgarden@huanchaco.zzn.com; d US$10; P ⌨) At the far north end of town, this place is good value. Rooms have hot showers and cable TV, and a garden surrounds the small pool. Kitchen and laundry privileges are available,

Also recommended are:

Hostal Solange (☎ 46-1410; hsolange@yahoo.ed; Los Ficus 484; d with hot showers US$9) Friendly; breakfast costs US$1.50.

Hotel El Ancla (☎ 46-1030; La Rivera 101; d with hot showers US$15; P) Handsome stone building on waterfront; rooms have cable TV.

MID-RANGE

All these hotels have private hot showers.

Huanchaco International Hotel (☎ 46-1754; www.huanchacointernational.com; Autopista a Huanchaco Km13.5; s/d US$35/45, bungalows US$65; ⌨ P ⌨) Owned by a friendly, multilingual Belgian-Peruvian couple, this hotel is in a quiet spot across the road from the beach, a 10-minute walk south of Huanchaco (but walk there along the road). All rooms are bright and airy, with cable TV, fans, and direct-dial phones. The bungalows, which sleep up to four, have two bedrooms and a private terrace with sea views. Rates include an American breakfast in the hotel restaurant. Discounts are offered in the low season or in some rooms lacking sea views – ask. Next to the pool, a covered garden bar and grill invite relaxation, and the beach is just steps away.

Huankarute Restaurant & Hospedaje (☎ 46-1705; huankarute@huanchaco.zzn.com; La Rivera 233; d/tr US$20/23; ☒ ℗) This is a small, friendly place with light rooms that have a fan and cable TV. Some rooms have sea views. Its restaurant features seafood and has lunch specials starting at US$1.80.

Hostal Bracamonte (☎ 46-1162; hostalbracamonte@yahoo.com; Los Olivos 503; s/d/t US$17.50/27/37, bungalows US$40-48; ☒ ℗ ▣). Popular, friendly, welcoming and secure behind high walls and a locked gate, the Bracamonte has nice gardens, a game room, video room, barbecue, restaurant, bar, and toddlers' playground. The rooms include cable TVs, fans and phone. This is the oldest of Huanchaco's good hotels, and it remains among the best choices.

Also recommended are:

Hostal Caballito de Totora (☎ 46-1154; totora@terra.com.pe; La Rivera 219; s/d from US$18/27; ℗)
The varied rooms here sleep up to six; there's a sea-view terrace.

Hostal El Malecon (☎ 46-1275; hostal_elmalecon@yahoo.com; La Rivera 225; s/d US$15/20) Features a café, a terrace with views of surfers and a video pub.

Eating

Huanchaco has many seafood restaurants, especially near the *totora* boats stacked at the north end of the beach.

Restaurant Lucho del Mar (☎ 46-1460; Victor Larco 600; mains US$5-8; ☺ 9am-6pm) In a large, white, two-story building on the waterfront at the north end, this locally popular restaurant serves large and tasty seafood dishes and is one of the best of several in the area. It has a balcony with sea views.

Restaurant Big Ben (☎ 46-1378; Larco 836; mains US$6-9) At the far north end, the Big Ben specializes in lunch-time ceviches and also has a reputation for its top-notch seafood.

Mamma Mía (Victor Larco at Independencia; mains average US$6) This tiny café with just a handful of tables is an Italian place – can't you guess? It does the best pizzas and pastas in town, and also does cheaper sandwiches and ice creams.

The Huanakarute (see Sleeping earlier) is another option as are:

La Estrella Marina (☎ 46-1095; Larco 594; ☺ 9am-11pm) Next door to Lucho del Mar, it is similar, good, a hair cheaper and has sea views.

Club Colonial (Grau 272) On the plaza, this Belgian-run place serves French food and is locally recommended but is pricey.

La Barca (☎ 46-1052; Unión 209; mains US$4-5.50; ☺ 11am-9pm Wed-Mon) This one is the best of three La Barcas in town and features seafood.

Getting There & Away

Combis leave from Industrial at España in Trujillo at frequent intervals from 7am to 11pm. The fare is about US$0.30. The bus can drop you off near the hotel of your choice – ask the driver. To return, just wait on the beachfront road for the bus as it returns from the north end, picking up passengers along the way. A taxi from Trujillo is about US$2.50.

OTUZCO

☎ 044 / elevation 2627m

The small town of Otuzco is a two- or three-hour drive inland from Trujillo. There is a large modern church built next to a smaller, older one, which is usually closed. Outside, stairs lead to the shrine of **La Virgen de la Puerta**, the site of a major pilgrimage every December 15. During this time, the few hotels in Otuzco are usually full, and people sleep in the Plaza de Armas. Otherwise, this is a little-visited but typical town of the western Andean slopes. The drive through coastal sugarcane fields and other subtropical crops (irrigated by the Río Moche) and into the highland agricultural regions (irrigated by the Río Otuzco) is an interesting cross section that only a few travelers experience. It's a rough but scenic drive on unpaved roads. Don't confuse this place with the Ventanillas de Otuzco (see p342).

There are some basic places to stay. The best is the cheap **Hostal Los Portales** (Santa Rosa 6th block). A few inexpensive restaurants serve Peruvian food; none seem outstanding.

Empresa Antisuyo, which has a station in the north of Trujillo, has buses to between Trujillo and Otuzco.

PUERTO CHICAMA

☎ 044

This small port is famous for its surf, and it reputedly has the longest left-handed wave in the world. Surfers claim to get better than a kilometer-long ride if there is a big swell; otherwise, the waves aren't always good for surfing. May to August are the best months to try. There is no gear available here – you'll have to bring it all with you. The water is cold apart from during December to April, and bringing a wet suit is recommended.

Puerto Chicama is a surfer's hang-out, and there are few other visitors. **El Hombre** (☎ 64-0504; s/d from US$4/7) faces the ocean, has good simple meals and kitchen privileges, and has housed surfers for decades. Next door, the newer **Hostal Los Delfines** (☎ 65-0008; losdelfineschicama@hotmail.com; s/d US$14.50/23; 🔊) has a restaurant and rooms with ocean views.

Buses leave frequently from Trujillo's Terminal Interurbano to the town of Paiján, 40km north on the Panamericana (US$1, 1½hrs). From here, you can catch colectivos to travel the 16km to Puerto Chicama (US$0.40).

PACASMAYO & PACATNAMÚ
☎ 044 / pop 12,000

The small port of Pacasmayo is 105km to the north of Trujillo on the Panamericana. Surfers find the long left-breaking waves good from May to August.

The turn-off to Cajamarca is 11km east of Pacasmayo. A few kilometers further along the Panamericana, just before the village of Guadalupe, a track leads toward the ocean. The little-visited ruins of **Pacatnamú** lie several kilometers along this track. This large site has been inhabited by various cultures: Gallinazo, Moche and Chimu.

Buses running along the Panamericana pass near Pacasmayo but don't enter it.

Sleeping
There are several cheap, basic but clean hotels in Pacasmayo. **Hostal Duke** (☎ 52-2017; Ayacucho 44; s/d US$7/10; 🅿) is run by a Peruvian surfer who shows surf videos and rents boards. Rooms have TV and hot showers. **Hotel San Francisco** (☎ 52-2021; L Prado 21; s/d US$4.50/6, with shower US$6/9) is clean. The best hotels are **Hotel Pakatnamú** (☎ 52-1051; fax 52-3255; Malecón Grau 103; US$18/28; 🅿 🐾), on the waterfront, and **Hotel Las Tejas** (☎ /fax 52-1484; Pablo Céspedes 112; s/d US18/28; 🅿 🐾), inland by the cement factory, which dominates the town.

In Guadalupe village, try **Hotel El Bosque** (☎ 56-6490; s/d with bathroom US$12/20).

CHICLAYO
☎ 074 / pop 500,000 / elevation 50m

The next major coastal city north of Trujillo is Chiclayo, just over 200km away on the Panamericana. Founded in the 16th century, Chiclayo remained no more than an outlying district of the older town of Lambayeque through the 19th century. Today, however, Lambayeque plays second fiddle to Chiclayo, which has become one of Peru's fastest-growing modern cities. Although the city itself has little to see of historical interest, it is vibrant and thriving with good opportunities to meet Peruvians – residents call the city the Peruvian capital of friendship. It's an important commercial center and is the capital of the coastal-desert Department of Lambayeque

In 1987 a royal Moche tomb at **Sipán** (see p284), about 30km southeast of Chiclayo, was located by researchers. This find proved to be extraordinary, and has been called the most important archaeological discovery in Peru in the last 50 years. Peruvian archaeologists have recovered hundreds of dazzling and priceless artefacts from the site. Excavation at the site continues, and a tourist infrastructure is developing.

Sipán is best visited from Chiclayo. Some of the spectacular finds are displayed in a fabulous museum in **Lambayeque** (see p284), 11km north of Chiclayo. Other sites worth visiting from Chiclayo are the archaeological ruins at **Túcume** (see p285), a fine museum in **Ferreñafe** (see p285), as well as a number of coastal villages.

Chiclayo's **cathedral** was built in the late 19th century, and the Plaza de Armas (Parque Principal) wasn't inaugurated until 1916, which gives an idea of how modern the city is by Peruvian standards. The **Paseo de las Musas** is Chiclayo's showplace park and has statues of mythological figures in classical style.

The city's experiment with a 'Tourist Ticket' system to cover many of the local sites and museums was discontinued in 2003. It is not clear whether it will resume at a later date.

Information
The **Policía de Turismo** (☎ 23-6700; Saenz Peña 830) is useful for reporting any problems and also provides tourist information. The **Centro de**

CHICLAYO

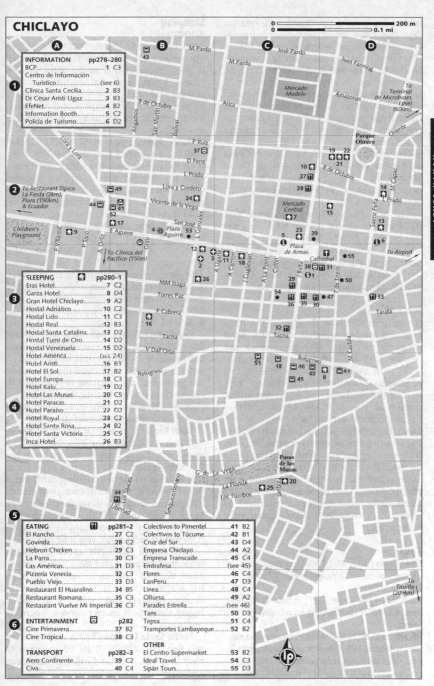

Informacíon Turístico (☎ 23-3132; Saenz Peña 838; ☒ 7:30am-4:30pm Mon-Fri) has limited information and there are information booths on Plaza de Armas and elsewhere that provide brochures, maps and guidance; they're open weekends and evenings.

The **post office** (E Aguirre 140; ☒ 8am-8:30pm Mon-Sat, 8am-2pm Sun) is west of Plaza Aguirre. **EfeNet** (E Aguirre 181; US$0.90/hr) has fast computers; many other Internet places are cheaper but slower.

For medical assistance you can try **Clínica del Pacífico** (☎ 23-6378; JL Ortiz 420) or **Clínica Santa Cecilia** (☎ 23-7154; L Gonzales 668). If you need a dentist, try **Dr César Aristi Ugaz** (☎ 23-8405; E Aguirre 374, office 205).

The **BCP** (J Balta 630) has a 24-hour Visa ATM and is one of several banks on the 600 block of J Balta. Shop around for the best rates for traveler's checks; cash rates, however, vary less. The moneychangers on the street outside the banks change cash quickly at rates similar to the banks.

Market

If you're in Chiclayo, don't miss the huge Mercado Modelo, which is one of the most interesting in Peru. Wander around and see the herbalist and *brujo* (witchdoctor) stalls with their dried plants, bones, bits of animals and other healing charms. This part of the market is inside the southwest corner of the Mercado Modelo. Other things to look for include heavy woven saddlebags called *alforjas*, items typical of the area that can be worn over the shoulder with one bag on your front and the other on your back. Woven straw items – such as hats, baskets, mats and ornaments – are also popular. And, of course, there is the usual cacophonous produce market. As always in a crowded market, watch your belongings.

Tours

Sipán Tours (☎ 22-9053, 22-9046; sipantours@terra .com.pe; 7 de Enero 772) Has guided tours in English, French or Spanish.

Ideal Travel (☎ 22-2991, 22-5751; indiantours@terra .com.pe, Colón 556) Does guided tours in English and Spanish.

InkaNatura (☎ 20-9948; postmaster@inkanatura.com .pe; Las Begonias 147) Works with InkaNatura agencies in Lima, Cuzco and Miami, and provides services both on the northern coast and in the rainforest of southeast Peru.

Sleeping

BUDGET

Hotel Paraíso (☎ 22-8161, 22-2070; hotelparaiso@ terra.com.pe; P Ruiz 1064; s/d US$10/13) This hotel is good value at this price, with modern rooms boasting decent furniture, a hot shower and cable TV. Breakfast is available in its café. It's the cheapest of three hotels on this block, but seems almost as good as any of them.

Hotel Kalu (☎ 23-9195, 22-9293, 22-8767; hotelkalu@terra.com.pe; P Ruiz 1038; s/d US$14/17; ☑) It's a spiffy-looking hotel with a doorman – hold on to your hats! Carpeted updated rooms have fan, cable TV and hot showers and some have a minifridge. The hotel restaurant provides room service.

Hotel Paracas (☎ 22-1611, ☎ /fax 23-6433; P Ruiz 1046; s/d US$14/17) Another OK choice with friendly staff and rooms with fans, hot showers, cable TV and writing desks. The owners were planning to open a café. A traveler reported that while surfing the package of over 60 cable channels, he stumbled across one showing porn; don't let the kids work the controls.

Hotel Santa Victoria (☎ /fax 22-5074; La Florida 586; s/d US$12/17.50; ☑) Overlooking the pleasant Paseo de las Musas, this quiet, modern hotel is a longish walk from the center, but is a great deal. Rooms have fans, cable TV, phones and private hot showers, and a restaurant with room service is available. Rates include a continental breakfast.

Hotel Royal (☎ 23-3421; San José 787; s/d US$6.50/ 9.25) This is the choice for aficionados of old, run-down, characterful hotels right on the Plaza de Armas. The only thing royal about this hotel is its elegant visiting card, but it does have large rooms, hot water in private bathrooms, and a TV room downstairs. Some rooms overlook the plaza, which is fun but noisy. If you enjoyed the Hotel Americano in Trujillo, you'll fit right in.

Hotel Europa (☎ 23-7919, 22-2066; hoteleuropac hiclayo@terra.com.pe; E Aguirre 466; s US$4.50, s/d with shower US$10/13) This clean but aging hotel has a spacious feel to it. The rooms with electric showers and cable TV are much bigger than most budget rooms. There's a restaurant.

Hostal Santa Catalina (☎ /fax 27-2119; Vincente de la Vega 1127; s/d US$10/13) Its 10 rooms with electric hot showers and cable TV are clean and quiet.

Hostal Tumi de Oro (☎ 22-7108; fax 23-7767; L Prado 1145; s/d US$6/9.50) This simple but clean and decent hotel has rooms with private hot showers, and a lobby with cable TV.

Hostal Real (☎ 23-7829; fax 22-7697; E Aguirre 338; s US$5, s/d with shower US$7.25/10) Couples can rent a single room and use one bed – a budgeteers' bargain indeed. This basic but clean, hot-water hotel offers TV in some of the rooms and seems fair value. It has a café.

Hostal Lido (☎ 23-6752; E Aguirre 412; s/d US$3/4.50, with shower US$4.50/7.25) The friendly Lido has a nice city view from the top floor. The water is hot in the shared bathrooms but tends to be tepid in the private ones. Nevertheless, it's a good shoestring choice.

Hostal Venezuela (☎ 23-2665; Lora y Cordero 954; s/d US$6/10) This clean and secure hotel has rooms with private bathrooms and hot water in the cooler months. The friendly staff say you don't need hot showers during the heat of January to April! The rooms at the back are quiet.

Hostal Adriático (☎ 24-0065; Balta 1009; s/d US$3/5) It has desperate digs for the truly impecunious. Rooms are quite big, but don't contain much more than a beat-up old bed.

MID-RANGE

All these hotels have private hot showers.

Hotel Santa Rosa (☎ 22-4411, fax 23-6242; L Gonzales 927; s/d US$17/22; P) This quiet, clean and pleasant hotel has comfortable rooms with fan, cable TV and phones. The size of the bathrooms varies from unit to unit, so look around. A continental breakfast is included and there's a good restaurant.

Hotel El Sol (☎ 23-2120, 23-1070; hotelvicus@hotmail.com; E Aguirre 119; s/d US$17/22; 🛒 P) The clean and comfortable El Sol has rooms with cable TV, fans and phones, but they vary in quality and size, so look around. It has a restaurant.

Hotel Aristi (☎ /fax 22-8673; F Cabrera 102; s/d US$17/25; P) The Aristi has a restaurant attached and decent rooms with fan, cable TV, phone and minifridge.

Hotel America (☎ 22-9305, 27-0664; americahotel@latinmail.com; L Gonzales 943; s/d US$17/24; 🖵) The America's nicely appointed, good-sized rooms have fans, cable TV, and minifridge. Its restaurant is open Monday to Saturday; on those days a continental breakfast is included in the rates.

Eras Hotel (☎ 23-6333, 23-5712; negotur@terra.com.pe; Vicente de la Vega 851; s/d US$20/25; 🖵) New and modern, the hotel has comfortable, carpeted rooms with cable TV, chairs and table, minifridge, sound-resistant windows, and a bathtub in some of the double rooms. The rates include breakfast, served in the hotel's brightly lit chicken restaurant. Chiclayo loves chicken!

Inca Hotel (☎ 23-5931, 23-7803; incahotel@cpi.udep.edu.pe; L Gonzales 622; s/d US$30/40; P 🛒) Finally, air-con! The carpeted rooms have sound-proofed windows and some have nice city views. Other features include direct-dial phones, hairdryer, minifridge and cable TV. Rates include a continental breakfast, and may be discounted if things are slow. The hotel has a restaurant, elevator and small casino.

TOP END

Hotel Las Musas (☎ 23-9884, 27-3445, 27-3450; lasmusas@terra.com.pe; Faiques 101; s/d US$40/55; P 🛒 🖵) Overlooking the peaceful Paseo de las Musas, this hotel has modern, spacious rooms, with cable TV, phone and minifridge. The bathrooms all have bathtubs as well as showers – a rarity in Peru. Some rooms have good views of the Paseo de las Musas park. A restaurant is open 7am to 11pm, and room service is available 24 hours. There is a karaoke-disco, small casino and tourist information, and tours are available. Rates include a continental breakfast.

Garza Hotel (☎ 22-8171/2; Bolognesi 756; s/d US$49/70; ste with Jacuzzi US$125; 🛒 🛒 P) This is a good but busy hotel with efficient services for businesspeople; there's a travel agency, a fine restaurant and bar, casino, and comfortable rooms with minifridge, cable TV and phone. The rates include breakfast.

Eating

Restaurant Romana (☎ 22-3598; J Balta 512; breakfast US$2.25, mains US$3-6; 🕑 7am-11pm or later) This locally popular place serves a wide variety of food with plenty of local dishes. If you're feeling brave, try the *chirimpico* for breakfast; it's stewed goat tripe and organs, and is guaranteed to cure a hangover (and maybe make you swear off booze altogether). Otherwise, you can have pastas, steaks, seafood, chicken or pork *chicharrones* with yucca. Cheap sandwiches and *menús* (set lunches) are also available.

Las Américas (☎ 20-9381, 23-7294; E Aguirre 824; sandwiches US$1, mains US$2.25-5; ☺ 7:30am-11:30pm) This bright, clean and popular place off the southeast corner of the plaza, is a perennial favorite. Choose from a varied menu of soups, meats and fish dishes – try the *criollo* (spicy Peruvian fare with Spanish and African influences) fish in a savory onion and tomato sauce.

Pueblo Viejo (☎ 20-6701, 22-9863; MM Izaga 900; mains US$2.50-5; ☺ noon-4:30pm) Chiclayano lunches are served under lazy overhead fans in a rustic ambiance of faded elegance. Recorded *criollo* songs of a bygone era and black-and-white photos of old Chiclayo help you while away the wait for lunch, which can include goat, seafood, or ceviche, including the local speciality, *chingirito*, a ceviche made out of dried dogfish. (Chewy!)

Hebron Chicken (☎ 22-2709; Balta 605; mains average US$4; ☺ 7:30am-midnight) This is one of Chiclayo's best chicken restaurants. It's brightly lit and extremely popular, and does a variety of meats other than just chicken.

El Rancho (☎ 27-3687; Balta 1115; breakfast US$1.50, sandwiches US$1-2, mains US$2-4.50; ☺ 7:30am-midnight) This is another of Chiclayo's best chicken restaurants. It cranks up the grill at midday, and also has some local dishes such as pork with yucca.

Govinda (☎ 22-7331; Balta 1029; menú US$1.50; ☺ 8am-9:30pm Mon-Sat, 8am-4pm Sun) If the goat's tripe and dried dogfish don't tickle your taste buds, the various vegetarian offerings, lovingly prepared by the Hare Krishna, probably will.

Pizzería Venecia (☎ 20-9453; Balta 413; large pizzas US$8; ☺ noon-late) This rip-roaring pizzeria attracts a young crowd that listens to rock and Latin favorites while they chug beer with their food.

Restaurant Vuelve Mi Imperial (☎ 23-5305; Balta 535; mains US$1.50-6.60) It's an unlovely hole-in-the-wall that is cheap and cheerful, has been around for ages and is locally popular. It specializes in grills, from a quarter chicken (US$1.50) to *cuy* (guinea pig; US$5) to your own huge personal mixed grill (US$6.60).

La Parra (☎ 22-7471, 22-5198; MM Izaga 752; mains US$2.50-6.50) There are two restaurants side by side; one is a *chifa* and the other is a grill, but they share an entrance and a kitchen. Both menus are available in each dining room.

Restaurant El Huaralino (☎ 27-0330; Libertad 155; mains US$5-10) One of Chiclayo's most upscale restaurants that serves good local and international cuisine and owns some of the cleanest bathrooms in Peru.

Restaurant Típico La Fiesta (☎ 20-1970; Salaverry 1820; mains US$5-12; ☺ 9:30am-11pm) Perhaps the best in Chiclayo, La Fiesta is in the Residencial 3 de Octubre suburb, about 2km west of the Gran Hotel Chiclayo. It's expensive by Peruvian standards, but the food is a delicious variety of local meats and seafood.

Entertainment

Travelers with kids might want to check out the **playground** at the west end of E Aguirre. **Cine Tropical**, on the Plaza de Armas, often has English-language films. **Cine Primavera** (☎ 20-7471; L Gonzales 1235) has five screens, often showing some Hollywood flicks. There are several **casinos**, some with discos, on Balta south of the Plaza de Armas.

Getting There & Away
AIR

The **airport** (☎ 23-3192) is 2km southeast of town; a taxi ride there is US$1. **Aero Continente** (☎ 20-9916, 22-6241, airport 20-9919; S José 867) has flights from Lima, continuing to Piura, every morning and evening. These services change often. There's a US$3.50 airport departure tax. **Tans** (☎ 22-6546; 7 de Enero 638) and **LanPeru** (☎ 27-4875; MM Izaga 770) have offices in town but no current flights to Chiclayo.

Charter and sightseeing flights in small aircraft are available from **Aero Servicio Andino** (☎ 23-3161).

BUS

Most, if not all, buses going north, travel up the New Panamericana.

Linea (☎ 23-3497; Bolognesi 638) has buses to: Trujillo (US$3, three hours), every hour from 6am to 8pm; Lima (US$11.50 to US$17, 11 hours) at 8pm and 8:30pm; Chimbote (US$4.50, five hours) at 9:15am and 3:15pm; Piura (US$3, three hours), every hour from 6am to 8pm; Cajamarca (US$6 to US$7.50, 5½ hours) at 10pm and 10:45pm; and Jaén (US$4.50 to US$5, six hours) at 1pm and 11pm.

Cruz del Sur (☎ 22-5508, 23-7965, 22-1181; Bolognesi 888) has various levels of service to Lima (US$10 to US$30) four times a day. **Oltursa**

(☎ 23-7789) has a ticket office at J Balta 598, but buses depart from Vincente de la Vega 101. Its bus-camas go to Lima (US$18 to US$25) at 8pm and 10 pm. **Civa** (☎ 24-4671; Bolognesi 714) has buses to: Lima at 8pm; Jaén at 10am and 9pm; Bagua Chica at 9pm; and Chachapoyas (US$6, 12 hours) at 5:30pm. **Emtrafesa** (☎ 23-4291; J Balta 110) goes to Trujillo and Lima.

Empresa Chiclayo (☎ 23-7984; JL Ortiz 010) has 15 daily buses to Piura, with the 9pm departure continuing to Tumbes.

Empresa Transcade (☎ 23-2552; 20-4945; J Balta 110) has morning and night buses to Jaén and Bagua Grande (US$4.50, six hours).

Tepsa (Bolognesi at Colón) has buses up and down the coast. Inside the Tepsa terminal are about 12 smaller agencies with buses to inland towns such as Cajamarca, Chachapoyas, Tarapoto, Huancabamba, Jaén, Celendín, Cajabamba and others.

Flores (J Balta 178) has buses up and down the coast. **Paredes Estrella** (☎ 20-4879), in the Flores terminal, has buses to Tarapoto (US$12, 18 hours) at 5am, 2pm and 4pm; and to Yurimaguas (US$15, 24 hours) at 2pm and 9pm.

Getting Around

Transportes Lambayeque (San José) minibuses to Lambayeque leave every few minutes. They'll drop you off right in front of the Bruning Museum (see p285) for US$0.25. A block away, there are frequent buses to Pimentel.

Buses for Ferreñafe, Sipán, Monsefú and Zaña leave frequently from the **Terminal de Microbuses Epsel** (Nicolás de Píerola at Oriente), northeast of downtown. Many other small local towns are serviced by this terminal.

Buses to Túcume leave from Angamos near M Pardo – it's hard to find this bus stop, so ask. Bus stops for small local towns change often; keep asking around.

AROUND CHICLAYO

For transport details to these localities from Chiclayo, see Getting Around under Chiclayo.

The Coast

☎ 074

Two coastal villages, Pimentel and Santa Rosa, can be conveniently visited from Chiclayo. Most beachgoers stay in Chiclayo,

because accommodations elsewhere are very limited. Simple rooms, however, can be rented in the villages – ask around.

Pimentel, 14km from Chiclayo, has a good sandy beach that gets very crowded on summer weekends (January to March) but is quiet during the off season. Stay at **Hostal Garuda** (☎ 45-2964; Quiñones 109; s US$7, s/d with shower US$11.50/17.25). The *hostal* is a block back from the coast and breakfast is available on request.

A few kilometers south of Pimentel is **Santa Rosa**, a busy fishing village where a few *caballitos* may still be seen. There is also a modern fishing fleet. (Pimentel also has *caballitos*.) You can walk from Pimentel to Santa Rosa in less than an hour or take a local bus. Both villages have seafood restaurants, though most are closed in the off season.

Colectivos operate from Santa Rosa to the small port of **Puerto Etén** to the south. Here, you can see a 19th-century train engine in the (disused) train station before heading down to the beach.

From Puerto Etén or Santa Rosa, you can return to Chiclayo via the village of **Monsefú**, 15km south of Chiclayo. Monsefú is known for its handicrafts. Several stores sell basketwork, embroidery and woodwork, and a craft festival called **Fexticum** is held in the last week of July. The village has a few simple restaurants, of which the simple and rustic Restaurant Tradiciones is recommended for good local food.

Transport to Pimentel leave from Chiclayo (see p283); during summer (January to March), they continue on from Pimentel along the so-called *circuito de playas* (beach circuit) through Santa Rosa, Puerto Etén and Monsefú before returning to Chiclayo the same day.

Sipán

This archaeological **site** (☎ 80-0048; adult/student US$2/0.75; ♥ 8am-5pm), also known as Huaca Rayada, was discovered by *huaqueros* (see the boxed text on p274) from the nearby village of Sipán. When local archaeologist Dr Walter Alva became aware of a huge influx of beautiful objects on the black market in early 1987, he realized that a wonderful burial site was being ransacked in the Chiclayo area. Careful questioning led Dr Alva to the Sipán pyramids, which, to the untrained eye, look like earthen hills with holes excavated in them.

By the time Dr Alva and his colleagues found the site, at least one major tomb had been pillaged by looters. Fast protective action by local archaeologists and police stopped the plundering. Scientists were then fortunate to discover several other, even better, tombs that the graverobbers had missed, including an exceptional royal Moche burial, which became known as The Lord of Sipán. One *huaquero* was shot and killed by police in the early, tense days of the struggle over the graves. The Sipán locals were obviously unhappy that this treasure trove had been made inaccessible to them and were not friendly to archaeologists. To solve this problem, the locals were invited to train to become excavators, researchers and guards at the site, which now provides steady employment to many of them.

The story, an exciting one of buried treasure, *huaqueros*, police, archaeologists and at least one killing, is detailed in articles by Dr Alva in the October 1988 and June 1990 issues of *National Geographic* magazine, and in the May 1994 issue of *Natural History* magazine. Also interesting is the book *Royal Tombs of Sipán* by Walter Alva and Christopher B Donnan.

Archaeologists continue to work at the site. Some of the tombs have been restored with replicas to show what they looked like just before being closed up over 1500 years

ago. The actual artefacts went on a world tour, and most returned to Lambayeque's Museo Tumbas Reales De Sipán, where they are now displayed. Opposite the entrance is a small on-site **museum**, which is worth a visit. Nearby are simple snack bars and gift shops, and guides can be hired (US$3). Climb the hill behind the museum for a good view of the entire site and surrounding area.

Daily guided tours are available from tour agencies in Chiclayo (see p280). Tours take about three hours.

Lambayeque

☎ 074 / pop 39,000 / elevation 50m

About 11km north of Chiclayo, Lambayeque was once the main town in the area but has now been completely overshadowed by Chiclayo. The town's museums (see following) are its best feature, but some colonial architecture can be seen, especially **La Casa de Logia** (2 de Mayo), a block south of the main plaza, which locals say has the longest balcony in Peru – you can see it from the street only. Continue past it to a popular, local restaurant with typical food and good service: **El Cantaro** (☎ 28-2196, 2 de Mayo 180; mains US$2.50-5.50; ♥ 10am-6pm). The museums are both within a 15-minute walk of the plaza, or you can grab a taxi. Everyone knows where the museums are. If traveling with children, note that a nice children's playground is near the Bruning museum.

MUSEO TUMBAS REALES DE SIPÁN

Opened in November 2002, this **museum** (☎ 28-3977/8; adult/student US$2/0.75; ♥ 9am-noon & 2:30-4pm Tue-Sun, museum stays open one hour after last admission; ☒ ℗) is the pride of northern Peru, as well it should be. It's a world-class facility designed specifically to showcase the marvelous finds of the Royal Tombs of Sipán. The director of the museum is Dr Walter Alva, who was responsible for the discovery, protection and archaeological investigation of Sipán. Photography is not permitted and all bags must be checked.

Visitors enter through the 3rd floor and enter a hall containing fabulous ceramics representing gods, people, plants, llamas and other animals. Large photos and models show what Sipán is and was like: in AD 300 there were two huge truncated pyramids, constructed over several generations, of millions of adobe bricks. Descending into the 2nd floor, visitors see how the archaeologists worked at excavating, preserving and restoring the royal finds. Objects include three pairs of turquoise-and-gold ear ornaments showing ducks, deer and the Lord of Sipán himself. The painstaking and advanced techniques necessary to create this jewelry place them among the most beautiful and important objects of the pre-Columbian Americas. Finally, the ground floor is reached, featuring exact reproductions of how the tombs were found. Numerous dazzling objects are displayed, most remarkable among them being gold pectoral plates representing sea creatures such as octopus and crab.

The lighting and layout is exceptional, but the signage is all in Spanish. Guides are available for US$3; some speak English. Each guide can accompany up to 20 visitors.

BRUNING MUSEUM

The modern **museum** (☎ 28-2110, 28-3440; adult/student US$2/0.75; 🕑 9am-5pm) houses a good collection of archaeological artefacts from the Chimu, Moche, Chavín and Vicus cultures. Students of archaeology will enjoy the exhibits showing the development of different phases of ceramics from different cultures, and the exhibits explaining how ceramics and metalwork were made. There are models of several important sites. The labels are in Spanish, but even if you don't read Spanish, the museum is worth a visit. English-speaking guides charges US$3. Buses from Chiclayo drop you off a block from the museum.

Ferreñafe

☎ 074 / pop 31,000

This old town, 18km northeast of Chiclayo, is worth visiting for its excellent **Museo Nacional Sicán** (☎ 28-6469; adult/student US$2/0.75; 🕑 9am-5pm Tue-Sun). Sicán (not to be confused with Sipán) is an archaeological site pertaining to the Lambayeque culture (AD 750–1375), which was contemporary with, but unrelated to, the Chimu. The site lies in remote country to the north and is hard to visit. The splendid museum (inaugurated in November 2001) displays replicas of the 12m-deep tombs found at the site, among the largest tombs found in South America.

Enigmatic burials were discovered within – the Lord of Sicán was buried upside down, in a fetal position with his head separated from his body. Another important burial was of a nobleman in a cross-legged sitting position, arms folded, gazing east and wearing a mask and headdress of gold and feathers, surrounded by smaller tombs and niches containing the bodies of young women. Go have a look; it's worth the ride out. And it's never crowded.

Túcume

This vast and little-known **site** (☎ 80-0052; adult/student US$2/0.75; 🕑 8am-4:30pm) can be seen from a spectacular cliff-top *mirador* (lookout) around 30km to the north of Lambayeque on the Panamericana. It is worth the climb to see over 200 hectares of crumbling walls, plazas and no fewer than 28 pyramids. This was the capital of the Lambayeque culture (see Ferreñafe). Little excavation has been done, and no spectacular tombs have been found (although some later Inca burials have been found), but it is the sheer size of the site that makes it a memorable visit. More details are found in *Pyramids of Túcume: The Quest for Peru's Forgotten City*, by Thor Heyerdahl, Daniel H Sandweiss and Alfredo Narváez. This book is currently out of print, but is available at many public libraries.

There is a small but attractive and interesting on-site **museum**. Nearby is a snack bar and guides are available (US$3).

At Túcume, you have to walk almost a kilometer from where the bus from Chiclayo drops you off. Buses from Lambayeque also go here (ask at the Bruning museum). Guided tours are available from Chiclayo (see p280).

Chiclayo to Chota via Chongoyape

About halfway to Chongoyape, a few kilometers beyond Tumán, a minor road on your left leads to the ruins of **Batán Grande**, 31km away. (Some exhibits from this site are in Ferreñafe's Museo Nacional Sicán; see opposite for details.) This is a major archaeological site where about 50 pyramids have been identified and several burials have been excavated. With the urging of Dr Walter Alva, among others, the site has recently become the **Santuario Histórico Bosque de Pomac**, but there is no tourist infrastructure. The reserve protects a forest of *algarrobo* (mesquite) trees.

As there is almost no public transport to Batán Grande, you will have to find a taxi or tour to take you. There are also poor roads to Batán Grande from the villages of Chongoyape and Ferreñafe.

Chongoyape is an old village about 65km east of Chiclayo, in the foothills of the Andes. Buses from Terminal de Microbuses Edsel in Chiclayo take about 1½ hours for the journey. The village has a cheap, basic hotel. The **Chavín Petroglyphs of Cerro Mulato** are 3km away, and there are a few other minor archaeological sites. The irrigation complex of **Tinajones** forms a large reservoir just before Chongoyape.

A rough but scenic road climbs east from Chongoyape into the Andes until it reaches **Chota** (at an altitude of around 2400m), a 170km journey that takes about eight hours. Two or three buses a day from Chiclayo go through Chongoyape and continue on to Chota, where there are basic hotels. From Chota, a daily bus makes the rough journey via Bambamarca and Hualgayoc to Cajamarca.

Zaña
☎ 074

Also called Saña, the old site of the village is a ghost town about 50km southeast of Chiclayo. Founded in 1563, Zaña once held a wealth of colonial architecture, with a number of rich churches and monasteries. At one time, it was even slated to become the nation's capital. During the 17th century, it survived attacks by pirates and slave uprisings, only to be destroyed by the great flood of 1720. Today, great walls and the arches of four churches poke eerily out of the desert sands. Nearby, the present-day village of Zaña houses about 1000 people. Stay at the **Centro Vacacional Santa Ana** (☎ 43-1025). Buses go to the new town from Chiclayo's Terminal de Microbuses Edsel, or you can take a tour.

PIURA
☎ 073 / pop 342,000

Piura is the capital of its department. Intense irrigation of the desert has made it a major agricultural center, with rice and cotton being the main crops. Corn and plantains (type of bananas) are also cultivated.

The department's petroleum industry, based around the coastal oil fields near Talara, is as valuable as its agriculture.

Piura's economic development has been precarious, buffeted by extreme droughts and devastating floods. The department was among the hardest hit by the disastrous El Niño floods of 1983, which destroyed almost 90% of the rice, cotton and plantain crops, as well as causing serious damage to roads, bridges, buildings and oil wells in the area, and many people were left with no food, homes or jobs. The El Niño of 1992 washed out roads and bridges north of Piura, and going by bus to Tumbes involved a relay of buses. Passengers frequently had to wade through rivers to meet a successive bus. This was repeated during the 1998 El Niño, when the Bolognesi bridge in central Piura collapsed, killing several people.

Piura is referred to as the oldest colonial town in Peru. Its original site, on the north banks of the Río Chira, was called San Miguel de Piura and was founded by Pizarro in 1532, before he headed inland and began the conquest of the Incas. The settlement moved three times before construction at its present location began in 1588. Piura's cathedral dates from that year, and the city center still has a number of colonial buildings, though many were destroyed in the earthquake of 1912. Today, the center of the city is the large, shady and pleasant Plaza de Armas.

The center of the Vicus culture – which existed around the time of Christ – was roughly 30km east of Piura. Although no buildings remain from that period, tombs have yielded a great number of ceramics, which can be seen in the museums of Piura and Lima.

Information
Tourist information is available at the **Consejo Provinicial** (☎ 30-3208; Plaza de Armas; 8am-1pm & 4-8pm Mon-Fri, 8am-1pm Sat). BCP (with Visa ATM), Banco Wiese (MasterCard ATM) and Banco Continental are all on the Plaza de Armas. *Casas de cambio* are at the Ica and Arequipa intersection.

Internet access is available at **Piura@online** (Arequipa 728), **KFE Net** (S Cerro 273) and others on S Cerro.

The best medical attention is at **Clínica San Miguel** (☎ 30-9300, 33-5913; Los Cocos 111; ⏲ 24hr).

Piura Tours (☎ 32-8873; piuratours@mail.udep.edu.pe; Ayacucho 585) is a recommended travel agency that's registered with IATA.

Museums

The small **Museo de Oro Vicus** (☎ 30-9267; Huánuco 893; US$0.90; ☺ 9am-5pm Tue-Sun) has an underground gold museum from nearby Vicus culture sites. Some excellent pieces are displayed, including a gold belt decorated with a life-sized, gold cat head that puts modern belt-buckles to shame. Upstairs are local archaeology and changing art exhibits (free of charge).

Casa Grau (☎ 32-6541; Tacna 662; entry by donation; ☺ 8am-noon & 3-6pm Mon-Fri, 8am-noon Sat & Sun) is the house where Admiral Miguel

Grau was born on July 27, 1834. The house was almost completely destroyed by the 1912 earthquake; it was later restored by the Peruvian navy and is now a naval museum. Admiral Grau was a hero of the War of the Pacific against Chile (1879–80) and captain of the British-built warship *Huáscar*, a model of which can be seen in the museum.

Churches

The **cathedral** on the Plaza de Armas is Piura's oldest church. Parts of it date from 1588, but the main altar was built in 1960. The side altar of the Virgin of Fatima, built in the early 17th century, was once the main altar and is the oldest. Famed local artist,

NORTH COAST

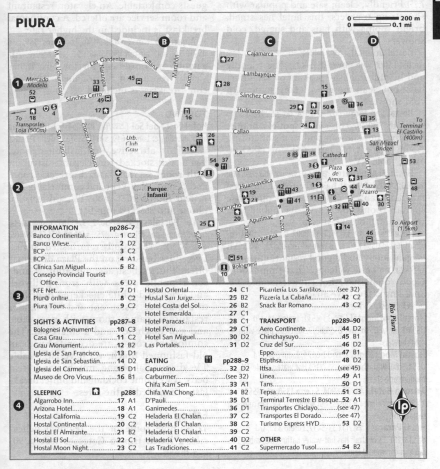

PIURA

0 — 200 m
0 — 0.1 mi

INFORMATION	pp286–7
Banco Continental	1 C2
Banco Wiese	2 D2
BCP	3 C2
BCP	4 A1
Clínica San Miguel	5 B2
Consejo Provincial Tourist Office	6 D2
KFE Net	7 D1
Plur@ online	8 C2
Piura Tours	9 C2

SIGHTS & ACTIVITIES	pp287–8
Bolognesi Monument	10 C3
Casa Grau	11 C2
Grau Monument	12 B2
Iglesia de San Francisco	13 D1
Iglesia de San Sebastián	14 D2
Iglesia del Carmen	15 D1
Museo de Oro Vicus	16 B1

SLEEPING	p288
Algarrobo Inn	17 A1
Arizona Hotel	18 A1
Hostal California	19 C2
Hostal Continental	20 C2
Hostal El Almirante	21 B2
Hostal El Sol	22 C1
Hostal Moon Night	23 C2

Hostal Oriental	24 C1
Hostal San Jorge	25 B2
Hotel Costa del Sol	26 B2
Hotel Esmeralda	27 C1
Hotel Paracas	28 C1
Hotel Peru	29 C1
Hotel San Miguel	30 D2
Las Portales	31 D2

EATING 🍴	pp288–9
Capuccino	32 D2
Carburmer	(see 32)
Chifa Kam Sem	33 A1
Chifa Wa Chong	34 B2
D'Pauli	35 D1
Ganimedes	36 D1
Heladería El Chalan	37 C2
Heladería El Chalan	38 C2
Heladería El Chalan	39 C2
Heladería Venecia	40 D2
Las Tradiciones	41 C2

Picantería Los Santitos	(see 32)
Pizzería La Cabaña	42 C2
Snack Bar Romano	43 C2

TRANSPORT	pp289–90
Aero Continente	44 D2
Chinchaysuyo	45 B1
Cruz del Sur	46 D2
Eppo	47 B1
Etipthsa	48 D2
Ittsa	(see 45)
Linea	49 A1
Tans	50 D1
Tepsa	51 C3
Terminal Terrestre El Bosque	52 A1
Transportes Chiclayo	(see 47)
Transportes El Dorado	(see 47)
Turismo Express HYD	53 D2

OTHER	
Supermercado Tusol	54 B2

Ignacio Merino, painted the canvas of San Martín de Porres in the mid-19th century.

Other churches worth seeing are the **Iglesia de San Francisco**, where Piura's independence was declared on January 4, 1821, and the colonial churches of **El Carmen**, with a religious art museum and the chair used by the pope in 1985, and **San Sebastián**.

Jirón Lima
This street, a block southeast of the Plaza de Armas, has preserved its colonial character more than most in Piura.

Sleeping
BUDGET
Hostal California (☎ 32-8789; Junín 835; s/d US$4/7.25) Friendly, clean, safe and popular with shoestring travelers, this hotel has small, bright rooms with fans and shared, cold showers.

Hostal Oriental (☎ 30-4011, 30-8891; Callao 446; s/d US$3.50/7, with shower US$5/8.75) The friendly and helpful English-speaking owner offers basic but clean rooms with fans; some with cold showers.

Hostal San Jorge (☎ 32-7514; fax 32-2928; Loreto 960; s/d US$7.30/10) This small, spotless, homey hotel has hot showers and so it's often full. Rooms have table fans and, for US$1.50 extra, cable TV.

Hostal El Almirante (☎ 32-9137, ☎ /fax 33-5239; Ica 860; s/d US$10/13) It has private hot showers, fans and cable TV in clean but otherwise spartan rooms; there's a large public area with a small breakfast café.

Hotel Peru (☎ 33-3421, 33-5007; fax 33-1530; Arequipa 476; s/d US$11.30/17, d with air-con US$23; 🟈) An elegant lobby and a good restaurant (*menú* US$2) make a welcome first impression. Good rooms have hot showers, cable TV and fans; a few have air-con.

Also consider:

Hostal Continental (☎ 33-4531; Junín 924; s/d US$4/5.80, with shower US$5.80/7.30) Clean place with cold showers.

Hostal Moon Night (☎ 33-6174; Junín 899; s/d US$4/5.80, with showers US$7/10) Hot water, cable TV, modern and clean.

Arizona Hotel (☎ 30-6904; S Cerro 1350; s/d US$9/11.50) Convenient for buses, hot shower, a TV, fan and restaurant.

Hotel Paracas (☎ /fax 33-5412; Loreto 339; s/d US$13/18) It's central; has hot-water bathrooms, cable TV, fan and communal laundry.

MID-RANGE
These hotels all have private hot showers.

Hostal El Sol (☎ 32-4461, 32-6307; elsol@mail.udep.edu.pe; S Cerro 455; s/d US$14/20; 🟈 P) Rooms here are good-sized and are good value with a ceiling fan and cable TV. A restaurant is available for breakfast and a US$1.50 *menú*.

Hotel San Miguel (☎ 30-5122; Apurímac 1007; s/d US$11.50/20) A modern hotel overlooking a quiet park, this hotel is a good choice for its spotless standard rooms. There's a café on the premises and the staff are helpful.

Hotel Esmeralda (☎ 33-1205, 33-1782; reservas@hotelesmeralda.com.pe; Loreto 235; s/d US$20/25, with air-con US$37/48; P 🟈) The carpeted rooms with cable TV, phone and minifridge keep guests comfortable. An elevator, restaurant and room service are offered. A continental breakfast is included in the higher rate.

Algarrobo Inn (☎ 30-7450; Los Cocos 389; s/d US$10/20, with air-con US$35/45; 🟈 P) The Algarrobo is convenient for the bus; it has shabby rooms but two of them have air-con. Breakfast is included.

TOP END
Hotel Costa del Sol (☎ /fax 30-2864; hotelcostasol@mail.udep.edu.pe; Loreto 649; s/d US$55/65; 🟈 P 🟈 🟈) This attractive, old-fashioned hotel has a well-stocked bar, elegant restaurant with room service, Jacuzzi, exercise room and casino. Well-kept and comfortably furnished rooms offer cable TV, a direct-dial phone and stocked minibar.

Los Portales (☎ 32-3072, 32-1161; losportales@cpi.udep.edu.pe; Libertad 875; s/d/ste US$65/85/105; 🟈 🟈 P 🟈) A fully refurbished, attractive, older building on the Plaza de Armas offers Piura's best accomodation. Handsome public areas with iron grillwork and black-and-white checkered floor lead to a poolside restaurant and bar, indoor restaurant, games room with pool table and slot machines, and a smart bar. The comfortable rooms are decorated with an old-fashioned touch, yet have large cable TV, direct-dial phone, minibar and great beds. A welcome cocktail and buffet breakfast is included in the rates.

Eating
To sample some of the regional delicacies, a lunch trip to Catacaos (see p290) is a must.

Picantería Los Santitos (☎ 33-2380; Libertad 1014; mains US$2.50-6; 11am-3pm;) Inside a small mall, this cool and pleasingly old-fashioned restaurant has wooden floors, mud-plastered walls, cane ceilings and coastal music playing quietly in the background. It's the best place in town for a typical lunch; ask for their *piqueo*, a sampler platter of several local dishes.

Carburmer (☎ 33-2380; Libertad 1014; mains average US$6, large pizza US$8; 6-11pm;) Next door to, and under the same management as Los Santitos, this cozy, romantic place is the best Italian restaurant in town.

Capuccino (☎ 30-1111; Libertad 1048; sandwiches US$2.50) Adjoining the same small mall, this is an excellent place for coffees and desserts.

Heladería Venecia (Libertad at Apurímac) Opposite the Capuccino, this corner shop does a good ice-cream trade.

Heladería El Chalan (Tacna 520; Grau 173; Grau 453; US$1.50-3; 7:30am-10pm) This popular fast-food place has several outlets. All burgers and sandwiches are freshly prepared, and it has a good selection of juices and cakes, and over a dozen ice creams.

Ganimedes (☎ 32-9176; Lima 440; menú US$1.50, mains US$2-3; 7:30am-9:30pm Mon-Sat, 11am-8pm Sun) This is Piura's purest vegetarian restaurant. No goat-head soups here, but plenty of refreshing fruit juices and yummy yogurts.

Snack Bar Romano (☎ 32 3399; Ayacucho 580; menú US$1.70; 8am-10pm; mains US$2-6) This is a local favorite and has been recommended several times by readers. The seafood is good here.

Other recommendations:

Pizzería La Cabaña (Ayacucho 598) Good Italian food.

Las Tradiciones (☎ 32-2683; Ayacucho 579; menú US$1.70) Serves Peruvian standards.

Chifa Wa Chong (Loreto 652; mains US$2-3) Small, locally popular *chifa* with large, tasty portions.

D'Pauli (Lima 451) Great cake shop.

Chifa Kam Sen (☎ 32-2407; S Cerro 1238) Cheap *chifa* that's convenient for bus stations.

Supermercado Tusol (Plaza Grau) For self-catering.

Getting There & Away
AIR
The **airport** (☎ 34-4505) is on the southeastern bank of the Río Piura, 2km from the city center. Schedules change often. The usual US$3.50 airport tax is charged. **Aero Continente** (☎ 32-5635; Libertad 951) has daily

morning and evening flights to Lima via Chiclayo. **Tans** (☎ 30-6886; Libertad 442) has an office here – but no Piura flights.

BUS
International
The standard route to Ecuador goes via Tumbes to Machala, Ecuador, along the Panamericana. **Transportes Loja** (☎ 30-9407; S Cerro 228) has direct buses to Machala (US$7.50, seven hours) at 10:30pm, and also via La Tina to Macará (US$3.50, four hours) and Loja (US$7.25, eight hours) at 9:30am and 9pm. These buses stop for border formalities, then continue. (Transportes Loja is based in Ecuador.)

Domestic
The best services to Lima (12 to 16 hours) are with **Cruz del Sur** (☎ 33-7094; Bolognesi at Lima), which has several afternoon and evening departures for US$11, plus a Bus-cama service for US$24 to US$30. **Tepsa** (☎ 32-3721, Loreto 1198) also has buses to Lima.

Several companies have offices on the 1100 block of S Cerro. **Eppo** (☎ 30-4543, S Cerro 1141) has buses to Sullana (US$0.50) and Talara (US$2) every 30 minutes, and slow, frequently stopping buses to Máncora (US$3.20, 3½ hours) six times a day. **Transportes El Dorado** (☎ 32-5875, 33-6952; S Cerro 1119) has buses for Tumbes (US$4.50, five hours) eight times a day. **Ittsa** (☎ 33-3982; S Cerro 1142) has buses to Trujillo (US$4.50 to US$7.50), Chimbote, and bus-camas to Lima (US$20). **Transportes Chiclayo** (S Cerro 1121) has almost hourly buses to Chiclayo (US$3, three hours). **Linea** (☎ 32-7821; S Cerro 1215) has 17 buses between 5am to 7:30pm to Chiclayo, an 11pm bus to Trujillo and a 6pm bus to Cajamarca (10 hours). It may have some buses to Jaén. For Cajamarca and across the northern Andes, it's usually best to go to Chiclayo and get a connection there. **Chinchaysuyo** (S Cerro 1156) has overnight buses to Huaraz via Trujillo.

A few blocks east of the San Miguel pedestrian bridge over the river on Huancavelica, Terminal El Castillo has buses for departmental towns east of Piura. **Turismo Express HYD** (☎ 34-5382; Tacna 104) and **Etipthsa** (☎ 34-5174; Tacna 277) have buses to Huancabamba (US$7, eight to 10 hours), usually around 7am and 7pm. These buses stop at Terminal El Castillo.

Buses and combis for the departmental towns on the coast (such as Catacaos, Sullana and Paita) leave from **Terminal Terrestre El Bosque** (1200 block of S Cerro).

Catch buses for Chulucanas opposite the Eppo and El Dorado bus terminals.

CATACAOS

☎ 073 / pop 66,000

The village of Catacaos, 12km southwest of Piura, is famous for its **crafts market** and for its local restaurants, which are particularly recommended for lunch. Reach it by colectivo from the Terminal Terrestre in Piura.

The crafts market sells a good variety of products, including gold and silver filigree ornaments, wood carvings, leather work and panama hats.

There are several little *picanterías* (local restaurants) serving *chicha* (a fermented maize beer) and dishes typical of the area. Most *picanterías* are only open two or three days a week, but as there are so many of them, you won't have any difficulty finding several open on the day you visit. They open for lunch rather than dinner, and live music is sometimes played. Typical *norteño* (northern) dishes include *seco de chabelo* (a thick plantain and beef stew), *seco de cabrito* (goat stew), *tamales verdes* (green corn dumplings), *caldo de siete carnes* (a thick soup with seven types of meat), *copus* (made from dried goat heads cured in vinegar and then stewed for several hours with goat meat and vegetables such as turnips, sweet potatoes and plantains), *carne aliñada* (dried and fried ham slices served with fried plantains) and many other dishes, including the familiar seafood ceviches of the Peruvian coast.

Catacaos is famous for its elaborate **Semana Santa** (Holy Week) processions and celebrations.

PAITA

☎ 073 / pop 53,000

The main port of the Department of Piura is the historic town of Paita, 50km due west of Piura by paved road. There are several banks and a basic hospital.

Paita's secluded location on a natural bay surrounded by cliffs did not protect it from the seafaring conquistadors; Pizarro landed here in 1527 on his second voyage to Peru. Since then, Paita has had an interesting history. It became a Spanish colonial port and was frequently sacked by pirates and buccaneers. According to local historians:

In 1579, Paita was the victim of the savage aggression of the English filibuster, Francis Drake. Apparently, he heard that the Spanish galleon *Sacafuego* was in the area, laden with treasure destined for the Spanish crown. With shooting and violence, he attacked the port, reducing its temple, monastery and houses to ashes, and fleeing with his booty.

Sir Francis Drake was not the only one making life miserable for the Spaniards. Numerous privateers arrived during the centuries that followed, with another notable episode occurring in the 18th century, when the Protestant buccaneer George Anson attempted to decapitate the wooden statue of Our Lady of Mercy. The statue, complete with slashed neck, can still be seen in the church of **La Merced**. The feast of **La Virgen de La Merced** is held annually on September 24.

Paita is also famous as the **home of Manuela Sáenz**, the influential mistress of Simón Bolívar. She was Ecuadorian, and arrived here upon Bolívar's death in 1850. Forgoing the fame and fortune left to her by her lover, she worked as a seamstress until her death over 20 years later. Her house still stands (people live there), and a plaque commemorates its history. Across the street is La Figura, a wooden figurehead from a pirate ship.

To the north and south of the port are good beaches, which are popular with holidaymakers from Piura during the summer season. A few kilometers to the north is the good beach of **Colán**, home to the oldest colonial church in Peru. The beach of **Yasila**, some 12km to the south, is also popular.

Sleeping & Eating

Despite the town's historic interest and beaches, Paita has only a few hotels, and most visitors stay in Piura. The best in town is **Hostal Las Brisas** (☎ 61-1023; fax 61-2175; Ayurora 201 at A Ugarte; s/d from US$11.50/17.30), which has rooms with phones, cable TV and hot-water bathrooms. **Hostal Miramar**

(☎ 61-1083; Jorge Chávez 418; s/d US$8.50/11.50) is in an attractive, though somewhat run-down colonial building. Cheaper options include **Hostal El Mundo** (☎ 61-1401; Bolívar 402; s/d US$5.80/8.80), which has rooms with showers, and a few other basic places to stay.

There are a few basic restaurants on or near the Plaza de Armas. The best place is in **Club Liberal** (☎ 61-1173; Jorge Chávez 162), where the public can eat seafood on the 2nd floor, which has views of the ocean.

On Colán beach, **Playa Colán Lodge** (http://pagina.de/colanlodge; 2-/4-/5-person cabin US$55/65/75; ☎ ℗) has tennis, a restaurant and bar. In the low season, there is a US$20 discount. Colán lacks phones so make reservations online or at **Piura Tours** (☎ 32-8873; Ayacucho 585, Piura). There's a couple of cheaper places nearby.

Getting There & Away

Transportes Dora (S Cerro 1387, Piura) has buses to Paita from near Terminal Terrestre in Piura every 20 minutes.

SULLANA

☎ 073 / pop 174,000 / elevation 90m

A modern city 38km north of Piura, Sullana is a busy commercial and agricultural center, and therefore has several hotels. There's little to see in Sullana except the hustle and bustle of a Peruvian market town and most travelers stay in Piura. Transportation from the Ecuadorian border at Macará/La Tina (see p293) arrives here (and may continue to Piura).

Sleeping & Eating

Decent budget hotels include the **Hostal Santa Julia** (☎ 50-2714; Grau 1084; s/d US$6/9) with private, cold-water bathrooms. Better is **Hostal Turicamari** (☎ 50-2899; San Martín 814; s/d US$5.80/7.30 with shower US$8.50/11.50) Some rooms have hot water. The best is **Hostal La Siesta** (☎ /fax 50-2264; Av La Panamericana 404; s US$21-30, d US$25-38; ℗ ✖ ☎), on the outskirts of town.

Restaurant ParPlaza (Plaza de Armas) is a good place with a Peruvian menu.

CHULUCANAS

☎ 073 / pop 65,000 / elevation 95m

This village is about 55km east of Piura, just before the Sechura Desert starts rising into the Andean slopes. It is locally known for

its distinctive **ceramics** – rounded, glazed, earth-colored pots that represent people. These pots are becoming famous outside of Peru and can be purchased in Chulucanas and Piura, as well as in Lima, and even abroad.

There are a few basic hotels, including **Hostal Chulucanas Soler** (☎ 37-8576; Ica 209; s/d US$7/10), which is two blocks from the plaza and has rooms with bath and TV.

The village is reached by taking the Panamericana Vieja (Old Panamerican) due east for 50km, then north on a side road for about 5km more. There are direct buses from Piura.

HUANCABAMBA

☎ 073 / pop 30,000 / elevation 1957m

The eastern side of the Department of Piura is mountainous, has few roads and is infrequently visited by travelers. Huancabamba, 210km east of Piura by rough road, is one of the most important and interesting of the department's highland towns – it's a major center of *brujería*, which is loosely translated as witchcraft or sorcery.

Traveling east from Chullucanas, the road soon becomes dirt all the way to Huancabamba. Along the way you pass citrus groves, sugarcane fields and coffee plantations. Beyond **Canchaque** (which has some basic *hostals*), the road climbs steeply over a 3000m-high pass, before dropping to Huancabamba. This last 70km stretch is very rough, and subject to delays in the rainy season.

Huancabamba is an attractive country town in a lovely setting at the head of the long, narrow Río Huancabamba valley and surrounded by mountains. Although only 160km from the Pacific Ocean, the waters of the Huancabamba empty into the Atlantic, some 3500km away as the macaw flies. The banks of the Huancabamba are unstable and constantly eroding. The town itself is subject to frequent subsidence and slippage, and so has earned itself the nickname *la ciudad que camina*, or 'the town that walks'.

Although a few *curanderos* (medicine men) live in Huancabamba, those with the best reputation are found in the highlands north of town in the Huaringas lake region, almost 4000m above sea level. The main lake is **Shumbe**, 35km north of Huancabamba,

BRUJERÍA

Traditional *brujería* (witchcraft or sorcery) methods are used both to influence a client's future and to heal and cure. The use of local herbs or potions (including the hallucinogenic San Pedro cactus and home-made sugar-cane alcohol) is combined with ritual ablutions in certain lakes said to possess curative powers.

People from all walks of life and from all over Peru (and other Latin American countries) visit the *brujos* (shamans) and *curanderos* (medicine men or healers), paying sizable sums in their attempts to find cures for ailments that have not responded to more modern treatments, or to remedy unrequited love, bad luck or infertility. A typical healing ceremony will last all night and can cost roughly US$50 per person. Costs vary depending on how well known the healer is and how many people are being healed.

though the nearby **Laguna Negra** is the one most frequently used by the *curanderos*. Trucks from Huancabamba go as far as Sapalache, some 20km to the north, and you can hire mules from there. There's also a bus that leaves Huancabamba before dawn for the village of Salala, about a 45-minute walk from Sapalache. Many locals (but few gringos) visit the area, so finding information and guides is not difficult. The tradition, however, is taken very seriously, and gawkers or skeptics will get a hostile reception. This is not a trip for the faint of heart.

Also of interest is a dirt road that heads roughly west of Sapalache, over Cerro Chinguela, and gives access to *páramo* (grasslands) and montane cloud forests – good for serious **bird-watching**. A hummingbird called the Neblina Metaltail was discovered here, and it is the only known Peruvian site for the Red-faced Parrot (*Hapalopsittara pyrrhops*). Colonists are discovering the area, but ProAvesPeru, a nongovernmental organization, is trying to protect the area.

Information

Tourist information is available at the bus station. There you can get a list of certified *brujos* and *curanderos*. There are no facilities for credit cards or traveler's checks. There's a basic **hospital** (☎ 47-3024).

Sleeping & Eating

Hotels are all basic with shared bathrooms, usually with cold water. **Hostal El Dorado** (☎ 47-3016; Medina 116; s/d US$4/6) is on the Plaza de Armas. It has one of the best restaurants and a helpful owner. **Hostal Danubio** (☎ 47-3200; Grau 206; s/d US$4/6), on the corner of the plaza, has TVs available. There are others.

Restaurants to try include **Casa Blanca**, which serves Peruvian food. The local beverage is *rompope*, a concoction of sugarcane alcohol with raw egg, honey, lemon and spices – a pauper's pisco sour.

Getting There & Away

At the bus terminal, **Etipthsa** (☎ 47-3000) and **Turismo Express HYD** (☎ 47-3320) have morning and evening buses to Piura (US$7, eight hours). Combis for local destinations leave from the terminal as well.

AYABACA

☎ 073 / elevation 2715m

Ayabaca, a small colonial highland town in an isolated, rarely visited region close to the Ecuadorian border, gives access to the Ecuadorian village of Amaluza (five hours by various combis).

Credit cards and traveler's checks aren't negotiated in Ayabaca. Information is available at the **municipalidad** (Cáceres 578), on the Plaza de Armas.

The Inca site at **Ayapate** (2½ hours by truck, then three hours on foot) contains walls, flights of stairs, ceremonial baths and a central plaza, but is overgrown. Other Inca and pre-Inca sites, many unexplored, are found in the region, as well as mysterious caves, lakes and mountains, some of which are said to be bewitched. Ornithologists report excellent **bird-watching** habitats.

Visit the area in the mountain dry season when the trails are passable; avoid the wettest months of December to April. **Raul Bardales** (☎ 47-1043, leave message; Piura 331) guides tourists to Ayapate (US$30). Celso Acuña Calle has been recommended as a knowledgeable guide; ask around for him. Other recommendations are for orchid specialist Angel Seminario and Esteban Aguilera, in the adjoining village of Llacupampa.

The colorful religious festival of **El Señor Cautivo** (October 12 to 15), rarely seen by tourists, packs every hotel, and fiesta-goers sleep in the streets.

Sleeping & Eating

Hotel Samanaga Municipal (☎ /fax 47-1049; s/d US$8/11.50), on the Plaza de Armas, is the best option, with friendly staff, a decent restaurant and rooms with TV and hot showers. Cheaper choices include **Hotel Samanaga** (Tacna), **Hostal San Martín** (Cáceres 192) and **Hostal Alex** (Bolívar 112).

Getting There & Away

Ask at Piura's Terminal Terrestre about daily buses to Ayabaca.

TO/FROM ECUADOR VIA LA TINA

The border post of **La Tina** lacks hotels, but the Ecuadorian town of **Macará** (3km from the border) has adequate facilities. La Tina is reached by colectivo taxis (US$3, two hours) leaving Sullana throughout the day. Alternatively, **Transportes Loja** (☎ 30-9407; S Cerro 228, Piura) buses from Piura go straight through here and on to Loja – a convenient trip that minimises border hassles.

The border is the international bridge over the Río Calvas and is open 24 hours. Formalities are relaxed as long as your documents are all in order. There are no banks, though you'll find moneychangers at the border or in Macará, Ecuador. They'll change cash, but traveler's checks are hard to negotiate.

Travelers entering Ecuador will find taxis (including colectivos) to take them to Macará, where the Ecuadorian Immigration building is found on the 2nd floor of the municipalidad, on the plaza. Normally, only a valid passport is required. You are given a tourist card, which must be surrendered when leaving. See Lonely Planet's *Ecuador & the Galápagos Islands* for further information on Ecuador.

After crossing the international bridge, travelers entering Peru will find the migraciónes office on the right and the police on the left. There is a Peruvian Consulate in Macará.

TALARA

☎ 073 / pop 101,000

Forty years ago, Talara was a small fishing village. Today, it is the site of Peru's largest oil refinery, producing 60,000 barrels of petroleum a day. Talara is a desert town, so everything – including water – must be imported. During the 120km desert drive

along the Panamericana from Piura, you'll see the automatic pumps used in oil extraction. Although there are some good beaches near Talara, the town has little to interest the tourist, and its few hotels are often full of oil workers and businesspeople. Authorities, however, are promoting the beaches in an attempt to attract tourists. One of the better beaches is at **Las Peñitas**, 3km to the north.

Negritos, 11km south of Talara by road, is on Punta Pariñas, the most westerly point on the South American continent. The **tar pits** of La Brea, where Pizarro dug tar to caulk his ships, can be seen on the Pariñas Peninsula.

On the northern side of Talara are the **Pariñas Woods**. According to a local tourist-information booklet, the woods 'are perhaps the city's major tourist attraction, where one can encounter magnificent examples of wild rabbits and squirrels, etc, as well as a diversity of little birds that belong to the fauna of the place.' Don't miss them.

BCP (☎ 38-2671) and other banks are near the Centro Cívico.

Sleeping & Eating

Some 20 hotels house oil workers, but water supply is an ongoing problem. Try the following.

Hostal Grau (☎ 38-2841; Grau; A-77; s/d US$8/11) has rooms with bathrooms that have hot water for limited hours, and TV. **Hostal Charito** (☎ /fax 38-1600; Av B 143; US$25/35; ☒) has rooms with relatively reliable water supplies, minifridge and cable TV, and its restaurant offers room service. **Gran Hotel Pacifico** (☎ 38-2780, 38-5449; www.ghotelpacificotala ra.com.pe; s/d US$38/57; ☒ ☒ P) is the best place in town and has a café for snacks as well as a restaurant.

Getting There & Away

A few years ago, there were daily flights to Lima. Now, nothing. Check locally for the latest situation.

Many buses go to Talara from Piura or Tumbes.

CABO BLANCO

☎ 073

From Talara, the Panamericana heads northeast for 200km to the Ecuadorian border. The road parallels the ocean, with frequent views of the coast – a number of beaches, resorts and small villages are passed on the drive to Tumbes. Buses between the two towns (except for direct express services) can drop you off wherever you want. This area is also one of Peru's main oilfields, and oil pumps are often seen both on land and on platforms in the sea.

The ocean is fairly warm, staying at around 18°C year-round, although few Peruvians (except for the fishers) venture into the sea outside the hottest months of January to March. Women are advised not to visit the beaches alone.

About 40km north of Talara is Cabo Blanco, famous for sport fishing. Ernest Hemingway fished here in the early 1950s. The largest fish ever landed here on a rod was a 710kg black marlin, caught in 1953 by Alfred Glassell Jr. The angling is still good, though 20kg tuna are a more likely catch than black marlin, which have declined and are rarely over 100kg, although 300kg specimens are still occasionally caught on a catch-and-release basis. Mahi mahi is another frequent catch. During November to January, magnificent 3m waves attract hard-core surfers, some of whom camp on the beach for free. **Hostal Merlin** (☎ 85-6188, in Lima ☎ 01-442-8318; s/d US$20/30) has 12 huge rooms with handsome, stone-flagged floors, private cold showers and balconies with ocean views. Rates include a continental breakfast; other meals are available on request.

Fishing
The *La Cristina*, a 32-foot deep-sea fishing boat with high-quality Penn tackle, can be rented through Hostal Merlin and other area hotels for US$450 per eight-hour day, including drinks and lunch. Up to four anglers can be accommodated. Fishing is available year-round, though January, February and September are considered the best months.

MÁNCORA
☎ 073 / pop 13,000
The small fishing village of Máncora, about 30km further north, has a lovely beach that is popular with surfers and beach lovers, and is the most visited coastal resort on the north coast. It is unique in the area because it is directly accessible from the

Panamericana, is far enough south of Tumbes to avoid humidity and mosquitoes, and is sunny year-round. Although Peruvians and Ecuadorians flock here, it's not yet well-known by international travelers, but during the best surfing months of November to February it's 'quite a scene' according to one reader.

Other, remote, **deserted beaches** can be visited; ask your hotel to arrange a taxi or give you directions by bus and foot – be prepared to walk several kilometers. A good one is about 3km south of the unkempt fishing village of El Ñuro (itself 15km south of Máncora along the Panamericana). Here, there is a pier that used to be part of a now-defunct desalination plant, and which is excellent for **fishing**. A short way south of the pier, ringed by multihued hills where fossils may be found, **caves** attract the adventurous traveler. You can spend the day on the beach, completely alone. Taxi drivers will pick you up at a prearranged time (US$15 from Máncora).

Orientation & Information
The Panamericana, called Calle Piura at the south end and Calle Grau at the north, is the main drag through the center and most businesses are along it. From the bridge at the south end, the 'Antigua' (old) Panamericana, as it's known here, is a dirt road following the coast for several kilometers and passing upscale hotels. The beach is separated from the Panamericana by a block of businesses.

There is no information office, but a useful website is www.vivamancora.com. Two ATMs (no bank) accept Visa cards; otherwise money exchange is difficult, although the pricier hotels accept payment in US dollars cash. Several places offer Internet access. **Roviluz** (☎ 85-8276; Piura 509) is the best general store, sells phonecards and has several telephone booths. Addresses are not much used – just look for signs in the center.

Activities
SURFING
This is best from November to February, although good waves are found periodically year-round. Several budget hotels rent surfboards (US$4 per day) or you can try **Soledad** (Piura 316).

MUD BATHS

About 11km east of town, up the wooded Q Fernandez valley, a natural hot spring offers bubbling water and powder-fine mud that is perfect for a face pack. The slightly sulfurous water and mud is said to have curative properties. Development is limited to two clean pit toilets, which provide shelter for changing. The hot spring can be reached by mototaxi (US$8 including a wait) and admission is US$0.60.

TREKKING

To see some of the interior of this desert coast, hire a pickup to take you up the Q Fernandez valley, past the mud baths, and on until the road ends (about 1½ hours). Continue for two hours on horseback or foot through mixed woodlands with unique birdlife to reach *Los Pilares*, pools ideal for swimming. Local hotel owners can arrange guides and horses, or you can make arrangements in advance with **Peru Chasquitur** (in Lima ☎ 01-441-1455).

Sleeping

Rates for accommodations in Máncora are seasonal; the cheapest are from around mid-March to mid-December, depending on the hotel. January to mid-March is the high season, with rates approximately 50% higher, especially at weekends. The three major holiday weeks, Christmas–New Year, Semana Santa and Fiestas Patrias, can command rates triple or more than that of the low season, require multi-night stays, are very crowded, and are best avoided. School holidays in May and October may also command higher rates. Low-season rates are given here. Most hotels readily give discounts for travelers staying for several nights.

BUDGET

Cheap sleeps are found in the center of town, all close to the beach.

HI La Posada (☎ 85-8328; Panamericana Km1164; beds US$4.50-6, camping per person US$1.50; P) By the bridge at the south end of town, this quiet place is close to the beach. Safe, with a pleasant garden, hammocks and basic kitchen facilities, this HI-affiliated *hostal* attracts both overnight guests and long-stay travelers. Owner-manager Luisa goes out of her way to make guests feel comfort-able. Most rooms have bathrooms and vary from two to six beds. Recommended.

Hospedaje Don Carlos (☎ 85-8007; Piura 641; r per person US$3-4.50; d with shower US$11.50) Of many cheap places in the center of Máncora, this is among the best run with helpful owners. Bathrooms have only cold water, which is not a major problem in this climate. Rooms sleep two to six, some have TVs, all have fans, and there is a public sitting room.

Hostal Sausalito (☎ 85-8058; in Lima 01-479-0779; jcvigoe@terra.com.pe; Piura 4th block; s/d with shower US$9/11.50) Clean, quiet and well-run, but with tiny rooms, this hotel is popular because of its ceiling fans and TV in the rooms. Showers are cold and a restaurant is available.

Hostal Sol y Mar (☎ 85-8106, 85-8088; Piura 220; r per person from US$4.50, d with bathroom US$13; P 🍴) With 67 rooms, this sprawling place close to good waves attracts surfers and a party crowd. The huge speakers in front of the hotel can tell you what to expect – loud music and dancing till late at night. Table tennis, table football and a bar/restaurant complete the picture. Rooms vary widely; those at the back are quieter but tend to have saggier beds. All have cold showers and some sleep up to six. Keep your valuables in a safe place, though; some thefts have been reported from rooms.

Hostal Las Olas (☎ 85-8109; fax 85-8212; lasolasmancora@terra.com.pe; s/d US$15/30) The price includes a continental breakfast; snacks and other meals are available. This small hotel is right on the beach in front of surfing waves and it rents boards. Rooms vary in size and decor so look around before making a choice. Visa cards are accepted with a 6% fee.

Other suggestions include:

Hospedaje Casablanca (☎ 85-8337; in Lima 01-247-7641; casablanca63@hotmail.com; Piura 229; r per person US$6, d with shower US$14.50) Rooms feature fans and cold water; nicer doubles have TV. A surfers' noticeboard and book exchange are offered in the on-site restaurant.

Hostal El Angolo (☎ 85-8212; Piura 262; s/d with shower US$9/11.50) Guests can sit out on the hotel terrace.

Hospedaje Crillón (☎ 85-8131; Paita 168; r per person US$4.50) One block back from the 6th block of Piura (the Panamericana), this place has mainly quadruple rooms with cold showers.

Del Wawa (☎ 85-8289; www.delwawa.com; s/d US$15/20) This nine-room, beach-front hotel offers good showers with hot water.

MID-RANGE

South of Máncora, along La Antigua Pana-mericana, are several pleasant hotels spread out over several kilometers. All are on the beach, have a restaurant and are reached by mototaxi (US$1 to US$2 from town). They are described in the order they are reached. Many places offer discounts for pre-teen children staying with parents.

Punta Ballenas Inn (☎ 85-8136; puntaballenas@ yahoo.com; Panamericana Km1164; d US$50; P ☂) At the bridge at the south end of town where the Antigua Panamericana branches off, this quiet hotel is owned and managed by the friendly and irrepressible Harry Schuler, who speaks English and aims to please. The rates include breakfast. Situated on a point between a rocky and sandy beach, the inn offers both tide-pooling and swimming. It has a restaurant with international food, a colorful bar, a book exchange, two cats, free bottled drinking water in the rooms and plenty of local art gracing the walls. The showers are cold.

Casa de Playa (☎ 85-8005; in Lima 01-241-0889; casadeplayamancora@yahoo.com; d US$50 to 6-person room US$120; ☂) About a kilometer further along the old Panamericana, these bright yellow bungalows catch the visitor's eye. The green-and-red restaurant/bar continue the cheerful theme. Ocean kayaks are available for loan, and there are both sandy and rocky beachfronts. All 22 rooms have cool pastel interiors, wall art, hot showers, ceiling fans, and a terrace with a hammock and varying degrees of ocean view. A continental breakfast is included, and the restaurant (average mains US$6) is recommended. Look for the unique models of three-masted man-o'-wars, made entirely from bird bones. Recommended.

Sunset (☎ 85-8111; www.hotelsunset.com.pe; s/d US$58/66; ☂) Further along the old Pana-mericana, the Sunset has nine good-sized rooms that offer solid mattresses, good hot showers, balconies and sea views. Red-stone floors are attractively set with a checkered pattern, and high mosquito-netted windows allow air flow. The pool is tiny, and ocean access is rocky, though a short walk brings you to gentle sandy access. The hotel's Italian restaurant is excellent.

Puerto Palos (☎ 85-8199; fax 85-8198; www .puertopalos.com; s/d US$35/50; P ☂) Its pleasant rooms have colored, stone-flagged floors,

light walls with art, large bathrooms and hot water. Most rooms have balconies with sea views; those that don't have a TV. Two rooms have an entrance right onto the beach, and some sleep up to five. Rates include a continental breakfast and all major credit cards are accepted. The Argentine owners often prepare barbecues.

Las Pocitas (☎ 61-6070, 69-2033; www.laspocitas mancora.com; d US$50; P ☂) Las Pocitas' 17 rooms – with white-stone walls timbered with bamboo – are cool and inviting. All have patios with a hammock and sea view. A children's playground, table tennis, table football, *sapo* and a grassy lawn are featured. Pocitas means 'little pools' and refers to the beach, with many rocky tide pools, that fronts the hotel, about 2km along the old Panamericana. Rates include a continental breakfast.

Los Corales (☎ 85-8309, 969-9170; fax 85-8124; sandrapqr@yahoo.com; d US$40; ☂) This small hotel is tightly arranged to make maximum use of space. The 11 rooms have balconies and hammocks (some with sea views), firm mattresses and hot showers. Some sleep up to five. The pool is tiny, there is a small children's playground, and the beachfront is rocky. A continental breakfast is included.

Máncora Beach Bungalows (☎ 85-8125, in Lima 01-241-6116; fax 241-6115; www.hotelmancorabeach .com; s/d US$25/40; P ☂) Almost 4km south of Máncora, this well-run hotel has both an 'adults only' beachside pool with bar, and a separated, second, large family pool with a waterslide. Other features include a Jacuzzi, a good restaurant serving both north Peruvian and Mexican specialities (US$5 to US$7) and sandwiches, a children's playground, games area with table tennis, table football and *sapo*, and beach volleyball. Inviting guests to linger are 32 comfortable one- and two-bedroom units with private furnished terraces or balconies facing the beach, hammocks, quality mattresses, ceiling fans, king-sized beds and large bathrooms with hot water. The beach has both sandy and tide-pool areas and body boards can be borrowed. Local tours, including horse rides, are arranged. Rates include a continental breakfast. Recommended.

Las Arenas (☎ /fax 85-8240, in Lima 01-441-1542; www.lasarenasdemancora.com; d US$40; P ☂) A 5km mototaxi ride from Máncora brings you to this pleasant little resort with six double and two quadruple bungalows, all with ceiling fans and patios with hammocks and sea views. Featured are a nice pool, grassy landscaping, children's playground beach bar on a pier with panoramic views of the sandy beach. Air-con is planned for 2004 (US$10 extra). A continental breakfast is included. Sea kayaks, bicycles and horse rides are available.

Vichayito (☎ 64-1046, in Lima 01-446-5737; www .vichayito.com; s/d US$25/50; P ☒) About 8km south of Máncora, this attractively constructed hotel with rustic-looking cane, bamboo and wood bungalows, is set back about 200m from the beach – perfect if the noise of waves outside your door keeps you awake. A continental breakfast is included. Travelers with cars can reach the hotel by turning off the Panamericana at Km1155 (2km north of the village of Los Organos), and following the old Panamericana for 3km to the hotel.

Eating
Máncora has to import most of its food, or fish for it. If you love seafood, you'll be happy. If not... there isn't much else. Try *majarisco*, mixed seafood cooked with plantains – it's a local dish. Otherwise, there is all manner of ceviches, *chicharrones*, *sudados* and just plain *pescado*. It's good and it's always fresh! There aren't any special local restaurants – some of the mid-range hotels (see p296) have excellent eateries. New restaurants serving something other than seafood come and go. Look around for the current happening place.

Regina's (☎ 85-8246; Piura 6th block; breakfast US$2; mains US$2.50-5.50; ☽ 6:30am-9pm-ish) The ceviches are good at this simple but friendly place, which also serves a few meat dishes.

Las Gemelitas (Micaela Bastidas 154; mains US$3-5) Two blocks off the Panamericana – ask anyone – this cane-walled restaurant does great seafood and nothing else. Portions are big.

Juguería Mi Janett (Piura 5th block; juices US$1-2) Yup. The best juices in town.

El Espada (Piura 5th block; mains US$3-6) Two locations close to one another are among the most tourist-oriented seafood eateries in the center. Other places are nearby.

Karamba (Piura 230; US$1.50-5) This new place offers sandwiches and Mexican food – let's hope it lasts!

Sunset (☎ 85-8111; mains average US$11) In the hotel of the same name, this is the most gourmet restaurant in town with a short menu of excellent Italian food when the Italian chef is on; disappointing when he isn't.

Peña Parada (☎ 85-8125; most mains US$4.50-7; ☽ 8am-10pm) In the Máncora Beach Bungalows, this ocean-side restaurant has a great variety of well-prepared plates. Try some of the local seafood (of course), or one of several types of *chicharrones*. Pastas, Mexican food, the best chicken in town, and steak are on the menu. Vegetarians will enjoy a salad, cream soup or a *quesadilla* (Mexican tortilla-and-cheese dish), while kids find their own menu complete with hot dogs and chicken nuggets.

Getting There & Away
Many bus offices are in the center and most southbound trips originate in Tumbes, so departure times are approximate. Seats can be reserved. Bus-camas go direct to Lima; others can drop you in intermediate cities. In addition to these, there are combis that leave for Tumbes (US$1.50, two hours) about every hour – they drive along the main drag until they are full.

Cruz del Sur (☎ 964-0647; Piura 5th block) Economy buses to Lima at 3:30pm and 9pm (US$12, 18 hours), and bus-cama at 6:30 pm (US$32 to US$39, 16 hours).

Ormeño (☎ 85-8304; Piura 5th block) Afternoon buses to Lima for US$29 to US$40.

Eppo (Grau 4th block) Many slow buses to Talara, Sullana and Piura (US$3, 3½ hours).

El Dorado (Grau 4th block) Six buses a day to Piura (US$3.50, three hours) with fast transfers to Chiclayo (US$7.50, six hours) and Trujillo (US$10, nine hours) Also has buses to Tumbes.

Flores (Grau 1st block) To Lima at 2:30pm (US$12, 18 hours), 5:30pm (US$18 to US$22, 17 hours) and 7:30pm (US$15, 18 hours).

Tepsa (Grau 197) Buses north and southbound.

Civa (☎ 85-8026; Panamericana Sur s/n) Has a 6pm service to Lima.

PUNTA SAL
☎ 072
This beach is about 25km north of Máncora and 70km south of Tumbes, making it a popular spot for Tumbeños who enjoy the year-round warm waters. Minibuses run between Máncora and Punta Sal, which is a couple of kilometers off the Panamericana.

NORTH COAST

Hotel Bucanero (☎ 60-6910, 69-3017; htlelbucaner optasal@hotmail.com; d from US$30; P ⚲) It has 14 rooms by the beach, each with cold shower, fan and a patio or balcony. The hotel has a games room, TV room, restaurant, two bars, a grassy garden and a lookout with ocean views. Rates include a welcome drink and breakfast.

Hua Punta Sal (☎ 60-8365, 54-0043; huapuntasal@ hotmail.com; s/d with bathroom from US$10/20 in low season, from US$20/35 in high season) This is a friendly, rustic, family-run hotel. Rooms with and without sea views are available; those with are more expensive. Rooms have terraces, a restaurant is on the premises and the hotel rents canoes and fishing boats.

Sunset Punta Sal (☎ 54-0041; puntasunset@hot mail.com; s/d US$15/30) Tidy rooms with private cold showers and terrace, red-tiled floors, pastel-painted walls and cane ceilings are attractive, but few have sea views. Rates include breakfast; full board is US$10 extra. The staff will arrange inexpensive coastal fishing trips in small boats.

Hotel Caballito de Mar (☎ 54-0048, in Lima 01-446-3122; www.hotelcaballito.com.pe; r per child/adult with meals US$25/35; ⚲ P) This is a beach resort with 23 ocean-view rooms that have private patios and bathrooms, plus a restaurant, bar, Jacuzzi, TV room and games room. Activities such as fishing, boating, horseback riding, water skiing and surfing can be arranged.

Punta Sal Club Hotel (☎ 60-8373, in Lima 442-5992; www.puntasal.com.pe; r per person with meals US$55-82; ✄ ⚲ P) Off the Panamericana at Km1192, this seaside resort hotel offers a variety of rooms and activities, including deep-sea fishing for US$500 per day in a boat that will take up to six anglers.

ZORRITOS
☎ 072

About 35km south of Tumbes, Zorritos is the biggest fishing village along this section of coast, and its beaches are frequented by the people of Tumbes. The village is interesting for **fishing** activities and for the coastal **birdlife**. You can see frigate birds, pelicans, egrets and many migratory birds around here.

A few kilometers south of central Zorritos, at Panamericana Km1236, is **Hostel Casa Grillo** (☎ /fax 54-4222; casagrillo@yahoo.es; Los Pinos 563; s/d US$7/14, with bathroom US$10/18; P).

The rooms here are quite basic with cold showers, but members of Hostelling International, students and groups receive discounts. It has a restaurant with vegetarian specials (sandwiches US$1 to US$2, mains US$3 to US$5) and information about tours to nearby national parks and reserves (see p302). Horse riding and hiking to nearby mud baths can be arranged. Its day tours include a guide, transport and meals and start at US$20 per person. The hostel also does multi-day *hostal*-and-camping tours into the nearby parks (see p300) for up to nine days for US$280 per person including everything – a great deal! Ask the staff about volunteer positions. See the website http://usuarios.lycos.es/casagrillo for details of these activities.

About 1km away at Km1235 is **Tres Puntas Ecological Tourist Center** (see Hostal Casa Grilla for contact info and room rates; P). This place has been constructed (mainly by volunteers) completely of natural materials such as bamboo and cane. Everything is recycled, including water – shower water is saved for flushing toilets, which is then used for irrigation. Rustic cabins with balconies and hammocks are on the beach. You can camp for US$3 per person (using your tent) or US$5.50 per person (their tent), again with discounts available. Camp sites have electricity and a shade roof, and showers are available. If you like dogs, get the owner to show you his 17 Peruvian hairless dogs – he breeds them.

Mid-range choices include the beachfront **Punta Cocos** (☎ in Lima 447-6415; punta cocos@millicom.pe; Panamericana Km1243; s/d US$30/40; ⚲ P), which also does full board for US$40 per person. The rooms, which were being renovated at the time of research, are spacious and all have a ceiling fan, large bathroom with a tub and hot water, and patio or balcony with hammocks. There's also a children's playground and a games room.

Another option is the quiet, beachfront **Hostal Punta Camerón** (☎ 960-8366, 9608-0778; in Lima 01-445-6592; puntacamaron@terra,com.pe; r per person US$20; ⚲ P). The rates include breakfast; other meals are available on request, though service can be slow. Rooms are plain but big, with fans and hot showers, and there are terraces with hammocks. There is an attractive, old-fashioned bar with nautical paraphernalia, a TV room with 52 channels and beach volleyball.

Bungalows Costa Azul (☎ 54-4268; costaazul zorritos1@yahoo.com; from s/d US$15/20; Ⓟ) The Costa Azul has various-sized, simple rooms, some sleeping up to six people, right on the beach. It has a restaurant, bar and a tiny pool

Colectivos to Zorritos (US$1, about one hour) leave from the market in Tumbes, as do buses, which are cheaper but slower. Coming from the south, just catch a bus heading to Tumbes.

TUMBES
☎ 072 / pop 91,000

Tumbes was an Ecuadorian town until Peru's victory in the 1940–41 border war; it is now about 30km south of the border. A garrison town with a strong military presence, it is also the capital of Peru's smallest department. It's hot and (depending on season) dusty or mosquito-bugged, and most travelers don't stay long. Some nearby national reserves are unique and of interest to nature buffs.

History
Most travelers pass through Tumbes without realizing that the city has a long history. Ceramics found in the area are up to 1500 years old.

At the time of the Spanish conquest, Tumbes was an Inca town on the coastal highway. It was first sighted by Pizarro in 1528 during his second voyage of exploration (the first voyage never reached Peru). Pizarro invited an Inca noble to dine aboard his ship and sent two of his men ashore to inspect the Inca city. They reported an obviously well-organized and fabulously rich civilization. Pizarro returned a few years later and began his conquest of Peru.

Present-day Tumbes is about 5km northeast of the old Inca city, which is marked on maps as San Pedro de los Incas. The Panamericana passes through the site, but there is little to see.

Information
IMMIGRATION
The **Ecuadorian Consul** (Bolívar 123; ☯ 9am-1pm & 4-6pm Mon-Fri) is on the Plaza de Armas.

TUMBES

Scale	
0	200 m
0	0.1 mi

INFORMATION	pp299–300
Banco Continental	1 A2
BCP	(see 1)
Ecuadorian Consul	2 A3
EFE Net	3 A2
Micro Tecni	4 B3
Ministerio de Turismo	5 B3

SLEEPING	🛏 p302
Hospedaje Amazonas	(see 6)
Hospedaje Chicho	6 A2
Hospedaje El Estoril	7 B3
Hospedaje Florian	8 A2
Hospedaje Franco	9 B2
Hospedaje Sudamericano	10 B2
Hospedaje Tumbes	11 B3
Hostal Lourdes	12 C2
Hostal Roma	13 B2
Hotel Costa del Sol	14 B1

EATING	🍴 pp302–3
Classic Restaurant	15 A3
Restaurant Latino	16 A3
Restaurant Menova	17 A1
Restaurant Sí Señor	18 A3
Studio 307	19 D2

TRANSPORT	pp303–4
Aero Continente	20 A2
Colectivos to Aguas Verdes & Ecuadorian Border	(see 26)
Colectivos to Máncora	21 A2
Colectivos to Puerto Pizarro	22 C2
Colectivos to Zorritos & Caleta La Cruz	23 C3
Colectivos to Zorritos	24 C2
Cruz del Sur	25 A2
Ormeño	26 A2
Tepsa	27 A2
Transportes Chiclayo	28 B1

OTHER	
Cocodrilos Tours	29 B2
Preference Tours	(see 13)
Tumbes Tours	30 A1

To FCPN Office, Inrena, Flores, Civa, Cial, Cifa (1 block), Hotel Chilimasa & Airport (8km)

Abad Puell

Plaza Bolognesi

Paell

Plaza de Armas

Cathedral

Market

Tarapaca
Arica
Piura
Tumbes (Teniente Vázquez)
Tacna
Bolívar
San Martín
Bolognesi
Los Andes
Grau
Huáscar
Navarrete
A Ugarte
Mayor Bodero
Ramón Castilla
Piura
José Gálvez
Filidm

7 de Enero

To Museo de Cabeza de Baca (5km) & Lima (1264km)

Panamericana
Malecón Ushner
Río Tumbes

General Vidal

DOLLAR DOLDRUMS

Moneychangers at the border or in Tumbes will sometimes hope to mislead you into accepting a low rate, thinking you may have just arrived from Ecuador and won't know any better. Ask around before changing money. Try to find out what the dollar is worth in Peru from travelers going the other way. Beware of 'fixed' calculators, short-changing and other rip-offs.

If leaving Peru, it's best to change excess nuevos soles to dollars in Peru to get the best rates. And remember – the Ecuadorian currency is now the US dollar.

INTERNET ACCESS & POST
The **post office** (San Martín 208) is on the block south of Plaza Bolognesi. There are many Internet places; try:
Micro Tecni (Bolognesi 116)
EFE Net (Bolívar 227)

MONEY
BCP (☎ 52-5060; Bolívar 261) Changes traveler's checks and has an ATM.
Banco Continental (☎ 52-3914; Bolívar 129)

TOURIST INFORMATION
The **Ministerio de Turismo** (☎ 52-3699, 52-4940; Bolognesi 194, 2nd floor; ☻ 7:30am-1pm & 2-4:30pm Mon-Fri) provides useful information. The local tour companies (see p302 for details of some), apart from offering tours, can also help.

Sights
East of the Plaza de Armas, on Grau, there are several **old houses** dating from the early 19th century. The plaza itself has several outdoor restaurants and makes for a nice place to relax. The **pedestrian streets** north of the plaza (especially Bolívar) have several large, modern monuments and are favorite hang-outs for young and old alike. They are lined with chicken restaurants, ice-cream shops and hamburger stands, and are full of vibrant Peruvian life. During the day, you can walk along the **Malecón** for views of the Río Tumbes. Although the Malecón was destroyed during the most recent El Niño, it is being rebuilt.

Museo de Cabeza de Baca (☻ 9am-2pm Mon-Sat; adult/student US$0.60/0.30) About 5km south of town, off the Panamericana, is an overgrown, archaeological site where the Tumpis people lived and, later, the Incas built a fort that was visited by Pizarro on his way to beginning the conquest. The story is told in a tiny site museum, which also displays ceramics discovered by workers on the site of the Hotel Costa del Sol. These pottery vessels have been tentatively dated at about 1500 years old.

Puerto Pizarro
About 14km north of Tumbes, the character of the oceanfront changes from the coastal desert, which stretches over 2000km north from central Chile to northern Peru to the mangrove swamps that dominate much of the Ecuadorian and Colombian coastlines. This change of environment also signals a different variety of **birdlife**. Boats can be hired to tour the area; one tour is to a **crocodile sanctuary** where these reptiles are raised (US$18, two hours). The nearby **Isla de Aves** can also be visited (but not landed on) by boat to see the many nesting seabirds (US$8, one hour). This is especially interesting from 5 to 6pm when huge flocks of birds return to roost for the night. The **Isla del Amor** has lunch restaurants. Boats for hire line the waterfront and will take several people for the same cost, so get a group together. The tour companies (see p302) can also provide guided tours to the area.

Although the water is a bit muddier it is still pleasant enough for swimming and is less crowded with fishers than the beaches to the south. Most visitors stay in Tumbes and visit Puerto Pizarro on a day trip; however, accommodation is available at **Hotel Puerto Pizarro** (☎ 54-3045; s US$10-35, d US$15-40; ☒ ☒ ☒) on the waterfront. Boats can be rented here for personal use.

You can catch combis to Puerto Pizarro from Tumbes (see p303).

Reserva de Biosfera del Noroeste
The Northwestern Biosphere Reserve consists of four protected areas (which are detailed following) that cover a total of 2344 sq km in the Department of Tumbes and in northern Piura, abutting the Ecuadorian border. Although the four areas are protected by the government, a lack of funding means that there is relatively little infrastructure, such as ranger stations or

Chavín bas-relief, **Chavín de Huántar** (p327)

ERIC WHEATER

ALFREDO MAIQUEZ

Llanganuco valley (p322), Cordillera Blanca

Sunset on the southern face of **Alpamayo** (p323), Cordillera Blanca

GRANT DIXON

GREG CAIRE

Trekker, **Cordillera Blanca** (p318)

GF

Mountaineers crossing a glacier on **Alpamayo** (p323), Cordillera Blanca

Sunset, **Cordillera Blanca** (p318)

GF

tourist facilities. Much of what is available is funded by private organizations such as the Fundación Peruana para la Conservación de la Naturaleza (FPCN, also called ProNaturaleza), with assistance from international bodies such as the World Wide Fund for Nature and the International Union for the Conservation of Nature.

Information about all four areas is available from the Tumbes **FPCN office** (☎ /fax 52-3412, ptumbes@mail.cosapidata.com.pe, Av Tarapaca 4-16, Urbanización Fonavi), a short taxi ride from the town center. FPCN can help set up a visit if you have spare time and money. Applying insect repellent is strongly advised. The areas are under the administration of **Inrena** (☎ 52-6489; Urb José Lisner Tavela, Manzana A, Lote 19), another short taxi ride. The biologist in charge is Fernando Cuadras Villanueva, who can also provide information. It is best to call ahead, as this office may have changed address by the time you get here. Finally, the tour companies listed on p302 have guides who can arrange tours, and Hostal Casa Grillo in Zorritos (see p298) also arranges tours; there are also local guides described under the specific areas following.

There are few roads into the areas, which is a blessing in disguise because as roads go in, timber comes out.

PARQUE NACIONAL CERROS DE AMOTAPE

The tropical, dry, forest ecosystem of Cerros de Amotape is protected by the 913-sq-km national park that was created in 1975. The interesting flora and fauna include jaguars, condors and anteaters. You are unlikely to see much in the way of wildlife without a guide. More common sightings are parrots, deer, squirrels and peccaries. Large-scale logging, illegal hunting and overgrazing are some of the threats facing this habitat, of which there is very little left anywhere.

Guides are available from the village of Rica Playa, just within the park. Two have been recommended: Manuel Porras Sanchez and Roberto Correo. The FPCN suggests the Mellizos Hidalgo family as a good source of local information. There is a national-park control post at Rica Playa.

During the dry season, a morning bus leaves for Rica Playa from the Tumbes market (taking about two hours). Most of the route is paved, but the last 18km are unpaved and may be difficult going during the wet months (January to April). Trucks also make the trip – one is Señor Esteban Hidalgo's truck 'Flecha de Oro.' Señor Hidalgo can be contacted at San Ramon 101 in Tumbes.

Rica Playa is a small, friendly village. Although there are no hotels, you can camp, and local families will sell you meals. It's a good idea to bring some of your own food.

Another way to visit the park is to go to the village of **Casitas** near Caña Veral, where there's a ranger station. The park chief comes into Tumbes every week and can help you get out there. Buses go to Casitas once a day from the market in Tumbes.

ZONA RESERVADA DE TUMBES

This 751-sq-km reserve adjoins Cerros de Amotape to the northeast. The forest here is similar to the tropical dry forest of Cerros de Amotape, but because it lies more on the easterly side of the hills, it is wetter and has a slightly different flora and fauna, including crocodiles, monkeys and nutria. Visiting during the wet months of December to April is very difficult. During the dry months, visits can be arranged, but there is no public transport and you'll have to hire a truck or jeep.

COTO DE CAZA EL ANGOLO

This 650-sq-km extension at the southwest border of Cerros de Amotape is the most remote section of the tropical dry forest. It is a hunting preserve where hunting is allowed by permit.

SANTUARIO NACIONAL LOS MANGLARES DE TUMBES

This national sanctuary is on the coast and not linked to the other three dry-forest areas. Only about 30 sq km in size, it plays an essential role in conserving Peru's only region of mangroves and was established in 1988.

Los Manglares de Tumbes can be visited by going to Puerto Pizarro and taking a dirt road northeast for a few kilometers along the coast to the tiny community of **El Bendito**. There, ask for Agustín Correa Benites, who has a canoe and can show you the mangroves. Access depends on the tides. Guided tours are available from Puerto Pizarro as well.

Tours

The following companies run local tours:

Cocodrilos Tours (☎ 52-4133; cocodrilostours@terra mail.com.pe; Huáscar 309)

Preference Tours (☎ 52-5518; turismomundial@terra .com.pe; Grau 427)

Tumbes Tours (☎ 52-2481; tumbestours@terra.com.pe; Tumbes 351)

Sleeping

Almost all of Tumbes' many hotels are in the budget range. The large amount of border traffic means that the hotels tend to be crowded, and during the major annual holidays and occasional trade fairs, they are often full by early afternoon. During the rest of the year, it can be difficult to find single rooms by mid-afternoon, though doubles are usually available into the evening. Rates can vary considerably from day to day – often it's a seller's market.

Most hotels have only cold water, but that's no problem in the heat. All but the most basic hotels have fans – ask at the front desk. Rooms with air-con or fans are recommended during the hottest months (December to March). Readers have reported lots of mosquitoes at irregular times during the year, during the wet season and during the twice-yearly rice harvests when rice paddies provide breeding grounds – a fan helps repel them. There are frequent water and electricity outages.

BUDGET

Hospedaje Chicho (☎ 52-2282, ☎ /fax 52-3696; Tumbes 327; s/d US$8.50/13.50) It has small but neat rooms with private hot shower, cable TV, fan, minifridge, phone and helpful staff. Mosquito nets are also provided on request.

Hostal Roma (☎ 52-4137, 52-2494, 52-5879; hotel romatumbes@hotmail.com; Bolognesi 425; s/d US$11.50/ 17.30) A modern hotel with a great Plaza de Armas location, the Roma offers clean, comfortable rooms with private hot shower, fans, phone and cable TV.

Hostal Lourdes (☎ 52-2126, 52-2966; fax 52-2758; Mayor Bodero 118; s/d US$11.50/17.30) Clean, safe and friendly, the Lourdes includes a top-floor restaurant among its amenities. Fairly simple rooms have fans, phones, TV and hot showers.

By municipal law, the cheapest hotels are locally called *hospedajes*. The following are friendly and reasonably clean hotels and are among the best of about 30 registered places.

Hospedaje Amazonas (☎ 52-5266; Tumbes 317; s/d US$6/9) Rooms have cold showers and fans. A TV lounge offers entertainment.

Hospedaje El Estoril (☎ 52-4906; Huáscar 361; s/d US$5/7.50) Has small rooms with hot showers.

Hospedaje Florian (☎ 52-2464; Piura 414; s/d US$6/9) Has private warm showers, fans and cable TV for US$1.25 extra.

Hospedaje Franco (☎ 52-5295; San Martín 107; s/d US$6/9) Private cold showers and fan; upper rooms are larger.

Hospedaje Sudamericano (no phone; San Martín 130; s/d US$3/4, with bathroom US$4/5) Spartan shoestring choice; cold showers at odd hours.

Hospedaje Tumbes (☎ 52-2203; Grau 614; s/d US$4.50/7.50) Good-sized rooms with cold showers and fans.

MID-RANGE

Hotel Costa del Sol (☎ 52-3991, 52-3992; fax 52-5862; www.costadelsolperu.com; San Martín 275; s/d US$55/65; ⌨ P ⌨) This is by far the best hotel in town, with a decent restaurant, a pleasant bar and a garden, plus Jacuzzi, adult and children's swimming pools, a small casino and exercise equipment. The comfortable rooms have cable TV, a direct-dial phone, fans, mini-fridge, and bathroom with hot shower and hair drier.

Hotel Chilimasa (☎ 52-4555; fax 52-1946; Urb Andrés Araujo, Manzana 2A; s/d US$23/29; ⌨ P) About 2km north of town en route to the airport, this hotel offers comfortable rooms and a restaurant.

Eating

There are several bars and restaurants on the Plaza de Armas, many with shaded tables and chairs outside – a real boon in hot weather. It's a pleasant place to sit and watch the world go by as you drink a cold beer and wait for your bus. North of the plaza, the pedestrian street of Bolívar has inexpensive chicken restaurants, *chifas* and *heladerías*.

Classic Restaurant (☎ 52-2622; Tumbes 185; breakfast or menú US$1.80, sandwiches US$1, mains US$3-5; ⏰ 7:30am-5pm; ⌨ ⌨) Small, quiet and dignified, this is a wonderful place to escape torrid Tumbes and relax with a long lunch, as many of the town's better-connected locals do. Food is mainly coastal.

Studio 307 (52-4052; Grau 307; sandwiches US$1-3; mains US$2.50-5; 8am-midnight) On the north side of the plaza, this hip and hopping place attracts a younger crowd who enjoy desserts, ice creams, burgers, pizzas, and beers late into the night. It does decent breakfasts as well.

Restaurant Latino (52-3198; Bolívar 165; mains US$3-6; 7am-11pm) This popular place may have live *folklórica* music on weekends. It serves from a long menu of Peruvian food, especially seafood, and you can eat in or outside on the shaded pavement. Travelers arriving from Ecuador should try the ceviche – this marinated seafood dish is much spicier than the Ecuadorian version and goes down very well with a cold beer.

Also try:

Restaurant Sí Señor (Bolívar 119; menú US$1.50) Serves Peruvian food; a cheaper version of Restaurant Latino.

Restaurant Menova (52-3550; Tumbes 362; menú US$1) Within a block of most bus terminals; sells good, cheap food.

Getting There & Away

AIR

The **airport** (52-5102) is 8km north of town. The usual US$3.50 airport departure tax is charged. **Aero Continente** (52-2350; Tumbes 217) has daily flights to and from Lima stopping in Trujillo. Flights are often full, so reconfirm. Schedules, carriers and routes change frequently.

BUS

Most long-distance bus company offices are on Tumbes, especially around the intersection with Piura. You can usually find a bus to Lima within 24 hours of your arrival in Tumbes, but they're sometimes (especially major holidays) sold out a few days in advance. In that case, take a bus south to any major city and try again from there. Carry your passport with you – there are several passport-control stops south of Tumbes.

Buses to Lima take 18 to 20 hours and fares vary from US$12 to US$40, depending on the season and class of bus. Some companies offer limited-stop special service, with air-con, bathrooms and video, and some have bus-camas. There are several buses a day; most stop at Piura (five hours), Chiclayo (eight to nine hours), Trujillo (10 to 12 hours) and other intermediate cities.

If you arrive in Tumbes early in the morning, there's a reasonable chance you'll get out the same day if you are in a hurry; otherwise be prepared to spend the night. Most major companies have at least two departures a day.

If you're going to Ecuador, the best service is with Cifa, an Ecuadorian company that stops at the border for you to complete passport formalities.

Cial (52-6350; Tumbes 556) To Lima.

Cifa (52-7120; Tumbes 572) To Machala, Ecuador (US$2, two hours) and Guayaquil (US$5, five hours) about every two hours.

Civa (52-5120; Tumbes 518) Various services to Lima.

Cruz del Sur (52-4001; Tumbes 319) To Lima (US$12) at 1:30pm and 7:30pm; bus-cama (US$39) 9am and 5pm.

Flores (52-5346; Tumbes 570) To Lima 1pm, 4pm and 6pm.

Ormeño (52-2288, 52-2228; Tumbes 314) To Lima, various services, 11:30am, 1pm, 6pm and 7pm.

Tepsa (52-2428; Tumbes 199) To Chiclayo (US$6), Trujillo (US$7.50), Lima (US$12) at noon and 8:30pm.

Transportes Chiclayo (52-5260; Tumbes 466) Several daily to Talara, Sullana, Piura, Chiclayo and Trujillo.

Getting Around

TO/FROM THE AIRPORT

The **airport** (52-5102) is north of town, about US$2 to US$4 by taxi depending on your bargaining abilities. If you have confirmed flights and are coming from Ecuador, it's faster and cheaper to go direct from the border to the airport and avoid Tumbes altogether. There are no combis to the airport.

LOCAL TRANSPORT

If you're heading for Puerto Pizarro, Zorritos or Máncora, there are combi stops in Tumbes. Ask locals, as the stops aren't always marked. The market area is the place for colectivo taxis, buses and trucks to most other local destinations.

TO/FROM THE BORDER

Colectivos for the border leave from Tumbes (by the Ormeño terminal), and cost about US$1 per person for the 26km journey. If you're in a group, hire a car to take you to the border. A taxi to the border charges about US$5 to US$7. However, unless you have a real need to spend time at the border, it is far better to take a Cifa bus straight through to Machala or Guayaquil in Ecuador; the bus stops for all border formalities.

TO/FROM ECUADOR VIA TUMBES
Departing Peru

The Peruvian immigration office (*El Complejo*) is in the middle of the desert at Aguas Verdes, about 3km from the border .

Travelers leaving Peru must surrender their Peruvian tourist cards and obtain exit stamps from the immigration office. Assuming your documents are in order, exit formalities are quick and easy. Immigration is open 24 hours. From the immigration office, mototaxis take you to the border town of Aguas Verdes (US$0.50).

Aguas Verdes is basically a long street full of stalls selling consumer products. It has a bank and a few simple restaurants, but no hotels. The long market street continues into the Ecuadorian border town of **Huaquillas** via an international bridge across the Río Zarumilla. You may have to show your documents again as you cross the bridge. Huaquillas, on the Ecuadorian side, has similar stalls of consumer products.

The Ecuadorian immigration office is about 4km to the north of the international bridge. Taxis charge about US$1.30. The office is open 24 hours. Ecuadorian entrance formalities are usually straightforward. Few tourists need a visa, but everyone needs a T3 embarkation card, available free at the immigration office. You must surrender your T3 when you leave Ecuador, so don't lose it. Exit tickets out of Ecuador and sufficient funds (US$20 per day) are legally required, but rarely asked for. Stays of up to 90 days are allowed, but often only 30 days are given. Extensions are easily and freely obtained in Guayaquil or Quito. Tourists are allowed only 180 days per year in Ecuador. If you've already been in Ecuador for 180 days and try to return, you'll be refused entry. If you have an international flight from Ecuador, you can usually get a 72-hour transit visa to get you to the airport and out of the country.

There are a few basic hotels in Huaquillas, but most people make the two-hour bus trip to the city of Machala, where there are much better facilities. See Lonely Planet's *Ecuador & the Galápagos Islands*.

At the border, many people offer their services as porters and guides. Most are very insistent and usually overcharge, so unless you really need help, they're more of a hassle than they're worth. Even if you do need help, bargain hard. Readers have written that not only porters, but border guards, taxi drivers and moneychangers all try to rip you off. There are no entry fees into either country, so be polite but insistent with border guards, bargain hard with drivers, and find out exchange rates ahead of time before changing money.

Arriving in Peru

Travelers arriving in Peru essentially do the above in reverse. They surrender their Ecuadorian T3 card at the immigration office north of the border and obtain an Ecuadorian exit stamp in their passports. Take a taxi to the international bridge, where guards usually inspect but don't stamp your passport. The bridge is crossed on foot, and Peruvian immigration can be reached by continuing for a short distance or by taking a mototaxi.

North Americans, Australians, New Zealanders and most European nationals don't need a visa to visit Peru, but are given a tourist card at the border. Keep this card, as you must surrender it when leaving Peru. Visas are not available at the border, and you have to go back to the Peruvian Consulate in Machala to get one if you need one.

Although an exit ticket out of Peru is officially required, gringo travelers are rarely asked for one unless they look thoroughly disreputable. Latin American travelers are often asked for an exit ticket, so be prepared for this eventuality if you're a non-Peruvian Latin American (or if you are traveling with one). A bus office in Aguas Verdes sells (nonrefundable) tickets out of Peru. The immigration official can tell you where it is.

Huaraz & the Cordillera Blanca

CONTENTS

Huaraz is the most important climbing, trekking and backpacking center in Peru, arguably in all of South America. Although the city itself has been demolished several times by massive earthquakes and is not particularly attractive, the surrounding mountains are exceptionally beautiful, and many travelers come to Peru specifically to see, trek around or climb them.

The mountains offer a wide range of attractions, the most evident of which are the many permanently glaciated peaks jutting up to over 6000m. Hidden among them are glistening glacial lakes, ice caves, relaxing hot springs, and Inca and pre-Inca sites, foremost among them the fascinating 3000-year-old Chavín de Huántar, which is the most important site in the Americas from that period. The people living in remote villages, accessible only by mule or on foot, are friendly, interesting and interested in you. And the flora and fauna are fascinating, including vicuñas, vizcachas, and the magnificent Andean condor.

HIGHLIGHTS

■ **Trekking**

Wandering around the Cordillera Blanca, South America's loveliest range (p318), or the Cordillera Huayhuash (p326)

■ **Archaeology**

Going underground at the monumental Chavín de Huántar (p327)

■ **Botany**

Marvelling at *Puya raimondii*, the tallest flower spike on the planet (p326)

■ **Feasting**

Gorging on a rural *pachamanca* (meat and potato feast; (p320)

■ **Activities**

Mountaineering (p318) and mountain biking (p312) offer the traveler other options to trekking

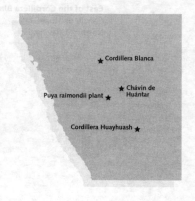

★ Cordillera Blanca

★ Chávín de Huántar

Puya raimondii plant ★

Cordillera Huayhuash ★

THE ANDES AROUND HUARAZ

Huaraz lies in the Río Santa valley, flanked to the west by the Cordillera Negra and to the east by the Cordillera Blanca. The valley between these two mountain ranges is popularly referred to as El Callejón de Huaylas, after the district of Huaylas at the northern end. A paved road runs the valley's length, linking the main towns and providing spectacular views of the mountains.

The Cordillera Negra, though an attractive range in its own right, is snowless and is completely eclipsed by the magnificent snowcapped mountains of the Cordillera Blanca. The lower range is sometimes visited by road from the coast en route to the Cordillera Blanca.

The Cordillera Blanca is about 20km wide and 180km long. In this fairly small area, there are more than 50 peaks of 5700m or higher. In contrast, North America has only three mountains in excess of 5700m (Pico de Orizaba in Mexico, Logan in Canada and Denali in Alaska), and Europe has none. Only Asia can boast mountain ranges that are higher than those in the Andes. Huascarán, at 6768m, is Peru's highest mountain and the highest peak in the tropics anywhere in the world. However, this string of statistics does not do the Cordillera Blanca justice. Its shining glaciers, sparkling streams, awesome vertical walls and lovely lakes have to be seen to be appreciated.

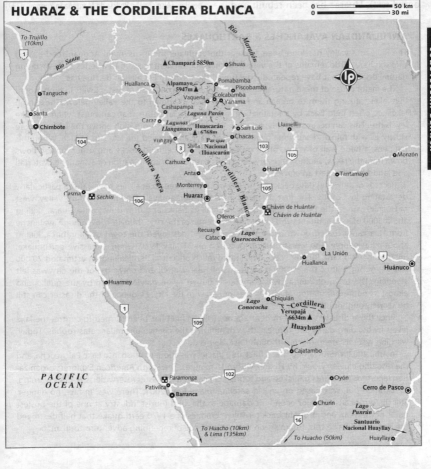

HUARAZ & THE CORDILLERA BLANCA

South of the Cordillera Blanca is the smaller, more remote, but no less spectacular Cordillera Huayhuash. It contains Peru's second-highest peak, the 6634m Yerupajá, and is a more rugged and less frequently visited range. The main difference between the two ranges, for the hiker at least, is that you walk *through* the Cordillera Blanca surrounded by magnificent peaks and you walk *around* the smaller Huayhuash, one of the world's most spectacular mountain circuits. Both ranges are highly recommended.

HUARAZ

☎ 043 / pop 79,000 / elevation 3091m

Since the 1970 earthquake disaster (see the boxed text), Huaraz has been rebuilt and is now the flourishing, if not especially attractive, capital of the Department of Ancash. Its renown as the center for visiting the Cordillera Blanca has led to the development of a thriving tourist industry, with a multitude of hotels and other facilities, full during Easter and the May to September dry season, but sadly suffering the rest of the year.

INFORMATION
Emergency

Casa de Guías (☎ 72-1811; Plaza Ginebra 28-G) It can arrange mountain rescue; register with them before heading out on a climb. All trekkers and climbers should carry rescue insurance, best purchased before leaving home. A helicopter rescue will cost several thousand dollars. A guided evacuation by land will cost several hundred dollars per day. (Also see the Policía de Montaña in Yungay, p322)

AWFUL ANDEAN AVALANCHES & EARTHQUAKES

The Río Santa valley has long been a major thoroughfare; the Incas' main Andean road passed through here. Little remains of the valley's archaeological heritage due to a series of devastating natural disasters that have repeatedly destroyed the towns of El Callejón de Huaylas.

The major cause of these natural disasters has been the build-up of water levels in high mountain lakes, causing them to breach and water to cascade down to the valley below. These high lakes are often held back by a relatively thin wall of glacial debris that can burst when the lake levels rise. This can occur suddenly, as when an avalanche falls from high above the lake, or more slowly, as with rain and snow melt. Earthquakes have also caused the lakes to breach. When this happens, a huge wall of water, often mixed with snow, ice, mud, rocks and other matter, flows down from the lakes, wiping out everything in its path. Such a combination of avalanche, waterfall and landslide is named an *aluvión*.

Records of *aluviónes* date back almost 300 years, and three recent ones have caused particularly devastating loss of life. The first occurred in 1941, when an avalanche in the Cojup valley, west of Huaraz, caused the Laguna Palcacocha to break its banks and flow down onto Huaraz, killing about 5000 of its inhabitants and flattening the center of the city. Then, in 1962, a huge avalanche from Huascarán roared down its western slopes and destroyed the town of Ranrahirca, killing about 4000 people. The worst disaster occurred on 31 May 1970, when a massive earthquake, measuring 7.7 on the Richter scale, devastated much of central Peru, killing an estimated 70,000 people. About half of the 30,000 inhabitants of Huaraz died, and only 10% of the city was left standing. The town of Yungay was completely buried by an *aluvión* caused by the quake, and almost its entire population of 18,000 was buried with the city. Evidence of the disaster can still be seen throughout the valley.

Since these disasters, a government agency (Hidrandina) has been formed to control the lake levels by building dams and tunnels, thus minimizing the chance of similar catastrophes. Today, warning systems are in place, although false alarms do occur.

In April 2003 NASA warned that a fractured glacier was about to crash into Lake Palcacocha, and the resulting *aluvión* would hit Huaraz within 15 minutes. The South American Explorers organization reported: 'Residents panicked and tourists cancelled their Easter reservations. NASA's warning, as it turned out, was based on an old satellite image from 2001. There was, in fact, no danger. Still the error caused major economic damage to the local tourist industry at one of the busiest times of the year, and brought back terrible memories of a 1970 earthquake that half-destroyed the city. With PR like this, Huaraz is on the cutting edge of redefining adventure-tourism.'

Local Police (☎ 72-1221, 72-1331; Sucre at San Martín)

National Police (☎ 72-1021; 28 de Julio 701)

Policía de Turismo (☎ 72-1341; ☺ 9am-1pm Mon-Sat, 4-6pm Mon-Fri) On an alley on west side of Plaza de Armas. Some officers speak limited English.

Internet Access

There are about 10 places on Plaza Ginebra and the corresponding block of Luzuriaga has many others.

Laundry

Both of these are good for down gear and dry-cleaning:

B&B/Pressmatic (☎ 72-1719; José de la Mar 674; US$1.25/kg)

Lavandería Dennys (☎ 72-9232; José de la Mar 561)

Medical Services

There are pharmacies along Luzuriaga.

Clínica San Pablo (☎ 72-8811, 72-8805; Huaylas 172; ☺ 24 hr) Some doctors speak English. Best care in town.

Farmacia Recuay (☎ 72-1391; Luzuriaga 497) Will restock expedition medical kits.

Hospital Regional (☎ 72-1861; 72-1290; Luzuriaga 13th block) At south end of town; for basic medical care.

Money

BCP (formerly Banco de Credito; ☎ 72-1692; Luzuriaga 691) Has a Visa ATM.

Banco Wiese (☎ 72-1500; José Sucre 760) MasterCard ATM.

Interbanc (☎ 72-1502; José Sucre 687) Visa ATM.

Oh NaNa Casa de Cambio (northeast cnr Plaza de Armas) Changes US dollars at good rates, but euros, yen, UK pounds and Canadian dollars attract a hefty commission.

Post

The **post office** (☎ 72-1031; Luzuriaga 702; ☺ 8am-8pm Mon-Sat) is on the Plaza de Armas.

Tourist Information

Mountain Bike Adventures (see Café Andino, p315). The owner specializes in Cordillera Huayhuash travel information, maps etc.

Parque Nacional Huascarán (☎ 72-2086; Sal y Rosas 555; ☺ 8:30am-1pm & 2:30-6pm Mon-Fri) Staff have limited information about visiting the park.

Policía de Turismo (see Emergency earlier). Has general information about the area.

DANGERS & ANNOYANCES

Time to acclimatize is important. Huaraz's altitude will make you feel breathless and may give you a headache during your first few days, so don't overexert yourself. The surrounding mountains will cause altitude sickness if you venture into them without spending a few days acclimatizing in Huaraz. (See the Health chapter p423 for advice.)

Unfortunately, during late 2002 and early 2003, there were a series of armed robberies of tourists going on day trips by foot to Laguna Churup, Rataquenua, the bouldering area at Huancha, the *mirador*/cross above Huaraz and the ruins at Wilcahuaín. Usually the tourists were alone or in small groups. No injuries have been reported. Ask locally what the situation is. A suggestion is to hire somebody to go with you; ask at your hotel or the tourist police for advice.

SIGHTS

The **Museo Regional de Ancash** (☎ 72-1551; adult/student US$1.50/0.60; ☺ 9am-5pm Mon-Sat, 9am-2pm Sun) is on the Plaza de Armas. It's small but quite interesting with a few mummies, some trepanned skulls and a garden of stone monoliths from the Recuay culture (400 BC to AD 600) and the Wari culture (AD 600 to 1000). Spanish-speaking guides will take you around for a nominal fee.

At a trout hatchery, **Piscigranja de Truchas** (admission US$0.40; ☺ 9am-5pm), you can see the stages of the trout-hatching process from eggs to adults. By the entrance, the **Recreo de Los Jardínes** serves trout for lunch. Get there by walking east on Raimondi to Confraternidad Este, then turn left and cross the bridge over the Río Quilcay. The hatchery is just beyond (a half-hour walk from the center).

Jirón José Olaya, also east of town, is on the right-hand side of Raimondi a block beyond Confraternidad. It's the only street that remained intact through the earthquakes and shows what old Huaraz looked like; go on Sunday when a street market sells regional foods.

Mirador de Retaquenua is about a 45-minute walk southeast of the city. This lookout gives a view of the city, as well as the mountains behind it. Ask locally for directions, and also ask if it is safe to walk up there.

Monumento Nacional Wilcahuaín

This small Wari **ruin** (adult/student US$1.20/0.60; ☺ 7am-5pm), about 8km north of Huaraz, is in quite a good state of preservation. Dating

HUARAZ & THE
CORDILLERA BLANCA

HUARAZ

INFORMATION	pp308–9
B&B/Pressmatic	1 C4
BCP	2 C5
Banco Wiese	3 C5
Farmacia Recuay	4 C4
Interbanc	5 C5
Lavandería Dennys	6 C4
Oh NaNa Casa de Cambio	7 C5
Parque Nacional Huascarán Office	8 B6

SIGHTS & ACTIVITIES	pp309–11
Iglesia de la Soledad	9 E6
Mountain Bike Adventures	10 C4
Museo Regional de Ancash	11 C5

SLEEPING	pp311–15
Albergue Churup	12 E5
Alojamiento El Farolito	13 A6
Alojamiento Soledad	14 E5
B&B My House	15 B5
Caroline Lodging	16 A6
Casa de Guías	17 C4
Casa de Jaime	18 A5
Edward's Inn	19 A4
Familia Meza Lodging	20 C4
Grand Hotel Huaraz	21 D5
Hospedaje La Cabaña	22 E5
Hostal Quintana	23 B4
Hostal Raimondi	24 C3
Hostal Schatzi	25 D4
Hotel Colomba	26 C1
Hotel Gyula	27 C5

Hotel Los Portales	28 D3
Hotel Samuel's	29 D4
Hotel Santa Victoria	30 D5
Hotel Tumi	31 B6
Jo's Place	32 D1
La Casa de Zarela	33 E6
Olaza's Guest House	34 E6
Pensión Galaxia	35 B4
Piramide Hotel	36 C5
San Sebastian	37 F4

EATING	pp315–17
Baby Donkey	38 C4
Bistro de los Andes	39 D4
Café Andino	(see 10)
Chez Pepe	40 C3
Chifa Min Hua	41 C6
Crêperie Patrick	42 C4
El Fogón	43 B6
El Rinconcito Minero	44 C4
Fuente de Salud	45 C4
La Brasa Roja	46 C6
Limón, Leña y Carbón	47 B6
Mercado Ortiz	48 C3
Monte Rosa/Inka Pub	49 C4
Pachamama	50 B5
Piccolo	51 C4
Pizza B&B	52 C4
Pizza Bruno	53 B6
Sabor Salud Pizzería	54 C5
Siam de los Andes	55 D4

Carhuaz

To Monumento
Nacional
Wilcahuain,
Clínica San
Pablo,
Carhuaz,
Yungay
& Caraz

Villazón

To Hospedaje
Ezama (2 blocks)

Francisco de Zela

M Melgar

Centenario

V Veles

Rio Quilcay

13 de Diciembre

Caraz

Américas

Conecio

Cajamarca

Gamarra

Stadium

To Casma

Bolognesi

M Cáceres

27 de Noviembre (Tarapacá)

Mercado
Central

Huallán

San Cristóbal

Raimondi

Fitzcarrald

Cruz Romero

José de la Mar

Lúcar y Torre

Morales

San Martín

Luzuriaga

Park

Park

A Gridilla

Confraternidad Internacional Oeste

Huascar

Romero

Grau

Plaza
Ginebra

Plaza
de
Armas

Cathedral

Bolívar

Larrea y Loredo

José Sucre

Amadeo Figueroa

28 de Julio

Farfán

Uribe

Sal y Rosas

To Lima

To Hospital

To Tebac

to about AD 1100, it's an imitation of the temple at Chavín done in the Tiahuanaco style. Wilcahuaín means 'grandson's house' in Quechua. The three-story temple has a base of about 11m by 16m, and each story has seven rooms, some of which are filled with rubble. The rooms are now lit, and kids in the area will take you inside the ruin and show you around for a tip. (These kids are a lot of fun – hire them!)

Taxis cost a few dollars, or ask for combis at the bus stops by the Río Quilcay in town. If planning to walk, ask locally if it is safe.

Instead of returning to Huaraz, you could walk down to the hot springs at Monterrey (see p320) along a footpath that takes about an hour. Locals will show you the way or you can hire a kid to walk down with you. From Monterrey, take a bus back to Huaraz.

ACTIVITIES
Hiking & Mountaineering
Many outfitters arrange trips in this, Peru's premier mountain area. Of course, many experienced backpackers go camping, hiking and climbing in the mountains without any local help, and you can too. Just remember, though, that carrying a backpack full of gear over a 4800m pass requires much more effort than hiking at low altitudes. People hike year-round, but the dry season of mid-May to mid-September is the most popular and recommended. December to April is the wettest. Climbers pretty much stick to the dry season for serious mountaineering.

Other Activities
If you want to go **mountain biking**, talk to Julio Olaza (see Tours & Guides p312) for useful information and tours. Skiers will not find ski lifts in the Cordillera Blanca, but there is limited mountain **skiing** for diehards who want to climb with skis. The glaciers have been receding in recent years, and skiing is difficult. Ask locally for current conditions. **River running** is offered on the Río Santa, but it's a very polluted river (mine-tailings upstream) and it's not recommended, though someone will offer it most years. **Horse riding** is a possibility; nobody does it specifically, but horses can be hired by asking around. **Parapenting** (hang-gliding) has just begun here – ask at Montrek. **Surfing** – OK, just kidding.

COURSES

Sierra Verde Spanish School (☎ 72-1203; sierraverde
_sp@hotmail.com; Lucar y Torre 530) offers Spanish
lessons.

TOURS & GUIDES

Trekkers and climbers will find that the
travel agencies and guides mentioned here
are good sources of information. During
the May-to-September season, international
climbers and trekkers are also great source
of up-to-date information.

Local Tours

Many agencies provide local tours. **Pablo
Tours** (☎ 72-1145; pablotours@terra.com.pe; Luzuriaga
501) has received several recommendations
for its bus tours. Other experienced agencies on the same block are **Huaraz Chavín
Tours** (☎ 72-1578; hct@chavintours.com.pe; Luzuriaga
502), which has several minibuses, and **Milla
Tours** (☎ 72-1742; Luzuriaga 528), but these are
by no means the only ones. Prices are fixed
and include transport (usually in minibuses) and a guide (who may or may not
speak English). You should bring a packed
lunch, warm clothes, drinking water and
sunblock. Admission fees are extra. Tours
depart daily during the high season, but at
other times, departures depend on passenger demand. Often, different agencies will
pool their passengers.

The four most popular trips around
Huaraz each take a full day and cost US$8 to
US$10, depending on the tour and number
of passengers. One tour visits the ruins at
Chavín de Huántar (see p327); another
passes through Yungay to the beautiful
Lagunas Llanganuco (p322), where there
are superb views of Huascarán and other
mountains; a third takes you through Caraz
to Laguna Parón (p323), which is spectacularly surrounded by glaciated peaks; and a
fourth goes through Catac to see the giant
Puya raimondii plant (p326) and continues
to Nevado Pastoruri, where there are glaciers and mineral springs.

Trekking & Mountaineering Tours

Make sure your guide is qualified and experienced, particularly if you are hiring a
mountain guide: You are putting your life
in their hands. Even experienced mountaineers would do well to add a local guide
to their group; the locals know exactly what

has been happening in the mountains an
are a great safety precaution.

Mountaineers and trekkers should chec
out the hostel **Casa de Guías** (☎ 72-1811; Plaz
Ginebra 28G). It has a list of certified guides an
staff here are a good source of hiking an
climbing information. It is the headquar
ters of the **Mountain Guide Association of Per**
(agmp@terra.com.pe).

One of the best outfitters is **Pyrami
Adventures** (☎ /fax 72-3443; moralesf@terra.com.pe
run by the Morales family. The compan
specializes in providing full service to inter
national trekking and climbing groups. Th
staff here are knowledgeable, hardworking
honest and friendly, and they provide a ver
high level of service at fair prices. They ar
also accomplished mountaineers and hav
been involved in new ascents as well a
mountain-rescue activities. Eudes Morale
speaks English.

Montrek (☎ 72-1124; monttrek@terra.com.pe; 2n
fl, Luzuriaga 646) is another good source fo
service and information, and has bee
recommended. It also offers adventure
such as river running and parapenting. **Sky
line Adventures** (☎ 968-2774; skylineadventures@
hotmail.com; San Martín 637) offers guides for trek
and mountain climbs. It also does two
and three-day mountaineering courses
Some gear is available for rent. **Montañer**
(☎ 72-6386; Parque Ginebra) arranges treks an
climbs and rents or sells a wide variety o
quality gear.

Some cheaper guide services are availabl
if you shop around, but try to get reference
from other travelers before contracting wit
them. The cheapest option is to hire *arriero*
(mule drivers) directly, though this involve
speaking Spanish and perhaps bargaining
Again, get references and check credential
first. The Parque Nacional Huascarán (se
Tourist Information p309) has a list of cer
tified *arrieros*.

See also Equipment & Rentals opposite.

Mountain Biking

Mountain Bike Adventures (☎ 72-4259; julio.ol
za@terra.com.pe; 2nd fl, Lúcar y Torre 530) has bee
in business for over a decade and receive
repeated visits by mountain bikers becaus
it has decent bikes and knowledgeable
friendly service. The owner is a lifelon
resident of Huaraz who speaks Englis
and has spent time mountain-biking i

the USA, and he knows the region's single-track possibilities better than anyone. The company offers bike rentals for independent types or guided tours ranging from an easy five-hour cruise to multiday circuits of the Cordillera Blanca. Rates start at US$20 per day for independent rentals.

Equipment & Rentals

The better guide services (see earlier) can supply everything from tents to ice axes, and may rent gear without selling a guided tour. Another reliable rental agency is **MountClimb** (☎ 72-6060; M Cáceres 421), which has high-quality climbing gear. **Restaurant Monte Rosa** (☎ 72-1447; José de la Mar 661) sells and buys high-quality climbing gear and skis, and is the official Swiss Army knife outlet. **Andean Kingdom** (Luzuriaga 522) rents gear at competitive rates and has a bouldering cave. Several other places along Luzuriaga rent equipment, perhaps a bit more cheaply, but check what you are getting carefully.

If you bring your own equipment, *kerex* (kerosene, paraffin) can be purchased from gas stations, and *bencina* (white gas, stove alcohol) is found in hardware stores and pharmacies. Expensive Camping Gaz canisters are usually available in rental places (please carry them out after use). Firewood is not available and chopping down live trees is illegal. It often freezes at night, so bring an adequately warm sleeping bag. It can rain even in the dry season, so rain gear and a waterproof tent are needed. Wear a brimmed hat and sunglasses, and bring strong sunblock with you, as it is difficult to find in Huaraz. The same applies to effective insect repellent.

Food is no problem. Expensive, lightweight, freeze-dried food is occasionally left over from mountaineering expeditions and can be bought at trekking and rental agencies. You can easily make do with oatmeal, dried soups, fast-cooking noodles and the usual canned goods, all of which are readily available.

Logistics

Some folks prefer to trek or climb on their own without joining a group. Companies that will provide information and make arrangements for transportation, renting gear, hiring an *arriero* or a high-altitude guide or a cook (whatever you need) include:

La Casa de Zarela (☎ 72-1694; zarelaz@hotmail.com; Arguedas 1263)

La Cima Logistics (☎ 72-1203; lacima_peru@hotmail .com) US owner guides in Huayhuash.

Tebac (☎ 72-3557; tebac@yahoo.com; Sal y Rosas 368) Ask for Miguel Chiri.

FESTIVALS & EVENTS

Semana Santa (Holy Week) is very busy with many Peruvian tourists flooding to town. On the Tuesday before Easter) there is a day of intense water fights – stay inside your hotel if you don't want to get soaked. **Ash Wednesday** is much more interesting and colorful, with funeral processions for *Ño Carnavalon* converging on the Plaza de Armas. Here, his 'will' is read, giving opportunity for many jabs at local politicians, police and other dignitaries, before the procession continues to the river where the coffin is thrown in. Participants dress in colorful costumes with papier-mâché heads, some of which are recognizable celebrities.

Huaraz pays homage to its patron, **El Señor de la Soledad**, beginning 3 May. This weeklong festival involves fireworks, music, dancing, elaborately costumed processions and much drinking.

Semana de Andinismo is held annually in June. This attracts mountaineers from several countries, and various competitions and exhibitions are held.

Many Peruvians like to spend **Fiestas Patrias**, 28 to 29 July, in the Huaraz area.

SLEEPING

The prices given here are average high-(dry-) season rates. Hotel prices can double during the holiday periods (see Festivals & Events) and rooms become very scarce. However, bargains can be found or made in the remaining October-to-April low season. Perhaps because Huaraz is seen as a trekking, climbing and backpacking center, budget hotels predominate. Some hotels have Internet access, but don't want to advertise it. Make friends and ask.

Budget

Especially during the high season, locals meet buses from Lima and offer inexpensive accommodations in their houses. Hostels also employ individuals to meet buses, but beware of incorrect information or overpricing, and don't pay anybody until you have seen the room.

Albergue Churup (☎ 72-2584; www.churup.com; A Figueroa 1257; dm US$4; d/tr/4-bed room with bathroom US$15/22/25) A super-popular hotel favored by international travelers, it has a pretty garden with mountain views, a comfortable sitting room with fireplace and tables, book exchange, laundry facilities, and a travel office that rents trekking gear and arranges Spanish lessons. Downstairs, the four dorm rooms sleep up to four people; upstairs, five rooms with bathrooms all have hot water. Two more rooms with bathrooms are in the garden. It's a small place and usually full in the high season; reservations are advised. The friendly owners live around the corner (Pedro Campos 735) where they provide varied homemade breakfasts for US$3 and allow use of their kitchen in the evenings.

Casa de Guías (☎ 72-1811; casa_de_guias@hotmail .com; Plaza Ginebra 28G; dm US$5) There's a large dorm room with 14 beds and several hot showers. Kitchen and laundry facilities and a popular pizza restaurant (which serves breakfasts) are also on the premises. This is a youth hostel and climbers' meeting place; it has bulletin boards of information. The Mountain Guide Association has an office here.

Caroline Lodging (☎ 72-2588; Urb Avitentel Mz-D, Lt 1; dm US$3) Budget travelers repeatedly rave about this friendly place, southwest of the center. Call – they'll pick you up and give you free continental breakfast as well. Once you find out where it is (beyond the west end of 28 de Julio) you won't have any problem finding it again. Kitchen and laundry facilities, hot showers – a deal for US$3.

Jo's Place (☎ 72-5505; josplacehuaraz@hotmail.com; D Villazon 278; dm US$3, s/d US$5/10) An informal and charmingly chaotic place with a huge grassy yard (camping allowed, or dry out your gear here), this *hostal* attracts trekkers and climbers. Some rooms have bathrooms. English expat Jo provides the Sunday papers (arriving a few days late) and makes bacon and eggs for breakfast. Free coffee is available and there's a common room with cable TV and a fireplace.

Hospedaje Ezama (☎ 72-3490; ezama_623@yahoo .es; M Melgar 623; dm US$3, s/d with bathroom US$4.50/8.50) Going north of town on Centenario

for five blocks to Corongo, then right two blocks to Melgar, brings you to this quiet, super-friendly, seven-room place that has spacious rooms and good hard beds. Hot water and tourist information is available. There's a TV lounge and breakfast costs just US$1.50.

Olaza's Guest House (☎ 72-2529; info@andean explorer.com; J Arguedas 1242; s/d US$10/15) This small, spotless guest house has excellent hot showers in every room, a book exchange, laundry facilities and wonderful views from the rooftop terrace. Breakfast (continental US$2.50, full US$5) is served up here – a great place to start the day. The owners can arrange mountain biking trips and have an excellent gift shop. Bus station pick-up is free with reserved rooms.

La Casa de Zarela (☎ 72-1694; zarelaz@hotmail.com; J Arguedas 1263; d/tr US$15/18) Another popular choice; Zarela's helpfulness is legendary. Her 18 double and triple rooms have hot showers, and breakfast, kitchen facilities and expedition planning are offered. Check out the rooftop terrace or try Zarela's famous 'megaburrito' in her café.

Alojamiento Soledad (☎ 72-1196; ghsoledad@ hotmail.com; A Figueroa 1267; d US$11.50, d with bathroom US$14.50; 🖳) This cozy family house has eight rooms, six with bathrooms and hot showers. Its rooftop terrace has one of the best views in town, and has a barbecue for sunset cook-outs. The friendly and helpful owners speak English and German, have a book exchange, cable TV room, kitchen and laundry facilities, will arrange treks (see www.peru-adventure.de) and have gear for rent. (Other small family-run places are listed at the end of this section.)

Hostal Raimondi (☎ 72-1082; Raimondi 820; s/d US$6/9) This older property has rooms with comfy beds, writing desks and showers; hot water is available during certain hours only. It's convenient for buses and has a small café for 7am breakfasts.

Other recommendations are:

Casa de Jaime (☎ 72-2281; A Gridilla 267; dm US$2, s/d with bathroom US$3/6; 🖳) Basic, friendly, crowded and noisy, it has a kitchen, laundry and tepid showers.

Hospedaje La Cabaña (☎ 72-3428; José Sucre 1224; s/d US$4.50/9) A patio, information and rooms with hot shower.

Alojamiento El Farolito (☎ 72-5792, Tarapaca 1466; d US$5, d with bathroom US$9) Friendly, family-run and noisy, it has a TV room, café and laundry service.

Edward's Inn (☎ 72-2692; edwardsinn@viabcp.com; Bolognesi 121; dm US$3-5, s/d with bathroom US$10/20) Solar showers; perennially popular.

Hostal Quintana (☎ 72-6060; M Cáceres 411; s/d US$6/10) Family-run, friendly; basic clean rooms; hot water.

Pensión Galaxia (☎ 72-2230; fax 72-6535; Romero 633; d US$8.50, d with bathroom US$12) Spartan but warm and welcoming.

Familia Meza Lodging (☎ 72-6763; Lucar y Torre 538; s/d US$5/10) Shared hot showers. Bike tours arranged. Helpful family.

Hostal Gyula (☎ 72-1567; hostal_gyula_inn@yahoo .com; Plaza Ginebra 632; s/d US$4/8) Hot showers; gear rental.

Hotel Samuel's (☎ /fax 72-6370; Bolívar 504; s/d US$9/16) Simple but adequate rooms with TVs and phone; there's a restaurant.

Mid-Range

B&B My House (☎ 72-3375; bmark@ddm.com.pe; 27 de Noviembre 773; s/d with breakfast US$12/20) A small, bright patio and six rooms decorated like they belong to a family member welcome you to this hospitable B&B. Rooms have a writing desk and hot shower. English and French are spoken.

Steel Guest House (☎ 72-9709; steelguehouse@ yahoo.com; Pje A Maguina 1467; s/d US$14/24; 💻) It's a four-story hotel with just nine rooms. The ground floor has a restaurant (breakfast US$1.80), book exchange, TV room, billiards, foosball, laundry, kitchen and sauna (US$4). The rooftop terrace has good views and a café. Rooms are plain with comfy beds and hot showers. Israeli, French and English are spoken.

Hotel Tumi (☎ 72-1784, 72-1852; hottumo@terra .com.pe; San Martín 1121; s/d US$16/29; P 💻) Clean, comfortable and quiet, many of the Tumi's rooms have great mountain views and cable TV – your choice. A good and inexpensive hotel restaurant provides room service, and there is a 'business center', making this the hotel of choice for many Peruvian business-people visiting town.

Piramide Hotel (☎ 72-8250, 72-5801; filiberto@terra .com.pe; Parque Ginebra U-22; s/d/ste US$25/30/60; ✗) It's a new modern hotel with phones and TVs, some rooms have a balcony looking out into the plaza or towards the mountains. There's a restaurant with room service and rates include an American breakfast.

Hotel Los Portales (☎ 72-8184; Raimondi 903; s/d US$20/35; P) Rooms are clean, carpeted and comfortable in a generic motel style, but a games room (pool and table tennis) and a continental breakfast included in the price add some attraction. There is a restaurant and a sauna.

Hotel Colomba (☎ 72-7106, 72-1241; colomba@ terra.com.pe; Francisco de Zela 278; s/d US$33/45; P) Bungalows with cable TV and telephones are set in a large, lush garden full of plants and birdcages. A restaurant provides all meals and includes vegetarian requests; room service is available.

San Sebastian (☎ 72-6960.72-6386; andeway@terra .com.pe; Italia 1124; s/d US$45/53; P) A beautiful white-walled and red-roofed building with balconies and arches overlooking a grassy garden and an inner courtyard with a soothing fountain – this four-story hotel is a pleasing neocolonial architectural surprise. The 2nd-floor and rooftop terrace have the best views. All rooms have a writing desk, good beds, hot shower and TV on request. A few rooms have balconies. Rates include a full breakfast; the attractive restaurant is also open for dinner.

Other recommendations include:

Hostal Schatzi (☎ /fax 72-3074; schatzihs@yahoo.com; Bolívar 419; s/d US$15/19) Ten rooms around a pleasant courtyard. Reliable and recommended.

Hotel Santa Victoria (☎ 72-2422; fax 72 4870; Gamarra 690, s/d US$12/23) Simple but spacious rooms with hot shower, cable TV and phone.

Grand Hotel Huaraz (☎ 72-2227, 72-6536; grand hotel@terra.com.pe; Larrea y Loredo 721; s/d US$20/35; P 💻) This new hotel looks good; check it out.

Top End

Hotel Andino (☎ 72-1662; www.hotelandino.com; Pedro Cochachin 357; s/d US$77/85, with balcony US$85/100; P 💻) This Swiss-run hotel southeast of town has one of the best restaurants in Huaraz. It's very popular with international trekking and climbing groups; reservations are a good idea for the high season.

EATING

Many restaurants cut back their hours or days of operation in the low season. Also, closing hours vary; they'll stay open later if they have clients and close if they're empty. Some restaurants add a 28% tax and tip.

Café Andino (☎ 72-1203; cafeandino@hotmail.com; 3rd fl, Lucar y Torre 530; breakfast US$2-4; 🕗 8am-10pm) This coffee-drinkers' paradise is the best java-joint in town and one of the best in Peru. They roast and grind their own and sell it as well. Good teas and other drinks, yummy breakfasts and snacks all day, and a superb place to meet people. Great vistas, board games, and a huge lending/reference library, with map and guidebook sales. Especially knowledgeable about everything to do with the Cordillera Huayhuash.

Casa de Guías (☎ 72-1811; Plaza Ginebra 28G; breakfasts US$2-3, mains US$3-5, pizzas US$6-9; ☺ 7-11am, 5-11pm) Breakfasts include granola, yogurt and fruit, as well as the more usual fare. The evening menu is varied and the pizzas will feed four; the pisco sours have been recommended.

Piccolo (☎ 72-7306; Morales 632; mains US$3-6; ☺ 7am-midnight) Very popular with young foreign visitors attracted to the outdoor pavement seating, friendly service and reasonable prices, the Piccolo is a café, pizzería, restaurant all in one. It has a good Italian and international menu, but make sure you see its Peruvian menu.

Fuente de Salud (☎ 72-4469; José de la Mar 562; meals US$1-4; ☺ 7:30am-10:30pm) A good option for vegetarians, the 'Fountain of Health' offers yogurts, vegetable soups, a vegetarian set lunch, as well as some dishes with meat.

Sabor Salud Pizzería (2nd fl, Luzuriaga 672; meals US$1.50-4; ☺ 7am-11pm) 'Flavor and Health' are the bywords for this vegetarian pizzería, which also offers spinach lasagne and other pastas, soy burgers, yogurt, fruit salads, vegetable salads, omelettes, garlic bread, muesli – vegetarianism sounds tasty here!

La Brasa Roja (☎ 72-7738; Luzuriaga 919; sandwiches US$1-2, mains US$2.50-5; ☺ noon-11pm) Although the 'Red-Hot Coals' is primarily a grilled chicken restaurant, it's the best in town and also has a few other dishes including sandwiches, pastas and beef. Peruvians love this place.

El Fogón (☎ 72-1267; 2nd fl, Luzuriaga 928; mains average US$3; ☺ lunch & dinner) This agreeable grill offers the usual chicken, trout and great *anticuchos* (kebabs), as well as rabbit and soups. There's a nice little bar and it does deliveries as well. Good value.

Bistro de los Andes (☎ 72-6249; Morales 823; mains average US$5; ☺ 7am-10pm Tue-Sun, 6-10pm Mon) This restaurant with a European air is owned by a multilingual Frenchman and serves an international and Peruvian menu ranging from pancakes to pastas. Good coffees, delectable desserts, fabulous fish

dishes; there's something here for everyone at any time of day. It has a book exchange, the ambience is as elegant as you'll find in Huaraz and the service is obliging.

Pachamama (☎ 72-1834; San Martín 687; snacks & mains US$1.50-6) This warm and delightful restaurant-bar features a glass roof, plant-filled interior garden, fireplace, pool table, table tennis, art on the wall and giant chessboard on the floor. It's a hip, fun and popular locale that may have live music and dancing at weekends (not *folklórica*!). The menu is Peruvian and international with a Swiss twist.

Siam de los Andes (☎ 72-8006; Gamarra 560; mains US$7-11; ☺ 6-10pm) The friendly Thai chef serves up superb (and authentic) Thai food. It's pricier than other downtown restaurants, but every diner says 'It's worth it!'. This is a great choice for vegetarians as well.

Monte Rosa/Inca Pub (☎ 72-1447; José de la Mar 661; mains US$5-8; ☺ 10am-11pm) Excellent Swiss-run restaurant with an Alpine vibe; does an international menu including fondue and raclette as well as pizzas and Peruvian plates. Service is good.

Chez Pepe (☎ 72-6482; Raimondi 624; ☺ 7:30am-11pm; mains average US$4) Pepe is an institution on the Huaraz scene. His tartan-table-clothed establishment is warm and welcoming and the pizzas, Italian and international dishes are well prepared and good value. There's a decent wine list as well.

Crêperie Patrick (☎ 72-3364; Luzuriaga 422; mains average US$5; ☺ 8am-10pm) This is a French-influenced place recommended for crepes, ice cream and continental dinners (trout, fondue, pasta). It has a rooftop patio open in the mornings for enjoying breakfast under the sun.

Limón, Leña y Carbón (☎ 80-9243; Luzuriaga 1014; mains US$4.50-6; ☺ lunch & dinner) You go along a funky, graffiti-covered tunnel into a surprisingly good eatery. It specializes in seafood for lunch, including Huaraz's best ceviche. In the evening, it becomes a wood-fired grill and pizza joint.

Other recommendations are:

Chifa Min Hua (Luzuriaga 849; menú US$1.30; mains US$2-3) Best Chinese food in town.

Recreo de Los Jardines (☎ 72-1100; in front of the trout hatchery; meals US$3; ☺ lunch) A locally popular place for fresh trout dishes.

Baby Donkey (San Martín Plaza; ☺ summer only) Good Mexican vegetarian and meat dishes; cheap beer.

Pizza B&B (☎ 72-1719; José de la Mar 674; ☻ noon-10pm; mains US$3-4) Popular wood-fired pizza oven; has pastas as well.

El Rinconcito Minero (Morales 757) Open all day and has a popular outdoor patio.

Pizza Bruno (☎ 72-5689; Luzuriaga 834; mains US$3-7; ☻ 5 -11pm) Serves pizza and has good steaks, salads and seafood.

Mercado Ortiz (Luzuriaga at Raimondi) Best store for self-catering.

Hotel Andino (see Sleeping; mains US$6-10; dinner by reservation) The Swiss kitchen in this hotel prepares first-class dishes.

ENTERTAINMENT

There are several bars, discos and *peñas* (bar featuring folkloric music) and their names and levels of popularity are everchanging. Several restaurants are popular for hanging out, including Café Andino, Pachamama and Piccolo (see Eating opposite).

Vagamundo Travel Bar (Morales 753) Opens late morning and has erratic hours. Come in for a beer, snack and a game of foosball. Enjoy rock and blues and peruse the many maps on the walls, or sit outside on the patio. At the time of writing, world food (Asian, Mediterranean etc) had been added to the menu.

X-treme Bar (☎ 72-3150; upstairs cnr Uribe & Luzuriaga; ☻ dusk-late) A wild and woolly atmosphere is accomplished with bizarre art, drunken graffiti, strong cocktails and good rock and blues; popular with international backpackers.

El Tambo Bar (☎ 72-3417; José de la Mar 776; cover US$3; ☻ 9pm-4am) The longest-lasting and best-known of the dance clubs, El Tambo is popular with both gringos and Peruvians. Music varies from techno-cumbia to Top 20, with salsa to spice it up. Occasional live bands play (higher cover). Dancing gets under way at about 10pm or 11pm. There's a downside: it's the smokiest bar in town.

Makondos (José de la Mar 812; cover varies) Large, airy Latin and Top 40 disco with many different corners to hide away in; prides itself on having good security personnel to prevent unwanted attention etc.

Las Kenas Pub (☎ 72-7101; Uribe 620; happy hour 8-10pm) Crowded with young Peruvians overflowing from the entrance, bent on the techno-cumbia craze and lack of a cover most nights.

SHOPPING

Inexpensive thick woolen sweaters, scarves, hats, socks, gloves, ponchos and blankets are available for travelers needing warm clothes for the mountains; many of these are sold from stalls on the pedestrian alleys off Luzuriaga. Tooled leather goods are also popular souvenirs. There is a sprinkling of other souvenirs for those who aren't planning to spend time in Cuzco or Lima, where the selection is better.

High-quality, attractive T-shirts with appropriately mountainous designs are made by **Andean Expressions** (☎ 72-2951). They are sold in several outlets in town, or you can get them from the home-factory where they are made at J Arguedas 1246, under the Olaza's Guest House.

GETTING THERE & AWAY
Air
The Huaraz-area airport at Anta, 23km north of town, takes only chartered flights.

Bus
Buses heading north along the length of El Callejón de Huaylas stop near the corner of Fitzcarrald and Raimondi when coming from Lima. Local transport goes as far as Caraz. Minibuses for Caraz (US$1.30, 1½ hours) leave every few minutes during the day from Centenario on the north side of the river. These will drop you in any of the towns between Huaraz and Caraz. Minibuses south along El Callejón de Huaylas to Recuay, Catac and other villages leave from the Transportes Zona Sur terminal on Gridilla at Tarapaca.

A plethora of companies have departures for Lima (US$6 to US$12, seven to eight hours), so shop around for the price/class/time you prefer. Most depart mid-morning or late evening. Price hikes of 50% and more do occur leading up to and during major national holidays, and companies will run extra buses to Lima during those dates. For the cheapest tickets, look for companies advertising along Raimondi. Some companies begin in Caraz and stop in Huaraz to pick up passengers, but if you have a numbered ticket, there should be no problem.

Three bus routes reach Chimbote (US$5 to US$7, eight hours) on the north coast. Most buses take the paved road to Pativilca (the same route as Lima-bound buses) and then head north on the Panamericana. A second route follows El Callejón de Huaylas and passes through the narrow, spectacular Cañón del Pato before descending to the coast at Chimbote. A third route crosses the 4225m-high Punta Callán, 30km west of Huaraz, and provides spectacular views of the Cordillera Blanca before dropping to Casma, but the road is in rough shape. Most companies that service Chimbote continue on to Trujillo (US$6 to US$9, 10 hours).

For services across the Andes to the towns east of Huaraz, there are many small companies with brave, beat-up buses. The information here is not exhaustive and is subject to frequent change. Recommended companies are Cruz del Sur and Movil Tours.

Chavín Express (☎ 72-4652; M Cáceres 338) Has 7:30am, 11am and 2pm services to Chavín, San Marcos and Huari. Ask about Llamelin, Sihuas and Huacracucho.

Chinchaysuyo (☎ 72-6417; Morales 650B) Has a 9pm bus to Trujillo.

Civa Cial (☎ 72-1947, 72-9253; Morales 650) Good mid-priced night buses to Lima.

Cruz del Sur (☎ 72-8726; Raimondi 242) 11am and 10pm Imperial nonstop service to Lima for US$12.

El Amigo de Milenium (south side of market) Departs 12:45pm to Huallanca, 1pm to Chiquián.

Empresa 14 (☎ 72-1282; Bolívar 407) Leaves 8:30pm via Pativilca to Trujillo.

Expreso Ancash (☎ 72-1102; Raimondi 835) Subsidiary of Ormeño; services to Lima 2pm, 9:30pm and 10pm.

Linea (☎ 72-6666; Bolívar 450) 9:30pm via Pativilca, Chimbote to Trujillo; might have Lima buses.

Movil Tours (☎ 72-2555; Bolívar 542) Several daily; nightly buses to Lima, various classes. Night buses to Chimbote and Trujillo.

Renzo (☎ 72-9673; Raimondi 835) Departs 6am to Chacas, San Luis (US$5, five hours) 6:30am to Yanama, Piscobamba, Pomabamba (US$6, eight hours).

Transportes El Rápido (☎ 72-2887, M Cáceres at Tarapaca) Leaves 6am and 1pm to Chiquián (US$3, three hours); 6am and 12:30pm to Huallanca (US$4, five hours); La Unión (eight to 10 hours).

Transportes Flores (☎ 72-6598; Raimondi 813) Cheapish buses to Lima.

Transportes Río Mosna (opposite El Rápido) To Chiquián at 6am and 1pm.

Transportes Rodríguez (☎ 72-1353; Tarapaca 622) Decent night buses to Lima and Chimbote.

Transvir (☎ 72-5356, 72-7744; Caraz 604) Early bus to Chacas, San Luis, Piscobamba, Pomabamba and Sihuas.

Yungay Express (☎ 72-4377; Fitzcarrald 237) Morning buses to Chimbote via Cañón del Pato or Casma; night bus via Pativilca.

GETTING AROUND

A taxi ride around Huaraz costs under US$1. A taxi ride to Caraz is about US$20. Other rides can be arranged. Look for taxis at the bridge on Fitzcarrald or along Luzuriaga.

PARQUE NACIONAL HUASCARÁN

Protecting the beauty of the Cordillera Blanca was first suggested by the Peruvian mountaineer César Morales Arnao in the early 1960s, but didn't become reality until 1975, when Parque Nacional Huascarán was established. The 3400-sq-km park encompasses the entire area of the Cordillera Blanca above 4000m, except for Champará, which is in the extreme northern part of the range.

The park was established to protect the flora, fauna, archaeological sites and scenic beauty of the area, and to raise living standards of the people within its boundaries. Unlike in national parks in many countries, in Peru, native people who have lived here for generations continue to eke out an agricultural livelihood.

Visitors to the park should bring their passports to register at the park office (see Tourist Information p309 under Huaraz) and pay the park fee. This is about US$2 per person for a day visit, or US$20 for a multiday visit if you plan on trekking or climbing. The US$20 fee is officially valid for 30 days, but it could be accepted for the entire season. It is best to pay in soles. You can also register and pay your fee at one of the control stations (not always staffed in the low season) at the Lagunas Llanganuco, Pastoruri glacier or Musho village, west of Huascarán. (The tiny community of Collón is charging US$5 to enter Quebrada Ishinca; it's not clear whether the park will set up an official station here. There may be other stations in the future.) The money from the fees is used to help maintain trails, pay park rangers (there are a few) and offset the effects of so many visitors in the area. Some oppose regulation; however, the number of visitors to the Cordillera Blanca, while still relatively small by North American or European standards, is ncreasing fast enough to warrant some sort of governance if the inherent attraction of the mountains is to be protected. It makes sense that as foreign visitors are the ones who get the most joy out of the Cordillera Blanca, and are among those causing the greatest change within the area, they should contribute to the financing of the national park with their user fees.

Unfortunately, this hasn't been the case. Alarming numbers of trekkers have changed their routes or arrived at the park gates in the middle of the night just to avoid paying fees. Travelers should remember that the cheapest option isn't always the correct one. Parque Nacional Huascarán and the Cordillera Blanca are some of the most magical places on the planet; make sure your visit contributes to preserving the longevity of this mountain paradise.

Present park regulations are largely a matter of courtesy and common sense. 'Do not litter' is the most obvious one – obvious, that is, to almost all of us. There are always a few visitors who leave a trail of yellow film cartons, pink toilet paper, broken bottles and jagged tin cans to mark their path. This is thoughtless, rude and illegal. It's true that locals are among the worst offenders, but 'When in Rome…' is not a sensible reason for imitating the offense. It is also true that people tend to litter more where litter already exists, so each candy wrapper contributes to the overall problem by beginning or continuing this chain reaction. Don't do it. Remember, if you carry it in, you can carry it out. If you can pick up and carry out some extra garbage, you'll start a chain reaction that will benefit everybody.

Other park regulations include: don't disturb the flora or fauna; don't cut down trees or live branches for fires or other use (open fires are illegal); don't destroy or alter park signs; don't use off-road vehicles; don't hunt; don't fish during the off season (September to May); don't fish with explosives or nets and don't take fish less than 25cm in length.

Visiting the Mountains

Basically, there are two ways to visit the mountains. One is to stay in the towns of El Callejón de Huaylas and take day trips by bus or taxi. A glance at the map reveals that the summit of Peru's highest peak is a mere 14km from the main valley road, and spectacular views can certainly be obtained from public transport or day tours. For many people, that is enough. The more adventurous will want to take their backpacks and trek, camp or climb in the mountains. This book gives details of public transport and mentions some of the major hikes, but does not pretend to be a trail guide (see Trail Guidebooks & Maps on p320).

When to Go

The best months for hiking, climbing and mountain views are the dry months of June, July and August. May and September are also usually quite good. For the rest of the year, the wet season makes hiking difficult, especially from December to March, because the trails are so boggy, and the weather is frequently overcast and very wet. Despite this, you may be lucky and see some spectacular mountain views between the clouds, especially in the days around a full moon. Even during the dry season, however, you should be prepared for occasional rain, hail or snow.

Mountain Guide Services

Guiding services range from a single *arriero* (mule driver), with a couple of pack animals for your camping gear, to a complete trekking expedition, with *arrieros*, *burros* (mules), cooks, guides, food and all equipment provided. You can also hire high-altitude porters and guides for mountaineering expeditions. These are available in Huaraz and, to a much lesser extent, in Caraz. Guides and arrieros with ID cards are recommended.

If your Spanish is up to it and you're not in a great hurry, you can hire *arrieros* and mules in trailhead villages, particularly Cashapampa, Colcabamba and Vaquería, among others. The going rate for an *arriero* is about US$10 a day, a mule is US$5 a day (cheaper mules are likely to be old and decrepit), but this does not include the cost of the *arriero's* meals (which you provide). You may need to rent a tent for the *arriero* as well. You also have to pay for the days the *arriero* and mules are walking back, unloaded, to the point of origin. It's difficult to hire a pack animal for yourself; the arrieros will not send out *burros* without experienced drivers. Horses and mules for riding purposes are also available at about US$10 per day. Bear in mind that it is easier to make arrangements in Huaraz than anywhere else in the area, and that in some towns and villages, arrieros are difficult to find. If you want a guide, the official rates are US$30 to US$50 per day for a trekking guide and US$50 to US$75 for a climbing guide, depending on the route, plus food.

As you enter a valley, you often find a locked gate. The locals will unlock it for you and charge you to go through 'their' valley. The fees have been variously reported as US$2 an animal or US$5 to US$15 per group. Ask the arrieros about these fees. Backpackers without animals can often just climb over the gate.

Trail Guidebooks & Maps
Lonely Planet's *Trekking in the Central Andes* covers the best hikes in the Cordillera Blanca and a 12-day circuit of the Cordillera Huayhuash (of which you might choose to do only a portion). Felipe Díaz's 1:286,000 *Cordilleras Blanca & Huayhuash* is a useful map with major trails and town plans; it may not be detailed enough for remote treks. The Alpine Mapping Guild's 1:65,000 *Cordillera Huayhuash* topographic map is excellent. Both are available in Caraz, Huaraz and at South American Explorers' clubhouses (see p56). Note that detailed 1:100,000 IGN topographical maps are hard to find and very expensive in Huaraz; get them in Lima.

NORTH OF HUARAZ

The stupendous El Callejón de Huaylas road north of Huaraz follows the Río Santa valley and is completely overshadowed by Andean peaks, including Huascarán, which is only 14km away from the road as the condor flies. The road is paved.

MONTERREY
☎ 043 / pop 1000 / elevation 2800m
Just 5km north of Huaraz is this small village, famous for its natural **hot springs** (admission US$1; ☼ 8am-6pm, Tue-Sun). The bus terminates right in front of the springs, so there's no difficulty finding them. The hot springs are divided into two sections;

the lower pools are more crowded than the upper pools, where there are private rooms (20 minutes for US$1.60 per person). The pools are very busy on weekends and are closed Monday for cleaning, so Tuesday is the cleanest day. Despite this, the pool is naturally a chocolate color.

Sleeping & Eating
The hotels are near the springs – ask anyone for directions. Restaurants are a little further afield, but within walking distance.

Hostal El Nogal (☎ 72-5929; s/d US$8.50/17) has rooms with hot showers and rather beat-up beds, though the garden is pleasant.

Real Hotel Baños Termales Monterrey (☎ /fax 72-1717, 72-7690; d US$58, bungalow US$81-116; **P** 🖳) This is a pleasant older building with creaky wooden floors but a certain dated charm in the public areas. It is set in gardens right next to the hot springs and rates include access to them. There is a simple restaurant with outdoor dining (overlooking the pool) and reasonably priced meals. Rather spartan rooms have hot showers and a TV that shows local channels. The four bungalows sleep either two or four. You needn't stay at the hotel to use the pool or the restaurant.

El Patio (☎ 72-4965; elpatio@terra.com.pe; s/d US$40/55; **P**) The nicest option has colonial-style architecture that is nicely complemented by the colonial-style furniture in the rooms, most of which are spacious and have bathtubs and showers, phones and local TV. Some rooms (US$85) sleep up to four and a few have a fireplace. Most rooms look out onto a pleasant garden or around an attractive patio with a restful fountain; some have a balcony. Breakfast (US$4.50) and dinner (mains US$8) are available in the cozy restaurant-bar with fireplace.

Apart from the hotel restaurants, there's the nice little **Monterrey Café & Bar** (☼ 10am-5pm) just below the Real Hotel. There are also several good rural places serving local food, especially grills such as *cuy* (guinea pig), *chicharrones*, trout and *pachamanca*, the latter normally on Saturday and/or Sunday or by special arrangement. These are along the main Huaraz–Caraz road. **Recreo Mochica** (☎ 72-9074. 72-3072; Km2.5; mains US$2.50-5; ☼ 8am-8pm) is a small but locally popular place serving local food; specialties are *cuy* or mixed platter containing *chicharron de chancho, rocotto relleno, tamal* and *mote*.

You can't miss the rock model of the Cordillera Blanca outside **Recreo Buongiorno** (☎ 72-7145; Km2.5; meals US$3-6), which serves local and national food and has superb pastries. Outside is a nice garden with a playset for children that attracts families. **El Cortijo** (☎ 72-3813; in Monterrey; mains US$4-9; ✆ 7am-dusk) This is an excellent grill offering ostrich along with *cuy* and other meats, as well as 'ordinary' food. Outdoor tables are arranged around a fountain in a grassy flower-filled garden, with swings for children. There is also an indoor restaurant and an outdoor terrace for a choice of ambience. **Restaurant Cordillera Blanca** (near El Cortijo) is also good and slightly cheaper. **El Ollon de Barro** (☎ 72-3364; Km7; meals US$3-9) has a large, pretty garden with a fronton court, children's swings and trees, all hidden behind a wall – a safe place for kids to play while adults feast. Several typical plates such as *rocotta relleno* and *ají de gallina* are on offer, as well as the usual country grills.

Getting There & Away

Monterrey is reached by local buses from Huaraz, which go north along Luzuriaga, west on 28 de Julio, north on 27 de Noviembre, east on Raimondi and north on Fitzcarrald. Try to catch a bus early in the route, as they soon fill up. The fare for the 15-minute ride is US$0.30. A taxi ride between Huaraz and Monterrey is US$1.50.

MONTERREY TO CARHUAZ

About 16km north of Huaraz, the road goes through the little village of **Taricá**, which is famous as a local pottery center. You can stop at the friendly **Hostal Sterling** (☎ 79-1277, 79-0299; s/d US$6/11.50; **P**), which has funky, concrete block rooms with electric showers, a small restaurant and a bar that looks like it hasn't been changed or even dusted since the 1950s. Behind the hotel is a mountain, Aparac, which is used for hang-gliding.

About 23km north of Huaraz is tiny Anta airport, and 2km beyond is the small village of **Marcará**. From here, minibuses and trucks leave regularly for the hot springs of **Chancos**, 4km to the east, and occasionally continue another 4km to **Vicos**. It's a 5km walk from here to the ruins of **Joncapampa**. Beyond Vicos, the Quebrada Honda trail (for hikers

<table>
<tr><td>

MOUNTAIN REFUGES

Three refuges have been constructed by **Don Bosco en Los Andes** (☎ 74-3061; andesbosco@virgilio.it), an Italian relief organization based in Marcará. The refuges are heated, have 60 beds each and charge US$30 per night for bed, breakfast and dinner. Profits go to local aid projects.

Refugio Perú (4765m) is a two-hour walk from Llanaganuco and a base for climbing Pisco. **Refugio Ishinca** (4350m) is a three-hour walk from Collón village in the Ishinca valley. **Refugio Huascarán** (4670m) is a four-hour walk from Musho. Trekkers, mountaineers, and sightseers are welcomed.

</td></tr>
</table>

only) continues across the Cordillera Blanca. The rustic Chancos hot springs are popular with locals on weekends, when they tend to be crowded. Steam baths in natural caves are US$1.50 for 15 minutes, private tepid pools are US$0.60 and the pool is US$0.30.

Marcará has the basic **Hostal Los Jazmines** (main plaza; r per person US$5) with shared bathrooms.

CARHUAZ

☎ 043 / pop 6000 / elevation 2638m
This small town, 35km north of Huaraz, is the best entrance or exit into the Cordillera Blanca via the beautiful Quebrada Ulta. Vehicles from Carhuaz to Shilla leave from near the plaza many times a day; some continue through the Quebrada Ulta and may go over the Punta Olimpica pass. Ask locally. This trekking route is becoming increasingly popular.

Carhuaz's annual **La Virgen de La Merced fiesta** is celebrated 14 to 24 September with processions, fireworks, dancing, bullfights and plenty of drinking; it's one of the area's best and wildest festivals.

Sleeping & Eating

Hostal El Abuelo (☎ 79-4456; hostalelabuelo@terra .com.pe; 9 de Diciembre 257; d US$40; **P** **▣**) It's a spotless hotel with comfortable beds and hot showers; breakfast is included. Several family *hostals* offer simple, clean rooms with hot-water bathrooms for US$6/12 a single/double. Try **Hostal Río Santa** (☎ 79-4128), **Hostal Las Bromelias** (☎ 79-4033; Brazil 208) or **Hostal Las Torrecitas** (☎ 79-4213; Amazonas 412).

The older **Hotel La Merced** (☎ 79-4241; Ucayali 724; s/d US$3/6; s/d with bathroom US$4.50/9) has hot showers and offers group discounts. The simple rooms are clean and some are brightened by a balcony.

Café Heladería El Abuelo (☎ /fax 79-4149; meals US$1-4; ☻ 8am-9pm), on the Plaza de Armas, is owned by local cartographer Felipe Díaz (you probably have his map; everyone does!). It serves breakfast, snacks and ice cream made from local fruits, and provides local information.

El Mirador (☎ 79-4244; meals US$2-4), about 2km south of Carhuaz on the south of a hill with views, is a lunchtime restaurant with typical food. Just north is **La Cabaña** (☎ 79-4292; meals US$2-4), a grill with outdoor tables in a bucolic garden with a small pool and playground.

YUNGAY

☎ 043 / pop 9000 / elevation 2458m

The rubble-strewn area of old Yungay, about 2km south of the new town is the site of the single worst natural disaster in the Andes. The earthquake of May 31, 1970 loosened 15 million cubic meters of granite and ice from the west wall of Huascarán Norte and the resulting *aluvión* reached a speed of 300km/h as it dropped over three vertical kilometers on its way to Yungay, 14km away. The town and almost all of its 18,000 inhabitants were buried. The earthquake also killed about 50,000 people in other parts of central Peru.

Today the quake site, **Campo Santo** (admission US$0.60; ☻ 8am-6pm), is marked by a huge white statue of Christ on a knoll overlooking old Yungay. The path of the *aluvión* can plainly be seen from the road. Flower-filled gardens top the site, with occasional gravestones and monuments commemorating the thousands of people who lie buried beneath your feet. At the old Plaza de Armas, you can see just the very top of the cathedral tower and a few palm trees, which are all that remain of the devastated village. A replica of the cathedral's facade has been built in honor of the dead.

New Yungay has been rebuilt just beyond the *aluvión* path, about 59km north of Huaraz. A stark, hastily built town, it offers no attraction in itself, but is the entry point for the beautiful and popular excursion to the Lagunas Llganuco.

The annual festival is 28 October.

Emergency

Policía de Montaña (☎ 79-3327, 79-3333, 79-3291 usam@pnp.gob.pe) has two helicopters, trained search-and-rescue dogs, and police officers who have taken mountaineering courses. They may work with experts from the Mountain Guide Association at the Casa de Guías (p308) in Huaraz.

Sleeping & Eating

Hostal Gledel (☎ 79-3048; s/d US$3/6) is a basic but clean and friendly backpackers hotel that has long been popular. Thirteen rooms share two hot showers, three toilets and three sinks. Breakfast is available. The decent **Hostal Yungay** (☎ 79-3053; s/d US$4.50/7.30) has 25 basic rooms that have electric showers. **Hostal Sol de Oro** (☎ 79-3116; s/d US$4.50/9) has firm mattresses and hot showers. All three are close to the plaza.

There are several cheap and simple places to eat in Yungay's market, next to the plaza. **Restaurant Turístico Alpamayo** (☎ 79-3090; meals US$1-3; ☻ 7am-7pm), off the main highway at the north end of town, is the best restaurant.

Getting There & Away

Minibuses run from the Plaza de Armas to Caraz (US$0.50, 15 minutes), and buses en route from Caraz will pick up passengers to Huaraz (US$1.20, 1¼ hours) from the southwest side of the plaza. Buses from Caraz to Lima and buses from Huaraz to Chimbote pick up passengers at the Plaza de Armas.

Dawn departures on beat-up buses to Pomabamba via the Lagunas Llganuco run daily. Ask where to find them.

LAGUNAS LLGANUCO

A dirt road climbs the Llganuco valley to the two lovely lakes of the same name, 28km east of Yungay. There are killer views of the giant mountains of Huascarán (6768m), Chopicalqui (6354m), Chacraraju (6112m), Huandoy (6395m) and others, particularly if you drive a few kilometers beyond the lakes. The road continues over the pass beyond the lakes and down to Yanama on the other side of the Cordillera Blanca; there is often an early-morning vehicle from Yungay going to Yanama and beyond.

It is also from Yungay that hikers begin the Llganuco-to-Santa Cruz loop – the most popular and spectacular trek of the Cordillera Blanca. This takes five leisurely days (though is often done in four) and is a good hike for everybody, especially beginners, because the trail is relatively well defined. Note that there is a US$2 day-use and US$20 multiday-use fee. See Lonely Planet's *Trekking in the Central Andes* for this and other hike descriptions, or use the adequate maps available in Huaraz.

The Llanganuco road also provides access to the Pisco base camp, where the ascent of Nevado Pisco (5752m) begins. Though considered one of the most straightforward high-snow ascents in the range, it is not to be taken lightly and requires snow and ice-climbing equipment and experience.

To reach Lagunas Llanganuco, you can take a tour from Huaraz or use buses or taxis from Yungay. During the June-to-August high season, minibuses leave from Yungay's Plaza de Armas. The round trip costs about US$5 and allows about two hours in the lake area. A national-park admission fee of around US$2 is also charged. During the rest of the year, minibuses do the trip if there is enough demand, and taxis are also available. Go in the early morning for clear views; it's often cloudy in the afternoon. A daily morning bus links Yungay with Yanama, passing the lakes without stopping there.

CARAZ

☎ 043 / pop 22,000 / elevation 2270m

The pretty little town of Caraz is one of the few places in the area that has managed to avoid total destruction by earthquake or *aluvión*. The town has an attractive Plaza de Armas and you can take pleasant walks in the surrounding hills. It lies 67km north of Huaraz and is the end of the road as far as regular and frequent transport is concerned, although the paved road now continues to Huallanca and is slowly being extended.

Caraz is both the end point of the time-honored Llanganuco-to-Santa Cruz trek which can also be done in reverse starting here) and the point of departure for rugged treks into the remote northern parts of the Cordillera Blanca. The town makes a good base for treks to the north side of Alpamayo 5947m), often called the most beautiful mountain in the world for its knife-edged perfectly pyramidal northern silhouette. Ex-

cursions can be made by road to stunning Laguna Parón and to the Cañón del Pato.

The bright-blue **Laguna Parón**, 32km east of Caraz, is surrounded by spectacular snowcapped peaks, of which Pyramide (5885m), at the end of the lake, looks particularly magnificent. The road to the lake goes through a canyon with 1000m-high granite walls and this drive is as spectacular as the better-known Llanganuco trip.

The spectacular **Cañón del Pato** is at the far north end of El Callejón de Huaylas and is its narrowest point. Buses en route to Chimbote take this road every day, or you can take a pickup truck or taxi from Caraz. There is a cheap, clean hotel in Huallanca at the north end of the Cañón (not to be confused with Huallanca at the southeast end of the Cordillera Blanca).

Punta Winchus, a remote 4157m pass in the Cordillera Negra 45km west of Caraz, reached by tour vehicles, is the center of a huge stand of *Puya raimondii*, with an estimated 5000 plants – the biggest known stand of the Andean giants. Additionally, a clear day gives an astounding 145km view of the Cordillera Blanca, as well as the Pacific Ocean.

Although much smaller than Huaraz, Caraz is beginning to develop some infrastructure for tourism.

Information

A source of extensive information, Alberto Cafferata speaks English, French and Spanish and runs the recommended **Pony Expeditions** (☎ /fax 79-1642, 968-2848; www .ponyexpeditions.com; José Sucre 1266; ⏰ 8am 10pm). He's a great source for all local information, and provides equipment rental (including 17 bicycles), transport, guides, *arrieros*, and various excursions. Books, maps, fuels and other items are for sale at the shop. This is the place to get up-to-date trekking information as well as directions for local day hikes. The **Municipalidad** on the Plaza de Armas also has limited tourist information and useful brochures.

Internet Satelital, at the northwest corner of the Plaza de Armas, provides Internet access.

BCP (☎ 79-1010; Daniel Villar 217) changes cash and traveler's checks but lacks an ATM. Pony Expeditions can change US cash and euros and arrange Visa advances.

CARAZ

0 ——— 0.1 km
0 ——— 0.1 mi

To Grand Hostal
Caraz Dulzura (8 blocks)

To Hostal Chamana,
Hostal Tumshukaiko (2 blocks),
Hostal La Alameda (5 blocks),
Laguna Parón & Tumshukaiko Ruins (2km)

16

Santa Cruz

Plaza

Mercado Central

La Mar

Cordova

San Martín

José Sucre

Grau

Bolognesi

14

A Ugarte

Santa Rosa

Manco Cápac

10 13 5   15

2
@
1
S

18

Daniel Villar

Plaza de
Armas

Raimondi

12

11

9

To
Alojamiento
Caballero,
Albergue Los Pinas
& La Punta

6

M Cáceres

19
i
4

7

8

3

L Prado

José Galvez

SLEEPING		pp324–5
Alojamiento Ramírez	6	A2
Hostal Chavín	7	B3
Hostal Familiar Aguilar	8	B3
Hostal La Casona	9	C2
La Perla de Los Andes	10	B2

EATING		p325
Café de Rat	11	B2
El Mirador	12	B2
Heladería Caraz Dulzura	13	B2
La Esmeralda	14	B1
Pollería Jeny	15	B2

TRANSPORT		p325
Colectivos to Cashapampa	16	D1
Minibuses to Yungay & Huaraz	17	B3
Transportes Rodríguez & other Bus companies	18	A2
Yungay Express	19	A2

OTHER		
Pony Expeditions	(see 11)	

INFORMATION	pp323–4
BCP	1 A2
Internet Satelital	2 B2
Lavandería Marshall	3 B3
Municipalidad	4 B2

SIGHTS & ACTIVITIES	
Church	5 B2

Cemetery

Luriuraga

Carretera Central

To o'Pal Inn (1.5km),
Yungay & Huaraz

Lavandería Marshall (San Martín 11th block; 8am-2pm & 4-8pm) gives back your washing washed and folded.

Tumshukaiko

The partially excavated Chavín ruins of Tumshukaiko are about 2km on a dirt road north of Caraz. Take José Sucre until it becomes 28 de Julio, and continue about 1km to the site on your left. There is no sign or fee. The extensive walls (now in poor condition) and buried underground chambers indicate this was once an important Chavín site.

Sleeping

Apart from the independence holidays at the end of July, hotel prices remain quite stable throughout the year, probably because Caraz has not yet been overrun by visitors.

Grand Hostal Caraz Dulzura (79-1523; Saenz Peña 212; s/d US$7.50/13; P) About 10 blocks north of town along San Martín, this is an attractive, modern rural retreat. Rooms are bright and have hot showers and comfy beds. There's a patio, TV room, book exchange and res taurant for breakfast (US$1.50) and dinne (mains US$1 to US$3); lunch is availabl on request.

Hostal Tumshukaico (79-2212; tumshukaico@ hotmail.com; Melgar 114; d US$14) Five blocks north of town is this hotel with modern 2nd-floo rooms that are decorated in a rustic theme and feature excellent mattresses and ho showers. Downstairs is a garden and a Spanish-influenced restaurant that serve bonzer buffet breakfasts (US$2). The room cost US$10 in low season.

Hostal La Alameda (79-1177; laalameda@huara online.com; Bazán Peralta 262; d US$17; P) Thi pretty hotel, set in a flourishing garden, i run by friendly older ladies who'll mothe you. Parquet-floored rooms are spotless have comfy mattresses and hot showers Breakfast is available.

La Perla de Los Andes (/fax 79-2007; Plaza d Armas 179; d US$17) This great location righ on the plaza is special because the Cara plaza is much quieter than in most towns Although rooms are a mite small, they al have cable TV, solid mattresses and ho showers, and some have balconies with plaza views. A restaurant serves breakfast on the premises and the staff is helpful.

Alojamiento Caballero (☎ 79-1637; Daniel Villar 485; s/d US$3/6) It's a small, simple, clean, friendly, family-run place with shared hot showers and good views (inquire at Pony Expeditions).

Albergue Los Pinos (☎ 79-1130; lospinos@terra .com.pe; Parque San Martín 103; camping per person US$2.50; s/d US$8/16, s/d with bathroom US$10/20; P ⬜) Five blocks southwest of the plaza and affiliated with the International Youth Hostel Federation, this popular *hostal* has hot water, kitchen and laundry privileges, travel information, café and a garden. Rates can halve in the low season.

Hostal La Casona (☎ 79-1334; Raimondi 319; s/d US$4/6; s/d with bathroom US$6/8) An attractive patio makes this place a favored budget choice.

Hostal Chavín (☎ 79-1171; hostalchavin@latin mail.com; San Martín 1135; s/d US$8/11) The friendly owner knows the area and provides information, tours and local transportation. Rooms are simple but all have hot showers. Breakfast is available.

Hostal Chamana (☎ 969-1645; Nueva Victoria 185; s/d US$15/25; P) It's less than 2km from the center on the road to Cashapampa (ask locals for directions and take a taxi at night). The Chamana has six pleasant cabins, all with hot showers, set in a pretty garden. Food is German-influenced and good; a full breakfast is US$6.

Other recommendations are:

Alojamiento Ramírez (☎ 79-1368; Daniel Villar 407; s/d US$3/5) Basic, noisy but clean and cheap; there's shared cold showers.

Hostal Familiar Aguilar (☎ 79-1161; San Martín 1143; s/d US$3/6) Friendly family, basic rooms and shared showers with hot water in the morning.

O'Pal Inn (☎ 79-1015; d US$30-60; P) Several kilometers south off the road to Huaraz. Nicely furnished rooms and apartments. Breakfast is available.

Eating

Café de Rat (above Pony Expeditions; meals US$1-3; large pizzas US$6-8; ☯ 7am-10pm Mon-Sat) This atmospheric wood-beamed restaurant serves breakfasts, sandwiches, pastas, coffees and drinks throughout the day. It also has a book exchange, darts, a bar and music; it's a good place to hang out. It has a fireplace and plaza views.

Pollería Jeny (☎ 79-1101; on plaza; meals US$1-3; ☯ 7am-10:30pm) Good set lunches and the best chicken in town bring in the impecunious; slightly pricier à la carte items include steak and trout. Breakfast, snacks and sandwiches are also available.

La Punta (☎ 79-1320; Daniel Villar 595; meals US$1-3) A short walk from the town center, this is definitely the place for a typical highland lunch. It serves dishes (including *cuy*) and there is a plant-filled garden to eat in, which includes a pond, gazebo and *sapo* game. If you don't feel like *cuy*, try a hearty bowl of soup, *lomo saltado* (grilled strips of beef mixed with french fries) or *tamales*.

Other recommendations include:

El Mirador (José Sucre 1202; meals US$1-2.50) Serves *menús* (set meals) and grilled chicken; has nice plaza views from its balcony.

Heladería Caraz Dulzura (next to the church) This is the place for ice cream.

La Esmeralda (A Ugarte 404; meals US$1-2) Good for *lomo saltado* and *menús*.

Getting There & Away

Caraz is often the final destination for buses heading from the coast to El Callejón de Huaylas, and there is frequent transport from here to other points in the area and the coast. Most coastal buses go via Huaraz.

LONG DISTANCE

Transportes Rodríguez (☎ 79-1184; Cordova 141), **Expreso Ancash** (☎ 79-1023), **Movil Tours** (☎ 79-1922) and other companies go to Lima (about US$7, 10 hours). They are to be found on the 1st block of Cordova. **Yungay Express** (☎ 79-1693; Daniel Villar 316) has two buses a day to Chimbote (US$6, nine hours), one via the Cañón del Pato leaving at 8:30am.

CARAZ AREA

Minibuses to Yungay and Huaraz leave from the station on the Carretera Central. Colectivo taxis for Cashapampa (US$1.50, two hours), for the northern end of the Llanganuco-to-Santa Cruz trek, leave when full from the corner of Ramón Castilla at Santa Cruz. Also from here are 5am and 1pm buses to Pueblo Parón (US$1.50, one hour) for the famous Laguna Parón, which is about 9km further on foot or by truck if you can find one. Buses return from Pueblo Parón at 6am and 2pm. Note that the hours may change on Sunday.

PUYA RAIMONDII

The giant *Puya raimondii* is the largest member of the bromeliads, or the pineapple family, and grows as a spiny rosette of long, tough, waxy leaves that reaches 2m in diameter and takes about 100 years to grow to full size. It then flowers by producing a huge spike, often 10m high, which is covered by approximately 20,000 flowers – a magnificent sight. This spiky inflorescence is the largest in the world; the plant remains in flower for about three months, and is pollinated by hummingbirds. After flowering once, the plant dies. Puyas tend to flower in groups about every three or four years, so make local inquiries to find out where they are flowering at any particular time.

This giant bromeliad is one of the world's most ancient plant species and is considered a living fossil. It is found only in a few isolated areas of the Peruvian and Bolivian Andes. The sites in the Cordillera Blanca are among the best known and receive protection as part of the Parque Nacional Huascarán. Other sites are found in the Cordillera Negra (see Caraz p323).

The best-known site is in the Carpa sector of the national park, reached by turning off the main road 10km south of Catac and following a dirt road for 18km to the Quebrada Raria, where the *puyas* are to be seen. These areas are also the best place in the Cordillera Blanca to watch for the beautiful vicuña, an infrequently seen wild relative of the alpaca and llama. Tour companies in Huaraz make trips to this site.

Taxis (US$0.60) and mototaxis (US$0.30) trundle around town.

SOUTH OF HUARAZ

This area covers the southern extent of the Cordillera Blanca and the majestic **Cordillera Huayhuash**, the less-known but no less lovely mountain range to the south. It is a tightly bound range looking up to **Yerupajá** (6634m), Peru's second-highest mountain. The Huayhuash is the main reason for travelers to head south from Huaraz (apart from heading to Lima). Hiking in the Huayhuash usually involves making a circuit of the entire range – this is fairly strenuous and takes almost two weeks. (Lonely Planet's *Trekking in the Central Andes* fully describes the trail and various shorter options available.) Because it is less accessible than the Blanca, the Huayhuash has fewer visitors. For details of trekking companies servicing the area see p312.

The first place of interest south of Huaraz is the Puente Bedoya, a bridge about 18km away. From here, a dirt road leads 2km east from the highway to the village of **Olleros**, the starting point for the easy three-day trek across the Cordillera Blanca to Chavín. **Recuay** is a village 25km from Huaraz and is one of the few towns to have survived the 1970 earthquake largely unscathed. **Catac**, 10km south of Recuay, is an even smaller town and the starting point for trips to see the remarkable *Puya raimondii* (see the boxed text for details).

CHIQUIÁN

☎ 043 / pop 5000 / elevation 3400m

This town is the center for visiting the Cordillera Huayhuash. There are great views of the Huayhuash as you drive to the village.

Trekking services can be arranged here through a couple of small agencies in town. Daily rates are the same as in Huaraz. It is possible to privately hire an *arriero* and *burros* for a little less, but you have to provide them with food and something to sleep in. Trekkers should also be prepared for aggressively territorial dogs along the way; bending down to pick up a rock is usually enough to keep them off.

The annual festival here is **Santa Rosa de Lima**, held in late August, with dances, parades, music and bullfights. There is also a **Semana Turística** in early July.

Sleeping & Eating

Clean and attractive **Hotel Los Nogales** (☎ 74-7121; hotel_nogales_chiquian@yahoo.com; Comercio 1301; s/d US$3/6, with bathroom US$6/12) is about three blocks from the central plaza. Rooms surround a pretty, colonial-style courtyard and meals are available on request. There is not hot water. Also good is the more modern **Gran Hotel Huayhuash** (☎ 74-7049, 74-7183; 28 de Julio 400; s/d US$3/6, with bathroom from US$6/12). Some rooms have cable TV and offer good views; hot water is available, and the hotel has the town's best restaurant (menú

US$1.20, mains US$1.80 to US$4.50). The hotel owner here is a good source of local information. Cheaper and adequate, **Hostal Chavín** (San Martín 1st block; d US$5) is an attractive option for shoestring travelers.

Getting There & Away

If you are interested in Chiquián and the Cordillera Huayhuash, you'll find direct buses from Lima. However, Chiquián is not a particularly exciting town in which to acclimatize, and spending a few days in Huaraz is more fun. El Rápido buses go from Chiquián to Huaraz at 5am and 2pm, leaving from Gran Hotel Huayhuash (opposite).

Transfysa (☎ 74-7063; 2 de Mayo 1109) has an 8:30am bus to Lima (US$5, nine hours), or try **Turismo Cavassa** (☎ 74-7036; Bolognesi 421), with an 8:30pm departure; times change frequently.

Ask at the Gran Hotel Huayhuash to arrange transportation to Pacllón or Llamac to get closer to the Cordillera Huayhuash. It is also possible to get from Chiquían to Huallanca although service is irregular. Ask. Huallanca has a basic hotel, and transport continues on from here to La Unión and Huánuco.

CAJATAMBO

☎ 01 / pop 3000 / elevation 3400m

This village on the far side of the Cordillera Huayhuash is reached by trekking or by going along a poor road from Lima; because it is at the north end of the Department of Lima it has Lima-style seven-digit phone numbers.

Sleeping & Eating

Of several basic cold-water cheapies, **Hotel Miranda** (Tacna 141; s/d US$4/8) is probably as good as any. **Tambomachay** (☎ 244-2046; Bolognesi 140; r per person from US$10) offers better service and hot water and arranges local bus tickets. The most upscale place in the Huayhuash area is the overpriced **International Inn** (☎ 244-2071; international.inn@hostal.net; Benavides 4th block; s/d US$40/50; **P**) The small rooms have comfortable beds, hot water and TV. Bargain hard for a discount. There's an expensive restaurant here as well. Budget travelers will find cheap chicken places on or near the Plaza de Armas.

Getting There & Away

Empresa Andia (Plaza de Armas) has 6am buses to Lima (US$8, nine hours).

EAST OF THE CORDILLERA BLANCA

The Conchucos valley (to the east of the Cordillera Blanca) is much more remote, traditional and lacking in contact with foreigners than the popular western side. Transport in this area becomes erratic and difficult during the wettest months. But the views of the mountains remain gorgeous, and travelers prepared for potentially difficult conditions and able to remain open-minded and sensitive will find fabulous off-the-gringo-trail travel opportunities here.

CHAVÍN DE HUÁNTAR

☎ 043 / pop 2500 / elevation 3250m

The best-preserved site from the Chavín culture should not be missed. Many visitors come here on day trips from Huaraz; locals wish people would use local buses and spend a night to leave some money in Chavín. Food for thought.

Chavín town is about 1km north of the ruins. The main drag is 17 de Enero, which leaves the pleasant Plaza de Armas southbound, passing several restaurants and the entrance to the archaeological site. You can't change money in town.

For some details on the Chavín culture, see the boxed text on p328.

Visiting the Site

This **site** (admission US$1; ⏰ 8am-4pm), which represents a stupendous achievement of ancient engineering is, at first sight, not particularly prepossessing; most of the site's more interesting parts were built underground, and the area was covered by a huge landslide in 1945. To get the most from your visit you must enter the underground chambers (which are electrically lit). It is worth hiring a guide to show you around; they usually speak Spanish only. Recommended guides include Celestino Tacilla, Martín Justinianao and Alejandro Espinoza.

The site contains a huge central square, slightly sunken below ground level, with an intricate and well-engineered system

THE CHAVÍN CULTURE

Named after its type site at Chavín de Huántar, this is the oldest major culture in Peru, existing from about 1000 to 300 BC and, incredibly, predating the Incas by two millennia. The major period of influence was from about 800 to 400 BC, and the Chavín certainly were influential. Its people didn't conquer by warfare; they influenced the artistic and cultural development of all of northern Peru by example – perhaps a lesson to us all today. Archaeologists formerly referred to this cultural expansion as the Chavín Horizon, though Early Horizon is now the preferred usage. Signs of Chavín influence are evident in sites throughout northern Peru, though none of them are as well preserved or as frequently visited as Chavín de Huántar.

The principal Chavín deity was feline (jaguar or puma), and lesser condor, snake and human deities also existed. Highly stylized representations of these deities are carved in Chavín sites. The experienced eye can see similarities in the precise yet fluid lines of these carvings, while the nonexpert can be amazed and admires such fine work done 3000 years ago.

The artistic work of Chavín is much more stylized and cultist than the naturalistic art of the later Moche and Nazca cultures. Because of this, archaeologists lack an accurate picture of life in Chavín times. However, excavations of ancient garbage dumps (archaeologists' treasure) indicate that corn became a staple food, and agriculture improved with the introduction of squash, avocados, yucca and other crops. Better agriculture meant allowed more leisure time. Thus, art and religion could develop, and so the Early Horizon, linking art and religion in its feline-worshipping cults, was able to influence a large part of Peru.

For detailed information, read the excellent *Chavín and the Origins of Peruvian Civilization* by Richard Burger.

of channels for drainage. From the square, a broad staircase leads up to the single entrance of the largest and most important building – the Castillo. With an area of about 75 sq m and height of up to 13m, the Castillo was built on three different levels, each of dry stone masonry. At one time, the walls were embellished with tenons (keystones of large projecting blocks carved to resemble a stylized human head). Only one of these remains in its original place; the others have been moved inside the Castillo in the underground chambers or to museums.

The underground tunnels are an exceptional feat of 3000-year-old engineering; they are so well ventilated that the air is not musty, yet the main entrance is the only doorway. In the heart of the underground complex is an exquisitely carved rock known as the Lanzón de Chavín. It is a thrilling and distinctly mysterious experience to come upon this 4m-high, dagger-like rock stuck into the ground at the intersection of four narrow passageways, deep within the Castillo. (There is now a metal grille to protect the Lanzón, though the view is undiminished.)

The site is best visited in the morning before the crowds from Huarez arrive.

Sleeping & Eating

All hotels are on or near the plaza.

The hot water is erratic at **La Casona de JB** (☎ 75-4020; Plaza de Armas 130; s/d US$3/6; s/d with showers US$4.50/8.50; **P**), an old house with a traditional courtyard. However, it is a friendly and recommended budget choice. Some rooms have TV or a plaza balcony and there's a restaurant.

Hotel Chavín Arqueológico (☎ 75-4055, 75-4009; Inca Roca 141; s/d US$8/14) is modern, has hot water and TV in all rooms and a restaurant. Around the corner is the affiliated but cheaper and more basic **Hostal Chavín**; between the two of them you'll find a room to suit and guests bargain for the best deal.

Hostal Turístico Rickay (☎ 75-4068; 17 de Enero 600; s/d US$8/15) with a patio, restaurant (serving pastas) and modern rooms with hot showers and TV is also good. There are several other cheaper choices.

Camping by the ruins is possible with permission of the guard.

The restaurants have a reputation for closing soon after sunset, so eat early. For lunch, **Chavín Turístico** (☎ 75-4051, 75-4029; 17 de Enero 439; meals US$1-2.50) is considered the best option with a chalkboard of traditional plates and rickety tables around a tiny courtyard. The food is tasty and popular with tour groups.

Other decent eateries can be found along 17 de Enero, and in the hotels.

Getting There & Away

The scenic drive across the Cordillera Blanca via Catac passes the Laguna Querococha at 3980m; from here, there are views of the peaks of Pucaraju (5322m) and Yanamarey (5237m). The road deteriorates as it continues climbing to the Cahuish tunnel at 4178m above sea level. The tunnel cuts through the Cahuish Pass, which is over 300m higher, before the road descends to Chavín.

Tour buses make day trips from Huaraz. Also see Huaraz (p317) for details of Chavín Express and other companies that have several daily departures to Chavín (US$2.80). Returning to Huaraz is straightforward with Chavín Express (on the Plaza de Armas).

Continuing north along the east side of the Cordillera Blanca involves asking around. Several buses a week from Lima pass through Chavín on their way to Huari and more remote villages further north. Trucks and minibuses leave Chavín to the north most days.

Hikers can walk to Chavín from Olleros in about three days; its a popular but uncrowded hike.

NORTH OF CHAVÍN

☎ 043

The road north of Chavín goes through the villages of San Marcos (after 8km), Huari (40km, two hours), San Luis (100km, five hours), Piscobamba (160km, eight hours), Pomabamba and Sihuas. The further north you go, the more difficult transport becomes, and it may stop altogether during the wet season.

From Sihuas, it is possible to continue on to Huallanca (at the end of Cañón del Pato, see p323) via Tres Cruces and thus return to El Callejón de Huaylas. This round trip is scenic, remote and rarely made by travelers. It shouldn't be too difficult to find transport during the dry season if you really want to get off the beaten track and enjoy highland hospitality.

Side roads also cross the Cordillera Blanca to El Callejón de Huaylas.

Huari

This small market town has good mountain views and an annual fiesta on the days around October 4. Market day here is Sunday. A good hike is to **Purhuaycocha**, a beautiful lake about 5km away. A two- or three-day backpacking trip continues past the lake emerging at the village of Chacas (see later).

There are half a dozen basic cheap hostels, of which the best are **Hostal Paraíso** (☎ 75-3029; Bolívar 263; r per person US$3-7) and the nearby, similarly priced, **Hostal Huaganku** (☎ 75-3078). Both have hot showers and some rooms have bathrooms. There are several restaurants; try **Restaurant Turístico El Milagro** (San Martín 589).

Buses for Huaraz and for Lima leave most days from the Plaza Vigil.

San Luis

This village is reached by infrequent buses from Huaraz via Yungay and Yanama, or by buses between Huari and Pomabamba (you get some super views coming from Huari). San Luis suffers from water and electricity shortages. The best of several basic hotels here is **Hostal San Lucho**, near the market.

Chacas

This village, to the southwest of San Luis, is reached by a fairly good road from Carhuaz (see p321). The Chacas fiesta is held on August 15. The very basic **Hostal Saragoza** (r per person US$2.80) is on the Plaza de Armas. Pilar Ames (owner of El Cortijo restaurant in Monterrey; p321) has a comfortable *hostal* with modern facilities, open upon reservation (r per person with shared bathroom US$20, d with bathroom US$60). This place is used as part of a local tour.

Yanama

A daily morning bus links Yungay (p322) with Yanama, passing the famous Lagunas Llanganuco (p322) and within 1km of the village of **Colcabamba**, the starting point for the Llanganuco-to-Santa Cruz trekking circuit. In Yanama, which has electricity from 6pm to 9pm only, a good place to stay is at the basic **Hostel Los Pinos**, which is behind the church and has a huge pine tree outside. In Colcabamba, stay with the Calonge family, where Elvis offers beds with dinner for US$5 per person. Who's Elvis? Elvis is well known by everyone in town, just ask for him.

Piscobamba

There are nice views of the montains from this place, which is next village north of San Luis. It has a couple of basic places to stay and eat.

Pomabamba

This is the largest village north of Huari and can be the end point for various remote cross-Cordillera treks. There is a small **museum** by the plaza and natural **hot springs** (US$0.40), a few minutes walk away on the outskirts of town.

There are several basic hotels, of which the friendly **Alojamiento Estrada** (☎ 75-1048; r per person US$4), by the church, is the best but lacks hot water. Also try the cheaper **Hostal Pomabamba**.

Buses from Pomabamba head to Yungay daily. Buses also go to Huaraz and even Lima. There are daily combis to Sihuas and Piscobamba.

Northern Highlands

These areas receive few travelers but provide much excitement. Most of the places described in this chapter are off the 'gringo trail', but that isn't to say that foreigners aren't welcomed here – they are! Lovers of ruins will not want to miss the huge pre-Inca site of Kuélap. For the adventurous, there are remote but impressive ruins rarely visited by tourists; visit them on a trek or on horseback if you desire. Followers of Inca history will be drawn to Los Baños del Inca, where Atahualpa bathed, and El Cuarto del Rescate (the Ransom Chamber) in Cajamarca, where Atahualpa was imprisoned by Pizarro.

Traveling through this area used to be very difficult and it was often easier to go from one place to another via the coast. But things are gradually changing. A new paved road to Tarapoto makes access easier, and with undiscovered treasures awaiting the intrepid traveler, just go for it!

HIGHLIGHTS

■ **Archaeology**

Being awestruck at Kuélap – with no crowds! (p348)

■ **Adventure**

Mounting an expedition from Chachapoyas (p345)

■ **Cloud Forest**

Discovering waterfalls, lakes and rivers around Tarapoto (p349)

■ **Historical Soak**

Steaming in the hot springs where Atahualpa bathed (p341)

■ **Lose Yourself**

Enjoying traveling in a lovely area that's *off* the gringo trail

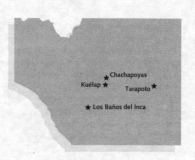

Pre-Inca cemetery, **Ventanillas de Otuzco** (p342)

Relaxing warm waters, **Los Baños del Inca** (p341)

Puya raimondii, **Parque Nacional Huascarán** (p318)

Street singers in the main plaza, **Chachapoyas** (p345)

Cruising along, **Río Tambopata** (p366)

ALFREDO MAIQUEZ

SHANNON NACE

Sunset, **Amazon basin** (p354)

Floating market on the Upper Amazon, **Amazon basin** (p354)

JOHN BC

CAJAMARCA

☎ 076 / pop 111,000 / elevation 2650m

Cajamarca and its environs are steeped in history. Once a major Inca city, Cajamarca played a crucial role in the Spanish conquest. It was here that Pizarro tricked, captured, imprisoned and finally assassinated the Inca Atahualpa. The city remains important today as the capital of its department and a major city of Peru's northern Andes. It has attractive colonial architecture, excellent Andean food and interesting people and customs. In the last decade, foreign-operated gold mines in the area have given the city a new air of prosperity. The surrounding countryside is green and attractive, particularly during the wet season.

History

Little is known about the area's pre-Inca sites, which are attributed to the Chavín-influenced Cajamarca culture. In about 1460, the Incas conquered the Cajamarca people, and Cajamarca became a major Inca city on the Inca Andean highway, which linked Cuzco with Quito.

After the death of the Inca Huayna Capac in 1525 the Inca Empire, which then stretched from southern Colombia to central Chile, was divided between the half brothers Atahualpa and Huáscar. Atahualpa ruled the north, and Huáscar ruled the south. Civil war soon broke out, and Atahualpa, who had the support of the army, gained the upper hand. In 1532 he and his victorious troops marched southward toward Cuzco to take complete control of the Inca Empire. During this march south, Atahualpa and his army stopped at Cajamarca to rest for a few days. The Inca emperor was camped at the natural thermal springs, known today as Los Baños del Inca, when he heard the news that the Spanish were nearby.

Pizarro and his force of about 160 Spaniards arrived in Cajamarca on November 15, 1532. The city was almost deserted; most of its 2000 inhabitants were with Atahualpa at his encampment by the hot springs, 6km away. Pizarro sent a force of about 35 cavalry and a native interpreter to Atahualpa's camp to ask where the Spaniards were to stay. They were told to lodge in the *kallankas*

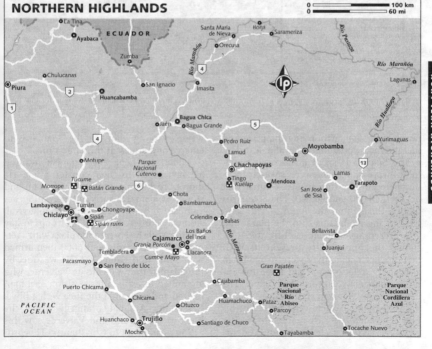

NORTHERN HIGHLANDS

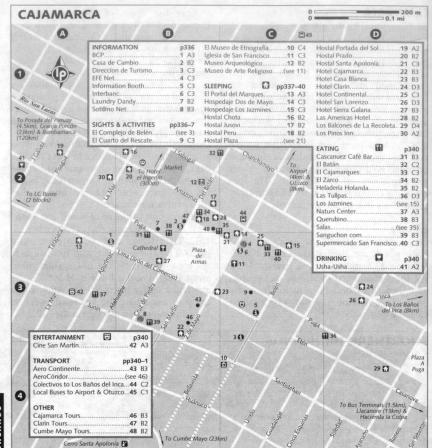

CAJAMARCA

0   200 m
0   0.1 mi

Río San Lucas
To Posada del Punay
(4.5km), Granja Porcón
(23km) & Bambamarca
(120km)

Market
To Hotel
el Ingenio
(300m)

To Airport
(4km) &
Otuzco
(8km)

To LC Busre
(2 blocks)

Cathedral

Plaza
de
Armas

To Los Baños
del Inca (8km)

Plaza
A
Puga

Cerro Santa Apolonia

To Cumbe Mayo (23km)

To Bus Terminals (1.5km),
Llacanore (13km) &
Hacienda la Colpa

(assembly halls) surrounding the plaza and that the Inca would join them the next day.

The Spaniards spent an anxious night, fully aware that they were severely outnumbered by the Inca troops, estimated at between 40,000 and 80,000. The Spaniards plotted throughout the night, deciding to try enticing Atahualpa into the plaza and, at a prearranged signal, capture the Inca, should the opportunity present itself. If this did not occur, they were to maintain a 'friendly' relationship and hope for another chance to capture Atahualpa. The next morning, Pizarro stationed his troops in the *kallankas*, which were perfect for his plan. The *kallankas* surrounded three sides of the plaza, and each had about 20 door-

ways, enabling many of the Spaniards to emerge and attack at the same time.

Atahualpa kept the Spanish waiting all day, much to their consternation. He didn't break camp until the afternoon and reached Cajamarca early in the evening, accompanied by his vast army. Upon arrival, Atahualpa ordered most of his troops to stay outside while he entered the plaza with a retinue of nobles and about 6000 men armed with slings and hand axes. He was met by the Spanish friar Vicente de Valverde, who attempted to explain his position as a man of God and presented the Inca with a Bible. Reputedly, Atahualpa angrily threw the book to the ground and Valverde saw this action as an insult to Christianity. This provided the excuse he needed to absolve the Spaniards in advance for an attack upon the Inca. He rushed back to the *kallankas* and prevailed upon Pizarro to order the firing of his cannons into the group of Indians. This was the prearranged signal to attack.

The cannons were fired, and the Spanish cavalry attacked. The Indians, who had never seen cannons or horses before, were terrified and bewildered by the fearsome onslaught. Their small hand axes and slings were no match for the well-armored Spaniards, who were swinging razor-sharp swords from the advantageous height of horseback. The Indians tried to flee, but the plaza entrance was too narrow to allow escape. By sheer weight of numbers, they knocked down a section of wall 2m thick and swarmed out of the plaza in total disarray. Pizarro's horsemen charged after them, hacking down as many Indians as they could. Meanwhile, Pizarro himself led a small contingent that succeeded in capturing Atahualpa. As the sun set over Cajamarca on the evening of November 16, the course of Latin American history was changed forever. With an estimated 7000 Indians dead and Atahualpa captured, the small band of Spaniards had succeeded beyond their wildest hopes. Now they literally were conquistadors.

After his capture, Atahualpa became aware of the Spaniards' lust for gold, and offered to fill a large room once with gold and twice with silver in return for his freedom. Astounded by their good fortune, the conquistadors agreed to the offer and led Atahualpa to believe that they would release him after the ransom was paid and allow him to return to his northern lands around Quito.

This was a wily move by Pizarro. By promising Atahualpa's return to Quito, he effectively controlled the northern part of the Inca Empire. And by holding Atahualpa captive, Pizarro also maintained control of the southern half of the empire, whose inhabitants, having just been beaten by Atahualpa in a civil war, considered Pizarro a liberator rather than an invader. Playing one Inca faction against the other in this way was Pizarro's strongest weapon. If the Inca Empire had been united when the Spanish arrived, the story of the conquest would have been entirely different.

Gold and silver began to arrive at Cajamarca. Pizarro sent some of his men to Cuzco to ensure the collection of the ransom. Meanwhile, Atahualpa was held as a royal prisoner, with the servants and comfort to which he was accustomed. The Spanish were in no great hurry to collect the ransom; they were also waiting for reinforcements. On April 14, 1533, Diego de Almagro arrived from the coast with 150 soldiers, almost doubling the Spanish force at Cajamarca. Atahualpa began to suspect that the Spaniards were lying to him and that he wouldn't be released and allowed to return to Quito upon payment of the ransom.

By mid-June of 1533 the ransom was complete, and Pizarro ordered the melting down and distribution of the treasure. Careful records were kept, and about 6000kg of gold and 12,000kg of silver were melted down into gold and silver bullion. At today's prices, this would be worth almost US$60 million, but the artistic value of the ornaments and implements that were melted down is impossible to estimate or recover. The gold and silver were distributed among the conquistadors in strictly controlled quotas.

Atahualpa, still a prisoner, now knew he was not going to be released. He sent desperate messages to his followers in Quito to come to Cajamarca and rescue him. The Spaniards heard of the rescue attempt and became panic-stricken. Although Pizarro was not anxious to kill the Inca emperor, intending instead to further his own aims by continuing to hold Atahualpa hostage and using him as a puppet ruler, the other leading Spaniards insisted on the Inca's death. Despite the lack of a formal trial, Atahualpa was sentenced to death for attempting to arrange his own rescue. On July 26, 1533, Atahualpa was led out to the center of the Cajamarca plaza to be burned at the stake. At the last hour, Atahualpa accepted baptism, and his sentence was changed to a quicker death by strangulation.

Immediately after Atahualpa's death, the Spaniards crowned Tupac Huallpa, a younger brother of Huáscar, as the new Inca emperor. With this puppet ruler, the Spaniards were free to march into Cuzco as liberators. During the march, the new emperer died of an unknown illness, and the Spanish arrived in Cuzco on November 15 without an Inca ruler.

Today, little remains of Inca Cajamarca. Most of the great stone buildings were torn down and the stones used in the construction of Spanish homes and churches. The great plaza where Atahualpa was captured and later killed was in roughly the same location as today's Plaza de Armas, though in Atahualpa's time it was a much larger plaza. The Ransom Chamber, or El Cuarto del Rescate, which some will tell you is the building that Atahualpa purportedly filled once with gold and twice with silver, is the only building still standing.

Information

See the **Dirección de Turismo** (☎ 82-2903; El Complejo de Belén; ☿ 7:30am-1:30pm & 3:30-5:30pm Mon-Fri) for tourist information. There's also an **information booth** (Lima at Belén).

You can access the Internet at **EFE Net** (2 de Mayo 568) and **Sot@no.Net** (Junín at Cruz de Piedra). The **post office** (☎ 82-4065; Amazonas 443) is to the west of the market.

Laundry Dandy (☎ 92-3454; Puga 545) charges US$1.40 per kg. **Clínica Limatambo** (☎ 82-4241; Puno 265), west of town, has the best medical service.

Interbanc (☎ 82-2460; 2 de Mayo 546 on the Plaza de Armas) changes traveler's checks and it has an ATM. There is also a **BCP** (formerly Banco de Crédito; ☎ 82-2742; on Lima, also called Jirón del Comercio, at Apurímac). You can change US cash quicker at **Casa de Cambio** (Del Batán on Plaza de Armas) or with moneychangers near the Plaza de Armas; heed the usual precautions with the moneychangers.

Sights & Activities

All these places are officially open 9am to 1pm and 3pm to 6pm daily, but take this with a grain of salt. They don't have addresses but are in the center of town. A US$1 ticket to El Cuarto del Rescate includes El Complejo de Belén and Museo de Etnografía if they are all visited on the same day. See the Dirección de Turismo for information.

EL CUARTO DEL RESCATE

The Ransom Chamber is the only Inca building still standing in Cajamarca. Although called the Ransom Chamber, the room shown to visitors is where Atahualpa

was imprisoned, not where the ransom was stored. The small room has three trapezoidal doorways and a few trapezoidal niches in the inner walls – a typical sign of Inca construction. Although well constructed, it does not compare with the Inca buildings in the Cuzco area. In the entrance to the site are a couple of modern paintings depicting Atahualpa's capture and imprisonment.

EL COMPLEJO DE BELÉN

Construction of the church and hospital of Belén began in the latter part of the 17th century. The hospital was run by nuns. Inside, 31 tiny, cell-like bedrooms line the walls of the T-shaped building. In what used to be the women's hospital, there is a small archaeology museum. The kitchen and dispensary of the hospital now houses an unimpressive art museum.

The church next door has a fine cupola and a well-carved and painted pulpit. There are several interesting wood carvings, including an extremely tired-looking Christ sitting cross-legged on his throne, propping up his chin with a double-jointed wrist and looking as though he could do with a pisco sour after a hard day's miracle-working. The outside walls of the church are lavishly decorated.

MUSEO DE ETNOGRAFÍA

This small museum, just a few meters from El Complejo de Belén, has limited exhibits of local costumes and clothing, domestic and agricultural implements, musical instruments and crafts made of wood, bone, leather and stone, as well as other examples of Cajamarca culture.

PLAZA DE ARMAS

The plaza is pleasant and has a well-kept topiary garden. The fine central **fountain** dates from 1692 and commemorates the bicentennary of Columbus' landing in the Americas. The town's inhabitants congregate in the plaza every evening. Strolling and discussing the day's events are traditionally popular activities, more so in this area of northern Peru than other parts of the country.

Two churches face the Plaza de Armas: the **cathedral** (☿ hours vary) and the **Iglesia de San Francisco** (admission US$0.50; ☿ 9am-noon & 5pm Mon-Fri). Both are often illuminated in the evening, especially on weekends. The cathedral is a squat building that was begun in the late 17th century and has only recently been finished. Like most of Cajamarca's churches, the cathedral has no belfry. This is because the Spanish crown levied a tax on finished churches and so the belfries were not built, leaving the church unfinished and thereby avoiding taxes.

San Francisco's belfries were finished in the 20th century – too late for the Spanish crown to collect its tax. Visit the small **Museo de Arte Religioso** and **catacombs**. The intricately sculpted **Capilla de la Dolorosa** (to the right of the church) is considered one of the finest chapels in the city.

MUSEO ARQUEOLÓGICO
This small **museum** (Del Batán 289; admission free; 8am-2:30pm Mon-Fri) is worth visiting. Knock on the door to enter. Its varied ceramics collection includes a few examples of Cajamarca pots and an unusual collection of ceremonial spears, also from the same culture. The Cajamarca culture, which existed in the area before the Inca Empire, is little studied and not very well known. The museum also has black-and-white photographs of various historic and prehistoric sites in the Cajamarca area; its director is knowledgeable and willing to talk about the exhibits. The museum is run by the Universidad de Cajamarca.

CERRO SANTA APOLONIA
This **hilltop** (admission US$0.50) overlooks the city from the southwest and is a prominent Cajamarca landmark. It's easily reached by climbing the stairs at the end of 2 de Mayo. The pre-Hispanic carved rocks at the summit are mainly Inca, but some are thought to originally date back to the Chavín period. One of the rocks, known as the Seat of the Inca, has a shape that suggests a throne and the Inca is said to have reviewed his troops from here. There are pretty gardens around the carved rocks.

Tours & Guides
Tour companies provide tourist information and inexpensive guided tours of the city and surrounds. They claim to have English-speaking guides, but only a few guides speak passable English. The companies will often pool tours. There are many tour companies

---

FEAST DAYS IN CAJAMARCA

Like most Peruvian Andean towns, Cajamarca is famous for its **Carnaval** – this one is a particularly wet affair, and its water fights are worse (or better, depending on your point of view) than you'd encounter elsewhere. Local teenagers don't necessarily limit themselves to soaking one another with water – paint, oil and urine have all been reported! The action begins on the Saturday preceding Lent and continues through Shrove Tuesday. The Corpus Christi processions are also very colorful.

Both of these are Catholic feast days and the dates vary each year, depending on the dates for Easter. Carnaval is the last few days before Lent (which, in turn, is 40 days before Easter Sunday). Corpus Christi is the Thursday after Trinity Sunday, which is the Sunday after Whitsunday (Pentecost), which is the seventh Sunday after Easter. Confused fiesta-goers would do well to buy a Catholic calendar for the year they plan on being in Peru.

---

on the Plaza de Armas. These ones have received recommendations:

Cajamarca Tours (82-2813, 82-5674; 2 de Mayo 323)

Clarín Tours (82-6829; clarintours@yahoo.com; Del Batán 161)

Cumbe Mayo Tours (82-2938; Puga 635)

Festivals & Special Events
Carnaval and **Corpus Christi** are popular feast days in Cajamarca (see the boxed text). **Independence Day** celebrations at the end of July may include a bullfight. Cajamarca's **Tourist Festival** is around the second week in August. The various cultural events include art shows, folkmusic and dancing competitions, beauty pageants and processions. Hotel and other prices rise during all these events and are also usually slightly higher in the dry season (May to September).

The lobby of Interbanc has free changing art shows.

Sleeping
BUDGET
Some of the cheapest hotels have only cold water, but you can get a hot bath at Los Baños del Inca (p341). Cheap hotels that

claim to have hot water usually have it for only a few hours a day.

Hotel San Lorenzo (☎ 82-2909, 82-6433; Amazonas 1060; s/d US$10/16) Helpful, friendly owners provide good-sized rooms (though the street-side ones can be noisy), cable TV, hot showers and a café.

Los Balcones de La Recoleta (☎ /fax 82-3302, 82-4446; Puga 1050; s/d US$14.50/17.50) This 19th-century building has 12 well-presented rooms around a grassy, plant-filled courtyard. Private hot showers all day, cable TV and comfortable beds with a candy on the pillow at night – what more do you need? OK, add a small restaurant, crafts on most of the walls, and friendly staff and you have a winner.

Hostal Santa Apolonia (☎ 82-7207, ☎ /fax 82-8574; Puga 649; s/d US$14.50/23) The best budget hotel on the plaza, the smart Santa Apolonia features comfortable, carpeted rooms with solid mattresses, 24-hour hot showers, cable TV and minifridges. Two rooms have plaza views. The attractive public areas and small plant-filled courtyard are restful.

Hostal Chota (☎ 82-8704; La Mar 637; s/d US$3/4.50) Shoestringers find this basic place acceptable and nicely priced; communal showers have hot water on request.

Hostal Plaza (☎ 82-2058; Puga 669; s/d US$4.50/8.50, s/d with bathroom US$7.25/13) This is an old and colorful building on the Plaza de Armas. Rooms are creaky and basic, but the eight with bathrooms are fun, with plaza views and some with balconies. Hot water is available from 7am to 10am and 7pm to 10pm. Some rooms, priced midway, have private toilets but shared showers; two of these have balconies with views.

Hospedaje Dos de Mayo (☎ 82-2527; 2 de Mayo 585; s/d US$6/11) Basic rooms have private sink and toilet; the communal showers have hot water in the evening.

Hostal Peru (☎ 82-4030; Puga 605; s/d US$8/13) Capitalizing on its plaza location, this hotel has private bathrooms with hot showers all day, but is rather rundown and open to bargaining. It's popular with gringos.

Hospedaje Los Jazmines (☎ /fax 82-1812; Amazonas 775; s/d US$8.50/13, s/d with bathroom US$11.50/17) This six-room German-run *hospedaje* isn't much to look at but its excellent café, comfortable beds, hot showers and practice of hiring disabled people keep attracting altruistic travelers.

Hostal Jusovi (☎ 82-2920; Amazonas 637; s/d US$8.50/14.50) This clean hotel has tidy if small rooms with private showers. Hot water is available from 6am to 9am and sometimes later by request. Some rooms have TVs. A nice feature is the rooftop terrace with views of the cathedral spire.

Hostal Prado (☎ 82-6093, ☎ /fax 82-4388; La Mar 582; s/d US$7.25/10, s/d with bathroom US$12/20) This well-kept, clean property has a café and hot water all day. Rooms have TVs, but cable is restricted to the higher-priced ones. Some of the staff speak English.

MID-RANGE

All hotels in this range have 24-hour hot water.

Hotel Casa Blanca (☎ 83-0509, ☎ /fax 82-2141; 2 de Mayo 446; s/d US$20/29) This thick-walled, creaky-floored, interesting old building on the Plaza de Armas has maintained an old-world charm while providing modern services. Rooms are good-sized, with cable TV, direct-dial telephones and minifridges. The hotel café provides room service, and they also arrange car rental and have a small casino (off to the side so it doesn't disturb guests). Some rooms are larger and have bathtubs (double US$37), while a family room with five beds is US$58. Rates include breakfast and airport transfers are provided.

El Portal del Marques (☎ /fax 82-8464; portaldelmarques@terra.com.pe; Lima 644; s/d US$24/34; P 🖥) A pretty, colonial-style hotel in a renovated mansion, offering 14 rooms overlooking a central courtyard. Rooms have cable TV, minifridges, bright bedspreads and Andean wall art; the restaurant provides room service.

Los Pinos Inn (☎ /fax 82-5992, 82-5991; pinoshostal@yahoo.com; La Mar 521; s/d US$18.50/28.50) Small and elegantly colonial, with pretty tile-work in the inviting entrance, this hotel features 21 large rooms, all different, with distressed floorboards, antique flourishes and solid beds. Continental breakfast is served in a pleasing courtyard café covered with a stained-glass roof. This is a good hotel that is often full, so call ahead.

Hostal Portada del Sol (☎ 82-3395; portadadelsol@terra.com.pe; Pisagua 731; s/d US$20/29; P) Another welcoming small hotel with colonial ambience, the Portada del Sol features rooms with polished wooden floors and beams, and all the usual services. Its recommended restaurant offers room service and breakfast is included. The owners also have a rammed-earth **hacienda** (☎ 82-3395; portada delsol@terra.com.pe; Pisagua 731) 5.5km away in the countryside on the unpaved road to Cumbe Mayo. The 15 rooms here are tranquil, private and many have good country views. A tree house and playground make this an ideal getaway for families and groups.

Las Americas Hotel (☎ 82-8863, ☎ /fax 82-3951; Amazonas 618; s/d US$30/42; **P**) This modern property makes a change from all those colonial hotels! It's a four-story building with a central atrium bedecked with plenty of plants and a rooftop terrace giving plaza and church views. The 28 rooms are all carpeted and have a direct-dial phone, minifridge, cable TV and excellent mattresses; five of them have Jacuzzi tubs and three have balconies, so it pays to check around. A restaurant provides room service.

Hacienda San Antonio (☎ /fax 83-8237; www .hsanantonio.cjb.net/; s/d US$35/45; **P**) This hacienda is 5km out on the road to Los Baños del Inca, then 1.5km left (just past the El Porongo gas station) to San Antonio (a US$2.50 cab ride). It's an ideal rural getaway, especially for those with children. It's a lovely rustic-looking hacienda, but the rooms are recently built (though with antique touches), all with hot showers and one with a fireplace. The property has a kids' playground and horse rides are available. An artificial stream and pond have fishing and canoeing, and nice country walks can be taken. The rural restaurant is popular with Cajamarqueños on weekends. Rates include a breakfast of homemade breads and jams, as well as a horse or canoe ride. Fun!

Complejo Turístico Baños del Inca (☎ /fax 83-8249; bungalow US$35; **P**) Right behind Los Baños del Inca are eight spacious bungalows, each with sitting room, bedroom, minifridge and cable TV. Too bad they don't have a kitchenette. Views are of reservoirs of 78°C (120°F) water, steaming Dantesquely – this water must be mixed with cold water before it flows into the spa complex. (Don't fall in – you'll be scalded to death!)

Also consider:

Hotel Cajamarca (☎ 82-2532; fax 82-2813; 2 de Mayo 311; s/d US$24/35) Good, clean hotel in colonial house, with a restaurant.

Hotel Clarín (☎ 83-1275; Amazonas 1025; s/d US$29/37; **P**) Large rooms with bathtubs and direct-dial phones; there's also a restaurant.

Hotel Sierra Galana (☎ 82-2470, ☎ /fax 82-2472; Lima 773; s/d US$30/40) On the Plaza de Armas, this was the town's first good hotel, but is now jaded but clean.

Hotel Continental (☎ 82-2758, 82-3063; fax 82-3024; hotelcontinental@terra.com.pe; Amazonas 760; s/d from US$33/43; **P**) Business hotel over a small shopping mall.

Hostal Jose Galvez (☎ /fax 83-8396; s/d US$15/20; **P**) Near Los Baños del Inca; clean rooms with hot thermal showers.

TOP END

Hotel El Ingenio (☎ /fax 82-7121; ingeniocaj@terra .com.pe; Vía de Evitamiento 1611-1709; s/d US$40/50, ste US$75; **P**) This modern, quiet and attractive property built in colonial style is the best in town. Rooms are large and comfortable, with cable TV, direct-dial telephones, minifridges and tubs in the bathrooms. Some have patios or balconies, and the six minisuites each have a Jacuzzi. The staff are attentive and helpful, and the grounds are nicely landscaped, with two pleasant courtyards and an expansive lawn. There is also a good restaurant and bar. It's a 10-minute walk into town

Posada del Puruay (☎ 82-8318; fax 82-7928; www.puruayhotel.com.pe; s/d US$70/90, ste US$100-130; **P**) This 19th-century mansion, 4.5km out of Cajamarca on the road to Porcón, has been converted into a 12-room country hotel and exudes elegance. It's surrounded by lovely gardens and organizes horse and bicycle rides and guided walks. But you're here for the high-ceilinged beamed rooms full of period furniture and with extra amenities like VHS players and a video library (cable doesn't make it out here), clock radios, direct dial phones and heaters. Spring for the balconied suites if possible; they are sumptuous and vast. The exclusive restaurant attracts visitors on weekends to sample the varied international menu (mains US$6 to US$12). The room rates include airport transfer, welcome drink, American breakfast and a horse ride.

Hostal Laguna Seca (☎ 82-4600; fax 89-4646; hotel@lagunaseca.com.pe; s/d US$76/92, ste US$105-139; **P**) Situated 6km from Cajamarca near Los Baños del Inca, this resort hotel has a huge heated swimming pool, Jacuzzi, Turkish bath, and the hot water in all rooms is fed by the natural thermal springs nearby.

Rooms have large bathrooms with deep tubs for soaking, direct-dial phones, cable TV, minifridge and radio alarm. Horseback riding, bicycle rental, massages and spa health treatments can be arranged. There is a pleasant garden with a children's playground and a decent restaurant.

Eating

El Batán (☎ 82-6025; anabufet@hotmail.com; Del Batán 369; menú US$3.50, mains US$4-8; ☺ often closed Mon) One of the town's best places, this gallery-restaurant-*peña*–cultural center serves varied Peruvian and international dishes and has a decent wine list. The set menú (one of eight appetizers, one of seven main courses, dessert and a drink) is an excellent deal. On Friday and Saturday nights, it has live shows of local music – anything from folk songs to traditional Andean music to Afro-Peruvian dance rhythms. There is a full bar. Upstairs, there is an art gallery with changing shows every month. Paintings are for sale and the quality is surprisingly high.

Heladería Holanda (☎ 83-0113; Puga 657; double scoop US$0.60; ☺ 9am-7pm) Don't miss the tiny entrance on the Plaza de Armas; it opens into a large, bright café selling the best ice cream in northern Peru. About 20 changing flavors are offered, including some made of local fruit. Add excellent espressos, creamy cappuccinos and homemade pies – this place isn't to be missed.

Spaghetti Om-Gri (☎ 82-7619; San Martín 360; mains US$2.25-5; ☺ 1:45pm-late Mon-Sat, 6:30pm-when clients leave Sun) This friendly, five-table Italian place serves the best lasagne in town. The kitchen is behind the counter and the chef chats with guests as he cooks.

Salas (☎ 82-2867; Puga 637; menú US$2.25, mains US$2.25-6) This barn of a place on the Plaza de Armas has been a local favorite since 1947; diners all seem to know one another. Various local dishes such as goat, delicious corn tamales and *sesos* (cow brains) are on offer, as well as more standard plates.

El Cajamarques (☎ 82-2128; Amazonas 770; mains US$4-7; ☺ 8:30am-11pm) This is an elegant upscale restaurant adjoining a colonial courtyard containing tropical birds; it can't be beat for an arresting ambience. Both Peruvian and international food are presented on spiffy white tablecloths.

Cascanuez Café Bar (☎ 82-6089; Puga 554; desserts US$1-2; ☺ 8am-10pm) This café sells snacks and meals, but people flock here for the delectable choice of fine desserts and good coffee.

Querubino (☎ 83-0900; Puga 589; mains US$4-7.50; ☺ 9am-11pm) This stylish but cheerfully colorful place has a wide menu of Peruvian and international dishes; the steaks and seafood are among Cajamarca's best.

Other recommendations are:

Naturs Center (Apurímac 614; mains US$2) A small vegetarian restaurant, though meat dishes are also served.

Los Jazmines (Amazonas 775; US$0.60-3; ☺ 9am-noon & 4-9pm Mon-Sat, 4-9pm Sun) Great snacks, sandwiches, cakes and breakfasts.

Sanguchon.com (Junín 1137; average US$2; ☺ noon-late) Popular hamburger and sandwich joint; excellent bar.

Las Tullpas (☎ 82-3516; Puga 946; mains US$2.50-5; ☺ 7am-11pm) Small, bright restaurant; huge menu; reliable standard.

El Zarco (☎ 82-3421; Del Batán 170; mains US$3.50; ☺ 7am-11pm, closed Sat) Has *cuy* (roast guinea pig) and some vegetarian specialties.

Supermercado San Francisco (☎ 82-2128; Amazonas 780) For self-catering.

Entertainment

Cine San Martín (☎ 82-3260; Junín 829; US$1.50) is a two-screen cinema that often shows English-language movies. **Usha-Usha** (Puga 142; cover US$1.50; ☺ closed Sun) is a very local, hole-in-the-wall bar, run by a local musician who likes to tell stories. It serves only strong mixed drinks or colas, has impromptu musical evenings, and can be a blast or a bust. Worth a look. *Discotecas* come and go, and are usually on the outskirts. Ask locally. El Batán and Sanguchon.com, under Eating, are other options.

Getting There & Away

AIR

Schedules are subject to change, as well as occasional cancellations and delays, so reconfirm and arrive early at the **airport** (☎ 82-2523). **AeroCóndor** (☎ 82-2813, 82-5674; 2 de Mayo 323) has a daily morning flight from Lima, returning via Trujillo on demand. Recently, **Aero Continente** (☎ 82-3304; 2 de Mayo 381) and **LC Busre** (Lima 1020) have added flights to Lima.

BUS

Long-Distance Buses

Cajamarca is an ancient crossroads dating back many centuries before the Incas. Nowadays, buses leave Cajamarca on roads heading for all four points of the compass.

Most bus terminals are close to the 3rd block of Atahualpa, about 1.5km southeast of the center (not to be confused with the Atahualpa in the town center), on the road to Los Baños del Inca.

The major route is westbound, paved to the Panamericana near Pacasmayo on the coast. From here, you travel north to Chiclayo or south to Trujillo and Lima. Services to Trujillo (US$5 to US$9, six hours), Chiclayo (US$4.50 to US$7, six hours) and Lima (US$9 to US$30, 13 hours) are provided by many companies. Most buses to Lima travel overnight; change in Trujillo for daytime travel.

The southbound road is the old route to Trujillo via Cajabamba (US$3, five hours) and Huamachuco. The trip to Trujillo takes two or three times longer on this rough dirt road than it does along the newer paved road via Pacasmayo, although the old route is only 60km longer. The scenery is supposedly prettier on the longer route, but most buses are less comfortable and less frequent beyond Cajabamba. For Huamachuco and on to Trujillo, change at Cajabamba.

Note that companies provide services beyond those outlined here, and departure times change often.

Cial (☎ 82-8701, 82-3270; Atahualpa 300) Cheap buses to Lima and Trujillo.

Civa (☎ 82-1460; Atahualpa 753) Good buses to Lima 9am.

Cruz del Sur (☎ 82-4421, 82-2488; Via de Evitamiento 750) Luxury bus-cama to Lima 7pm.

El Cumbe (☎ 82-3038; Atahualpa 300) Cheap buses to Chiclayo 7am, 11am, 3pm and 9pm.

Empresa Atahualpa (☎ 82-3060; Atahualpa 322) Cheap buses to the coast, Cajabamba, Celendín and Bambamarca.

Flores (☎ 83-1294; Atahualpa 248) Cheap bus to Lima at 6:30pm.

Linea (☎ 82-3956; Atahualpa 318) High-quality bus-cama services. Goes to Lima 7pm, Chiclayo 10:45pm and 11pm, and Trujillo 10:30am, 10pm and 10:30pm.

Ormeño (☎ 82-9889; Via de Evitamiento 740) Good buses to coastal destinations.

Palacios (☎ 82-5855; Atahualpa 312) Cheap buses to the coast, Celendín and Cajabamba.

Royal Palacios (Atahualpa 337) Celendín at 5am and Bambamarca at 11:30am.

Transportes Nuevo Milena (Atahualpa 306) Cajabamba 1:30pm and 1am.

Transportes Rojas (☎ 830548; Atahualpa 405) Cajabamba 1:30pm and 2am.

Tepsa (☎ 82-3306; Atahualpa 300) Cheap buses towards the coast.

Turismo Diaz (☎ 82-8289; Sucre 422) Chiclayo, Chota via Bambamarca and Celendín.

Turismo Nacional (☎ 83-0357; Atahualpa 309) Cajabamba at 1pm.

Local Buses

The rough northbound road to Chota (US$6, nine hours) passes through wild and attractive countryside via the towns of Hualgayoc (US$5) and Bambamarca (US$5.50). Hualgayoc is a mining village in a beautiful setting and Bambamarca has a colorful market on Sunday morning. (It has simple hotels, as does Chota.) Buses run from Chota to Chiclayo along a very rough road.

The very scenic eastbound road heads to Celendín (US$3, five hours), then across the Andes, past Chachapoyas and down into the Amazon lowlands. The road between Celendín and Chachapoyas is very bad, though, and transport is unreliable; if you're going to Chachapoyas, you are advised to travel from Chiclayo via Bagua, unless you have plenty of time and patience.

Buses for Ventanillas de Otuzco (US$0.50) leave from the north end of Del Batán, 500m north of the Plaza de Armas.

Getting Around

Buses for Ventanillas de Otuzco pass the airport (US$0.30), or take a taxi (US$1.50).

Colectivos (small buses) for Los Baños del Inca leave frequently from 2 de Mayo near Amazonas (US$0.50). Cheaper buses travel along Lima and through the Plaza de Armas to the baños.

AROUND CAJAMARCA

Places of interest around Cajamarca are reached by public transport, on foot, by taxi or with a guided tour. Tour agencies (see p337) pool their clients to form a group for any trip, although more expensive individual outings can be arranged.

Los Baños del Inca

Atahualpa was camped by these natural hot springs when Pizarro arrived, hence the name. They are 6km from Cajamarca and have a few hotel possibilities (see p337). Hot water is channeled into many private cubicles (US$0.50 to US$1.50 per hour), some large enough for up to six people at a time.

There is a public pool (US$0.50), which is cleaned on Monday and Friday. Locals pack the place on weekends; join them!

Cumbe Mayo
The name is supposedly derived from the Quechua term *kumpi mayo*, or 'well-made water channel.' The site, 23km from Cajamarca, has well-engineered **pre-Inca channels** running for several kilometers across the bleak mountaintops. Some nearby caves contain **petroglyphs**. The countryside is high, windswept and slightly eerie. Superstitious stories are told about the area's eroded rock formations, which look like groups of shrouded mountain climbers.

The site can be reached on foot via a signposted road from the Cerro Santa Apolonia. The walk takes about four hours if you take the obvious shortcuts and ask every passerby for directions. Guided bus tours (US$6) are offered in Cajamarca (see p337): these last four to five hours and are a good idea.

Ventanillas de Otuzco & Combayo
These pre-Inca necropolises have hundreds of funerary niches built into the hillside, hence the name *ventanillas*, or 'windows.' Otuzco is in beautiful countryside, 8km northeast of Cajamarca and easily walked from either Cajamarca or Los Baños del Inca (ask for directions); or take local buses or tours (US$5). The larger and better preserved Ventanillas de Combayo are 30km away and are visited on a US$10 tour.

Llacanora & Hacienda la Colpa
The picturesque hamlet of Llacanora is 13km from Cajamarca. Some inhabitants still play the traditional 3m-long bamboo trumpet called the *clarín*. A few kilometers away is the Hacienda la Colpa, often visited on a tour combined with Llacanora (about US$5 per person). The hacienda is a working cattle ranch; in the afternoons, ranchhands herd cows into their stalls by calling out each animal by name. This is a locally famous tourist attraction.

Granja Porcón
Located about 23km by road from Cajamarca, this is a successful 7th Day evangelical cooperative. Overlooked by 'God loves you' billboards, about 800 residents work

in fields, a dairy, wood mill, looms, craft shop, simple restaurant, local zoo, and even a **lodge** (☎ 82-5631; granjaporcon@yahoo.com). It's an interesting ongoing project and visited by daily tours (US$6). A highlight is the herd of vicuñas running free.

CAJABAMBA
☎ 076 / pop 2500 / elevation 2655m
The old route from Cajamarca to Trujillo takes at least 15 hours along 360km of dirt road via Cajabamba and Huamachuco. Although this route passes through more interesting scenery and towns than the new road, the bus trip is very rough, and few tourists come through.

Cajabamba is a pleasant small town with a 19th-century atmosphere and a pretty plaza. You'll see more mules than cars in the streets, and the whitewashed houses and red-tiled roofs give the place a colonial air. The **feast of La Virgen del Rosario** is celebrated around the first Sunday in October with bullfights, processions, dances and general bucolic carousing.

Sleeping
The simple hotels fill before Sunday (market day) and for La Virgen del Rosario. They suffer from periodic water shortages and dim lighting. **Hostal Flores** (☎ 85-1086; L Prado 137; s/d US$3/6) has rooms with a balcony onto the plaza, private toilets and shared showers. **Hostal Caribe** (☎ 80-1486; Cárdenas 784; s/d US$3/6; with bathroom US$4.50/8.50) has rooms with TV and hot water. **Hostal La Casona** (☎ 85-1300; Ugarte 586; d US$9) is a plaza hotel, and among the best with TV and private hot shower.

Getting There & Away
Palacios (☎ 85-1348; Lara 551) has a daily bus for Cajamarca and another for Huamachuco. **Transportes Rojas** (☎ 85-1399; Bolognesi 700) has buses to Cajamarca. Also ask for Transportes Atahualpa, Transportes Anita and Transportes Horna.

HUAMACHUCO
☎ 044 / pop 5000 / elevation 3160m
This small colonial town is 53km beyond Cajabamba (reached in three hours by poor road) and 190km from Trujillo (seven hours). It has an impressive Plaza de Armas, said to be Peru's largest.

The massive ruins of the pre-Inca hilltop fort of **Marcahuamachuco** lie 10km away via a track passable only by 4WD or a truck. Other archaeological sites nearby can be explored.

Hostal San José (Bolívar 361; s/d US$3/5) is a clean, basic hotel. The recommended **Hostal Huamachuco** (☎ 44-1393; Castilla 354; s/d US$4/6, with bathroom US$7.25/10) is on the plaza, and has hot water and TV. **Hostal Colonial** (☎ 51-1101, 44-1334; Castilla 347; s/d US$10/15; P) has a restaurant.

Vuelos Lider, in Trujillo (ask at travel agencies), sometimes flies to Huamachuco. Several bus companies in the center leave for Trujillo or Cajabamba.

CELENDÍN

☎ 076 / pop 15,000 / elevation 2625m

This friendly little town is 118km from Cajamarca and receives few travelers except those taking the wild and scenic route to Chachapoyas. **Hot springs** and mud baths at Llanguat are reached by a 30-minute drive. Market day is Sunday. The annual fiesta (July 29 to August 3) coincides with Fiestas Patrias and features **bullfighting** with matadors from Mexico and Spain. The fiesta of **La Virgen del Carmen** is celebrated on July 16.

Sleeping & Eating

Hostal Celendín (☎ 85-5041; fax 85-5239; Unión 305; s/d with shower US$4.75/8.50) This clean *hostal* on the Plaza de Armas has one of the town's best restaurants. Some rooms have plaza views and are being remodeled; expect a price increase. Hot water takes about five minutes to come through – be patient! Staff are helpful with travel arrangements.

Hostal Amazonas (☎ 85-5093; 2 de Mayo 316; r per person US$4.50) Another clean *hostal*, this place has rooms with private electric showers and cheerful bedspreads. It also has a café.

Hostal Loyers (☎ 85-5210; fax 85-5354; J Gálvez 440; s/d US$3/5, with shower US$4.50/8.50) has a nice courtyard and hot electric showers. **Hostal Imperial** (☎ 85-5492; 2 de Mayo 568; s/d US$4/7, with shower US$4.50/8; P) is a new hotel that looks OK. **Hostal Maxmar** (☎ 85-5414; 2 de Mayo 349) is being remodeled but has been recommended. **Hotel José Gálvez** (2 de Mayo 334; r per person US$2.75) is a basic hotel that has cold water only.

The best restaurants are **La Reserva** (J Gálvez 420) and **Hostal Celendín** (Plaza de Armas).

Getting There & Away

The rough road from Cajamarca is far better than the one from Chachapoyas.

Transportes Atahualpa and **Palacios** (☎ 85-5322) are on the Plaza de Armas and have departures at about 6am and 1pm to Cajamarca (US$3, four hours). Virgen del Carmen has buses to Chachapoyas (US$7.50, 12 to 14 hours) at noon on Sunday and Thursday. A taxi charges US$60 to US$80. Ask around; trucks or private vehicles will happily carry paying passengers.

FROM CELENDÍN TO CHACHAPOYAS

This rough but beautiful route may be temporarily impassable during the wet season. It's worth finding transportation other than the bus and leaving at about 6am so you can see the route in daylight.

The road climbs over a 3085m pass before dropping steeply to the Río Marañón at the squalid village of **Balsas** (975m), 55km from Celendín. There's a miserable hotel here. The road climbs again, through spectacular cloud forests, emerging 57km later at the 3678m high point of the drive, aptly named **Abra de Barro Negro** (Black Mud Pass), which indicates road conditions during the rainy season. Then the road drops 32km to Leimebamba at the head of the Río Utcubamba valley and follows the river as it descends past Tingo (near Kuélap) and on to Chachapoyas. Travelers should carry water and food, as the few restaurants en route are poor and unhygienic.

The normal route to Chachapoyas is from Chiclayo via Bagua; a much easier, and less spectacular, route.

LEIMEBAMBA

pop 1000 / elevation 2050m

Also spelt Leymebamba, this remote, attractive little colonial highland town is surrounded by many little-known archaeological sites. Leimebamba has no bank or post office. Two phone offices and a police station are on the plaza.

One of the most interesting sites is on a cliff above Laguna de los Cóndores, where a **tomb** containing 217 mummies was investigated in 1997. It takes a strenuous nine- to 12-hour day to hike there, or you can hire horses. The mummies are now being studied in the **Museo Leymebamba** (admission US$1.50; ☉ 9am-5pm Mon-Sat), 3km south of town. Most of the mummies are wrapped in bundles and can be seen in a glass case; two have been unwrapped. Other objects on display include ceramics, textiles, wood figures, *quipus* and photos of the site. There is a also small **Tourist Center and Museum** open erratically on the main plaza. A new **tomb**, three day's walk south from Leimebamba, was discovered in 1999.

Tours & Guides

Local guides (ask at the museums) will arrange trips to the tombs and other sites, some of which are easily visited on a day trip, while others require several days. Homer Ullilen, the son of the owner of the Albergue Turístico de la Laguna de los Cóndores, can guide you to sites on their land. Horses cost about US$6 per day, plus another US$6 for the *arriero* (mule driver).

Sleeping & Eating

Albergue Turístico de la Laguna de los Cóndores
(Amazonas 320; s US$4.50, s/d with shower US$8.75/14.50)
Half a block from the plaza, this small, spotless hotel with hot showers has information and can arrange tours. There are a couple of other cheaper, basic *hospedajes*.

The best of the simple restaurants are **Cely's Café** (La Verdad 530), which does pizzas,

while **El Caribe** (menú $1.20), on the plaza, does a poor set lunch.

Getting There & Away

Minibuses for Chachapoyas (four hours) leave at 3am and 5am from in front of one of the telephone offices on the plaza; there is a sign. Reserve a seat the night before. A taxi to Chachapoyas costs US$23. The two weekly buses to Chachapoyas pass through at about 8pm on Sunday and Thursday, to Cajamarca at 11am on Tuesday and Friday. There are occasional trucks and private vehicles to Chachapoyas and Celendín.

FROM CHICLAYO TO CHACHAPOYAS

This is the usual route for travelers to Chachapoyas. From the old Panamericana 100km north of Chiclayo, a paved road heads east over the Andes via the 2145m Porculla Pass, the lowest Peruvian pass going over the Andean continental divide. The route then drops to the Río Marañón valley. About 190km from the Panamericana turn-off, you reach the town of **Jaén**, the beginning of a newly opened route to Ecuador (see the boxed text below). Continuing east, a short side road reaches the town of **Bagua Chica** in a low, enclosed valley (elevation about 500m), which Peruvians claim is the hottest town in

---

ECUADOR – THE BACK WAY

From Jaén, a good northbound road heads 107km to San Ignacio near the Ecuadorian border. Since the peace treaty was signed with Ecuador in late 1998, it has become possible to cross into Ecuador at this remote outpost.

Begin at the fast-growing agricultural center of **Jaén** (☎ 076; pop 50,000; elevation 725m), where there are now a couple of banks and over a dozen hotels. Good ones include the budget **Hostal Jaén** (☎ 73-1333; San Martín 1528; s/d US$4.50/7.25), with friendly staff and private cold showers, or the family-run **Hostal Diana Gris** (☎ 73-2127; Urreta 1136, 2nd fl; s/d US$7.25/11.50), which has private hot showers, fans, cable TV and restaurant. Also try the recommended **Prim's Hotel** (☎ 73-2970; Palo-mino 1353; s/d US$20/24; ☒ ℗), which has a *chifa* (Chinese restaurant), or the town's best option, **Hotel El Bosque** (☎ 73-1492; M Muro 632; s/d US$23/31; ☒ ℗ ☒), with bungalows set in gardens.

From Jaén, colectivos leave for **San Ignacio** (US$4.50, 2½ hours), where there's a simple hotel and places to eat. Change here for another colectivo on the rough road to **La Balsa** (US$4.50, 2½ hours) on the Río Blanco dividing Peru from Ecuador. There used to be a ferry here (hence the name 'La Balsa') but a new international bridge has been built linking the countries. Border formalities are straightforward if you have your papers in order, although the immigration officers won't have seen many gringos coming through yet!

Once in Ecuador, curious and typical *rancheras* (trucks with rows of wooden seats mounted on them) await to take you on the uncomfortable 10km drive to Zumba. From here, buses go to the famed 'valley of longevity' of Vilcabamba (US$4, three hours) where you'll be ready to relax in one of the comfortable hotels and read Lonely Planet's *Ecuador & the Galápagos Islands* book. If you leave Jaén at dawn, you should be able to make it in to Vilcabamba in one day.

NORTHERN HIGHLANDS

the country. The bus usually goes through **Bagua Grande** on the main road about 20km away from Bagua Chica, and follows the Río Utcubamba valley to the crossroads town of **Pedro Ruíz** (see p348), about 90 minutes from Bagua Grande. From here, a bumpy and rough southbound road branches to Chachapoyas, 54km and about 90 minutes away.

CHACHAPOYAS

☎ 041 / pop 25,000 / elevation 2335 m

The pleasant capital of the Department of Amazonas is not in the Amazon basin but in a mountainous area (it formerly included the lowland Department of Loreto). The town has always been difficult to reach, and even today Chachapoyas is reached exclusively by rough unpaved roads or irregular flights. It's a quiet, friendly town that provides an excellent base for visiting remote archaeological sites. The best known and most accessible of these is the magnificent site of Kuélap (see p348). The traditional evening pastime of strolling around the Plaza de Armas is a favorite way of relaxing and socializing.

The area contains vast tracts of little-explored cloud forest containing some of Peru's most fascinating and least-known archaeological ruins. Although the ravages of weather and time, as well as the more recent attentions of grave robbers and treasure seekers, have caused damage to many of the ruins, some have survived remarkably well and can be visited by the adventurous traveler.

Travelers wishing to visit one of the scores of other sites in the area should seek further information in Chachapoyas. Many trips will require at least sleeping bags, and sometimes tents and food as well. The dry months (May to September) are the best for hiking and to organize a group to share costs. October to December isn't too wet, but January to April can be very rainy.

History

The Chachapoyan culture was conquered but not subdued by the Incas a few decades before the Spaniards arrived. When the Europeans showed up, local chief Curaca Huáman supposedly aided them in

CHACHAPOYAS

0 — 200 m
0 — 0.1 mi

To Mirador Guayamil (3 blocks)

INFORMATION	p346
BCP	1 B2
Cyber Club	2 C3
Lavandería Clean	3 C2
Tourist Information	4 C3

SIGHTS & ACTIVITIES	p346
Church	5 C2
Instituto Nacional de Cultura (INC) Museum	6 C2

SLEEPING	pp346–7
Casa Vieja Hotel	7 B2
Hostal Belén	8 B2
Hostal El Tejado	9 C2
Hostal Johumaji	10 C2
Hostal Kuélap	11 B2
Hotel Continental	12 B2
Hotel El Dorado	13 B2
Hotel Gran Vilaya	14 C2
Hotel Puma Urco	15 C2
Hotel Revash	16 C2

EATING	p347
Chacha	17 C2
Chifa Chuy Xien	18 C2
El Tejado	(see 9)
Las Rocas	19 C2
Panificadora San José	20 C2
Restaurant Matalacha	21 D2

DRINKING	p347
La Noche	22 B3
No Limits	23 C1

TRANSPORT	pp347–8
Civa	24 C1
Colectivos to Tingo	25 C1
LC Busre	26 A1
Minibuses to Leimebamba	27 C1
Movil Tours	28 B1
Pedro Ruiz	(see 25)
Transervis Kuélap	29 B1
Transportes Roller	30 C1
Transportes Zelada	31 B1
Virgen del Carmen	32 C1

OTHER	
Gran Vilaya Tours	33 C2

their conquest. Because of the relative lack of Inca influence, the people didn't learn to speak Quechua and today Spanish is spoken almost exclusively here. Local historians claim that San Juan de la Frontera de las Chachapoyas was the third town founded by the Spaniards in Peru (after Piura and Lima) and, at one time, was the seventh-largest town in Peru.

Information

For information on local attractions, visit **Dirección Regional de Industria y Turismo** (Junín 801; ⏲ 8am-1pm & 2-5pm Mon-Fri). The **Hotel & Restaurant Association** website (www.chachapoyasperu.com) has links to several local hotels, restaurants and businesses.

You can email your friends from **Cyber Club** (Triunfo 769; ⏲ 8am-midnight). The post office is on the Plaza de Armas.

Clean you clothes at **Lavandería Clean** (Amazonas 813; ⏲ 9am-1pm & 3-9pm Mon-Sat) for US$0.90 per kilo.

BCP (Plaza de Armas) changes US cash and traveler's checks and has a Visa/Amex ATM. Several stores on the plaza will change US cash at reasonable rates.

Sights & Activities

There's not much to see at **Instituto Nacional de Cultura Museo** (INC; Ayacucho 904; admission free; ⏲ 9am-noon & 3-5pm Mon-Sat) half a dozen mummies and ceramics from several pre-Columbian periods.

A 10-minute stroll northwest along Salamanca brings you to **Mirador Guayamil**, a lookout with city views. About three blocks beyond it is a well, the **Pozo de Yanayacu**, where visitors are said to become enchanted, so they will always return to Chachapoyas.

One good center for exploration is **Levanto**, a small village three- to four-hours' walk south along an Inca road, or 1½ hours by minibus in the early morning. Ask the mayor for a place to sleep. Another popular trip is the four- or five-day Gran Vilaya trek from Choctemal to the Marañón canyon through pristine cloud forest and past many ruins.

Tours & Guides

Gran Vilaya Tours (☎ 77-7506; fax 77-8154; Grau 624; info@vilayatours.com) has native, English-speaking guides who arrange day and also multiday excursions for those interested in archaeology, trekking, climbing and horseback riding. Co-owner Englishman Rob Dover is very enthusiastic and knowledgeable about the area.

Martín Chumbe (☎ 77-7712, 77-8158; m_chumbe@yahoo.com.mx; Bolivia 620 interior) is a recommended local guide who can take you to many nearby ruins, including an expedition to see the enigmatic sarcophagi (coffins in the shape of human beings) high on a cliff wall in the jungle. Most trips last from four to 10 days and many include overnight stays with local people, making it a cultural experience rarely found in Peru. Rates for his popular six-day Gran Vilaya trek are US$30 per day for groups of two to 10 people, plus food – an incredible bargain. Martín speaks Spanish, but he doesn't have any spare gear, so you need to be self-sufficient with equipment or rent it in advance (a sleeping bag, boots and rain gear are sufficient for most trips, but some require a tent.)

Hotel Revash (below) arranges day tours to Kuélap and sites in the Lamud area. **Lamud** is a tiny village with a basic hotel, almost 40km northwest of Chachapoyas, in the Río Utcubamba valley. Tours are about US$10 per person plus entry fees, with a minimum of four people.

Several other agencies are found on the plaza; they pool their clients.

Sleeping

Cable TV is offered in most hotels, but only Spanish-language stations come through.

Hostal El Tejado (☎ 77-7654; eltejado@viabcp.com; Grau 534; s/d with showers US$9/13) Well-kept rooms with hot water are quiet and include breakfast in the adjoining restaurant (opposite). Enthusiastically recommended by LP readers.

Hotel Revash (☎ 77-7391; fax 77-7356; Grau 517; s/d with showers US$10/14) The showers seem endlessly hot in this older, classic Chachapoyas hotel. The thickly forested courtyard and wooden floors add plenty of character, and the owner, Carlos Burga, arranges local tours. Laundry costs US$1.50 per kg and US cash can be exchanged. The front four rooms are large and offer small balconies with plaza views.

Hostal Johumaji (☎ 77-7279; fax 77-7819; olvacha@terra.com.pe; Ayacucho 711; s/d US$4.50/6) The best of the cheap hotels. The small, tidy rooms have good lighting and electric hot showers. Laundry service for US$1 per kg is offered, as is a TV for US$1.50 extra per night.

Hostal Kuélap (☎ 77-7136; kuelaphotel@hotmail .com; Amazonas 1057; s US$3; s/d with shower US$6/8; **P**) This is currently the only place with on-site parking. Rooms are clean enough with hot water, though mattresses are a bit saggy.

Casa Vieja Hostal (☎ /fax 77-7353; casavieja@viabcp .com; Chincha Alta 569; s/d US$9/15;) Comfortable rooms in a converted mansion make this a special choice. The private showers are hot and breakfast is available.

Hotel Gran Vilaya (☎ 77-7664; fax 77-8154; hotelvilaya@viabcp.com; Ayacucho 755; s/d US$18/23) It's a modern hotel which includes continental breakfast in the adjacent café. Rooms are spacious, showers are hot, but the ambience is rather unexciting.

Other choices include:

Hotel Continental (☎ 77-8352, fax 77-7150; Arrieta 431; s US$4.50; s/d with showers US$6/8) Modern, cheap and adequate.

Hotel El Dorado (☎ 77-7047; Ayacucho 1062; s/d US$7.50/9) An older house with some electric hot showers.

Hotel Puma Urco (☎ /fax 77-7871; Amazonas 833; s/d with showers US$9/13) New and modern.

Hostal Belén (☎ 77-7830, fax 77-8518; Arrieta 540; s/d with showers US$9/14.50) Small tidy rooms with good mattresses.

Eating

Moving east across the Andes, Chachapoyas is the first place where you begin finding Amazonian dishes, with local variations. *Juanes* (steamed rice with fish or chicken, wrapped in a banana leaf) are made with yucca here instead of rice, and taste different. *Cecina*, a smoked pork dish in the lowlands, is often made with beef here.

El Eden (Grau 505; menú US$0.90; 8:30am-5pm) This tiny and friendly vegetarian restaurant does a veggie-noodle soup and rice-and-lentils set lunch, but other food is prepared on request.

Panificadora San José (Ayacucho 816; breakfast US$1-2; from 6:30am) This bakery features tables where you can enjoy a *humita*, *tamal* (corn dough usually stuffed with meat, beans or chilies) or sandwich with coffee for breakfast, and snacks and desserts all day. Pick up some bread and cheese for a picnic.

El Tejado (☎ 77-7554; Grau 534, 2nd fl; menú US$2) It's an atmospheric restaurant with a plaza view (unfortunately there's only one table by the window), recommended for its set lunches; the service can be slow, though.

Las Rocas (☎ 77-8158; Ayacucho 932; mains US$1.50-3.50; 7:30am-9pm Mon-Sat, 6-9pm Sun) The inexpensive meals here aren't fancy, but they are excellent value.

Chacha (☎ 77-7107; Grau 545; set menú US$1; mains US$2-4; 7am-10pm) This is an old standby on the plaza – it's a toss up whether this or Las Rocas is better.

Restaurant Matalacha (☎ 77-8325; Ayacucho 616; mains US$1.50-4.50; 7am-10pm) This bright, locally popular restaurant has large, tasty portions of the usual Peruvian fare and good juices, as well as *cuy* (guinea pig).

Chifa Chuy Xien (☎ 77-8587; Amazonas 840; mains US$2-5) This is the town's best *chifa* (Chinese restaurant).

Entertainment

The evening promenade around the plaza is the main entertainment here. Young people dance to loud music at **La Noche** (Triunfo 1061) and **No Limits** (Grau at La Libertad).

Getting There & Away

AIR

Services are erratic and carriers change often. The current one is **LC Busre** (☎ 77-7610; Puno 368), with flights to Lima on Tuesday and Saturday morning (US$79). The airport is a 20-minute taxi ride away. There's a US$3.50 airport tax.

BUS

The frequently traveled route to Chiclayo (US$7 to US$10, 10 to 12 hours) and on to Lima (US$17 to US$22, 20 to 25 hours) starts along the unpaved but spectacular route to Pedro Ruíz, and then is paved throughout. Major towns en route are Bagua and Jaén. **Transervis Kuélap** (☎ 77-8128; Arrieta 412) has a daily bus to Chiclayo at 7:30pm. **Civa** (☎ 77-8048; La Libertad 812) has a daily 6pm bus to Chiclayo and buses for Lima on Monday, Wednesday and Friday. **Transportes Zelada** (☎ 77-8066; Arrieta 310) goes to Chiclayo and Lima at 11am and **Movil Tours** (☎ 77-8545; La Libertad 1084) leaves at noon.

Virgen del Carmen (Salamanca 650) goes to Celendín on Tuesday and Friday only.

Transportes Roller (Grau 302) has buses to Kuélap (US$3.50, 3½ hours) at 4:30am. This block also has colectivo cars for Tingo

(US$1.75, 1½ hours) which may continue on to María (US$3). Minibuses to Leimebamba take four hours.

To continue further into the Amazon Basin, take a colectivo to the crossroads at Pedro Ruíz (US$3, 1½ hours) and wait for an eastbound bus. Ask around for trucks and minibuses to other destinations.

AROUND CHACHAPOYAS

In **Tingo** (elevation 1900m), there's the basic **Albergue Léon** (d US$6) behind Restaurant Kuélap. On the outskirts, the attractive **Valle Kuélap Hotel Inn** (☎ 77-8433; contact in Chachapoyas at Grau 62-3627; vallekuelap@hotmail.com; s/d US$12/24; **P**) is irregularly open (call ahead); visitors enjoy bungalows with private hot showers, and a bar-restaurant (breakfast US$1.50, lunch *menú* US$3). Tours can be arranged.

Hacienda Chillo (r per person incl meals US$30), 5km south of Tingo, is a nice rustic place to stay, get information about local ruins and arrange mule hire. The owner is Oscar Arce, a good Spanish-speaking guide. On offer is simple accommodation, with no hot water.

Choctemal, closer to Kuélap, has the simple **Choctemal Lodge** (r per person incl meals US$10), 3km above the village; it's usually open June to August only. Minibuses go about twice a day to **María**, from where it's a two-hour walk to Kuélap. Locals in María can provide a bed and meal.

KUÉLAP
elevation 3100m

This fabulous ruined city in the mountains southeast of Chachapoyas is the best preserved and most accessible of the major ruins in the area. Remarkably, the site receives only a few small groups of visitors per day.

In common with the area's other sites, **Kuélap** (admission US$3; ◷ 8am-5pm) is a pre-Inca city, though little is known about the people who built it. The Chachapoyas area was the center of a highland people known as the Chachapoyans (Sachupoyans) who were incorporated into the Inca Empire by Huayna Capac in the late 15th century. They left massive walled cities and fortresses on many of the area's mountaintops. The stonework of these sites is somewhat rougher looking than Inca stonework, but is embellished with patterns and designs not found in Inca work.

Kuélap, perched on a ridge high above the left bank of the Río Utcubamba, is an oval-shaped city about 600m long and entirely surrounded by a massive **defensive wall** 6m to 12m high. Three entrances pierce this wall. The principal entrance, still used today, leads into an impressive, funnel-shaped, high-walled passageway. This is a highly defensible entrance; it would have been almost impossible for attackers to scale these high walls without being repulsed by projectiles from the defenders poised above them. Inside are more than 400 buildings, most of which are round. One, named **El Tintero** (Inkpot), is a mysterious underground chamber where, locals claim, pumas were kept and thrown human sacrifices. Another of the buildings is a lookout tower with excellent views.

The guardians at Kuélap are very friendly and helpful; one is almost always on hand to show visitors around and answer questions. Don José Gabriel Portocarrero Chávez has been there for years, can guide you and is a good source of information on this and other ruins in the area. Tip a few soles.

The small **hostel** (r per person US$2.25) on site is run by the guardians. It has a few beds, but if there are more of you, sleeping on the floor is no problem (bring sleeping bags). Tent camping is permitted. You should carry or purify water, though soft drinks are usually for sale. Basic food is available, but bringing your own is a good idea.

Getting There & Away

A trail climbs from the south end of Tingo to the ruins about 1200m above. There are some signposts on the way and the trail is not difficult to follow, but it is breathlessly steep; allow five to six hours. Remember to bring water, because there is little available at Kuélap and none on the trail. During the rainy season (October to April), especially the latter half, the trail can become very muddy and travel can be difficult.

From Choctemal Lodge, you can hike to Kuélap in about three hours, and from María in about two hours. The Transportes Roller bus reaches within a kilometer of the site.

PEDRO RUÍZ
☎ 041 / elevation 1400m

This village marks the junction of the Chiclayo–Tarapoto road with the turn-off to Chachapoyas. When traveling from Chachapoyas, you can board eastbound buses here. **Casa Blanca Hotel** (s/d with bathroom US$9/15), by the road junction, has a restaurant below it. **Hostal Amazonense** is cheaper.

Buses from the coast pick up passengers to Rioja, Moyobamba (US$4.25) and Tarapoto (US$7, seven hours). Several come through daily, but may be crowded. A colectivo taxi to Moyobamba charges US$5.75 and is quicker than the bus. Ask where they leave from. The road is paved to Tarapoto. If coming from Tarapoto, you'll find plenty of colectivos for Chachapoyas (US$3, 1½ hours) leaving from the junction.

The journey east from Pedro Ruíz is spectacular, climbing over two passes and dropping into fantastic high-jungle vegetation in between.

RIOJA
☎ 042 / pop 4500 / elevation 1400m
Rioja is a small but busy town with an airport that services both Rioja and nearby Moyobamba.

There is a **BCP** (Grau 711). Three or four basic hotels are found, mainly on Avenida Grau, but Moyobamba, 25km away, has a better selection.

Aero Continente (☎ 55-8622, 56-2199) and **AeroCóndor** (☎ 55-8098, 55-8651) have offices, although there were no flights at the time of research. Small local aircraft can be chartered. Tarapoto has the nearest large airport.

Minibuses and colectivos leave every few minutes from the plaza for Moyobamba (US$1.50, 30 minutes). Larger long-distance companies stop in Rioja when they have space available.

MOYOBAMBA
☎ 042 / pop 32,000 / elevation 860m
Moyobamba, the capital of the Department of San Martín, was founded in 1542, but earthquakes (most recently in 1990 and 1991) have contributed to the demise of any historic buildings. Nevertheless, Moyobamba is a pleasant enough town, though there's not much to do. **Hot springs**, about 4km south of town (taxi US$1 or walk) are crowded with locals at weekends who know that the waters are curative; they'd love to see travelers. Some impressive **waterfalls** are publicized locally.

Information
Dirección Regional de Industria y Turismo (☎ 56-2043; San Martín 301) has limited tourism information. **Instituto Nacional de Cultura** (INC; ☎ 56-2281; admission US$0.30; ☼ 9am-noon & 2-5pm Mon-Fri) is a small museum and has information as well.

Money can be changed at the **BCP** (☎ 56-2572; A Alvarado 903). Email your folks at **Internet Moyobamba** (☎ 56-2891; A Alvarado 961).

Sleeping & Eating
Country Club Hostal (☎ 56-2110, ☎ /fax 56-3139; countryclub@moyobamba.net; M de Aguila 667; s/d US$7.50/10; ℗) Spartan, clean, tiled rooms have private hot showers and a garden with a tiny pool. Good value.

Hostal Royal (☎ 56-2662; A Alvarado 784) This hostal is cheaper and OK.

Hostal Marco Antonio (☎ 56-2045, ☎ /fax 56-2319; P Canga 488; s/d US$18/28) A modern hotel with restaurant and room service, and decent rooms with cable TV and private hot showers. Staff arrange local tours.

Hotel Puerto Mirador (☎ /fax 56-2050; pmiradorhotel@terra.com.pe; s/d US$26/43, bungalows US$50/70; ☒ ℗) Located on Jirón Sucre, 1km northeast of town, this hotel has fine views over the Río Mayo. Rates include breakfast. A restaurant provides room service.

La Olla de Barro (☎ 56-1034; P Canga at S Filomeno; mains US$1.50-5) For local jungle dishes, try this well-known place. Good and cheaper food is available elsewhere, but this is the best.

Getting There & Away
There's an office of **Aero Continente** (☎ 56-2199, 56-21472; A Alvarado 726) in town, though there were no flights to Moyobamba at the time of research.

Colectivos to Rioja (US$1.50, 30 minutes) and Tarapoto (US$3, two hours) leave frequently from or near Callao, three blocks east of the Plaza de Armas.

The bus terminal on Avenida Grau, about 1km from the center, has daily departures for Chiclayo and Tarapoto. Buses from Tarapoto to Chiclayo stop here as well.

TARAPOTO
☎ 042 / pop 94,000 / elevation 356m
On the edge of the eastern Andean foothills, Tarapoto is the largest and busiest town in the Department of San Martín, and it's the center for the northern lowlands'

NORTHERN HIGHLANDS

expanding agricultural colonization. Some of this expansion has come from coca-growing in the middle and upper Río Huallaga valley to the south, but tourists don't encounter problems (except in the Saposoa region; the trip through there to Tingo María is not recommended). The route from Moyobamba through Tarapoto and on to Yurimaguas is safe. A tourism industry is now developing in the Tarapoto area to take advantage of the lakes, forests and white-water rivers in the Andean foothills.

Information

INTERNET ACCESS

There are plenty in this area.

Cibernautas.com (San Pablo de la Cruz 114)
Viajeros.com (Pimentel 136)

LAUNDRY

Make sure you've got plenty of clean socks for your expedition by popping into **Lavandería El Churre** (☎ 52-7133; La Cruz 140; ☼ 7:30am-9pm Mon-Sat, 8am-1pm Sun), which charges US$1.50 per kg.

MEDICAL SERVICES

The best medical care is probably at the **Clínica San Martín** (☎ 52-3680, 52-7860; San Martín 274; ☼ 24 hr).

MONEY

BCP (☎ 52-2682; Maynas 130)
Banco Continental (☎ 52-3228; Hurtado 149)
Interbanc (☎ 89-5092; Grau 119)

TOURIST INFORMATION

Casa de Turista (northeast side of Plaza de Armas) A craft shop that also provides some information. Otherwise, check the travel agencies.
Tarapoto Travel (☎ 52-5148; www.geocities.com /tarapototravel/index; San Martín 213) English-speaking owner Martín Zamora is a wealth of information.

Sights & Activities

There is not much to do in Tarapoto itself, apart from just hanging out in the Plaza de Armas (also called the Plaza Mayor) or visiting the tiny **Museo Regional** (Maynas 174; admission US$0.30; ☼ 8am-noon & 12:30-8pm Mon-Fri), but there are several local excursions. Tarapoto's geography is rugged, and waterfalls and lakes are abundant.

Lamas is an Indian village with a few colonial buildings, and is a standard tour

destination. The large indigenous population here has an annual **Fiesta de Santa Rosa** in the last week of August. Although buses and colectivos go to Lamas (US$1, 28km) it's best to go on a guided tour (per person US$6 to US$8, four hours) to get the most out of your visit. There is a small museum and some crafts on offer.

Laguna Azul (also called Laguna de Sauce, because it is near the village of Sauce) is a popular local destination reached by crossing the Río Huallaga on a raft ferry (it takes vehicles). It's 40km to the ferry and then another 45-minute drive. Day tours (per person US$20 to US$26) and overnight excursions are offered. There is good swimming, boating and fishing here, and accommodation, ranging from camping to upscale bungalows, is available. Several combis a day go to Sauce (US$4, four hours) from a bus stop in the Banda de Shilcayo district, east of the town. Taxi drivers know it.

Laguna Venecia and the nearby **Cataratas de Ahuashiyacu** are about 45 minutes away on the road to Yurimaguas. There's a small restaurant nearby, and a 10-minute walk takes you to a locally favored swimming spot. Five-hour tours cost US$11 to US$15 per person. Also popular is a similarly-priced trip to the **Cataratas de Huacamaillo**, which involves two hours of hiking, and wading across the river several times. These places can be reached by public transport and then on foot, but get detailed information to avoid getting lost or go with a guide.

River running on the Río Mayo, 30km from Tarapoto, and on the lower Río Huallaga (not to be confused with the best-avoided middle and upper Huallaga, where the coca-growing industry is centered) is offered mainly from June to November. The shorter trips (half- and full-day trips, from US$20 per person) are mainly Class II and III white-water, while the longer trips (up to six days, from July to October only) include Class III and Class IV rapids and camping on the river. Inflatable kayaks are available for rent for US$15/25 for a half/full day. Longer tours to the Reserva Nacional Pacaya-Samiria lasting about 10 days and shaman and Ayahuasca ceremonies can also be arranged. Check with **Los Chancas Expeditions** (☎ 52-2616; chancas.tripod.com; Rioja 357), which specializes in river rafting.

TARAPOTO

Fishing is reportedly excellent from July to September on the Río Huallaga.

Festivals

The **Aniversario de Tarapoto** (August 20) is the city's biggest fiesta, with music and dancing in the streets. *Uvachado*, made by steeping macerated grapes in cane liquor, keeps the party fueled. The fiesta lasts for an entire week around the anniversary.

The **Patronato de Tarapoto** is a similar festival in mid-July, celebrating the town's Indian heritage.

Sleeping

BUDGET

El Mirador (☎ 52-2177; La Cruz 517; s/d US$13/16) This spotless, super-friendly hotel has 13 rooms, all with a bathroom, big fan and great mattresses. Some of the rooms have hot showers; TV is available. Being a few blocks away from the center cuts down most of the mototaxi (three-wheeled motorcycle rickshaw) noise. Breakfast (US$2) is served on the rooftop terrace ('El Mirador') with views of the city one way and treetops

the other; hammocks make this a perfect place to kick back.

La Patarashca (☎ 52-3899, 52-7554; lapatarashca@hotmail.com; Lamas 261; s/d US$10/13) A tropical vibe encompasses this cute 11-room *hospedaje*, which connects to the similarly-named restaurant (see p352). A plant-filled courtyard and alley has hammocks, while rooms have private cold showers and cable TVs.

Hospedaje Misti (☎ 2-2439; L Prado 341; s/d US$4.50/7) The rooms have tiny bathrooms (where the cold shower splashes the toilet) but you get a TV and ceiling fan; good shoestring value.

Hostal San Antonio (☎ 2-5563, ☎ /fax 52-2226; Pimentel 126; s/d US$7.50/11) Good value is provided in standard clean rooms with private hot showers, fans and cable TV. A restaurant is attached and there's a small courtyard; the Plaza de Armas is just steps away.

Alojamiento July (☎ 2-2087; A Morey 205; s/d US$8.50/10) Cheerfully painted rooms with electric shower, cable TV, minifridge and fan are OK for the price.

Alojamiento Arevalo (☎ 52-5265, 52-7467; Moyobamba 223; US$9/13; P) The best thing about this quiet hotel is the large rooms – space to spread your gear out. Each has a private cold shower, cable TV, fan and minifridge. A large public area with tables (game of cards, anyone?) adjoins a lush courtyard.

Hostal Luna Azul (☎ 52-5787, 52-7604; lunaazul hotel.tripod.com; Manco Cápac 262; s/d US$10/15, d with air-con US$30; P ⊠ ☐) The Luna Azul is a modern hotel with comfortable rooms; only two have air-con, but this may change. Hot water, direct-dial phones and cable TV put this close to the mid-range class. It has a snack bar.

Also try:

Hospedaje Las Palmeras (☎ 52-5475; M Grau 229; s US$2, d with bathroom US$4.50) Basic cold-water place at a minimal price.

Hostal Pasquelandia (☎ 52-2290; Pimentel 341; s/d US$3/4; with bathroom US$4/6) Another basic cold-water option.

Hostal Miami (☎ /fax 52-2038; Urzua 257; s/d US$5/8) Private cold showers and TV in rooms.

Hostal San Martín (☎ 52-2108; M de Compagnon 273; s/d US$7.25/11.50) A satisfactory option.

MID-RANGE

All hotels in this range have cable TV and hot water.

La Posada Inn (☎ 52-5557, 52-2234; San Martín 146; d US$18-29; ⊠) This charming hotel has beamed ceilings and traditional ironwork, but contains a modern infrastructure with a decent restaurant. Rooms are an eclectic mix: some have balconies onto the street, some have air-con and some have electric showers. Look around before choosing.

Hotel Monte Azul (☎ 52-2443, 52-3145; fax 52-3636; C Morey 156; s US$18-31, d US$23-36; ⊠ P) Clean, bright, quiet and hospitable, this is a good choice. All rooms have quality mattresses, direct-dial phones and minifridges. You choose whether you want air-con. A continental breakfast is included.

Hotel Lily (☎ 52-3154, 52-3341; fax 52-2394; Pimentel 405; s/d US$32/43; ⊠ ⊠ P) Unpretentious but secure and restful, this hotel features a sauna and a breakfast room by the pool (buffet breakfast is included). Rooms are spacious with writing desks, minifridge and direct-dial phones. Street-side rooms have balconies, but can be noisy.

Hotel Nilas (☎ 52-7331/2; nilas-tpto@terra.com.pe; Moyobamba 173; s/d US$37/52; ⊠ ⊠ P ☐) This contemporary, central hotel has exercise equipment and a restaurant-bar. The good-

sized rooms have art on the walls, a mini-fridge and phone. Businesspeople like it.

Hotel Río Shilcayo (☎ 52-2225, ☎ /fax 52-4236; hotelrsh@terra.com.pe; Pasaje La Flores 224; s/d US$45/55, bungalows US$65; ⊠ ⊠ P) Almost 2km east of town, this hotel is quiet, cool and has a sauna, good restaurant, bar, and rooms with the usual modern amenities. Rates include breakfast and airport transfer.

Eating

Las Terrazas (☎ 52-6525; Hurtado 183; mains US$1.50-5; ⊠ 8:30am-11:30pm) A good economical choice on the Plaza de Armas, serving standard Peruvian meals and some local dishes.

Real Grill (☎ 52-2183; Moyobamba 131; mains US$2.50-7.50; ⊠ 8am-midnight) On the Plaza de Armas, this place has some (noisy) outdoor tables and an indoors area serving pastas, Chinese meals, local dishes, meat, seafood, burgers and so on. A huge middle-of-the-road menu.

El Brassero (☎ 52-2700; Lamas 231; mains US$3-4; ⊠ 7pm-whenever) Carnivores congregate at this great grill. Choose your cut and it's grilled for you; pork ribs are the specialty. The owners love to chat – they close when the coals die down and people leave. Burgers cost US$1.75.

La Collpa (☎ 52-2644, 52-6954; Circunvalación 164; mains US$3-8; ⊠ 10am-11pm) A great balcony view over the river and forest; best for lunch to appreciate the views, though candlelit dinners are also a treat. Food is local and Peruvian.

La Patarashca (☎ 52-3899; Lamas 261; mains US$4-8) It connects with La Patarashca hotel. Regional Amazon cuisine is featured, as well as standard chicken, fish and meat dishes. The 2nd floor, with street views and tropical ambience, is popular on weekends. See and be seen.

Also try:

Las Tinajas (Moyobambo at Manco Cápac; menú US$1.20) Good set lunches and reasonably priced Peruvian dishes.

Banana's Burgers (☎ 52-3260; AA de Morey 102; US$1-2) Excellent burger joint; always open.

Chifa Tai Pai (☎ 52-4393; L Prado 250) This inexpensive Chinese restaurant draws local families.

Natur Micuna (☎ 52-7904; Maynas 257; menú US$2) This Hare Krishna restaurant is a good choice for vegetarians.

La Pizzería (cnr San Pedro de la Cruz & Lamas; mains US$2-3) This corner spot probably has better pizzas and pastas than anywhere else in town.

Supermercado La Inmaculada (☎ 52-7598; M de Compagnon 126) This is the best option for self-catering.

Entertainment

Stonewasi Taberna (☎ 52-4681; Lamas 222) Lamas near the intersection with La Cruz is a good place to hang out, with several good people-watching restaurants and bars. This is the best of the bars, with sidewalk tables and rock music.

Whisky Bar (☎ 52-3034; AA de Morey 157) Classic rock (think *Whisky Bar* sung by The Doors), a great drinks selection and outdoor seating attract locals and travelers.

La Alternativa (☎ 52-7898; Grau 401) This 'alternative' hole-in-the-wall bar has shelves of dusty bottles containing *uvachado* and various homemade natural concoctions based on soaking roots, lianas etc in cane liquor. Amazon aphrodisiac, anyone? Not for the faint-hearted.

Papillón (☎ 52-2574; Peru 209; cover US$2; ✆ Fri-Sat nights only) This nightclub occasionally has live salsa bands, otherwise there's dancing to DJs. Popular with young locals and travelers, it's in the Morales district, by the Río Cumbaza about 3km west of the center. Mototaxis go out there for under US$1; drivers know several other nightclubs in this area, usually open weekends only and with a small cover. Try **Sapo Enamorado** (Toad in Love!), **Bajú** and **El Monasterio**.

Getting There & Away

AIR

The **airport** (☎ 52-2278) is about 3km southwest of the center. **Aero Continente** (☎ 52-4332, 52-3704; Moyobamba 101) has a daily nonstop flight to and from Lima. **Tans** (☎ 52 5339, 52-4839; Plaza Mayor 491) has daily flights each way to Lima and Iquitos. **LC Busre** (www.lcbusre.com.pe; at the airport) flies from and to Lima via Juanjui on Monday and Thursday. **Saosa** (☎ 52-4185, 52-9107; at the airport) has daily flights in small aircraft to Pucallpa and possibly other jungle destinations. **Saeta** (☎ 52-7399; at the airport) also has similar flights. **AviaSelva** is another local airline, with a Saturday flight to Iquitos via Yurimaguas (this is a new start-up and likely to change).

Just show up in the morning and see what is available. Planes fill up fast. You can also charter a flight to most jungle destinations – you have to pay for all five passenger seats, but that's no problem if you can get a group together. Tarapoto Travel (p350) is a good agency to contact about the less common flights.

BUS

Several companies head west on the paved road to Lima (about US$25, 25 to 30 hours) via Moyobamba, Chiclayo (about US$15, 15 to 17 hours) and Trujillo, generally leaving between 8am and 4pm. Most companies are along Salaverry in the Morales district. The best companies, with onboard toilets and infrequent stops, are **Movil** (☎ 52-9193; Salaverry 858) and **El Sol Peruano** (☎ 52-8322).

Cheaper companies with more stops include **Paredes Estrella** (☎ 52-8552/71), **Expreso Huamanga** (☎ 52-7272) and **Turismo Tarapoto** (☎ 52-6161), all on Salaverry 7th block, and **Ejetur** (☎ 52-6827; Levau 338). If you're going to Moyobamba, ask about the frequent and faster minibuses and colectivos. If you're heading to Chachapoyas, you'll need to change in Pedro Ruíz (p348).

Minibuses, pickup trucks and colectivo taxis for Yurimaguas (US$4 to US$7) leave when full from the *mercado* in the eastern suburb of Banda de Shilcayo and take six hours in the dry season, more in the wet. Paredes Estrella and Expreso Huamanga have buses to Yurimaguas. The unpaved road is in terrible shape, though it's one of the most beautiful drives in the area. The 130km road climbs over the final foothills of the Andes and emerges on the Amazonian plains before continuing on to Yurimaguas (p383).

The southbound journey via Bellavista to Juanjuí (145km) and on to Tocache and Tingo María (485km) is dangerous and not recommended because of drug-running and problems with bandits. If you go, avoid traveling at night, and see if any flights are available. Bellavista, Juanjuí and Tocache all have basic hotels. Tingo María (p252) is safe enough.

NORTHERN HIGHLANDS

Amazon Basin

Travelers experience a dramatic sense of remoteness and get a glimpse of the frontier spirit when exploring this region. There are animals and birds galore in this natural habitat, though they take some finding at times – but that is half the fun! Glide your way by boat down tranquil waterways and enjoy the natural splendours of the Amazon and its tributaries and see locals going about their daily lives.

About half of Peru is in the Amazon basin, but this wilderness is penetrated by few roads, and not many towns of any size have been built. Those that exist started as river ports and were connected with towns further downstream, usually in Brazil or Bolivia. Only a few decades ago, travelers from Peru's major jungle port of Iquitos had to travel thousands of kilometers down the Río Amazonas to the Atlantic and then go either south around Cape Horn or north through the Panama Canal to reach Lima – a journey of several months. With the advent of roads and airports, these jungle areas have slowly become a more integral part of Peru. Nevertheless, this vast area contains only about 5% of the nation's population and they all seem to enjoy seeing new faces. Perhaps you'll be one of them.

HIGHLIGHTS

■ **Cultural Adventure**
Visiting the Ashaninka people from Puerto Bermúdez (p377)

■ **Coolest Time**
Witnessing a dawn; wonderful anywhere on a rainforest lake or river

■ **Watching Wildlife**
Spotting Amazonian animals and birds at Manu (p369), Pacaya-Samiria (p386) and the upper Río Tambopata (p366)

■ **River Tripping**
Swinging in a hammock on a riverboat to/from Iquitos (p393)

■ **Craft Shopping**
Buying Shipibo ceramics and cloth near Yarinacocha (p382), near Pucallpa

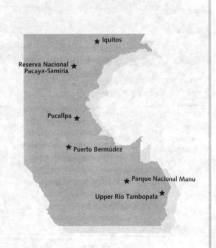

★ Iquitos
Reserva Nacional ★ Pacaya-Samiria
Pucallpa ★
★ Puerto Bermúdez
★ Parque Nacional Manu
Upper Río Tambopata ★

AMAZON BASIN

GEOGRAPHY & CLIMATE

Four main jungle areas of Peru are accessible to the traveler. In the southeast, near the Bolivian border, there's Puerto Maldonado, a port at the junction of the Ríos Tambopata and Madre de Dios. Puerto Maldonado is most easily reached by air (particularly from Cuzco) or by an atrociously bad dirt road (an uncomfortable two- or three-day journey by truck). South of Puerto Maldonado are numerous lodges and camp sites in the Reserva Nacional Tambopata and in the Parque Nacional Bahuaja-Sonene.

North of Cuzco, and fairly easily accessible from there, is Parque Nacional Manu, one of the best areas of protected rainforest in the Amazon.

In central Peru, east of Lima, is the area known as Chanchamayo, which consists of the two small towns of San Ramón and La Merced, both easily accessible by road from Lima, and several nearby villages including Puerto Bermúdez and Oxapampa. From La Merced a paved road continues to the boomtown of Satipo, until recently a no-go zone because of terrorism but now a major coffee-growing area.

A very rough jungle road goes north from La Merced, and past Puerto Bermúdez, to the important port of Pucallpa, the capital of the Department of Ucayali. Most travelers going to Pucallpa, however, take the better roads from Lima via Huánuco and Tingo María, or fly.

AMAZON BASIN

Further north, in the Department of Loreto, is the small port of Yurimaguas, reached from the North Coast by road (much of the long journey is described in the Northern Highlands chapter on p000) or by air from Lima. Further northeast, and accessible only by river boat from Pucallpa or Yurimaguas, or by air from Lima and other cities, is Peru's major jungle port, Iquitos.

Wherever you go in the Amazon basin, you can be sure of two things: there will be rainforest and it's going to rain. Even in the drier months of June to September, the area gets more rain than the wettest months in the mountains.

MADRE DE DIOS

PUERTO MALDONADO

☎ 082 / pop 44,000 / elevation 250m

Founded a century ago, Puerto Maldonado has been important as a rubber boom-town, a logging center and more recently as a center for gold and oil prospectors. It is also a major centre for the production of jungle crops such as Brazil nuts and coffee, and there is some ranching done in the area. Because of the logging industry, the jungle around Puerto Maldonado has been mostly cleared. Inhabitants involved in gold panning, Brazil-nut harvesting, and logging come and go for long periods of time, and the city's population fluctuates dramatically from month to month.

The various commercial enterprises centered on Puerto Maldonado have made it the most important port and capital of the Department of Madre de Dios. It is a fast-growing town with a busy frontier feel and, though it is interesting to experience this boomtown atmosphere, there isn't much to see otherwise. Puerto Maldonado is used as a starting point for trips into the jungle, especially to nearby jungle lodges.

Information

IMMIGRATION

There is a **Bolivian consulate** (Loreto 268, upstairs) on the Plaza de Armas.

To leave Peru via Puerto Heath for Bolivia (see p368), check first with officials at **migraciónes** (immigration office; ☎ 57-1069; 26 de Diciembre 356) in Puerto Maldonado. Here

travelers can also extend their visas or tourist cards for the standard US$28 fee. The border town of Iñapari (see p368) now has a border post but you can't get a visa there.

INTERNET ACCESS

UnAMad (2 de Mayo 287; US$1.50/hr) University-run, it's the best of several places downtown.

ZonaVirtual.com (Velarde near Plaza de Armas) Another popular choice.

LAUNDRY

There's a **lavandería** (Velarde 898) to wash your mud-caked, sweat-soaked, repulsive jungle rags.

MEDICAL SERVICES

Hospital Santa Rosa (☎ 57-1019, 57-1046; Cajamarca 171) Provides basic services.

Social Seguro Hospital (☎ 57-1711) At Km3 on the road to Cuzco. It's newer.

MONEY

Brazilian cruzeiros and Bolivian pesos are hard to negotiate anywhere.

BCP (formerly Banco de Crédito; ☎ 57-1210; Plaza de Armas) Changes US cash or traveler's checks; has Visa ATM.

Banco de la Nación (Plaza de Armas) Limited facilities.

Casa de Cambio (Puno at G Prada) Has good rates for US dollars.

POST

The **post office** (Velarde) is southwest of the Plaza de Armas.

TOURIST INFORMATION

Ministerio de Industria y Turismo (☎ 57-1413, 57-1164; Fitzcarrald 252) Has tourist information, and an airport booth that provides limited information.

Inrena (☎ 57-1604; Cuzco 135) The national park office gives information and collects entrance fees; currently US$8.50 if you stay on the north side of the Río Tambopata, but US$20 if you enter the south side.

Sights & Activities

The strangely cosmic, blue **Obelisco** (US$0.30, with use of elevator US$1; ☉ 10am-4pm) is at the intersection of Fitzcarrald and Madre de Dios. Designed as a modern *mirador* (look-out tower), its 30m-height unfortunately does not rise high enough above the city for viewers to glimpse the rivers, though plenty of corrugated-metal roofs can be admired! Locals say that the tower is closed during rainstorms because water from the

AMAZON BASIN

PUERTO MALDONADO

0 ————————— 200 m
0 ————————— 0.1 mi

INFORMATION	p357	
Banco de la Nación	1	C1
BCP	2	C2
Bolivian Consulate	3	C1
Casa de Cambio	4	B2
Inrena	5	C2
Laundry	6	B3
Migraciones (Immigration) office	7	C2
Ministerio de Industria y Turismo	8	A3
UnAMad	9	B2
ZonaVirtual.com	10	C1

SLEEPING	pp359–60	
Corto Maltes office	11	C1
Hospedaje Rey Port	12	C2
Hospedaje Royal Inn	13	B2
Hostal Cabaña Quinta	14	B1
Hostal Cahuata	15	A3
Hostal El Solar	16	B2
Hostal Moderno	17	C1
Hotel Wilson	18	B2
Inkaterra office	19	B1
Rainforest Expeditions office	20	C2
Tambopata Jungle Lodge office	21	B2
Wasai Lodge	22	C1

EATING	p360	
Chifa Wa-Seng	23	C2
El Califa	24	C1
El Tigre	25	A2
La Casa Nostra	26	B2
La Estrella	27	B2
Pizzeria El Hornito/Chez Maggy	28	C1
Pollería Astoria	29	B3

DRINKING	p360	
Discoteca Anaconda	30	C2
Discoteca Witite	31	C1
Unnamed Nightclub	32	C2

TRANSPORT	pp360–1	
Aero Continente	33	B2
Buses to Laberinto	34	A3
Colectivo taxi to Iñapari	35	A2
Empresa Transportes Imperial	(see 35)	
Ferry Crossing Dock	36	D1
River-Boat Hire	(see 22)	
Tans	37	C1
Trucks to Cuzco	(see 34)	

OTHER		
Agencia Moto	38	B2
Municipalidad	39	C1

roof drains down the stairwells, making them impassable.

The **Madre de Dios ferry** (⏰ dawn-dark; US$0.15) is a cheap way of seeing a little of this major Peruvian jungle river, which is about 500m wide at this point. The river traffic is colorfully ramshackle: *peki-pekis* (canoes powered by two-stroke motorcycle engines with outlandishly long propeller shafts) leave from the dock several times an hour, and simple wooden catamarans take vehicles across to continue on the road to Iberia and Iñapari.

Courses

Tambopata Language Centre (☎ 57-6014; www .tambopata-language.com; Cajamarca 895) offers you Spanish classes one-on-one or in small groups, and also family homestays, cultural and jungle tours, and an English book exchange. Cajamarca is parallel to and southwest of Fitzcarrald.

Tours & Guides

Many visitors arrive with prearranged tours and stay at one of the jungle lodges described later in this chapter. You can arrange a tour when you arrive, either by going to the lodge offices where you might get a small discount on a tour that would cost more in Lima or Cuzco, or by looking for a guide. Beware of guides at the airport, who often take you to a 'recommended' hotel (and collect a commission) and then hound you throughout your stay. There are crooked operators out there – shop around, don't prepay for any tour and if paying an advance deposit, insist on a signed receipt. If you agree to a boat driver's price, make sure it includes the return trip. When not working, guides hang out in restaurants in town; La Casa Nostra is one such gathering spot.

There are about 30 guides with official licenses granted by the local Ministerio de Industria y Turismo. Unfortunately, many of the best ones work full time for one of the local jungle lodges, and getting a license is not a very demanding process. Still, having a licensed guide does give you some recourse in the unlikely event of a disastrous trip. In almost all cases boat rides are needed to get out of Puerto

Maldonado, and boats use a lot of gas and are notoriously expensive to run. Guides charge from US$25 to US$60 per person per day depending on the destination and number of people, plus park fees.

Victor Yohamona (☎ 968-6279; victorguideperu@ hotmail.com) is a well-known local guide who can be contacted through Hostal Cabaña Quinta (see details later). Another recommended guide is **Hernán Llavé** (☎ 57-2243), who speaks some English. If he's not on a tour, you'll find him in the baggage reception area of the airport waiting for incoming flights. Another honest freelance guide is **Willy Wither** (☎ 57-2014; compured@compured.lim aperu.net), who speaks some English and German and is very enthusiastic. Readers have recommended **Nadir Gnan** (☎ 57-1900), who speaks English and Italian, and has firsthand expertise on mining activities. The *motorista* (boat driver) Victor Yarikawa and guide Arturo Balarezo Revilla (ask at Hotel Wilson) are other possibilities.

Sleeping

Puerto Maldonado has about 20 hotels, most in the budget range. The better ones may fill by late morning in the high season and foreigners may be overcharged. Expect cold showers unless stated otherwise.

BUDGET

Hostal Moderno (☎ 57-1063; Billinghurst 359; s/d/tr US$4.50/6/7.50) Despite the up-to-date name, this family-run place has been around for decades. Rooms are simple but clean and the owners invest in a new coat of paint every few years to keep this quiet budget choice presentable and popular. Meals are served on request.

Hostal Cahuata (☎ 57-1526; Fitzcarrald 517; s/d US$3/6, with bathroom US$6/9) The market-side location won't give you much sleep during the day, but it quiets down at night. Rooms are small but neat, have fans and are good value for the price. Rooms with bathrooms even offer a TV.

Hostal El Solar (☎ 57-1634; G Prada 445; s/d US$4.50/7.50, with bathroom US$6/10) The rooms are fairly basic but do have fans, and a TV is provided on request if you want to practice your Spanish.

Hotel Wilson (☎ 57-2838; G Prada 355; s/d US$4.50/ 7.50, with bathroom US$7.50/10.50) The rooms with bathroom also boast fans, which makes

them more comfortable, though still quite basic. The owners offer discounts for groups and multi-night stays, and a simple café and air-travel agency are on the premises.

Hospedaje Royal Inn (☎ 57-1048; 2 de Mayo 333; s/d with bathroom US$7.50/10.50) Large, clean rooms with fans make this a good choice for travelers needing to spread out their gear.

Hospedaje Rey Port (☎ 57-1177; Velarde 457; s/d US$6/9, with shower US$10/14) The rooms are clean and have fans, but aren't remarkable. The upper floors do have good views though, which is the hotel's best feature.

Iñapari Lodge (☎ 57-2575; fax 57-2155; r per person US$6) Five kilometers away from the center, near the airport, this rustic but pleasant and friendly *hostal* has rooms with communal showers, restaurant and bar. Inexpensive horseback, bicycle and other tours can be arranged.

There's also Brombus (see Eating p360).

MID-RANGE

Hotel Don Carlos (☎ 57-1323, 57-1029; hdoncarlosm aldonado@viabcp.com; León Velarde 1271; s US$20-29, d US$25-36; ✿ ✿) The wood-paneled rooms are reasonably sized and have hot showers, minifridge and TV. The location – about 1km southwest of the center – is quiet, and the Río Tambopata can be seen from the grounds. A little restaurant opens on demand, has an outdoor dining balcony and room service, and a continental breakfast and airport transfer is included in the rates. The promotional lower rates are for walk-in guests or in the low season.

Hostal Cabaña Quinta (☎ 57-1045, 57-3336; Cuzco 535; s/d standard US$13/18.50, superior US$26/35; ✿) This is the hotel of choice for folks wanting economical comfort in the town center. Standard rooms have cold showers, fans and TV; superior rooms boast air-con, minifridge and hot shower as well. A decent and moderately priced restaurant saves you walking into the town center, and the staff try to please. Room service is available.

Wasai Lodge (☎ 57-2290, 57-1335; reservas@ wasai.com; Billinghurst at Arequipa; s/d US$36/48; ✿ ✿) This small lodge has an exotic entrance, and rooms are in bungalows overlooking the Madre de Dios. A few rooms offer air-con; those that do cost an extra US$10. However, minifridge, hot showers, cable TV and a river view of the Madre de Dios are standard. There is a good restaurant (mains

AMAZON BASIN

US$5 to US$6), room service and bar. The lodge arranges one-day and overnight trips into the area (see www.wasai.com).

Outside Puerto Maldonado are a dozen jungle lodges (see p362 and 366).

Eating

There are no fancy restaurants in Puerto Maldonado; most are fairly basic. Despite this, prices are comparatively pricey because of high food-transportation costs. Regional specialties include *juanes* (rice steamed with fish or chicken in a banana leaf), *chilcano* (a broth of fish chunks flavored with the native cilantro herb) and *parrillada de la selva* (a barbecue of marinated meat, often game, in a Brazil-nut sauce). A *plátano* (plantain) is served boiled or fried as a side dish to many meals.

Pizzería El Hornito/Chez Maggy (☎ 57-2082; D Carrión 271; individual/family pizzas US$3.50/8.50; ☽ 6pm-late) This popular hang-out on the Plaza de Armas serves pasta and wood-oven, thin-crust pizza – the best in town. There's no lunches – the oven makes it too hot during the day!

Chifa Wa-Seng (Cuzco 244; mains US$4-6; ☽ noon-2pm Tue-Sun, 6-11pm daily) The Peruvian Amazon version of Chinese food is actually quite tasty, though somewhat different from the fare in Shanghai. Come with an open mind and mouth – portions are big.

El Califa (☎ 57-1119; Piura 266; mains US$2-5; ☽ 10am-4:30pm Mon-Sat) This is a rustic place serving good regional specialties including heart of palm salad, *juanes*, fried *plátano* and game meat. It's sultry and a few blocks away from the center, but still attracts daily diners who consider it the best lunch in town.

El Tigre (☎ 57-2286; Tacna 456; mains average US$4) Recommended for its ceviche (marinated fish dish), this place is popular in the morning and for lunch. Other local fish dishes are also offered.

La Casa Nostra (☎ 57-2647; Velarde 515; snacks & breakfast US$1-3; ☽ 7am-1pm & 5-11pm) The best café in town, it serves varied breakfasts, *tamales*, great juices, snacks, desserts and coffee. It is a meeting spot for travelers and guides.

La Estrella (☎ 57-3107; Velarde 474; meals US$2; ☽ 11am-10pm) This neon-lit chicken restaurant looks like a US fast-food outlet and its clean bright decor attracts locals happy to spend US$2 for a quarter-chicken, fries

and chicken broth – the standard and most popular menu item. It's one of the best-value budget options in town.

Pollería Astoria (☎ 57-1422; Velarde 701; meals US$2) This is exactly the same yet precisely opposite to La Estrella, above. Same food, same price, same value, yet served in a dimly lit wooden restaurant that has more of an Amazonian feel and has an equally large local following. Your choice!

Other good options include the satisfactory Hotel Cabaña Quinta (p359) restaurant, and the pricier, well-recommended Wasai Lodge (see p359). Also consider **Brombus** (☎ 57-3230), 4km out on the way to the airport. In a peaceful setting that combines adobe walls and thatched roofs, Fernando Rosemberg and his wife serve local delicacies and international dishes. A few simple rooms are available for rent – call ahead.

In the Mercado Modelo, look for freshly squeezed fruit juices and other jungle staples, such as *fariña,* a muesli-like yucca concoction eaten fried or mixed in lemonade. Also in the market, look out for children selling hot, fresh *pan de arroz* in the early morning (7am to 8am). This bread is made from rice flour, yucca and butter and takes three days to prepare.

Drinking

A handful of nightclubs sputter into life late on weekend nights, usually with recorded and occasionally live music. The best known is **Discoteca Witite** (☎ 57-2419, 57-3861; Velarde 153). Also try **Discoteca Anaconda** (Loreto 2nd block) on the Plaza de Armas and an **unnamed place** (Arequipa) at the southeast corner of the plaza. Listen around for other possibilities.

Getting There & Away

Most people fly here from Cuzco. The long road or river trips are only for travelers prepared to put up with discomfort and delay.

AIR

The airport is 7km out of town. Scheduled flights leave every morning to and from Lima via Cuzco with **Aero Continente** (☎ 57-2004; Velarde 584) and **Tans** (☎ 57-1429; Velarde 147). LanPeru has three flights a week. Schedules and airlines change every year and numerous travel agents in the center have the latest details. At the time of writing rates are US$160 return from Lima and US$80 return from Cuzco.

Light aircraft to anywhere can be chartered as long as you pay for five seats and the return trip. Ask at the airport.

BOAT

Hire boats at the Río Madre de Dios ferry dock for local excursions or to take you downriver to the Bolivian border. It's difficult to find boats up the Madre de Dios (against the current) to Manu, and though it is possible to fly to Boca Manu (also called Manu) on chartered light aircraft, this is normally done from Cuzco. Cuzco is a better place than Puerto Maldonado from which to reach Manu. Occasionally, people reach Puerto Maldonado by boat from Manu (with the current) or from the Bolivian border (against the current), but transportation is infrequent. Be prepared for waits of several days.

At the Tambopata dock, several kilometers south of town and reached by *motocarros* (three-wheeled motorcycle rickshaw), there are public boats up the Tambopata as far as the community of Baltimore. The *Tiburon* leaves twice a week (currently Monday and Thursday, but subject to change) and can drop you off at any of the lodges between Puerto Maldonado and Baltimore. The fare is US$5 or less, depending on how far you go. Also ask for *El Gordo*, a portly gentleman who regularly boats up the Tambopata. All passengers must stop at La Torre Puesto de Control (checkpoint) where passports and Inrena permits (US$8.50) are needed. (See Tourist Information, p357, for more details on Inrena permits.)

Some Río Tambopata lodges avoid the first two hours of river travel when transporting visitors upriver, by taking the side road to the Indian community of Infierno (which means 'Hell'), almost an hour away, and continuing by boat from there. Going to Hell needs to be arranged ahead of time because there is nowhere to stay there and no boats awaiting passengers.

LOCAL TRANSPORT

Trucks, minibuses and colectivo taxis leave Puerto Maldonado for Laberinto (US$2, 1½ hours), passing the turn-off to Baltimore at Km37 on the road to Cuzco. They leave

---

FRIAJES

Although the Puerto Maldonado region is hot and humid year-round, with temperatures averaging 27°C and often climbing above 32°C, there are occasional cold winds from the Andes. Known as *friajes*, these winds can make temperatures plunge to 9°C or even lower. It's worth having a light jacket or sweater in case this happens. The *friaje's* effect on the wildlife contributes to the high species diversity and endemism of the region.

---

frequently during the morning and less often in the afternoon from the corner of Ica and E Rivero. Colectivo taxis to Iñapari (US$8, four hours), near the tri-border with Brazil and Bolivia, leave from **Empresa Transportes Imperial** (☎ 57-4274; Ica 5th block) when they have four passengers. Some other companies on the same block also advertise this trip.

TRUCK

Ha! You noticed – the heading doesn't read 'Bus'. During the highland dry season, trucks to Cuzco leave from the Mercado Modelo on E Rivero, or from outside the public swimming pool, which is two blocks south of the mercado on the same street. Although it's only about 500km, the road is so rough that the trip takes 60 hours or more, depending on weather conditions (see Cuzco to Puerto Maldonado on p220). During the rainy season, the trip can take days.

Getting Around

Motocarros take two or three passengers (and light luggage) to the airport for US$2. Short rides around town cost under US$1.

There are also *taximotos*: Honda 90s that will take one passenger around town for about US$0.25, but don't expect a motorcycle helmet.

MOTORCYCLE RENTAL

You can rent motorcycles if you want to see some of the surrounding countryside; go in pairs in case of breakdowns or accident. There are several motorcycle-rental places, mainly on G Prada between Velarde and Puno. They charge US$1.20 per hour and have mainly small, 100cc bikes. Bargain for all-day discounts.

AROUND PUERTO MALDONADO

Laberinto

A bus trip to the nearby gold-rush town of Laberinto enables you to see the countryside around Puerto Maldonado. You can leave in the morning and return in the afternoon, but don't miss the last bus, as the one hotel in Laberinto is a real dive and usually full of drunk miners. Laberinto itself is a shantytown. However, you can take trips up and down the Río Madre de Dios from here to nearby communities. You may see buyers blowtorching gold to melt and purify it. The miners come into Laberinto to sell their gold at the Banco de Minero. If the bank runs out of money, the miners may barter their gold in exchange for gas, food and other supplies. See Getting There & Away (p360) for transport details.

Along the Río Madre de Dios

This important river flows past Puerto Maldonado, eastbound, heading into Bolivia and Brazil, and the Amazon proper.

Apart from fishing and nature trips, visits to beaches, Indian communities, salt licks and gold-panning areas can be made along the Madre de Dios. Some excursions involve camping or staying in simple thatched shelters, so bring a sleeping pad and bag and/or hammock. Be prepared for muddy trails – two pairs of shoes are recommended, a dry pair for camp use and a pair that can get thoroughly wet and covered with mud. Insect repellent, sunblock and a means of purifying water are essential.

SIGHTS & ACTIVITIES

New in 2003, the **ATI Aceer Tambopata en Inkaterra** (to stay here see Reserva Amazonica Lodge p364) has the potential of becoming the area's most important research center. Almost opposite Cuzco Tambo Lodge (see later), it was built on the site of a 19th-century house formerly occupied by one of the first doctors to practice in this part of the Amazon. ATI retains parts of the original house while providing modern research facilities in the new construction. Although the modern accommodation is mainly for researchers, ATI can be visited by ecotourists who examine the small exhibit about local conservation issues, and attend lectures.

You can reach **Lago Sandoval** (see p365) from some of the lodges here.

SLEEPING

Lodges are listed as you travel away from Puerto Maldonado, irrespective of price.

The closest lodge to Puerto Maldonado is the reader-recommended **Corto Maltes** (☎ /fax in Puerto Maldonado 57-3831; www.cortomaltes -amazonia.com). Only 5km from town, this lodge offers 15 comfortable, fully-screened, high-ceilinged bungalows with solid mattresses, eye-catching Shipibo Indian wall art, patios with two hammocks, bathrooms with unusual wooden sinks and cheerful decorative touches in the public areas. Electricity is available from dusk till 10:30pm and showers have hot water. The French owners pride themselves on the excellent food, and remind visitors that they can take a boat back to Puerto Maldonado to go dancing at night if the urge grabs them. Despite the lodge's proximity to the city, good day tours further into the rainforest are provided.

About 9km from town is the Cuzco Tambo Lodge, with six habitable bungalows and more being reconstructed. Poorly run and frequently changing ownership, this place occasionally gets used under the guise of being a better lodge than it actually is. Beware. It's OK if you get low rates and tours are included.

Further down the Madre de Dios, almost 16km away from Puerto Maldonado, the comfortable **Reserva Amazonica Lodge** (run

---

CASAS DE HOSPEDAJE

If you ask around the riverfront or at the Ministerio de Industria y Turismo in Puerto Maldonado, you'll hear about these cheap places that are often run by local farmers and their families. Small, very rustic and reached by boat or on foot, they offer the cheapest places to stay (meals are available) and are geared toward travelers on a very tight budget. We don't necessarily recommend them, because guides are rarely provided and the rainforest nearby is usually secondary growth and sometimes degraded, but they may be suitable for some folks. At least using them puts money into the economy at a grassroots level. They are found on Lago Sandoval (p000) near the Río Madre de Dios and near the village of Baltimore (p000) on the Río Tambopata.

AROUND PUERTO MALDONADO

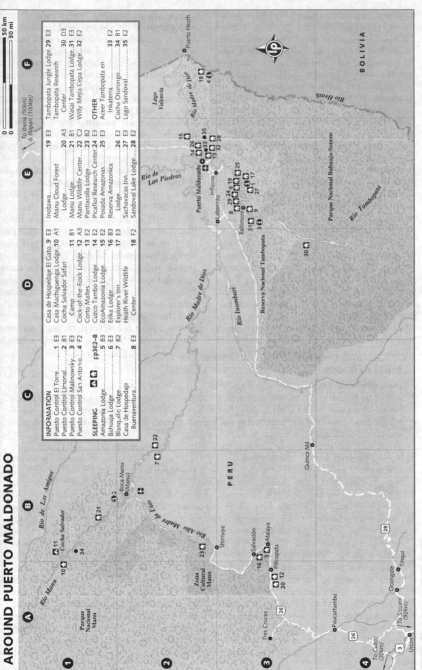

by Inkaterra; www.inkaterra.com; 3 days & 2 nights s/d US$183/314, ste US$292/480; Cuzco ☎ 084-24-5314; Lima ☎ 01-610-0404) offers local tours and a better look at the jungle. Tours include a visit to a nearby farm and hiking on 10km of private trails; a canopy climbing platform is planned for 2004. Longer packages are available. A huge, traditionally thatched, cone-shaped two-story reception/restaurant/bar/library/relaxation area greets the arriving traveler. Downstairs, beautifully presented, delicious set meals are served from one of the largest and best-equipped kitchens in the southern Amazon; travelers with special dietary needs can be accommodated. Upstairs, four separate sitting areas complete with couches and private balconies invite conversation and lingering with binoculars to enjoy the fine views and birdlife outside. On occasion, a barbecue is served alfresco with guests stuffing their own choice of food into bamboo tubes and leaving them on hot coals to roast to juicy perfection, while enjoying a jungle sundowner accompanied by a guitar. A separate building houses an interpretation center (with maps, photos, casts of mammal footprints

– ask about making your own – and occasional slide shows) and one of the largest collections of rubber boots on the river (even imported size 12), which are useful for sloshing through the rainforest accompanied by a guide who may speak English, French or Italian. About 40 rustic individual cabins have bathrooms and porches with two hammocks. Three suites (three more are planned for 2004) boast huge bathrooms with double vanities, two queen beds each, a writing desk, and one has a warm shower.

Roughly 30km from Puerto Maldonado is **EcoAmazonia Lodge** (www.ecoamazonia.com.pe; 3 days & 2 nights s/d US$240/320; Cuzco ☎ 084-23-6159, 084-24-2244; Lima ☎ 01-242-2708; Puerto Maldonado ☎ 57-3491), another lodge boasting a huge, thatched-roof restaurant and bar, with fine river views from the 2nd floor. Most visitors are European and guides speak English, French and Italian; the knowledgeable manager also speaks Japanese. Forty-seven identical, rustic, completely screened bungalows (many newly built or reconditioned in 2003) each have a bathroom and a small sitting room. There are several trails of varying length from this lodge, including a tough

---

JUNGLE LODGES

The area's jungle lodges can only be reached by boat and give visitors a rustic jungle experience, as well as providing guides and tours with the highest chances of seeing local wildlife. Lodge reservations should be made in Cuzco or Lima, as it can be difficult to contact the offices in Puerto Maldonado, where rates aren't much cheaper. These lodges do deal with international tour groups and can be full at any time, but are often fairly empty.

Although two-day/one-night packages are available, a minimum stay of three days/two nights is recommended, because the first and last day are largely consumed by air travel from and to Cuzco. The last day involves leaving the lodge after a predawn breakfast to catch the late-morning flight to Cuzco. All prices should include round-trip transportation from Puerto Maldonado airport to the river and the lodge, plus meals, accommodations and some local guided tours. An airfare to Puerto Maldonado is extra. All bottled drinks (including water) and tips are extra. Tea, coffee and cold water for your own bottle are normally available all day at no charge. The guides come and go, and the quality and depth of their knowledge varies. Discounts can normally be arranged if it's the low season (December to April) and you are traveling as a group (usually five or more) or planning a long stay. All the lodges will happily arrange longer stays.

Accommodations are rustic but comfortable enough. Unless indicated otherwise, lodges normally lack electricity, except to run a refrigerator in the kitchen. Lighting is by kerosene lantern or candle, so pack a flashlight. Showers are cold, shocking the body, but refreshing at the end of a sweaty day, and beds usually have mosquito netting. Some lodges have several rooms in one building, with minimal acoustic privacy, while others have separate bungalows, which lowers neighbors' noise. Visitors will see a large variety of tropical plants, insects and birds, but mammals are elusive and hard to see in the rainforest. Don't go with high expectations of seeing jaguars and tapirs. Monkeys, sloths and bats are the most frequently sighted mammals.

14km hike to a lake, and shorter walks for all levels of fitness. Boat tours to local lakes and along the rivers are also offered, and shamanism and *ayahuasca* ceremonies can be arranged by advance request.

Lago Sandoval

An attractive jungle lake, Lago Sandoval is surrounded by different types of rainforest and is about two hours from Puerto Maldonado down the Madre de Dios. The best way to see wildlife is to stay overnight and take a boat ride on the lake, though day trips to the lake are offered. Half the trip is done by boat and the other half on foot. Bring your own food and water. For about US$25 to US$30 (bargain – several people can travel for this price), a boat will drop you at the beginning of the trail and pick you up later. The boat driver will also guide you to the lake on request. With luck, you might see caiman, turtles, exotic birds, monkeys and maybe the rare endangered giant river otters that live in the lake.

You can also reach the lake by hiking along a 3km trail from the jungle lodges here. Between Reserva Amazonica Lodge and EcoAmazonia Lodge (see p364) but on the opposite (south) side of the river, is the trail leading to Lago Sandoval. The flat trail has boardwalks and gravel and is easily passable year-round. From the end of this trail, you can continue 2km on a narrower, less-maintained trail to an inexpensive lodge, or take a boat ride across the lake to the best lodge in this area.

SLEEPING

The inexpensive lodge is the family-run **Willy Mejía Cepa Lodge** (book in Puerto Maldonado at Velarde 487; r per person US$20). Willy's father, Don César Mejía Zaballos, homesteaded the lake 50 years ago and has been offering basic accommodations to budget travelers for 16 years. The lodge has room for 20 people, showers and bathrooms are shared and are separate from the sleeping areas. Mosquito nets and meals are included; bottled drinks are sold. For groups of 10 or more, rates are US$15 per person per day including transportation from Puerto Maldonado, simple family meals, a bed and excursions (in Spanish).

The best lodge is **Sandoval Lake Lodge** (book with Inkanatura, www.inkanatura.com; 3 days & 2 nights s/d with bathroom US$260/380, extra nights per person US$70; Cuzco ☎ 084-25-1173; Plateros 361; Lima ☎ 01-440-2022; Manuel Bañón 461, San Isidro), which is on the other side of the lake to Willy Mejía. Getting there is half the fun. After hiking the 3km to the lake (bicycle rickshaws are available for luggage and for people with walking difficulties), you board canoes to negotiate narrow canals through a flooded palm-tree forest inhabited by hundreds of nesting red-bellied macaws. Emerging from the flooded forest, you are silently paddled across the beautiful lake to the lodge. With luck, you may spot the endangered giant river otter, of which several pairs live in the lake and can sometimes be seen during early morning boating excursions. Various monkey species and a host of birds can also be spotted, as well as caiman, frogs and lizards. Hikes into the forest are offered, and guides are multilingual and knowledgeable.

The spacious lodge is built on a hilltop about 30m above the lake and is surrounded by primary forest. The hilltop was a former farm, and the lodge was built from salvaged driftwood, so the owners pride themselves on the fact that no primary forest was cut during construction. (This is also true of some other lodges, though not always mentioned.) The rooms (with heated and tiled showers and ceiling fans) are the best in the area, and the restaurant/bar area is huge, airy and conducive to relaxing and chatting. Rates include transport from Puerto Maldonado and all meals.

LAGO VALENCIA

Lago Valencia, just off the Río Madre de Dios and near the Bolivian border is about 60km from Puerto Maldonado. At least two days are needed for a visit here, though three or four days are recommended. This lake reportedly offers the region's best **fishing**, as well as good **bird-watching** and **wildlife-watching** (bring your binoculars). There are trails into the jungle around the lake.

ALONG THE RÍO HEATH

About two hours south of the Río Madre de Dios and along the Río Heath (the latter forming the border between Peru and Bolivia), the **Parque Nacional Bahuaja-Sonene** (US$8.50) has some of the best wildlife in Peru's Amazon region, though much of it is hard to see. Infrastructure in the park, one of the nation's largest, is limited, and wildlife-watching trips have only just started up here. The Heath River Wildlife Center (see following) arranges guided tours to a nearby *colpa* (clay lick), a popular attraction for macaws and parrots (binoculars are recommended). The entrance fee into the park should be paid at Inrena (p357) in Puerto Maldonado, because the checkpoints along the way don't have tickets.

Sleeping

InkaNatura has built the simple, six-room **Heath River Wildlife Center** (contact InkaNatura www .inkanatura.com; Cuzco ☎ 084-251-173; Plateros 361; Lima ☎ 01-440-2022; Manuel Bañón 461, San Isidro; 5 days & 4 nights, with first and last night at Sandoval Lake Lodge s/d US$800/1320). The lodge is owned by the Ese'eja Indians of Sonene who provide guiding and cultural services. Trails into the new Parque Nacional Bahuaja-Sonene are available, and field biologists have assessed this area as one of the most biodiverse in southeastern Peru. Capybaras are a frequent highlight along the river.

ALONG THE RÍO TAMBOPATA

This river is a major tributary of the Río Madre de Dios, joining it at Puerto Maldonado. Boats go up the river, past several good lodges, and into the **Reserva Nacional Tambopata** (US$8.50, US$20 if visiting the Tambopata Center), an important protected area divided into the reserve itself and into **Zona de Amortiguamiento** ('buffer zone'). The entrance fee needs to be paid for at Inrena (p357) in Puerto Maldonado, unless you are on a guided tour, in which case you will pay at the lodge office.

Travelers heading up the Río Tambopata must register their passport numbers at the Puesto Control (guard post) El Torre next to the Explorer's Inn (opposite) and show their national-park entrance permits obtained in Puerto Maldonado. Visiting the reserve is quite easy if you book a guided stay at one of the lodges within the reserve. One of the highlights of the reserve is the Colpa de Guacamayos (macaw clay lick), one of the largest natural clay licks in the country. It attracts hundreds of birds and continues to be a spectacular sight (see the January 1994 *National Geographic* for a photographic story).

Sleeping

The **Posada Amazonas** (book with Rainforest Expeditions; www.perunature.com; 3 days & 2 nights s/d US$225/ 390; Cuzco ☎ /fax 084-23-2772; cusco@rainforest.com.pe; Calle El Triunfo 350; Lima ☎ 01-421-8347; postmast@ rainforest.com.pe; fax 01-421-8183; Aramburú 166, Miraflores, Lima 18; Puerto Maldonado ☎ /fax 57-1056; pdeza@rainforest.com.pe; Arequipa 401) is about two hours from Puerto Maldonado along the Río Tambopata, followed by a 10-minute uphill walk. The Posada is on the land of the Ese'eja Native Community of **Infierno**, and tribal members, as well as local *mestizos*, are among the guides. (Several other lodges use 'native' guides, but these are often *mestizos* rather than tribal members.) Harpy eagles used to nest around the community (see the July/August 1998 edition of *International Wildlife* magazine for the story of Ese'eja involvement in protecting this endangered bird), and although harpy sightings are now rare, there are excellent chances of seeing macaws and parrots on a small salt lick nearby, and giant river otters are often found swimming in lakes close to the lodge. Guides at the lodge are mainly English-speaking Peruvian naturalists with varying interests. One day you might go on a hike with a bird-watcher and the next with a botanist. Ese'eja villagers, accompanied by translators, guide ethnobotanical walks with explanations of how the products of the rainforest are used by Indian communities. A 30m-high observation platform gives views of the rainforest canopy. The lodge has 30 large double rooms with private showers and open (unglassed) windows overlooking the rainforest. Mosquito nets are provided. Rainforest Expeditions also operate the Tambopata Research Center (see p368).

Inotawa (www.inotawaexpeditions.com; 3 days & 2 nights per person US$120, extra nights per person US$35; Lima ☎ 01-467-4560; Puerto Maldonado ☎ /fax 57-2511; Fonavi J9) lies a few kilometers beyond Posada Amazonas and is a good budget option. Rates include transfers from Puerto Maldonado, meals, guided walks and boat rides. The lodge features a high roof with an unusual transparent window at the ceiling apex, allowing more light than most other lodges. Most of the 10 rooms have shared bathrooms, but there are plenty of them. A large, cool hammock room invites relaxation and the Swiss-Peruvian owners promise excellent food with a European flair.

AMAZON BASIN

German-, French- and English-speaking guides are available on advance request.

Explorer's Inn (www.peruviansafaris.com; 3 days & 2 nights s/d including meals and guided tours excluding tours to the salt lick US$195/360; Cuzco ☎ 084-23-5342, Plateros 365; Lima ☎ 01-447-8888, 447-4761; safaris@ amauta.rcp.net.pe; fax 01-241-8427; Alcanfores 459, Miraflores, Lima 18; Puerto Maldonado ☎ 57-2078; Fitzcarrald 136) is 58km from Puerto Maldonado (three to four hours of river travel) and features 15 rustic double and 15 triple rooms, all with bathroom and screened windows. The central lodge room has a restaurant, a TV room, a football table, and a small museum. It is located in the former 5500-hectare Zona Preservada Tambopata (itself now surrounded by the much larger Reserva Nacional Tambopata). Over 600 species of birds have been recorded in this preserved zone, which is a world record for bird species sighted in one area. There are similar records for other kinds of wildlife, including over 1200 butterflies. Despite these records (which are scientifically documented), the average tourist won't see much more here than anywhere else during the standard two-night visit. The 38km of trails around the lodge can be explored independently or with naturalist guides. The latter are usually British or American university students who may or may not know much about the area, depending on how long they have worked there. Most of them are enthusiastic and try hard, but a few find guiding to be an imposition on their studies. Some guides are local or from Lima. The area is more pristine than that surrounding the lodges on the Madre de Dios.

Some 10km beyond Explorer's Inn is a low-key, ecolodge/research station called **Bahuaja Lodge** (Contact Tambopata Language Center for further information), which is now being used by foreign student groups (who sleep on the floor) almost year-round. Just a few kilometers further down the river is **Sachavacas Inn** (☎ 57-3129; book through Eoindari Tours; 2 de Mayo 937, Puerto Maldonado; 3 days & 2 nights per person US$100). This place has 10 small, hot, stuffy rooms with bathrooms, and offers tours of local farms as well as wildlife watching. The comfort-level is low but the price is right for budgeteers.

Picaflor Research Center (www.picaflor.org; 74km from Puerto Maldonado) is a real find for budget travelers wanting to get into the rainforest,

and has received repeated recommendations from volunteers and researchers. Owners are Dr Laurel Hanna (a British biologist) and her boat-captain Peruvian husband, 'Pico' Maceda-Huinga. Visitors can volunteer, research or take guided tours. Volunteers work three hours daily and pay US$140 for 10 nights of food and accommodation (plus park fees and US$3 transportation from Puerto Maldonado). Researchers pay about US$20 a night and tourists pay US$190 for an all-inclusive three-day/two-night tour. The center is small (six rooms with solar lights) but replete with guidebooks and trails. The library has a power outlet for laptops. Check out their website for ongoing research projects and volunteer opportunities.

Next is **Tambopata Jungle Lodge** (☎ 084-22-5701, 084-24-5695; fax 084-23-8911; Suecia 343, Cuzco; www.tambopatalodge.com; 3 days & 2 nights, s/d US$247/422). Set mainly near secondary forest and some farms, this lodge is still within the Reserva Tambopata, and a short boat ride will get you out into primary forest. Tours to nearby lakes and to the salt lick are offered, and naturalist guides are available. There are 10km of well-marked trails, which you can wander at will without a guide. The lodge was being completely renovated at the time of research and will consist of bungalows, each with two bedrooms and private bathroom, some with hot showers and electricity. The pastel-colored walls and modern bathroom tiles look cool and inviting after a sweaty day in the rainforest.

A little further up the Tambopata, near the community of **Baltimore**, are several small *casas de hospedaje*; inquire in Puerto Maldonado about these or just show up and hope for the best (maybe bring some food). Baltimore is reached by a twice-weekly passenger boat from Puerto Maldonado, or by bus and foot. Take any vehicle from Puerto Maldonado heading to Laberinto, and ask to get off at Km37. From there, a footpath goes to Baltimore (about five hours). In Baltimore is the **Casa de Hospedaje Buenaventura** (r per person US$6-10) with seven two- and three-bed rooms, mosquito nets, two showers and an attractive octagonal communal room with river views and a few English novels to read. Food is extra. This seems the best option. Across the river, **Casa de Hospedaje El Gato** (r per person US$20), owned by the Ramirez family, has basic beds, showers at waterfalls in the river, and includes meals and walks in the forests. There are several other places but they seemed deserted when we visited.

Shortly past Baltimore is the small **Wasai Tambopata Lodge** (contact Wasai Lodge in Puerto Maldonado, see p359; 3 days/2 nights from US$265). Like all the other lodges, it can be reached by river, or you can take a truck for about an hour and hike in for about four hours (guides are provided). A macaw lick is an hour away by boat; there is a nearby jungle waterfall and numerous jungle trails. Volunteers can stay for 10 days and pay US$250; they work four hours a day. The lodge has 16 rooms with bathroom, and a three-story tower over the dining room. There are two 3km trails leading to the macaw lick.

About seven hours from Puerto Maldonado, the **Tambopata Research Center** (see Posada Amazonas p366; 6 days & 5 nights US$1560) is known for a famous salt lick nearby that attracts four to 10 species of parrots and macaws on most mornings. Research here included breeding and reintroducing macaws into the wild, and the successful project is currently being monitored for long-term results. The lodge is fairly simple, with 13 double rooms sharing four showers and four toilets, but because of the distances involved, rates are higher than the other places. If you're interested in seeing more macaws than you ever thought possible, it's worth the expense, although the owners point out that occasionally, due to poor weather or other factors, the macaws aren't found at the lick. Still, about 75% of visitors get good looks at macaw, though you shouldn't expect to get the kinds of photos in the *National Geographic* article. Travel time to the lodge varies, depending on river levels and the size of your boat motor, and a stopover is usually made at Posada Amazonas on the first and last nights. The last section of the ride is through remote country with excellent chances of seeing capybara and maybe more unusual animals. Have your passport ready at the Puesto de Control Malinowsky.

TO/FROM BRAZIL VIA PUERTO MALDONADO

An unpaved but well-maintained road goes from Puerto Maldonado to Iberia and on to Iñapari, on the Brazilian border. Along the road are small settlements of people involved in the Brazil-nut industry, some cattle-ranching and logging. After 170km, you reach **Iberia**, which has a couple of very basic hotels. The village of **Iñapari** is another 70km beyond Iberia.

Peruvian border formalities can be carried out in Iñapari if your passport is in order. Stores around the main plaza will accept and change both Peruvian and Brazilian currency; if leaving Peru, it's best to get rid of your soles here. Small denominations of US cash are often negotiable. A block north of the plaza, **Hostal Milagritos** (☎ 57-4274; s/d US$8/16) has the best rooms. From Iñapari, it is about 1km on foot to **Assis Brasil** in Brazil; the Río Acre must be waded, although a bridge is planned. It's hard to change Peruvian currency in Assis, which has better hotels; rates start at US$7 per person. There is no Brazilian immigration in Assis, and you need to travel 118km by bus on good road to **Brasiléia** (a small town with hotels on the Brazilian border with Bolivia) to get passport stamps. Neither Iñapari nor Brasiléia is set up to issue visas (US citizens need to get one in Lima). From Brasiléia, it's a further 244km by paved road to the important Brazilian city of Rio Branco.

TO/FROM BOLIVIA VIA PUERTO MALDONADO

There are two ways of reaching Bolivia from the Puerto Maldonado area. One is to go to Brasiléia in Brazil (see earlier), and cross the Río Acre by ferry or bridge to **Cobija** in Bolivia, where there are hotels and an airstrip with erratically scheduled flights further into Bolivia. There is also a gravel road to the city of **Riberalta** (12 hours in the dry season).

Alternatively, hire a boat at Puerto Maldonado's Madre de Dios dock to take you to the Peru/Bolivia border at **Puerto Pardo** (Puerto Heath is on the Bolivian side, a few minutes away from Puerto Pardo by boat). The trip takes half a day and costs about US$100 – the boat will carry several people. With time and luck, you may also be able to find a cargo boat that's going there anyway and will take passengers more cheaply.

It's possible to continue down the river on the Bolivian side, but this can take days (even weeks) to arrange and isn't cheap. Travel in a group to share costs, and avoid the dry months of July to September (when the river is too low). From Puerto Heath, continue down the Río Madre de Dios as far as **Riberalta** (at the confluence of the Madre de Dios and Beni, far into northern Bolivia), where road and air connections can be made. Basic food and shelter (bring a hammock) can be found en route. When the water is high enough, a cargo and passenger boat plies from Puerto Maldonado to Riberalta and back about twice a month, but this trip is rarely done by foreigners.

The Peruvian and Bolivian border guards can stamp you out of and in to their respective countries if your passport is in order. Visas are not available, however, so get one ahead of time if you need it. Formalities are slow and relaxed – they don't see many travelers, so be prepared to sit around for an hour, chatting about your trip.

MANU AREA

The Manu area encompasses the **Parque Nacional Manu** (see p371) and much of the surrounding area. The park covers almost 20,000 sq km (about the size of Wales) and is one of the best places in South America to see a wide variety of tropical wildlife. There is much talk of 'reserved zones' and 'park zones' etc; in 2002 most of the area simply became a national park, and the status of different zones is an ongoing bureaucratic mess. Entry to most of the park is restricted to a few Indian groups, mainly the Machiguenga, some of whom continue to live here as they have for generations; some groups have had almost no contact with outsiders and do not seem to want any. Fortunately, this wish is respected. A handful of researchers with permits are also allowed in to study the wildlife. Small sections of the park are open to guided camping and there are two lodges. A small 'multiple use zone' along parts of the river allows the establishment of lodges, farms and other interests. In addition, the areas around the park proper provide good wildlife-watching opportunities, especially near the Manu Wildlife Center (see p373), which is outside the park.

TOURS TO THE MANU AREA

It's important to check exactly where the tours are going, because Manu is a catch-all word that includes the national park and much of the surrounding area. Some tours, such as to the Manu Wildlife Center, don't actually enter the Manu park at all (although the Wildlife Center is recommended for wildlife watching, nevertheless). Some companies aren't allowed to enter the park, but offer what they call 'Manu Tours' either outside the park or act as agents for other operators. Other companies work together and share resources such as lodges, guides and transportation services. Most will combine a Manu experience with a full Peru tour on request. Confusing? You bet! The companies listed in this section were recently all authorized to operate within Manu by the national-park service and maintain some level of conservation and low-impact practices. The number of permits to operate tours into Parque Nacional Manu is limited, and allow only about 3000 visitors annually.

Tour costs depend on whether you camp or stay in a lodge, and whether you arrive/depart overland or by air. The more expensive companies offer more reliable and trained multilingual guides, better-maintained equipment, a wider variety of food and intangibles such as local experience, suitable insurance and emergency procedures. All companies provide transportation, food, purified drinking water, guides, permits and camping equipment or screens in lodge rooms. Personal items such as a sleeping bag (unless staying in a lodge), insect repellent, sunblock, flashlight with spare batteries, suitable clothing and bottled drinks are the client's responsibility. Binoculars are highly recommended.

Manu Expeditions (☎ 084-22-6671, 084-23-9974; www.manuexpeditions.com; Pardo 895, Cuzco) comes highly recommended, with over two decades of Manu experience, owners of the only tented camp within the national park, and co-owners of the Manu Wildlife Center. Their guides are excellent, experienced and highly knowledgeable, but if you are lucky enough to go with the owner, British ornithologist and long-time Cuzco resident, Barry Walker, you will really be in excellent hands, particularly if birding is your main interest. (Barry was featured in Michael Plain's *Full Circle* travel series on the BBC.) The most popular trip leaves Cuzco every Sunday (except January, February and March when it's the first Sunday of month only) and lasts nine days, including overland transportation to Manu with two nights of camping, three nights at Manu Wildlife Center, three nights at other lodges and a flight back to Cuzco. This costs US$1595. The overland section can include a mountain-biking descent if arranged in advance. Shorter, longer and customized trips are offered.

Manu Nature Tours (☎ 084-25-2721; www.manuperu .com; Pardo 1046, Cuzco) operates the respected Manu Lodge, which is open year-round. The lodge has 12 double rooms (bathrooms are planned) and a dining room/bar next to a lake, which is home to a breeding family of giant otters. A 20km trail network, and guided visits to lakes and observation towers are also provided. A five-day tour, flying in or out, is US$1650 per person, double occupancy, with fixed departures every Friday. The trip has a bilingual naturalist guide and all meals are provided. For an extra fee, mountain-biking or river running (whitewater rafting) can be incorporated into the road descent. Longer tours are available. This company also has departures to its Manu Cloud Forest Lodge (opposite).

Pantiacolla Tours (☎ 084-23-8323; www.pantiacolla .com; Plateros 360, Cuzco) is often recommended by budget travelers. Pantiacolla Tours' owners were raised in the area and are knowledgeable; they offer a variety of tours including the opportunity to study Spanish at their jungle lodge. Trips start at US$750 per person for five days, flying out, or US$800 per person for nine days, all overland, and include a mixture of camping and lodge accommodations. More expensive options are available. The company also works with local Indian groups in their Yine Project as outlined in their website.

InkaNatura (www.inkanatura.com; Cuzco ☎ 084-25-1173; Plateros 361; Lima ☎ 01-440-2022; Manuel Bañon 461, San Isidro; in USA Tropical Nature Travel ☎ 1-877-888-1770, 1-352-376-3377; POB 5276, Gainesville FL32627-5276) is a highly respected international agency is co-owner of Manu Wildlife Center, and can combine a visit here with visits to other parts of the southeastern Peruvian rainforest, including the Puerto Maldonado area and the Pongo de Manique area (see p219), where it has a lodge.

Manu Ecological Adventures (☎ 084-26-1640; www.manuadventures.com; Plateros 356, Cuzco) has camping trips using tents on the beaches

of the national park; an eight-day trip costs US$610 per person. There are bilingual guides, and all gear and bus transportation is provided.

Expediciones Vilca (☎ 084-24-4751; manuvilca .terra.com.pe; Plateros 363, Cuzco) is a company that offers rather a mish-mash of inexpensive camping and pricier lodge tours. It has been around for years but seems to lack a sense of direction and will book anything they can at any price.

FROM CUZCO TO MANU

This journey provides opportunities for some excellent **bird-watching** opportunites at the lodges en route.

If traveling overland, the first stage of the journey involves taking a bus or truck from Cuzco via Paucartambo (see p220 in the Cuzco chapter) to **Shintuya** (p371). Buses run by Gallito de las Rocas leave from Cuzco's Avenida Angamos at 10am for Pilcopata (US$6, 12 hours in good weather) along the one-way road on Monday, Wednesday and Friday. Cheaper trucks leave the same days and possibly Sunday from the Coliseo Cerrado in Cuzco. In the dry season they take about 24 hours to reach Shintuya. Breakdowns, flat tires, extreme overcrowding and delays are common, and during the rainy season (and even during the dry) vehicles slide off the road. It's safer, more comfortable and more reliable to take the costlier tourist buses (which are basically heavy-duty trucks) offered by Cuzco tour operators. Many tour companies in Cuzco offer trips to Manu (see p369).

Sleeping

There are two lodges between Paucartambo and Pilcopata. **Cock-of-the-Rock Lodge** (contact Inka Natura www.inkanatura.com; Cuzco ☎ 084-251-173; Plateros 361; Lima ☎ 01-440-2022; Manuel Bañon 461, San Isidro; 3 days & 2 nights d US$900) is just a few minutes' walk from a *lek* (mating ground) for cocks-of-the-rock (brightly colored rainforest birds that live on rock cliffs and outcrops; they conduct elaborate communal mating 'dances'). This lodge offers exceptional cloud-forest **birding** at a pleasant 1600m elevation. The owners claim you can get photos of male cocks-of-the-rock displaying about 7m from your camera. The lodge has a restaurant and 10 rustic double cabins with hot showers. Normally, visitors overnight here en route to Manu, but the lodge can be used as a destination in itself for cloud-forest birding. Rates include meals and round-trip transportation from Cuzco, which can take six to 10 hours. Discounts are available for longer stays and larger groups.

Nearby, **Manu Cloud Forest Lodge** (☎ 084-25-2721; www.manuperu.com; Pardo 1046, Cuzco; including meals d US$196) is near the same stretch of road. The lodge provides six rooms with hot showers, a restaurant, a sauna (US$10) and birding opportunities in the high cloud forest. Transportation is extra. Nearby, is the **Manu Cloud Forest Tented Camp** (☎ 084-25-2721; www.manuperu.com; Pardo 1046, Cuzco; d US$76). Five large tents on platforms sleep two people each (bedding, showers, toilets and meals provided).

The truck trip to these lodges is often broken at **Pilcopata**, which is the biggest village along the road and is currently the end of the public bus route. There are a couple of basic hotels and a few stores in town. A bed costs about US$5, or floor/hammock space is US$2.50. Pickup trucks leave early every morning for Atalaya and Shintuya (US$3, about five hours).

About 40km before Shintuya is the village of Atalaya (not to be confused with the village of the same name on the Río Ucayali, see p377) on the Río Alto Madre de Dios. Across the river is the very pleasant **Amazonia Lodge** (☎ /fax 084-23-1370; www.amazonialodge.com; Matará 334, Cuzco; r per person US$60), in an old hacienda in the foothills of the Andes. The lodge offers clean, comfortable beds and communal hot showers; simple but satisfactory meals are also included. There is no electricity, but that is more than compensated for by the low number of mosquitoes. There are trails into the forest, and the birding is excellent. Birders could profitably spend a few days here in relative comfort, or fully guided birding tours are offered. The lodge can make transportation arrangements on request, or the tour agencies in Cuzco can make reservations. From Atalaya, boats leave for **Erika Lodge** (contact Ernesto Yallico ☎ 084-22-7765; Casilla 560, Cuzco; r per person US$40). Within a private reserve on the banks of the Alto Madre de Dios, this lodge provides simple accommodations and meals, and camping is allowed.

The village of **Salvación**, about 10km closer to Shintuya, has a national park office and

a couple of basic hotels. Ask here for boats continuing down the river but note that park entry is restricted to tour groups and there are very few other boats available.

Shintuya is the end of the road at this time and is the closest village to the park, but it has only a few places to stay. You may be able to camp at the mission station by talking to the priest.

The Ecuadorian-Dutch Moscoso family lives 30 minutes downriver from Shintuya and operates **Pantiacolla Lodge** (contact Pantiacolla Tours ☎ 084-23-8323; www.pantiacolla.com; Plateros 360, Cuzco; r per person US$55). There are 14 double rooms with shared bathrooms here. Rates include meals but not transportation or tours, though you can hike on the forest trails nearby. Various transportation and guided tour options are available starting at US$750 per person for five days. The lodge is on the fringe of the national park, and good wildlife sightings have been reported.

Boats can travel from Pilcopata, Atalaya, Salvación or Shintuya toward Manu. People on tours often start river travel from Atalaya after a night in a lodge. The boat journey down the Alto Madre de Dios to the Río Manu takes almost a day, depending on how fast the boat is. At the junction is the village of **Boca Manu**, with simple stores and bars. This village is known for building the best river boats in the area, and it is interesting to see them in various stages of construction. There is an inexpensive lodge here, but reservations are hard to make – just show up and hope for the best. A few minutes from the village is the Boca Manu airstrip, often the starting or exit point for commercial trips into the park. **Trans Andes** (☎ 084-22-4638; Cuzco airport) and **Malu Servicios Aereos** (☎ 084-24-2104; Cuzco airport) fly small aircraft here most days for US$120. Most seats are taken up with tour groups, but empty seats are often available. A US$10 airport fee is charged.

PARQUE NACIONAL MANU

The great biodiversity of this national park is due to it starting in the eastern slopes of the Andes and plunging down into the lowlands, thus covering a wide range of cloud forest and rainforest habitats. The most progressive aspect of the park is the fact that so much of it is very carefully protected – a rarity anywhere in the world.

AMAZON BASIN

After Peru introduced protection laws in 1973, Unesco declared Manu a Biosphere Reserve in 1977 and a World Natural Heritage Site in 1987. One reason the park is so successful in preserving such a large tract of virgin jungle and its wildlife is that it is remote and relatively inaccessible to people, and therefore has not been exploited by rubber tappers, loggers, oil companies or hunters.

It is illegal to enter the park without a guide. Going with an organized group can be arranged in Cuzco (see p180) or with international tour operators. It's an expensive trip; budget travelers should arrange their trip in Cuzco and be very flexible with travel plans. Travelers often report returning from Manu three or four days late. Don't plan an international airline connection the day after a Manu trip!

Permits, which are necessary to enter the park, are arranged by tour agencies. Transportation, accommodations, food and guides are also part of tour packages. Most visits are for a week, although three-night stays at a lodge can be arranged.

The best time to go is during the dry season (June to November); Manu may be inaccessible or closed during the rainy months (January to April), except to visitors staying at the two lodges within the park boundaries (see later).

Virgin jungle lies up the Río Manu northwest of Boca Manu. At the Puesto Control Limonal (guardpost), about an hour from Boca Manu, you pay a park entrance fee of US$20 per person. Continuing beyond is only possible with a guide and permit. Near Limonal are a few trails.

Six hours upstream is **Cocha Salvador**, one of the park's largest and most beautiful lakes, where there are guided camping and hiking possibilities. With patience, wildlife is seen in most areas. This is not a wide-open habitat as is the African plains. The

thick vegetation will obscure many animals, and a skilled guide is very useful in helping you to see them.

During a one-week trip, you can reasonably expect to see scores of different bird species, several monkey species and possibly a few other mammals. Jaguars, tapirs, giant anteaters, tamanduas, capybaras, peccaries and giant river otters are among the common large mammals of Manu. But they are elusive, and you can consider a trip very successful if you see two or three large mammals during a week's visit. Smaller mammals you might see include kinkajous, pacas, agoutis, squirrels, brocket deer, ocelots and armadillos. Other animals include river turtles and caiman (which are frequently seen), snakes (which are less often spotted) and a variety of other reptiles and amphibians. Colorful butterflies and less-pleasing insects also abound.

Sleeping

There are two lodges within the park, however some tour operators include camping options.

Manu Lodge (contact Manu Nature Tours ☎ 084-25-2721; www.manuperu.com; Pardo 1046, Cuzco) A row of 14 simple double rooms are screened and have comfortable beds; a separate building has cold showers and toilets. The lodge is on Cocha Juarez, a 2km-long oxbow lake, and is about 1km from the Río Manu; a breeding family of giant river otters is often encountered. For an extra fee, a climb up to a canopy platform or river running can be arranged. A 20km network of trails from the lodge around the lake and beyond provides ample opportunities for spotting monkeys and birds.

Cocha Salvador Safari Camp (contact Manu Expeditions ☎ 084-22-6671, 084-23-9974; www.manu expeditions.com; Pardo 895, Cuzco) Beyond Manu Lodge, this camp has raised platforms supporting large walk-in screened tents containing cots and bedding. Modern showers, toilets and meals are available. Manu Expeditions occasionally use the more rustic Casa Machiguenga Lodge, which was built in traditional style by Machiguenga Indians in 1998.

More primitive camping, usually on the sandy beaches of the Río Manu or on the foreshore of a few of the lakes, is another possibility. Tour operators can provide all

---

FULL BINOCULARS!

During a recent stop at the Limonal guard post, author Rob saw a Muscovy duck, green ibis, rufescent tiger-heron and white-winged swallow all at the same time in a single binocular field – ie without moving the binoculars.

necessary equipment. During the rainy season (January to April), these beaches are flooded and the park is closed to camping. Campers should come prepared with plenty of insect repellent.

Manu Wildlife Center & Around

A two-hour boat ride southeast of Boca Manu on the Río Madre de Dios takes you to **Manu Wildlife Center** (s/d 5 days/4 nights US$1250/ 2100). The center is a jungle lodge jointly owned by Manu Expeditions and InkaNatura, both of which accept reservations (see p181). Although the lodge is not in Manu Biosphere Reserve, it is recommended for its exceptional wildlife-watching and birding opportunities. There are 22 screened double cabins with hot showers, a dining room and a bar/hammock room. The lodge is set in tropical gardens.

There are 48km of trails around the wildlife center, where 12 species of monkeys, as well as other wildlife, can be seen. Two canopy platforms are a short walk away, and one is always available for guests wishing to view the top of the rainforest and look for birds that frequent the canopy.

A 3km walk through the forest brings you to a natural salt lick, where there is a raised platform with mosquito nets for viewing the nightly activities of the tapirs. This hike is for visitors who can negotiate forest trails by flashlight. Visitors may wait for hours to see the animals. Nothing is guaranteed, but the chances are excellent if you have the patience. Note that there isn't much happening at the lick during the day.

A short boat ride along the Madre de Dios brings visitors to another well-known salt lick that attracts various species of parrots and macaws. Most mornings you can see flocks in the hundreds. The largest flocks are seen from late July to September. As the rainy season kicks in, the numbers diminish, though there are usually some birds all year except June when birds don't visit the salt lick at all. May and early July aren't reliable either, though ornithologists report the presence of the birds in other nearby areas during these months, and birders will usually see them.

The macaw lick is visited on a floating catamaran blind, with the blind providing a concealed enclosure from which 20 people can view the wildlife. The catamaran is stable enough to be able to use a tripod and scope or telephoto lens, and gets about halfway across the river. The boat drivers are experienced and won't bring the blind too close to disturb the birds.

In addition to the trails and salt licks, there are a couple of nearby lakes where paddled catamarans provide transportation and giant otters may be seen (as well as various birds and other animals). Visitors wishing to see the macaw and tapir lick, lakes and canopy, and to hike the trails in search of wildlife should plan on a three-night stay at the Manu Wildlife Center, though shorter and longer stays are workable.

Near the Manu Wildlife Center, the rustic Blanquillo Lodge has rooms with shared bathrooms. Some companies in Cuzco combine this cheaper option with a tour including other lodges in the Manu area, but prices vary. Staying at just Blanquillo itself isn't offered.

If you continue down the Madre de Dios, past gold-panning areas to Puerto Maldonado, you won't see much wildlife. This takes 14 hours to two days and may cost as little as US$10 if you can find a boat heading that way. But transportation to Puerto Maldonado is infrequent, and almost all visitors return to Cuzco.

CENTRAL AMAZON

The region of Chanchamayo has the most accessible jungle area east of Lima. It comprises the neighboring towns of La Merced and San Ramón. Chanchamayo and the surrounding jungle regions are popularly called La Selva Central. The area is noted for coffee and fruit production.

LA MERCED & SAN RAMÓN

☎ 064 / pop 40,000 / elevation 800m

San Ramón is 295km east of Lima and La Merced is 11km further along. All buses terminate in La Merced, the more important of the two towns and the center for ground transportation in the region, including the surrounding jungle areas. La Merced has a greater choice of hotels and restaurants, though the quieter San Ramón boasts the regional airstrip nearby.

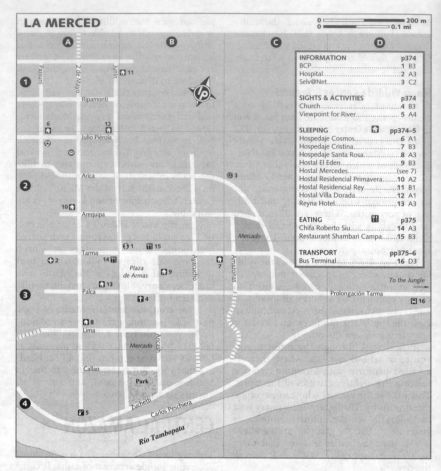

LA MERCED

INFORMATION	p374
BCP...1	B3
Hospital..2	A3
Selv@Net..3	C2

SIGHTS & ACTIVITIES	p374
Church...4	B3
Viewpoint for River.....................5	A4

SLEEPING	pp374–5
Hospedaje Cosmos.......................6	A1
Hospedaje Cristina.......................7	B3
Hospedaje Santa Rosa.................8	A3
Hostal El Eden...............................9	B3
Hostal Mercedes.....................(see 7)	
Hostal Residencial Primavera...10	A2
Hostal Residencial Rey..............11	B1
Hostal Villa Dorada....................12	A1
Reyna Hotel..................................13	A3

EATING	p375
Chifa Roberto Siu......................14	A3
Restaurant Shambari Campa......15	B3

TRANSPORT	pp375–6
Bus Terminal...............................16	D3

Information

Both towns have a BCP with an ATM, and plenty of public telephones. La Merced has a **post office** (2 de Mayo), Internet access at **Selv@Net** (☎ 53-1760; Arica 307) and a small **hospital** (☎ 53-1002, 53-1408). La Merced's police station is on Julio Piérola at Passuni.

Sights & Activities

There is a colorful daily **market** in La Merced. A weekend **market** at San Luis de Shuaro, 22km beyond La Merced, is also interesting – local Indians visit it. Ashaninka Indians occasionally come into La Merced to sell handicrafts.

Avenida 2 de Mayo is good for **views** of La Merced; the stairs at the northwest end

afford a good view of the town, and from the balcony at the southeast end there's a photogenic river view.

An interesting **botanical garden** is on the grounds of El Refugio Hotel (see p375) in San Ramón.

Sleeping

LA MERCED

Hospedaje Santa Rosa (☎ 53-1012; 2 de Mayo 447; s/d US$3/5, s/d with shower US$5/7) The cleanest of the cheapest hotels, the Santa Rosa boasts light rooms with large windows but cold shower.

Hostal Residencial Primavera (☎/fax 53-1433; Arequipa 175; s or d with cold/hot shower US$7/9) Singles cost the same as doubles at this bright, tidy but bland hostel. Rooms have a fan and cable TV.

Hospedaje Cosmos (☎ 53-1051; Julio Piérola at Passuni; s/d US$9/11.50) A large lobby with eclectic furniture invites hanging out. The rooms are somewhat spartan with cold showers, but certainly clean.

Hospedaje Cristina (☎ 53-1276; Tarma 582; s/d US$7.50/10.50; **P**) Good-sized rooms feature cable TV and decent mattresses, but the decor is plain and the cold-shower bathrooms cramped.

Hostal Residencial Rey (☎ 53-1185; Junín 103; s/d US$13/16) Bright, inviting hallways decorated with flowers and pictures lead to attractive rooms with fan, cable TV and hot shower complete with towels and soap. A restaurant on the top floor serves good breakfasts; it plans to serve other meals in future. Climb up for a view of the town.

Reyna Hotel (☎ /fax 53-1780, 53-2196; rchareyna@ hotmail.com; Palca 259; s/d US$15/17.50; **P**) It's a new, modern and brightly tiled hotel with a sparkling cafeteria. Rooms feature direct-dial phone, fan, cable TV, excellent beds and hot shower.

Other choices include:

Hostal Villa Dorada (☎ 53-1221; Julio Piérola 265; s/d US$3/6, s/d with bath US$6/8) Large rooms but small, cold showers.

Hostal Mercedes (☎ /fax 53-1304; Tarma 576; s/d US$10/13; **P**) Rooms seem charmless but the hot showers and TVs make up for that.

Hostal El Eden (☎ 53-1183, 53-2340; Ancash 347; US$12/23) You pay for the plaza location; rooms are OK with TV, fan and cold shower.

SAN RAMÓN
El Refugio Hotel (☎ /fax 33-1082; Ejército 490; s/d US$23/29; **P** 🛏) About a 10-minute walk from the town center, this hotel features grounds containing a small, well-designed botanical garden. The various exotic plants are labeled and tend to attract butterflies and birds. The rooms are comfortable bungalows with hot shower, fan and TV; rates include breakfast.

Hospedaje Chanchamayo (☎ 33-1008; Progreso 291; s/d US$3/6, s/d with shower US$6/9) A good budget choice, this hotel has hot water and TV in the rooms.

Hotel Conquistador (☎ /fax 33-1157; Progreso 298; s/d US$7.50/12; **P**) This modern hotel with motel-like rooms complete with TV and hot shower doubles its rates when busy.

Hospedaje El Parral (☎ 33-1128, ☎ /fax 33-1536; Uriarte 355; s/d US$12/15) This modern hotel has a locally popular restaurant serving jungle specialties. Rooms are simple but comfortable with hot shower, fan and cable TV.

Eating
LA MERCED
Restaurant Shambari Campa (☎ 53-1138, 53-1153; menú US$3, mains US$3-5; ☽ 6:30am-12:30am) On the plaza, this famous, graffiti- and photo-covered hole-in-the-wall restaurant has been serving good local food for decades. The menu, including the set lunches, is extensive, but service can be slow and unenthusiastic.

Chifa Roberto Siu (☎ 53-1207; Junín 310; mains US$3-4.50; ☽ 11am-2pm & 6-11pm) Also on the plaza, this is the best *chifa* in town.

Also consider any one of many chicken restaurants on Ayacucho at Tarma, where a quarter-chicken with fries will set you back US$1.30. The *mercado* at Tarma and Amazonas has plenty of stalls selling juice and cake – for travel-hardened stomachs.

SAN RAMÓN
Chifa Felipe Siu (☎ 33-1078; Progreso 440; ☽ 11am-2pm, 6:30-11pm) is good, and the hotel restaurants are worth a visit.

Getting There & Away
AIR
The Chanchamayo airstrip is a 30-minute walk from San Ramón. Colectivos and taxis go there.

Air service is provided by local companies with light aircraft. There are daily flights to Puerto Bermúdez. For other destinations, go to the airport early in the morning and ask around for a flight. Planes carry five to nine passengers and leave when they are full. Planes can be chartered to almost anywhere in the region.

BUS
The bus terminal is a 1km downhill walk east of the center of La Merced. Most buses arrive/leave from here. Schedules are haphazard – go down there as early as you can and ask around.

Direct buses go from Lima to Chanchamayo, though some travelers find it convenient to break the journey at Tarma. It is worth trying to travel the 70km stretch from Tarma to San Ramón in daylight for the views during the 2200m descent. Companies going to Lima (US$7, eight hours) include **Transportes Chanchamayo** (☎ 53-1259, 53-2051), considered the most reliable, **Expreso Satipo**, **Transportes Lobato** and others. There are several daily departures. **Empresa de Transportes San Juan** (☎ 53-1522) charges US$4 for the five-hour journey to Huancayo (with stops at Tarma and Jauja). Frequent buses (various companies) go to Tarma (US$2, 2½ hours).

Most transportation into the jungle is by large minibus. The minibuses leave for Pichanaqui (US$1.50, one hour) about every half hour. Change at Pichanaqui for another minibus to Satipo. **Empresa Santa Rosa** (☎ 53-1084) has frequent minibuses to Oxapampa (US$3, three hours), with a few continuing to Pozuzo (US$5, six to seven hours). For Puerto Bermúdez (US$9, seven to 12 hours), **Empresa Fisel** and **Transdife** leave at 4am; these are trucks with seats in the cabin. The journey depends on weather and road conditions.

Colectivo taxis seating four passengers go to Tarma (US$3) and Pichanaqui (US$2.25). Ask at the terminal.

Getting Around

Minibuses link La Merced with San Ramón every few minutes (US$0.25; 15 minutes), leaving from outside the bus terminal. Mototaxis charge US$0.30 to drive you from the terminal up into La Merced center.

PICHANAQUI

☎ 064 / pop 25,000 / elevation 500m

Almost 70km east of La Merced on the newly paved road to Satipo, Pichanaqui is a fast-growing center for coffee production. Sitting on the Río Perené, the town attracts some local tourism during the April to August dry months when water levels drop and sandy beaches are revealed. **Playa El Pescador** is a favorite beach, with several restaurants serving mainly fish. **El Bambú** (☎ 34-7047) and **El Parralito** (☎ 34-7655) are locally recommended. Hotels are popping up almost overnight in this booming town; try **Hospedaje Brice's** (☎ 34-7745; 7 de Junio 375; d US$6-9; **P**), which has a private shower and fan, plus cable TV in the better rooms.

Frequent minibuses from Pichanaqui run to Satipo (US$1.25, 45 minutes).

SATIPO

☎ 064 / pop 25,000 / elevation 630m

This jungle town is the center of a coffee- and fruit-producing region and lies about 130km by road southeast of La Merced. This road was paved in 2000 to provide an outlet for produce, and as a result Satipo is growing quickly. It is also linked by a poor road to the highlands of Huancayo. There is a BCP (ATM) and an Internet café which was temporarily off-line at the time of writing.

Sleeping

Hotel Majestic (☎ /fax 54-5762; Colonos Fundadores Principal 408; s/d US$10/15; **P**) On the Central Plaza, this is a simple but clean choice with private cold showers and cable TV.

Hostal Palermo (☎ 54-5020, 54-5543; Manuel Prado 229; s US$4.50-7.50; d US$7.50-11.50; **P**) Half a block from the plaza, this place has varied rooms at varied rates. The best ones have private cold shower, fan and cable TV, while the cheapest have communal showers and no TV. A restaurant is attached.

Hostal San José (☎ 54-5105, 54-5990; AB Leguía 684; s/d US$9/13; **P**) Modern, clean and the best in town, this hostel has cool tiled floors, hot water and cable TV.

There are several other cheap and more basic hotels.

Getting There & Away

AIR

The nearby airport has light aircraft for charter. Flights to Pucallpa and other jungle towns leave irregularly, when there are enough passengers.

BUS

Minibuses leave many times a day for Pichanaqui, where you can change for La Merced. A few slower, larger buses leave every morning and evening for La Merced, some continuing on to Lima. **Selva Tours** (☎ 54-5631; Manuel Prado 455) has several daily buses to Huancayo (US$5, 10 hours) via the spectacular but difficult direct road through Comas.

EAST OF SATIPO

It's possible to continue east into the jungle. A fairly good unpaved road goes through **Mazamari**, 20km away, where there's the clean **Hospedaje Divina Montaña** (☎ 54-8042). It offers hot showers, a sauna and a popular restaurant serving jungle and game dishes. Another 40km futher and you'll come to **Puerto Ocopa**, reached by colectivo from Satipo in a couple of hours. Beyond Puerto Ocopa, a rough road continues to **Atalaya** at the intersection of the Ríos Urubamba, Tambo and Ucayali. The road may be impassable, in which case boats go down the Río Tambo to Atalaya, taking a full day.

In Atalaya, there are simple hotels and an airstrip with connections to Satipo. Boats can be found to Pucallpa every few days (US$14, one to three days). Atalaya is two or three days away by boat from Sepahua (see p219) to the east, though there are few boats.

OXAPAMPA

☎ 063 / pop 10,000 / elevation 1800m

This is a ranching and coffee center, 75km north of La Merced. Look around at your fellow passengers on the bus north from La Merced – occasional blond heads and blue eyes attest to the several hundred German settlers who arrived in the mid-19th century. Their descendants inhabit Oxapampa or smaller, lower **Pozuzo** (three to four hours north of Oxapampa by daily minibus; longer in the wet season), and have preserved many Germanic customs. Buildings have a Tyrolean look to them, Austrian-German food is prepared and an old-fashioned form of German is still spoken by some families. Although the area has been long settled, it is remote and rarely visited. The people are friendly and interested in talking with tourists.

Oxapampa has a BCP and several simple and cheap hotels. The cold-water hostels **Rocio** (☎ 76-2163), **Santa Isolina** (☎ 76-2305/6), Arias and Liz have been recommended as clean and charge about US$3 to US$6 per person. Pozuzo also has several hotels, of which El Tirol is the best at about US$10 per person including meals.

PUERTO BERMÚDEZ

☎ 063 / pop 1000 / elevation 500m

Looking at the huddle of dugout canoes tied up to the mud bank of the little Río Pachitea flowing past sleepy Puerto Bermúdez, it is difficult to imagine that one can embark here on a river journey that would eventually lead down the Amazon to the Atlantic.

The area southeast of Puerto Bermúdez is the home of the Ashaninka Indians, the largest Amazon Indian group in Peru. In the late 1980s and early '90s, Sendero Luminoso guerrillas attempted to indoctrinate the Ashaninka. When the guerrillas were unable to get the Indians' total support, they tried intimidation by massacring dozens. Thankfully, Sendero activity has been reduced since the capture of the guerrilla leaders. People interested in learning more about the Ashaninka can get information in Puerto Bermúdez. Contact Albergue Humboldt (see following) if you want to visit the Ashaninka.

Sleeping & Eating

Albergue Humboldt (☎ 72-0267; www.geocities.com/ puerto_bermudez; r US$4) Located near the river, this is the best place to stay in the region. You can enjoy rustic rooms with shared cold showers and electricity from 6pm to 11:30pm, or sleep in a hammock, or camp. Three meals, plus drinking water, tea and coffee, are US$5 a day. The friendly and hospitable owner will arrange all manner of trekking, wildlife and cultural expeditions into Ashaninka territory for US$18 to US$30 per person per day, depending on group size and including food, boat and accommodation in simple shelters. Highly recommended for budget adventurers!

Hostal Tania (r per person US$3) This is another basic hotel right by the river; it offers four walls and a river view. The river view is pretty, especially at dawn and dusk.

The town's main street has a few simple eateries.

Getting There & Away

Trucks carrying passengers go to La Merced daily. Continuing north the road deteriorates, and erratic transportation to **Ciudad Constitución**, **Zungaro**, **Puerto Inca** and Pucallpa is often by truck. This trip is very rough and can take two days. Boats go north to Ciudad Constitución and Puerto Inca, but do not have particular schedules. During the dry season, the river may be too low for passage, and the road is the better bet. During the wet months, the road can be badly passable, and boats are better. You can also fly from the airstrip near Puerto Bermúdez. The folks at Albergue Humboldt know what's going on.

PUCALLPA

☎ 061 / pop 222,000 / elevation 154m

The capital of the Department of Ucayali, Pucallpa is Peru's fastest-growing jungle town and the biggest to be linked directly with Lima by road. Apart from a few contemporary banks and hotels, and a modern Plaza de Armas with a new city hall, many buildings have been hastily constructed in concrete with tin roofs. Its roads are slowly being paved, but those away from the town center are still red mud quagmires in the wet season and choking red dust in the dry. Sidewalks are incredibly uneven; watch your step! Huge flocks of vultures circling lazily over the markets, plazas and docks are one

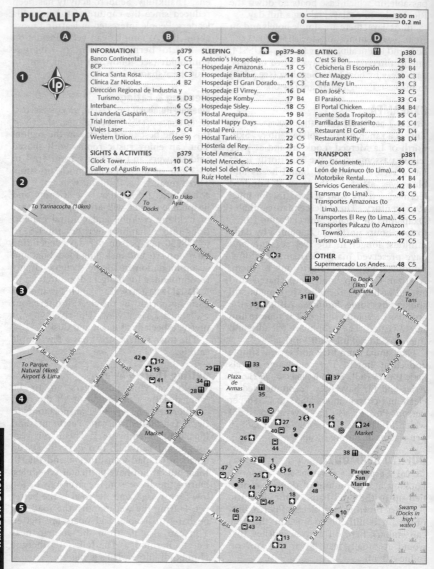

PUCALLPA

0 ——— 300 m
0 ——— 0.2 mi

INFORMATION	p379
Banco Continental	1 C5
BCP	2 C4
Clínica Santa Rosa	3 C3
Clínica Zar Nicolas	4 B2
Dirección Regional de Industria y Turismo	5 D3
Interbanc	6 C5
Lavandería Gasparin	7 C5
Trial Internet	8 D4
Viajes Laser	9 C4
Western Union	(see 9)

SIGHTS & ACTIVITIES	p379
Clock Tower	10 D5
Gallery of Agustín Rivas	11 C4

SLEEPING	🛏 pp379–80
Antonio's Hospedaje	12 B4
Hospedaje Amazonas	13 C5
Hospedaje Barbtur	14 C5
Hospedaje El Gran Dorado	15 C3
Hospedaje El Virrey	16 D4
Hospedaje Komby	17 B4
Hospedaje Sisley	18 C5
Hostal Arequipa	19 B4
Hostal Happy Days	20 C4
Hostal Perú	21 C5
Hostal Tariri	22 C5
Hostería del Rey	23 C5
Hotel America	24 D4
Hotel Mercedes	25 C5
Hotel Sol del Oriente	26 C4
Ruíz Hotel	27 C4

EATING	🍴 p380
C'est Si Bon	28 B4
Cebichería El Escorpión	29 B4
Chez Maggy	30 C3
Chifa Mey Lin	31 C3
Don José's	32 C4
El Paraíso	33 C4
El Portal Chicken	34 B4
Fuente Soda Tropitop	35 C4
Parrilladas El Braserito	36 C4
Restaurant El Golf	37 D4
Restaurant Kitty	38 D4

TRANSPORT	p381
Aero Continente	39 C5
León de Huánuco (to Lima)	40 C4
Motorbike Rental	41 B4
Servicios Generales	42 B4
Transmar (to Lima)	43 C5
Transportes Amazonas (to Lima)	44 C4
Transportes El Rey (to Lima)	45 C5
Transportes Palcazu (to Amazon Towns)	46 C5
Turismo Ucayali	47 C5

OTHER	
Supermercado Los Andes	48 C5

To Yarinacocha (10km)

To Usko Ayar
To Docks

Inmaculada
Atahualpa
Tarapaca
Huáscar
Carmen Cabrejos
A Morey
Bolívar
Saenz Peña
7 de Junio
Zavalo
Tacna
Salaverry
Ucayali
Progreso
Libertad
Independencia
Sucre
San Martín
Raimondi
A Vargas
Portillo
9 de Diciembre
Tacna
Aríca
2 de Mayo
M Castilla
M Cáceres

To Parque Natural (4km), Airport & Lima

Plaza de Armas

To Docks (3km) & Capitania

To Tans

Parque San Martín

Swamp (Docks in high water)

Market

AMAZON BASIN

of Pucallpa's most startling sights. Although the town seems grubby and noisy, locals take pride in Pucallpa's progress and growth.

Information

The **Dirección Regional de Industria y Turismo** (☎ 57-1303; 2 de Mayo 111) has limited tourist information. **Trial Internet** (Portillo 398; ☼ 8am-11pm) has fast machines.

Lavandería Gasparin (☎ 59-1147; Portillo 526; ☼ 9am-1pm & 4-8pm Mon-Sat) provides both self-service and drop-off laundry services.

The **Clínica Santa Rosa** (☎ 57-1689; Inmaculada 529; ☼ 24 hr) is quite good for stool, urine or blood tests. **Clínica Zar Nicolas** (☎ 57-2854; Saenz Peña 166) is also good.

Several banks change money and traveler's checks and have ATMs. Foreign-exchange houses are found along the 4th, 5th and 6th blocks of Raimondi. Western Union is at **Viajes Laser** (☎ 57-1120; fax 57-3776; Raimondi 470), which is one of the better travel agencies in Pucallpa, but for jungle guides go to Yarinacocha.

Sights & Activities

Many visit nearby Yarinacocha (see p382), which, although it is more interesting than Pucallpa, is far from touristy.

About 4km from the center of Pucallpa, off the road to the airport, is **Parque Natural** (US$0.70; ☼ 9am-5pm). Here, you'll find an Amazon zoo, a museum displaying Shipibo pottery and a few other objects, a small children's playground and a snack bar. Buses heading to the airport can drop you here, or a *motocarro* is about US$1.

Usko Ayar (☎ 57-3088; Sánchez Cerro 465) is the gallery of the visionary local artist Pablo Amaringo, whose work and biography can be accessed at www.egallery.com/pablo .html. Other promising Amazonian artists study, work and display here – it's well worth a visit. Tell drivers it's near the Iglesia Fray Marcos.

Agustín Rivas (☎ 57-1834; Tarapaca 861, 2nd fl) is a famed local woodcarver whose work graces the lobbies of some of Pucallpa's best hotels and businesses. Ring the bell to enter his house/gallery.

Sleeping

BUDGET

Hostería del Rey (☎ 57-5815; Portillo 747; s/d US$5/6) High ceilings indicate this hotel was built

---

> **PRONOUNCING PUCALLPA**
>
> One hint: just as you've become used to remembering that 'll' is always pronounced 'y' in Spanish, you arrive at one of the very few exceptions to this rule; Pucallpa is pronounced 'pu-*kal*-pa'.

---

for the tropics – hot air rises. Cold showers and fans keep you cool, and a TV can be added for US$1.50.

Hospedaje Sisley (☎ 57-5137; Portillo 658, upstairs; s/d US$8.50/12) Friendly older ladies run this decent budget hotel. Tidy rooms include private cold shower, fan and TV.

Hospedaje Barbtur (☎ 57-2532; Raimondi 670; s/d US$4/5.50, s/d with shower US$7.25/10) Small, friendly, well maintained and family run, this hotel has cold showers and includes cable TV in its en-suite rooms.

Hostal Perú (☎ 57-5128; Raimondi 639; s/d US$4.25/5.50, s/d with shower US$5.50/7.25 or US$9/11.50) A Shipibo pot collection brightens the faded entry stairs of this large, older property. Rooms are tiny but clean with small fan. The more expensive rooms have been refurbished. Showers are cold and TVs are an extra US$1.50.

Also consider:

Hospedaje Amazonas (☎ 57-1080; Portillo 729; s/d US$4.50/6) Basic, dingy rooms have a cold shower and fan, and the price is right.

Hostal Tariri (☎ 57-5147; Raimondi 733; s US$4.50-6, d US$6-9) Rooms with cold shower vary substantially in size and quality.

MID-RANGE

All the following have rooms with bathroom, fan and cable TV.

Hospedaje Komby (☎ 57-1562; fax 59-2074; Ucayali 360; s/d US$10/13; ☼) Rooms are clean but basic, though the small pool and restaurant make up for that.

Hostal Happy Days (☎ 57-2067; fax 57-3263; Huáscar 440; s US$10-17.25, d US$13-20; ☼) Rooms are tiny but on a quiet side street; continental breakfast is included.

Hospedaje El Gran Dorado (☎ /fax 57-4592; Independencia 204; s/d US$11.50/17.30) The electric-blue tiled reception and hallways ooze hygiene. Rooms are smallish but spotless and have a minifridge. Rates include a continental breakfast daily except Sunday. Discounts are readily available for longer stays.

AMAZON BASIN

Antonio's Hospedaje (☎ 57-3721, 57-4721; Progreso 545; s US$14.50-20, d US$17.30-23; 🅿️) Rooms here are huge and have hot shower, comfortable mattresses and minifridge. A small garden with armchairs allows outdoor relaxation.

Hospedaje El Virrey (☎ 57-5611; ☎ / fax 59-0579; elvirrey@terra.com.pe; Tarapaca 945; s US$13-25, d US$16-35; ❄️) Rooms are neat and well kept. The pricier rooms have warm shower and air-con and include a continental breakfast in the hotel restaurant.

Hostal Arequipa (☎ 57-3171, 57-3112; hostalarequipa@viabcp.com; Progreso 573; s US$16-26, d US$18.80-31.50; ❄️ 🅿️) It's a popular and often full mid-range choice, with attractive public area, hot water, minifridges, restaurant and airline ticket sales and reconfirmation. The pricier rooms with air-con include a continental breakfast.

Ruíz Hotel (☎ 57-1280, 57-2771; hotelruiz@terra.com.pe; San Martín 475; s/d including continental breakfast US$26/33; ❄️) Rooms are spartan but bigger than average, and have phone, warm shower and minifridge.

Hotel America (☎ /fax 57-5989; hotelamerica@viabcp.com; Portillo 357; s US$13-28.50, d US$19-37, minisuites US$37-43; ❄️ 🖥️) Rooms are modern but small and amenities vary; minifridges, telephones and hot showers are available. There is a small restaurant, and continental or American breakfast is included.

Hotel Mercedes (☎ 57-5120; ☎ /fax 57-1191; Raimondi 610; s US$20-22, d US$26-29, ste US$46; 🖥️ 🅿️ ❄️) This was Pucallpa's first good hotel and has a certain dated charm and character. Rooms, though faded, are well looked after and have comfortable beds and minifridge. The pool is set in a lush garden and there is a good restaurant/bar on the premises. Some rooms can be noisy. The four suites have a full sitting room.

TOP END

Hotel Sol del Oriente (☎ 57-5154; ☎ /fax 57-5510; hsoloriente@qnet.com.pe; San Martín 552; s/d/suite US$65/80/130, s/d with Jacuzzi tub US$75/90; ❄️ 🖥️ 🅿️) Rates

---

PUCALLPA PILSENER

The local beer, San Juan, has the distinction of being Peru's only beer brewed in the Amazon. It's light and refreshing on a hot day.

---

in this large modern hotel include breakfast and a welcome cocktail. Rooms are spacious and coolly tiled, and the public areas invite lounging with shaded deck chairs, patios, palms and life-sized carved wooden statues.

Eating

The town abounds with cheap and mid-range restaurants, though few are noteworthy. The heat in the middle of the day means that restaurants tend to open by 7am for breakfast. Many are closed Sunday.

Don José's (☎ 57-2865; Ucayali 661; menú US$1.50, mains US$1.50-5; ⏰ 7am-10:30pm) For cold, freshly squeezed fruit juices, this traditional place is the old standby. In addition to juices, they serve reasonably priced meals and sandwiches.

C'est Si Bon (☎ 57-1893; Independencia 560) and **Fuente Soda Tropitop** (☎ 57-2860; Sucre 401; ⏰ 7am-11pm) On opposite corners of the plaza, these bright spots serve ice creams, snacks, breakfasts and sandwiches for US$1 to US$3.

Cebichería El Escorpión (☎ 57-4516; Independencia 430; meals US$3-6) It has a prime plaza location, with (noisy) sidewalk tables, and serves good seafood for breakfast and lunch.

Restaurant Kitty (☎ 57-4764; Tarapaca 1062; menú US$1.50) The Kitty is clean and popular and brings in local lunch crowds. Join 'em!

El Portal Chicken (☎ 57-1771; Independencia 510; ⏰ 5pm-midnight; mains about US$3) This three-story restaurant with open-air plaza views is the best of several chicken restaurants in the area. They also serve a few other meaty dishes.

Parrilladas El Braserito (San Martín 498; mains US$5-8; ⏰ 11:30am-4pm daily, 6-11pm Mon-Sat) For good grills (steak, fish and venison) in an elegant atmosphere, this is a good choice.

Chez Maggy (☎ 57-4958; Inmaculada 643; large pizza US$7, mains US$3) Maggy has pizza from a wood-burning oven and tasty pastas – yum!

Chifa Mey Lin (☎ 57-4687; Sucre 698; mains US$3) The best Chinese restaurant in town.

El Paraíso (☎ 57-5878; Tarapacá 653; menú US$1; ⏰ closed Sat) This plaza-side vegetarian restaurant uses soy to make typical Peruvian meat dishes and also has vegetable plates.

Restaurant El Golf (☎ 57-4632; Huáscar 545; mains US$3.50-7; ⏰ 10am-5pm; ❄️) An upscale seafood restaurant with a variety of ceviches – try the local *doncella* rather than the endangered *paiche*.

Shopping

The local Shipibo Indians wander the streets of town selling souvenirs. More of their work is seen near Yarinacocha. For details on their handicrafts, see the boxed text on p383.

For long trips, stock up at **Supermercado Los Andes** (Portillo 545).

Getting There & Away

AIR

Pucallpa's small, busy airport is 5km northwest of town. **Aero Continente** (☎ 57-5643; 7 de Junio 861) has daily direct flights to and from Lima (US$79), while Iquitos (US$69) is served by **Tans** (☎ 59-1852; Arica 500). Departure tax is US$3.50.

Other towns (including Tarapoto, Juanjuí, Atalaya, Sepahua, Contamaná, Bellavista, Tingo María, Cruzeiro do Sul in Brazil) are served by small local airlines using light aircraft. Servicios Aereos del Oriente, or **Saosa** (☎ 57-2637, 57-8637), flies most days to Tarapoto; also try **Servicios Generales** (☎ 57-8003; Progreso 564). These and other small airlines provide charter services. Note that luggage is limited to 10kg per passenger.

BOAT

Pucallpa's port moves depending on water levels. During high water (January to April) boats dock at the town itself, southeast of Parque San Martín. As water levels drop, the port moves to about 3km northeast of the town center, reached by minibuses from the center (US$0.50).

Anyway, wherever the port is, river boats sail the Río Ucayali from Pucallpa to Iquitos (US$15 to US$25 including basic meals, three to five days). Cabins with two or four bunks cost an extra US$1.50 per bunk per day, and come with better food service. Boats announce their departure dates and destinations on chalkboards near the docks, but these are unreliable. Talk to the captain or the cargo loadmaster for greater dependability. They must present boat documents on the morning of their departure day at the **Capitanía** (☎ 57-2517; M Castilla 860). Many people work here, but only the official in charge of documents knows the real scoop and can give you accurate sailing information. Passages are daily when the river is high, but in the dry season low water levels result in slower, less frequent passages.

This is not a trip for everyone; see p419 for more details. Come prepared – the market in Pucallpa sells hammocks, but the mosquito repellent is of poor quality. Bottled drinks are sold on board, but it's worth bringing some large bottles of water or juice.

Jungle 'guides' approaching you on the Pucallpa waterfront are usually unreliable and sometimes dishonest. For jungle excursions, look for a reliable service in Yarinacocha. For a river-boat passage, ask at any likely looking boat, but don't pay until you and your luggage are aboard the boat of your choice. Then pay the captain and no one else.

The river journey can be broken at various villages, including Contamaná (15 to 20 hours) and Requena, and continued on the next vessel coming through. Or ask around for speedboats to Contamaná (US$22, about five hours). The return trip (US$27, six to seven hours) goes against the current. Boats leave daily about noon in each direction.

BUS

A direct bus to and from Lima (US$13) takes 20 hours in the dry season; the journey can be broken in Huánuco (US$8, 12 hours) or Tingo María (US$5).

León de Huánuco (☎ 57-2411, 57-9751; Tacna 655) serves Lima at noon and 5:30pm, as does **Transportes El Rey** (☎ 57-5545, 57-6793; Raimondi at 7 de Junio) at 10am; **Transmar** (☎ 57-4900, 59-2264; Raimondi 793) at 10:30am and 4:30pm; and **Transportes Amazonas** (☎ 57-1292; Tacna 628) at 11am.

Turismo Ucayali (☎ 59-3002, 57-7158; 7 de Junio 799) has cars to Aguaytía and Tingo María (US$11.50, six hours) leaving about every hour from 4am to 3pm. At the same crossstreet, small companies have cars and minibuses to Aguaytía and Tingo María.

Transportes Palcazu (☎ 57-1273; Raimondi 730) has trucks and buses to Puerto Bermúdez.

Getting Around

Motocarros to the airport or Yarinacocha are about US$2. Taxis are not much more expensive, except for the usual airport markup. Colectivos to Yarinacocha (US$0.25) leave from 9 de Diciembre near the market, San Martín at Ucayali, and other places.

Motorcycles can be rented in the town center for about US$2 per hour or US$15 to US$20 for 12 hours (6am to 6pm).

AMAZON BASIN

YARINACOCHA

About 10km northeast of the center of Pucallpa, Yarinacocha is a lovely oxbow lake where you can go canoeing, observe wildlife, and visit Indian communities and purchase their handicrafts. The lake, once part of the Río Ucayali, is now entirely landlocked, though a small canal links the two bodies of water during the rainy season. Boat services are provided here in a casual atmosphere. It's well worth spending a couple of days here.

A part of the lake has been set aside as a reserve. There is also a **botanical garden** (US$0.60; 8am-4pm), which is reached by a 45-minute boat ride followed by a 30-minute walk. Go early in the morning to watch birds on the walk there.

The village of **Puerto Callao** provides simple accommodation and food; boats are also hired here. Internet is available at the Restaurant Latino. Wildlife to watch out for include freshwater dolphins, sloths, meter-long green iguanas, as well as exotic birds such as the curiously long-toed wattled jacana (which walks on lily pads) and the metallic-green Amazon kingfisher.

If you like **fishing**, the dry season is said to be the best time

SHIPIBO INDIANS

The matriarchal Shipibo Indians live along the Río Ucayali and its tributaries in small loose villages of simple, thatched platform houses. San Francisco, at the northwest end of Yarinacocha and accessible by dirt road from Pucallpa, and the boat-access-only village of Santa Clara, are often visited. San Francisco even has simple lodging (from US$3 per person).

Shipibo women craft delicate pots and textiles, decorated with highly distinctive, geometric designs. In Puerto Callao they run a fine craft store, Maroti Shobo, which collects work from about 40 villages. Each piece is handmade, so though patterns are similar, each one is unique. They range from inexpensive small pots and animal figurines to huge urns valued at hundreds of dollars (and more, internationally). The friendly staff arrange international shipping if you buy a large piece. Prices are fixed but fair.

Tours & Guides

Whatever your interests, you'll find plenty of *peki-peki* boat owners ready to oblige. Take your time in choosing a tour; there's no point in going with the first offer unless you are sure you like your boat driver. Guides are also available for walking trips into the surrounding forest including some overnight hikes.

A recommended guide is **Gilber Reategui Sangama** (www.sacredheritage.com/normita; or leave message with sister-in-law ☎ 57-9018), who owns the boat *La Normita* on Yarinacocha. He has expedition supplies (sleeping pads, mosquito nets, purified drinking water) and is both knowledgeable and environmentally aware of the wildlife and people. He speaks some English, is safe and reliable, and will cook most of your meals for you. He charges about US$35 per person per day, with a minimum of two people, for an average of three to five days. Gilber works with Arcesio Morales and Roberto 'Jungle Man' Tamani, who don't speak English. He also recommends his uncle and nephew, Nemecio and Daniel Sangama, with their boat *El Rayito*.

Others who have been recommended for local day tours include the friendly **Miguel 'Pituco' Tans** (☎ 59-7494) and his boat *Pituco*; **Eduardo Vela** (message ☎ 57-5383) who lives on 2 de Mayo at Nuevo Eden, with *The Best*; Gustavo Paredes with *Poseidon*; Mauricio (nicknamed 'Boa'); and Jorge Morales.

Note that other guides will claim that the above are unavailable or don't work there. Don't believe all you hear. A good boat driver will float slowly along, so that you can look for birdlife at the water's edge, or sloths *(perezosos)* in the trees. Sunset is a good time to be on the lake.

Trips to the **Shipibo villages** of either San Francisco (which is now reached by road) or, better, Santa Clara, which is reached by boat, are also popular. For short trips, boat drivers charge about US$5 an hour for the boat, which can carry several people. It's always worth bargaining over the price.

Sleeping & Eating

PUERTO CALLAO

Hotel El Pescador (s/d US$4/6) This hotel has waterfront location; otherwise it's pretty basic with an erratic water supply.

Hostal Los Delfines (☎ 59-6423, 57-1129, 59-6761; r per person US$4-12) Better and larger than the

El Pescador, this *hostal* has rooms of varying quality and size, some with fan, TV and shower.

Several inexpensive restaurants and lively bars line the Puerto Callao waterfront.

NUEVA LUZ DE FATIMA

This village of about 50 families is a 20-minute boat ride from Puerto Callao. **Gilber Reategui Sangama** (junglesecrets@yahoo.com; or leave message with sister-in-law ☎ 57-9018; r per person US$15) and his family offer rustic home hospitality, including all meals and very basic shared showers. Gilber's father is a shaman with over 50 years experience who conducts ceremonies.

LAKESIDE LODGES

La Cabaña (☎ 57-1689; per person including meals US$35) A 10-minute *peki-peki* ride from Puerto Callao, this lodge has 15 simple bungalows with private bathroom and electricity.

La Perla (☎ /fax 61-6004; www.eproima.net/laperla; per person including meals US$25) A few minutes beyond La Cabaña is this German-Peruvian-run lodge with four rooms sharing showers and solar-powered electricity in the evening. An extra US$5 gets an airport pickup.

Both places arrange tours, and are within an hour's walk of the botanical gardens.

Pandisho Albergue (☎ 57-5041, 962-0030; including meals dm US$3, s/d US$25/50) About 30 minutes from Puerto Callao in a different direction, this place has eight rooms with bathroom, and electricity from 6am to 10pm. Its bar is popular with locals on weekends when there's music, but it's quiet otherwise.

CONTAMANÁ TO REQUENA

Contamaná has a colorful waterfront market, a frontier-town atmosphere and, like most river towns, is settled mainly by *mestizo* colonists. It also boasts an airstrip, 24-hour electricity and some Internet cafés. Stay in 10-room **Hostal Augusts** (☎ 065-85-1008; s/d US$9/12) on the plaza. It's the best in town and rooms have a shower, fan and TV. **Hotel Venezia** (☎ 065-85-1031, 065-85-1047; s/d US$3/6, s or d with shower, TV, fan US$9) has friendly staff who service 40 rooms with shared bathroom and nine with bathroom. There are several other cheaper and dingier options.

The next major port is **Orellana**, which has electricity from 6:30pm to 10:30pm and half

a dozen basic hotels charging US$3/5 or less for singles/doubles with shared bathroom. Rooms with bathroom are under construction. Further on, the village of **Juancito** has some very basic rooms.

In the town of **Requena** (two to four days from Pucallpa), with 24-hour electricity, the nicest sleeps are tiny but cute **Hostal Jicely** (☎ 065-41-2216, 065-41-2493; M Manaos 292; s/d US$9/10) and friendly **Hotel Río Seco** (☎ 065-41-2242; s/d US$7/10) with private shower, TV, fan and the **Palo Alto** restaurant next door. There's several other more basic places. Boats to Iquitos leave on most days, taking 12 to 15 hours.

LARETO

YURIMAGUAS
☎ 065 / pop 35,000 / elevation 181m

Yurimaguas is a quiet, pleasant town little changed in the last decade – quite different from the bustling boomtown atmosphere of Pucallpa. There are signs of the rubber days, such as the expensive imported tiles decorating buildings at the end of Avenida Arica, but generally it is a sleepy port where you may wait a day or two for a river boat to Iquitos. Locals call Yurimaguas 'the pearl of the Huallaga.' It is the major port on the Río Huallaga, and is also reached by road (see p353) or air from Lima.

Information

The **Consejo Regional** (Plaza de Armas) can give information. **Manguare Expediciones** (Lores 126) arranges tours, sells handicrafts and gives information. BCP and Banco Continental (with a Visa ATM) will change US cash and traveler's checks. **JC's Internet** (Plaza de Armas; ☒ 8am-midnight; US$1.20 per hr) is conveniently located. **Paraíso Azul** (Huallaga at M Castilla) has a public pool.

Sleeping

Few hotels have hot water, though most have bathrooms.

Quinta Lucy (☎ 35-1575; Jáuregui 305; s US$3, s/d with shower US$3.50/4.50) This cheap place is decently run, although it is basic and rooms look like jail cells.

Hostal César Gustavo (☎ 35-1585; Atahualpa 102; s/d with showers US$4.50/6) The best of the basic places, this is clean and quiet. It has decent

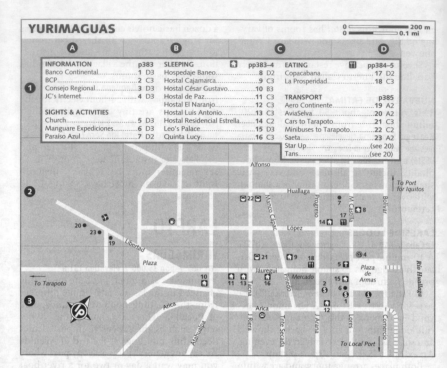

YURIMAGUAS

INFORMATION	p383
Banco Continental	1 D3
BCP	2 C3
Consejo Regional	3 D3
JC's Internet	4 D3

SIGHTS & ACTIVITIES	
Church	5 D3
Manguare Expediciones	6 D3
Paraíso Azul	7 D2

SLEEPING	pp383-4
Hospedaje Baneo	8 D2
Hostal Cajamarca	9 C3
Hostal César Gustavo	10 B3
Hostal de Paz	11 C3
Hostal El Naranjo	12 C3
Hostal Luis Antonio	13 C3
Hostal Residencial Estrella	14 C2
Leo's Palace	15 D3
Quinta Lucy	16 C3

EATING	pp384-5
Copacabana	17 D2
La Prosperidad	18 C3

TRANSPORT	p385
Aero Continente	19 A2
AviaSelva	20 A2
Cars to Tarapoto	21 C3
Minibuses to Tarapoto	22 C2
Saeta	23 A2
Star Up	(see 20)
Tans	(see 20)

beds, ceiling fans and is recommended by readers.

Hostal de Paz (☎ /fax 35-2123; Jáuregui 431; s/d with shower US$6/8) The hotel lacks a sign but is good value, with ceiling fan and TV in the rooms.

Leo's Palace (☎ 35-1499, ☎ /fax 35-2213; Lores 108; s/d with shower US$6/9) The oldest of the better hotels and now a bit run down, it has a few simple but spacious rooms with fan and a balcony overlooking the Plaza de Armas, (some rooms are smaller or lack balcony). TV is available on request and there is a restaurant serving decent cheap lunches (US$1).

Hostal El Naranjo (☎ 35-2650, 35-1560; elnaranjo_yms@hotmail.com; Arica 318; s/d with shower US$10/15) This clean, quiet and recommended hotel has rooms with ceiling fan and cable TV, but was being extensively remodeled at time of writing; a pool, hot water, air-con and Internet access are all planned. It has a good restaurant.

Hostal Luis Antonio (☎ 35-2065, ☎ /fax 35-2061; Jáuregui 407; s US$10-20, d US$20-30; 🖨 🖥) Prices here vary depending on whether you want

cable TV and/or air-con. There is a decent restaurant and small pool, and all standard rooms have a ceiling fan; all are well maintained.

Porta Péricos (☎ 35-2009; San Miguel 720; s/d with shower & including continental breakfast US$30/40; 🅿 🖥) On the northern outskirts, overlooking the Río Paranapura, this hotel's breezy location negates the necessity for air-con, the staff claim. Rates include use of a games room (table tennis and foosball) but seem a tad high.

Other options include:

Hostal Residencial Estrella (☎ 35-2218; López 314; s/d with shower US$3/4.50) Request a table fan.

Hospedaje Baneo (☎ 35-2406; M Castilla 304; s/d with shower US$4.50/7) Basic rooms have fan.

Hostal Cajamarca (☎ 35-2380; Manco Cápac 114; s/d with shower US$6/9) Nothing special, but you get a ceiling fan and TV in the room.

Eating

Many restaurants close between meals. The hotel restaurants are among the best, but they aren't anything special. Also OK is **Copacabana** (M Castilla at López) for standard food and **La Prosperidad** (☎ 35-2057; Progreso 107) for tropical juices, burgers and chicken.

Shopping
Stores selling hammocks for river journeys are on the north side of the market.

Getting There & Away
AIR
Tans, Star Up and **AviaSelva** (☎ 35-2387, 35-2825; Libertad 221) share an office in front of the airport. AviaSelva, which is affiliated with Star Up, flies the Iquitos–Yurimaguas–Tarapoto–Yurimaguas–Iquitos route on Saturday (highly likely to change). Connections from Tarapoto can be made for Lima and other cities. **Aero Continente** (☎ 35-2592; Libertad 139) and Tans do not have flights from Yurimaguas but sell tickets for flights from Tarapoto. **Saeta** (☎ 35-2614; Libertad 209) is one of several companies flying light aircraft to various nearby towns on demand. Carriers, schedules and routes change frequently.

BOAT
The main port 'La Boca' is 13 blocks north of the center. Cargo boats from Yurimaguas follow the Huallaga to the Río Marañón and on to Iquitos. The trip takes about two days with numerous stops for loading and unloading cargo. There are usually departures daily, except Sunday, at about 6pm (though captains may claim they leave earlier). Passages cost US$12 on deck (sling your own hammock and receive very basic food) or US$24 for a bunk in double or quadruple cabins on the top deck, where the food is better and your gear is safer. Bottled water, soft drinks and snacks are sold aboard. Bring insect repellent and ask the locals if the mosquitoes are bad enough to require a net. Boat information is available from the **Bodega Davila store** (☎ 35-2477) by the dock. The *Eduardo* ships (of which there are five) are considered the best. The journey can be broken at Lagunas (10 hours), just before the Río Huallaga meets the Marañón.

About every three or four weeks, the *MV Arca* cruise ship sails for Iquitos, taking five days (see p397).

BUS
For Tarapoto (US$3, six hours) Paredes Estrella and Expreso Huamanga usually leave at 7am from their offices on the outskirts of town on the road to Tarapoto. Through tickets to Chiclayo and the Lima area are available.

Minibuses and pickup trucks (US$4) leave town from Tacna when full several times daily from 4am to 6pm. Cars (US$7, five hours) leave when they have four passengers. The trip takes longer in the wet season.

Getting Around
Mototaxis charge US$0.30 to take you anywhere around town.

LAGUNAS
☎ 065
This village is the best point from which to begin a trip to the Reserva Nacional Pacaya-Samiria (see p386). Lagunas is small and remote, so you should bring most supplies with you. There are no money-changing facilities, and food is limited and expensive.

Tours & Guides
Spanish-speaking guides are locally available to visit Pacaya-Samiria (see p386). It is illegal to hunt within the reserve, but you may need to remind the guides of that (though fishing for the pot is OK). The going rate is about US$15 per passenger per day for guide, boat and accommodation in huts, tents and ranger stations. Food and park fees are extra. Often, the guides will cook for you.

To avoid harassing competition and price cutting, there is now an official guides' association, **Estpel** (☎ 40-1007), which gives guides jobs in turn, so it is harder to get a particular guide. That said, the organization is currently headed by **Gamaniel Valles** (☎ 40-1005) who is himself a recommended and experienced guide with a good knowledge of wildlife. Other recommended guides are Job Gongora and his nephews, and also Edinson and Kleber Saldaña, Juan Huaycama and Genaro Mendoza. However, you don't know whom you will get until you arrive.

Sleeping & Eating
Hotels are very basic, but choice is limited.
Hostal Miraflores (☎ 40-1001; Miraflores 249; s/d US$3/5) This is the best option, with clean rooms and a shared shower.
Hostal La Sombra (☎ 40-1063; r per person US$2) There are hot, stuffy little rooms with a shared shower at this hostel.

Hostel (☎ 40-1009; r per person US$2) Above the Farmacia, this clean place doesn't have showers (buckets of water are provided).

The hostels provide cheap meals and are your best bet for food.

Getting There & Away

Boats from Yurimaguas to Lagunas take about 10 hours and leave around 6pm most days. This means an arrival in the wee hours, so make sure you ask the crew to wake you. The boat usually docks for about 20 minutes to load/unload passengers and cargo. To continue to Iquitos or return to Yurimaguas, ask which radio station is in contact with the boat captains to get an expected time of arrival. Asking at the port will get you wildly differing answers!

BRETAÑA

☎ 065

On the east side of Pacaya-Samiria, this village is another entry point into the reserve, reached from Pucallpa (three days) or Iquitos (1½ days). There are simple eateries and one basic hotel.

To plan ahead, **Shapshico Tour** (☎ 59-7059; csjhu@yahoo.com) in Pucallpa is run by the Galan family (Marcos, Edgar, Cesar). They will help with the logistics of getting to Bretaña and provide accommodation and well-organized services for US$40 per person per day, including food but not park fees.

RESERVA NACIONAL PACAYA-SAMIRIA

At 20,800 sq km, this is the largest of Peru's parks and reserves. Typically, Pacaya-Samiria provides local people with food and a home, and protects ecologically important habitats. In this case, an estimated 42,000 people live on and around the reserve. Juggling the needs of the human inhabitants while protecting wildlife is the responsibility of 20 to 30 rangers. Staff also teach inhabitants how to best harvest the natural renewable resources to benefit the local people and to maintain thriving populations of plants and animals. Despite this, three rangers were murdered by poachers in late 1998.

The reserve is the home of aquatic animals such as Amazon manatees, pink and grey river dolphins, two species of caiman, giant South American river turtles and many others. Monkeys and birds are abundant.

The best way to visit the reserve is to go by dugout canoe with a guide from Lagunas (see p385) or Bretaña (p386) and spend several days camping and exploring. Alternately, comfortable ships visit from Iquitos (see p393). The nearest lodge is the Pacaya-Samiria Amazon Lodge (see p396). The area close to Lagunas has suffered from depletion by hunting, so you need several days to get deep into the least disturbed areas. Ranger stations charge US$20 to enter the reserve and you can then stay as long as you want. Official information is available at the reserve office in Iquitos.

The best time to go is during the dry season, when you are more likely to see animals along the riverbanks. Although rains ease off in late May, it takes a month or so for water levels to drop, making July and August the best months to visit (with excellent fishing). September to November aren't too bad, and December and January often have fairly low water. The heaviest rains begin in January, and the months of February to May are the worst times to go. February to June tend to be the hottest months.

Travelers should bring plenty of insect repellent and plastic bags (to cover luggage), and be prepared to camp out.

IQUITOS

☎ 065 / pop 400,000 / elevation 130m

Linked to the outside world by air and by river, Iquitos is the world's largest city that cannot be reached by road. It has a unique personality: friendly, noisy, sassy and slightly manic. Travelers come here for an excursion into the rainforest or a river trip along the Amazon, but they often stay a few days to relish this remote jungle capital of the huge Department of Loreto.

Iquitos was founded in the 1750s as a Jesuit mission, fending off attacks from Indian tribes who didn't want to be converted. The tiny settlement survived and grew slowly until, by the 1870s, it had 1500 inhabitants. Then came the great rubber boom, and by the 1880s the population had increased 16-fold. For the next 30 years, Iquitos was at once the scene of ostentatious wealth and abject poverty. The rubber barons became fabulously rich, and the rubber tappers (mainly local Indians and poor *mestizos*) suffered virtual enslavement and sometimes death from disease or

IQUITOS

0 — 200 m
0 — 0.1 mi

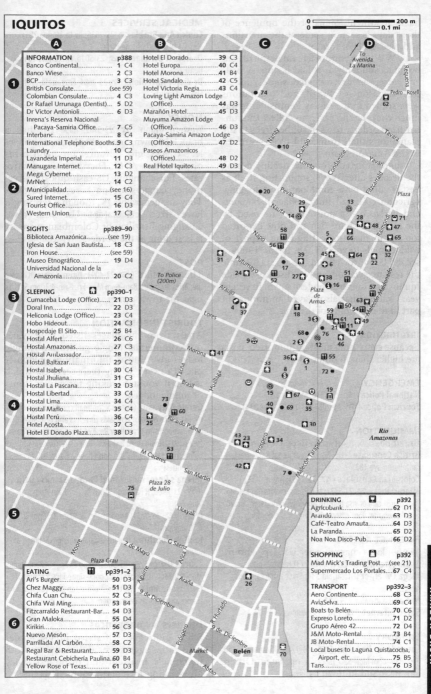

harsh treatment. Signs of the opulence of those days is seen in some of the mansions and tiled walls of Iquitos.

By WWI, the bottom fell out of the rubber boom as suddenly as it had begun. A British entrepreneur smuggled some rubber-tree seeds out of Brazil, and plantations were seeded in the Malay Peninsula. It was much cheaper and easier to collect the rubber from orderly rows of rubber trees in the plantations than from wild trees scattered in the Amazon basin.

Iquitos suffered economic decline during the decades after WWI, supporting itself as best it could by a combination of logging, agriculture (Brazil nuts, tobacco, bananas and *barbasco* – a poisonous vine used by the Indians to hunt fish and now exported for use in insecticides) and the export of wild animals to zoos. Then, in the 1960s, a second boom revitalized the area. This time the resource was oil, and its discovery made Iquitos a prosperous modern town. In recent years tourism has also played an important part in the economy of the area.

Information

Because everything must be 'imported' costs are higher than in other cities.

EMERGENCY
National Police (☎ 23-3330; Morona 126)
Tourism Police (☎ 24-2081, 23-1852; Lores 834)

IMMIGRATION
Brazil has a consul in Leticia, Colombia.
British Consulate (☎ 22-2732; at Regal Bar & Restaurant, Putumayo 182)
Colombian Consulate (☎ 23-1461; Araujo 431)
Migraciónes (☎ 23-5371; M Cáceres, cuadra 18) Extend your tourist card or visa here. (If arriving/leaving from Brazil or Colombia, get your entry/exit stamp at the border.)

INTERNET ACCESS
Many places charge under US$1 per hour:
Manugare Internet (Próspero 273) Fast machines.
Mega Cybernet (Fitzcarrald 334) Serves snacks; plays music.
MrNet (Condamine 259; 🖳)
Sured Internet (☎ 23-6119; Morona 213; 🖳)

LAUNDRY
Lavandería Imperial (☎ 23-1768; Putumayo 150; 🕑 8am-8pm Mon-Sat) is coin-operated. Others can be found in town as well.

MEDICAL SERVICES
Clínica Ana Stahl (☎ 25-2535; Av La Marina 285; 🕑 24 hr) Good private clinic.
Dr Rafael Urrunaga (☎ 23-5016, Fitzcarrald 201) Dentist.
Dr Victor Antonioli (☎ 23-2684; Fitzcarrald 156) Speaks English.

MONEY
Western Union (☎ 23-5182; Napo 359) has a branch in town. Several banks change traveler's checks, give advances on credit cards or provide an ATM. They have competitive rates. For changing US cash quickly, street moneychangers are on Lores at Próspero. They are generally OK, though a few might have 'fixed' calculators. Use your own. Changing Brazilian or Colombian currency is best done at the border.

POST
The **post office** (☎ 23-4091; turismo.mpm@tvs.com.pe; Arica 402; 🕑 8am-6pm Mon-Fri, 8am-4:30pm Sat) is near the town center.

TOURIST INFORMATION
Apart from the places listed here, various commercial jungle guides and jungle lodges give tourist information, obviously biased toward selling their services, which is fine if you are looking for guides, tours or jungle lodges.
Gerald Mayeaux (cajafesa@hotmail.com) Former tourist-office director now aids travelers and dispenses information from his Yellow Rose of Texas restaurant/bar (see p391). If you need a shower or a place to hang out before your late flight, and don't have a hotel, ask to use its facilities!
Inrena's Reserva Nacional Pacaya-Samiria Office (☎ 23-2980; R Palma 113, 4th fl; 🕑 8am-4pm Mon-Fri)
iPeru (☎ 26-0251; Airport; 🕑 8:30am-1:30pm & 4:30-8:30pm)
Iquitos Monthly A free newspaper in English aimed at tourists.
Tourist Office (☎ 23-5621; Napo 232; 🕑 8am-8pm Mon-Fri, 9am-1pm Sat) In a poorly signed back room on the Plaza de Armas, the tourist office can give you maps of the area, as well as information.

Dangers & Annoyances
Street touts and self-styled jungle guides tend to be aggressive, and many are both irritatingly insistent and dishonest. They are working for commissions. It is best to

make your own decisions by contacting hotels, lodges and tour companies directly. That said, crime is relatively uncommon in Iquitos.

Sights

IRON HOUSE

Every guidebook tells of the 'majestic' Iron House designed by Eiffel (of Tower fame). It was made in Paris in 1860 and imported piece by piece into Iquitos around 1890, during the opulent rubber-boom days, to beautify the city. Although three different iron houses were imported, only one, at the southeast corner of the Plaza de Armas, survives. It looks like a bunch of scrap-metal sheets bolted together and was once a store and the Iquitos Club. Now, there is a café downstairs and upstairs it houses the British consul and the Regal Bar & Restaurant.

AZULEJOS

Other remnants of those rubber-boom days include *azulejos*, handmade tiles imported from Portugal to decorate the mansions of the rubber barons. Many buildings along Raimondi and Malecón Tarapaca are lavishly decorated with *azulejos*. Some of the best are various government buildings along or near the malecón.

LIBRARY & MUSEUM

On the malecón, at the corner with Morona, is an old building housing the Biblioteca Amazónica and the small Museo Etnográfico. Both are open on weekdays. The museum includes life-size fiberglass casts of members of various Amazon tribes.

BELÉN

A walk down Raimondi (which turns into Próspero) and back along the malecón is interesting, not only to see some of the tile-faced buildings, but also because you can visit the Belén **market** area at the southeast end of town. Belén itself is a floating shantytown with a certain charm to it (the locals call it the Venice of the Amazon, but others would call it a slum). It consists of scores of huts built on rafts, which rise and fall with the river. During the low-water months, these rafts sit on the river mud and are dirty and unhealthy, but for most of the year they float on the river – a colorful and exotic sight. Seven thousand people live here, and

canoes float from hut to hut selling and trading jungle produce. If you speak a few words of Spanish, you can find someone to paddle you around for a fee. Ask at the end of 9 de Diciembre. The area seems reasonably safe in daylight.

The market, within the city blocks in front of Belén, is a raucous, crowded affair common to most Peruvian towns. All kinds of strange and exotic products are sold among the mundane bags of rice, sugar, flour and cheap plastic and metal household goods. Look for the bark of the *chuchuhuasi* tree that is soaked in rum for weeks and used as a tonic (served in many of the local bars). *Chuchuhuasi* and other Amazon plants are common ingredients in herbal pain-reducing and arthritis formulas manufactured in Europe and the USA. All kinds of medicinal and culinary offerings are on sale: piles of dried frogs and fish, armadillo shells, piranha teeth and a great variety of tropical fruits. Pasaje Paquito is the block where they sell medicinal plants. It makes for exciting shopping and sightseeing, but remember to watch your wallet.

LAGUNA MORONACOCHA

This lake forms the town's western boundary. To get there, take the colectivo (15 minutes) that departs from 2 de Mayo and leaves the city center along Ejército. There isn't much to see but there are a couple of ramshackle bars with lake views – a good place to relax with a cold beer and watch the sunset.

NEARBY VILLAGES & LAKES

About 16km from town, past the airport, **Santo Tomás** has a few bars overlooking Mapacocha, a lake formed by an arm of the Río Nanay. You can rent boats (paddle or motor) by asking around. A motorboat with driver is US$5 to US$10 an hour, or you can paddle your own canoe for less. **Santa Clara** is about 15km away, on the banks of the Río Nanay. Boats can also be rented, and locals swim off the beaches formed during low water levels (July to September). Both villages can be reached by *motocarros* (about US$4) and taxis.

Corrientillo is a lake near the Río Nanay. There are a few bars around the lake, which is locally popular for swimming on weekends and has good sunsets. It's about

15km from town; a *motocarro* will charge about US$3.

LAGUNA QUISTACOCHA

This lake, 15km south of Iquitos, is served by minibuses several times an hour from Plaza 28 de Julio. A small **zoo** of local fauna has been improved under an Australian director who is sometimes available to show you around.

An adjoining **fish hatchery** has 2m-long *paiche* (a river fish), which tastes excellent, but its popularity and loss of habitat has caused a severe decline in its numbers. An attempt to rectify the situation is being made with the breeding program here. A pedestrian walk circles the lake (in which people swim, though it looks murky) and paddleboats are for hire. It's fairly crowded with locals on the weekend but not midweek. Admission is US$1.

Sleeping

Mosquitoes are rarely a serious problem in town, so mosquito netting is not provided.

The best hotels tend to be booked up on Friday and Saturday. The busiest season is from May to September, when prices may rise slightly.

BUDGET

All these hotels have bathrooms and fans unless otherwise indicated.

Hostal Alfert (☎ 23-4105; G Saenz 001; s/d US$4.50/ 7.30) With a view of the river and warm showers, this place attracts shoestringers, though the neighborhood is dodgy.

Hobo Hideout (☎ 23-4099; hobohideout@yahoo .com; Putumayo 437; dm/s/d US$5/7.50/9, with shower s/d US$10/11.50) A cool travelers' vibe reaches out through the iron-grill gate, and kitchen privileges, laundry area, bar, cable TV room and 2-sq-meter plunge pool with waterfall draw international hobos. One (pricier) room towers above the rest on jungle-style stilts; others are small and dark. Expeditions can be arranged.

Hostal Lima (☎ 23-5152, 22-1409; fax 23-4111; Próspero 549; s/d US$7.50/10) A small courtyard opens onto small, clean rooms (the fans are window-mounted for lack of space) with small bathroom (the hot shower sprays the toilet). TVs are available on request and upstairs rooms are better and breezier. It's one for the budget traveler.

Hospedaje El Sitio (☎ 23-4932, 22-3103; R Palma 545; s/d US$7.50/10) Clean, extra-large rooms with TV are the draw here.

Hostal Maflo (☎ 24-1257, 23-1256; hostalmaflo@ mixmail.com; Morona 177; s/d including continental breakfast US$7.50/11) Simple, plain rooms are set back from the street and feature hot water and cable TV – a good deal.

Hostal Libertad (☎ 23-5763; Arica 361; s/d US$7.50/11.50; d with air-con US$15; ⌘) Rooms are fairly simple with electric shower, though some have cable TV. Only two rooms have air-con.

Hostal La Pascana (☎ 23-1418; pascana@tsi.com .pe; fax 23-3466; Pevas 133; s/d/t US$9/12/15) With a small plant-filled garden, this safe and friendly place is deservedly popular with travelers and often full. A book exchange and breakfast area add to the attraction.

Also consider:

Hostal Baltazar (☎ 23-2240; Condamine 265; s/d US$7.50-12/10-17; ⌘) Quiet, clean and decent.

Hostal Isabel (☎ 23-4901; Brasil 164; s/d US$4.50/6) Rooms vary from poor to quite good.

Hostal Perú (☎ 23-1616; Próspero 218; s/d US$4.50/ 6.50) Old and basic but adequate.

Hotel Morona (☎ 22-1055; Morona 420; US$6/9) Clean but basic and noisy.

MID-RANGE

All of the hotels listed here have fairly generic rooms with air-con and private bathroom, normally with hot water. Walk-in rates for standard rooms are given; advance reservations or holiday rates may be higher.

Hotel Sandalo (☎ 23-4761; sandalo@iquitos.net; Próspero 616; s/d US$20/25; ⌘) Modern, motel-style carpeted rooms with cable TV, mini-fridge and phone. Breakfast is included.

Hostal Ambassador (☎ /fax 23-3110; Pevas 260; s/d US$20/30; ⌘) Comfortable rooms, cable TV, continental breakfast and free airport transfers are provided and a restaurant offers room service.

Marañón Hotel (☎ 24-2673, 23-3918; hotel.mara non@terra.com.pe; Nauta 285; s/d US$30/35; ⌘ ⌘) Sparklingly new at press time, this hotel has light tiles everywhere and a restaurant with room service. The rooms have notably good-sized bathrooms by Iquitos standards, as well as the usual amenities. A continental breakfast is included. Good value.

Hostal Amazonas (☎ /fax 24-2431; amazonas@tvs .com.pe; Arica 108; s/d US$30/40; ⌘) A prime location on the Plaza de Armas and popular with Peruvian businesspeople. A restaurant is on the premises; rooms are carpeted and have cable TV, minifridge and phone.

Hostal Europa (☎ 23-1123, 23-4744; heuropa@ mnet.com.pe; Próspero 494; s/d US$30/40; ☒) This modern block hotel rises five floors above Próspero with good views from the top. Breakfast is included, a restaurant is available and the bright new rooms have cable TV and minifridge.

Doral Inn (☎ 24-3386, ☎/fax 24-1970; doralinn hotel_iquitos@hotmail.com; Raimondi 220; s/d including continental breakfast US$25-35/35-45; ☒) This new hotel has a 5th-floor restaurant with a view where you can enjoy your breakfast. Neat rooms have the usual amenities plus room service, and the hotel arranges tours to its Amazon Adventure Lodge.

Real Hotel Iquitos (☎/fax 23-1011; s/d US$45/55; ☒) On Malecón Tarapaca, this is the grand dame of Iquitos' hotels. Rooms are spacious but slightly shabby, though the river view compensates for the deteriorated decor. Hot water is by request, which makes these rates a bit steep. Cheaper rooms without river view are almost half price.

Also consider:

Hotel Acosta (☎ 23-5974; chasa@meganet.com.pe; on Huallaga at Araujo; s/d including continental breakfast US$30/40; ☒)

Hostal Jhuliana (☎/fax 23-3154; Putumayo 521; s/d US$25/35; ☒ ☒) This strangely spelled hotel has cafeteria and bar, room service and carpeted rooms with minifridge, cable TV and phone.

TOP END

Note that these top-end hotels have only a few dozen rooms and are often full, so reservations aren't a bad idea.

Hotel Victoria Regia (☎/fax 23-1983; info@victoria regiahotel.com; Ricardo Palma 252; s/d including breakfast US$50/60, ste US$70/90; ☒ ☒ ☐) It has excellent beds and comfortable rooms with all the usual amenities, plus hairdryers in the bathroom. The well-maintained pool is indoor. A fine restaurant and bar attract upscale guests and businesspeople. Their cappuccinos are excellent.

Hotel El Dorado Plaza (☎ 22-2555; iquitos@eldorado plazahotel.com; Napo 258; s or d US$130; ☒ ☒) With a prime plaza location, this modern hotel is easily the town's best, with 64 well-equipped spacious rooms (some with plaza views, others overlooking the pool). Jacuzzi, sauna,

gym, restaurant, 24-hour room service, two bars and attentive staff make this a five-star hotel. Breakfast is included.

Also consider **Hotel El Dorado** (☎ 23-1742, ☎/fax 22-1985; dorado@tvs.com.pe; Napo 362; s/d including breakfast US$66/80, deluxe d US$90; ☒ ☒) Airport transfer is included.

Eating

Chifa Wai Ming (☎ 23-3649; San Martín 464; mains about US$6) There are several inexpensive *chifas* and other restaurants near the Plaza 28 de Julio, of which the Wai Ming is a little more expensive but worth it.

Chifa Cuan Chu (Huallaga 173; mains US$3) It's a good budget *chifa*. Try the house speciality: sweet-and-sour chicken prepared with fresh pineapple.

Restaurant Cebichería Paulina (☎ 23-1298; Tacna 591; menús US$3, mains US$3-6) A huge menu of ceviches and local food (including caiman) attracts a Peruvian lunch crowd.

Kirikiri (☎ 23-2020; Napo 159; 1/4 chicken & chips US$2) How does a Peruvian cock crow? 'Kirikiri.' This is the best place in town for grilled chicken.

Parrillada Al Carbón (☎ 22-3292; Condamine 115; mains US$2-5) This grill serves tasty cuts of meat, as well as chicken and fish.

Lidia's (Bolognesi 1181 at Abtao; mains from US$2; ☒ 6-9pm Mon-Sat) This is pretty much inside Lidia's living room. She and her family grill meats, fish, *cecina*, *tamales* and plantains on a barbecue outside the house. No sign, but plenty of sizzle and full of locals. Come early for the best food selection – when they're done, they close.

Chez Maggy (☎ 24-1816; Raimondi 181; pastas US$3, large pizza US$7.50; ☒ 6-11:30pm) A wood-burning oven produces fresh pizzas, just like its sister restaurants in Cuzco and other cities.

Ari's Burger (☎ 23-1470; Próspero 127; meals US$2-6; ☒ 7am-3am) On the corner of the Plaza de Armas, this clean, brightly lit joint is known locally as 'gringolandia.' Two walls are open to the street allowing great plaza- and people-watching. They are open almost always, serve American-style food as well as some local plates and ice creams, change US dollars and are generally helpful and popular with tourists.

Yellow Rose of Texas (☎ 24-1010; Putumayo 180; breakfast from US$1.50, mains US$5-7.50; ☒ 24 hr) Run by ex-tourism director Gerald Mayeaux (see p388) this restaurant and bar specializes in

Texas barbecue, but has a varied menu of international and regional dishes. Eat on the sidewalk, inside, or in a tiny lantern-lit courtyard in the back. The bar has comfortable Adirondack chairs you can fall asleep in, board games, darts, sports TV, an excellent book exchange and beers kept ice-cold in unique balsa-wood holders.

Regal Bar & Restaurant (☎ 22-2732; Putumayo 182; mains US$4-9) It's on the 2nd floor of the famous Iron House on the plaza. The British consul, Mr Phill Duffy, owns the Regal and conducts consular business in the bar over pints and darts. The plaza-view balcony is a great place for a snack or (slightly overpriced?) meal, and you can examine parts of the restored Iron House.

Fitzcarraldo Restaurant-Bar (☎ 24-3434; Napo 100; mains US$3-7; ☺ noon-late) The Fitzcarraldo anchors a whole block of riverside restaurants and is the most upscale of them, with good food and service. Dine indoors or on the street-side patio. It does good pizzas (delivery available) and various local and international dishes. Sitting and just having a drink is perfectly acceptable in this friendly place.

Nuevo Mesón (☎ 23-1857; Malecón Maldonado 153; mains US$3-8; ☺ lunch till late) Another choice on riverside row, this place serves local specialties (including jungle animals); the local turtles are protected and should not be served, but deer and peccary are fair game.

Gran Maloka (☎ 23-3126; Lores 170; menú US$3.50, mains US$7-9; ☺ noon-10pm; ✗) Enjoy elegant and quiet dining in this atmospheric Amazonian restaurant inside a tiled mansion from rubber-boom days. The menu can be adventurous (curried caiman) but has plenty of well-prepared and less startling meat and fish dishes. Locals consider this to be the town's best restaurant.

Drinking

There are several places to meet for a cold beer or other drinks and hear music, both recorded and live. Several places are found along the pedestrian blocks of the malecón north of Napo. A good beer bar here is **Arandú**, next to the Fitzcarraldo.

Café-Teatro Amauta (☎ 23-3109; Nauta 250) has live Peruvian music on most nights and has a well-stocked bar with local drinks as well as a café. **Regal Bar**, on the Plaza de Armas,

is good for a quiet drink and chat. Around the corner, **Jungle Jim's** is a bar totally surrounded by the **Yellow Rose of Texas** (see p391). It's about darts, beer, chat.

For dancing, the most locally popular place is **Agricobank** (Condamine at Pablo Rosell). It's a huge outdoor place where hundreds of locals gather for drinking, dancing and socializing; a US$1.75 cover is charged. The more upscale **Noa Noa Disco-Pub** (☎ 23-2902; Pevas 292) charges a US$6 cover and is a very trendy disco. Also popular for dancing, **La Paranda** (Pevas 174) fills up with locals strutting their stuff on weekends.

Shopping

There are a few shops on the 1st block of Napo selling jungle crafts, some of high quality and pricey. A good place for crafts is Mercado de Artesanía San Juan on the road to the airport – bus and taxi drivers know it. Although items made from animal bones and skins are available, we discourage their purchase. It is illegal to import many of them into North America and Europe.

For a jungle expedition, stop by **Mad Mick's Trading Post** (michaelcollis@hotmail.com; Putumayo 184; ☺ 8am-8pm) where you can buy, rent or trade almost anything. Don't need it afterwards? Mick will buy anything back (if it's in good nick) for half price. For food supplies, stop by **Supermercado Los Portales** (Próspero at Morona).

Getting There & Away
AIR

Iquitos has a small international airport with flights to Colombia as well as local flights. There have been flights to Miami and Brazil in the past, but none at the time of writing. Direct Miami–Iquitos flights may be offered in the future.

Aero Continente (☎ 24-3489, 24-2995; airport 26-0874; Próspero 232) and **Tans** (☎ 23-1071; Próspero 215) are the main airlines serving Lima, with two or more flights a day. Tans flies daily to Pucallpa. Some Lima flights stop at Tarapoto, Chiclayo or Trujillo. **AviaSelva** (Próspero 439) is a new airline with flights to Leticia, Colombia, on Monday and Friday, and Yurimaguas and Tarapoto on Saturday; though this is definitely likely to change. There has been ongoing talk of direct Iquitos–Cuzco flights for many years; don't hold your breath. **Grupo Aéreo 42**

(☎ 23-4632, 23-4521; Lores 127) is a military airline with flights to several small jungle towns. Flights are often full and subject to cancellation or postponement. Schedules, destinations and fares change frequently, so check locally.

Charter companies at the airport have five-passenger planes to almost anywhere in the Amazon. Rates are around US$300 an hour. Other small airlines may have offices at the airport.

The airport departure tax is US$10 for international flights and US$3.50 for domestic flights.

BOAT

Iquitos is Peru's largest and best-organized river port, and it accepts oceangoing vessels as it did in the rubber-boom days. Most boats today, however, ply only Peruvian waters, and voyagers change boats at the border (see p419).

Cargo boats normally leave from Puerto Masusa, on Avenida La Marina about 2km or 3km north of the town center (maybe closer if the water is very high in May to July). Chalkboards tell you which boats are leaving when, for where, and whether they are accepting passengers. Although there are agencies in town, it's usually best to go to the dock and look around; don't trust anyone except the captain for a rough estimate of departure time. Be wary: the chalkboards have a habit of changing dates overnight! Boats often leave many hours or a few days late.

Upriver passages to Pucallpa (four to seven days) or Yurimaguas (three to six days) cost about US$20 to US$30 per person. It takes longer when the river is high and the boat is going against the current. Boats leave about three times a week to Pucallpa, more often to Yurimaguas, and there are more frequent departures for the closer intermediate ports. Some boats have cabins and charge more for those (see p385).

Downriver boats to the Peruvian border with Brazil and Colombia leave about twice a week and take two days. Fares are US$15 to US$20 per person.

You can often sleep aboard the boat while waiting for departure; this enables you to get the best hammock space (away from the engine, and not under a light that attracts insects and keeps you awake).

Never leave gear unattended; ask to have your bags locked up when you sleep.

If you're in a hurry, **Expreso Loreto** (☎ 23-4086, 24-3661; Loreto at Raimondi) has fast motor launches to the border at 6am every two days. The fare is US$50 for the 12-hour trip, including lunch. Other companies nearby offer similar trips.

Amazon Tours & Cruises (see p397) has weekly cruises on comfortable ships that go from Iquitos to Leticia, Colombia, leaving on Sunday. Most passengers are foreigners on a one-week, round-trip tour, but cheaper one-way passages are sold on a space-available basis.

Getting Around
BUSES & TAXIS

The ubiquitous *motocarros* cost less than a taxi and are fun to ride, though they don't provide much protection in an accident. Most rides around Iquitos cost a standard US$0.70.

Taxis are relatively few and are pricier than in other Peruvian cities. A taxi ride to the airport costs about US$5. *Motocarros* are about half that.

Buses and trucks for several nearby destinations, including the airport, leave from the Plaza 28 de Julio.

A road is being pushed through the jungle as far as **Nauta** on the Río Marañón, just beyond its confluence with the Río Ucayali. When this road is passable for buses, it will cut the boat passenger route from Yurimaguas by six hours. Ask locally for the latest information.

MOTORCYCLE
JB Moto-Rental (Yavari 702) and **J&M Moto-Rental** (Tacna at R Palma) rent motorcycles for US$2.50 an hour.

EXPLORING THE JUNGLE AROUND IQUITOS

Excursions into the jungle are of three types: visits to jungle lodges (which is what most visitors opy for) mostly for wildlife viewing; a cruise on a river boat outfitted for tourism (an increasingly popular option) to observe the way of life along the river; and the more demanding camping and walking trips. Some cruises or lodges offer dedicated fishing trips. July to September are by far the best months for this.

AMAZON BASIN

Jungle Lodges

A wide range of options at varying prices can be booked from abroad or in Lima, but if you show up in Iquitos without a reservation, you can certainly book a lodge or tour and it'll cost you less. Bargaining is not out of the question if you are on a tight budget, even though operators show you fixed price lists. If the lodge has space and you have the cash, they'll nearly always give you a discount, sometimes a substantial one. If planning on booking after you arrive, avoid the major Peruvian holidays, when many places are filled with Peruvian holidaymakers. June to September (the dry months and the summer vacation for North American and European visitors) are also quite busy, though bargains can be found if you're flexible with time. It's worth shopping around.

The lodges are some distance from Iquitos, so river transport is included in the price. Most of the area within 50km of the city is not virgin jungle, and the chance of seeing big mammals is remote. Any Indians will be acculturated and performing for tourism. Nevertheless, much can be seen of the jungle way of life, and birds, insects and small mammals can be observed. The more remote lodges have more wildlife.

A representative two-day trip involves a river journey of two or three hours to a jungle lodge with reasonable comforts and meals, a 'typical' jungle lunch, a guided visit to an Indian village to buy crafts and perhaps see dances (though tourists often

---

JUNGLE DOCTOR

In 1990 Linnea Smith, MD, gave up her Wisconsin medical practice to provide medical services to the indigenous people of the Peruvian Amazon. Initially she operated out of a small thatched-roof room without electricity, running water, staff, funding or lab services. Volunteers built a six-room clinic complete with well, solar panels, a hammock house for patients and their families, and adjacent rooms for clinic workers and visiting medical staff. The clinic is next to Explorama Lodge, which provides Dr Smith with meals and river transportation. Explorama guests are welcome to tour the clinic or leave donations. For more information, see www.amazonmedical.org.

---

outnumber Indians), an evening meal at the lodge, maybe an after-dark canoe trip to look for caiman by searchlight, and a walk in the jungle the following day to see jungle vegetation (and if you are lucky, monkeys or other wildlife). A trip like this will set you back about US$60 to US$150, depending on the operator, the distance traveled and the comfort of the lodge. On longer trips, you'll get further away from Iquitos, and see more of the jungle, and the cost per night drops.

SLEEPING

There are many good lodges in the Iquitos area that will give you a rewarding look at the rainforest. All prices quoted here are approximate; bargaining is often acceptable, and meals, guided tours and transportation from Iquitos should be included. Bottled drinks (including water) are extra; however, every lodge will provide large containers of purified water for you to fill your own water bottle, as well as 24-hour hot water with instant coffee and tea bags. Meals normally include juice.

Explorama Lodges (☎ 25-2526; www.explorama .com; fax 25-2533; Av La Marina 340; 8 days & 7 nights, departing Tuesday, s/d US$1069/1788, any-day departure s/d US$1400/2200) This well-established and recommended company owns and operates lodges (see following) and is an involved supporter of ACTS, Amazon Conservatory of Tropical Studies, which has a lab at the famed Canopy Walkway (opposite). You could arrange a trip to visit one or more lodges (each of which is very different) combined with a visit to the walkway. Sample rates are given; contact Explorama for other options and combinations. Explorama serves all-you-can-eat lunch and dinner buffets, has fast boats (50km/h) and half-price rates for under-12s. Ask about group discounts. Their well-trained, friendly and knowledgeable guides are locals who speak English (other languages on request).

Ceiba Tops (3 days & 2 nights, departing Friday s/d US$248/396, any-day departure s/d US$335/570; 🕾 🕾 🖳) Forty kilometers northeast of Iquitos on the Amazon, this is Explorama's and the area's most modern lodge and resort. There are 75 luxurious rooms and suites, all attractively decorated and featuring comfortable beds and furniture, fan, screened windows, porches and spacious bathroom with hot shower. A satellite TV room is available. Landscaped grounds surround the pool complex, complete with hydromassage, waterslide and hammock house. The restaurant (with better meals than at Explorama's other places) adjoins a bar with live Amazon music daily. Short guided walks and boat rides are available for a taste of the jungle; there is some primary forest nearby. One highlight is the *Victoria regia*, or giant Amazon water lily, which has 2m-diameter leaves which a child could sleep on without sinking. This lodge is a recommended option for people who really *don't* want to rough it. It even hosts business incentive meetings.

Explorama Lodge (3 days & 2 nights s/d US$325/570) Eighty kilometers away on the Amazon, near its junction with the Río Napo, this was one of the first lodges constructed in the Iquitos area (1964) and remains attractively rustic. The lodge has several large palm-thatched buildings with 75 rooms with shared cold-water bathroom; covered walkways join the buildings, and lighting is by kerosene lantern. Guides accompany visitors on several trails that go deeper into the forest.

Explornapo Lodge (5 days & 4 nights s/d US$1135/1760) On the Río Napo, 157km from Iquitos, this simple lodge has 30 rooms with shared cold-shower facilities. The highlights are guided trail hikes in remote primary forest, bird-watching, ReNuPeRu ethnobotanical garden of useful plants (curated by a local shaman) and a visit to the nearby Canopy Walkway (half-hour walk). Because of the distance involved, on five-day/four-night packages, you spend the first and last night at the Explorama Lodge.

ExplorTambos (5 days & 4 nights s/d US$1160/1804) This lodge is a two-hour walk from Explornapo. Guests (16 maximum) sleep on mattresses on open-sided sleeping platforms covered with a mosquito net; don't plan a passionate honeymoon here! Basic toilets and washing facilities are provided, and wildlife-watching opportunities here are better than at the lodges. A Canopy Walkway visit (see the boxed text) is included.

ACTS Field Station (s/d US$140/240) (Note that the old name Aceer is still used by some companies.) Near the Canopy Walkway, the 20 rooms here are in buildings similar to those at Explorama Lodge. Book ahead, because accommodations are often used by researchers and workshop groups.

CANOPY WALKWAY

Until the 1970s, biologists working in the rainforest made their observations and collected specimens from the forest floor and along the rivers, unaware that many plant and animal species spent their entire lives in the canopy. When scientists ventured into the treetops, they discovered so many new species that the canopy became known as the new frontier of tropical biology. Until recently, it was difficult to visit the canopy unless you were a researcher, but it is now possible for travelers to get to the top of the rainforest.

This awesome hanging walkway stretches over 500m through the rainforest canopy, reaching 35m above the ground. It is about a 10-minute walk from ACTS Field Station. The canopy is reached by stairs and is accessible to any able-bodied visitor. The views are excellent, and birders spend hours up there. Some warnings, though. Visiting the Canopy Walkway involves a lot of travel if you are not staying nearby, and it may terrify you if you are afraid of heights. It can get hot on top of the trees, so bring sun protection and a water bottle. Also, go with realistic expectations. Binoculars and an expert guide will enable you to see scores of tropical bird species, but you are not likely to spot many mammals in the canopy.

Muyuna Amazon Lodge (☎ 24-2858; amazonas@muyuna.com; Putumayo 163, Iquitos; 3 days & 2 nights per person US$300, 6 days & 5 nights per person US$520) About 130km upriver from Iquitos on the Río Yanayacu, this intimate, eight-bungalow lodge in a remote area gives visitors a good look at the jungle, which tends to be less traveled and colonized upriver than downriver. The helpful owners live in Iquitos and have a very hands-on approach to maintaining their lodge, ensuring recycling, encouraging staff and keeping guests happy. Each stilted, thatched bungalow has a private cold shower, two or three comfortable beds, is large enough for a writing desk and is fully screened. There is also a balcony with hammock. During high water the river rises up to the bungalows, which are connected to the lodge/dining building with covered, raised walkways. Lighting is by kerosene lanterns. The bilingual guides are excellent and there are good possibilities of seeing several monkey species and other animals, as well as birds galore. Muyuna has received many readers' and travelers' recommendations. Unlike most other lodges, the owners do not pay commissions, so street touts don't recommend them.

Loving Light Amazon Lodge (Iquitos ☎ 24-3180; Putumayo 128; USA ☎ 425-836-9431; info@junglelodge .com; 7016 248th Ave NE, Redmond, WA 98053; 5 days & 4 nights per person US$570; ayahuasca ceremonies US$35). About 120km from Iquitos on the Río Yanayacu, it has a circular thatched dining room/reception lodge that is connected by walkways to seven bungalows with private shower and screens. Each sleeps up to four people, and book-sized solar panels in the thatched roofs are used for lighting. The usual jungle tours are available, and there are opportunities to listen to musicians in the evening, or take part in spiritual ceremonies conducted by a local shaman. Walk-up discounts are offered, but when the lodge is empty, it looks woebegone.

Amazon Yarapa River Lodge (☎ 22-3376; www.ya rapariverlodge.com; La Marina 124, Iquitos; 4 days & 3 nights per person US$600, with bathroom per person US$675; ▢) Approximately 130km upriver from Iquitos on the Río Yarapa, this lodge is simply stunning. It has a huge and well-designed tropical biology laboratory, regularly used by the US Cornell University for research and postgraduate classes. The lab is powered by an expansive solar-panel system, which also provides electric power throughout the lodge (bring your laptop). The lodge has satellite phone connections. The facilities are beautifully maintained, with an impressive entrance pier, elaborate wood carvings in the restaurant/bar and even on the bed heads, and fully screened rooms linked by screened walkways. Eight huge bedrooms with oversized private bathroom are available (professors stay here when Cornell is in residence) and 16 comfortable rooms share a multitude of well-equipped, modern bathrooms. Of course, with its scientific agenda, the lodge offers top-notch guides for its jungle tours, which visit remote areas. Their boats take about three to four hours from Iquitos but have a bathroom aboard. Recommended.

Paseos Amazonicos (☎ /fax 23-3110; www.paseos amazonicos.com; Pevas 246, Iquitos; r per person US$50-140) This company runs three lodges. One of the oldest and best established is Amazonas Sinchicuy Lodge, on a small tributary of the Amazon, 25km northeast of Iquitos. The 32 rooms have private cold shower, can sleep up to four, and are lantern-lit. Some rooms are wheelchair-accessible. This lodge can be visited on a day trip from Iquitos. The palm-thatched Tambo Yanayacu Lodge is 50km northeast of Iquitos and has 10 rustic rooms with private bathroom. Here, the staff can supply tents for jungle expeditions. Stays at these two lodges can be combined into one trip. Finally, the Tambo Amazonico Lodge is about 150km upriver on the Río Yarapa. It is less a lodge and more of a camping place, with two open-air dormitories sleeping up to 20 people, with beds and mosquito nets. Camping trips can be arranged, including into the Pacaya-Samiria reserve.

Pacaya-Samiria Amazon Lodge (☎ /fax 23-4128; www.pacayasamiria.com.pe; Raimondi 378, Iquitos; 3 days & 2 nights per person, 4-person minimum, from US$299). About 190km upriver on the Marañón, this new lodge is past Requena and on the outskirts of the Pacaya-Samiria reserve. It's four hours from Iquitos and can arrange overnights within the reserve. Rooms feature private shower and a porch with river view, and the lodge has electricity in the evening.

Amazon Jungle Camp (see Amazon Tours & Cruises p397) This camp is near the mouth of the Río Momón, an Amazon tributary just north of Iquitos. It provides optional first/last nights near Iquitos for passengers on one of the many river cruises offered by this company. The lodge has about two dozen rooms with private toilet, and is lit by kerosene lanterns. Cold showers are provided in a separate building.

Cumaceba Lodge (☎ /fax 23-2229; Putumayo 184, Iquitos; 2 days & 1 night US$85, 3 days & 2 nights US$125) About 35km downriver from Iquitos, this lodge has 15 screened rooms with private shower and can arrange more adventurous trips where you would stay in simple, open-sided shelters. This is a popular, nearby, quick budget option.

Heliconia Lodge (☎ 23-1959; www.heliconialodge .com.pe; R Palma 242; 4 days & 3 nights s/d US$310/580, discounts available) Approximately 80km down-river from Iquitos, this comfortable lodge is associated with Iquitos' Hotel Victoria Regia and provides 21 good-sized rooms with private, tiled hot showers. Covered walkways connect rooms to the lobby, restaurant, bar and hammock room. Electricity is available in the evenings, kerosene lanterns later at night. The usual boat and foot tours are offered to see both wildlife and Indian villages.

Cruises

Amazon Tours & Cruises (☎ 23-3931, 23-1611; www.amazontours.net; fax 23-1265; Requena 336; USA ☎ 305-227-2266, 800-423-2791; info@amazontours.com; 275 Fontainebleau Blvd, Suite 173, Miami, FL 33172) Off Avenida La Marina, this company has been operating comfortable cruises for over two decades.

The *MV Río Amazonas* is their largest ship (146 feet) and has 21 air-conditioned cabins with private shower and two or three beds. Three of the cabins are larger suites (two junior and one senior). There is also a dorm cabin with communal showers for student or backpacker use. The 29-passenger *MV Arca* has 10 cabins with air-con that have upper/lower bunks, and three cabins with three beds. All cabins have private showers. In addition, there is a dorm bunk room. Both ships have air-conditioned restaurants. The new *MV Amazonia* should go into service in 2004 and will have 20 upscale cabins and eight suites and an on-deck swimming pool. It will attract a cruise-ship market. No dorms!

The 20-passenger *MV Delfin* has 10 cabins with upper/lower bunks, fans and four shared showers/toilets. The 16-passenger *MV Amazon Explorer* has eight cabins with air-con that have upper/lower bunks and private showers. All these are typical three- or four-decked Amazon river boats with a lot of romantic charm, and they are comfortable but not luxurious (with the exception of the *MV Río Amazonas* suites). All have dining areas and bars and plenty of deck space for watching the river go by. Each is accompanied by a full crew, including an experienced bilingual local naturalist guide. Small launches are carried for side trips. The *MV Delfin* and *MV Amazon Explorer* are available for private charter. Two smaller boats with eight bunks each are also available for tours or charter.

The *MV Río Amazonas* leaves Iquitos almost every Sunday, often with a complement of passengers who arrived from Miami

on a flight the day before. They spend three days sailing downriver to Leticia/Tabatinga and three days returning to Iquitos. Stops are made at jungle towns, Indian villages (for dancing and crafts sales), and almost a day is spent looking around the colorful Colombian port of Leticia and neighboring Tabatinga in Brazil. Short side trips are made to lagoons and up tributaries, and hikes in the jungle last from one to a few hours. This trip is on a well-traveled and long-settled part of the Amazon and gives a good look at the river and its inhabitants today. Wildlife enthusiasts will see dozens of bird species, pink dolphins, beautiful butterflies and other insects, but there's no guarantee you'll see other mammals. Rates start at US$1165 per person, double occupancy, for the six-day round trip, with suites at US$1455 and US$1870. The dorm beds are US$365 on a space-available basis. If just going one-way, the rate is a little over half price.

The *MV Arca* leaves about twice a month, on Sundays, for a five-day cruise of the Pacaya-Samiria reserve. Some tours return to Iquitos, while others end in Yurimaguas. Side trips, bilingual guides, birding trips, fishing excursions etc, are offered. This is currently the most comfortable way of seeing Pacaya-Samiria. Rates are US$795 per person, double occupancy, or US$195 in dorms on a space-available basis. For exact departure dates, see the website.

The *MV Amazonia*, when it begins sailing, will charge roughly 50% more than the *MV Río Amazonas*.

Explorations (☎ 941-992-9660, 800-446-9660; goxploring@aol.com; 27655 Kent Rd, Bonita Springs, FL 34135) This is a US tour agency that sells complete eight-day packages in Miami for travel to Iquitos and Leticia and return on the *MV Río Amazonas*, for visiting Pacaya-Samiria on the *MV Arca*, or doing fishing expeditions. Packages cost about US$1595 and include domestic airfare from Lima, an American biologist guide who accompanies you throughout the trip (in addition to the onboard local naturalist guide), predeparture information, all meals and hotel nights at either end. International flights from most US cities are US$600 to US$850. This is a convenient way to go.

International Expeditions (☎ 205-428-1700, 800-633-4734; nature@ietravel.com; 1 Environs Park, Helena,

AL 35080, USA) This company operates a fleet of boats (all named after gems) and can arrange weeklong cruises from Iquitos. These are elegant boats with three decks, air-conditioned double cabins with private showers, good dining and viewing facilities; and experienced guides. Contact the company for details; you need advance reservations.

Roughing It
Jungle guides in Iquitos will approach you at the airport, in restaurants and on the street. Their quality and reliability varies considerably, so get references for any guide, and proceed with caution. Some guides have criminal records – some for robbing tourists. All guides should have a permit or license; if they don't, check with the tourist office. Readers and travelers have had mixed experiences with private guides, and none are especially recommended. The better jungle-lodge companies snap up the best guides and can arrange wilderness trips.

PEVAS
About 145km downriver from Iquitos, Pevas is Peru's oldest town on the Amazon. Founded by missionaries in 1735, Pevas now has about 3000 inhabitants but no cars, post office or banks (or attorneys!); the first telephone was installed in 1998. Most residents are *mestizos* or Indians from one of four tribes and are friendly and easygoing. Pevas is the most interesting town between Iquitos and the border and is visited regularly (if briefly) by the cruise boats traveling to Leticia.

Sleeping
The rustic but attractive Casa de la Loma lodge on a hill in the outskirts of Pevas offers Amazon views and interesting activities. With its hilltop breezes and views, it is the best place to stay between Iquitos and Leticia. This is a place to spend a few days and get to know the town and the inhabitants, join in a fiesta or shop at the market. There are five screened rooms, which share three clean showers. There is no phone, and reservations are problematical, though Scott at **Amazon Tours & Cruises** (scottpevas@hotmail.com) has good contacts with Pevas and can help. Room rates are low mid-range, but not fixed. Be adventurous and show up.

There is also the basic **Hospedaje Rodríguez**, near the Pevas Plaza, which offers beds and food for a few dollars. Artists have been known to stay at fellow-artist **Francisco Grippa's house**. Grippa handmakes his canvases from local bark, similar to that formerly used by local Indians for cloth.

Getting There & Away
If you haven't arranged transportation with one of the agencies, just go down to the Iquitos docks and get on a boat to Leticia – stops are made at Pevas. (The same applies if you are coming from Leticia.)

THE TRI-BORDER
Even in the middle of the Amazon, border formalities must be adhered to, and officials will refuse passage if documents are not in order. With a valid passport and visa or tourist card, border crossing is not a problem.

When leaving Peru for Brazil or Colombia, you'll get an exit stamp at a Peruvian guard post just before the border (boats stop there long enough for this, ask the captain).

The ports at the three-way border are several kilometers apart and connected by public ferries. They are reached by air or boat, but not road. The biggest town, **Leticia** in Colombia, boasts by far the best hotels and restaurants, and a hospital. You can fly from Leticia to Bogotá on almost daily commercial flights. Otherwise, infrequent boats go to Puerto Asis on the Río Putumayo; the trip takes up to 12 days. From Puerto Asis, buses go further into Colombia.

The two small ports in Brazil are **Tabatinga** and Benjamin Constant; both have basic hotels. Tabatinga has an airport with flights to Manaus. Tabatinga is a continuation of Leticia, and you can walk or take a taxi between the two with no immigration hassles, unless you are planning on traveling further into Brazil or Colombia. Boats leave from Tabatinga downriver, usually stopping in Benjamin Constant for a night, then continuing on to Manaus, Brazil, a week away. Brazilian entry formalities are in Tabatinga. It takes about an hour to reach Benjamin Constant by public ferry. US citizens need a visa to enter Brazil.

Peru is on the south side of the river, where currents create a constantly shifting bank. Most boats from Iquitos will drop you at Santa Rosa, with Peruvian immigration facilities. Motor canoes reach Leticia in about 15 minutes. If you are heading for Colombia or Brazil, Lonely Planet has guidebooks for both countries.

If you are arriving from Colombia or Brazil, you'll find boats in Tabatinga and Leticia for Iquitos. You should pay US$20 or less for the three-day trip on a cargo river boat, or US$50 for an *expreso* (12 to 14 hours), which leave daily. The cruise

ships leave Wednesday and arrive in Iquitos on Saturday morning. You can also ask in Leticia about flights to Iquitos (see p414 for details).

With three borders and four ports to choose from, the best place to base yourself is in Leticia. Remember that however disorganized things may appear, you can always get meals, beds and boats, and money changed simpily by asking around. The locals are used to the different way of doing things on the river, so ask them.

Directory

CONTENTS

ACCOMMODATIONS

Hotels are the norm. Campgrounds aren't to be found, except when trekking. A few youth hostels exist, but are similar value to budget hotels. Homestays may be offered to people taking Spanish courses, but are otherwise a rare option, as are B&Bs. So let's look at those hotels!

Recent regulations require places to have rooms with private hot showers, telephones and other facilities such as a restaurant before they can be called hotels. This has caused many former hotels to change their names to *hospedaje* or *hostal*. This system hasn't entirely caught on but, as a general rule, usually hotels provide the best quality accommodations.

Room rates vary depending on season and city. Cuzco is by far the most expensive town for hotels, even though it's full of them. This is travelers' central, and during the high season (June to August) demand is very high. The busiest times are Inti Raymi, Semana Santa and Fiestas Patrias (see Festivals & Events p407), when advance reservations might be a good idea. Other cities and towns that are pricier than average are Lima, Iquitos, Trujillo and, during the high season, Huaraz. On the other hand, out of prime time you can find incredibly good deals, especially in less visited towns. The rates mentioned here are, therefore, very approximate.

Budget hotels may not accept phone reservations, or may not honor them if you

---

PRACTICALITIES

- Use the **metric** system except for gas/petrol, which is in gallons

- Don't fry your 110V gadgets on the Peruvian 220V, 60 cycles AC **electricity** supply

- Plug your hairdryer into two-pronged **outlets**, which accept both flat (North American) and round (European) plugs

- Ask if your hotel **TV** has cable, or you will be stuck with a poor selection of local soap operas

- Buy or watch **videos** on the NTSC system (compatible with North America)

- Bring a tripod or high-speed **film** to photograph in the low light of the rainforest

- The **camera's** 'evil-eye' can bring bad luck or steal a person's soul – always ask permission before pointing and shooting

- Be up-to-date with Lima's *El Comercio* – dry, conservative but considered the best Spanish-language **newspaper** – and read opposing viewpoints in the mildly left-wing *La Republica*

arrive late in the day. Call them when you arrive in town to see if they have a room available, then head over right away. Better hotels will tell you what time you have to arrive by; others may want a prepayment by means of a deposit into their bank account.

While making reservations by email or websites is convenient, expect to pay for the privilege. Rates secured this way are guaranteed, but walk-in rates off the street can be much lower, as long as rooms are available.

Budget

These hotels are the cheapest, but not necessarily the worst. Rates range from about US$5 to US$20 for a double, and rooms can vary remarkably in quality and facilities.

Budget hotels are often basic but can be clean and well kept, and are good places to meet other budget travelers. Some have rooms of varied quality, often at the same price. Always ask to see a room before accepting it to avoid rooms either overlooking noisy streets, lacking a window, lacking something you need (such as a writing desk and chair), or appearing insecure. Looking around might yield a much more suitable room for about the same rate.

Budget hotels usually have hot showers at least some of the time. Often they are shared, but some rooms with private facilities may be available. There are some excellent bargains to be had in this price range if all you need is a clean bed.

Mid-Range

Mid-priced places range from US$25 to US$70 a double, up to US$100 in Cuzco, although the cheapest mid-range places may sometimes be worse than the best budget choices, so it pays to look around.

At this level, rooms usually have private showers (remote jungle lodges are often an exception) and hot water is the norm. In warm areas, air-conditioning is often, but not always, included. Rooms frequently have amenities such as cable TV, minifridge (sometimes stocked) and telephone. Note that the phones usually connect with reception and can only receive incoming calls. To make outgoing calls, guests have the minor irritation of giving the number to reception, hanging up, and waiting to get called back.

STRANGE SHOWERS

Some showers are heated electrically, with a single cold-water showerhead hooked up to an electric heating element that is switched on when you want a hot (more likely, tepid) shower. Although these may look and sound dangerous, they are quite safe, although mild electric jolts are very occasionally reported.

The cheapest hotels don't always have hot water, or it may be turned on only at certain hours of the day, or may be available upon request with an hour's notice, or even at an extra cost. Ask about this before checking in.

At the other end of the spectrum, the better mid-range hotels and all top-end hotels have modern bathrooms.

Top End

These cost from US$75 upwards. Many conform to international standards, with direct-dial phones, hairdryers in the bathroom, alarm radios by the bed, restaurants with room service, and obliging staff. Most towns don't have top-end hotels; these hotels are found in major cities or tourist centers. Top-end hotels charge a tax of 18% on the rates for their rooms, however, they are allowed to refund this 18% to a non-Peruvian traveler if they can keep a photocopy of your passport.

ACTIVITIES

Most travelers are interested in three main activities – visiting archaeological sites, trekking and/or watching wildlife. But there are more possibilities, as outlined here. You can indulge in these at any time, though trekking in the highlands is a very wet and muddy proposition from December to April.

Diving

Scuba diving is limited. The water is cold except from December to March, and the water is cloudiest then because of run-off from mountain rivers as it's the wet season. There are dive shops in Lima (see p65). The best diving areas are the warm waters near the Ecuadorian border and the clear waters around the Península de Paracas.

Mountain Biking

In Peru mountain biking is a fledgling sport. See under Cuzco (p177) and Huaraz (p311) for options. Be aware that, with the exception of Huaraz, rental mountain bikes tend to be pretty basic, so if you are planning on some serious biking, it's best to bring your own. Domestic flights may charge from US$10 to US$50 extra for a bike. Even with your own bike, it's worth hiring a guide or getting local information about the best biking routes. Most of them aren't very well known.

Mountaineering

The Cordillera Blanca, with dozens of peaks exceeding 5000m, is arguably the most inspiring climbing area in South America. Huaraz has tours, guides, information and climbing equipment for hire (p312), though it's best to bring your own gear for more serious ascents.

Ishinca (5530m) and Pisco (5752m) are snow peaks considered easy enough for relatively inexperienced climbers. These mountains are good warm-up climbs for experienced climbers who are acclimatizing for bigger adventures, such as Huascarán (6768m), the highest peak in Peru and a fairly challenging climb. In between are many more difficult peaks, including the knife-edged Alpamayo (5947m), considered by many to be the most beautiful mountain in Peru, and dozens of possible new routes for highly experienced climbers. South of the Cordillera Blanca, the Cordillera Huayhuash offers many other possibilities, including Yerupajá (6634m), Peru's second-highest peak.

High-altitude climbing is best done during the dry season, with mid-June to mid-July considered the best time. Acclimatization to altitude is essential (see p429 for details).

River Running

Also known as white-water rafting, river running is a popular activity year-round. Adventurers are discovering the unspoiled rivers plunging from the Andes into the lush canyons of the upper Amazon. Commercial rafting trips and kayaking are both possible; trips can range from a few hours to over two weeks.

Cuzco is undoubtedly the main town in which to find the greatest variety of river possibilities (p177), ranging from a few hours of mild rapids on the Urubamba to several days on the Apurímac (technically the source of the Amazon and with some world-class rafting) or Tambopata (a river-running trip that tumbles down the eastern slopes of the Andes, culminating in a couple of days of floating in unspoiled rainforest). Other areas include Arequipa (p135) and Lunahuaná (p91).

On the more difficult Apurímac and Tambopata rivers, paying customers and guides have died in accidents in recent years. These and other rivers are remote, and rescues can take days. It is therefore worth investing in a well-run expedition with a reputable company and avoiding the cut-price trips.

A good operator will have insurance, provide you with a Boleta de Venta (a legal document indicating the operator is registered), have highly experienced guides with certified first-aid training who carry a properly stocked medical kit, and provide top-notch equipment including self-bailing rafts, US Coast Guard–approved life jackets, 1st-class helmets and spare paddles. Many good companies raft rivers accompanied by a kayaker who is experienced in river rescue.

As with the cheaper trekking outfitters, some river-running companies are not environmentally sensitive, resulting in dirty camping beaches. The only way to protect yourself and the river is to ask the tough questions and inspect equipment.

Surfing

In Peru surfing is enjoyed mainly by a few local middle- and upper-class young people and a handful of international surfers. The surfing is good, uncrowded and with plenty of new places to explore.

The water is cold from April to December (as low as 13°C or 55°F), when locals wear wet suits to surf. Indeed, many surfers wear wet suits year-round, even though they could get away with not using them in the January to March period, when the water is a little warmer (around 20°C in the Lima area). The far north coast (north of Talara) stays above 21°C most of the year. The surfing is quite challenging, but available facilities and equipment are limited and expensive; see p65 in the Lima chapter for a list of surf shops.

Going from north to south: Máncora and Zorritos have good lefts, but the left at Cabo Blanco can be tricky when conditions are intimidating. The most famous wave is at Puerto Chicama, where rides of over a kilometer in length are possible, on a wave considered the world's longest. Pacasmayo, just to the north, is also good.

In Lima, surfers can be found on the crowded Miraflores and Costa Verde beaches. Slightly south, Herradura, with an outstanding left, gets crowded when there is a strong swell. In-the-know surfers prefer the smaller crowds further south at Punta Hermosa. Near here is Punta Rocas, where international and national championships are held annually. Isla San Gallán, off the Península de Paracas, is accessible only by boat (ask local fishermen or at the hotels) and provides an excellent right.

Swimming

This is popular from January to March, when the ocean is warm, although the beaches are contaminated near the major coastal cities and there are many dangerous currents. Only north of Talara does the water stay warm year-round.

Trekking

Trekking is very rewarding during the May to September dry season in the Andes. It is certainly possible to hike during the wet season; just be prepared for rain!

The main trekking centers are Cuzco (for the world-famous Inca Trail to Machu Picchu and exploring Ausangate) and Huaraz (for the spectacular Cordillera Blanca and Cordillera Huayhuash). Both towns have outfitters who will provide rental equipment and guides.

Visiting Archaeological Sites

Peru's main attractions are its Inca ruins, especially Machu Picchu (p207). However, there is also a wealth of sites from other cultures; we recommend the following.

Trujillo is an excellent base for seeing Chan Chan (the huge adobe capital of the Chimu, p269), as well as ongoing excavations in the Moche pyramids (p274). If you have time in Huaraz, the 2500-year-old ruins of the Chavín (p327) are worth a trip. The wonderfully woven artefacts of Paracas are best seen in museums – Lima's Museo

de la Nación (p57) and Museo Larco (p63) in particular, and the Nazca Lines (p104) can only be appreciated properly from the air. The excavated site of El Señor del Sipán (p284) near Chiclayo is interesting but the highlights are in the Sipán Museum in Lambayeque (p284). The funerary towers of the Colla people at Sillustani (p155), near Lake Titicaca, are worth seeing if you have a spare day in Puno. Kuélap (p348) is great if you have the time and energy to go to such a remote area.

Watching Wildlife

Sea lions, seabirds, vicuñas, condors, scarlet macaws, hummingbirds, sloths, leaf-cutter ants, monkeys, caimans, toucans, iguanas, parrots, freshwater dolphins – the list of Peruvian wildlife seems endless, and there are many opportunities to see these animals. Many people come specifically to spend their days watching wildlife, and many companies arrange guided natural-history tours.

The national parks and reserves are all good places for observation, but private areas such as jungle lodges can also yield a good number of birds, insects, reptiles and even monkeys. Early morning and late afternoon are the best times to watch for wildlife activity anywhere; the hot middle part of the day is when many animals rest – out of sight. A lightweight pair of binoculars will improve wildlife observation tremendously.

Have realistic expectations. The desert has limited wildlife – go to the Península de Paracas and Islas Ballestas for the best experience. The rugged highlands have Andean wildlife, but much of it has been hunted out, so visit more remote trekking areas. The rainforest is a fantastic environment with plenty of wildlife, but animals are hard to see because the vegetation is so thick. You could be 15m from a jaguar and not even know it is there. Don't expect to see jaguars, ocelots, tapirs, and many other mammals, which are shy, well camouflaged and rare. Concentrate on wildlife that is easier to observe and enjoy them – most of the animals listed earlier can be seen fairly easily if you visit different parts of the country. Walk slowly and quietly; listen as well as look. And be patient.

BUSINESS HOURS

Hours are variable and liable to change. Some places may have posted hours and not adhere to them. Many shops and offices close for an extended lunch break, but banks and post offices stay open. Weekend hours are limited or nonexistent for government offices. Recently a few 24-hour supermarkets have opened in Lima and some other major cities. Taxi drivers often know where late-night stores are. Be flexible and patient when needing to get things done as service can be slow and official opening hours aren't always kept.

CHILDREN

If they occupy a seat, children pay full fare on buses but often ride free if they sit on a parent's knee. Children under 12 pay half fare on domestic flights and get a seat, while infants under two pay 10% but don't get a seat.

In hotels, children shouldn't be charged as much as an adult, but the rate is open to discussion. Cots are rarely available.

While 'kids' meals' are not offered in restaurants, it is perfectly acceptable to order a meal to split between two children or an adult and a child. High chairs are rarely available.

Foreigners traveling with children are a curiosity in Peru and will meet with extra, generally friendly, attention and interest.

For more information, see Lonely Planet's *Travel with Children*.

CLIMATE CHARTS

June to August is the dry season in the highlands; the wettest months are from January to April. The coast is arid and some parts see rain rarely, if at all. It rains all the time in the eastern rainforest but the wettest months are December to April. However, it rarely rains for more than a few hours at a time. See When to Go (p13) for more information.

COURSES

Peru is less well known for its Spanish-language courses than some Latin American countries. However, there are schools in Lima (p67), Puerto Maldonado (p358), Huancayo (p233) and, best of all, Cuzco (p179).

CUSTOMS

Peru allows duty-free importation of 3L of alcohol and 400 cigarettes. You can import

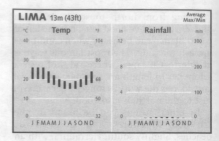

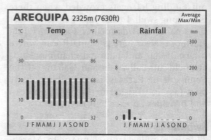

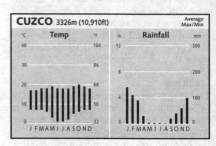

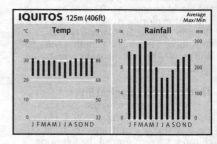

US$300 of gifts and bring items for personal use. Legally, you are allowed to bring in a laptop, cameras, bicycles, kayaks, climbing gear etc for personal use, though don't draw attention to it.

It is illegal to take pre-Columbian artefacts out of Peru, and it is illegal to bring them into most countries. Bringing home animal products from endangered species is also illegal. Coca leaves are legal in Peru, but not in most other countries – even in the form of tea bags, which are freely available in Peruvian shops. People subject to random drug testing should be aware that coca, even in the form of tea, may leave trace amounts in their urine.

DANGERS & ANNOYANCES
Theft

Peru has a reputation for thievery. Every year we hear from travelers who have been robbed. However, by taking basic precautions and exercising a reasonable amount of vigilance, you probably won't be robbed. Often travelers are so involved in their new surroundings and experiences that they forget to stay alert – and that's when something is stolen. It's good to know that armed theft is not as frequent as sneak theft. Remember that crowded places are usually the haunts of pickpockets – badly lit bus and train terminals or bustling markets and fiestas. Hotels and hotel staff aren't entirely safe either; lock your valuables inside your closed luggage, or use safety deposit services where they are offered.

Thieves look for easy targets. Tourists carrying a wallet or passport in a hip pocket are asking for trouble. Leave your wallet in a secure place at your hotel, otherwise it's an easy mark for a pickpocket. A small roll of bills loosely wadded under a handkerchief in your front pocket is as safe a way as any of carrying your daily spending money. The rest should be hidden. Always use at least a closable inside pocket (or preferably a hidden body pouch, money belt or leg pouch) to protect your money and passport.

Carry some of your money as traveler's checks. These can be refunded if lost or stolen, often within a few days in Lima. However, exchange rates for traveler's checks are quite a bit lower than for US cash. Airlines may reissue a lost ticket for a fee, if you have a receipt. Stolen passports can be reissued at your embassy. For this, you need a police report of the theft and positive identification.

Snatch theft is also common, so don't wear gold necklaces, cameras and expensive wristwatches. Snatch theft can also occur if you place a bag on the ground for just a second.

COPIES

All important documents (passport, credit cards, travel insurance policy, driving license etc) should be photocopied before you leave home. Leave one copy at home and keep another with you, separate from the originals.

Another way of storing your travel documents is with Lonely Planet's free online Travel Vault. Create your own vault at www.ekno.lonelyplanet.com.

Thieves often work in pairs or groups. While your attention is being distracted by one, another is robbing you. The distraction can take the form of a bunch of kids fighting in front of you, an old lady 'accidentally' bumping into you, someone dropping something in your path or spilling something on your clothes and so on.

Razor-blade artists may slit open your luggage when you're not looking. All luggage is vulnerable; a pack on your back or luggage in the rack of a bus – or even your trouser pocket. Many travelers carry their day packs on their chests to avoid having them slashed during day trips to markets and other crowded public spaces. It is always a good idea to walk purposefully wherever you are going, even if you are lost.

One of the best solutions to the rip-off problem is to travel with a friend and to watch one another. If you see a suspicious-looking character, look them directly in the eye and point them out to your traveling companions.

Take out traveler's insurance (see p409 later), but don't get paranoid. Stay alert and you can spend months in Peru without anything being stolen.

Drugs

Definitely avoid having any conversation with someone who offers you drugs. In fact, talking to any stranger on the street can hold risks. It has happened that travelers have been stopped soon after by plainclothes police officers and accused of talking to a drug dealer. Never get into a vehicle with the 'police,' but insist on going to a bona fide police station on foot. Be wary of false or crooked police who prey on tourists. Note that the Policía de Turismo, listed in major cities, is usually helpful with legal problems.

Be aware that there are draconian penalties for the possession of even a small amount of drugs for personal use. Minimum sentences are several years in jail.

DANGEROUS DRUG AREAS
It is best to avoid the Río Huallaga valley between Tingo María and Juanjui. This is where the majority of Peru's illegal drug-growing takes place, and the area is somewhat dangerous.

Environmental Hazards
Some of the hazards you might encounter in Peru include altitude sickness (see p429), earthquakes and avalanches (p429), animal bites (p429), hypothermia (p430) and heat exhaustion (p431). You can take precautions for most of these, while the rest are, thankfully, rare.

Terrorism
There are two guerrilla groups in Peru, the MRTA and the Sendero Luminoso. The main leaders of both groups were captured in 1992 and, since then, travel safety has improved dramatically. Occasional attacks by a few remaining Senderistas are still reported, but these happen in remote areas and are not generally aimed at tourists.

DISABLED TRAVELERS
Peru's official tourism organization, **Prom-Peru** (www.promperu.gob.pe) has a link to Accessible Tourism. It lists wheelchair-accessible hotels, restaurants and attractions in Lima, Cuzco, Aguas Calientes, Iquitos and Trujillo, with more to come.

Peru offers few conveniences for disabled travelers. Wheelchair ramps are few and far between, and pavement is often badly potholed and cracked. Bathrooms and toilets are often barely large enough for an able-bodied person to walk into, so few are accessible to wheelchairs. Features such as signs in braille or phones for the hearing-impaired are virtually nonexistent. Nevertheless, there are disabled Peruvians who get around, mainly through the help of others. It is not particularly unusual to see disabled travelers being carried bodily to a seat on a bus, for example. If you need assistance, be polite and good natured.

Apumayo Expeditions (☎ 084-24-6018; www.apumayo.com; Garcilaso 265, Interior 3, Cuzco) An adventure-tour company that takes disabled travelers to Cuzco, Machu Picchu, other historical sites, river running and to the rainforest.
Society for Accessible Travel & Hospitality (SATH; ☎ 212-447-7284; fax 212-725-8253; www.sath.org; 347 5th Ave, Suite 610, New York, NY 10016, USA) is a good resource for information.

DISCOUNT CARDS
Official International Student Identity Cards (ISIC), with a photograph, can get you a 50% discount in some places. Senior discount cards are not recognized.

EMBASSIES & CONSULATES
For details of the location of migraciónes (immigration) offices in Peru, which issue entry cards, provide exit stamps and extend the period of your stay, see Visas (p412).

Your Own Embassy
It's important to realize what your embassy – the embassy of the country of which you are a citizen – can and can't do to help you if you get into trouble. Generally speaking, it won't be much help if the trouble you're in is remotely your own fault. Your embassy will not be sympathetic if you end up in jail after committing a crime locally, even if such actions are legal in your own country.

In genuine emergencies, you might get some assistance, but only if other channels have been exhausted. If you need to get home urgently, a free ticket is exceedingly unlikely – the embassy would expect you to have travel insurance. If all your money and documents are stolen, it should assist you with getting a new passport, but a loan for onward travel is out of the question.

Peruvian Embassies & Consulates
For countries not listed here, refer to the government website www.rree.gob.pe.
Australia (☎ 02-6273-8752; embassy@embaperu.org.au; 40 Brisbane Ave, Suite 8, Barton, ACT 2600)
Bolivia (☎ 02-244-0631; conperlp@ceibo.entelnet.bo; Av 6 de Agosto 2455, Edificio Hilda, Oficina 402, Sopocachi, La Paz)
Brazil (☎ 61-242-9435; fax 61-244-9344; www.embperu.org.br; SES, Av das Nações, Lote 43, 70428-900, Brasília DF)
Canada (☎ 613-238-1777; emperuca@bellnet.ca; 130 Albert St, Suite 1901, Ottawa, Ontario K1P 5G4)

Chile Santiago (☎ 2-235-2356; fax 2-235-8139; embstgo@entelchile.net; Av Andrés Bello 1751, Providencia 9, Casilla 16277, Santiago) Arica (☎ 58-23-1020; fax 58-23-1433; Conperarica@entelchile.net; San Martín 235, Arica)

Colombia Bogotá (☎ 1-257-0505; fax 1-249-8581; lbogota@cable.net.co; Carrera 80A; 6-50, Bogotá DC) Leticia (☎ 98-592-7204; fax 98-592-7402; Calle 13, No 11-48, Leticia)

Ecuador (☎ 04-228-0114; conperu@gye.satnet.net; Av Francisco de Orellana Kennedy Norte, 14th fl, Oficina 02, Edificio Centrum, Guayaquil)

France (☎ 331-53-70-42-00; amb.perou@noos.fr; Av Kleber, 75116 Paris 50)

Germany (☎ 030-206-4103; eprfa@aol.com; Mohrenstrasse 42, 10117 Berlín)

Japan (☎ 3-346-4243; fax 3-3409-7589; embperu tokyo@embperujapan.org; 4-4-27, Higashi 1-Chome, Shibuya-ku, Tokyo)

Netherlands (☎ 70-365-3500; fax 70-365-1929; info@embassyofperu.nl; Nassauplein 4, 2585 EA, The Hague)

New Zealand (☎ 04-499-8087; embassy.peru@ xtra.co.nz; Level 8, Cigna House, 40 Mercer St, Wellington, PO Box 2566)

UK (☎ 0207-235-1917; postmaster@peruembassy -uk.com; 52 Sloane St, London SW1X 9SP)

USA (☎ 202-833-9860-9; lepruwash@aol.com; 1700 Massachusetts Ave NW, Washington DC 20036)

Embassies & Consulates in Peru

The following principal representatives are in Lima (unless stated otherwise), and are open Monday to Friday. Other consuls are listed under the relevant cities.

Australia (☎ 222-8281; fax 221-4996; losani@ibm.net.pe; Victor Belaúnde 398, San Isidro) There's limited services only at the Honorary Consul.

Bolivia Lima (☎ 422-8231; fax 222-4594; Los Castaños 235, San Isidro; ☽ 9:30am-12:30pm)
Tacna (☎ 71-5792; Bolognesi 1721, Tacna; ☽ 9am-2pm Mon-Fri) Puerto Maldonado (Loreto 268 on the Plaza de Armas)

Brazil (☎ 421-5650; fax 445-2421; José Pardo 850, Miraflores; ☽ 9:30am-1pm & 2-5pm)

Canada (☎ 444-4015; lima@dfait-maeci.gc.ca; Federico Gerdes 130, Miraflores; ☽ 8am-5pm)

Chile (☎ 221-2817, 221-2818; Javier Prado Oeste 790, San Isidro; ☽ 9am-1pm)

Colombia (☎ 441-0954; fax 441-9806; Jorge Basadre 1580, San Isidro; ☽ 9am-1pm)
consulate (☎ 23-1461; Araujo 431, Iquitos)

Ecuador Lima (☎ 440-9991; fax 442-4182; Las Palmeras 356, San Isidro; ☽ 9am-1pm & 3-6pm)
Tumbes (Bolívar 123, Tumbes; ☽ 9am-1pm & 4-6pm Mon-Fri)

France (☎ 215-8400; embajada@ambafrance-pe.org; Arequipa 3415, San Isidro; ☽ 9-11am)

Germany (☎ 212-5016; kanzlei@embajada-alemana .org.pe; Arequipa 4202, Miraflores; ☽ 9am-noon)

Israel (☎ /fax 433-4431; Natalio Sánchez 125, 6th fl, Santa Beatriz; ☽ 10am-1pm)

Netherlands (☎ 476-1069; fax 475-6536; Principal 190, Santa Catalina; ☽ 9am-noon)

New Zealand (☎ 222-5022; Alfonso.Rey@newzealand milk.com; New Zealand Milk (Peru) SA, Av Victor Andres Belaunde 147, Edificio Real Tres-Oficina 1102, San Isidro)

UK (☎ 617-3000; britemb@terra.com.pe; José Larco 1301, 22nd fl, Miraflores; ☽ 8am-noon)

USA (Map p53; ☎ 434-3000; usembassy.state.gov/lima; Av Cuadra 17, Surco; ☽ 8am-5pm)

FESTIVALS & EVENTS

Many of Peru's festivals favor the Roman Catholic liturgical calendar and are celebrated with great pageantry, especially in highland Indian villages, where Catholic feast days are often linked with some traditional agricultural festival (such as harvest time). These days provide an excuse for a fiesta, with much drinking, dancing, rituals and processions. Other holidays are of historical or political interest, such as Fiestas Patrias (National Independence) on July 28 and 29. See Holidays (p408) for details of days that are public holidays in Peru.

In addition to these, local fiestas and festivals are held somewhere in Peru every week. Many are mentioned in the individual town descriptions.

JANUARY

Año Nuevo (New Year's Day; January 1) This holiday is particularly important in Huancayo, where a fiesta continues until January 6.

FEBRUARY

La Virgen de la Candelaria (Candlemas; February 2) This highland fiesta is particularly colorful around Puno.

Carnaval Held on the last few days before Lent, this holiday is often 'celebrated' with water fights, so be warned. It's a popular fiesta in the highlands, with the Carnaval de Cajamarca being one of the biggest. It's also busy in beach towns, where the water is still warm.

MARCH-APRIL

Semana Santa (Holy Week) The week before Easter Sunday is celebrated with spectacular religious processions almost daily, with Ayacucho being recognized as having the best in Peru. Cuzco is also good for Easter processions. Again, beach towns do good business.

MAY
Labor Day (May 1)

JUNE
Corpus Christi (9th Thursday after Easter) Processions in Cuzco are especially dramatic.
Inti Raymi (also St John the Baptist and Peasant's Day; June 24) Inti Raymi celebrates the winter solstice and is the greatest of the Inca festivals. It's certainly the spectacle of the year in Cuzco and attracts thousands of Peruvian and foreign visitors. Despite its commercialization, it's still worth seeing the street dances and parades, as well as the pageant held in Sacsayhuamán. It's also a big holiday in many of the jungle towns.
San Pedro y San Pablo (June 29) More fiestas, especially in the highlands.

JULY
La Virgen del Carmen (July 16) This holiday is mainly celebrated in the southern sierra, with Paucartambo and Pisac near Cuzco, and Pucara near Lake Titicaca, being especially important.
Fiestas Patrias (Peru's Independence; July 28-29) This is celebrated nationwide; in the southern sierra festivities begin three days ahead with the feast of St James (July 25).

AUGUST
Santa Rosa de Lima (August 30) This involves major processions held in Lima to honor the patron saint of Lima and of the Americas.

OCTOBER
El Señor de los Milagros (Lord of the Miracles; October 18) Major religious processions in Lima; celebrants wear purple.

NOVEMBER
Todos Santos (All Saint's Day; November 1) A religious precursor to the following day.
Día de los Muertos (All Soul's Day; November 2) Celebrated with gifts of food, drink and flowers taken to family graves; especially colorful in the sierra. Some of the 'gift' food and drink is consumed, and the atmosphere is festive rather than somber.
Puno Day (November 5) Several days of spectacular costumes and street dancing to celebrate the legendary emergence of the first Inca, Manco Capac.

DECEMBER
Inmaculada (Fiesta de la Purísma Concepción; Feast of the Immaculate Conception; December 8) A national holiday celebrated with religious processions to the Virgin Mary.
Christmas Day (December 25) Less secular and more religious than in developed countries.

GAY & LESBIAN TRAVELERS

Gay rights in a political or legal context don't even exist as an issue for most Peruvians. Sexuality is more stereotyped in Peru (and in many Latin countries) than it is in other countries, with the man playing a dominant macho role and the woman tagging along with that. This attitude spills over into homosexuality: 'Straight-acting' macho men are not considered to be gay, even if they are, while an effeminate man, even if he is straight, may be called a *maricón* – a derogatory term for a homosexual man. Public displays of affection are very rarely seen, even with hetero couples, and may be treated with derision, indifference, hostility or laughter. Relatively few gay men in Peru are exclusively homosexual. This means that AIDS is often transmitted heterosexually and is a growing problem in Peru (see HIV/AIDS p426).

Lesbians are a largely ignored segment of the population; most Peruvians realize they exist but don't think much about them.

Lima is by far the most accepting of gay people; Cuzco is getting there.

Organizations

Peru's best-known gay organization is **Movimiento Homosexual-Lesbiana** (MHOL, ☎ 01-433-6375; fax 01-433-5519; mhol@terra.com.pe; Mariscal Miller 828, Jesús María, Lima). Its phone line is open 24 hours, and it has English-speaking staff in the evenings.

The best website for gay travelers is the excellent gaylimape.tripod.com, with regularly updated information about the best places to stay, eat and play throughout gay Lima, with some links to other cities.

HOLIDAYS

On major holidays, banks, offices and other services are closed, and transportation tends to be very crowded, so book ahead if possible. If an official public holiday falls on a weekend, offices close on the following Monday. If an official holiday falls midweek, it may or may not be moved to the nearest Monday to create a long weekend. Major holidays may be celebrated for days around the official date. Fiestas Patrias is the biggest national holiday, and the whole nation seems to be on the move then. Buses and hotels are booked long in advance for the major holidays and hotel prices can triple.

Official holidays are: January 1; Good Friday; May 1; June 24; June 29; July 28-29; August 30; November 1; December 25. See Festivals & Events (p407) earlier for more details.

INSURANCE

Having a travel-insurance policy to cover theft, loss and medical problems is a very good idea. Some policies specifically exclude 'dangerous activities', which can include scuba diving, motorcycling, even trekking.

You may prefer a policy that pays doctors or hospitals directly rather than you having to pay on the spot and claim later. If you have to claim later make sure you keep all documentation. Check that the policy covers ambulances or an emergency flight home.

INTERNET ACCESS

Accessing the Internet is exceptionally easy in Peru. Even the tiniest of towns has an Internet café, and larger cities have dozens of them. Some are listed under each town in this book, but you will find many more. In most cities, connection rates are under US$1 per hour and it is only in the more remote towns that you may pay a little over US$1. Most places are open till late in the evening. If you use any of the many free web-based email accounts (such as Hotmail or Yahoo!) you can easily access your email anywhere.

Using your own laptop for access is generally an expensive hassle because ISPs don't have dialups in Peru, so you have to make an international call. It's far better to rely on Internet cafés.

See Internet Resources (p17) for some useful Peruvian sites.

LAUNDRY

Self-service laundry machines are available in only a few major cities. This means that you have to find someone to wash your clothes or else wash them yourself. In most towns, there are *lavanderías* (laundries) where you leave your clothes for a full day or overnight. Some *lavanderías* only do dry-cleaning and/or charge by the number of items rather than weight, so check.

LEGAL MATTERS

Be aware that some police are corrupt (see Drugs on p405 earlier). Also be aware that your own embassy is of limited help if you get into trouble with the law (see Embassies & Consulates on p406). Should you be stopped by a plainclothes policeman, don't hand over any documents or money, and insist on going to a police station. Don't get into the policeman's car.

Bribery is illegal. However, you'll often see a Peruvian driver slipping a policeman some money in order to smooth things along. The idea here is not to offer an (illegal) bribe, but simply a 'gift' or 'on-the-spot fine' so that you can get on your way. For most travelers, who won't have to deal with traffic police, the most likely place that you'll be expected to pay officials a little extra is (sometimes) at land borders. This too is illegal, and if you have the time and fortitude to stick to your guns, you'll eventually be allowed in without paying a fee.

If you are driving and are involved in an accident that results in injury, know that drivers are routinely imprisoned for several days or even weeks until innocence has been established. If you are imprisoned for any reason, make sure someone knows about it. Prison food is extremely poor, and Peruvians routinely bring food to family members who are in prison.

MAPS

For general travel, the maps in this book are probably quite sufficient. The best (and most recent) road map of Peru is the 1:2,200,000 *Mapa Vial* published by Lima 2000 and available in better bookstores. For topographic hiking maps, the best source is the Instituto Geográfico Nacional (IGN; see p51) in Lima.

MONEY

Peru uses the nuevo sol, which has traded at US$1 per S/3.40 to S/3.50 for several years. For more details on exchange rates, see the Quick Reference page on the inside cover of this book.

The nuevo sol comes in bills of S/10, S/20, S/50, S/100 and (rarely) S/200. It is divided into 100 céntimos, with copper-colored coins of S/0.05, S/0.10 and S/0.20, and silver-colored S/0.50 and S/1. In addition, there are attractive bimetallic S/2 and S/5 coins with a copper-colored center surrounded by a silver-colored metal.

When receiving local currency, ask for some small bills, as S/100 bills are hard to change in small towns for small purchases. The best places to exchange money are normally *casas de cambio* (foreign-exchange houses), which are fast, have longer hours, and give slightly better rates than banks.

See also Costs (p16).

ATMs

Most cities and many small towns have ATMs on the Plus (Visa) or Cirrus (MasterCard) system and will accept your debit card. This is a convenient way of obtaining cash at rates usually about 2% lower than at *casas de cambio*. Both US dollars and nuevo soles are available. Check the ATM locators on www.visa.com or www.mastercard.com. Your bank will charge a fee (usually US$2) for each foreign ATM transaction. ATMs are normally open 24 hours.

Cash

This is the best way to carry your money for receiving the top exchange rates quickly. The best currency for exchange is the US dollar, although the euro is starting to gain increasing acceptance. Other hard currencies can be exchanged, but with difficulty except in the major cities and tourist centers. All foreign currencies must be in excellent condition; worn, torn or damaged bills are not accepted.

Credit Cards

Many top-end hotels and shops accept credit cards but usually charge you a 7% (or greater) fee for using them.

Moneychangers

Street moneychangers hang out near banks and *casas de cambio* and give competitive rates (you may need to bargain), but are not always honest, so be careful if using them. Officially, they should wear a vest and badge identifying them as legal. Their main use is after hours or at borders where other sources are unavailable.

Taxes & Refunds

International (p415) and domestic (p419) departure taxes are charged in airports. Upmarket hotels and restaurants may charge a tax; if so, they are included in prices listed in this book (but see Top End on p401).

Top-end restaurants will charge a tax and service charge which, combined, can be as high as 31%. If on a budget, ask before ordering to avoid unpleasant surprises. There is no system of tax refunds.

Traveler's Checks

Although they are safer in the event of loss, commissions mean that you can lose from 3% to 12% of the checks' value when you exchange them, and they may be hard to change in small towns. Some *casas de cambio* don't deal with them, so you may need to use a bank. American Express checks are the most widely accepted, followed by Visa and Thomas Cook.

POST

The privatized postal system is now run by Serpost. The service is quite efficient but more expensive than in more developed nations. Airmail postcards and letters cost about US$1 to most foreign destinations and arrive in about seven to 10 days from Lima, and longer from the provincial cities.

Lista de correos (general delivery or poste restante) can be sent to any major post office. Make sure your last name is clearly printed and underlined to avoid confusion; it's worth checking under your first and middle names in case.

SHOPPING

Arts and crafts are sold wherever tourists gather. Bargaining is the norm at street stalls and small markets; prices are fixed in the most upscale stores in Lima. Popular items include clothes of alpaca wool, tapestries, ceramics, masks, and gold and silver jewelry.

SOLO TRAVELERS

The undeniable advantage of being able to do what you want when you want usually outweighs any problems that solo travelers may have. However, it can be a good idea to briefly hook up with other travelers, eg when returning to your hotel late at night or trekking. Solo females may be the target of unwanted attention – see Women Travelers (p412).

TELEPHONE

Public phones are available in even the smallest towns and often villages. Most work with phonecards, many with coins.

PERU'S DEPARTMENTAL CODES

There are 24 departmental (area) codes within the country.

Lima	☎ 01
Amazonas	☎ 041
Ancash	☎ 043
Apurímac	☎ 083
Arequipa	☎ 054
Ayacucho	☎ 066
Cajamarca	☎ 076
Cuzco	☎ 084
Huancavelica	☎ 067
Huánuco	☎ 062
Ica	☎ 056
Junín	☎ 064
La Libertad	☎ 044
Lambayeque	☎ 074
Loreto	☎ 065
Madre de Dios	☎ 082
Moquegua	☎ 053
Pasco	☎ 063
Piura	☎ 073
Puno	☎ 051
San Martín	☎ 042
Tacna	☎ 052
Tumbes	☎ 072
Ucayali	☎ 061

Each government region (called a department) has its own area code which is listed immediately after each town entry in this book and in the boxed text. If you are dialing within the department, you don't need to dial the area code. To dial another department, you'll need to dial the area code first.

Note that any phone number beginning with a 9 is a mobile-phone number.

If calling Peru from abroad, dial your access code, Peru's country code (51), then the area code *without the 0*, then the local number.

If making international calls from Peru, dial the access code (00), the country code, the area code (without the initial 0) and then the phone number.

There's an online telephone directory at www.amarillastelefonica.com. See the Quick Reference page inside the front cover of this book for details on how to make collect calls in Peru, or contact an operator or information.

Phonecards

Called *tarjetas telefonicas*, these cards are widely available and are made by many companies in many price ranges. Some are designed specifically for international calls. Some have an electronic chip that keeps track of your balance when the card is inserted into an appropriate phone.

Other cards use a code system whereby you dial your own personal code to obtain balances and access; these can be used from almost any phone. The most common are the 147 cards; you dial 147, then enter your personal code (which is on the back of the card), listen to a message telling you how much money you have left on the card, dial the number, and listen to a message telling you how much time you have left for this call. The drawback is it's in Spanish. The 147 card is best used for local calls. For long-distance calls, the Hola Peru card is cheaper, and works the same way except that you begin by dialing 141.

There are numerous other cards – ask around for which ones offer the best deal.

TIME

Peru is five hours behind Greenwich Mean Time. Daylight savings time is not used.

It is appropriate here to mention that punctuality is not one of the things that Latin America is famous for. Be prepared for some serious waiting.

TOILETS

Peruvian plumbing (except in top-end hotels and restaurants) leaves something to be desired. Flushing a toilet can lead to an overflow, so you should avoid putting anything other than human waste into the toilet. Even putting toilet paper into the bowl can clog up the system and so a waste receptacle is routinely provided for the paper. This may not seem particularly sanitary, but is better than clogged bowls and water on the floor. A well-run hotel or restaurant, even a cheap one, will ensure that the receptacle is emptied and the toilet cleaned every day.

Public toilets are rare outside of transportation terminals and restaurants. Those in transportation terminals usually have an attendant who charges you about US$0.10 and provides a few sheets of toilet paper. Toilet paper is provided only in the better restaurants, and travelers should carry a supply of their own.

TOURIST INFORMATION

Peru doesn't have international tourist offices, but their official tourism website (www.promperu.gob.pe), in Spanish, English and German, is an excellent way to obtain tourist information before you depart. Peruvian embassies sometimes supply tourist information as well.

Once in Peru, you'll find that PromPeru runs information offices called iPeru in Lima, Arequipa, Ayacucho, Cuzco, Iquitos, Puno and Trujillo. There is a 24-hour **iPeru hotline** (☎ /fax 01-574-8000; iperu@promperu.gob.pe), which can assist if you feel you were ripped off by a hotel or tour operator. Municipal tourist offices are found in many other cities and listed in the text.

VISAS

With very few exceptions (a handful of Asian, African and communist countries), visas are not required for travelers entering Peru. Travelers are permitted a 30- to 90-day stay, stamped into their passports and onto an embarkation card that you keep and return upon leaving the country. Extensions can be obtained in the migraciónes (immigration) offices of the major cities, with Lima (p54) being the easiest place to do this. They cost about US$28 and you can keep extending your stay up to 180 days total. When your time is up, you can leave the country overland and return a day later to begin the process again.

Apart from in Lima, migraciónes offices are in Arequipa, Cuzco, Iquitos, Puno and Puerto Maldonado, as well as on or near the Chilean and Ecuadorian borders.

WOMEN TRAVELERS

The majority of female travelers to Peru will encounter no serious problems, though they should come mentally prepared for being the center of attention. Machismo is alive and well in Peruvian towns and cities, where it's not uncommon for fast-talking charmers to attach themselves to gringas and be surprisingly oblivious to a lack of interest from their quarry. Curious staring, whistling, hissing and catcalls in the streets are also run-of-the-mill. Many Peruvian men make a pastime of dropping *piropos*

(compliments) such as *linda* (pretty) or *guapa* (good-looking) at passing women, which can feel threatening at first, especially if you don't understand Spanish.

Women with light-colored hair and skin often attract more attention, partly because gringas are considered to be more liberated and sexually available than Peruvian women. Ignoring provocation and staring ahead is generally the best response, but in the case of persistent harassment, keep in store a number of ardor-smothering phrases such as *soy casada* (I'm married) or a sharper *déjame en paz* (leave me in peace). Appealing to locals is also recommended, as you'll find most Peruvians to be extremely warm and protective towards lone women, commonly expressing surprise and concern if you tell them you're traveling without your family or husband. However, it's best to use common sense and develop friendships with men in public places to start with, making it clear if only friendship is intended.

Traveling in a group significantly reduces risks and wearing a ring on the wedding finger is also a good deterrent. Stick to centrally located hostels where possible and avoid pirate taxis flagged down on the street; take only official taxis with a lit company number on their roof and take note of the registration number. Also, avoid dark streets and take care in remote places when traveling solo as these are where rapes occasionally do occur. Carry a whistle or rape-alarm to scare away would-be attackers, and if possible, take a self-defense course prior to your trip.

WORK

Officially you need a work visa to work in Peru. You can, however, possibly get a job teaching English in language schools without a work visa, usually in Lima. This is, however, illegal and becoming increasingly difficult to secure without a work visa (though some travelers take a chance and do it anyway). Schools occasionally advertise for teachers in the newspapers, but more often, jobs are found by word of mouth. They expect you to be a native English speaker, and the pay is usually low – US$100 per week is quite good, if you are an unqualified teacher.

If, in addition to speaking English like a native, you actually have a bona fide teaching credential, so much the better; we have heard a few reports of much higher pay rates for qualified teachers. American and British schools in Lima will sometimes hire teachers of math, biology and other subjects and can often help you get a work visa if you want to stay. They also pay much better than the language schools. Members of the South American Explorers may find that their Lima office (see p56) has contacts with schools that are looking for teachers.

Some enterprising travelers make money selling jewelry or art in crafts markets. Most other jobs are obtained by word of mouth (eg bartenders, jungle guides), but the possibilities are limited.

Volunteering

General advice for finding volunteer work is to ask at language schools; they usually know of several programmes suitable for their students. South American Explorers (SAE) also has reports left by many foreign volunteers, especially in Lima and Cuzco. The following organizations may be able to provide opportunities for volunteers if you contact them in advance. We particularly recommend ProPeru.

Adevas (☎ 084-963-6959; dianajuez@yahoo.com; Y'llary-Habitat Mz C, Lt 17, Ccotohuincho) It's a small NGO based in a village just outside Urubamba that has a physical and psychotherapy clinic for children. It will provide food and basic lodging for volunteers with physiotherapy skills or those with economic know-how.

ADRA Peru (☎ 01-213-7700 ext 3710; www .adra .org.pe; Angamos 770, Miraflores) ADRA is a development and relief agency based in Lima with various projects regarding health, education and agriculture throughout Peru.

Ann Sullivan Center (☎ 01-263-6296; annsullivan@tsi.com.pe; Calle Petronila Alvarez 180, San Miguel) This is a good contact in Lima for those wanting to help out with kids who have Down's Syndrome or autism.

Centro Educativo de Niños (☎ 01-470-1070; Pasaje Condurcunca 118, Lince) Based in Lima, the center accepts Spanish-speaking volunteers to work as teacher assistants for mentally disabled school children.

Hope Foundation (☎ 084-24-9462, in the Netherlands 0413-47-3666; www.stichtinghope.org/english/index.html; Casilla 59, Correo Central, Cuzco) The Hope Foundation gives support in the areas of education and health care.

Inka Porter Project (Porteadores Inka Ñan; www .peruweb.org/porters; ☎ 084-24-6829; South American Explorers, office 4; Choquechaca 188, Cuzco) Peruvian and foreign volunteers work for porters' rights on the Inca Trail and other areas, where porters have traditionally been underpaid, overworked and abysmally treated. Various volunteer skills are needed.

ProPeru Student Service Corporations (☎ 084-20-1340, 084-974-9256; www.properu.org; Grau 654, Urubamba) The ProPeru Service Corps offers two- to 26-week cultural, service and academic experiences in the Sacred Valley or the Peruvian Amazon. It has links with 40 affiliated NGOs throughout Peru and with advance warning can organize placements for individuals or groups.

Teaching & Projects Abroad (info@teaching -abroad.co.uk; www.teaching-abroad.co.uk) This is a UK-based gap-year organization that arranges long-term archaeological projects for volunteers in the Sacred Valley, biological research in the jungle and English teaching in various locations.

Transport

THINGS CHANGE

The information in this chapter is particularly vulnerable to change. Check directly with the airline or a travel agent to make sure you understand how a fare (and ticket you may buy) works and be aware of the security requirements for international travel. Shop carefully. The details given in this chapter should be regarded as pointers and are not a substitute for your own careful, up-to-date research.

GETTING THERE & AWAY

ENTERING THE COUNTRY

Arriving in or departing from Peru either by air or overland is straightforward as long as your passport is valid for at least six months beyond your departure date. When arriving by air or a border crossing, officials sometimes stamp only 30 days into your passport; if this happens, tell the official how many days you need, supported by your exit ticket if possible. For general information see Visas (p412).

AIR

From the USA, there are direct (nonstop) flights to Lima from Miami, New York, Los Angeles, Dallas–Fort Worth and Houston. There are also direct flights from Amsterdam and Madrid in Europe. Many South American capitals have direct flights to Lima as well. There are international flights between Cuzco and La Paz (Bolivia) and between Iquitos and Leticia (Colombia). See individual departure countries/continents (below) for further details.

Airports & Airlines

Lima's **Aeropuerto Internacional Jorge Chávez** (☎ 595-0606; Callao) is a major South American hub, serviced by many flights from North, Central and South America, and a few direct flights from Europe. Travelers from other continents normally change services in the USA or a South American city.

The main Peruvian carrier is **Aero Continente** (www.aerocontinente.com), with flights from Lima to Miami in the USA and many Latin American capitals. International flights with **LanPeru** (www.lanperu.com) are mainly operated by **LanChile** (www.lanchile.com) and go to Miami, Los Angeles and New York, as well as Latin American cities. Other international airlines have offices in Lima (see p81).

Cuzco's **Aeropuerto Alejandro Velasco Astete** (☎ 22-2611) has international flights to/from La Paz in Bolivia for US$106 one-way on **Lloyd Aereo Boliviano** (LAB; ☎ 22-2990; Santa Catalina Angosta 160, Cuzco). Flights leave and arrive in Cuzco on Tuesday and Saturday mornings, with more services in the high season.

Iquitos has international flights to Leticia in Colombia on Monday and Friday with **AviaSelva** (Próspero 439). From Leticia you can cross the border to the Brazilian town of Tabatinga and take flights into other parts of Brazil from there. Direct flights to Brazil and to Miami from Iquitos were suspended at the time of writing.

Tickets

The high season for air travel to and within Peru is June to early September and also December to mid-January. Lower fares may be offered at other times.

Students with international student ID cards and anyone aged under 26 can get discounts with most airlines. Those paying

DEPARTURE TAX

Lima's international departure tax is US$28, payable in cash (dollars or nuevos soles) when you check in. At Cuzco and Iquitos it is US$10.

student fares may also be eligible for a free international stopover and tickets are often valid for a year. Tickets bought in Peru are subject to 18% tax.

It is essential to reconfirm your return flights 72 hours in advance or you may well get bumped off the list. If you are going to be in the boonies, have a travel agent do this for you.

Many travelers now buy tickets online. This is safe, but web prices vary tremendously; shop around. Tickets for Monday to Thursday flights are cheaper than on other days. The following international online sites are good, but there are many others. Check the weekend travel sections of major newspapers for more companies. Also see other suggestions under specific countries (below).

Expedia (www.expedia.com)
Flight Centre International (www.flightcentre.com)
Flights.com (www.eltexpress.com)
STA (www.sta.com)
Travelocity (www.travelocity.com)

COURIER FLIGHTS

If you are flexible with dates and can manage with only carry-on luggage, you can fly to Lima as a courier. This is most practical from major US gateways. Some of the largest US-based courier operators are:

Air Courier Association (☎ 800-282-1202; www.aircourier.org)
Air Courier International (☎ 800-682-6593)
International Association of Air Travel Couriers (☎ 308-632-3273; www.courier.org)

From the USA

Discount travel agents in the USA are known as consolidators (although you won't see a sign on the door saying 'Consolidator'.) San Francisco is the ticket consolidator capital of America, although some good deals can be found in Los Angeles, New York and other cities.

The following online booking agencies are recommended:

www.cheaptickets.com
www.exitotravel.com (☎ 800-655-4053) A Latin America specialist.
www.itn.net
www.lowestfare.com
www.orbitz.com
www.sta.com (☎ 800-329-9537)

From Canada

Canadians will need to take a connecting flight to a US city. **Travel CUTS** (☎ 800-667-2887; www.travelcuts.com) is Canada's national student travel agency.

From the UK

Discount air travel is big business in London. Advertisements for many travel agencies appear in the weekend newspapers, *Time Out*, the *Evening Standard* and in the free magazine *TNT*.

Recommended travel agencies include:
Bridge the World (☎ 0870-444-7474; www.b-t-w.co.uk)
Flightbookers (☎ 0870-010-7000; www.ebookers.com)
Flight Centre (☎ 0870-890-8099; www.flightcentre.co.uk)
North-South Travel (☎ 01245-608-291; www.northsouthtravel.co.uk) North-South Travel donate part of its profit to projects in the developing world.
Quest Travel (☎ 0870-442-3542; www.questtravel.com)
STA Travel (☎ 0870-160-0599; www.statravel.co.uk)
Trailfinders (www.trailfinders.co.uk)
Travel Bag (☎ 0870-890-1456; www.travelbag.co.uk)

From Continental Europe

There are direct flights to Lima from Amsterdam and Madrid, but most European travelers will find it cheaper if they take flights that have connections in one or more of the UK, USA, the Caribbean or Colombia.

The following European agencies are recommended:

FRANCE

Anyway (☎ 0892-89-38-92; www.anyway.fr)
Lastminute (☎ 0892-70-50-00; www.lastminute.fr)
Nouvelles Frontiéres (☎ 0825-00-07-47; www.nouvelles-frontieres.fr)
OTU Voyages (☎ www.otu.fr) Specializes in student and youth travelers.
Voyageurs du Monde (☎ 01-40-15-11-15; www.vdm.com)

FLYING WITH FILM

Always carry film with you onto airplanes; the X-ray scanners used for hand luggage are supposedly safe for film. If you place all your rolls into a clear plastic bag you may be able to get it hand-checked (though this may be refused since September 11, 2001). *Never* put film into checked luggage because the scanners used for those bags are much stronger and likely to damage your film.

GERMANY
Expedia (☎ www.expedia.de)
Just Travel (☎ 089-747-3330; www.justtravel.de)
Lastminute (☎ 01805-284-366; www.lastminute.de)
STA Travel (☎ 01805-456-422; www.statravel.de)

OTHER
Airfair (☎ 020-620-5121; www.airfair.nl) A Dutch agency.
Barcelo Viajes (☎ 902-116-226; www.barcelo viajes.com) A Spanish agency.
CTS Viaggi (☎ 06-462-0431; www.cts.it) Italian agency that specializes in student and youth travel.
Nouvelles Frontiéres (☎ 90-217-09-79) Also operates in Spain.

From Australia & New Zealand

Flights are usually via the USA or a South American capital such as Santiago or Buenos Aires.

In Australia there are many branches of **STA** (☎ 1300-733-035; www.statravel.com.au); New Zealand also has **STA** branches (☎ 0508-782-872; www.statravel.co.nz). **Flight Centre** (☎ 133-133; www.flightcentre.com.au) and (☎ 0800-243-544; www.flightcentre.co.nz) have many offices. Also try **Travel.com** (www.travel.com.au) in Australia and **Travel.co** (www.travel.co.nz) in New Zealand.

From Asia

Visitors from Asia mostly connect via the USA.

STA Travel offices proliferate in Asia, with branches in many major cities. Another resource in Japan is **No 1 Travel** (☎ 03-3205-6073; www.no1-travel.com); in Hong Kong, try **Four Seas Tours** (☎ 2200-7760; www.fourseastravel.com /english). In India **STIC Travels** (www.stictravel.com) has offices in dozens of cities. The **Israel Student Travel Association** (ISSTA; ☎ 02-625 7257) is in Jerusalem.

From Africa

Travel is normally via the USA. **Rennies Travel** (www.renniestravel.com) and **STA Travel** (www.sta travel.co.za) have offices throughout Southern Africa. Check their websites for branch locations.

From South America

Flights from Latin American countries are usually subject to high tax, and good deals are not often available.

Many Latin American airlines fly to Lima. These include Aerolíneas Argentinas, Aeroméxico and Mexicana (Mexico), Servivensa (Venezuela), Avianca (Colombia), Copa (Panama), Grupo Taca (Central America), LanChile (Chile), LAB (Bolivia), Ecuatoriana and Saeta (Ecuador) and Varig (Brazil). In addition, several US companies and Peru's Aero Continente have flights between some Latin American cities and Lima.

Recommended travel agencies include:
ASATEJ (☎ 011-4114-7595; www.asatej.com) Argentina
Student Travel Bureau (☎ 3038-1555; www.stb .com.br) Brazil
IVI Tours (☎ 0212-993-6082; www.ividiomas.com) Venezuela

LAND

Because no roads cross the Darien Gap, it is not possible to travel to South America by land from the north (unless you spend a week hiking through drug-dealer-infested jungle). Because of this, bringing your own vehicle to Peru from North America is a costly undertaking.

Bus, Train & Boat

It is always much cheaper to buy tickets to the border, cross, and then buy onward tickets on the other side. If traveling with a bus service that crosses a border, check carefully with the company about what is included, and whether the service is direct or involves a transfer at the border. **Ormeño** (☎ 01-472-1710; www.ascinsa.com/ORMENO; Av Javier Prado Este 1059, Central Lima) is the main bus company offering across-border bus travel.

The only train service that crosses the Peruvian border is the train between Tacna on the south coast and Arica in Chile.

Boat travel is possible from points on the Amazon in Brazil and from Leticia in Colombia.

TO/FROM BOLIVIA

Peru is normally reached from Bolivia via Yunguyo or Desaguadero to Puno. There are many bus options for these routes, almost all of which involve changing buses at the border. Bus services can also connect you with pricey hydrofoil and catamaran services in Bolivia. For more details on each of these options, see p161.

It's also possible, but difficult, to reach Bolivia by river from Puerto Maldonado (see p368) or going along the northern shore of Lake Titicaca from Juliaca (p147).

TO/FROM BRAZIL

You can travel between Peru and Brazil across land (not easily) via Iñapari (p368).

Traveling to/from Iquitos, it's straightforward to voyage along the Amazon to/from Tabatinga in Brazil via Leticia in Colombia (see p393 for details of trips downstream and The Tri-border on p398 for details on trips upsteam).

TO/FROM CHILE

Traveling on the Panamericana, the major crossing point is Tacna to Arica, Chile (see p118 for more details).

Most people take buses to or from the border. There are buses to Tacna from Cuzco, Puno and Arequipa, as well as from Lima. Ormeño (see contact details earlier) runs buses from both Lima and Arequipa to Santiago in Chile (2¼ days).

It is also possible to cross between Tacna and Arica by train; border formalities are done at the respective stations.

TO/FROM COLOMBIA

It is easier to get to Peru via Ecuador. It's far better to do the trip in stages, but Ormeño (see contact details earlier) has buses between Lima and Bogotá, Colombia (three days) via Ecuador.

It is straightforward to voyage up/down the Amazon by boat between Iquitos (see p393) and Leticia in Colombia, from where there are flights to Bogotá. For more details on Leticia and border formalities there, as well as details of traveling from Leticia to Iquitos, see The Tri-border on p398.

TO/FROM ECUADOR

The usual way to get to/from Ecuador is along the Panamericana Norte via Tumbes (see p303 for more details). Another route is via La Tina to Loja in Ecuador (see p293). A third route is via Jaén (see p344).

While most people take buses to and from the border and catch an ongoing service from the other side, **Cifa** (☎ 072-52-7120; Tumbes 572, Tumbes) runs buses between Tumbes in Peru and Machala or Guayaquil in Ecuador. Tranportes Loja runs buses between Piura and Machala or Loja in Ecuador. Ormeño (see contact details earlier) has weekly buses between Lima and Quito in Ecuador (1½ days).

GETTING AROUND

AIR

Domestic flights are competitively priced with several major and minor carriers. Most cities are served by modern jets; some smaller towns are served by propeller aircraft. The major companies have good reputations. A useful site is www.traficoperu.com, which gives air schedules between major cities.

Airports & Airlines

Domestic-flight schedules and ticket prices change frequently. Also, new airlines open and close every year. Many domestic air lines have sprung up recently, and at the time of writing competition was fierce, with special offers as low as US$59 from Lima to Arequipa and Cuzco. Two one-way tickets cost the same as a round-trip ticket so you can travel one way overland and save time by returning by air.

Important destinations for travelers are Lima, Arequipa, Ayacucho, Cajamarca, Chiclayo, Cuzco, Huánuco, Iquitos, Juliaca, Piura, Pucallpa, Puerto Maldonado, Tacna, Tarapoto, Trujillo and Tumbes. The more remote towns require connecting flights, and smaller towns are not served every day. Many of the airports for these places are often no more than a grass strip in the jungle. They can be reached on some of the small airlines or by chartered light aircraft.

The best companies with the most extensive services are **Aero Continente** (www.aero continente.com) and **LanPeru** (www.lanperu.com). **Tans** (www.tans.com.pe) is good for Cuzco and the jungle cities. **AeroCóndor** (www.aerocondor.com.pe) flies to Ayacucho, Andahuaylas, Cajamarca and Trujillo. Airline offices are listed in the

TRANSPORT

PERU AIR ROUTES

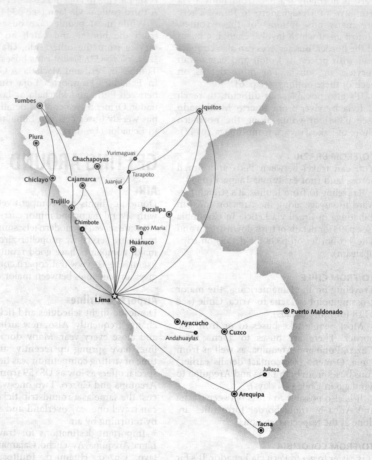

text under the appropriate cities, along with other smaller airlines.

Be at the airport at least 60 minutes early; 90 minutes for Lima. This is a precaution as your flight may be overbooked, baggage handling and check-in procedures tend to be chaotic, and it's not unknown for flights to leave *before* their official departure time because predicted bad weather might cancel the flight later. Be aware too that flights are frequently late.

Buying Tickets & Reconfirming Flights

Getting flight information, buying tickets and reconfirming flights are best done at the airline offices; in remote areas, find a responsible travel agent to do this for you. You can sometimes buy tickets at the airport on a space-available basis, but don't count on it. Note that it is almost impossible to buy tickets for just before the major holidays of Semana Santa (the week before Easter) and Fiestas Patrias (last week in July). Also, overbooking is the norm, not underbooking.

Ensure all reservations are *confirmed and reconfirmed* 72 and 24 hours in advance; airlines are notorious for bumping passengers off flights. Flights are changed or canceled with depressing frequency, so it's even worth calling the airport or airline just before leaving for the airport. Members of the South American Explorers can have the club reconfirm for them. Confirmation is especially necessary during the busy months of July and August.

AIR PASSES

Aero Continente and LanPeru sell passes abroad, which are not available in Peru. The passes cost about the same as if you buy the tickets in Peru. Travelers have a greater choice of flights and airlines if they wait till they are in Peru.

DOMESTIC DEPARTURE TAX

There's a US$3.50 domestic departure tax, payable when you get your boarding pass. At Lima and Cuzco it's US$5.

BICYCLE

Cycling will be more enjoyable and safer off the main roads. Mountain bikes are recommended as road bikes won't stand up to the poor roads.

Renting bikes is described under Huaraz (p312), Huancayo (p233) and Cuzco (p177). These are rented for people to bike locally, though, not travel all over the country. For long-distance touring, bring your own.

Airlines' bicycle-carrying policies vary, so shop around. Some airlines will fly your bike as checked baggage if it's boxed. However, boxing the bike gives baggage handlers little clue to the contents, and the box may be roughly handled. If it's OK with the airline, try wrapping it in heavy-duty plastic; baggage handlers can see the contents.

BOAT

There are no coastal passenger services.

In the highlands, there are boat services on Lake Titicaca; small motorized vessels take about 20 passengers from Puno (p155) to visit various islands on the lake.

In Peru's Amazon basin, boat travel is of major importance. Dugout canoes powered by an outboard engine act as a water taxi on the smaller rivers. Some are powered by a strange arrangement that looks like an inboard motorcycle engine attached to a tiny propeller by a 3m-long propeller shaft. Called *peki-pekis*, these canoes are a slow and rather noisy method of transportation. In some places, modern aluminum launches are used.

RIVER BOAT

On wider rivers, larger river boats are available. This is the classic way to travel down the Amazon – swinging in your hammock aboard a banana boat piloted by a grizzled old captain who knows the waters better than the back of his hand. You can travel from Pucallpa or Yurimaguas to Iquitos and on into Brazil this way (see p385).

Cargo boats carrying passengers leave most days. The boats have two or three decks; the lower deck is for cargo, and the upper for passengers and crew. Bring your own hammock, or rent a cabin. At ports, there are chalkboards with ship's names, destinations and departure times displayed; the departure times are usually optimistic. The captain has to clear his documents with the *capitanía* (harbor master) on the day of departure, so asking the person in charge of documents at the *capitanía* can yield information. Asking the captain is also good – nobody else really knows. Departure time often depends on a full cargo, and *mañana* may go on for several days if the hold isn't full. Usually you can sleep on the boat while you are waiting for departure if you want to save on hotel bills. Never leave your luggage unattended.

If using a hammock (rather than a cabin) hang it away from the noisy engine room and not directly under a light, as these are often lit late at night, precluding sleep and attracting insects. The cabins are often hot, airless boxes, but are lockable (for your luggage) and not too hot at night. Basic food is usually included in the price of the passage, and may be marginally better on some of the bigger and better ships, or if you are in cabin class. Finicky or sensitive eaters should bring their own food. Bottled soft drinks are usually available and priced very reasonably. Sanitary facilities are basic but adequate if you're not too fussy, and there's usually a pump shower on board.

BUS

Buses are frequent and comfortable on the major routes and are the normal form of transport for most Peruvians and many travelers. Less traveled routes are served by older and less comfortable vehicles, some with inadequate leg-room for long-legged travelers. Fares are relatively cheap. There is no bus-pass system.

Scores of bus companies exist and no one company covers the whole country. Some companies cover most of Peru's major cities. The two biggest companies are **Cruz del Sur** (www.cruzdelsur.com.pe) and **Ormeño** (www.ascinsa.com/ORMENO). Other reputable companies are **Civa** (www.civa.com.pe), Móvil Tours, and the new **Linea** (www.transporteslinea.com.pe). That isn't to say that other companies aren't reputable!

The scores of competing bus companies have their own offices. In some towns, the companies have their offices in one main bus terminal. In many cities, bus companies are clustered around a few city blocks, while elsewhere, the terminals may be scattered all over town. Slowly, cities are moving toward having one long-distance bus terminal. Schedules and fares change frequently and vary from company to company; therefore, we give only approximations. Students with international student cards may be able to get a 10% discount.

At low travel periods, some companies offer discounted fares; conversely, fares can double around holidays such as Christmas, Easter or Fiestas Patrias (around 28 July), when tickets may be sold out several days ahead of time. Buses can be much delayed during the rainy season, especially in the highlands and jungles. From January to April, journey times can double because of landslides and bad road conditions.

Try to avoid seats at the back of the bus, because the ride is bumpier. When waiting in bus terminals, watch your luggage very carefully. See Dangers & Annoyances (p405) for more information on playing it safe.

Luggage

During the journey, your luggage will travel in the luggage compartment unless it is small enough to carry on board. This is reasonably safe. You are given a baggage tag in exchange for your bag, which should be securely closed or locked if possible. Your hand luggage is a different matter. If you're asleep with a camera around your neck, you might wake up with a neatly razored strap and no camera at the end of it. Hide valuables!

Some travelers prefer to bring their luggage on the bus with them, because there are occasional reports of theft from the luggage compartment. This works if your pack is small enough to shove it between your legs or on your lap.

Classes of Bus

The bigger companies often have luxury buses (called Imperial or similar), charging 30% to 100% more than *económico* buses and providing express service, with toilets, snacks, videos and air-conditioning. Some companies offer Bus-Camas (bed buses) on which the seat reclines almost fully – you can sleep quite well on them. These can cost two or three times more than the cheapest buses. Note that the toilets are, as one company announces during their 'in-flight announcements,' for 'urination only.' On trips over six hours, bathroom stops are made. Details of available services are given under each city.

Long-distance buses stop for three meals a day (unless you travel on luxury buses, which serve snacks and don't stop). Many companies have their own special rest areas, sometimes in the middle of nowhere, so you don't have any choice but to eat there. The food is inexpensive but not particularly appetizing. Some travelers prefer to bring their own food.

CAR & MOTORCYCLE
Car Rental

The major car-rental companies are found in Lima (see p84), and a few are found in the other major cities. Car rental averages US$50 a day with hidden charges for mileage (per kilometer), insurance and so on, so understand the rental agreement before you sign up. Vehicles such as 4WD jeeps are very expensive to rent. A credit card is required, and renters normally need to be aged over 25. Your own driving license is accepted for driving in Peru.

It's a long way from Lima to most destinations; it's suggested that you use bus or air to travel to wherever you want to go and rent a car when you get there.

ROAD HAZARDS

Bear in mind that the condition of the rental vehicles is often poor, roads are badly potholed (even the paved Panamericana) and drivers are extremely aggressive. Road signs are often small and unclear. Gas stations are few and far between. Driving at night is not recommended because of poor road conditions, speeding buses, and slow-moving, poorly lit trucks. Theft is all too common, so you should not leave your vehicle parked in the street. When stopping overnight, park the car in a guarded lot (the better hotels have them). Consider renting taxis at your destination instead (see below).

Motorcycle Rental

Renting a motorcycle is an option mainly in jungle towns, where bikers can go for short runs around town and into the surroundings, but not much further.

HITCHING

Hitchhiking is never entirely safe in any country in the world and is not recommended. Travelers who decide to hitch should understand that they are taking a small but potentially serious risk. People who do choose to hitch will be safer if they travel in pairs and let someone know where they are planning to go.

Hitching is not very practical in Peru because there are few private cars, public transport is cheap, and trucks are used as public transport in remote areas.

LOCAL TRANSPORT

Bus

Local buses are slow and crowded but cheap. Ask locally for help, as there aren't any obvious bus lines in most towns.

Taxi

For short hops around a city, flag down one of the many taxis that seem to be everywhere. They have a small red taxi sticker in the windshield and aren't regulated. Safer, regulated taxis called by telephone are available in Lima and some of the other major cities, and are listed in applicable chapters. These are more expensive than taxis flagged down on the street, but are more reliable. Single women should stick to regulated taxis, especially at night.

Fares are cheaper than in North America or Europe. Always ask the fare in advance, as there are no meters. It's quite acceptable to haggle over a fare; try to find out what the going rate is before taking a cab. The standard fare for short runs in most cities is under US$1. Tipping is not the norm.

Renting a taxi for long-distance trips costs little more than renting a car and takes care of many of the problems outlined under Car Rental earlier. Not all taxi drivers will agree to drive long distances, but if one does, you should check the driver's credentials before hiring.

TRAIN

The privatized Peruvian rail system, **Perúrail** (www.perurail.com) runs from Cuzco to Aguas Calientes (for Machu Picchu) several times a day (see p194), and between Cuzco and Puno three times a week (see p155 or p194). The passenger train between Arequipa and Puno has been suspended, but will run as a charter.

The lovely central railroad line, which reaches altitudes of 4781m, runs from Lima to Huancayo a few times a year, usually around holidays. See Huancayo (p237) for details. In Huancayo, you can change train stations and continue to Huancavelica. This train runs daily.

TOURS

The following overseas companies (and there are scores more) offer organized tours for travelers who don't like to travel on their own or have a limited amount of time and who prefer to maximize their Peruvian experience. Usually these tours travel with knowledgeable guides but be aware that you pay a great deal extra for this privilege. For details of Peruvian companies, see Tours under the town and cities. The best places to look for tours are Cuzco, Huaraz and Lima, because they have the most companies.

For specialized tours for individuals or small groups, you can hire a good Spanish-speaking guide for about US$25 a day plus expenses; tours in English or other languages are more expensive. Some students or unregistered guides are cheaper, but the usual caveat applies – some are good, some aren't. Some recommended guides are listed in this book.

From North America

Because of the easy flight connection to Peru, the USA has far more companies offering tours than the rest of the world put together. You can find their addresses in advertisements in outdoor and travel magazines such as *Outside, National Geographic Adventure* and *Arthur Frommers Budget Travel*, as well as more general magazines, such as *Natural History* and *Smithsonian*. The following are some of the best and longest-established companies:

Adventure Center (☎ 510-654-1879, 1-800-227-8747; www.adventurecenter.com; 1311 – 63rd St, Suite 200, Emeryville, CA 94608) This is a clearing house for numerous operators offering various trips at different costs to Peru and other countries.

Backroads (☎ 510-527-1555, 800-462-2848; goactive@backroads.com; 801 Cedar St, Berkeley, CA 94710) It organizes cycling tours in the Cuzco area.

eXito Latin America Travel Specialists (☎ 800-655-4053; fax 510-868-8306; www.exitotravel.com) Specializes in Latin America only and can provide inexpensive short- and long-term air tickets with multiple stopovers if desired, as well as various tours of all kinds.

Explorations (☎ 239-992-9660, 800-446-9660; www.ExplorationsInc.com; 27655 Kent Rd, Bonita Springs, FL 34135) Offers Amazon trips including Amazon cruises, lodge-based expeditions, and fishing trips in the Iquitos and Pacaya-Samiria area. Extensions to Cuzco and Machu Picchu are always offered.

GAP Adventures (☎ 1-800-465-5600; www.gap.ca) It's the premier Canadian agency for long- and short-distance budget tours, including hotel-based, trekking, rafting and Amazon trips.

International Expeditions (☎ 205-428-1700, 800-633-4734; amazon@ietravel.com; One Environs Park, Helena, AL 35080) Offers Amazon tours to both the northern and southern Peruvian rainforests, staying in jungle lodges or on river boats, with an emphasis on natural history. It can combine Amazon trips with visits to other parts of Peru, especially the archaeological sites of the northern coast.

Southwind Adventures (☎ 303-972-0701, 800-377-9463; www.southwindadventures.com; PO Box 621057, Littleton, CO 80162) Has varied trips in South America, ranging from jungles to highlands. Some are hotel-based.

Wilderness Travel (☎ 510-558-2488, 800-368-2794; www.wildernesstravel.com; 1102 Ninth St, Berkeley, CA 94710) This company has been sending small groups (four to 15 participants) to Peru (and many other countries) since the 1970s, and is one of the best in the business. It offers many treks – ranging from four nights on the Inca Trail to two weeks in the remote Cordillera Huayhuash –

combined with hotel portions in the Cuzco–Machu Picchu area. Wilderness Travel also offers comfortable hotel-based tours to the most interesting areas of Peru.

Wildland Adventures (☎ 206-365-0686, 1-800-345-4453; www.wildland.com; 3516 NE 155th St, Seattle, WA 98155-7412) Prides itself on environmentally sound treks to Machu Picchu, Ausangate and the Cordillera Blanca.

From the UK & Continental Europe

Amazonas Explorer (☎ 01437-891743, 015395-52281; in Peru ☎ 084-22-7137, 65-3366; www.amazonas-explorer.com; Riverside, Black Tar, Llangwm, Haverfordwest, Pembs, Wales, UK SA62 4JD) It does rafting, cycling and trekking trips, including the Inca Trail and custom private itineraries.

Club Aventure (☎ 0825-30-60-32, fax 496-15-10-59; www.clubaventure.fr; 18 rue Séguier 75006, Paris, France) Club Adventure, a French company, organizes treks in Peru.

Exodus (☎ 08772-3822; www.exodus.co.uk; 9 Weir Rd, London, UK SW12 0LT) Has long-distance overland trips and shorter cultural and trekking adventures.

Explore Worldwide (☎ 01252-760144; www.explore worldwide.com; 1 Frederick St, Aldershot, Hants, UK GU11 1LQ) Explore has various tours of Peru.

Hauser (☎ 8923-50060, fax 8929-13714: www.hauser -exkursionen.de; Marienstrabe 17, Munich D-80331, Germany) Hauser is among the best of the German companies offering Andean treks.

Journey Latin America (☎ 0208-747-3108; www .journeylatinamerica.co.uk; 12 & 13 Heathfield Terrace, Chiswick, London, UK W4 4JE) This is an excellent all-round company and arranges cultural, hotel-based trips and treks in the Cordillera Blanca, Huayhuash and to Machu Picchu.

From Australia & New Zealand

Adventure World (☎ 02-8913-0755, 800-221-931; www.adventureworld.com.au; 73 Walker St, North Sydney, NSW 2060) Provides a variety of Peruvian trips, concentrating mostly on the gringo trail.

Contours (☎ 03-9670-6900; www.contourstravel.com .au; 310 King St, Melbourne, VIC 3000) Specializes in Latin American travel and can arrange a variety of trips in Peru.

Peregrine Adventures (☎ 03-9663-8611; www .peregrine.net.au; 258 Lonsdale St, Melbourne, VIC 3000) Peregrine has both hotel-based and trekking trips in Peru.

Health by Dr David Goldberg

Prevention is the key to staying healthy while abroad. Travelers who receive the recommended vaccines and follow some common-sense precautions usually come down with nothing more than a little diarrhea.

Medically speaking, Peru is part of tropical South America, which includes most of the continent except for the southernmost portion. The diseases found in this area are comparable to those found in tropical areas of Africa and Asia. Particularly important are mosquito-borne infections, including malaria, yellow fever and dengue fever, which are not a significant concern in the temperate regions of the country.

BEFORE YOU GO

Since most vaccines don't provide immunity until at least two weeks after they're given, visit a physician four to eight weeks before departure. Don't forget to take your vaccination certificate on your travels (otherwise known as the yellow booklet); it is mandatory for countries that require proof of yellow-fever vaccination upon entry.

Bring medications in their original, clearly labelled, containers. A signed and dated letter from your physician describing your medical conditions and medications (including their generic names), is also a good idea. If carrying syringes or needles, be sure to have a physician's letter documenting their medical necessity.

If your health insurer doesn't cover you for medical expenses incurred abroad, get some extra travel insurance – check p409 and the links under www.lonelyplanet.com/subwwway for more information. Find out in advance if your travel insurer will make payments directly to providers or reimburse you later for overseas health expenditures. (Many doctors in Peru, though, expect payment in cash.)

INTERNET RESOURCES

There is a wealth of travel health advice on the Internet. For further general information, the links at Lonely Planet website (www.lonelyplanet.com/subwwway) is a good place to start. The World Health Organization publishes a superb book called *International Travel and Health*, which is revised annually and is available online at no cost (www.who.int/ith/). Another website of general interest is the MD Travel Health website (www.mdtravelhealth.com), which provides complete travel health recommendations for every country and is updated daily.

FURTHER READING

For more detailed information on health matters, see *Healthy Travel Central & South America*, published by Lonely Planet. If you are traveling with children, Lonely Planet's *Travel with Children* may provide some useful advice. The *ABC of Healthy Travel*, by E Walker et al, is another valuable resource.

David Goldberg MD completed his training in internal medicine and infectious diseases at the Columbia Presbyterian Medical Center in New York City, where he has also served as voluntary faculty. At present, he is an infectious diseases specialist in Scarsdale NY and the editor-in-chief of the website www.mdtravelhealth.com.

IMMUNIZATIONS

The only required vaccine for Peru is yellow fever, and that's only if you're arriving from a yellow-fever-infected country in Africa or the Americas. A number of vaccines are recommended.

vaccine	recommended for	dosage	possible side effects
chickenpox	travelers who have never had chickenpox	two doses one month apart	fever, mild case of chickenpox
hepatitis A	all travelers	one dose before trip; booster six to 12 months later	soreness at injection site, headaches, body aches
hepatitis B	travelers who will have long-term contact with the local population	three doses over six months	soreness at injection site, long-term fever
measles	travelers born after 1956 who've never had measles and had only one measles vaccination	one dose	fever, rash, joint pains, allergic reactions
rabies	travelers who have contact with animals or won't have access to medical assistance	three doses over a four-week period	soreness at injection site, headaches, body aches
tetanus/diphtheria	all travelers who haven't had a booster in 10 years	one dose every 10 years	soreness at injection site
typhoid	all travelers	four capsules by mouth – one taken every other day	abdominal pain, nausea, rash
yellow fever	travelers to jungle areas at altitudes below 2300m	one dose every 10 years	headaches, body aches, severe reactions are rare

IN TRANSIT

DEEP VEIN THROMBOSIS

Blood clots may form in the legs (deep vein thrombosis or DVT) during plane flights, chiefly because of prolonged immobility. The longer the flight, the greater the risk. Though most blood clots are reabsorbed uneventfully, some may break off and travel through the blood vessels to the lungs, where they could cause life-threatening complications.

The chief symptom of DVT is swelling or pain of the foot, ankle or calf, usually – but not always – on just one side. When a blood clot travels to the lungs, it may cause chest pain and difficulty breathing. Travelers with any of these symptoms should immediately seek medical attention.

To prevent the development of DVT on long flights, you should walk about the cabin, flex the leg muscles while sitting, drink plenty of fluids and avoid alcohol and tobacco.

JET LAG

The onset of jet lag is common when crossing more than five time zones, resulting in insomnia, fatigue, malaise or nausea. To minimize jet lag try drinking plenty of (nonalcoholic) fluids and eating light meals. Upon arrival, get exposure to natural sunlight and readjust your schedule (for meals, sleep etc) as soon as possible.

IN PERU

AVAILABILITY OF HEALTH CARE

There are several high-quality medical clinics in Lima open 24 hours for medical emergencies (for details see p54). They also function as hospitals and offer subspecialty consultations. For a guide to clinics in Lima, check out the **US embassy website** (usembassy.state.gov /lima/wwwsmedical-e.shtml). There are also many English-speaking physicians and dentists in private practice in Lima (listed on the same website). Good medical care may be more difficult to find in other cities and impossible to locate in rural areas.

Many doctors and hospitals expect payment in cash, regardless of whether you have travel insurance. If you develop a life-threatening medical problem, you'll probably want to be evacuated to a country with state-of-the-art medical care. Since this may cost tens of thousands of dollars, be sure you have insurance to cover this before you depart. You can find a list of medical evacuation and travel insurance companies on the website of the **US State Department** (www.travel.state.gov/medical.html).

The pharmacies in Peru are known as *farmacias* or *boticas* and are identified by a green or red cross in the window. They're generally reliable and offer most of the medications available in other countries. Inka Farma and Superfarma are two well-known pharmacy chains.

INFECTIOUS DISEASES
Of the diseases listed below, malaria, yellow fever and dengue fever are spread by mosquitoes. For information about protecting yourself from mosquito bites, see p430.

Cholera
An intestinal infection, cholera is acquired through ingestion of contaminated food or water. The main symptom is profuse, watery diarrhea, which may be so severe that it causes life-threatening dehydration. The key treatment is drinking oral rehydration solution. Antibiotics are also given, usually tetracycline or doxycycline, though quinolone antibiotics such as ciprofloxacin and levofloxacin are also effective.

Cholera occurs regularly in Peru, but it's rare among travelers. Cholera vaccine is no longer required to enter Peru, and is in fact no longer available in some countries, including the USA, because the old vaccine was relatively ineffective and caused side effects. There are new vaccines that are safer and more effective, but they're not available in many countries and are only recommended for those at particularly high risk.

Dengue Fever
This is a viral infection found throughout South America. Dengue is transmitted by Aedes mosquitoes, which usually bite during the daytime and are often found close to human habitations, often indoors. They breed primarily in artificial water containers, such as cans, cisterns, metal drums, plastic containers and discarded tires. As a result, dengue is especially common in densely populated, urban environments, including Lima and Cuzco.

MEDICAL CHECKLIST

- antibiotics
- antidiarrheal drugs (eg loperamide)
- acetaminophen (Tylenol) or aspirin
- anti-inflammatory drugs (eg ibuprofen)
- antihistamines (for hay fever and allergic reactions)
- antibacterial ointment (eg Bactroban; for cuts and abrasions)
- steroid cream or cortisone (for poison ivy and other allergic rashes)
- bandages, gauze, gauze rolls
- adhesive or paper tape
- scissors, safety pins, tweezers
- thermometer
- pocketknife
- DEET-containing insect repellent for the skin
- permethrin-containing insect spray for clothing, tents and bed nets
- sun block
- oral rehydration salts
- iodine tablets (for water purification)
- syringes and sterile needles
- acetazolamide (Diamox; for altitude sickness)

Dengue usually causes flu-like symptoms, including fever, muscle aches, joint pains, headaches, nausea and vomiting, often followed by a rash. The body aches may be quite uncomfortable, but most cases resolve uneventfully in a few days. Severe cases usually occur in children aged under 15 who are experiencing their second dengue infection.

There is no treatment available for dengue fever except to take analgesics such as acetaminophen/paracetamol (Tylenol) and drink plenty of fluids. Severe cases may require hospitalization for intravenous fluids and supportive care.

Hepatitis A
A viral infection of the liver, hepatitis A is usually acquired by ingestion of contaminated water, food, or ice, though it may also

be acquired by direct contact with infected persons. Hepatitis A is the second most common travel-related infection (after travelers' diarrhea). The illness occurs throughout the world, but the incidence is higher in developing nations. Symptoms may include fever, malaise, jaundice, nausea, vomiting and abdominal pain. Most cases resolve without complications, though hepatitis A occasionally causes severe liver damage. There is no treatment; to aid recovery, avoid alcohol and eat simple, nonfatty foods.

The vaccine for hepatitis A is extremely safe and highly effective. If you get a booster six to 12 months later, it lasts for at least 10 years. You really should get it before you go to Peru or any other developing nation. Because the safety of hepatitis A vaccine has not been established for pregnant women or children aged under two, they should instead be given a gammaglobulin injection.

Hepatitis B

Like hepatitis A, hepatitis B is a liver infection that occurs worldwide but is more common in developing nations. Unlike hepatitis A, the disease is usually acquired by sexual contact or by exposure to infected blood, generally through blood transfusions or contaminated needles. The vaccine is recommended only for long-term travelers (on the road more than six months) who expect to live in rural areas or have close physical contact with the local population. Additionally, the vaccine is recommended for anyone who anticipates sexual contact with the local inhabitants or a possible need for medical, dental, or other treatments while abroad, including transfusions or vaccinations.

Hepatitis B vaccine is safe and highly effective. However, a total of three injections are necessary to establish full immunity. Several countries added hepatitis B vaccine to the list of routine childhood immunizations in the 1980s, so many young adults are already protected.

HIV/AIDS

The Human Immunodeficiency Virus (HIV) may develop into Acquired Immune Deficiency Syndrome (AIDS; SIDA in Spanish). HIV/AIDS has been reported in all South American countries. Be sure to use condoms for all sexual encounters. Exposure to blood or blood products and bodily fluids may put an individual at risk. Fear of HIV infection should never preclude treatment of serious medical conditions as the risk of infection remains very small.

Malaria

Cases of malaria occur in every South American country except Chile, Uruguay and the Falkland Islands. It's transmitted by mosquito bites, usually between dusk and dawn. The main symptom is high spiking fevers, which may be accompanied by chills, sweats, headaches, body aches, weakness, vomiting, or diarrhea. Severe cases may affect the central nervous system and lead to seizures, confusion, coma and death.

Taking malaria pills is strongly recommended for all areas in Peru except Lima and its vicinity, the coastal areas south of Lima and the highland areas (including around Cuzco, Machu Picchu, Lake Titicaca and Arequipa). The number of cases of malaria has risen sharply in recent years. Most cases in Peru occur in Loreto in northeast Peru, where malaria transmission has reached epidemic levels.

There is a choice of three malaria pills, all of which work about equally well. Mefloquine (Lariam) is taken once weekly in a dosage of 250mg, starting one to two weeks before arrival at an area where malaria is endemic and continuing through the trip and for four weeks after returning. The problem is that some people develop neuropsychiatric side effects, which may range from mild to severe. Atovaquone/proguanil (Malarone) is a newly approved combination pill taken once daily with food starting two days before arrival and continuing through the trip and for seven days after departure. Side effects are typically mild. Doxycycline is a third alternative, but may cause an exaggerated sunburn reaction.

In general, Malarone seems to cause fewer side effects than mefloquine and is becoming more popular. The chief disadvantage is that it has to be taken daily. For longer trips, it's probably worth trying mefloquine; for shorter trips, Malarone will be the drug of choice for most people. None of the pills is 100% effective.

If you may not have access to medical care while traveling, you should bring along additional pills for emergency self-treatment, which you should take if you can't reach a doctor and you develop symptoms that suggest malaria, such as high spiking fevers. One option is to take four tablets of Malarone once daily for three days. However, Malarone should not be used for treatment if you're already taking it for prevention. If taking Malarone, take 650mg of quinine three times daily and 100mg doxycycline twice daily for one week. If you start self-medication, see a doctor at the earliest possible opportunity. If you develop a fever after returning home, see a physician, as malaria symptoms may not occur for months.

Ensure you take precautions to minimize your chances of being bitten by mosquitoes (see Mosquito Bites on p430).

Rabies

A viral infection of the brain and spinal cord, rabies is almost always fatal unless treated promptly. The rabies virus is carried in the saliva of infected animals and is typically transmitted through an animal bite, though contamination of any break in the skin with infected saliva may result in rabies. Rabies occurs in all South American countries. In Peru, most cases are related to bites from dogs or vampire bats.

Rabies vaccine is safe, but a full series requires three injections and is quite expensive. Those at high risk for rabies, such as animal handlers and spelunkers (cave explorers), should certainly get the vaccine. Those at lower risk for animal bites should also consider asking for the vaccine if they might be traveling to remote areas and might not have access to appropriate medical care if needed. The treatment for a possibly rabid bite consists of rabies vaccine with rabies immune globulin. It's effective, but must be given promptly.

All animal bites and scratches must immediately be thoroughly cleansed with large amounts of soap and water, and local health authorities contacted to determine whether or not further treatment is necessary (see Animal Bites, p429, for more details).

Tetanus

This potentially fatal disease is found in undeveloped tropical areas. It is difficult to treat, but it is preventable with immunization. Tetanus occurs when a wound becomes infected by a germ that lives in the feces of animals or people, so clean all cuts, punctures or animal bites. Tetanus is also known as lockjaw, and the first symptom may be discomfort in swallowing, or stiffening of the jaw and neck; this is followed by painful convulsions of the jaw and whole body.

Typhoid Fever

This fever is caused by ingesting food or water contaminated by a species of Salmonella known as Salmonella typhi. Fever occurs in virtually all cases. Other symptoms may include headaches, malaise, muscle aches, dizziness, loss of appetite, nausea and abdominal pain. Either diarrhea or constipation may occur. Possible complications include intestinal perforation or bleeding, confusion, delirium or, rarely, coma.

Unless you expect to take all your meals in major hotels and restaurants, getting typhoid vaccine is a good idea. It's usually given orally, but is also available as an injection. Neither vaccine is approved for use in children under two.

The drug of choice for typhoid fever is usually a quinolone antibiotic such as ciprofloxacin (Cipro) or levofloxacin (Levaquin), which many travelers carry for treatment of travelers' diarrhea. However, if you self-treat for typhoid fever, you may also need to self-treat for malaria, since the symptoms of the two diseases may be indistinguishable.

Yellow Fever

A life-threatening viral infection, yellow fever is transmitted by mosquitoes in forested areas. The illness begins with flu-like symptoms, which may include fever, chills, headache, muscle aches, backache, loss of appetite, nausea and vomiting. These symptoms usually subside in a few days, but one person in six enters a second, toxic phase characterized by recurrent fever, vomiting, listlessness, jaundice, kidney failure, and hemorrhage, leading to death in up to half of the cases. There is no treatment except for supportive care.

Yellow-fever vaccine is strongly recommended for all those who visit any jungle areas of Peru at altitudes less than 2300m (7546 ft). Most cases occur in the departments in the central jungle. Proof of vaccination is required from all travelers arriving in Peru from an area where yellow fever is endemic in Africa or the Americas.

HEALTH

Yellow-fever vaccine is given only in approved yellow-fever vaccination centers, which provide validated vaccination certificates. The vaccine should be given at least 10 days before any potential exposure to yellow fever and remains effective for about 10 years. Reactions to the vaccine are generally mild (see the boxed text on p424), and severe reactions are rare. While you may not be required to have proof of a yellow-fever vaccination to enter Peru, after visiting a region where yellow fever occurs, you'll need to have the vaccination to get to most other countries – even your home country. So you're better off getting your jab before you leave home.

Other Infectious Diseases

Bartonellosis (Oroya fever) is carried by sand flies in the arid river valleys on the western slopes of the Andes in Peru, Colombia and Ecuador between altitudes of 800m and 3000m. The chief symptoms are fever and severe bone pains. Complications may include marked anemia, enlargement of the liver and spleen, and sometimes death. The drug of choice is chloramphenicol, though doxycycline is also effective.

Chagas' disease is a parasitic infection that is transmitted by triatomine insects (reduviid bugs), which inhabit crevices in the walls and roofs of substandard housing in South and Central America. In Peru, most cases occur in the southern part of the country. The triatomine insect drops its feces on human skin as it bites, usually at night. A person becomes infected when he or she unknowingly rubs the feces into the bite wound or any other open sore. Chagas' disease is extremely rare in travelers. However, if you sleep in a poorly constructed house, especially one made of mud, adobe, or thatch, you should be sure to protect yourself with a bed net and a good insecticide (see Mosquito Bites on p430).

Gnathostomiasis is an intestinal parasite acquired by eating raw or undercooked freshwater fish, including ceviche. (Note, though, that ceviche eaten on the coast will be, almost certainly, made from seafood.)

Leishmaniasis occurs in the mountains and jungles of all South American countries. The infection is transmitted by sand flies, which are about one-third the size of mosquitoes. In Peru, more cases have been seen recently in children aged under 15, due to the increasing use of child labor for brush clearing and preparation of farmlands on mountain slopes of the Andes. Most adult cases occur in men who've migrated into jungle areas for farming, working or hunting. Leishmaniasis may be limited to the skin, causing slow-growing ulcers over exposed parts of the body, or less commonly disseminate to the bone marrow, liver and spleen. There is no vaccine. To protect yourself from sand flies, follow the same precautions as for mosquito bites (see p430), except that netting must be finer-mesh (at least 18 holes to the linear inch).

Leptospirosis is acquired by exposure to water contaminated by the urine of infected animals. Outbreaks often occur at times of flooding, when sewage overflow may contaminate water sources. Initial symptoms, which resemble a mild flu, usually subside uneventfully in a few days with or without treatment, but a minority of cases are complicated by jaundice or meningitis. There's no vaccine. You can minimize your risk by staying out of bodies of fresh water that may be contaminated by animal urine. If you're visiting an area where an outbreak is in progress, as occurred in Peru after flooding in 1998, you can take 200mg of doxycycline once weekly as a preventative measure. If you actually develop leptospirosis, the treatment is 100mg of doxycycline twice daily.

Plague is usually transmitted to humans by the bite of rodent fleas, typically when rodents die off. Symptoms include fever, chills, muscle aches, and malaise, associated with the development of an acutely swollen, exquisitely painful lymph node, known as a bubo, most often in the groin. Cases of the plague are reported from Peru nearly every year, chiefly from the departments of Cajamarca, La Libertad, Piura and Lambayeque in the northern part of the country. Most travelers are at extremely low risk for this disease. However, if you might have contact with rodents or their fleas, especially in the above areas, you should bring along a bottle of doxycycline, to be taken prophylactically during periods of exposure. Those less than eight years old or allergic to doxycycline should take trimethoprim-sulfamethoxazole instead. In addition, you should avoid areas containing rodent burrows or nests, never handle sick or dead animals, and follow the guidelines for protecting yourself from mosquito bites on p430.

TRAVELERS' DIARRHEA

You get diarrhea from ingesting contaminated water or food. See Water (p431) and Food (p430) for ideas for reducing the risk of getting diarrhea. If you develop diarrhea, be sure to drink plenty of fluids, preferably an oral rehydration solution containing lots of salt and sugar. A few loose stools don't require treatment but if you start having more than four or five stools a day, you should start taking an antibiotic (usually a quinolone drug) and an antidiarrheal agent (such as loperamide). If diarrhea is bloody, persists for more than 72 hours or is accompanied by fever, shaking chills or severe abdominal pain you should seek medical attention.

ENVIRONMENTAL HAZARDS
Altitude Sickness

Those who ascend rapidly to altitudes greater than 2500m (8100ft) may develop altitude sickness. In Peru, this includes Machu Picchu (about 2500m), Lake Titicaca (3820m) and Cuzco (3326m). Being physically fit offers no protection. Those who have experienced altitude sickness in the past are prone to future episodes. The risk increases with faster ascents, higher altitudes and greater exertion. Symptoms may include headaches, nausea, vomiting, dizziness, malaise, insomnia and loss of appetite. Severe cases may be complicated by fluid in the lungs (high-altitude pulmonary edema) or swelling of the brain (high-altitude cerebral edema). If symptoms are more than mild or persist for more than 24 hours (far less at high altitudes), descend immediately by at least 500m and see a doctor.

To help prevent altitude sickness, the best measure is to spend two nights or more at each rise of 1000m. Alternatively, take 125mg or 250mg of acetazolamide (Diamox) twice or three times daily starting 24 hours before ascent and continuing for 48 hours after arrival at altitude. Possible side effects include increased urinary volume, numbness, tingling, nausea, drowsiness, myopia and temporary impotence. Acetazolamide should not be given to pregnant women or anyone with a history of sulfa allergy. For those who cannot tolerate acetazolamide, the next best option is 4mg of dexamethasone taken four times daily. Unlike acetazolamide, dexamethasone must be tapered gradually upon arrival at altitude, since there is a risk that altitude sickness will occur as the dosage is reduced. Dexamethasone is a steroid, so it should not be given to diabetics or anyone for whom taking steroids is not advised. A natural alternative is gingko, which some people find quite helpful.

When traveling to high altitudes, it's also important to avoid overexertion, eat light meals, and abstain from alcohol. Altitude sickness should be taken seriously; it can be life-threatening when severe.

Animal Bites

Do not attempt to pet, handle, or feed any animal, with the exception of domestic animals known to be free of any infectious disease. Most animal injuries are directly related to a person's attempt to touch or feed the animal.

Any bite or scratch by a mammal, including bats, should be promptly and thoroughly cleansed with large amounts of soap and water, followed by application of an antiseptic such as iodine or alcohol. The local health authorities should be contacted immediately for possible post-exposure rabies treatment, whether or not you've been immunized against rabies. It may also be advisable to start an antibiotic, since wounds caused by animal bites and scratches frequently become infected. One of the newer quinolones, such as levofloxacin (Levaquin), which many travelers carry in case of diarrhea, would be an appropriate choice.

Snakes and leeches are a hazard in some areas of South America. In the event of a venomous snake bite, place the victim at rest, keep the bitten area immobilized, and move the victim immediately to the nearest medical facility. Avoid tourniquets, which are no longer recommended.

Earthquakes & Avalanches

Peru is in an earthquake zone and small tremors are frequent. Every few years, a large earthquake results in loss of life and property damage. Should you be caught in an earthquake, the best advice is to take shelter under a solid object, such as a desk or doorframe.

Do not stand near windows or heavy objects. Do not run out of the building. If you are outside, attempt to stay clear of falling wires, bricks, telephone poles and other hazards. Avoid crowds in the aftermath.

There's not much you can do when caught in an avalanche. Be aware that the main danger times are after heavy rains, when high ground may subside.

Food

Salads and fruit should be washed with purified water or peeled when possible. Ice cream is usually safe if it is a reputable brand name, but beware of street vendors and of ice cream that has melted and been refrozen. Thoroughly cooked food is safest, but not if it has been left to cool or if it has been reheated. Shellfish such as mussels, oysters and clams should be avoided, as should undercooked meat, particularly in the form of minced or ground beef. Steaming does not make bad shellfish safe for eating. Having said that, it is difficult to resist Peruvian seafood dishes such as ceviche, which is marinated but not cooked. This is rarely a problem, as long as it is served fresh in a reputable restaurant.

If a place looks clean and well run, and if the vendor also looks clean and healthy, then the food is probably safe. In general, places that are packed with travelers or locals will be fine, while empty restaurants are questionable.

Hypothermia

Too much cold is just as dangerous as too much heat, as it may cause hypothermia. If you are trekking at high altitudes, particu-

larly in wet or windy conditions, or simply taking a long bus trip over mountains, mostly at night, be prepared.

It is surprisingly easy to progress from very cold to dangerously cold due to a combination of wind, wet clothing, fatigue and hunger, even if the air temperature is above freezing. It is best to dress in layers; silk, wool and some of the new artificial fibers are all good insulating materials. A hat is important, as a lot of heat is lost through the head. A strong, waterproof outer layer is essential, because keeping dry is vital. Carry basic supplies, including food containing simple sugars to generate heat quickly, and lots of fluid to drink. A space blanket – an extremely thin, lightweight emergency blanket made of a reflective material that keeps heat in – is something all travelers in cold environments should carry.

Symptoms of hypothermia are exhaustion, numb skin (particularly toes and fingers), shivering, slurred speech, irrational or violent behavior, lethargy, stumbling, dizzy spells, muscle cramps and violent bursts of energy. Irrationality may take the form of sufferers claiming they are warm and trying to take off their clothes.

To treat mild hypothermia, first get the person out of the wind and/or rain, remove their clothing if it's wet and replace it with dry, warm clothing. Give them hot liquids – no alcohol – and some high-calorie, easily digestible food. Do not rub victims, as rough handling may cause cardiac arrest.

Mosquito Bites

To prevent mosquito bites, wear long sleeves, long pants, hats and shoes (rather than sandals). Bring along a good insect repellent, preferably one containing DEET, which should be applied to exposed skin and clothing, but not to eyes, mouth, cuts, wounds, or irritated skin. Products containing lower concentrations of DEET are as effective, but for shorter periods of time. In general, adults and children aged over 12 should use preparations containing 25% to 35% DEET, which usually lasts about six hours. Children aged between two and 12 should use preparations containing no more than 10% DEET, applied sparingly, which will usually last about three hours. Neurologic toxicity has been reported from DEET, especially in children, but appears

---

THE MAN SAYS...

It's usually a good idea to consult your government's travel health website before departure, if one is available:

Australia
www.dfat.gov.au/travel/

Canada
www.travelhealth.gc.ca

UK
www.doh.gov.uk/traveladvice/

USA
www.cdc.gov/travel/

to be extremely uncommon and generally related to overuse. DEET-containing compounds should not be used on children under age two.

Insect repellents containing certain botanical products, including oil of eucalyptus and soybean oil, are effective but last only 1½ to two hours. DEET-containing repellents are preferable for areas where there is a high risk of malaria or yellow fever. Products based on citronella are not effective.

For additional protection, apply permethrin to clothing, shoes, tents, and mosquito nets. Permethrin treatments are safe and remain effective for at least two weeks, even when items are laundered. Permethrin should not be applied directly to skin.

Don't sleep with the window open unless there is a screen. If sleeping outdoors or in an accommodation where mosquitoes can enter, use a mosquito net, preferably treated with permethrin, with edges tucked in under the mattress. The mesh size should be less than 1.5mm. If the sleeping area is not otherwise protected, use a mosquito coil, which will fill the room with insecticide through the night. Repellent-impregnated wristbands are not effective.

Sunburn & Heat Exhaustion

To protect yourself from excessive sun exposure, you should stay out of the midday sun, wear sunglasses and a wide-brimmed sun hat, and apply sun block with SPF 15 or higher, with both UVA and UVB protection, before exposure to the sun. Sun block should be reapplied after swimming or vigorous activity. Be aware that the sun is more intense at higher altitudes, even though you may feel cooler.

Dehydration or salt deficiency can cause heat exhaustion. Take time to acclimatize

to high temperatures, and make sure you get sufficient liquids. You should drink plenty of fluids and avoid excessive alcohol or strenuous activity when you first arrive in a hot climate. Long, continuous periods of exposure to high temperatures can leave you vulnerable to heat stroke, when body temperature rises to dangerous levels.

Water

Tap water in Peru is not safe to drink. Vigorous boiling of water for one minute is the most effective means of water purification. At altitudes greater than 2000m (6500ft), boil for three minutes.

Another option is to disinfect water with iodine or water purification pills. You can add 2% tincture of iodine to one quart or liter of water (five drops to clear water, 10 drops to cloudy water) and let stand for 30 minutes. If the water is cold, longer times may be required. Otherwise you can buy iodine pills, available at most pharmacies in your home country. The instructions for use should be carefully followed. The taste of iodinated water may be improved by adding vitamin C (ascorbic acid). Iodinated water should not be consumed for more than a few weeks. Pregnant women, those with a history of thyroid disease, and those allergic to iodine should not drink iodinated water.

A number of water filters are on the market. Those with smaller pores (reverse osmosis filters) provide the broadest protection, but they are relatively large and are readily plugged by debris. Those with somewhat larger pores (microstrainer filters) are ineffective against viruses, although they remove other organisms. Manufacturers' instructions must be carefully followed.

TRAVELING WITH CHILDREN

It's safer not to take children aged under three to high altitudes. Also, children under nine months should not be brought to jungle areas at lower altitudes because yellow-fever vaccine is not safe for this age group.

When traveling with young children, be particularly careful about what you allow them to eat and drink, because diarrhea can be especially dangerous to them and because the vaccines for the prevention of hepatitis A and typhoid fever are not approved for use in children aged under two.

FOLK REMEDIES

Some common traditional remedies include the following:

problem	treatment
altitude sickness	ginko
jet lag	melatonin
mosquito-bite prevention	oil of eucalyptus/ soybean oil
motion sickness	ginger

The two main malaria medications, Lariam and Malarone, may be given to children, but insect repellents must be applied in lower concentrations (see Mosquito Bites on p430).

WOMEN'S HEALTH

Although travel to Lima is reasonably safe if you're pregnant, there are risks in visiting many other parts of the country. First, it may be difficult to find quality obstetric care, if needed, outside Lima, especially away from the main tourist areas. Second, it isn't advisable for pregnant women to

spend time at high altitudes where the air is thin, which precludes travel to many of the most popular destinations, including Cuzco, Machu Picchu and Lake Titicaca. (If you are still determined to visit these places regardless, then be sure to ascend more slowly than recommended under Altitude Sickness as described on p429.) Lastly, yellow-fever vaccine, strongly recommended for travel to jungle areas at altitudes less than 2300m (see p424), should not be given during pregnancy because the vaccine contains a live virus that may infect the fetus.

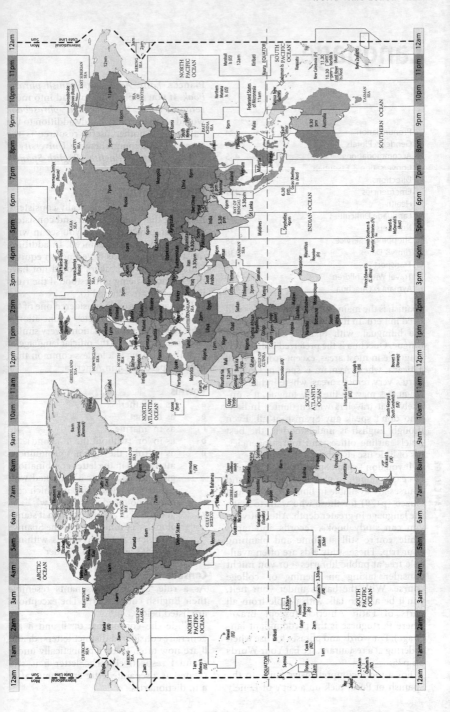

Language

CONTENTS

Spanish is the main language the traveler will need in Peru. In the highlands, most Indians are bilingual, with Spanish as a second tongue. Quechua is the preferred indigenous language in most areas, except around Lake Titicaca, where Aymara is spoken. Outside Peru's very remote areas, where indigenous languages may be the only tongue, it's unlikely that travelers will encounter Indians who don't speak any Spanish at all. Even though English is understood in the best hotels, airline offices and tourist agencies, it's of little use elsewhere.

If you don't speak Spanish, don't despair. It's easy enough to pick up the basics, and courses are available in Lima (see p67) and Cuzco (p179) for those who want to learn the language in greater depth. Alternatively, you can study books, records and tapes while you're still at home and planning your trip. These study aids are often available free at public libraries – or you might consider taking an evening or college course. With the basics under your belt, you'll be able to talk with people from all parts of Latin America (except Brazil, where Portuguese is the predominant language). For words and phrases for use when ordering at a restaurant, see Eat Your Words on p45.

For a more comprehensive guide to the Spanish of Peru, pick up a copy of Lonely Planet's *Latin American Spanish phrasebook*. If you're planning to head into more remote areas the *Quechua phrasebook* would also be a a very handy addition to the backpack. Another useful resource is the compact and comprehensive *University of Chicago Spanish-English, English-Spanish Dictionary*.

PRONUNCIATION

Spanish spelling is phonetically consistent, meaning that there's a clear and consistent relationship between what you see in writing and how it's pronounced. In addition, most Spanish sounds have English equivalents, so English speakers should not have much trouble being understood if the rules listed below are adhered to.

Peruvian Spanish is considered one of the language's 'cleanest' dialects – enunciation is relatively clear, pronunciation is very similar to Castilian Spanish (the official language of Spain), and slang is a lot less common than in other parts of Latin America.

Vowels

a	as in 'father'
e	as in 'met'
i	as in 'marine'
o	as in 'or' (without the 'r' sound)
u	as in 'rule'; the 'u' is not pronounced after **q** and in the letter combinations **gue** and **gui**, unless it's marked with a diaeresis (eg *argüir*), in which case it's pronounced as English 'w'
y	at the end of a word or when it stands alone, it's pronounced as the Spanish **i** (eg *ley*); between vowels within a word it's as the 'y' in 'yonder'

Consonants

As a rule, Spanish consonants resemble their English counterparts. The exceptions are listed below.

While the consonants **ch**, **ll** and **ñ** are generally considered distinct letters, **ch** and **ll** are now often listed alphabetically under **c** and **l** respectively. The letter **ñ** is still treated as a separate letter and comes after **n** in dictionaries.

b   similar to English 'b,' but softer; referred to as 'b larga'

c   as in 'celery' before **e** and **i**; otherwise as English 'k'

ch   as in 'church'

d   as in 'dog,' but between vowels and after **l** or **n**, the sound is closer to the 'th' in 'this'

g   as the 'ch' in the Scottish *loch* before **e** and **i** ('kh' in our guides to pronunciation); elsewhere, as in 'go'

h   invariably silent. If your name begins with this letter, listen carefully if you're waiting for public officials to call you.

j   as the 'ch' in the Scottish *loch* (written as 'kh' in our guides to pronunciation)

ll   as the 'y' in 'yellow'

ñ   as the 'ni' in 'onion'

r   a short **r** except at the beginning of a word, and after **l**, **n** or **s**, when it's often rolled

rr   very strongly rolled

v   similar to English 'b,' but softer; referred to as 'b corta'

x   as in 'taxi' except for a very few words, when it's pronounced as **j**

z   as the 's' in 'sun'

Word Stress

In general, words ending in vowels or the letters **n** or **s** have stress on the next-to-last syllable, while those with other endings have stress on the last syllable. Thus *vaca* (cow) and *caballos* (horses) both carry stress on the next-to-last syllable, while *ciudad* (city) and *infeliz* (unhappy) are both stressed on the last syllable.

Written accents will almost always appear in words that don't follow the rules above, eg *sótano* (basement), *América* and *porción* (portion). When counting syllables, be sure to remember that diphthongs (vowel combinations, such as the 'ue' in *puede*) constitute only one. When a word with a written accent appears in capital letters, the accent is often not written, but is still pronounced.

GENDER & PLURALS

In Spanish, nouns are either masculine or feminine, and there are rules to help determine gender (there are of course some exceptions). Feminine nouns generally end with -**a** or with the groups -**ción**, -**sión** or -**dad**.

Other endings typically signify a masculine noun. Endings for adjectives also change to agree with the gender of the noun they modify (masculine/feminine -**o**/-**a**). Where both masculine and feminine forms are included in this language guide, they are separated by a slash, with the masculine form first, eg *perdido/a*.

If a noun or adjective ends in a vowel, the plural is formed by adding **s** to the end. If it ends in a consonant, the plural is formed by adding **es** to the end.

ACCOMMODATIONS

I'm looking for ...	*Estoy buscando ...*	e·stoy boos·*kan*·do ...
Where is ...?	*¿Dónde hay ...?*	*don*·de ai ...
a hotel	*un hotel*	oon o·*tel*
a boarding house	*una pensión/ residencial/ un hospedaje*	oo·na pen·*syon*/ re·see·den·*syal*/ oon os·pe·*da*·khe
a youth hostel	*un albergue juvenil*	oon al·*ber*·ge khoo·ve·*neel*
I'd like a ... room.	*Quisiera una habitación ...*	kee·*sye*·ra oo·na a·bee·ta·*syon* ...
double	*doble*	*do*·ble
single	*individual*	een·dee·vee·*dwal*
twin	*con dos camas*	kon dos *ka*·mas
How much is it per ...?	*¿Cuánto cuesta por ...?*	*kwan*·to *kwes*·ta por ...
night	*noche*	*no*·che
person	*persona*	per·*so*·na
week	*semana*	se·*ma*·na

Does it include breakfast?
¿Incluye el desayuno?   een·*kloo*·ye el de·sa·*yoo*·no
May I see the room?
¿Puedo ver la habitación?   *pwe*·do ver la a·bee·ta·*syon*
I don't like it.
No me gusta.   no me *goos*·ta
It's fine. I'll take it.
OK. La alquilo.   o·*kay* la al·*kee*·lo
I'm leaving now.
Me voy ahora.   me *voy* a·o·ra

full board	*pensión completa*	pen·*syon* kom·*ple*·ta
private/shared bathroom	*baño privado/ compartido*	*ba*·nyo pree·*va*·do/ kom·par·*tee*·do
too expensive	*demasiado caro*	de·ma·*sya*·do *ka*·ro
cheaper	*más económico*	mas e·ko·*no*·mee·ko
discount	*descuento*	des·*kwen*·to

LANGUAGE

MAKING A RESERVATION
(for phone or written requests)

To ...	*A ...*
From ...	*De ...*
Date	*Fecha*
I'd like to book ...	*Quisiera reservar ...* (see the list under 'Accommodations' for bed/room options)
in the name of ...	*en nombre de ...*
for the nights of ...	*para las noches del ...*
credit card ...	*tarjeta de crédito ...*
number	*número*
expiry date	*fecha de vencimiento*
Please confirm ...	*Puede confirmar ...*
availability	*la disponibilidad*
price	*el precio*

CONVERSATION & ESSENTIALS

In their public behavior, South Americans are very conscious of civilities, sometimes to the point of ceremoniousness. Never approach a stranger for information without extending a greeting and use only the polite form of address, especially with the police and public officials. Young people may be less likely to expect this, but it's best to stick to the polite form unless you're quite sure you won't offend by using the informal mode. The polite form is used in all cases in this guide; where options are given, the form is indicated by the abbreviations 'pol' and 'inf.'

Hello.	*Hola.*	o·la
Good morning.	*Buenos días.*	bwe·nos dee·as
Good afternoon.	*Buenas tardes.*	bwe·nas tar·des
Good evening/night.	*Buenas noches.*	bwe·nas no·ches
Goodbye.	*Adiós.*	a·dyos
Bye/See you soon.	*Hasta luego.*	as·ta lwe·go
Yes.	*Sí.*	see
No.	*No.*	no
Please.	*Por favor.*	por fa·vor
Thank you.	*Gracias.*	gra·syas
Many thanks.	*Muchas gracias.*	moo·chas gra·syas
You're welcome.	*De nada.*	de na·da
Pardon me.	*Perdón.*	per·don
Excuse me.	*Permiso.*	per·mee·so
(used when asking permission)		
Forgive me.	*Disculpe.*	dees·kool·pe
(used when apologizing)		

How are things?		
¿Qué tal?	ke tal	
What's your name?		
¿Cómo se llama?	ko·mo se ya·ma (pol)	
¿Cómo te llamas?	ko·mo te ya·mas (inf)	
My name is ...		
Me llamo ...	me ya·mo ...	
It's a pleasure to meet you.		
Mucho gusto.	moo·cho goos·to	
The pleasure is mine.		
El gusto es mío.	el goos·to es mee·o	
Where are you from?		
¿De dónde es/eres?	de don·de es/e·res (pol/inf)	
I'm from ...		
Soy de ...	soy de ...	
Where are you staying?		
¿Dónde está alojado?	don·de es·ta a·lo·kha·do (pol)	
¿Dónde estás alojado?	don·de es·tas a·lo·kha·do (inf)	
May I take a photo?		
¿Puedo sacar una foto?	pwe·do sa·kar oo·na fo·to	

DIRECTIONS

How do I get to ...?	
¿Cómo puedo llegar a ...?	ko·mo pwe·do lye·gar a ...
Is it far?	
¿Está lejos?	es·ta le·khos
Go straight ahead.	
Siga/Vaya derecho.	see·ga/va·ya de·re·cho
Turn left.	
Voltée a la izquierda.	vol·te·e a la ees·kyer·da
Turn right.	
Voltée a la derecha.	vol·te·e a la de·re·cha
I'm lost.	
Estoy perdido/a.	es·toy per·dee·do/a
Can you show me (on the map)?	
¿Me lo podría indicar (en el mapa)?	me lo po·dree·a een·dee·kar (en el ma·pa)

north	*norte*	nor·te
south	*sur*	soor
east	*este/oriente*	es·te/o·ryen·te
west	*oeste/occidente*	o·es·te/ok·see·den·te

SIGNS

Entrada	Entrance
Salida	Exit
Información	Information
Abierto	Open
Cerrado	Closed
Prohibido	Prohibited
Comisaria	Police Station
Servicios/Baños	Toilets
Hombres/Varones	Men
Mujeres/Damas	Women

here	*aquí*	a·*kee*
there	*allí*	a·*yee*
avenue	*avenida*	a·ve·*nee*·da
block	*cuadra*	*kwa*·dra
street	*calle/paseo*	*ka*·lye/pa·*se*·o

EMERGENCIES

Help!	*¡Socorro!*	so·*ko*·ro
Fire!	*¡Incendio!*	een·*sen*·dyo
I've been robbed.	*Me robaron.*	me ro·*ba*·ron
Go away!	*¡Déjeme!*	*de*·khe·me
Get lost!	*¡Váyase!*	*va*·ya·se
Call ...!	*¡Llame a ...!*	*ya*·me a
the police	*la policía*	la po·lee·*see*·a
a doctor	*un médico*	oon *me*·dee·ko
an ambulance	*una ambulancia*	oo·na am·boo·*lan*·sya

It's an emergency.
Es una emergencia. es oo·na e·mer·*khen*·sya
Could you help me, please?
¿Me puede ayudar, por favor? me *pwe*·de a·yoo·*dar* por fa·*vor*
I'm lost.
Estoy perdido/a. es·*toy* per·*dee*·do/a
Where are the toilets?
¿Dónde están los baños? *don*·de es·*tan* los *ba*·nyos

HEALTH

I'm sick.
Estoy enfermo/a. es·*toy* en·*fer*·mo/a
I need a doctor.
Necesito un médico. ne·se·*see*·to oon *me*·dee·ko
Where's the hospital?
¿Dónde está el hospital? *don*·de es·*ta* el os·pee·*tal*
I'm pregnant.
Estoy embarazada. es·*toy* em·ba·ra·*sa*·da
I've been vaccinated.
Estoy vacunado/a. es·*toy* va·koo·*na*·do/a

I'm allergic to ...	*Soy alérgico/a a ...*	soy a·*ler*·khee·ko/a a ...
antibiotics	*los antibióticos*	los an·tee·*byo*·tee·kos
penicillin	*la penicilina*	la pe·nee·see·*lee*·na
nuts	*las fruta secas*	las *froo*·tas *se*·kas
I'm ...	*Soy ...*	soy ...
asthmatic	*asmático/a*	as·*ma*·tee·ko/a
diabetic	*diabético/a*	dya·*be*·tee·ko/a
epileptic	*epiléptico/a*	e·pee·*lep*·tee·ko/a

I have ...	*Tengo ...*	*ten*·go ...
altitude sickness	*soroche*	so·*ro*·che
diarrhea	*diarrea*	dya·*re*·a
nausea	*náusea*	*now*·se·a
a headache	*un dolor de cabeza*	oon do·*lor* de ka·*be*·sa
a cough	*tos*	tos

LANGUAGE DIFFICULTIES

Do you speak (English)?
¿Habla/Hablas (inglés)? *a*·bla/*a*·blas (een·*gles*) (pol/inf)
Does anyone here speak English?
¿Hay alguien que hable inglés? ai al·*gyen* ke *a*·ble een·*gles*
I (don't) understand.
Yo (no) entiendo. yo (no) en·*tyen*·do
How do you say ...?
¿Cómo se dice ...? *ko*·mo se *dee*·se ...
What does ...mean?
¿Qué quiere decir ...? ke *kye*·re de·*seer* ...

Could you please ...?	*¿Puede ..., por favor?*	*pwe*·de ... por fa·*vor*
repeat that	*repetirlo*	re·pe·*teer*·lo
speak more slowly	*hablar más despacio*	a·*blar* mas des·*pa*·syo
write it down	*escribirlo*	es·kree·*beer*·lo

NUMBERS

1	*uno*	*oo*·no
2	*dos*	dos
3	*tres*	tres
4	*cuatro*	*kwa*·tro
5	*cinco*	*seen*·ko
6	*seis*	says
7	*siete*	*sye*·te
8	*ocho*	*o*·cho
9	*nueve*	*nwe*·ve
10	*diez*	dyes
11	*once*	*on*·se
12	*doce*	*do*·se
13	*trece*	*tre*·se
14	*catorce*	ka·*tor*·se
15	*quince*	*keen*·se
16	*dieciséis*	dye·see·*says*
17	*diecisiete*	dye·see·*sye*·te
18	*dieciocho*	dye·see·*o*·cho
19	*diecinueve*	dye·see·*nwe*·ve
20	*veinte*	*vayn*·te
21	*veintiuno*	vayn·tee·*oo*·no
30	*treinta*	*trayn*·ta
31	*treinta y uno*	*trayn*·ta ee *oo*·no
40	*cuarenta*	kwa·*ren*·ta
50	*cincuenta*	seen·*kwen*·ta
60	*sesenta*	se·*sen*·ta

70	setenta	se·ten·ta
80	ochenta	o·chen·ta
90	noventa	no·ven·ta
100	cien	syen
101	ciento uno	syen·to oo·no
200	doscientos	do·syen·tos
1000	mil	meel
5000	cinco mil	seen·ko meel
10,000	diez mil	dyes meel
50,000	cincuenta mil	seen·kwen·ta meel
100,000	cien mil	syen meel
1,000,000	un millón	oon mee·yon

SHOPPING & SERVICES

I'd like to buy ...
Quisiera comprar ...   kee·sye·ra kom·prar ...
I'm just looking.
Sólo estoy mirando.   so·lo es·toy mee·ran·do
May I look at it?
¿Puedo mirar(lo/la)?   pwe·do mee·rar·(lo/la)
How much is it?
¿Cuánto cuesta?   kwan·to kwes·ta
That's too expensive for me.
Es demasiado caro   es de·ma·sya·do ka·ro
para mí.   pa·ra mee
Could you lower the price?
¿Podría bajar un poco   po·dree·a ba·khar oon po·ko
el precio?   el pre·syo
I don't like it.
No me gusta.   no me goos·ta
I'll take it.
Lo llevo.   lo ye·vo

Do you accept ...?	¿Aceptan ...?	a·sep·tan ...
American dollars	dólares americanos	do·la·res a·me·ree·ka·nos
credit cards	tarjetas de crédito	tar·khe·tas de kre·dee·to
traveler's checks	cheques de viajero	che·kes de vya·khe·ro

less	menos	me·nos
more	más	mas
large	grande	gran·de
small	pequeño/a	pe·ke·nyo/a

I'm looking for (the) ...	Estoy buscando ...	es·toy boos·kan·do
ATM	el cajero automático	el ka·khe·ro ow·to·ma·tee·ko
bank	el banco	el ban·ko
bookstore	la librería	la lee·bre·ree·a
embassy	la embajada	la em·ba·kha·da
exchange house	la casa de cambio	la ka·sa de kam·byo

general store	la tienda	la tyen·da
laundry	la lavandería	la la·van·de·ree·a
market	el mercado	el mer·ka·do
pharmacy/ chemist	la farmacia/ la botica	la far·ma·sya/ la bo·tee·ka
post office	el correo	el ko·re·o
supermarket	el supermercado	el soo·per·mer·ka·do
tourist office	la oficina de turismo	la o·fee·see·na de too·rees·mo

What time does it open/close?
¿A qué hora abre/cierra?   a ke o·ra a·bre/sye·ra
I want to change some money/traveler's checks.
Quiero cambiar dinero/   kye·ro kam·byar dee·ne·ro/
cheques de viajero.   che·kes de vya·khe·ro
What is the exchange rate?
¿Cuál es el tipo de   kwal es el tee·po de
cambio?   kam·byo
I want to call ...
Quiero llamar a ...   kye·ro lya·mar a ...

airmail	correo aéreo	ko·re·o a·e·re·o
black market	mercado (negro/ paralelo)	mer·ka·do ne·gro/ pa·ra·le·lo
letter	carta	kar·ta
registered mail	certificado	ser·tee·fee·ka·do
stamps	estampillas	es·tam·pee·lyas

TIME & DATES

What time is it?	¿Qué hora es?	ke o·ra es
It's one o'clock.	Es la una.	es la oo·na
It's seven o'clock.	Son las siete.	son las sye·te
midnight	medianoche	me·dya·no·che
noon	mediodía	me·dyo·dee·a
half past two	dos y media	dos ee me·dya

now	ahora	a·o·ra
today	hoy	oy
tonight	esta noche	es·ta no·che
tomorrow	mañana	ma·nya·na
yesterday	ayer	a·yer

Monday	lunes	loo·nes
Tuesday	martes	mar·tes
Wednesday	miércoles	myer·ko·les
Thursday	jueves	khwe·ves
Friday	viernes	vyer·nes
Saturday	sábado	sa·ba·do
Sunday	domingo	do·meen·go

January	enero	e·ne·ro
February	febrero	fe·bre·ro
March	marzo	mar·so
April	abril	a·breel
May	mayo	ma·yo

June	junio	khoo·nyo
July	julio	khoo·lyo
August	agosto	a·gos·to
September	septiembre	sep·tyem·bre
October	octubre	ok·too·bre
November	noviembre	no·vyem·bre
December	diciembre	dee·syem·bre

TRANSPORT
Public Transport

What time does	¿A qué hora ...	a ke o·ra ...
... leave/arrive?	sale/llega?	sa·le/ye·ga
the bus	autobus	ow·to·boos
the plane	el avión	el a·vyon
the ship	el barco/buque	el bar·ko/boo·ke
the train	el tren	el tren

airport	el aeropuerto	el a·e·ro·pwer·to
train station	la estación de ferrocarril	la es·ta·syon de fe·ro·ka·reel
bus station	la estación de autobuses	la es·ta·syon de ow·to·boo·ses
bus stop	la parada de autobuses	la pa·ra·da de ow·to·boo·ses
luggage check room	guardería/ equipaje	gwar·de·ree·a/ e·kee·pa·khe
ticket office	la boletería	la bo·le·te·ree·a

I'd like a ticket to ...
Quiero un boleto a ... kye·ro oon bo·le·to a ...
What's the fare to ...?
¿Cuánto cuesta hasta ...? kwan·to kwes·ta a·sta ...

student's	de estudiante	de es·too·dyan·te
1st class	primera clase	pree·me·ra kla·se
2nd class	segunda clase	se·goon·da kla·se
single/one-way	ida	ee·da
return/round trip	ida y vuelta	ee·da ee vwel·ta
taxi	taxi	tak·see

Private Transport

I'd like to	Quisiera	kee·sye·ra
hire a/an ...	alquilar ...	al·kee·lar ...
4WD	un todo terreno	oon to·do te·re·no
car	un auto	oon ow·to
motorbike	una moto	oo·na mo·to
bicycle	una bicicleta	oo·na bee·see·kle·ta

pickup (truck)	camioneta	ka·myo·ne·ta
truck	camión	ka·myon
hitchhike	hacer dedo	a·ser de·do

Is this the road to (...)?
¿Se va a (...) por esta carretera? se va a (...) por es·ta ka·re·te·ra

ROAD SIGNS

Acceso	Entrance
Aparcamiento	Parking
Ceda el Paso	Give way
Despacio	Slow
Dirección Única	One-way
Mantenga Su Derecha	Keep to the Right
No Adelantar/ No Rebase	No Passing
Peaje	Toll
Peligro	Danger
Prohibido Aparcar/ No Estacionar	No Parking
Prohibido el Paso	No Entry
Pare/Stop	Stop
Salida de Autopista	Exit Freeway

Where's a petrol station?
¿Dónde hay una gasolinera/un grifo? don·de ai oo·na ga·so·lee·ne·ra/oon gree·fo
Please fill it up.
Lleno, por favor. ye·no por fa·vor
I'd like (20) liters.
Quiero (veinte) litros. kye·ro (vayn·te) lee·tros

diesel	diesel	dee·sel
leaded (regular)	gasolina con plomo	ga·so·lee·na kon plo·mo
petrol (gas)	gasolina	ga·so·lee·na
unleaded	gasolina sin plomo	ga·so·lee·na seen plo·mo

(How long) Can I park here?
¿(Por cuánto tiempo) Puedo aparcar aqui? (por kwan·to tyem·po) pwe·do a·par·kar a·kee
Where do I pay?
¿Dónde se paga? don·de se pa·ga
I need a mechanic.
Necesito un mecánico. ne·se·see·to oon me·ka·nee·ko
The car has broken down (in ...).
El carro se ha averiado (en ...). el ka·ro se a a·ve·rya·do (en ...)
The motorbike won't start.
No arranca la moto. no a·ran·ka la mo·to
I have a flat tyre.
Tengo un pinchazo. ten·go oon peen·cha·so
I've run out of petrol.
Me quedé sin gasolina. me ke·de seen ga·so·lee·na
I've had an accident.
Tuve un accidente. too·ve oon ak·see·den·te

TRAVEL WITH CHILDREN

I need ...	Necesito ...	ne·se·see·to ...
Do you have ...?	¿Hay ...?	ai ...
a car baby seat	un asiento de seguridad para bebés	oon a·syen·to de se·goo·ree·da pa·ra be·bes
a child-minding service	un servicio de cuidado de niños	oon ser·vee·syo de kwee·da·do de nee·nyos
a children's menu	una carta infantil	oona kar·ta een·fan·teel
a creche	una guardería	oo·na gwar·de·ree·a
(disposable) diapers/nappies	pañoles (de usar y tirar)	pa·nyo·les de oo·sar ee tee·rar
an (English-speaking) babysitter	una niñera (de habla inglesa)	oo·na nee·nye·ra (de a·bla een·gle·sa)
formula (milk)	leche en polvo	le·che en pol·vo
a highchair	una trona	oo·na tro·na
a potty	una pelela	oo·na pe·le·la
a stroller	un cochecito	oon ko·che·see·to

Do you mind if I breast-feed here?
¿Le molesta que dé de pecho aquí?   le mo·les·ta ke de de pe·cho a·kee

Are children allowed?
¿Se admiten niños?   se ad·mee·ten nee·nyos

AYMARA & QUECHUA

The following list of words and phrases is obviously minimal, but it should be useful in areas where these languages are spoken. Pronounce them as you would a Spanish word. An apostrophe represents a glottal stop, which is the 'non-sound' that occurs in the middle of 'uh-oh.' In the following words and phrases, Aymara is the first entry, Quechua the second.

Hello.
Kamisaraki.   Napaykullayki.

Please.
Mirá.   Allichu.

Thank you.
Yuspagara.   Yusulipayki.

Yes/No.
Jisa/Janiwa.   Ari/Mana.

How do you say ...?
Cun sañasauca'ha ...?   Imainata nincha chaita ...?

It is called ...
Ucan sutipa'h ...   Chaipa'g sutin'ha ...

Please repeat.
Uastata sita.   Ua'manta niway.

How much?
K'gauka?   Maik'ata'g?

father	auqui	tayta
food	manka	mikiuy
mother	taica	mama
river	jawira	mayu
snowy peak	kollu	riti-orko
water	uma	yacu

1	maya	u'
2	paya	iskai
3	quimsa	quinsa
4	pusi	tahua
5	pesca	phiska
6	zo'hta	so'gta
7	pakalko	khanchis
8	quimsakalko	pusa'g
9	yatunca	iskon
10	tunca	chunca

Also available from Lonely Planet:
Latin American Spanish and *Quechua* phrasebooks

LANGUAGE

Glossary

See p45 in the Food & Drink chapter for useful words and phrases dealing with food and dining. See the Language chapter (p434) for other useful words and phrases.

A

abrazo – a backslapping hug exchanged between men

altiplano – literally high plateau or plain. It specifically refers to the high, desolate Andean flatlands of southern Peru, Bolivia, northern Chile and northern Argentina.

ambulantes – street vendors

aluvión – a fast-moving flow of ice, water, rocks, mud and debris caused by the bursting of a dam or an earthquake in a mountainous region

apacheta – pile or column of rocks built on mountain passes in honor of the *apus*

Apartado – post office box (also Apdo)

apu – mountain god

areneros – dune-buggies

Arequipeños – residents of Arequipa

arriero – mule driver

avenida – avenue

B

barrio – suburb

blanco/blanca – white

bodegas – wine shops and wine cellars

burro – donkey

bus-cama – long-distance double-decker buses with seats reclining into almost a bed; the 1st floor is the most spacious and expensive. Toilets, videos and snacks are provided.

C

caballitos – high-ended, cigar-shaped boats, or 'little horses', found near Huanchaco

caballo – horse

cajón – literally, a big box, used to describe a percussion instrument consisting of a box upon which the musician sits and which is drummed with the palms of the hands. Typically played by Afro-Peruvians.

calle – street

camión – truck; may be used for transport in remote areas

camioneta – pickup truck

campesino – peasant or rural inhabitant

capitanía – office of the port or harbor captain

carretera – highway

casa – home or house

casado/casada – married

cerro – hill or mountain without permanent snow

chasqui – a runner of Inca times, used for delivering messages

chicha – a fermented maize beer made by the Incas and still common in highland towns; also a modern fusion of Andean *huayno* and rock music, influenced by Colombian cumbia dance music

cocha – Quechua Indian name for a lake, often appended to many lake names, eg Conococha

colectivo – shared transportation, usually taxis or sometimes minibuses or even boats

colpa – clay lick usually found in the rainforest and used by mammals and birds to obtain minerals

combi – minibuses (usually with tiny seats, cramming in as many passengers as possible)

cordillera – mountain chain

criollo/criolla – Creole or native of Peru. It also applies to coastal Peruvians; *criollo* food refers to spicy Peruvian fare with Spanish and African influences.

cuadra – a city block

culebra – a generic term for snakes

Cuzqueños – residents of Cuzco

D

derecha – right

E

Escuela Cuzqueña – Cuzco school; colonial artists who combined Spanish and Andean artistic styles

F

flautas – flutes

G

garúa – coastal fog

gringo/gringa – a term generally utilized for all foreigners who are not from South or Central America and Mexico

guano – seabird droppings

guapo/guapa – good-looking

H

huaqueros – grave robbers

huayno – traditional Andean music using instrumentation with roots in pre-Colombian times

I

iglesia – church

IGN – Instituto Geográfico Nacional; the government agency that produces and sells topographic and other maps

impuestos – taxes
indígena – Indigenous person, male or female
Inrena – Instituto Nacional de Recursos Naturales (National Institute for Natural Resources); the government agency administering national parks, reserves, sanctuaries and other protected areas
isla – island
izquierda – left

J
jirón – road, usually several blocks with different names

L
lindo/linda – pretty
Limeños – residents of Lima

M
mestizo – person of mixed Indigenous and Spanish descent
migraciónes – immigration office
mirador – watchtower
mochila – backpack
motocarro, mototaxi – three-wheeled motorcycle rickshaw taxi
mula – mule

N
negro/negra – black
nevado – permanently glaciated or snowcapped mountain peak
niño/niña – boy/girl

P
pachamama – earth mother
pampa – a large, flat area
Panamericana – the Pan-American Highway, which is the main route joining Latin American countries and is called Interamericana in some countries
para llevar – to go
peki-peki – a wooden canoe powered by a two-stroke motor attached to a long propeller shaft. The name derives from the explosive coughing sound made by the engine.
peña – bar or club featuring live folkloric music

piropos – compliments, often used by men to try and pick up women
piruru – flute carved from the wing bone of a condor
piso – floor, ie as in 2nd floor
playa – beach
pongo – a narrow, steep-walled, rocky, jungle river canyon which can be a dangerous maelstrom during high water
puna – high Andean grasslands of the *altiplano*
puya – a spiky, rosette-like plant of the bromeliad family

Q
quebrada – literally, a break, usually referring to a steep ravine which may or may not have a river at the bottom of it
quenas – bamboo pennywhistles
queros – Inca wooden drinking vessels

R
río – river

S
sapo – a game in which brass disks are tossed onto a table with holes in it; holes are scored according to difficulty with the highest score for tossing your disk into the mouth of the *sapo* (toad) mounted in the center of the table
sillar – a light-colored volcanic rock
soroche – altitude sickness
SSHH – Servicios Higiénicos or public toilets

T
tambo – a resting place for the *chasquis*, where messages would get passed on to waiting runners
tinyas – hand drums

V
ventanas – windows

W
wankaras – larger drums

Z
zampoña – traditional Andean panpipes
Zona Arqueológica – archaeological zone

Behind the Scenes

THIS BOOK
The 5th edition of *Peru* was prepared in Lonely Planet's Melbourne office. The first four editions were written by Rob Rachowiecki.

THANKS FROM THE AUTHORS
Rob Rachowiecki Throughout northern, central and Amazonian Peru, I encountered much kindness, hospitality, friendship, help and interest in this book for which I am most grateful. I apologize for names I have missed. My research started rolling in the Huaraz area, where Huayhuash expert Chris Benway, the knowledgeable Olaza family, the hospitable Quirós family and always-cheerful Alberto Cafferata got me started on the right foot. Along the coast, David Wroughton quietly but convincingly made me relax in Máncora; here I owe a big gracias to Sandra Ratto-Risso, who freely turned her car over to me, complete with Willy, world-class super driver. A warm thanks to Michael and Clara, who opened their house and information services to me in Trujillo.

Then it was into the heart of Peru, where Fernando Maldonado was a gracious host and Pim Heijster was a great tour guide in Cajamarca. Lucho Hurtado introduced me to everyone in Huancayo (including a Polish-Peruvian couple with whom I had a surprise evening of conversation in my first language of Polish). I also thank Lily Acosta in Tarapoto. Heading into the jungle, Paul Wright opened his house to me in Iquitos, and Percy and Analia were a great source of information. Down in Puerto Maldonado, Kurt Holle made many things possible.

I also thank Adriaan Jansen, who accompanied me on a brief Chachapoyas adventure and went on to write many useful reports, and Jay Taylor, who has loved the Pucallpa area for years and keeps me abreast of river travel there. And Leo, in Lima, gets a special mention for retrieving packages of maps and notes that I sent back for safekeeping.

On the home front, I extend deepest love to and admiration of my children, Julia, Alison and David, to whom I dedicate this work.

Charlotte Beech In Lima, particular thanks go to Leo Rovayo and Monica Moreno of the Posada del Parque for their warm welcome and lessons in the finer points of Limeño cuisine, Simon Atkinson of Lima's South American Explorers club for all his tips and pointers, the guys at The Point in Barranco for an insider's guide to the local nightlife, and to Erwin of Pension Yolanda for his last-minute help. Thanks also go to William Nolasco Hernandez and Luis Herrera for ferrying me around Pisco and Paracas, Vlado Soto for his wealth of information in the White City, Tomás Tisnado Chura at Los Pinos and Victor Pauca at Allways for their hospitality in Puno, Orfa Corrales for so generously giving up a bed for a stranded traveler on a stormy night in Paucartambo, Ulrike Simic in Pisac, Carlos Milla and Russ Knutson in Cuzco.

Heartfelt thanks also to Emma Banks and Murray and Steve Fenwick for the memories, and to Michael Button, Monica Acosta and especially John

Beech and Alex Amelines for all their help back in London. I'd also like to thank the coordinating author, Rob, for sharing his copious knowledge, and Wendy Smith for first involving me in the project.

CREDITS

Editing was coordinated by Evan Jones with assistance from Helen Yeates, Carolyn Bain, Tom Smallman, Meaghan Amor, Bridget Blair, Brigitte Ellemor, Brigitte Barta, Imogen Bannister, Peter Cruttenden, Kate James, Francesca Coles, Stefanie Di Trocchio, Stephanie Pearson and Michelle Lewis. The cartography was coordinated by Karen Fry with assistance from Celia Wood and Daniel Fennessy. Karen also put together the color map. John Shippick prepared the rest of the color pages. Katie Cason laid out the book with assistance from John, Pablo Gastar and Laura Jane. The cover and the Quick Reference guide were designed by Yuki Kamimura. Layout checks were conducted by Adriana Mammarella, Kate McDonald and Rachel Imeson. The Language chapter was compiled by Quentin Frayne. Rachel Imeson was the project manager.

Series Publishing Manager Virginia Maxwell oversaw the development of the country guides series with help from Regional Publishing Manager Maria Donohue. Maria also steered the development of this title. The series was designed by James Hardy, with mapping development by Paul Piaia. This title was commissioned and developed in Lonely Planet's Oakland office by Wendy Smith. Cartography for this guide was developed by Graham Neale.

THANKS FROM LONELY PLANET

Many thanks to the travelers who used the last edition and wrote to us with helpful hints, useful advice and interesting anecdotes:

A Adriana Abreu, Anderson Abud, Dirk Achten, Bob Adams, Mitch Adams, Doug Adamson, Tamar Adelaar, Carlijn Adema, Peggy Aerts, Brion After, Dorianne Agius, Cristina Alcala, Lorraine Alcock, Ann Alderson, Alison Alessi, Karamat Ali, Thomas Allerstorfer, Milagros Alvarez-Calderon, Marycarmen Alzamora, Pat Amens, Ben Anderson, Matt Anderson, Corthout Andre, Jochen R Andritzky, Eduardo Angel, Niels Anger, Tine Ansbjerg, David Anthes, Rosemary Anton, Sayo Aoki, Carrie Appleton, Betty Arbulu, Wilfredo Ardito, Isabel Armendariz, Diana Armstrong, Egan Arnold, Dawn Arterburn, J Arthur Freed, Paola Artola, Hilmir Asgeirsson, Barbara Ashum, David Ashworth, Karen Askew, Will Askew, Rubu Askvik, Edouard Asselin, Caroline Atkinson, Philippe Aub, Nicole Avallone, Daniel Axelsson, James Ayres, Manola Azzariti **B** Joep B, Ceri Bacon, Henry Bacon, Werner Baer, Graham Bailey, Thomas Bailey, Adam Baird, Arash Bakhtari, Corina Bakker, David Balfour, Mandy Ball, Rod Ballantyne, Melinda Ballengee, Ute Balwaceda, Andrew Bambach, Paul Bannister, Bill Baragano, Ed Bardos, Monica Bargigli, Fleur Barker, Arnold Barkhordarian, Angie Barlow, Kim Baron, Richard Barragan, Manuel Barrenechea Solis, Daniel Barrera, Paul J Barrett, J Eugenio Barrios, Dom Barry, Robert Barth, Andrew Bassford, Laura Bassotti, Santiago Basualdo, Gemma Bath, Angela Bauer, Irmgard Bauer, Daniel Baum, Kelly Beairsto, Marc Beaudin, Jean-Pierre Beaufils, Bernd Becker, Clare Becker, Peter Beckmann, Perry Beebe, Gina Behrens, Jan-Willem Beijen, Mike Beishuizen, Anibal Bejar Torres, Ed Bekovich, Sheldon Belinkoff, Mary Bell, Yvonne Bell, Norma Viassone Beltrametti, Katie Bendall, Lisbet Bengtsson, John Bennett, Dr Kae Bennetts, Overli Bente, Brian Bentley, Alistair Beol, Frederic Bequet, Daniela Bercovitch, Elena Bergamini, Ralf Bergmann, Mauricio Bergstein, Alison Bermant, Molnar Bernadett, Tomas Berrin, Richard Berroa, Manuel Beschle, Jim Bethshares, Paul Beveridge, Karen Bevill, Alfred Beyer, Samantha Bianchi, Cathy Biggar, Iain Bird, Morten Bjerg, Veronique Blanc, Carolina Blanco, Bettina Blass, Patrick Blattman, Marita Blighman, Oswald Bloemen, Phillip Bloom, Nancy Bloomer, Mykel Board, Lynn Boatwright, Annette Bodier, Lenette and Joergen Boejgaard, Marile Bohm, Marc Bohn, Betina Bojaen, Inge Bollen, Robin Bollweg, Camilla Bolum, Claire Bonnet, Colin Bonnet, Justin Boocock, Nick Borg, Luis Borgeaud, Froukje Bosch, Robert Bough, Martin Bourgon, Kiki Bours, Joost Bouwmeester, Lisa Bowers, Michelle Bowlen, Bill Bowles, Edith Bowman, Simon Bowyer, Claire Boydell, Jean-Yves Boyer, Ran Boytner, Gracijela Bozovic, Petra Braam, Mikael W Braestrup, Gareth Brahams, Owen and Anna Brailsford, Oscar Brain, Kerstin Brandes, Philippe Branlant, Mike Brauner, Clara Bravo, Carl Bray, Kattis Brdnnlund, A Bregman, Gerlinde Breitschaft, Daniel Brenig, Kerry Breure, Oscar Brian, Mark Briggs, Derek Brill, Chuck Briscoe, Ian and Sally Britton, Graeme Brock, Evelien Broeder, Ulke Brolsma, Omer Brombery, Alan Brooke, Linda Broschofsky, Caroline Brouwer, Caryl A Brown, Hannah R Brown, Michael Brown, Ray Brown, Roger Brown, Simon Brown, Tim Browne, Angela Bruderer, Andrea Brugnoli, Thomas Bruhin, Lars C Brunner, Paul Brunner, Paul Christian Brunner, Christian F Bruns, Darrol Bryant, Thomas Bryson, Kristin Buchenhorner, Julia Buckell, Helene Budzinski, Patrick Buechel, Michael Buesing, Christian Bufnoir, Kay Buikstra, Kelly Buja, Werner Bull, Chris H Bumann, Claudia Burbaum, Bianca Burke, Emma Burke, Thomas Burkle, Tricia Burnett, Harold Burns, Agi and Shanf Burra, Matthew Burtch, Lois Burton, Bruce Busch, Jeanine Buschor, Oscar Buse, Luke Butcher, Melissa Butler, Mimi Butler, Bram Buunk, Jasper F Buxton, Stuart Buxton, Nic Bye **C** Lorena Cabrera, Marie Evelyn Cabrimol, Alberto Cafferata, Marcello Cafiero, Maximo Calla, Daniel Calvete, Bonnie Cameron, Eileen Cameron, Carlo Caminito, Alejandro Camino, Giulia Campanaro, Edward Canapary, Robert Candey, Saul Candib, Cecile Canivet, Eric Cantor, Margaret Cantrell, H Cardiff, Gavin Carey, Anna Carin Gustafson, J Carlucci, Alison Carney, Nigel Caro, Amanda Carpenter, Dan Carpenter, George Carstairs, Greg Carter, Ronan Carter, Miguel Carvalho, Salvatore Casari, Lucy Cass, Alan Casserly, Carmel Castellan, Roberto Castro, Laura Catleugh, Jeff Cenaiko, Sarah Cenaiko, Deivy Centeiro, Helena Cerin, Tanguy Ceulemans, Natalie Chambers, Steve

Chambers, Amitabh Chand, Carolynn Chaput, Graham Charles, Dominique Chauvet, Arun Chawla, Jonathan Cheek, Matthew Chell, Andrew Chenoweth, Ken Childs, Brad Chisholm, Daniel Christen, Ann Christian, William Christian, Yen Chuang, Felix-Leif Chue, Mark Churchill, Natalie Churnin, Genaro Saucedo Cienfuegos, Anilu Cigas, Cecilia Cincopil, Carolyn Cismoski, Liezy Claes, Kirsten Claiden-Yardley, Helene Clappaz, Lucy Claridge, Catherine Clark, Helen Clarke, Lisa Clarke, Ollie Clayton, Matt Cleary, James F Clements, Rachel Clemons, Mike Clulow, Mike Clyne, Sheelin Coates, Tim Cochrane, Karen Cockburn, Kevin Coghlan, Brett Cohen, Ellen Cohen, Shahar Cohen, Diana Cole, Helen Cole, Colette Colfer, Joke Collewijn, Christian Collins, Joe Collins, Marc Collis, Jessica Colp-Butler, Reid Colvin, Andrea Com, Megan Conaway, Emma Connell, Clare Conner, Annabelle Cook, Paul Cooke, Mairead Cooley, Crispin Cooper, Kit Cooper, Milton Copeland, Xavier Cordero Lopez, Arnaud Corin, Marieke Cornelissen, Robert Coronado, Briana Corso, Pascal Cosandier, Gregory J Cost, R Costigan, Theresa Costigan, Vanessa Cottle, Elisabeth Cox, John Cox, John P Coy, Chris Crabtree, Stuart Crane, Timothy P Crawfurd, Matthew Creeden, Penny Creswell, Tara Crete, Cheri Crider, Julia C Crislip, Daniel E Cronk, William Cropf, Hugh Cropp, Damien Croxton, Edmund Crozier, Alejandra Cuba, Jose Cuba, Denis Cullen, Terry Culver, Sandra Cunliffe, Benoit Cunningham, Mary Jean Currier, Derek Curtin, Daniel Curtis, Ted Custovich, Anna Czarnoccy, Karen Czulik **D** Inge Daemen, Jan Daems, Suheil Dahdal, Mara Dale, Francesco D'Alessandro, Beverly Dandurand, Adam Danek, Cristine D'Arthuys Lohman, Aaron Daub, GJ Davies, Sarah Davies, Vicky Davies, Elizabeth Davison, Julie Davison, Marcelle Dawson, Melanie Day, Koen de Boeck, Petra de Boer, Chris de Cat, Shahaira de Cuba, Ingrid de Graaf, Vincent de Groot, Martijn de Jong, Edu de la Combe, Sjoerd de Wit, Richard de Witts, Walter Deal, Emma Dean, Bil Deane, Silvia Decet, Chad and Gwen Deetkan, Aleonka del Aguila, Claude Deladoeuille, Ian Delahunt, Iris Delaney, Jean-Marc Delarte, Pascale Delhaye, Louis DeMaria, Rick DeMasi, CF den Hartog, Joanna Dench, CB Denning, Kurt Dennis, Claire Derrick, Werner Dettli, Danielle Deutscher, Thea Devers, Tarun Devraj, Remmert DeVroome, Anna M Di Ponio, Bark Diak, Rocio Diaz, Angel Diaz Mendez, Filippo Dibari, Jesus Dicartillo, Jesus Lopez de Dicastillo, Andrew Dick, Frank Van Dierendonck, Christa Dieterich, Marc DiGiacomo, Armin Dipping, Peter Ditlevsen, Marc Ditschke, Tara Dittrick, Anna Doab, Tiffany M Doan, Barbara Doersch, Debbie Dolar, Khamer Done, Gemma Dorritt, Brendon Douglas, Rob Dover, Paisley Drab, Marja Dral, Inga Drechsel, Jan Drescher, Adele Drexler, Kenneth Dreyfuss, D Dubbin, Ray Dubois, Natasja Dumay, Marlene Dunn, Mary Dunn, Ray Dunn, Anne Dupont, Augusto Durand, Suzanne DuRard, Owen Duxbury **E** Yasmin Ebrahim, Lutz Eckhardt, Christian Eckstein, Todd Edgar, Bruce Edmunds, Huw Edwards, Roland Ehrat, Mette Elf, Inge Ellenkammeshidt, Patricia Elmore, Bertha Elzinga, Colin Emmott, Elena Enache, Victor Englebert, Julia Epstein, Maren Erchinger, Chris Erhardt, Marisa Escudero, Peter Eshelby, Russ Essex, Jo Eustace, Dr Karl Evans, Karl Evans, Mark Evans, Dr Yair Even-Zohar **F** Edith Fällinger, Elisabetta Fabris, Brian Fagan, Caryll Fagan, Maria Antonietta Faina, Jonathan Falby, Roberto Falconi, Ralph Falkenburg, Heinz Falter, Jim and Carol Farmer, Esther Farrerons, Toni Farrugia, Lora Fasolino, Tessa Fayers, Michel Fecteau, Sven Feddern, Csaba Feher, Marian Feinberg, Toop

Felber, Judy Fennessy, Eckhard Ferber, Andrew Ferguson, Michael Ferguson, Juvenal Fernandes, Tonino Ferrara, Tracy Ferrell, Iggy Ferruelo, Stephane Ferry, Andreas Fertin, Eelco Fichtinger, Bjorn Fiedler, Lucia Cardenas Figueroa, Tara Findlay, Neal Firth, Jonas Fischer, Gloria Fisher, Diane and Gary Flannery, James Fletcher, Orlando Flores, Rosa Bustamante Flores, Donna Florio, Adam Folickman, Bruno Fontaine, Robert Ford, Noreen A Fordyce, Judy Forney, Katy Foster, Tim Foster, Guy Foux, Scott Fowler, Claudia Fraefel, Jonathan France, Paul Francescutti, George Frangakis, Sharon Frazzini, Bettina Fredrich, Bente K Fremmerlid, Audra French, Cash French, Erith French, Achim Freund, Caroline Fric, Beth Fridinger, Beth Fridinme, Gerry Friebe, Bruce Friedman, Robert Frizzo, Ondrej Frye, Tanya Frymersum, Werner Fuchs, Alejandro Fuentes, Rachel Fulcher, Dave Fuller, Dave and Lina Fuller, Erik Futtrup, Thomas Fux **G** SR Gage, Jos Ignacio Pichardo Galßn, Robert Galvan, Juan Galvan D, Marina Gama, Cesar Gamio Brou, Robert Gantner, Rebecca Garbett, Ferdinando Garbuglio, Miss Garcia, Joanna Gardner, Maria Gardner, Sarah Gardner, Juanito Garlitos, David Garrett, Maureen Garrigan, Samy Gasmi, Katie Gaudion, Miriam Gayoso, Marijn Gelderloos, Lorenzo Gennaro, Gabriel Genoves, Stephen George, Axarlis Georgios, Joe Geraci, Bjorn Gerritsen, Kathy Gerst, Mark Gertzberg, Matt Gervase, Christine Gesseney, Eva Geuder, Arthur GH Bing, Cecilia Ghione, Brooke Gibson, James Gibson, Sean Gibson, Annemarie Gielen, Marieke and Esther Gieteling, Julie Giguere, Beth Gilliam, Robert H Gillis, Charlie Gilmore, Michael Gimard, Werner Ginzky, Sonia Gipper, Sue Girling, Daniel Giroux, Malcolm Gladdish, Todd Glaesmer, Tina Glahr, Robyn Glaser, Jeremy Glass, Roswit Glaubitz, Katherine Glen, Martin Gluckman, Marc-Oliver Goebel, Matt Goff, V Gohl, Dan Goldberg, Philip Goldberg, Kevin Golde, Michael Goldfarb, Helen Goldfinch, Jane Golding, Piotr Golec, Petra Golja, Tone Golnar, Matthew Gomez, Marc Goncher, Natalia Gonzolez, Marne Good, Erik Goodbody, Diane B Goodpasture, Tress Goodwin, Patrick Goosen, Harry Goovaarts, Sandra Gordon, Cornel Grad, Andrea Graner, Sarah Gratton, Patricia Grau, Kay Greczkowski, Bob Greely, Julie Green, Alvaro Greene, Shiefra Greenwood, James Gregory, Alexander Grellmann, Jay Griffiths, David P Grill, Marie Elizabeth Griste-Rallis, Irena Grogan, Jeremy Grontesca, Friedhelm Grosch, Mario Grosso, Liz Groves, Carina Gudacker, Salvador Guerra, Dalinda Guerrero, Dean Guirguis, Alf Amund Gulsvik, Calum Gunn, Sergei Guschin, Lee Gwin **H** Roisin H, Ferdinand Hang, Stephan Haag, Emily Hadaway, Serena Hadi, Hans-Peter Hafner, Jon Hagen, Jochen Hahn, Alex Halbach, Melody Hall, Richard Hall, Karen Hammink, Greg Hampson, Christine Hancock, Eleanor Handreck, Gemma Handy, Roman Hanis, Maggie Hanlon, Yso Hardy, Anne Pernille Harlem Dyrbekk, Michelle Harmon, Frank Harmsen, Brian Harness, Lucy Harper, Andrew Harrington, Kate Harris, Steve Harris, Victoria Harrison, Colin Hart, JP Hart Hansen, Imke and Markus Hartig-Jansen, Bruce Hartnett, Philip Harvey, Zoe Harvey, Michael Haschka, Leslie Haskell, Jens Haubold, Sabine Hauptmann, Elvira Hautvast, Cindy Hayford, Andrew Haynes, Julie Haynes, Loona Hazarika, Oliver Headey, Mathew Heal, Annette Hebestreit, Louie Hechanova, Michelle Hecht, Gerrit Hecking, Shirley Heffron, Hendrik Heider, Matthias Heimberg, Oli Hein, Karl Heiss, Tim Helbo, Robert Heller, Consuela Hendriks, Tolima Hennighausen, Ann and Axel Henning-Ponnet, T Hennishausen, Jacob Henriksen, Anne Hernaes, Alexa Herrmann, Kathleen Hershner, Peter Hertrampf, Christiane Hess, Larry W Heuple, Klaus-Peter Heussler, Ernie Higgs, Belinda Hill, Michael Hill, Rebecca Hill, Matthias Hillenkamp, Nina Hillesund, Julie Hinckley, Jillian Hirasawa, Erich Hirtler, Andreas Hitzcar, Janet Hobbs, Jo Hobbs, Len Hobbs, Cary Hodgkinson, Tekla Hoehn, Liesbeth Hoek, Martine Hofstede, Ron Hohauser, Hasso Hohmann, Hillary Hohmann, Climmy Hoksbergen, Patrick Hoksbergen, Jenny Holden, Julie Hollar, Roos Hollenberg, Iris B Hollis, Andrew Holmes, Neil Holmes, Jeff Holt, Natasha Holt, Georg Holthausen, Kristen Holtz-Garcia, Miranda Hoogendoorn, Danielle Horneman, Peter Horsky, David Horton, Jozsef Horvath, Ayme Hosseini, GM Hosty, Patricia Houton, Trine Hovset, Jay Howarth, Gloria Huang, Sine Hudecek, Ed Hudson, Monica Hudson, Laura Hughes, R Huguet, Eelco Huizinga, David L Huntzinger, Cornelia Hurek, Fer Hurk, Andy Hurst, Lele Huss, Cameron Hutchison, Eva Huthoefer, Nick Hutton, Paul Hyman, Judith Hytrek **I** Trebor Iksrazal, Lani Imhof, Sonja Inderbitzin, Kris Inglis, Carlo Introzzi, Peter Irvine, Jim Isaacs, Irene Ivarsson, Roberto Frank Iza Mayorga, Oren Izhaky **J** Bastiaan Jaarsma, Toni Jackson, Morten Jacobsen, John E Jacobson, Jan James, James Jamison, Helena Janols, Jan Janousek, Juliette Jansen, Gisela Janson, Johana Janson, Andrea Janssen, Thomas Jansseune, Myles Jelf, Larry Jensen, Owen Jensen, Solveig Jeppesen, Sarah Jerebine, Barbara Jesser, Lars Johansson, Gerd Johnsen, Amanda Johnson, Carina Johnson, Carlotta Johnson, Denise Johnson, Kristen Johnson, Paul and Liz Johnson, Julie Johnston, Schona Jolly, Lobo Jon, Iestyn Jones, Milly Jones, Nicky Jones, Richard Jones, Dr Jennifer Jones-Cropf, Veronika Jonker, Rebecca Jonson, Karel Jonsson, Paul Jorn, John Jose, Catherine Joslyn, Stephanie Jud, Saskia Jukema, Cleve Justis **K** Hartmut Kähler, Claudia Kalin, Guenther Kalkofen, Melissa Kallas, Pamela Kalman, Inge Kampfen, Sabrina Kanji, Miso Kanlic, Ira Kaplan, Tuula Kareketo, Judith Karena, Pius Karena, Lisa Karolius, Peter Kars, George Karutz, Joanna Karwacka, Naoko Kato, Dave Katz, Dr Tobias Kaufmann, Mike Kaye, Susan Kealey, Chris Keavney, Ute Keck, Sonja Keckeis, Maryke Keet, Kirby Keeton, Adolf Kellermann, Lucas Kellet, Mandy Kells, Allan Kelly, Cathy Kelly, Helene Kelly, Jamie Kelly, Kristin Kelly, Keith Kemp, Abby Kennedy, Liz Kennedy, Mark Kennet, Judy Kenning, James Kenny, Patricia Kent, MC Kerby, Faiz Kermani, Monique Kerssens, Boris Keweloh, Sarah Kidd, Steve Kidd, Alfredo Kihien, Jiny Kim, Graham King, Jay King, Diana Kirk, Michael Kiwoor, Jutta Kiworr, Claus Kjaerby, Lucas Klamert, AMJ Klaver, April Klavins, Ken Klein, Hek Kleinberg, Roman Klotsvog, Manon Kluytmans, Kay Knightley Day, Brigitte Knoetig, Julia Knowles, Oliver Koeth, Axel Kohnen, Lynn Kohner, Milla Koistinen, Alexandra Konstantinoff, M Koo, Peter Koomen, Chris Korsten, Kees-Jan Korving, Ilkka Koskinen, Mieke-Ien Koster, Ryan Krake, Jeff and Diane Krans, Oliver Krause, Jonathan Kresge, Ulrich Kreuth, Jean-Luc Krieger, Emma Kristensen, Kirstine Kristensen, Sten Kristensen, Olga Kroes, Julianna Krolak, Susie Krott, Tamar Krupnik, Johan Kruseman, Hartmut Kuhne, Marjolein Kuijers, Annelies Kuipers, Eppo Kuipers, Agnieszka Kula, Nina Kulas, Timo Kuntzsch, Rosie Kunz **L** Marcelo Labre, Inga Labuhn, Denis Lachenal, Mikko Lahtinen, James Laird, Dagmar Lais, Emma Lakin, Jason Lamb, Vicky Lamb, Marjon Lambooij van Capelle, Christel Lammertink, Iuce Lamy, Mark Lander, Edoardo Lando, Christina Langton, Diana Laponder, Carl Lariviere, Samuel Larsson, Dr David Lasry, Julie Lassonde, Silvia Lavalle, Ian Lavoie, Aidan Lawrence, Mary Lawrence, Stephen Lawrence, Justin Lawson, Linda Layfield, Alexander Ledig, Bill Lee, Davis Lee, Edna Lee, Marcus Lee, Peter Lee, Rose Lee, Karine Lefas, Anneliese Lehmann, Julia Lehmann, Kristin Lehoullier, Mirja Leibnitz, Diane Leighton, Zoe Leighton, Nanci Leitch, Christoph Lenherr, Graham Lenton, D Leslie, Markus Lessky, Mikkel Levelt, Ellen-Karine Levesen, Daniel Levitt, Asaf Levy, Idan Levy, Jeff Levy, Stuart Levy, Pamela Lewis, Peter Lewis, Ralph Lewis, Colin Lewsi, Jeff Libman, Eleonore Lickl, Sigrid Liede, Verhofstadt Lieven, Nicholas Light, R Lightbulb Winders, Eliose Liles, Nick Lilley, Lianne van der Linden, Anne Lindley, David Lindner, Peter V Lindsay, Setha Lingam, Marianne Lipshutz, Coraleigh Listen, Jen Little, Dmitriy Litvak, Adam Livett, Shad Lloyd, Helen Lo, Martin Loebell, Paula Loeber, Andreas Loeffler, Martine Loffeld, Maribeth Long, Robie Loomer, Sam Loose, Maneola Lope, Manoela Lopez, Aimee Lord, Raynald Losier, Peter Loucks, Imogen Love, V Love, Deborah Lowe, Gary Lowe, Simone Ludwig, Diederik Lugtigheid, M Luiza, Karl Lundberg, Sergio Lupio, Robert Lupp, Tanja Lutolf, Dikrßn P Lutufyan, Val Lyon **M** Casper Maasdam, Maitu Mac Gabhann, Campbell Macdonald, Jane L Macdonald, Zack and Susan Macdonald, Ian Mace, JT Mack, Miki Maclean, Ken MacLennan, Karla Mader, Magisteele Magisteele, Christina Maile, Cedric Maizieres, Nadia Mallette, Gunnar Malmqvist, Philip Manchester, Chelsea Mannix, Liz Manship, Axel Manthey, Andrew Marcus, Anne Margrethe, Karen Marie Miller, Karen Marie Winterhalter, Lin Mario Ping-Cheng, Yvonne Markestein, Christine Markham, Will Markle, Margit and Folke Markwardt, M Marlen, Sunny Maroo, Armenio Marques, Nimer Marroquin, Mary Marsella, Saskia Marsh, Ove Martensson, Alix Martin, Trajan Martin, Kathryn Martys, Bo Maslanka, Dave Mason, Dr Barry R Masters, Cliff Matheson, David Mathews, Mario Mathieu, Kyle and Terri Mathis, Gerd Maxl, Con Maxwell, Gudrun Mayer-Ullmann, Thomas Mayes, Rupert Mclean and John Mayhead, Charles Mays, Wendy McCarty, Brendan McCauley, Shayne McCreadie, Ralph B McCuen, Tasha McDonald, Jennifer McGowan, Mike McKenna, Phil McKenzie, Patrick McKone, Sarah Mclean, Suzanne McParland, Anne-Marie McShannon, Joe McSpedon, Lee Mead, Peter Meaker, Bill Medhurst, Allan Mee, Kees Meerman, Sharon Meieran, Diane Melendez, Les Melrose, Chantal Melser, Miranda Men, Shirit Menashe, J Mentan, Jan Menzel, Silvia Merli, Don Merritt, Eli Merritt, Sally Merryman, Erik Mes, Claire Metherell, Astrid Metzger, Joshua Michaud, Claudia Michel, Alan Michell, Valerie Michon, Monica Middleton, MA Midson, Vanessa Migliosi, Trikaliotis Mihalis, Pavel Mikhlin, Birte Mikkelsen, Rebecca Millar, Becky Mills, Steven Mincin, Carolina Miranda, Kavita Misra, Haruo Miyata, Oded Mizrahi, Maryam Moayeri, Hank Moffat, Dennis Mogerman, Jock Moilliet, Karen Mojorovich, Elaine Mokey, Alexis Molho, Sarah Mollenkramer, Rich Molter, Danny Mommers, Andrew G Moncrieff, Paul Moore, Jaime Mora, Amalia Moran, Lorn Moran, Lucille Moreau, Ricardo Moreno, Leonard Thomas Morin, Hannah Morley, Dan Morris, Jim Morris, Michael Morris, Lars Mosbach, Asron Mozsowski, B Muldrow, Kerry Mullen, Georg Muller, Jerry Muller, Jutta Muller, Kitty Muller, Jorg Muller-Tows, Patrick Mundy-O'Toman, Carlos Muniz, Cristina Munoz, Harriet Murray, Gus Musto, Sara Myers, Jens Myhre **N** Marcie N,

Ray Naden, Ingrid Naden, Ishay Nadler, Pier Nado, Vandana Nair, Kiran Nandra, Gil Nashilevich, Kim Nearpass, Marcelo F Neira, Naomi Nestel, Alois Neumier, Richard Neurink, Nina Newhouser, Jay Newlin, Catherine Newman, Pete and Cath Newman, Michael Newton, Tom Newton Chance, Ryan Nice, Katie Nicholls, Stephen and Kathryn Nicol, Gitte Nielsen, Greg Nielsen, Sofie Nielsen, Laurens Nieuwenhuizen, Aernout Nieuwkerk, Corina Nigg, Manuel Ninapaitan, Holly Niner, Max Nish, Jerry Noble, Thomas Nordenholz, Christo Norman, Katharina Nothelfer, Andrzaj Nowak, Pieter Nuiten, Francesca Nurock **O** Sue Oakes, Stephen Oakley, Markus Oberli, William OConnell, Diane O'Connor, Klaus Oenning-Terhart, Karin Offer, Anthony O'Hehir, Deirdre O'Kelly, Michelle Okouneff, Ole Olesen, Enrique Olivares, Frank Oliver, Matt Oliver, Nick Oliver, Morten Olsen, Radek Ondrusak, Martijn Ophoff, Andre Oppe, Kara O'Reilly, Cathal O'Riordain, Erin O'Rourke, Sharon O'Rourke, Anne Ortegren, Otto Ortner, Jonathan Osborne, Sebastian Osenstetter, Brian O'Shea, Rosaleen O'Shea, Thomas Ostergaard, Ibon Ostolaza, Christian Osvald, Claudia Otero, Stefan Otti, Jeroen Overmars **P** Steve and Chris Page, Annie Pageau, Amarnath Pai, Graciela Pajuelo de Dahl Olsen, Daniel Palamara, Ed Palao, Jenny Paley, Arvind Pallan, Juliane Palm, Desiree Palmen, James Pan, Vijay Parbat, Lars Pardo, Jeremy Parker, Jessica Parker, Paolo Paron, Don Parris, Susan Parrow, Arnold Parzer, Jessica Pascoe, Alice Pater, Helen Paterson, Vikki Patino, Michael Patrikeev, Lynn H and Michele G Patterson, Stuart Pattullo, Connie M Payne, Daniel Payne, Sam Payne, Lucy Pearson, Morten Pedersen, Soeren Pedersen, CJ Peereboom, Elisabeth Peersen, Huub Peeters, Lucy Peile, Sabina Pensek, Carmen Pereda, Yara Perez, John C Perry, Marlo Perry, Lin Petry, Richard and Alison Pett, Dieter Pfeifer, Petr Pfeniq, Christophe Philippe, Jason Phillips, Peter Phillips, Fenny Pielage, Robert A Pierce, Matthew Piercy, Emmanuel Pierson, Katherine Pike, Cesar Piotto, Kurt Pläckinger, Mandy Planert, Tom A Plange, Marc Andre Plante, Joan Plested, Lidy van der Ploeg, Jens Poetsch, Daniela Pogliani, Francoise Pohu, Hans Polane, Chris Pollard, Pancho Poncho, Clive Ponsonby, Erik Poole, Helen Poole, Aase Popper, Helen Popper, Yvonne Post, Katja Potzsch, Alexandre Pouget, Andre Poulis, Jeremy Pounder, Donald Povey, William Powers, Daniela Prenger, Adam Price, Bart-Jan Prins, Miguel Pro, Mark Probst, Rachel Proctor, Cam Pulham, Pablo Pwoa Dallvorso **Q** Sacha Quadrelli, Margaret Quinlan Sharma, Margaret Quinlan-Sharma **R** Mark Rabine, Will Race, Sammy Radstone, Barbara Radweiske, Andy Sweet Nancy Rainwater, Marek Rajnic, Sriram Ramakrishnan, Giselle Ramirez, John Randall III, Duilio Vargas Ratto, Sanna-Leena Rautanen, Johann Rawlinson, John Reader, Robert Reagan, Albert Recknagel, Monique Reeves, Steven Reeves, Nora Regalado, Susan Regebro, Martijn Regelink, Andreas Rehberg, Franziska Reinhard, Tim Renders, Cami Renfrow, Abigail Reponen, J Reuther, Marco Antonio Reyes, Frank Rheindt, Heidi Rhodes, Eliana Ricalde, Jason Richard, Julia Richards, Julie Richards, Richard Richardson, Burt Richmond, Werner Richter, Robert Riesinger, Tim Rimington, Melanie Ringel, Branden Rippey, Kirsten Marie Risbjerg, Christine Rist, Henrik Risvang, Fernando Rivas, Martin Roberts, Nicola Robinson, Matt Robshaw, Cristiana Rodrigues, Lars Roennov, Michele Roessler, Lucy Rogerson, Luigi Romagnoli, David Romain, Megan Romano, C Romero, Edu Romero, Suzy Romero Treuiller, Udi Ron,

Ans Roovers, Sandy Rosas, Matthias Rose, Cecilia Rossel, Miga Rossetti, Adriano Rossi, David Roth, Catherine Rourke, Sonja and Marco Rouwenhorst, Karen Rowland, Simone Royer Yamashita, Ori Rub, Giovanni Rubbiani, Andrew Ruben, Debra Ruben, Sean Rubin, Audrey Rudofski, Michal Rudziecki, Dan Ruff, Alexandra Russell-Bitting, Nynke Rusticus, Richard Rykhus, Kaare Rysgaard Moller **S** Patrick Sagmeister, Amartya Saha, Marc Sajecki, Carmen Mabel Ahumada Salazar, Gabriela Salazar, Patricia Salazar, Monica and Noel Salazar Espinosa, Carolina Salmon, Gil Salomon, Wolfgang Salz, Andy Salzer, Bernabe Samaniego, Hamadi Samia, Paola Samoggia, Jodi Samuels, Stefan Samuelsson, Ian Samways, Grazyna Sanchez, Allen Sanderson, Jen Sands, Julie Sands, Karen Sangster, Paul Sap, Kim and Anna Saporito, Cathy Sarjeant, Paula Saunders, Jessica Savage, Louise Savenborg, Todd Savitz, Fortini Scarlatou, Michael Scarlett, Elisabeth and Frank Schaettgen, Natalie Schai, Emile Schenk, Mark Schiffner, Ralf Schmieder, Peter Schmeitz, Hauke Schmidke, Bernhard Schmidt, David Schmidt, Ernst Schmidt, Florian Schmidt, Robin Schmidt, Caroline Andrews and Schmutz, Erin Schneider, Irene Schneider, Thomas Schneider, Nancy Schneider-Deacon, Elizabeth Schofield, Ronald Schop, Mr and Mrs Gilbert Schouteet-Raes, Luc Schouten, Martin Schroeder, Liam Schubel, Melisa Schuette, Connie Schuler, Shon Schulte, Ingo Schultz, W Schuurman, Thomas Schwab, Eric Schwartz, Michael Schwartz, Falk Scleicher, Belinda Scotman, Alicia Scott, Lynda Seal, Tracy Seaton, Michel Secq, John Sedlander, Alex Seeley, Elana Sefton, Stephan Segers, Chris Seifert, Jacob Seligmann, Indranil Sen, Prof Gour C Sen, Franck Senghor, Miomir Serbinson, Pere

BEHIND THE SCENES

Serrat, Eric Sevrin, Gavin Sexton, Norman and Ruth Shanks, Nicole Uttama Sharma, Aileen Shaw, Peter and Florence Shaw, Walt Shaw, Betty Sheets, Mercedes Shelby, Rossie Shelty, Lisa Sherry, Steve Sherwood, Iain Shiels, Dennis Shilobod, Mykel Shlub, Mark Siaon, Jonathan Sibtain, Itay Sidar, Ricardo Sillicani, Amanda Silver, Charles Lustosa Silvestre, Marco Silvi, Oscar Silvius, Lydia Simbolon, Anthony Simmons, Jane Simon, Dean Simonsen, Deborah Sinay, Claire Sivacek, Lisel Sjogren, Luke Skinner, Reinhard Skinner, Diana Skroch, Malcolm Slater, James Sleeman, R Sleeman, Kristoffer Sletten, Jacilda Slevin, Tyrone Slothrope, John Smale, Carie Small, Brian Smith, Christopher Smith, Gary Smith, Iain Smith, Jason Smith, Michael Smith, Sally Smith, Stuart Smith, Judeth Marie Smith Nussbaum, Carol J Snaith, Hank Snell, Shawn Snowden, Rike Sohn, Martin Sohngen, Pascal Sommacal, Jennifer Sontag, Brent Sorensen, Jesse Sorrell, Julie Southworth, Martien Spanjer, Clare Spauls, Fred Spengler, Amanda Spice, David L Spiegelberg, Mark Stables, Martine Staepelaere, Tomasz Stafiej, Richard Stanaway, Espen Stangeland, Nicole Stania, Mitchell Staub, Nancy Staus, J Stavenuiter, Anna-Maree Van Der Steen, Miriam Gayoso Kate Stefanko, Fiona Steggles, Carl Stegman, Urs Steiger, Corri Stein, Bjorn Steinhaug, Gunhild Stenersen, Paul Steng, Martin Stengle, Elizabeth Stephens, Kent Stephens, Joachim Sterner, Joe Stickler, Herbert Stirmlinger, Michal F Stover, John Strang, Tim Strang, Christine Strasser, John Straube, EW Street, Miki Strong, Adrian Stuerm, Stephanie Stump, Penny Sturgess, Matthias Suenkler, Michael Suesskind, Stuart Sugarbread, Louise Sullivan, Daniel Suman, Steven Suranie, Patrick Suter, Esther Sutton, Gergo Sved, Judy and Ariana Svenson, Alex Swallow, Jeff Swartz, Peter Sweeny, Peter Symons, Andrew Szefler, Nagy Szilvia, Micole Sztanski **T** Cindy Taiclet, Simie Takashima, Nora Tam, Dave Tamblyn, Jeroen Tamsma, Andreas Tanberg, Shona Taner, Andrea Tavazza, Alexandra Tayler, Alexandra Taylor, Jeff Taylor, John Taylor, Shawn Teague, Mary Teahan, Ben Tellegen, Natascha Telling, Thijs ten Hag, Renske Terpstra, Annabel Terrill, Chris Terry, Ilan Tesler, Manuel Teunissen, Angelika Teuschl, Susanna Thatcher, Holger Theobald, Robert Thi, Belinda Thiele, Sabine Thielicke, Juliane Thiessen, David Thom, Andree Thomas, Jorens Thomassen, Jeremy Thompson, Alex Thorne, Alan Thornhill, Julie Tilghman, Sally Tillett, Marc Tissier, Yossi Tnaumi, Bill Toby, Juan Tohalino Vera, Dianne Tolentino, Mari Tomine Lunden, Catherine Tomkees, Paul Tonkin, Oskar Olav Topnes, Miriam Torres, Ryan Tott, Carl Townsend, Marisel Traverzo, Martin Tremblay, Doyle Trent, Jan Trien, Tu Trieu, Allegra Troiano, Petra Troost, Pauline Truman, Maria Trygger, Nickol Turak, John Tustin, Therese Tyacke **U** Alexander Uff, Silvia Ugarte, Marcela Ugaz, Andreas Ulrich, Kristin Ulsteen, BL Underwood **V** Jeroen Vahrmeijer, Cheyenne Valenzuela, Marcelo Vallejos, Wandy van Beek, Atle van Beelen Granlund, Marfa van Daal, Catherine van Daele, Louise van de dKop, Kaspar van den Berg, Sandra van den Berg, Floor van den Broek, Fer van den Hurk, Richard van der Baan, Jelmer van der Schaaf, Dave van der Spank, Jeanette van Ditzhuijzen, Loes van Dommelen, Erica van Drie, Natalie van Eckendonk, Jann van Gaal, Patti van Ham, Sofie van Hapert, Paul van Homelen, Carna van Hove, Dirk van Hoydonck, Ton van Maarsseveen, Alina van Maggelen, Bram van Regenmortel, Gisela van Sprang, Piet van Wesemael, David and Elizabeth van Wie, Kees van Zon, Guy Vanackeren, Francesco Vanoni, Bart VanOvermeire, Jozef Varnagy, Ray VarnBuhler, Carlos Vasquez, Susan Vaughan, Zoe Veater, Claudio Vecchi, Leigh Anne Vellacott, Andres Velole, Ann Venegas, Henk Veneman, Astrid Veninga, Rosa Vera, Teresa Mendez de Vera, Anony Verbaeys, Frits Verbeek, Gilbert Verbeken, Georges Verbinnen, Xavier Verdaguer, Karla Verhagen, Tjen Verheye, Jan Vermande, Margaret Vernon, Jason Verschoor, Gitte Vestergaard, Christian Vidal, Alexandre Videcoq, Vickie Villavicencio, Marcel Vink, Niels Vink, Claude-A J Visinand, Linda Visser, RW Visser, Nalini Viswanathan, Eric Vlaanderen, Arlinde Vletter, Cees Vletter, Martina Voelkel, Casper Vogel, Conny Vogel, John Vogel Jr, Barbara Vogeltanz, Martina Völkel, Marc-Andre Voll, Jan Vollebregt, Jan Voorhagen, Wim Vos, Leon Vroemen, Giuliette Vuerich **W** Jacob Waiman, Wolfgang Walch, Clive Walker, Michael J Walker, Richard C Walker, Michael Wall, Teena Wallis, Peter Walsh, Jimmy Walter, Anke Walzebug, Nina Wanendeya, Lillian Wang, Christopher Wanko, Michael Ward, Peter Ward, Tom Waring, Etienne Waterval, Patrick Watervoort, Neil Watson, Bram Wauters, Kris Wealand, Tom Webb, Karsten Weber, Barbara Wegman, Christian Weidner, Lauretta Weimer, Arthur Weinstein, Jutta Weisenburger, Heidi W Weiskel, Robin Weiss, Clark Weissinger, Kelly Wells, Mark Wenban, Anne Wendel, Sabine Wenig, Joel Werlen, Anja West, Ceinwen West, James West, Sharon Whalley, Dalma Whang, MC Whirter, Duanne White, Linda White, Matt White, Michaek White, Michael White, Stephen White, Ben Whiting, Pal Wibe, Julie Wichman, James Wigley, Dianne Wild, Anita Wildi, Claire Wilhelm, John D Wilkinson, Krsita Willeboer, Jennifer Williams, Jo Williams, John V Williams, Judy R Williams, Robin Williams, Sally Williams, Steve Williams, Russell Willis, Karsten Willmann, Lori Willocks, Janet Willoughby, Adam Wilson, Patricia Wim, Joanne Wimble, Julie Winans, Matthew Winer, Ralph Winkelmolen, Thea Wirds, Sheri Wisgerhof, Christophe Wittwer, Bogdan J Wnuk, Martin Woerner, Jim Wold, David Wong, Helen Wood, Katie Wood, Chris Woods, Nathan Woods, Kenneth J Woodside, Faeze T Woodville, AH Workman, Georgia Worrall, Allison Wright, Samantha L Wronski, Alexander Wuerfel, Jules Wyman, Tom Wynne-Powell **Y** Andrew Yale, Yuri Yamada, Henriikka Yliheljo, Josh Yolish, Kim Yongsoo, Scott T York, Bonnie Y Yoshida, Michaela Young-Mitchell, Tsui-Ling Yu, Simone Yurasek, Anthony V Yuro **Z** Gabriele Zacher, Zdenek Zadrapa, Katarina Zak, Stan Zalewski, Justin Zamen, Elles Zandhuis, Rosene Zaros, Jorge Zavaleta, Suana Zavaleta Escobedo, Petra Zellmer, Tymoteusz Zera, Helmut Zettl, Murray Zichlinsky, Paula Zimbrean, Joyce Zinbarg, Christine Zoller, Nicole Zuber, Magda Zupancic, Margot Zylicz

ACKNOWLEDGMENTS

Many thanks to the following for the use of their content.

Mountain High Maps® Copyright © 1993 Digital Wisdom, Inc.

Index

Index

LEGEND

ROUTES

Tollway	Walking Path
Freeway	Unsealed Road
Primary Road	Pedestrian Street
Secondary Road	Stepped Street
Tertiary Road	Tunnel
Lane	One Way Street
Walking Tour	Walking Tour Detour

TRANSPORT

Ferry	Rail
Metro	Rail (Underground)
Monorail	Tram

HYDROGRAPHY

River, Creek	Lake (Salt)
Intermittent River	Mudflats
Canal	Reef
Glacier	Swamp
Lake (Dry)	Water

BOUNDARIES

International	Ancient Wall
State, Provincial	Cliff
Regional, Suburb	Marine Park

POPULATION

○ CAPITAL (NATIONAL)	◉ CAPITAL (STATE)
○ Large City	● Medium City
○ Small City	○ Town, Village

AREA FEATURES

Area of Interest	Land
Beach, Desert	Mall
Building	Market
Cemetery, Christian	Park
Cemetery, Other	Sports
Forest	Urban

SYMBOLS

SIGHTS/ACTIVITIES	INFORMATION	SHOPPING
Beach	Bank, ATM	Shopping
Buddhist	Embassy/Consulate	**TRANSPORT**
Castle, Fortress	Hospital, Medical	Airport, Airfield
Christian	Information	Border Crossing
Confucian	Internet Facilities	Bus Station
Diving, Snorkeling	Parking Area	Cycling, Bicycle Path
Hindu	Petrol Station	General Transport
Islamic	Police Station	Taxi Rank
Jain	Post Office, GPO	Trail Head
Jewish	Telephone	**GEOGRAPHIC**
Monument	Toilets	Hazard
Museum, Gallery	**SLEEPING**	Lighthouse
Picnic Area	Sleeping	Lookout
Point of Interest	Camping	Mountain, Volcano
Ruin	**EATING**	National Park
Shinto	Eating	Oasis
Sikh	**DRINKING**	Pass, Canyon
Skiing	Drinking	River Flow
Taoist	Café	Shelter, Hut
Winery, Vineyard	**ENTERTAINMENT**	Spot Height
Zoo, Bird Sanctuary	Entertainment	Waterfall

NOTE: Not all symbols displayed above appear in this guide.

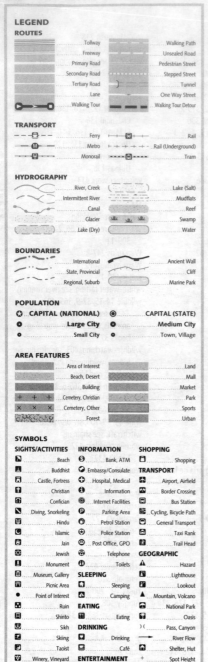

LONELY PLANET OFFICES

Australia
Head Office
Locked Bag 1, Footscray, Victoria 3011
☎ 03 8379 8000, fax 03 8379 8111
talk2us@lonelyplanet.com.au

USA
150 Linden St, Oakland, CA 94607
☎ 510 893 8555, toll free 800 275 8555
fax 510 893 8572, info@lonelyplanet.com

UK
72–82 Rosebery Ave,
Clerkenwell, London EC1R 4RW
☎ 020 7841 9000, fax 020 7841 9001
go@lonelyplanet.co.uk

France
1 rue du Dahomey, 75011 Paris
☎ 01 55 25 33 00, fax 01 55 25 33 01
bip@lonelyplanet.fr, www.lonelyplanet.fr

Published by Lonely Planet Publications Pty Ltd
ABN 36 005 607 983

© Lonely Planet 2004

© photographers as indicated 2004

Cover photographs by Lonely Planet Images: Boy in poncho, Cuzco, Richard I'Anson (front); Ruins at Machu Picchu, Woods Wheatcroft (back). Many of the images in this guide are available for licensing from Lonely Planet Images: www.lonelyplanetimages.com.